Kinship and Family Organization

Kinship and Family Organization

Edited by Bernard Farber

University of Illinois

John Wiley & Sons, Inc. New York / London / Sydney

Preface

This book depicts the family from a sociological perspective. First, it presents several definitions of the family in the sociological literature and shows how these definitions are related. It views the family as one of the kinship groups in society and indicates how the nuclear family is influenced by the structure of the kinship system. The book then relates the type of kinship and family system to the total community and society. Next, it focuses on kinship and family in contemporary society and then specifically on courtship and on relationships within the nuclear family. Materials on the socialization of children are included, for the transmission of the culture of the family and society depends on childrearing. In the concluding section change in family organization is discussed.

Although this book was not designed to accompany my *Family: Organization and Interaction*, much of the material supplements that book. The major difference between *Family* and this book is the increased emphasis on age-grading in American kinship relations.

Probably no one will agree with me that the papers in this volume are arranged in the most appropriate sequence. Articles on socialization appear next to articles on lineage characteristics; investigations based on limited samples are presented next to others resting on cross-cultural analysis. My only defense is that papers are arranged by chapter topics rather than by scope or technique of analysis.

The aid and advice of colleagues and friends should be acknowledged. David L. Harvey, William C. Jenne, Efrosini John, Harry M. Johnson, Aleksandras Kulikauskas, Jerry M. Lewis, and Michael Lewis, all of the University of Illinois, have commented on selections and introductory statements for various chapters. Louis Schneider provided invaluable assistance in the translation of the Schelsky paper. Credit for the clarity of the translation belongs to him; responsibility for ambiguities is mine. I wish also to express my appreciation to Daniel Glaser, Joseph Gusfield, Bernard Karsh and Joseph Meyerowitz for many stimulating discussions of family and society and to Jerry Lewis for preparing the index.

This book is dedicated to my wife Annette.

BERNARD FARBER

Urbana, Illinois
February, 1966

Contents

Kinship and Family Organization

Chapter 1

What is the Family?

Most people know intuitively what they mean by "the family." They have known families throughout their lifetime and intuitive definitions are sufficient for everyday conversation and action. When someone tries to analyze the family as a social institution, however, he finds that what he has considered as *the* family is inappropriate for systematic treatment. The characteristics of the families he has known do not fit "families" of other segments of his society. Family life in different societies exhibits even greater contrasts. In order to delimit his area of analysis of the family as a social institution, he must formulate a more rigorous definition.

Sociologists have developed several interpretive approaches to variations in family life, each one generating unique understanding about family organization while at the same time emphasizing a different aspect.[1] These variations in emphasis result in slightly modified definitions of the family in each approach. Some sociologists try to define the family in terms of a set of ends, others in terms of a kind of social structure organized to gain more general ends in societies, and still others in terms of structures and ends emerging in the unique history of each society. In this chapter several of these alternative sociological conceptions of the family are presented as background, and then the viewpoint of this book is described.

Viewpoints of the Family as an Institution

Sumner has defined an institution as a structure of regularized patterns of conduct of individuals organized around a concept or idea.[2] Such an idea may consist of values, goals, aims, ends, and any other kinds of forces stimulating organized activities. Although most sociologists agree with Sumner's general picture of an institution,

---

[1] For example, see classification of approaches in Reuben Hill and Donald A. Hansen, "The Identification of Conceptual Frameworks Utilized in Family Study," *Marriage and Family Living*, 22 (1960), pp. 299–311.
[2] William G. Sumner, *Folkways*, New York: Ginn, 1906, pp. 53–55.

they disagree about the way to interpret the words *idea* and *structure* in his definition. This disagreement has stimulated the development of at least three diverse viewpoints in the study of the family. The first of these viewpoints is that since the family exists as a recognizable institution in all societies logically the ends in family life must be universal.[3] The differences among families in various societies must lie in adaptations in the organization of family patterns of conduct to other developments in that society.

A second point of view claims that certain regularized patterns of conduct related to family life have developed historically.[4] For sociologists holding this view, each society is unique in the aims or ends accorded to the family, but parenthood, grandparenthood, and the other family positions are present in all historically relevant societies. They contend that the family is potentially the most powerful force in society for controlling the actions of individuals and suggest that in those societies in which the family controls the greatest number of aspects of its members' lives the degree of personal and social stability is greatest. Their view is that the traditional roles in the family (such as father, mother, grandfather, or grandmother) are capable of encompassing all of the society's activities in an efficient way.

Still a third group of sociologists claims that neither the ends nor the structures of regularized patterns of conduct approach universality. This group maintains that it is in the processes of interaction in a particular society that the characteristics of the family institution emerge.[5] However, because family membership is determined only by birth and marriage, there are some limitations placed on the kinds of social relationships possible. In the following discussion these three approaches to family sociology are termed the *universal-functions*, the *structural*, and the *interactionist*, respectively.[6]

The Universal-Functions Approach. Sociologists who use the universal-functions approach postulate that in all societies the family is organized to perform certain functions for the society.[7] A function is defined as an activity that is imperative if

[3] George P. Murdock, *Social Structure*, New York: Macmillan, 1949. Parsons and Bales complain of the failure of sociologists to develop a list of "root" functions of the family, but do not indicate the basis for this failure. Instead, they provide an arbitrary list of functions including procreation, child care, "economic" functions and religious functions. Talcott Parsons and Robert F. Bales, *Family Socialization and Interaction Process*, Glencoe, Ill.: Free Press, 1955.

[4] See Carle C. Zimmerman and Merle E. Frampton, *Family and Society*, New York: D. Van Nostrand, 1935 (based on LePlay), and Carle C. Zimmerman, *Family and Civilization*, New York: Harper and Brothers, 1947. Although the Zimmerman-LePlay approach is considered outmoded by some sociologists, others regard it as the most acceptable contemporary view of the family. See David Greenwood, *Essays in Human Relations*, Washington, D.C.: Public Affairs Press, 1956, pp. 44–46.

[5] Ernest W. Burgess, Harvey J. Locke, and Mary M. Thomes, *The Family*, New York: American Book, 1963, and Willard Waller, *The Family: A Dynamic Interpretation*, New York: Dryden, 1938.

[6] See Bernard Farber, *Family: Organization and Interaction*, San Francisco: Chandler, 1964, for a discussion of these approaches from the perspective of social change.

[7] For example, William J. Goode, "The Sociology of the Family," in Robert K. Merton, et al., *Sociology Today*, New York: Basic Books, 1959, pp. 178–196, and Bruno Malinowski, "Parenthood as a Basis for Social Structure," reprinted in Marvin B. Sussman (ed.), *Source Book on Marriage and the Family*, New York: Houghton-Mifflin, 1965, pp. 21–30.

the society is to continue to exist. The family performs these functions because it is the most efficient organization developed to undertake them. Each role (the organization of activities by an individual) is conceptualized around specific functions. Moreover, each role implies a reciprocal role; for example, the sexual functions of marriage reside both in the husband's role and in the reciprocating wife's role. To identify each function with a role it is necessary to regard not simply the functions but the roles themselves as universal. The specific content of the role may vary, but the formal aspects must be universal. Thus, although the particular rights and obligations of husband and wife differ from one society to the next, the essential character of sexual access is seen as universal.[8]

Sociologists who maintain this position define the nuclear family as a group composed of husband, wife, and their children. This group is the repository of family roles and corresponding functions and is universal, being the accepted form of family life in all societies. Murdock, who has compared family life in more than two hundred societies through the Human Relations Area Files, contends that the nuclear family exists as an identifiable unit in all societies.[9] Other anthropologists and sociologists, however, have found numerous exceptions to Murdock's generalization.[10]

Representing the universal-functions approach, Murdock posits four universal functions: sexual, reproductive, economic, and educational. Murdock argues that without the sexual and reproductive functions society would become extinct; without economic cooperation among family members, life would cease; without the education of children, culture would end.[11]

One of the major questions inherent in the universal-functions approach is simply: what are the relationships among functions? For the universal-functionalist, this question is answered by using the relationships among family roles. Thus Zelditch, studying the husband and wife roles in various societies,[12] found that the husband's primary role was to represent the family in the larger society. At the level of universal functions, this suggests that the father's major nonsexual role is economic. Because his tie with the family is essentially that of an outsider who represents society to his family, his authority is not supported, at least to the children, by sentimental and emotional bonds. It is the wife who must mediate between the husband and the children. She is related to the husband not simply by an economic bond but also by sexual functions. Her primary roles in the family are reproductive and educational. The wife's roles involve much sentiment and emotional attachment. Zelditch suggests that by this role specialization the husband becomes the instrumental leader in family relations, whereas the wife becomes the social-emotional leader. The social-emotional and instrumental classification found useful by the functionalists is thus derived from the more basic functions of the family.

[8] Recognizing logical difficulties in functionalism, Fletcher contends that functionalism is useful as a conceptual scheme only when not taken literally. Ronald Fletcher, "Functionalism as a Social Theory," *Sociological Review*, **4** (new serial, July, 1956), pp. 31–36.
[9] Murdock, *loc. cit.*
[10] William N. Stephens, *The Family in Cross-Cultural Perspective*, New York: Holt, Rinehart and Winston, 1963, pp. 12–33.
[11] Murdock, *loc. cit.*
[12] Morris Zelditch in Parsons and Bales, *loc. cit.*

A second question raised by the universal-functions position regards the effect of change in society on the performance of family functions. Parsons has suggested that certain imperatives are more powerful than others in controlling the functioning of a social system. He has tried to define this hierarchy of control in terms of four concepts, which he calls pattern maintenance, integration, goal attainment, and adaptation. To Parsons, change in the family results mainly from the influence of general values and norms on actions in a specific situation. In his view, values are the major controlling elements of groups in society, for they are pertinent to the maintenance of existing social patterns. Pattern maintenance is analogous to the concept of inertia in mechanics and is followed next in the control hierarchy by the integration of the norms in the society. Integration deals with the mutual adjustments of subunits of the society from the viewpoint of their contributions to the society as a whole. This means that the norms regulating family life must be integrated with norms of other major institutions of the society, including the economic and political systems. Third in the hierarchy of control is goal attainment. Unlike pattern maintenance, goal attainment is tied to specific situations and thus is variable. Although one of the general functions of the family is to produce children, goal attainment refers to their actual rate of production, which must be consistent with the norms (referring to integration) and with more general values (referring to pattern maintenance). Finally, at the base of the hierarchy of control of social action is adaptation by which Parsons means the provision of facilities or resources (which are ordinarily scarce) to attain goals. On this level, Parsons is concerned with such issues as the organization of facilities, for example, financial resources, or the separation of the place of work from residence. The absence of resources or facilities would affect the attainment of goals, and this failure in turn would affect conformity to norms and maintenance of values.[13]

Parsons has suggested that in modern society family roles are becoming increasingly more constricted. This constriction represents an increasing specialization in family functions. To be sure, the family retains its functions of procreation, child care, some "economic" functions, and sexual functions, but it shares some of them with other institutions. Presumably, as the nuclear family gives up or shares functions with other institutions, it loses some of the quality of "family" and changes the part it plays in the larger society.

The Structural Approach. Unlike the universal-functions approach, the structural view of the family encompasses a greater scope of family roles in its definition.[14] The structural approach is concerned more with kinship relations (i.e., those between all individuals related by birth or marriage) than with the nuclear family itself. The structural approach begins with the premise that in all societies there are grandparents, uncles and aunts, fathers and mothers, husbands and wives, nieces and nephews, siblings, and sons and daughters. Some societies have even sharper and more detailed distinctions in family statuses (or loci for roles), but, according to

[13] Talcott Parsons, "An Outline of the Social System," in Talcott Parsons, Edward Shils, Kaspar D. Naegele, and Jesse R. Pitts (eds.), *Theories of Society*, New York: Free Press of Glencoe, 1961, esp. pp. 36–41.
[14] See Footnote 4.

the structuralists, at least these family and kinship roles are found, especially in those societies historically related to the great Western and Eastern civilizations. Variations appear mainly in the content or functions of the roles associated with these statuses. Thus in some societies, for example, the grandfather may be entrusted with all of the property and personal rights of the members of the clan. In other societies the grandfather may have little or no authority.

The focus of the structuralist is on the content of the family roles associated with each status and on the controls instituted by the family and society to sustain this content. If the family is able to sustain the content of family roles in the younger generation, a stable and secure society will result. The criterion for effective family organization is its effect on the general state of society. Ruth Anshen indicates that the failure of contemporary modern society to identify the family as the institution basically in control of all other institutions has initiated many social problems.[15] She suggests that much of the aimlessness and tension in modern society results from the inability of the family to dominate moral and ethical life.

In a similar vein Evelyn Duvall suggests that the family is responsible for the development of the skills needed to carry on a "successful" existence in modern society.[16] She regards the family as the locus for a series of what she calls developmental tasks. Each status in the family has its appropriate developmental tasks. Elaborated mainly in terms of American middle-class society, this view is based on the assumption that each culture presents a maze which the individual members must learn. This maze is translated into a series of tasks which are actually norms of social relations. As the individual learns to conform to these norms, he achieves success in the family and the community. Here, again, the emphasis is on the ability of the family to control the individual and to prepare him for his existence in the larger society.

Using historical materials, Zimmerman has attempted to show how the decline of authority in the Roman family led to an atomization of family life and ultimately to the demoralization of the society.[17] This atomization was accompanied by a change in values and the content of roles. The earlier value of familism, in which individual wants and needs were subordinated to the needs of the family, gave way to values related to individualism, in which personal appetites were considered paramount. Zimmerman has suggested that American society may be approaching a similar state of demoralization in the development of atomistic family life.

The Interactionist Approach. Although the universal-functions approach assumes that certain ends of family life are found everywhere and the structural approach assumes a universality of family statuses in all historically relevant societies, the interactionists are concerned with the diversity of both structures and functions in family life. They are interested primarily in studying the way in which these variations affect the relations between members of the family group.[18] Most interactionist family sociologists have focused on contemporary Western society, which

[15] Ruth N. Anshen, *The Family: Its Function and Destiny*, New York: Harper and Brothers, 1959, pp. 3–19.
[16] Evelyn Millis Duvall, *Family Development*, New York: Lippincott, 1956.
[17] Zimmerman, *loc. cit.*
[18] See Footnote 5.

shows much variation in both family structure and function among various social classes and ethnic groups.

Burgess has claimed that the major problem confronting the contemporary family is the maintenance of unity in the face of an environment hostile to this unity.[19] By contrast, he considered the organization of rural societies conducive to the maintenance of family unity because of the operation of a variety of external pressures, including public opinion and the ability of relatives to apply sanctions. Burgess defined the family as a unity of interacting personalities. The specific statuses and functions in the family are important only as they affect this unity. Burgess suggested that the companionship family has developed to counteract the potentially disorganizing influences in modern society. He indicated that the parents themselves (rather than external forces) control the destiny of the family. The focus of the interactionist family sociologist is on the extent to which the husband and wife in contemporary families have developed a *modus operandi* to maintain a unity within the family.

The concept of "unity" has not been clearly defined by Burgess or other interactionists. The indices which Burgess and his associates have developed to study unity are concerned with personal adjustment of the husband and wife. The personal adjustment index indicates that (a) the husband and wife have developed ways of acting that are mutually satisfying and (b) there is little conflict in what they want out of life. Two kinds of marital adjustment indices have been developed, one focusing on the extent of general personal adjustment of each spouse[20] and the other on areas of adjustment in marriage such as finances, sex, and housework.[21] Both types of indices, however, equate personal satisfaction and lack of conflict with marital unity.

Three problems for investigation have developed from this emphasis on personal adjustment: the prediction of marital adjustment, kinds of family *modus operandi* favorable to adjustment, and factors in the discontinuities of family life (such as crisis and the family life-cycle) that force changes in patterns of conduct.[22] In prediction, the interactionists try to determine how far husband-wife interaction can be ascertained from characteristics of the couple before marriage. In describing the *modus operandi*, they attempt to discover which aspects of interaction are important for personal adjustment (e.g., equalitarian decision making and the presence of high empathy between husband and wife). In studying family crises, they investigate the development of an effective *modus operandi* in marriage and its modification by changes in the family situation.

[19] Ernest W. Burgess, "The Family in a Changing Society," *American Journal of Sociology*, **53** (1948), pp. 417–423.

[20] For example, Ernest W. Burgess and Paul Wallin, *Engagement and Marriage*, New York: Lippincott, 1953, and Harvey J. Locke, *Predicting Adjustment in Marriage*, New York: Holt, 1951.

[21] For example, Charles E. Bowerman, "Adjustment in Marriage: Overall and Specific Areas," *Sociology and Social Research*, **41** (1957), pp. 257–263, and Judson T. Landis, "Length of Time Required to Achieve Adjustment in Marriage," *American Sociological Review*, **11** (December, 1946), pp. 666–677.

[22] Burgess, Locke, and Thomes, *loc. cit.*

Viewpoint of the Book

The universal-functions, the structural, and the interactionist approaches to family sociology all contribute to the understanding of the operation of family life. The discussion which follows presents the viewpoint of this book in order to suggest the basis for later emphasis on theoretical writings on social process and the discussion of papers about cross-cultural comparisons and changes in contemporary society.

To sustain kinship groups in a changing environment family members must operate in certain ways. These family operations involve maintaining traditional patterns of family life, sustaining solidarity among members, establishing liaisons with other groups, and managing any contingencies that may arise. (These are defined briefly and discussed more fully in later chapters.)

Both maintenance of tradition and contingency management relate to permanence and change in family values and norms over time. Tradition maintenance refers to those activities that sustain the existing norms and values. These activities emerge from personal commitment to existent social patterns, belief systems (such as religious beliefs or ideologies), and the "tension management" mechanisms in the socialization of individuals (such as rituals and other aesthetic and emotional activities) that maintain family solidarity. Contingency management refers to the adjustment of values, norms, and tension-management mechanisms to changes in economic, political, and other institutions in the society.

Tradition maintenance can also be compared with establishment of liaisons. Whereas tradition maintenance refers to commitment to existing norms and values *within* the group, establishment of liaisons involves commitment to certain norms and values concerning interaction *outside* the group but still relevant for family life. For example, in modern society it is necessary to maintain successful economic and political relationships with others in order to sustain a particular set of family norms and values.

Solidarity is related to contingency management by the adjustment of norms and values to minimize conflicts and maximize personal gratification of individual family members. Internal consistency of norms, minimum conflict, and maximum personal gratification sustain the personal commitment of family members to one another and thereby promote solidarity. However, although contingency management is concerned with adjustment to conditions outside the group, sustaining family solidarity is concerned with the reciprocal adjustments within the group.

The definitions of the family as functional, structural, and interactional emphasize different aspects in the operation of family life which correspond to different processes emphasized by the particular definitions. The functional approach is concerned primarily with the maintenance of ends of family life (sex, reproduction, economic affairs, education of young) as contributions to the total society. The functionalists thereby emphasize the establishment and revisions of liaisons with other institutions. The structuralists are concerned with the different ends that maintain a similar organization of family statuses. The structuralists are thus interested in maintenance of traditional statuses when family functions in the society change. As noted earlier, their focus is on the extent to which commitment to traditional patterns of family organization influences other institutions in the society. The interactionists have been concerned specifically with the norms, values, and techniques of tension management related to solidarity in contemporary family life. Much of the concern of the interactionists has been with personal adjustment in the family and marital adjustment as indices of solidarity. Thus the universal functionalists emphasize liaisons, the structuralists, tradition maintenance, and the interactionists, solidarity.

Among these approaches to family sociology, this book adheres most closely to the interactionist view. However, concepts and viewpoints consistent with the functional and structural positions are also used. This book sees the family as a collective enterprise based on relationships defined by birth and marriage; in other words, the family is essentially a kinship organization mobilized to endure. The nature of this collective enterprise varies with historical circumstances; however, like other collective enterprises, the family and other kinship groups are involved in activities to ensure orderly replacement over the generations. The kin groups are concerned with the processes of maintaining tradition, providing for contingencies of changing external circumstances, developing procedures for sustaining solidarity of members, and evolving norms to permit liaison with other groups. These processes in family and kinship relations take place through the interaction of the family members within the particular historical circumstances. They do not imply that the functions of the family are basically the same everywhere or that *the* family is identified by a unique structure, departure from which is necessarily a decline in the importance of the family as a social institution. The viewpoint of this book and the description of general kinship processes are elaborated on in Chapter 2.

Readings on Sociological Approaches to the Family

The readings in this chapter are presented to illustrate the three approaches to family sociology described in the introductory statement. The functional position is indicated in a paper by Levy and Fallers. Positing socialization as the basic function of the family everywhere, Levy and Fallers discuss the variations in family organization required to carry out this function in different societies. Taking issue with Murdock, they question the assumption that the nuclear family exists as an identifiable unit in all societies. They contend that by focusing on the actual roles themselves, rather than on the person who carries out these roles, the relationship between family organization and socialization may be better understood.

The structural approach is illustrated by an excerpt from the work of LePlay. Historically, the structural approach was developed by LePlay between 1850 and 1875. He regarded the family as the basic unit in society. His concept of the stem family indicates how the variation in content of family roles may affect the personal destinies of family members. Whereas the Levy and Fallers paper pertains to a wide range of societies, the LePlay discussion focuses on family life in Western civilization. LePlay describes the historical situation conducive to the development of familism as a value in society.

The interactionist approach is described in the paper by Stryker. The Levy and Fallers paper is concerned with broad, cross-cultural generalizations of theoretical interest, but Stryker emphasizes the personal and social problems emerging from interaction in the family. He regards interactionist theory as appropriate to the study of, first, the acquisition of ways of behaving and, second, the organization of persistent behavior patterns. Specific areas of research interest include differential commitment of persons to their "family" identities, the consequences of this differential commitment for interaction both within and outside the nuclear family, effects of extra-family identities on family interaction, the relationship of crises to identity, and sequences in role-taking activity over the family life cycle.

1. The Family:

Some Comparative Considerations*

BY MARION J. LEVY AND LLOYD A. FALLERS

IN ORDER TO CARRY OUT comparative analysis, one clearly requires concepts on the most general level which are applicable to any society. The concept "family" is commonly used in this way; that is, it is commonly assumed that in every society there is something called "the family." We feel, however, that the concept as it is most often used is ill-adapted to comparative analysis. It is usually assumed, either implicitly or explicitly, that in every society there is a single social unit which is invariably associated with certain functions. It may even be assumed that this unit is everywhere structurally the same.

Now progress in the field of comparative analysis of societies has regularly involved clearer distinction between structure and function and between concrete social units and analytically distinguishable aspects of such units (Levy 1952). The political field provides a case in point. The term "political system" in its common-sense Western meaning refers to a series of specialized concrete social units (bureaucracies, legislatures, courts, parties) with particular structural forms

(hierarchical in the case of bureaucracies, collegial in the case of legislatures, and so on) and having particular functions with regard to the exercise of power and authority (adjudicating disputes, making decisions, securing consent). However, a concept like this is of little use comparatively. On the one hand, by this definition many societies simply do not have "political systems." In many societies a single social unit—perhaps a unilineal kinship group—may combine the functions of "church," "state," and "firm," and it will very likely differ greatly in structure from any of the specialized political units characteristic of the modern West. On the other hand, the above type of definition of "political system" tends to obscure as much as it reveals even within the systems to which it is indigenous. Even the specialized political units of the modern West have nonpolitical aspects, while other units, not of specialized political nature, nevertheless have political aspects. It is only when these distinctions are recognized that the political systems of the full range of human societies become commensurable.

As applied to the political field or to most other fields of comparative interest, distinctions of this kind are commonly made and, indeed, seem obvious, but in comparative studies of the family they seem to be considered unnecessary. Undoubtedly the reason for this is the apparent empirical ubiquity of small, kinship-structured

SOURCE: American Anthropologist, *Volume 61* (*August, 1959*), *pp. 647–651. Reprinted by permission of authors and American Anthropological Association.*

* This is a slight revision of a paper presented at the 1957 meeting of the American Anthropological Association in Chicago, in a symposium on "Models for the Study of Kinship" organized by Harry W. Basehart.

domestic units having reproductive, socialization, and sex-regulation functions. In most other respects human society is empirically so variable that distinction between structure and function, between social units and analytically distinguishable aspects of them, comes quite naturally to the social analyst. But the family, it seems to be felt, is an exception because a particular set of functions is so regularly associated with a particular type of unit. Murdock, in what is certainly the most extensive and influential comparative study yet undertaken, feels able to assert at the outset, on the basis of data from his sample of 250 societies, that "Either as the sole prevailing form or as the basic unit from which more complex familial forms are compounded, [the nuclear family] exists as a distinct and strongly functional group in every society" and that it universally performs "... four functions fundamental to human social life— the sexual, the economic, the reproductive and the educational" (Murdock 1949:2–3). Murdock's position has been widely adopted, perhaps most notably by Parsons and Bales (Parsons 1954; Parsons and Bales 1955).

It is not our purpose here to question the empirical ubiquity of small, kinship-structured domestic units with reproductive, sex-regulation, and socialization functions. That there are striking regularities in this sphere seems clear. Neither do we propose to take a stand on the question of whether or not these regularities are in any sense "biologically based." Rather we propose to argue that, in spite of such considerations —in a sense just *because* of the temptations to conceptual shoddiness to which apparent empirical regularities in the family sphere expose us—it is desirable to preserve in this field the conceptual distinctions which have proved so necessary in the comparative analysis of other aspects of human society.

Let us assume, then, that small, kinship-structured units are universal—are indeed structural requisites of any society. Functionally, socialization would appear to be the heart of the matter. Parsons and Bales have argued with great cogency that socialization requires small units and that completely non-kinship-structured small units are unlikely to carry out the function effectively (although of course human ingenuity may devise alternatives). Of the other "universal functions" attributed by Murdock to the family, reproduction and sexual regulation would appear to be associated with, and probably secondary to, socialization. Parsons' argument here seems to us convincing (Parsons 1954). Murdock's remaining "universal function"—the economic—seems to us to be on an entirely different level. It is not so much that families universally fulfill economic functions vis-à-vis other units and the society at large; clearly, the degree to which and the ways in which they do so are subject to enormous variation. Rather, the point would seem to be that families, like other social units, must make provision for the distribution of goods and services—that, like other units, they have economic aspects. If families are universal, probably because of their usefulness as socialization devices, then indeed in every society they have economic functions. It would appear to be the socialization function, however, which lies at the root of the requisite nature of families.

But, assuming that small, kinship-structured units are structural requisites of any society, and assuming that they are so because socialization requires it, it does not follow either that (a) there is a single such unit in every society ("*the* family") which carries out every aspect of the socialization function and its associated or derivative functions or, still less, that (b) in every society this unit is the nuclear family. We do not believe that either Murdock or Parsons has shown these statements to be true. If they are not true, then it becomes seriously misleading to use the term "family" as a comparative concept on the most general level to refer to a concrete unit, to a particular structural type and to an invariant set of functions taken together. It becomes necessary to distinguish these elements so that the ranges of variation which are thereby admitted may be discussed.

Let us first consider the universality of the nuclear family as the unit for socialization. Murdock argues that, even where the nuclear family is "enveloped" in more extended domestic units, it is always clearly distinguished as a separate subunit and he rather implies that it is always the more fundamental unit vis-à-vis the "universal functions of the family." We would not deny that in most, if not all, societies persons are typically able to distinguish their own parents and siblings from other kinsmen. We do not believe, however, that extended family households always "consist" of aggregations of nuclear families—that in such households children are always socialized primarily in terms of the nuclear family subunit. This is essentially the point made by Linton in his distinction between "conjugal" and "consanguineal" families (Linton 1936:159–160). We cannot in this paper undertake to test this notion on a wide range of empirical data, but we would cite data with which we are familiar from societies which are not particularly unusual in the relevant respects. One of us has pointed out that in the traditional Chinese family children are typically socialized in terms of the patrilineal extended family unit and that within this unit the nuclear family was by no means the "strongest" subunit for socialization purposes (Levy 1955). Among the Basoga of East Africa, the typical household is occupied by a nuclear family plus odd individual kinsmen. However, the solidarity of exogamous patrilineages is strong and nuclear families tend to be split by the conflicting loyalties of the spouses. Divorce is consequently very common and hence children are very often socialized in households where only one parent is present. More importantly, even where marriages remain intact, the conflict of lineage loyalties results in a primary orientation on the part of children to the lineages of the two parents rather than to the nuclear family as a unit (Fallers 1957). The Hopi would appear to represent an analogous situation on the matrilineal side, while among the famous Nayar, apparently, the nuclear family disappears altogether in favor of the consanguineal unit (Eggan 1950:113–114; Gough 1952a, 1952b). (Thus the Nayar seem to us, not an ethnographic oddity, but merely an extreme extension of a quite widespread pattern.)

Secondly, there is the question of whether in every society there is a single small, kinship-structured unit which carried out the socialization function. Again, the traditional Chinese extended family would seem to represent a relatively common contrary case. Young children tend to be socialized almost exclusively by mothers and grandmothers; later the sexes divide, boys associating primarily with adult males and girls with adult females. Thus, at various times and with regard to the two sexes, different subunits emerge as primary for socialization. Among the matrilineal Ashanti of Ghana, it is quite clear from Fortes' material, the typical child is primarily oriented during one phase of socialization to a consanguineal unit centering upon its mother and her brother, while during another phase it is associated primarily with a conjugal unit based upon father and mother (Fortes 1949).

We are well aware that this brief discussion is far from doing justice to Parsons' complex psychoanalytic argument concerning socialization and the nuclear family. From a psychogenetic standpoint, the kernel of the problem is whether adequate socialization requires the "Oedipus situation" in its full sexual sense—that is, the regular presence in the domestic unit of a cohabiting pair or "conjugal family"—or whether the mere presence in the domestic unit of adult male and female role models—an adult brother and sister, for example—is sufficient. An attempt to deal more fully with the psychogenetic argument must await another occasion, but we do feel that considerations of the sort put forward here suggest a restatement of the problem along the following lines:

It seems to us untenable to assume that the socialization function is invariably carried out primarily within a single kinship-structured unit—the nuclear family or any other—even though we assume that small, kinship-structured units are structural requisites of any society and that their requisite nature is bound up with the socialization function. This being so, we suggest that the concept "family," to be useful for general comparative purposes, should be used to refer not to a single social unit in each society, but rather to any small, kinship-structured unit which carries out aspects of the relevant functions. We suspect that, using the term in this way, one would find in most societies a series of "family" units. We cannot systematically spell out the possibilities here, but one would want to distinguish, among others, units for socializing each of the two sexes and units associated with distinguishable aspects and temporal phases of socialization. We have noted above that, while the requisite and universal nature of small, kinship-structured units probably rests upon the socialization function, once such units exist other functions come into the picture. Thus, for example, one would have to distinguish units which fulfill the economic functions arising from the existence of the socialization units; there is no reason to assume that these units would be the same. In Ashanti, a child and its mother may commonly live in the household of the mother's brother, but the mother may nevertheless send food to her husband living in another household.

We suggest that the concept of the family presented here facilitates a more differentiated analysis of small, kinship-structured units and their functions; that it brings the study of such units into more systematic relationship with other kinship studies; and that it facilitates the systematic comparison of such units with non-kinship-structured units. There is clearly something special about "the family"; we argue only that the study of it deserves the same conceptual care that we customarily apply to the study of other aspects of society.

REFERENCES

Eggan, Frederick, 1950, *Social Organization of the Western Pueblos*, Chicago: University of Chicago Press.

Fallers, L. A., 1957, "Some Determinants of Marriage Stability in Busoga: A Reformulation of Gluckman's Hypothesis," *Africa*, XXVII, pp. 106–123.

Fortes, Meyer, 1949, "Time and Social Structure: An Ashanti Case Study," in *Social Structure: Studies presented to A. R. Radcliffe-Brown*, Meyer Fortes (ed.), London: Oxford University Press.

Gough, Kathleen, 1952a, "Changing Kinship Usages in the Setting of Political and Economic Change among the Nayar of Malabar," *Journal of the Royal Anthropological Institute*, **52**, pp. 71–88. 1952b, "A Comparison of Incest Prohibitions and Rules of Exogamy in Three Matrilineal Groups of the Malabar Coast," *International Archives of Ethnography*, **46**, pp. 81–105.

Levy, M. J., Jr., 1952, *The Structure of Society*, Princeton: Princeton University Press. 1955, "Some Questions About Parsons' Treatment of the Incest Problem," *British Journal of Sociology*, VI, pp. 277–285.

Linton, Ralph, 1936, *The Study of Man*, New York: D. Appleton-Century.

Murdock, G. P., 1949, *Social Structure*, New York: Macmillan.

Parsons, Talcott, 1954, "The Incest Taboo in Relation to Social Structure and the Socialization of the Child," *British Journal of Sociology*, V, pp. 101–117.

Parsons, Talcott, and Robert F. Bales, 1955, *Family, Socialization and Interaction Process*, Glencoe: The Free Press.

2. Theories of Frederic Le Play

BY CARLE C. ZIMMERMAN AND MERLE E. FRAMPTON

THIS SECTION INTERPRETS and summarizes the passages of Le Play which set forth his ideas on the family most clearly.

Types of Families*

The family presents three principal types, which correspond to three distinct organizations of society.

Familism is necessary in all complete social organization to a degree even more imperative than the need for property. Many of the very persons who refuse to consider the family a direct creation of God see in it at least a necessary consequence of natural law.

There are regions, such as the steppes of the Orient, where an individual could not live if he were isolated. There are others where the law forbids individuals to separate themselves from the family. This was the condition among the Russian peasants up to the last reforms. The settled people of the West have pulled down these

SOURCE: *From Carle C. Zimmerman and Merle E. Frampton,* Family and Society, *Copyright, 1935, D. Van Nostrand Company, Inc., Princeton, N.J.. pp. 130–149. Reprinted by permission of Carle C. Zimmerman and publisher.*

* The remainder of the chapter is adapted from *La Reforme sociale*, Tours, 1887, 7th ed., Vol. I, section on the family, pp. 380–519.

prohibitions by degrees and one of the characteristics of their society is the passing of legislation to meet the demands of the individual rather than the requirements of the family.

The advantages which certain people derive from the unlimited extension of individual desires appear greater than they are in reality. Where individualism becomes dominant in social relations men rapidly move towards barbarism. On the contrary, in model societies, individuals desire to stay under the authority of the parents. Some leading European nations grant leeway to the exceptional desires of a few individuals for non-family life. But, at the same time, they continue to hold jurisdiction over the permanent needs of the masses by keeping most of them grouped in strong families.

The principles concerning possession and transference of property show that the best way of protecting the family is to bestow extensive powers upon the family head. Primogeniture seems to give complete satisfaction to the individualist, but in fact it seeks rather to insure the well-being of each of the members of the family.

Some societies have formed more extensive social groups to which the ordinary functions of the family have been partly delegated. A notable example is the subjecting of the Russian peasant families to the community and to the chief land owner of the area. Modern societies encourage large associations of individuals. It is evident that legislators have never lost sight of the benefits of non-family groups which have proved advantageous to the individual and to the family.

The family, in its accepted form is like religion and property, an imperishable institution; but its type undergoes considerable modification. Together with religion and property the family gives each social organization its essential character. One can distinguish two extreme types, i.e. the patriarchal and the unstable families. There is also an intermediary type—the stem-family.

The patriarchal form is common among the pastoral people of the Orient, among the Russian peasants and the Slavonic peasants of central Europe. The father keeps near him all his married sons and exercises over them, as well as over their children, a very extensive authority. Except for certain pieces of furniture the property remains undivided. The father directs the work and accumulates as savings the products not required for daily needs. Among nomadic tribes this family type exists during the lifetime of the father. Among settled agriculturists the family is divided when the paternal home is no longer able to house its members. Emigration from the home is also connected with the fertility of the soil. The emigrants may establish themselves nearby or migrate to another country.

It is then that the father, from the common savings, contributes to the creation of a new establishment. It is also the father who designates the member of the family who is to exercise the new patriarchal authority. The tendency that leads young couples to desire independence is neutralized among nomadic people by the struggle for survival. The necessities of life are not utilized so as to permit individuals or small groups to subsist in isolation. This individualist tendency is counteracted among settled agriculturists by the feudal organization of their society, and in both pastoral and agricultural families by the moral traditions.

Family beliefs are in part strongly religious or magical in origin. Religion maintains the respect for established order more than it develops the spirit of initiative. In this religious state of material as well as moral restraint, the community regulates the degree of social eminence that individuals can attain in an independent situation. It also enables the individuals who are less moral, less clever, and less willing to work to participate in the common well-being.

The unstable family prevails now among the working populations who live under the factory system of the West. It is multiplying among the wealthy classes of France under a group of influences, the most important of which is forced division of inheritance. The family increases at first, but decreases later as the children, freed from all obligations toward their parents and relatives, establish themselves outside the family. It dissolves finally at the death of the parents and the dispersal of the children. Each child disposes freely of his dowry and enjoys exclusively the fruits of his labor. Under this régime the individual, single or married, finding it no longer necessary to provide for the needs of his relatives, rapidly attains a high position, if he is capable. On the contrary, if he is incapable or unfortunate he is not able to call upon any family help in case of need. Thus, he falls more quickly into a miserable condition. Unhappily this depraved condition tends to perpetuate itself because parents can no longer contribute further to the establishment of their children or because the children are not under parental guidance. Thus is formed that peculiar social state which history has not often disclosed before—pauperism.

The stem-family develops among all people who combine the benefits of agriculture, industry, and settled life with the common-sense idea of defending their private life from the domination of legislators, from the invasion of bureaucrats, and the exaggerations of the manufacturing régime. This family organization joins one married child to the ancestral household and establishes all others independently with dowries. The patriarchal family does not give the others this freedom. It perpetuates habits of work, most of the property, and useful traditions at the paternal home. It forms a permanent center of protection to which all the members of the family may resort. Thus, it gives a security to the individuals which they do not find in the unstable family. The stem-family arises partly from traditional influences of patriarchal life but it finally forms itself under the influence of individual property. It satisfies both those who are happy in the situation of their birth and those who wish to advance socially or economically. It harmonizes the authority of the father and the liberty of the children. It is formed wherever the family is free, and it maintains itself throughout major disruptions of the established order. In the event of the premature death of the associate-heir, all the other offspring are willing to give up even brilliant outside prospects to fill the vacancy.

In brief, European people in becoming more free and more prosperous broke up the patriarchal family, which is too much given to the worship of tradition. They also attempted to repulse the unstable family with its desire for novelty. The stem-family satisfies both tendencies and harmonizes two equally imperative needs—the respect for tradition and the yearning for the new.

The Psycho-social Influence of the Domicile upon the Family

One of the most precious traditions of the European continent is that which assures in most regions home ownership to each family, rich or poor. Customs and institutions that maintain this wholesome practice contribute more than anything else to the prosperity of the nation. Even in a relatively backward social order, it gives families a dignity and an independence that others in some ways more advanced do not enjoy.

Ownership of the domestic establishment seems to have been one of the general traits of the old Europe. With rare exceptions it still exists among the Russians, among most of the Slavs of central Europe, and among the Hungarians. The sudden invasion of the manufacturing régime has destroyed this tutelary organization in several occidental countries. However, in many rural districts the principle of the possession of the home is still maintained. Every father worthy of the name refuses to marry his daughter to any suitor who does not possess a home in his own name or have good prospects. Those populations still impregnated with the old European spirit have a truer sentiment of dignity than those of our cities who seek instead the conspicuous consumption and the material enjoyments of the leisurely class. Marked social disorders have

been the characteristic of this urban non-home owning system in the Occident since the middle of the 18th century.

In England many eminent persons have already reacted against this tendency, and have undertaken to help workers obtain the possession of their habitations. Societies which stimulate thrift among the workers and enable them to purchase homes are being formed. On the continent several mining corporations have found that home ownership betters the intellectual and moral condition of the workers. When a house and garden are put up for sale, another worker is given preference over the capitalists, merchants, and political leaders of the locality. The buyer is able to borrow, if necessary, the total purchase price from the mining administration under a property mortgage. A portion of his salary is retained for interest and amortization. Even if he never succeeds in discharging the mortgage, the Hartz miner finds the means of rising to a better condition. It gives him dignity and he accepts habits of work and temperance more willingly. In France possession of the dwelling is one of the striking features of rural life, while renting has been introduced into the cities and the industrial centers as in England. The same remedies are being tried. Societies of Patronage, such as that of Mulhouse, stimulate home ownership among workers.

The natural instinct of possession has created a strong sentiment toward saving. The worker who has become a proprietor understands the dangers of political agitation. He dreams only of rising in the social ladder by thrift. Unhappily, our inheritance laws of forced division of property disorganize the small property owner. Many houses, upon the death of the owners, have been sold as a result of our inheritance laws. The capitalists now own them and the residents are tenants.

The sovereign who could by peaceful means direct the workers toward home ownership would found a stronger dynasty than did the well-intentioned king who three centuries ago wanted to put a "chicken in every family pot."

In England the rent régime imposed upon the middle and lower classes seems to be maintained by the system of emphyteusis. Persons who wish to build a dwelling for themselves ordinarily obtain use of the ground by stipulating that the entire building will return to the heirs of the present holder after a period of 99 years. Rented dwellings possessed by the large land owners have thus a tendency to multiply. But this dependence upon a numerous class of owners is lightened in practice by excellent traditions.

Many owners consider it a crime to modify the leases. Moreover, they do not feel that it is right to subject their tenants to the competition of new landlords. It not infrequently happens that generations of owners have been operating without written leases.

These traditions favorable to social harmony had also developed under the old French régime. Vestiges of them are found here and there in the provinces. In Paris these ideas are found only among the aged. Here, few owners of houses believe that rentals should not be at market rates. The new landlords change tenants very frequently. The rigorous application of the economic principle of temporary rentals, of supply and demand prices, disorganizes social relations with reference to renting and to salaries.

The complete isolation of the dwelling occupied by each family is one of the fundamental conveniences of every civilization. Model rural populations enjoy this convenience and satisfy the needs of the most efficient type of agriculture by placing the dwelling in the center of the domain. This condition of isolation is even met with in many European towns where the high cost of land bordering upon public highways requires that the houses be contiguous. The English particularly respect this principle. In London where soil is of considerable value, the smaller "bourgeois" and often the common workers each occupy separate houses. Under this régime a city dwelling is of the type still met with in the St. Marcian quarter of Paris. Small domiciles are subdivided into stories, the outlet for each of which is a small staircase. Each story has ordinarily three rooms with a toilet.

Wherever fecundity and other essentials to the family are being maintained the most modest dwellings consist of at least four rooms. These rooms generally are used as follows: the first room by the head of the family and his wife; the second by the associate-heir, his wife and child;

the other two by the children of the head of the family and the heir, by the "single" children and by the servants, separated according to sex. The hearth where the food is prepared, near which the meals are taken, and where meetings or evening gatherings are held is nearly always situated in the room of the head of the family.

Even in certain cities where space is scantiest, this minimum of rooms is always amplified by a few store rooms used for household provisions, laundry, and other domestic necessities. In the bread-eating region of Europe, there is generally a little workshop for grinding, sifting, and baking. However, in the West most of these milling and baking functions are performed outside the home. The use of coal for baking has set up an opposite tendency in recent Belgium and England.

In the country and in the outskirts of cities, dwellings have vegetable and fruit gardens as natural appurtenances, as well as a few outbuildings for the use of domestic animals. These animals, in order of frequency, are chickens, pigs, goats, milk cows, asses, and horses. When the household crafts require it the home is completed by a workshop. This organization of the home establishment is maintained among many rural craftsmen as well as among certain urban workers.

These uses of the home, once popular in all major parts of Europe and still important in the eastern region, are often discontinued in manufacturing regions. In certain cities of England and France the home is often reduced to a single room in a damp and dark cellar. These conditions are miserable. Such societies often given evidence of forms of suffering unknown among primitive peoples living in rigorous climates.

Increased wealth, when it goes with an understanding of social laws, raises the home above the level just described. The number of rooms is increased. Special rooms are used for the preparation of food, for meals, and for customary meetings.

The families of the upper classes set aside special places for domestic religion, for intellectual pursuits, and for traditional objects of their ancestors and their family. In all cases the number of rooms were proportional to the size of the principal dwelling. Near these various establishments is kept the family tomb, a pious custom maintained in all stable societies who are preoccupied with the future life or the memory of the ancestors. This custom has not been completely destroyed in France. Many Protestant communities of the region of Paitou have no interfamily cemeteries. Thus at St. Sauvant (Vienne) there is no cemetery for a town of 1500 Protestants. All the dead are buried in the ground reserved for this purpose on the family domains. These customs are becoming, however, more and more exceptional.

Among people with strong social constitutions each citizen finds satisfaction in living under the roof of his ancestors. In the system of unstable families the opposite state of things exists. It would be easy to demonstrate that this situation is very unwholesome for private life. The furniture, the utensils, and linen of the household are characteristic elements of the household. These are suited to the habits of the family and minister to its needs. They acquire great value among families desiring refined luxury. They amount to nothing among pauperized Western families. This total absence of furniture is usually the most manifest sign of poverty in the urban family.

Among the traditional people there exists a minimum of comfort and well-being, below which families do not consent to go. Young girls refuse to marry until, with the help of their future husbands and of their parents, they have succeeded in securing a normal amount of furniture, without which the new family could not aspire to public consideration.[1] Public opinion is very exacting. The youth feel inspired to work and save in order to marry. Possibly severe conditions imposed by the mores concerning marriage are the surest way to make all western workers desire to escape from the effects of pauperism, and, in general, to raise the living conditions of all classes of society.

The most commendable traits pertaining to the organization of the French home were met both in the cities and in the Provinces under the

old social régime. Even the most modest families lived alone in their own houses. Unfortunately, since the end of the 17th century, the relaxing of the mores and, since 1793, the new inheritance code have altered this tradition profoundly. Today, as in every other period, the man who has desires to rise in the social scale tends to build a dwelling proportionate to his fortune. But his children do not wish to live with their father and are still less capable of living in the home after his death. They are not financially able to live there alone. The usual solution is to sell the paternal home. Thus, many families are tenants in dwellings built by their ancestors. These old homes have fallen into the hands of the newly rich.

Further, coparceny has a tendency to lower the level of private living. The children when adult leave the paternal home. The non-traditional couples give birth to fewer children. The room required by these sterile families is more and more limited. Owners of old houses are interested in subdividing them in order to rent more rooms. This creates collective dwellings. It is understood that the general cost of this type of enterprise would be reduced by increasing the number of the tenants in each establishment. But these immense apartment houses violate all housing conditions from the familistic point of view.

A modern apartment house in Paris intended for a family of modest means is usually built with the luxury that was once used only for palaces. It is composed of floors, several stories high. Splendid staircases lead to an interior yard, to the rooms, and to the streets. Each story has several apartments lighted from the yard or the street. The families lose their privacy, not only by their proximity to one another and by the common use of the stairs, but by the dividing of each floor into two or three apartments. Often part of the service is located on the ground floor. In many cases the servants, and sometimes the young boys of the family, occupy rooms spread out here and there through the house and on the top floor.

The owner rarely lives in his apartment. He delegates his authority to a special agent called a "janitor," whose function is nearly unknown in the rest of the world. The janitors inconvenience

---

[1] The monographs published in *Les ouvriers européens* and in the volumes of *Les ouvriers des deux mondes* present detailed inventories of the furniture and the clothing as well as brief descriptions of the family dwellings.

the family by adding to the bothersome habits of the keeper and by promoting the sneaking ways of the dissatisfied servant.

This sort of promiscuity tends to influence the morals of the family and weaken the authority of its head. The servants corrupt one another. With the help of the janitor they often form a sort of clan which foments the spirit of insubordination. These feelings are bred in the children, who come in contact with the servants. Thus, the family tends to be weakened.

People of tradition are inspired by sentiment in the establishment of their dwellings. They do not give way to the spirit of speculation, to the fancies of fashion, and to the vagaries of architecture.

The Social History of the Stem-Family

Let us see how stem-families are founded, maintained, and how they contribute to the power of the state and to the expansion of the society. When young men see uncultivated and unoccupied territories close to the place of their birth, they wish to found new homes. They leave the paternal home as soon as they are able and with the help of the parents and the associate heir establish themselves anew. The clearing of the soil always offers work and generally some income from the sale of the timber. Under these conditions the United States has been developing rapidly for the past two centuries. Many writers have been led to see in the proximity of uncultivated territory the principal incentive of the expansion of a nation. This view is based upon a superficial appreciation of the causes of social development.[2]

The prosperity of 17th century New England was assured by those who, because of their religious beliefs, their understanding and their virtues, really formed the élite of Europe. In the conquest of civilization the predominance of moral over material force is once again seen here. The presence of timber or vacant land does not guarantee a strong society. If the proximity of vast uncleared territories does not bring about the development of the moral and intellectual

qualities of the family, the society never becomes great. But among the people that abandon themselves to the exaggerations of the democratic régime, this circumstance is a powerful factor in promoting stability and public order. Those who cannot get along with their neighbors simply leave for the frontier.

Upon land completely cleared local agriculture offers fewer resources for the separate establishment of young couples, but one cannot conclude, as do some economists, that the increase of population, one of the symptoms of prosperity of a nation, should be counteracted by systematic sterility in marriage. Observation of the most prosperous people shows, on the contrary, that fecundity is not less necessary in order to perfect powerful civilizations. Fecundity always remains an essential law of the family in the best social organizations.

Each year these people improve their agriculture and develop their industries. The remainder of the population is employed in the army and in the various occupations which deal with the intellectual and moral amelioration of the group. Some go to the colonies. This regulation emigration should not be considered a hardship or as a painful necessity imposed upon the population.

This belief in the bad influences of emigration or the objections which people raise against it, like many other false beliefs, prevail only among the French of this period. Everywhere else and especially in the countries where the old European fecundity has endured, families appreciate the benefits of emigration. They are eager to emigrate. Government must in general moderate rather than stimulate this propensity. There are no longer, moreover, any material obstacles against colonization; navigation establishes rapid and economic communication between the principal centers of civilization and territories that formerly remained subject to abandonment and barbarism. There are, so to speak, no more inaccessible areas on our globe, and already settlers from England go to Australia as easily as Russian settlers go to Siberia and American settlers to the Western prairies and the California forests.

These influences appear at their height in the stem-family; they endow the members with a

[2] Manchuria and the Japanese, for instance. (Editors.)

nobility which also distinguishes their offspring. Stem-families of central Europe are generally fecund and stable. They appear happy in their lot. They successfully keep at home in a state of celibacy young men who have little aptitude for marriage, and the new generation is thus obtained from a smaller number of better chosen procreators. When one compares the agglomerated populations of the West with the sparse populations of the steppes of the Far East, one sees a contrast in Europe. The stem-families of the Scandinavian states, of the northeast and the south of Germany, of the Alps, of the Apennines, of the Pyrenees, and of central France often have ten to twelve children per couple. It is rare to meet with more than four among patriarchal families in Russia and in the countries of Oremburg and Siberia, where the custom of precocious marriages prevails. In these countries of the north and of the west the new families have the most praiseworthy organization. These families of the stem type, once formed, resist the influences which tend to destroy them or to disperse their members.

The essential customs among successive generations of the stem-families of Europe are as follows: the stem unit dwells in the home built by the founder; the stem-family is preserved as a tangible continuous unit; and finally, the direct heirs tend to practice the same profession as their fathers.

The family increases with births. Within a period of 25 years, ten new children are often acquired. But death, emigration, and changes in the number of domestic apprentices, reestablish the equilibrium and thus keep the number of the members in proportion to the capacity of the house and the work. Some replace the vacancies left by death; and others seek positions in the army, the navy, industry, commerce, the clergy, and public administration. Among the best organized families at least one of the younger children goes to found a new home near the city or in the colonies.

If the heir dies prematurely, the widow keeps his place in the home. If the widow has no children, one of the youngest brothers, instead of emigrating, marries immediately in order to perpetuate the family. The home possesses a reserve in its emigrant members that easily fills the shortage produced by prolonged wars, epidemics, and other public calamities. This régime thus assures a head and support for the family in nearly all cases.

Thinkers who seek some new social combinations outside the family look afar for a happiness which humanity organized on the stem-family system has always had. The stem-family, indeed, answered all the legitimate instincts of humanity. This is the reason why public order prevails everywhere it exists in strength. Custom has founded it, and, where the corruption of the governing body and the law have not destroyed it, it satisfies various social aspirations. It provides a rightful place for tradition and for novelty, for liberty and for restraint, for association as well as for individualism. But the stem-family assures individuals what political parties and contemporary reformers hardly understand, namely, happiness in private life. Each member of the community enjoys in the midst of the tenderest affections the well-being acquired by the work of his ancestors. Those that are not satisfied by this certain but limited economic perspective can have their liberty; they even find help in seeking positions more in harmony with their taste and talents.

Unstable families are disorganized when the father dies leaving the children in infancy or when none of the adult children continues the paternal tradition. Stem-families, on the contrary, persist through these trials. For instance, the father who cannot at the approach of death be sure of an heir worthy of his ancestors, bequeaths the direction of the home to one of his single adult relatives.

The régime guarantees public interest as well as individual happiness; it relieves the state and community of all charges for assistance and assures help for unfortunates if there is any need. In a population organized upon the above bases, the families, after having chosen the members that are necessary to them, furnish the state their excess of young persons of both sexes, after the voluntary elimination of the feeble-minded and physically weak. These young people gifted with physical energy, moral aptitudes, professional education and even with necessary capital, are a real foundation for the enterprises of a great nation.

The régime of the stem-family developed in the Middle Ages in western Europe had not received in all our provinces the complete organization that these figures imply. Moreover, toward the end of the 18th century, it was profoundly stirred by skepticism and bad morals in the superior classes. Stem-families remained, nevertheless, in all parts of the territory. These keep the old tradition faithfully and offer the country nearly all the elements of social regeneration.

A good organization of the home not only satisfies the first needs of the individual and the sentiments of parenthood; it also establishes an excellent régime of work; and it gives birth to the richest associations in private relations and the best local form of government.

Stem-families are the basis of the northern populations. Here and there they are mingled with those that poverty has rendered unstable and very rarely with a few patriarchal families. The patriarchal types dominate only in the most northerly regions of the peninsula where the Laps wander with their reindeer herds.

Typologically, the stem-families of the north offer three principal traits. The father chooses as an heir one of his children judged the best fitted; he bequeaths the home and the work-shop by testament to the heir; and he imposes upon the heir the obligation to practice all the duties of the house father. Most families maintain fecundity so that the constant thought of the father and of the heir is how to keep up a steady flow of emigration.

The stem-families of the agriculturists are less well able to keep the social traditions pure than is the patriarchal family of the pastorals. Among the agriculturists, clergymen and public officials intervene in family action; but ordinarily this intervention is not excessive. The influence of the priest on the young is variable; it is nil during the years of infancy when moral habits are first established.

The parents repulse all persistent inclinations toward evil in their children. They take the initiative by remembering the example of the paternal home. The mother especially fights against the vicious propensities of the newly-born child. The parents then have recourse to the increasing use of reason, as the intelligence of the child develops. They take up force again when he resists. Finally, they complete the education of the adult by procuring for him, inasmuch as he depends on them, a situation fitted to his virtues and his talents. Among prosperous peoples government officials do not intervene in the family except by indirect means and by good example. The responsibility for behavior rests principally with the families. In the north family functions are the chief forms of social activity.

The stem-family type of England now shows slight symptoms of weakening. The change weighs especially heavily upon the working populations, but it tends to destroy one of the best customs of the stem-family among the wealthy classes. The fathers of families on the Continent associate during their lifetime with their heirs and thus train them by example in the practice of the best traditions of the family. In England the heir of a rich family leaves the paternal home by or before the time of his marriage and except for temporary visits re-enters it only after the death of the father and the departure of the widow. The custom of cohabitation of the father and of the heir was no longer practiced in England at the end of the 18th century.

The first three fundamental customs of the stem-family have maintained themselves for at least 14 centuries on the continental shores of the North Sea. They are altered somewhat in Norway and in Denmark, but they are maintained in their purity in Sweden and in Saxony. The large proprietors, the peasants, and the "bordiers" keep these stem-family customs in all their purity. The classes remain united by the bonds of an intimate solidarity. The city and manufacturing classes that are recruited in the country are inspired also by the feelings which come from family customs.

The Catalonian family presents all the general characteristics of the European stem-family. Here, as in other places, it wisely maintains itself *ab intestate*. A description of it will help to explain stem-family principles.

The father, conscious of his duties, directs the little society and develops its sentiments with his eyes on the future. If he has inherited nothing but the love of work, he tries with serene perseverance to acquire a patrimony. If, on the contrary, he has received possessions from his parents he feels obliged to keep and to better them. The one who neglects or loses the means of family subsistence is looked upon with disfavor and even with disdain.

Good example is the best teacher. The good conduct of the father of the family influences the work and position of the mother. The Catalonian woman, far from showing the indolence too common in other countries, is active, diligent, and thrifty. She reveals these qualities as soon as she marries and she is rewarded by the one who is her companion and husband.

In Catalonia marriage is not considered a commercial association, in which the death of one of the parties of the contract brings on a liquidation of the property. Neither of the survivors considers himself an ex-associate who asks for his due and the division of possessions acquired in common. These ideas are abhorred by the venerable traditions of the family. Sufficient evidence as to the truth of this is found in the classes of marriage contracts and those testaments given in the *Manual of the Notary*. Here we discover the terms under which a husband bequeaths an inheritance to his wife.

As a reward for the good services that I have received each day from my wife, I institute her major woman, mistress and heir of all my succession and of all my possessions during her natural life, upon the condition that she will live chaste without taking another husband, remaining in the habits of widowship and keeping her name; without taking her dowry from my succession nor from my possessions. For this reason I do not wish that my said wife should be obliged to furnish any surety as to the manner in which she will use said inheritance as a good proprietor should, nor any other which she should be called upon to furnish. As her right, she will not be obliged to prove any sort of employment, nor to give any account of the inheritance. I forbid my heir to ask her for any accounting or any pledge. Nevertheless, I wish that my said very dear wife be obliged to keep the sons and daughters which we have had in common and to pay the debts of my succession.

Besides these recommendations, the husband imposes upon his wife duties that belong only to the realm of her conscience and others that pertain to the children. He recommends especially that she close her ears to the words of corruption and obliges her, as head of the family, to give the best physical and moral education to the children.

In Catalonia the institution of an heir is in reality linked to the idea of work which must not cease. The heir is an authority who must be maintained at all cost, an auxiliary who permits the father to rest, an honored person who promises to accomplish his duties, and a depositary of venerable tradition without which there is no solid society: Finally, he is a guardian of the domestic home and a refuge for future generations.

The heir is the arm which assists the father during mature age and the stick which supports him during old age. He learns, under the paternal direction, to govern the family in whatever condition it may be. He never questions who will profit from the sweat of his brow and uses his own capital and the dowry of his wife for the dignity and prosperity of all.

Once the father is dead, there exists in the family two powers: the heir proprietor and the mother, the property heir. But these two powers, equally strong, know how to live together and function in harmony. The mother directs and the son must limit himself to executing her orders. If she wishes to rest and to keep only a nominal direction, she delegates all her powers to the heir.

Families formed on such strong bases can meet any event, and each one according to its rank fulfills its purpose. Under the direction of the father, of the mother beneficiary, or of the heir, the other sons and daughters gradually find positions; the former by taking up a profession, the latter by contracting, thanks to the patronage of the family, advantageous marriages. It is impossible to imagine more profitable customs for the future generations. For equality of sharing, even though it might offer a few advantages to the first generations, would bring about the indefinite breaking up of the inheritance and the dispersion of the family.

The father may choose one of his children who by his intelligence and conduct shows himself to be the most worthy. If he does not designate an heir, the eldest (son or daughter) who knows the century old custom[3] devotes himself to the home

---

[3] This custom was formulated into a law *ab intestate* dating from the year 1307. Catalonian law invites the testator to institute an heir having for his mission continuing the work of the family. This heir may be a stranger to the family. A legitimate part, forming one-fourth of all possessions must be equally divided among all the children not provided for. This law, respected by all Catalonians, points out the institution of an heir as the testament head and foundation.

and treats his younger brothers as his own children.

The brothers and sisters of the heir do not always marry. Those who remain single live and grow old in the paternal house which they consider as theirs. In case of the premature death of the first heir or of his children they naturally find themselves called upon to protect and direct the family. The younger single members live at first with their father, and after his death they keep the same relationship with the heir and his children; the goal of all being to increase the patrimony created by the ancestors. The heir always looks with pleasure upon a brother or an uncle living in the house; he becomes attached to the old bachelor through the family spirit, which fosters a feeling of gratitude for the care that he received from the family in his childhood. The bachelors find their happiness in the paternal house and are accustomed to bequeath to the heir the personal possessions they have acquired.

Catalonian legislators have shown a profound knowledge of the influence of the guidance of the father. The law *ab intestate*, allows the father testamentary liberty. They knew well that in his hands this liberty would not be a dangerous weapon. They thought that they should give it to him in order that he might fulfill his important duties in a better way. There are skeletons in family closets that the fathers alone know about.

Catalonia is the province of Spain which has maintained the stem-family in all its purity. It is this which unites in the highest degree the two conditions of a strong nation: the ancient devotion to the community, the province, and the country, with an energetic development of the best processes of agriculture, manufacturing industry, and commerce.

3. Symbolic Interaction as an Approach to Family Research*

BY SHELDON STRYKER

VARIOUS COMMENTATORS HAVE STATED that the ideas covered by the label *symbolic interaction* are part of the intellectual baggage of almost all who concern themselves with human behavior. On the other hand, persons identifying themselves as symbolic interactionists commonly hold that this theory suffers from general, albeit certainly undeserved, neglect. There is a good deal of validity in both views. Many social psychologists have made at least some of the ideas of symbolic interaction part of their theoretical equipment, whether or not they are aware of their debt. Yet the implications of this theoretical scheme are not always perceived and appreciated even by men calling themselves symbolic interactionists. The problem seems to be that at least some of the once-novel ideas of the theory have become for many simple commonplaces or platitudes and, like most platitudes, more likely to defeat thought than to stimulate it.

This paper is above all an attempt at a straightforward review of symbolic interaction theory. Its aim is to stimulate renewed interest in a simple, but relatively powerful, set of ideas which remain largely unexploited. It is perhaps particularly in the family field that these are open to exploitation.

The theory being dealt with has a venerable tradition, beginning at least as far back as Hegel. Modern formulations have their roots in American pragmatism, in the writings of Peirce and James. Suggestions contained here were elaborated and systematized by James Mark Baldwin, John Dewey, Charles Horton Cooley and, most important of all, George Herbert Mead. Specifically in the family field, Waller, Burgess, Hill, and Foote represent persons whose work, to important degree, stems from this framework.

There is no single orthodoxy which is symbolic interaction theory. There is certainly a hard core of agreement, and there are certainly important differences, among representatives of the position. Some see it as no more than a set of concepts serving to sensitize one to aspects of social life, some as a general theory of human behavior. The present discussion proceeds on another view, which sees the theory as addressing itself to a relatively modest series of questions.

Theory can be taken to mean a set of assumptions or postulates with which one approaches some part of the empirical world, a set of concepts in terms of which this part of the world is described, and a set of propositions, emerging from the assumptions and relating the concepts, about the way this part of the world "works" which are checked against observations of that

SOURCE: Marriage and Family Living, *Volume 21 (May, 1959), pp. 111–119. Reprinted by permission of the National Council on Family Relations.*

* A slightly amended version of a paper presented to the 21st Groves Conference on Marriage and the Family, Washington, D.C., April 15, 1958.

world. This presentation begins by noting briefly the general questions to which symbolic interaction theory is addressed, and turns successively to the assumptions underlying the theory, the concepts provided by the theory, and illustrative instances of the propositions which are the answers to its questions. It concludes by considering some of the implications of the theory for family research.

The Problems to Which the Theory is Addressed

As a social psychological theory, symbolic interaction addresses a set of interrelated questions, most of which take their place in the context of two major problems. The first is that of socialization: how the human organism acquires the ways of behaving, the values, norms and attitudes of the social units of which he is a part. The focus here is on development—that which happens over time to the human neophyte: the infant, the recruit entering the army, the student entering the university, the bride entering a new set of family relationships.

The twin of the problem of socialization is that of personality: the organization of persistent behavior patterns. Such organization cannot be assumed but must be demonstrated and accounted for. The task of a social psychology is to account for such organization insofar as it depends upon social relationships. It should be added that symbolic interaction addresses itself largely to the normal person—in the sense of the person without gross physical, physiological, or psychological defect.

To say that this position is oriented to the normal person is not to say that it is concerned only with personal organization for the theory seeks to explore personal disorganization as well. As a matter of fact, one of the strengths of this position is that it treats personal organization and personal disorganization as facets of the same problem, rather than different problems, and that it can provide answers to both without invoking principles lying outside its theoretical scheme.

These are the major problems which symbolic interaction theory seeks to resolve. They have been stated in general form, for more specific formulation depends on the assumptions and concepts with which the theory approaches the parts of the world in which it has interest.

Assumptions

The initial assumption is that, insofar as interests are social psychological, man must be studied on his own level. The position of symbolic interactionism is antireductionist; it argues that valid principles of human social psychological behavior cannot be derived from, or inferred from, the study of nonhuman forms. This assertion rests on the principle of emergence. Emergence suggests the existence of qualitative differences as well as quantitative continuities among the precipitates of the evolutionary process. If man is qualitatively different in some respects from other animal forms, it follows that principles derived from other forms cannot completely account for his behavior. The task of at least some social psychologists is to focus on that which is different in man.

A second assumption is that the most fruitful approach to man's social behavior is through an analysis of society. This assumption involves no assertion of some metaphysical priority of society over the individual. Social psychologists of one stripe have argued that society is *the* ultimate reality; social psychologists of another variety give ontological precedence to the individual, denying the reality of society. Either position leads to confusion and contradiction. Symbolic interaction has not resolved the argument; but it has bypassed it. It has done so by beginning its analyses with the social act. Its basic unit of observation is interaction, and from interaction both society and individual derive. It is worth noting that this formulation permits an articulation between sociology and social psychology which alternative frameworks can forge, if at all, only with great difficulty. Both begin with the same "building bricks": social actions. Sociology builds in one direction to the behavior of collectivities. Social psychology builds in another direction to the behavior of individuals. Those whose problems bridge the two fields, as is true of many students of the family, are provided with a framework facilitating movement from one level to the other, allowing systematic transactions between the two levels.

A third assumption concerns the equipment with which the newborn enters life. The human infant is, from this point of view, neither social nor antisocial, but rather asocial. It has the potentialities for social development. It is an active organism, it has "impulses," but these impulses are not channelled or directed toward any specific ends. Original nature is amorphous and plastic; it lacks organization.

A last assumption is that the human being is actor as well as reactor. The human being does not simply respond to stimuli occurring outside himself. In fact, what is a stimulus depends on the activity in which the organism is engaged; objects become stimuli when they serve to link impulses with satisfactions. The environment of the organism is a selected segment of the "real" world, the selection occurring in the interests of behavior which the human being himself has initiated. It is this assumption which leads to the fundamental methodological principle of symbolic interaction: the demand that the investigator see the world from the point of view of the subject of his investigation.

These seem to be the assumptions underlying symbolic interaction theory. Not an assumption, but closely related to those discussed, is predilection on the part of adherents of this theory to stay close to the world of everyday experience. The viewpoint develops out of such experience, and it is with such experience that it seeks to deal.

Major Concepts

An assumption of this theory, again, is emergence. The principal emergent on the human level is language behavior. The initial concern in this review of concepts thus must be with language and its correlatives.

The starting point is with the *act*: behavior by an organism stemming from an impulse requiring some adjustment to appropriate objects in the external world. A *social act* is one in which the appropriate object is another individual. But another individual does not "stand still"; he, too, acts with reference to the first actor. Thus every social act implicates at least two individuals, each of whom takes the other into account in the processes of satisfying impulses. Since such acts occur over time, they have a history. This makes possible the appearance of *gestures*, defined as any part of the act which stands for, or comes to be a sign of, those parts of the act yet to occur. Thus, in responding to one another, individuals may be involved in what Mead called a "conversation of gestures": they may come to use early stages of one anothers' acts as indicators of later stages. Such gestures have meaning. Vocal sounds can serve as gestures, and they too may have meaning. The meaning of a gesture (an early stage of an act) is the behavior which follows it (the later stages of the act): meaning is, by definition, behavior. Some gestures have an additional property. They may mean the same thing, imply the same set of subsequent behaviors, to the organism which produces the gesture and that which perceives it. When this occurs, the gesture becomes a *significant symbol*. To illustrate: the cry of the infant may serve as a sign of hunger to the mother, and she responds by feeding the infant. The cry is a gesture whose meaning lies in the parental response. At a later stage, the child may call out "milk!" and, unless the appropriate parental response is made, protest vigorously. The word "milk" is here a significant symbol. Language, basically, is a system of significant symbols. This is equivalent to asserting that language is a system of shared meanings, and this in turn implies that language is a system of shared behavior. Communication between human beings presupposes these characteristics of language symbols.

Retreat is necessary before going forward. Symbols arise in the context of social acts, and they function in completing acts: they reflect the interests from which the acts stem. We respond to symbols as predicters of further behavior, our own as well as that of others. Since these symbols predict later behavior, they provide a basis for adjusting our activity before that later behavior has occurred. Thus symbols may be said to function in the context of the act in place of that which they symbolize, and may further be said to organize behavior with reference to that which is symbolized. Symbols entail a plan of action. To illustrate and summarize:

Thus if one hunter shouts to another, "A duck!" the second hunter immediately looks into the air and makes appropriate preparations for shooting at a bird on the wing. If the first hunter shouts, "Rabbit!" his partner responds in a different manner. Language symbols do not merely stand for something else. They also indicate the significance of things for human behavior, and they organize behavior toward the thing symbolized.[1]

Some symbols represent generalizations of behavior toward objects; these are *categories*. To categorize is to apply a class term to a number of objects, to signify that a number of different things are, for certain purposes, to be treated as the same kind of thing. Classification or categorization is essential to activity, for life would be impossible if one were forced to respond to every object in the world as unique. Class terms, or categories, are of course symbols, and as such they share the characteristics of symbols. They have meaning, they are cues to behavior, and they organize behavior.

Humans respond to a classified world, one whose salient features are named and placed into categories indicating their significance for behavior. In short, humans do not respond to the environment as physically given, but to an environment as it is mediated through symbols —to a *symbolic environment*. Persons frequently enter situations in which their behavior is problematic. Before they can act, they must define the situation, that is, represent it to themselves in symbolic terms. The products of this defining behavior are termed "definitions of the situations."

A particularly important kind of category is that called "position."[2] Positions are socially recognized categories of actors, any general category serving to classify persons: father, sergeant, teacher are positions by this usage, as are playboy, intellectual, blacksheep.

The significance of such categories is that they serve to organize behavior toward persons so categorized. An equivalent assertion is that in attaching one of these position designations to a person we are led to expect certain behaviors from him and we behave toward him on the basis of these expectancies. To the expectations with regard to behavior attached to a position the term "role" is given. These expectations are social in the same sense symbolic behavior is always social: the ultimate meaning of the positions to which these expectations apply is shared behavior. They are social in another and most important sense, namely, that it is impossible to talk about *a* position without reference to some context of *other* positions: one cannot talk about the behavior of father except with reference to the positions of mother, child, and so on. Thus every position assumes some counterposition, and every role presumes some counter-role. To use the term "role" is necessarily to refer to an interpersonal relation.

The discussion of categories has been couched in terms of an actor responding to objects in the external world, including people, by classifying them in functionally relevant ways. Under certain circumstances, an actor may apply such categories to himself; he may respond to himself as he responds to other people, by naming, defining, classifying himself. To engage in this kind of behavior is to have a *self*. Self can be defined in various ways, each calling attention to slightly different aspects of the same activity. Mead defined the self as that which is an object to itself. Others have discussed the self as a set of responses of an organism serving to organize other responses of the same organism. It is useful in the present context to define the self in terms of categories one applies to himself, as a set of self-identifications.

However defined, self refers to activity, to reflexive activity, and not to an object, thing, or essence. It is a necessary concept, from the standpoint of the symbolic interactionist, but it is one fraught with the dangers of reification. As Robert W. White notes:

The necessity of using the concept of self does not confer the privilege of misusing it. As we use concepts in our thinking, they tend to get firmer and harder. Thought about fluid events tends to curdle and form solid clots. Before long we begin to think of the self as if it were a lump in the personality. It becomes a region, an institution, an

---

[1] Alfred R. Lindesmith and Anselm L. Strauss, *Social Psychology*, New York: Dryden Press, 1956, p. 63.

[2] Others have used the term "status" here. I prefer "position" in order to avoid the hierarchical implications of status. Positions may certainly be hierarchized, but hierarchy and position are conceptually distinct and it is important to distinguish between them.

entity. . . . In the end the self is standing like a solid boulder of granite in the midst of personality, and one's thinking about it is as flexible as granite.[3]

The self is defined in terms of socially recognized categories and their corresponding roles. Since these roles necessarily imply relationships to others, the self necessarily implies such relations. One's self is the way one describes to himself his relationships to others in a social process.

The discussion thus far has presumed but not made explicit the concept of "role-taking," or alternatively, "taking the role of the other." Role-taking refers to anticipating the responses of others implicated with one in some social act. The meaning of the concept can best be elucidated through illustration. Consider the class-room instructor who presents to his students an especially difficult conception. He perhaps finds that the words ordinarily used to cover the topic do not allow the discussion to proceed beyond the immediate issue. He then casts about for words which will allow him to clarify the conception, and so allow him to move beyond it to further materials. How shall he select such words? Presumably he will do so in terms of what he knows or guesses about the backgrounds or experiences of the students before him. He will, in other words, attempt to put himself in the place of the students; he will attempt to anticipate their responses to the words he will use. He takes the role of the other.

Role-taking may involve the anticipation of responses of some particular other. More frequently, it involves the anticipation of responses of what Mead called the "generalized other." To revert to the class-room illustration, the instructor must deal with the class not as discrete individuals but as an organized unit, the members of which can be expected to behave in differentiated yet related ways. To take the role of the generalized other is to see one's behavior as taking place in the context of a defined system of related roles. The concept of reference group, as it is currently used, represents partially a restatement and partially an extension of the generalized other concept.

In comparatively recent work, the concept of "significant other" has come into use. This concept represents the recognition that, in a fragmented and differentiated world, not all the persons with whom one interacts have identical or even compatible perspectives; and that, therefore, in order for action to proceed, the individual must give greater weight or priority to the perspectives of certain others. To speak, then, of significant others is to say that given others occupy high rank on an "importance" continuum for a given individual.

One last set of concepts must be mentioned. Symbolic interaction makes unashamed use of "mental" concepts such as thinking, volition, and self-consciousness. The case can be put in stronger fashion; its judgment is that any scheme which rules out such concepts distorts the facts of human experience. However, its usage of these terms is not traditional. Where frequently these concepts are defined in such way as to place them outside the bounds of scientific discourse, symbolic interaction defines these terms behavioristically and, in so doing, permits their treatment within the conventions of scientific procedure. Thus, thinking is defined as the internalized manipulation of language symbols. Volition becomes the process of selecting among alternatives symbolically present in the experience of the individual. And self-consciousness is the activity of viewing oneself from the standpoint of others.

The Answers Provided by the Theory: Illustrative Cases

It will be impossible, given limitations of space, to do full justice to the complexities of the problems raised or the explanations provided by symbolic interaction theory; all that can be done is to review these in barest outline.

The problem of socialization has a number of interrelated facets, among them questions of how meanings are obtained by the human infant, how the self develops and is structured, and how thinking and objectivity arises in the course of experience.

The human infant, active but unorganized, is born into an ongoing set of social relationships.

[3] Robert W. White, *The Abnormal Personality*, New York: Ronald Press, 1948, p. 140.

Such relationships are premised upon a set of shared meanings. The infant acts, but randomly; he thrashes his arms, he exercises his vocal cords. The adult responds to these actions, say the crying of the infant, by doing something to the infant—he feeds it, or changes it, or turns it over on its stomach. He will eventually find that response which will complete the act in a desired way, that is, stop the crying. There is in this situation an "impulsive" act which is, incipiently, a gesture, and there is incipient meaning as well. The incipient meaning is that part of the act supplied by the adult. In time, both the cry of the infant and the response of the adult become specialized; when this occurs, the cry is a gesture in the previously-defined sense. The significant point is that, since it is the adult who completes the act, it is he who supplies the meaning of the gesture. What kinds of completions will he supply? He is, of course, limited by the repertory of meanings available in the social unit of which he is a part. Further, the adult will have defined the situation, including his positional relationship to the infant, for example, that of father to son, and this definition will invoke the set of expected behaviors we call the role of the father. If the father is a middle-class American and if he takes the cry of the infant to mean that the infant is thirsty, his response will be to supply milk or water—but not wine or whiskey. The meanings attached to the gestures of the infant are social meanings, and they are supplied through his relationships with already socialized participants in an ongoing society.

The early activity of the child will include random vocalization. Eventually, too, he will imitate sounds others make. Others respond to the initially random vocalization by selecting out particular sounds and responding to these. They respond to the imitated sounds as well by acts which contain the adult meanings of these sounds. For the child, the correspondence between sound and meaning will be initially vague, but in the process of interaction over time the correspondence will become more pronounced. So, for example, the child may use the sound "ba" to refer to any approximately round object and, having played this game with daddy, may be led to roll any such object—ball, orange, egg— around the floor. The response of parent to the rolling of an egg—especially an uncooked one— will soon make clear that an egg is not a "ba" and thus is not to be rolled on the floor. In the course of time, child and parent will come to agree on what is and is not a ball, and thus a significant symbol will have come into existence. A sound, initially meaningless to the child, comes to mean for the child what it already means for the adult.

The "self" comes into existence in the same way. Just as the sound "ba" took on meaning through the responses of others, so too the human organism as an object takes on meaning through the behavior of those who respond to that organism. We come to know what we are through others' responses to us. Others supply us with a name, and they provide the meaning attached to that symbol. They categorize us in particular ways—as an infant, as a boy, et cetera. On the basis of such categorization, they expect particular behaviors from us; on the basis of these expectations, they act toward us. The manner in which they act towards us defines our "self," we come to categorize ourselves as they categorize us, and we act in ways appropriate to their expectations.

The evolution of the self is, of course, gradual; moreover, it is continual. This development is one of increasing complexity, in a sense, for as the child moves into the social world he comes into contact with a variety of persons in a variety of self-relevant situations. He comes, or may come, into contact with differing expectations concerning his behavior, and differing identities on which these expectations are based. Thus he has, through the role-taking process, a variety of perspectives from which to view and evalutate his own behavior, and he can act with reference to self as well as with reference to others. In short, the socialization process as described makes possible the appearance of objectivity. Furthermore, since these processes may be internalized through the use of language symbols, it also makes possible the appearance of self-control.

The individual, at the same time and through time as well, occupies a variety of positions in sets of social relationships. If he responded in each of these in terms of unique sets of role-expectations and self-definitions, his behavior would be discontinuous. Usually, however, there is continuity and organization among the behaviors of a given individual. The question is how such personal organization can be accounted for. The basic answer provided by symbolic interaction theory uses the concepts of self, role, and definition of the situation. On entering an ongoing social situation, one responds to that situation by defining it. This definition includes the assignment of positions to others, and thus the setting up of expectations concerning their behavior. It, further, includes an assessment of self, that is, the assignment of positional identities to oneself. Others in the situation are, of course, engaged in the same kind of activity. The behavior that ensues is a function of such definitions. A crucial question thus becomes one of the congruence of definitions, situation, role and self, of the interacting persons. Congruence permits efficient, organized behavior. Expanding this, again noting that the individual moves through a variety of interpersonal situations, the congruence of definitions, and so the behavioral expectations these imply, is fundamental to continuity of behavior. Personal organization is thus seen as a function, not simply of that which the individual carries around with him, but of the relationship between that which he carries with him—in the form of self-concepts—and the situations in which he interacts with others as these are mediated symbolically.

When one asks what kinds of social conditions foster or permit such congruence, the generalized answer is that when meanings are widely shared in a society, or among those persons within a society with whom one actually interacts, congruence is likely.

What happens when meanings are diverse among the others with whom one interacts? Reversing the above process, but maintaining the same explanatory principle, we may say that incongruities in definition and so incongruities in expectations will result, and that personal disorganization is the outcome. A number of possible types of incongruity may be suggested: conflicts or lack of coordination between self concepts and the expectations of others; conflicts among aspects of self called into play in the same situation; the temporal succession of expectations which do not articulate, and so on.

It may be worthwhile to take one type of incongruity, say lack of coordination between self concepts and expectations of others, and note more closely its relevance to personal disorganization. At the same time, the question can be raised: under what circumstances do identities change? Suppose one enters a situation with a set of self identifications which include the name "professor," and suppose he defines the situation—for example, as a classroom—in such a way that this identity is appropriate. He will then presumably conduct himself in ways indicated by that identity. He speaks in judicious, measured tones, he adopts a knowledgeable air, and so on. He can behave this way only so long as his audience accepts this definition of himself and so responds in such ways as validate his behavior, by taking notes, by concentrating attention upon him, by directing questions at him. Suppose, however, the audience fails to accept this definition; they think him a fool rather than a professor (although perhaps the two are not completely incompatible). They disregard what he is saying, they challenge his competency, they pay more attention to friends in class than they do to him. In short, they fail to validate his self-identification. How will he behave? It is highly probable that behaviors ordinarily inappropriate to the classroom will ensue. He will likely lose his judicious tones and become emotional. He is likely to act confused, uncertain, embarrassed, ambivalent. At the same time, since persons typically have considerable investment in identities, he very probably will attempt to defend himself. He may do so by redoubling his efforts to act the complete professor, by dismissing the incident as a joke, by regarding the audience as consisting of morons. But if, persistently, his identity as professor fails to be validated by others, he cannot retain that identity. Others validate identities by behaving in appropriate ways, ways which provide cues on the basis of which further performance in terms of the identity is possible. If these cues are not provided, then such performance is no longer possible, and the identity will fade.

Implications for Family Research

Rather than attempt to detail implications of symbolic interaction for family research, a few brief indications of researchable questions stimulated by this theory will be presented.

One question, or set of questions, has to do with differential commitment to family identities. It is obvious, for example, that not all persons who are objectively fathers are equally committed to such an identity. What accounts for such differentials, for the fact that for one man identity as father supersedes all other ways in which he sees himself, while for another the father identity is relatively low on the self totem pole? The theory suggests that this will be a function of the extent to which one is defined by significant others as a father. It also suggests that the degree of congruence of definitions by significant others will be of import. Borrowing a phrase from studies of political behavior, could the presence or absence of "cross-pressures" deriving from others with whom one interacts account for this differential commitment, at least in some degree?

Perhaps of greater significance to students of the family is the question of the consequences of differential commitment to familial identities. Foote[4] has contended that differences in motivation of role performances may fruitfully be seen in these terms. Political apathy seems to be in good part a consequence of lack of commitment to a clear-cut political identity; it seems reasonable to suspect that apathetic familial behavior has a similar source. It is also quite possible that, for example, the prediction of divorce would be on sounder ground when questions dealing with commitment to family identities are included in batteries of predictive items.

Closely related to these questions is another set. Are there extra-familial identities which are in varying degree compatible with familial identities? What are the effects of identities deriving from diverse spheres of activity on one another, and on behavior in these diverse spheres? Someone has suggested that the deviant behavior of a man in a work situation which appears to be idiosyncratic when viewed in this limited context, may rather be a consequence of his position and role within his family. That is, for example, the rate-buster on the job may not be acting "selfishly," but may simply be acting in accord with his conception of self as family breadwinner. It is certain that one's extra-familial identities operate within the family situation. Which identities so operate, their specific mode of articulation with family identities, and their consequences for family relationships are questions of obvious importance.

Another set of questions can be phrased around the relationship of crises to identity. Crises will always threaten identifications, for the latter depend on stable activities of others with reference to oneself; and crises are likely to be important in the process by which identities change. It may be that adaptation in crisis situations is a function of the ease with which identities alter; adaptation to the death of a spouse, for example, might profitably be approached in these terms. Yet that ease with which identities are altered is not always functional is suggested by Hill's research on war separation and return;[5] in such multi-phased crises it may be that, at least for some, easy alteration of identity at one point creates problems at still another point. Such questions, too, are worth the research energies of students of the family.

A different kind of question suggested by the theory may be prefaced by relating an overheard conversation. A young lady was speaking of her relationships with her boy friend. The two were, apparently sufficiently involved to talk about marriage and their future. But, it seems, they argued when they engaged in such talk. The basis for the argument was this: she labelled such talks "plans," he called them "dreams," and each bridled at the other's conception of their conversations. Nonsense? Arguing over mere words? Not when one has in mind the significance of defining behavior and the consequences of classification. Plan implies a greater stake in a projected course of action than does dream. Dreams suggest freedom of action, plans a commitment. Suggested here is the potential fertility of studying the courtship process, marital role relationships, parent-child relationships, and so on, in terms of role-linked symbolic behavior: for example, the investigation of possible sex-linked differences in defining family situations,

[4] Nelson N. Foote, "Identification as the Basis for a Theory of Motivation," *American Sociological Review*, **16** (February, 1951), pp. 14–21.

[5] Reuben Hill, *Families Under Stress*, New York: Harpers, 1949.

and the consequences of such differential definitions as may exist.

Finally, the theory suggests that studies focusing on the role-taking process may be rewarding. Role-taking is a variable; anticipation of the responses of others is not always correct. Foote and his associates have conducted an impressive series of studies[6] designed to uncover means by which role-taking ability can be improved, on the assumption that role-taking ability, or empathy in their language, is one aspect of interpersonal competence. While this may well be justified, some research[7] indicates that if one expects that interpersonal adjustment will always result from accurate role-taking, he is likely to be disappointed. But this still leaves open questions of the specific consequences under varying conditions, of role-taking accuracy. Are the consequences the same, for example, when husband and wife share the same value framework and when they do not? Might it not be that accurate role-taking differs in its consequences as role relationships change, when a couple moves through the sequential stages of courtship, early marital experience, and later family experience? These, too, are questions worth raising and answering.

One final remark: symbolic interaction is not a general theory of human behavior. That is, it does not incorporate all the variables presumably important in accounting for human behavior, but rather selects from these a few for concentrated attention. Thus it would not do to deny the contributions of alternative theoretical views from which human behavior can be approached. It is contended, however, that alternative views can be enriched by taking into account the set of ideas which have been developed.

[6] Nelson N. Foote (ed.), *Developing Interpersonal Competence: A Manual of Procedures for Family Life Educators*, unpublished manuscript.
[7] See, for example, Sheldon Stryker, "Role-Taking Accuracy and Adjustment," *Sociometry*, **20** (December, 1957), pp. 286–296.

Chapter 2

Kinship and Family

Sociologists and anthropologists often differ in their emphases on family and kinship. Sociologists have focused their studies of domestic institutions in twentieth-century industrial societies[1] on the nuclear family. The problems of marital instability and deviant socialization of children in urban settings are in part responsible for this focus. The breakdown of parental authority, the decline of the three-generation household, and extensive social and residential mobility have made the nuclear family the apparent social unit associated with birth and marriage in contemporary society.[2] Moreover, Murdock has suggested that the nuclear family is an identifiable unit in all societies.[3] These factors have caused many family sociologists to ignore kinship groups and to emphasize the father-mother-child as the basic structural unit in family life.

Most anthropologists, however, regard the nuclear family as only one of several possible kinship institutions in a society. They consider that the responsibility for replacing one generation by the next resides in the larger kinship group rather than in the nuclear family.[4] Various aspects of this responsibility may simply be delegated to the family. Positing the larger kinship group rather than the nuclear family as the basic domestic unit in a society means that the character of the individual family will vary with the type of kinship organization.

In order to retain the norms and values of one generation in the next, the kinship group must perpetuate traditional ways of life, sustain solidarity among its members, maintain liaisons with other groups, and manage any contingencies presented. The structure of the kinship group will determine how effectively it can perform these tasks.

[1] Ernest W. Burgess, Harvey J. Locke, and Mary Margaret Thomes, *The Family from Institution to Companionship*, New York: American Book, 1963; Talcott Parsons, "The Social Structure of the Family," in Ruth N. Anshen, ed., *The Family: Its Function and Destiny*, New York: Harper, 1959, pp. 241–274.
[2] Talcott Parsons and Robert F. Bales, *Family, Socialization and Interaction Process*, Glencoe: Free Press, 1955. See also Burgess, Locke, and Thomes, *op. cit.*, pp. 363–381.
[3] George Peter Murdock, *Social Structure*, New York: Macmillan, 1949.
[4] Bernard Farber, *Family: Organization and Interaction*, San Francisco: Chandler, 1964.

To the extent that there is a division of labor in these activities, the age, sex, and generation designations in the society are utilized in assigning kinship roles. The assignment of kinship roles varies with the structure of kinship groups. Those groups that emphasize membership in either the husband's or wife's kinship group (but not in both) with respect to distribution of kinship rights and obligations are considered as unilineal. In extreme unilineality, membership of an individual throughout his lifetime and sometimes long after death (through ancestor worship) resides in the kinship group into which he was born. In unilineal societies, marriage does not provide full membership in the spouse's kinship group. In bilateral systems, both the husband's and wife's kinship groups are given equal consideration in the assignment of kinship roles, and marriage gives an individual membership in his spouse's kinship group.

Unilineal and bilateral kinship systems differ in many ways. Bilateral kinship is discussed in papers on nonunilinear descent and on kinship laterality and emotional disturbance in children. In this introductory statement, first, general characteristics of unilineal kinship are discussed, then, patrilineal kinship, and third, matrilineal kinship.

Characteristics of Unilineal Kinship[5]

In unilineal kinship systems a single line of descent can be drawn from any ancestral mother or father. In matrilineal societies descent is traced through the mother; patrilineal systems trace descent through the father. These lines of descent provide a basis for common political interests, close identification, ownership of property, trust, reciprocities, and sociable interaction. They thereby facilitate the formation of groups based on common descent. The formalizing of rights and duties of descent group members gives rise to a lineage. A lineage is a corporate unit whose members are descended genealogically in a single line from a common ancestor.

Lineage organization is most developed in societies in which any government that exists depends on kinship ties for its legitimacy. In these societies the lineage is not only a corporate kinship unit but also the major political association. The more centralized and autonomous the government, the greater the tendency for the corporate strength of descent groups to be reduced. Even in those societies with strong central governments freed from kinship ties, however, social rank and property rights may still be vested in lineages. Unilineal descent groups are most in evidence in relatively homogeneous, preindustrial societies with some technological sophistication and considerable value attached to rights in durable property (as in an agricultural society like the Buganda of East Africa).

The lineage is regarded by its members as existing in perpetuity (as long as there are surviving members). This existence applies primarily to the "perpetual exercise of defined rights, duties, office and social tasks vested in the lineage."[6] When no

---

[5] The material in this section is based mainly on Meyer Fortes, "The Structure of Unilineal Descent Groups," *American Anthropologist*, **55** (1953), pp. 17–41.
[6] *Ibid.*, p. 27.

members (by birth) survive, the lineage rights may pass to affines, adopted members, or to a related lineage. The specific norms are organized to maintain the existing scheme of lineage offices, norms, rituals, and physical property intact from one generation to the next.

Although a lineage is normally regarded as a perpetual unit, actually it undergoes fission and accretion continually. "The general rule is that every segment is, in form, a replica of every other segment and of the whole lineage."[7] In reality, except for rifts and ideological differences, the segments are hierarchically organized. The older the lineage system the more elaborate the segmentation.

A lineage segment is conceptualized as a set of sibling groups related through a common ancestor. When descent is patrilineal, the paternal sibling group is vested with lineage rights and duties. When matrilineal descent is practiced, the maternal sibling group is the relevant one. This sibling group ordinarily continues as the primary reference for identity and rights of an individual throughout his lifetime. Exceptions occur when, as in the case of women in ancient Rome, lineage rights are given up at marriage.

Consistent with the segmentation principle, the structure of authority in lineages is hierarchical, with each segment having its own head. The longer the segment has been in existence, generally, the greater the authority. The segment head, who is advised by his lineage comembers, is the trustee for the whole group and its property (including the reproductive powers of its women). Lineages differ in the manner by which the head is chosen. Sometimes headship exists as a hereditary right; sometimes the head is chosen by the members of the lineage segment.

Although lineage membership has certain consequences for an individual, his domestic life is generally influenced by the lineages of both of his parents. For example, a child may belong to his father's lineage but may reside with his parents among his mother's people. In such instances especially it would be difficult to ignore the relatedness of the child to his mother's lineage even though he is not a member. Fortes calls the recognition of this relatedness complementary filiation. He considers complementary filiation as a basis for counterbalancing the authority of the descent group.[9] Although the descent group controls legal and property rights, the group of affiliation exerts its influence through sentiment, moral principles, and religious beliefs. Its effectiveness in balancing the control of the descent group is thereby influenced by its proximity and by the extent of interaction with the child and his parents.

The balance between the lineage of descent and lineage of affiliation in influencing the child has various consequences. First, the child develops loyalty toward the members of both lineages. Through this dual loyalty ultimately a network of political alliances between intermarrying lineages can be maintained. To sustain the network of lineage alliances through dual loyalties, the lineages must be responsive

---

[7] *Ibid.*, p. 31.

[8] Jack Goody, ed., *The Developmental Cycle in Domestic Groups,* Cambridge: Cambridge University Press, 1958.

[9] Complementary filiation may also become important when a lineage is in danger of dying out. An individual who is affiliated complementarily may assume the headship of the lineage. See Bernard Farber, *Family: Organization and Interaction,* San Francisco: Chandler, 1964, pp. 53–54.

to one another in the establishment of policies. Actions such as war with opposing groups, territorial expansion, creation of intermarriage ties with new lineages, and relationships with a central government must take into account the good will of lineages related through complementary filiation.

The reciprocal of the child's dual loyalty is that both lineages have a stake in maintaining stable and nonconflicting relations between the child's parents. Dissolution of the marriage would destroy the child's dual loyalty. To prevent this occurrence the lineages develop norms pertaining to marital rights and obligations of the parents and avoidance behavior of kin in situations of potential hostility.

The balance in influence between the descent and affiliation groups both forestalls conflict in domestic relationships and socializes the children to value cooperative interaction in family and kinship. The degree to which the influence of the lineage of affiliation balances that of the lineage of descent therefore affects the personal characteristics of children and, in the long run, the ability of intermarrying lineages to maintain their alliances.

Patrilineal Kinship. This section outlines the operation of patrilineages as devices for orderly replacement of family norms and values from one generation to the next. The patterns of authority, unity of the sibling group, dual loyalty, and minimizing potential conflict described in the preceding section are illustrated in terms of tradition maintenance, solidarity, liaisons between lineages, and contingency management in patrilineal systems.

TRADITION MAINTENANCE IN PATRILINEAGES. The responsibility for maintaining traditional patterns of norms and values in family life in a patrilineage generally falls to the patriarch. For example, in early Roman society the organization of the household was associated with religious activities. Each family has its own ancestral "gods," and the well being of the household depended on the patriarch's performances of rituals and ceremonies to appease these spirits.[10] In ancient Hebrew society, too, the patriarchs were charged with the responsibility for maintaining the family system and religion.[11] In these societies most emphasis was given to the socialization of male children, for they would carry on the family traditions and property rights. The major responsibilities for tradition maintenance resided in the male through his authoritarian relationship with the emerging generation.

In patrilineal societies, although the patriarch is generally responsible for socialization of all members of the patrilineage, often his wife or mother assumes responsibility for maintaining traditional norms among females.[12] The mother is frequently given a position of honor and respect and supervises the activities of the daughters-in-law. In doing so, she maintains the norms of the lineage and at the same time sustains the identity of the daughters-in-law as either outsiders or as second-class lineage members. Sometimes, however, this role is accorded the father's

[10] Numa Denis Fustel de Coulanges, *The Ancient City*, Garden City, N.Y.: Doubleday, n.d.
[11] Stuart A. Queen, Robert W. Habenstein, and John B. Adams, *The Family in Various Cultures*, New York: Lippincott, 1961.
[12] Shu-Ching Lee, "China's Traditional Family, Its Characteristics and Disintegration," *American Sociological Review,* **18** (1953), pp. 272–280; L. C. Faron, *Mapuche Social Structure,* Urbana: University of Illinois Press, 1961.

sister.[13] In any case, tradition maintenance in patrilineal societies appears to be sex-linked and intergenerational.

SOLIDARITY IN PATRILINEAGES. Norms regulating solidarity among members of a patrilineage appear to be based on membership in the agnatic group, which consists of males with common male ancestors. Although the criterion for membership is lineal and is defined by descent, families are integrated on an intragenerational basis. Brothers and male consanguinal cousins band together as extended families. Although relationships with the patriarch are ordinarily authoritarian, relationships between the extended families (such as the gens organization) rest on common activities. In Rome each gens was composed of related men and had its own gods and religious ceremonies. According to de Coulanges, the members of a gens were closely united in a way that extended beyond the celebration of the same sacred ceremonies. Members of the gens aided each other in all their needs. For example, the gens was responsible for the debts of any of its members; it would redeem prisoners and pay fines for condemned members. If any of its members became a magistrate, the gens would pay expenses incidental to this office, on the other hand, when a member was accused, he was accompanied to the tribunal by the members of his gens, and these members would not plead or bear witness against one another.[14]

Other societies utilize different means for maintaining sibling group solidarity. For example, the Nyakyusa maintain unity among brothers in common ownership of cattle. Each group of full brothers has a claim to the cattle coming from the marriages of their full sisters. Similarly, links with half brothers are developed by including the half brother in the cattle ownership group.[15] Among the Zulu the unity of the siblings is symbolized by a terminology in which all siblings and cousins of both sexes within the lineage are called "brother." Children of siblings and cousins are called "my child," and their children are called "grandchildren."[16] Thus, although patrilineal groups are united under a patriarch or a chief, the major elements of solidarity lie within the sibling and cousin group organized around the male members of the lineage.

LIAISONS BETWEEN PATRILINEAGES. The liaisons between patrilineages are organized by explicit reciprocities. Levi-Strauss has emphasized the reciprocities that have developed between kinship groups and tie them together in complementary relations.[17] The complementarity between lineages is also indicated by the taboos and practices limiting aggression and by religious beliefs permitting lineages to interact and occupy a common territory and yet remain separate in identity.

In lineage-dominated societies, the lineages generally constitute political and economic systems. Economic matters appear to be central in liaisons between lineages.

[13] Monica Wilson, "Nyakyusa Kinship," in A. R. Radcliffe-Brown and Daryll Forde (eds.), *African Systems of Kinship and Marriage*, New York: Oxford University Press, 1950, pp. 131–132.
[14] Fustel de Coulanges, *op. cit.*, esp. p. 104.
[15] Wilson, *op. cit.*, pp. 133–135.
[16] Max Gluckman, "Kinship and Marriage among the Lozi of Northern Rhodesia and the Zulu of Natal," in Radcliffe-Brown and Forde, *op. cit.*, p. 170.
[17] J. P. B. De Josselin De Jong, *Levi-Strauss' Theory on Kinship and Marriage*, Leiden: Brill, 1952.

Most economic relationships between lineages are concerned with reciprocities associated with marriages and with the maintenance of households. Since the husband and wife belong to different lineages, the household becomes a focal point for lineage interaction. For example, among the Zulu each exogamous clan obtains wives from other clans by payment of cattle. This exchange of wives for cattle transfers to the husbands and their agnates the rights to the children of these wives. The children are regarded as members of their father's lineage and their rights of inheritance are in this lineage, but they also have rights in the mother's lineage through affiliation. Although they cannot inherit in the mother's lineage or become associated with its ancestors, they are permitted to drink the milk from cattle in that lineage.[18]

The reciprocities between lineages also operate as a form of control in husband-wife relations. For instance, among the Swazi, even if a wife neglects her children or her household tasks such as cooking the husband may not beat her to the point of breaking the skin. If he does, the wife will return home and her lineage will exact a fine from the husband before permitting her to return. Similarly, a husband can "return his wife" if she continually acts improperly. On doing so, he can demand most of the marriage cattle paid for her. The payments of fines (usually in cattle) or a husband's gift of cattle to his wife act as forms of social control in the marriage.[19]

CONTINGENCY MANAGEMENT IN PATRILINEAGES. Lineages develop strategies to forestall conflict in potential crises. Husband-wife relationships are important in developing adaptations for meeting potential contingencies since lineages are related to one another primarily by marriage. The etiquette associated with marriage maintains the unity of the lineage by preventing certain interactions which might otherwise lead to conflict. For example, among the Swazi, a bride and her father-in-law avoid each other. Similarly, a groom must avoid his mother-in-law. With the emphasis upon relationships between parents-in-law and their children's spouses, norms of contingency management focus on intergenerational interaction. To sustain the unity of the lineage, taboos are frequently established for affines (relatives by marriage) of the same generation. Yet, since affines of the same generation but in different lineages are often potential spouses (through widowhood, polygyny, or divorce), restrictions on these relationships are ordinarily less strict. For instance, among the Swazi, because the wife's sisters can become secondary wives,[20] the husband can treat them in a familiar manner.

Matrilineal Kinship. In matrilineal societies, activities comparable to those in patrilineages occur. Appropriate modifications, however, must be made.

TRADITION MAINTENANCE IN MATRILINEAGES. Matrilineal kinship groups differ from patrilineages in that control over tradition maintenance is often *intra*generational rather than *inter*generational. Audrey Richards found that in some tribes among the Central Bantu a group of brothers and sisters form a corporate matrilineage under the rule of a senior brother. Frequently the married sisters and their eldest brother form

---

[18] Gluckman, *op. cit.*, p. 170.
[19] Hilda Kuper, "Kinship among the Swazi," in Radcliffe-Brown and Forde, *op. cit.*, p. 92.
[20] *Ibid.*, p. 108.

the core of a residential group.[21] The political authority, affecting both tradition maintenance and accommodation between lineage members, ordinarily rests with the senior brother. Among the Ashanti, however, the maternal grandmother is the "guardian of morals."[22]

SOLIDARITY IN MATRILINEAGES. Ties between members of a matrilineage are often maintained by joint ownership of land and other property. Generally, residential rules generate problems in solidarity among members of the matrilineage. In some societies the uterine brothers form the basic residential unit, although the descent is matrilineal. Such a society is matrilineal but patrilocal (with the wife and children residing in the husband's village). The combination of matrilineality and patrilocality generates conflict because the loyalty of women is split between their husbands and brothers.[23] On the other hand, when matrilocal residence is practiced along with matrilineality, the men of a community have difficulty maintaining authority over their own descent group because they are scattered in villages associated with their wives' lineages. In either case marriages are ordinarily easily broken and the unity of the matrilineages is maintained.

LIAISONS BETWEEN MATRILINEAGES. As in patrilineage, reciprocities connected with marriage develop between matrilineages. Sexual access to women in marriage as well as rights to their household services are exchanged for a substantial payment in money or goods by the husband and his lineage group. When patrilocal residence occurs in a matrilineal society, the woman generally occupies an inferior position as a stranger in her husband's village. Custom defines the services she must perform for her husband or his brothers. If she is asked to do anything beyond these tasks, she must be paid additionally for her work. Even when patrilocal residence occurs, the wife generally has her own gardens, and members of her own lineage are recipients of the goods she produces. Both in economic interest and in responsibilities she remains identified throughout her lifetime with her matrilineage.

CONTINGENCY MANAGMENT IN MATRILINEAGES. Compared with patrilineages, rules for handling contingencies between matrilineages appear to be less well defined. Among the Ashanti, as described by Fortes, the status of in-laws is not precisely defined. No specific forms of etiquette or obligation between parents-in-law and their son's wife or daughter's husband exist. The only general rule is that the parents-in-law must be treated with respect and given assistance whenever necessary. Because of a continual threat of friction with parents-in-law, both husband and wife tend to avoid frequent contact with them. Should the wife's brother require money, he can ask the husband at any time to lend him this money. In reality, this is a loan for an indefinite period. The loan serves as a pledge of the fidelity of the wife and is returnable only if the

---

[21] A. I. Richards, "Some Types of Family Structure amongst the Central Bantu," in Radcliffe-Brown and Forde, *op. cit.*, pp. 207–251.

[22] Fortes, *op. cit.*, p. 276. This Ashanti practice may be related to their political organization. The male head is commonly assisted by a "Queen Mother," whose duties are "to watch over the morals of the women and girls, to supervise such feminine matters as girls' puberty ceremonies, . . . and to help make peace in family quarrels." (pp. 256–257.)

[23] V. W. Turner, *Schism and Continuity in an African Society*, Manchester: Manchester University Press, 1957.

marriage is terminated by death of the wife or by divorce.[24] Note that it is the brother (rather than the husband or father) who controls the fidelity of the wife. Thus potential antagonism between the woman's husband and brother is minimized by the establishment of a set of mutual obligations between them.

Readings on Kinship and Family

The preceding discussion of unilineal kinship indicates the potential conflict between temporal continuity of descent groups and the establishment of congenial domestic relationships. Many students of kinship believe that this potential conflict exists in all types of kinship systems. They are interested in corporate lineages because the norms for dealing with descent and affiliation are most explicit in unilineal systems.

Contrasts between unilineal and nonunilineal systems are so obvious that similarities between them are often ignored. The readings in this chapter indicate both similarities and differences. For example, the paper by Davenport points out instances in which descent groups, ordinarily considered as characteristics of unilineal kinship organization, also appear in nonunilineal systems. (Davenport uses the term *nonunilinear*.) He indicates that nonunilineal systems with organized descent groups tend to have certain attributes. Like lineages, the nonunilineal descent groups have a name, hold property, and are associated with ritual. Membership in the nonunilineal descent group is based on a common ancestor (although genealogical ties to this ancestor are vague). There are also differences between lineages and nonunilineal descent groups which derive mainly from the greater prevalence of endogamy in nonunilineal descent groups. Endogamy permits the maintenance of descent group ties while discouraging alliances with other descent groups. Nonunilineal descent groups tend to be larger than lineage segments and are highly localized.

Davenport describes different kinds of nonunilineal systems associated with the presence of organized descent groups. He suggests that the utrolineal system is especially well adapted to the formation of descent groups. (In utrolineal systems the married couple may choose to belong to either the husband's or wife's lineage. As Davenport indicates, the name is derived from the Latin word *uter*, meaning *either*. This system is also called bilineal.) In contrast to utrolineal or bilineal systems, bilateral kinship is based primarily on affiliation (and only secondarily on descent).

The second paper, by Jack Goody, discusses incest and adultery in different societies. Goody describes the mechanisms employed to sustain the identity of the lineage and indicates that such concepts as incest, exogamy, and adultery have different meanings in bilateral and unilineal kinship systems. He suggests that in bilateral kinship groups incestuous adultery is prohibited as disruptive to the solidarity of the sibling group. Since no distinction is made between husband's and wife's siblings in bilateral kinship, the prohibition against incestuous adultery extends to both. Presumably, intergenerational incest would also be disruptive to the sibling group by stimulating competition for parental favor. Incestuous adultery in the

---

[24] Fortes, *op. cit.*, p. 281.

bilateral system would be more severely punished than other forms of adultery. Goody suggests that in the bilateral system incest must be discussed in terms of the solidarity of the sibling group, whereas in unilineal societies incest must be discussed in terms of the corporate descent groups. In either case, however, prohibitions against incest and adultery maintain the unity of the basic kinship group.

The crucial role of sibling solidarity in bilateral kinship is suggested in the third paper in this section. In a description of a study of the influence of kinship relations on socialization of children, Farber indicates the necessity of a bilateral sibling group to maintain family interaction conducive to healthy socialization. His finding supports the suggestion by Goody that solidarity with siblings of both the husband and wife is necessary for a bilateral system to operate effectively. In addition, his paper reinforces the statements by Davenport on the importance of filiation (rather than descent) in the bilateral kindred.

4. Nonunilinear Descent and Descent Groups[1]

BY WILLIAM DAVENPORT

FOR MANY YEARS, interest in social structure has been directed towards unilinear systems, while bilateral structures have been allowed to remain an unstudied residual category for everything that is not unilinear. Some writers (e.g. Fortes 1953:33) have stressed the universality of certain bilateral features, while others (e.g. Radcliffe Brown 1935:302) have considered the absence of a unilinear principle of some kind to be unusual or rare. Even the most cursory glance at the now voluminous literature on societies with bilateral structures reveals the great variation among them and suggests the need, not only for a better understanding of what these variations are, but also of what structural principles are being varied.

Murdock (1949:56–58), Pehrson (1954), and Spoehr (1950:3) have stressed the need for studies of bilateral social structure, and in his study of the Könkämä Lapps, Pehrson (1957) set

forth and defined the concept of "bilateralism." Also aware of the inadequacies in the current bilateral concept. Freeman (1955:7) has offered the term "utrolateral filiation" to describe some features of Iban social structure. Others have run into special problems in describing and classifying societies where the ordinary bilateral-unilinear distinctions are either inappropriate or inadequate. Most notable of these have been Boas (1920) with the Kwakiutl, Firth (1929:98) with the Maori, Gifford (1929:29–33) with the Tongans, McIlwraith (1948 I:117–162) with the Bella Coola, Gluckman (1951:71–76) with the Lozi, and Goodenough (1955:73–75) with the Gilbertese.

The plan of this paper is first to survey a number of selected examples of what Goodenough (1955:72) has called nonunilinear descent groups, and then to compare these with the well-known unilinear types and with variations in the so-called kindred type of structure. In comparing these systems, however, one does not get far before it also becomes clear that a new look at the concept of descent itself, as well as the related concepts of inheritance and succession, might be rewarding. The purpose of this paper is not just to set up a series of types or to study bilaterality as a special type, but to offer at least tentatively three structural features which seem to operate in all systems, and which in their various combinations produce the rich variety of kin groupings we find described.

SOURCE: American Anthropologist, *Volume 61 (August, 1959), pp. 557–572. Reprinted by Permission of the author and American Anthropological Association.*

[1] A portion of this paper, entitled "Bilateral Descent and Descent Groups," was read at the Annual Meeting of the American Anthropological Association, December 1957. I am particularly indebted to George P. Murdock for his helpful criticisms and valuable suggestions, and also to Paul Friedrich and Verne Carroll for their critical reviews of the manuscript. However, the author takes full responsibility for all statements contained in it.

Let us look briefly at the concept of descent. This has been variously defined, depending upon the interests of the investigator and the unit of analysis with which he starts. The most common American usage seems to begin with the existence of a kin group; descent is then defined as the manner in which persons affiliate with this group by birth (see Murdock 1949:15). A similar procedure is to start with society as the unit and to define descent as a means of grouping or of dividing the society into segments of kin (see Lowie 1948:7–9, 57–59). Another approach is to regard descent as a way of ascribing jural rights by means of kinship relationships (Radcliffe Brown 1935). These several usages do not really differ essentially from each other, and each has certain advantages when it comes to describing or comparing systems. It should be pointed out that, whatever else a kin group may be, its membership is characterized by some commonality of status with respect to other groups of kin, and that descent is as much a way of limiting a social unit and excluding some persons as it is of including others. As a minimal definition, therefore, let us consider descent as a way in which statuses are ascribed and/or withheld on the basis of kin relationships. Statuses can be defined either by their associated behavioral roles or in legal or quasi-legal terms.[2]

A rule of descent will be considered unilinear when ascription through a specified kin relationship approaches a frequency of 100 per cent and when the norms of the society do not under normal conditions provide alternatives. Emphasis is placed on normal conditions, for few if any societies are so rigid as not to provide alternatives for special situations (e.g. adoption, *ambil anak*). The matrilineal and patrilineal subtypes are well known, but it is well to keep in mind that these are not the only unilinear variations that have been described.[3]

Nonunilinear descent, then, is ascription or exclusion through specified kin relationships, but where societal norms provide more than one possibility or where no single alternative rule approaches a frequency of 100 per cent. However, nonunilinearity is not to be confused with double descent, where different statuses are ascribed by different unilinear rules (e.g., Ranon, Arunta; see Lowie 1948:58–59, 260; Murdock 1949:50–52).

A major step toward better understanding of bilateral social structure was taken by Goodenough (1955:71–72) when he differentiated between two types of groups on Onotoa in the Gilberts and at the same time untangled the terminological confusion in the use of the term "kindred." Following American usage and a precedent which seems to have been established by Phillpotts (1913:5) in her study of Teutonic kin groupings, Goodenough retained the term kindred for the kind of nonperpetuating kin grouping we have in the United States, namely, a set of kinsmen who are related through males and females within a specified degree of collaterality to a particular common relative. Different from the kindred is a group in which the members trace their relationship lineally through either or both sexes to a common known or unknown ancestor; Goodenough aptly called this the "nonunilinear descent group."

These nonunilinear descent groups resemble unilinear ones in several ways. For instance, the members believe they are descended from a

---

[2] Cf. Hoebel 1954, pp. 46–63; Linton 1936, pp. 113–131; Radcliffe-Brown 1935. It is to be noted that status by definition refers to a relationship between individuals and groups with respect to a single class of objects or persons. An individual's total participation, then, consists of a collection of these statuses (i.e. relationships), each of which may have been assigned by or assumed under a different principle or organization. Of particular value here are Hohfeld's (Hoebel 1954, p. 48) four fundamental legal relationships, with which the idea of ascription and exclusion can be simultaneously expressed.

[3] Chinnery (n.d. pp. 17–19, 71–73, 78–81) reports a descent system among the peoples around Moewe Haven of the south coast of New Britain in which the male children affiliate with the father's exogamous group and the female children affiliate with the mother's exogamous group. Nimendajú (1939, pp. 21–36) reports that the Apinayé have localized matrilineal moieties, regulating sports and names, while marriage is regulated by four exogamous "sides" or "parties," in which sons affiliate through their fathers and daughters through their mothers. Wagley and Galvão (1948, p. 171) also describe agamous ceremonial moieties and eight preferentially endogamous "feast groups" for the Tapirapé. In these latter groups males affiliate through their fathers and females through their mothers. These three systems might be termed "parallel descent."

common ancestor, though frequently they cannot state the precise genealogical connections; the groups are commonly named and have identifying emblems; land and other productive property are to be found under their collective control; and often myth, ritual, and religious beliefs are closely associated with them. Marriage may also be regulated by group membership, but more often than not exogamy does not prevail. To be sure, the Mangaian *kopu* is exogamous, with maximal extension to both mother's and father's groups,[4] but on the other hand, the Kwakiutl *numaym* is actually agamous, even though marriages are preferentially exogamous.[5] The Bella Coola *minmint* is also agamous, but with endogamic marriages preferred.[6]

The fact that these descent groups are not all exogamous divests them of a feature that has often been used to characterize the clan and sib (see Lowie 1948:9; Murdock 1949:47), but it must be remembered that there are many instances of agamous or even preferentially endogamous unilinear kin groups. The Tikopian *kainanga* (Firth 1936) and the Arab lineages are but two well-known instances. Admittedly, an endogamous kin group is quite different from an exogamous one, and the consequences of this difference become especially significant in the case of nonunilinear kin groups. Nevertheless, we should bear in mind that all or nearly all societies prescribe both exogamy and endogamy in accordance with various principles, including such diverse ones as age, race, social class, religion, and kinship.

Nonunilinear descent groups resemble unilinear ones in still other structural characteristics. One finds restricted segments of larger groups that seem to correspond to the lineage divisions of unilinear descent groups. For example, prior to 1746 the Highland Scottish clan, an endogamous nonunilinear descent group and not a unilinear clan, was frequently segmented into smaller lineage-like divisions called septs on the basis of descent from particular clan members (Adam 1952). The exogamous *'aiga sa* of Samoa has

similar segments based on the same principle,[7] and in both these cases the smaller divisions organize and control activities that the larger descent group does not. One also finds nonunilinear descent groups compounded into phratries or moieties for special purposes. The New Zealand Maori *iwi* is made up of constituent *hapu* on the basis of legendary associations,[8] while the Mangaian kopu are similarly linked into "right" and "left" moiety-like divisions.

Finally, nonunilinear descent groups, in combination with rules of postmarital residence, occur in localized and in dispersed or purely consanguineal forms. This is of course the distinction which Murdock (1949:65–78) has made between sib and clan for unilinear kin groups. It is pertinent to note here that it seems to be the localized forms of nonunilinear descent groups that are the more frequently described, since the kinds of activities, rights, and obligations most often regulated by them are those requiring residence and participation with other members of the group. Rules of postmarital residence, too, like those of inheritance and succession, can be thought of as systems of ascription that pertain to particular statuses or activities.

Let us now look at some of the varieties of nonunilinear descent itself. In Mangaia, affiliation with the exogamous kopu occurs through either the father or the mother, but the choice is not left to the individual. Children are assigned alternately to the father's then the mother's kopu, according to prearrangement between representatives of the two groups. In Nukuoro a similar system prevails. The descent groups, called *te-haka-sa-aluna*, do not regulate marriage, but in case of intergroup marriages the children are assigned first to one parent's group then to the other, beginning with the father's.[9]

With the Iban of the Baleh region of Sarawak, affiliation with the independent, corporate, exogamous three-generation apartment group, called *bilek*, is with that of either the husband or wife, depending upon with which the married couple chooses to reside. This means that rights

[4] All data on Mangaia from Buck 1934.
[5] All data on the Kwakiutl from Boas 1897, 1920; Drucker 1939; Ford 1941.
[6] All data on the Bella Coola from McIlwraith 1948.
[7] All data on Samoa from Ember 1958. See also Mead 1930.
[8] All data on the New Zealand Maori from Firth 1929.
[9] All data on Nukuoro from Eilers 1934, pp. 175–318; Kubary 1900.

in land, ritual obligations, and other activities which come under bilek control, as well as membership in the corporate longhouse village, are subject to some degree of choice at marriage. A couple which affiliates with one thereby relinquishes its potential claim on the other, so that there is no overlapping membership. Their children can belong only to the bilek with which their parents have affiliated, and like them, when they marry they must decide with which bilek (and longhouse group) they will live and affiliate (Freeman 1957).

On Onotoa one of the descent groups which controls land, feuding, and other economic activities, but does not regulate marriage in any way, is called the *kainga*. As in the case of the Iban bilek, affiliation is with either spouse's group, and only the one which is chosen by them becomes a possible choice for their children (Goodenough 1955). In both societies, economic factors exert some influence on the married couple's choice.

Among the Kwakiutl (southern branch) the descent groups are called numaym, and affiliation with one is dependent upon possession of a summer potlatch name that traditionally belongs to the group. Residence with and use of numaym lands are also contingent upon possession of the name. A man acquires his name from his father, from a close agnate such as a brother or a father's brother, or from his mother's father. Only one instance is recorded in which a man actually took a potlatch name from, and participated with, his wife's father's group instead of holding it and passing it on to his son. Marriage is not completely regulated by numaym affiliation, but exogamy is preferred. In Boas' time, individuals could be simultaneously affiliated with more than one numaym through the possession of several names.

The Bella Coola have a similar descent system, with groups called minmint. As with the Kwakiutl, affiliation depends upon having an ancestral name belonging to a group. A man may receive names from a number of his paternal and maternal relatives, and may thus possess more than one. However, having a name obliges him to validate it by potlatch, and it is difficult to fulfill this obligation for more than one name. Some men do so and thus belong to more than

one minmint, but most return unvalidated names to their respective groups and thereby relinquish their claims of affiliation. Here again a choice of descent is made among alternatives, and relative social and economic advantages seem to influence the choice. Since marriage is preferentially within the minmint, endogamy tends to reduce the number of different groups among which a man can exercise his choice of affiliation.

With the Lozi of Barotseland, each person is affiliated with a "descent name" group called *mishiku*. Each of these has an ancestral village site located on a small mound that rises above the flood level of the Zambezi River. Participation with one of these groups involves living in its ancestral village, and one may choose any of the villages where his or his spouse's parents or grandparents have lived. Since the mishiku does not regulate marriage in any way, intra-mishiku marriages frequently reduce the number of possible choices to less than the maximum. Since land is very limited on these mounds, a married couple's choice is partly influenced by the availability of space for a house.[10]

The Samoan 'aiga sa is a descent group controlling garden land, house sites, and certain ceremonials. It is exogamous, since the incest taboo is extended to all known relatives. Associated with each 'aiga sa is one or more titles, from the senior of which the group takes its name. Title holders are selected from among the eligible males participating with the group. Affiliation with a descent group is through either father or mother, and a married couple may affiliate with the groups of either spouse. A person is mainly associated with one group—that with which he lives—but he may participate to some extent in several. Living with and using lands belonging to a particular 'aiga sa, as well as the right to speak at meetings of the group, are dependent upon the consent of its members, and this may be denied if there is doubt about a person's genealogical relationship to the group or if he has failed to fulfill his obligations to it. Here, too, indefinitely extended relationships through consanguinity become limited by the obligations of participation. Even though there is considerable

[10] All data on the Lozi from Gluckman 1951.

overlapping membership, the number of potential affiliations is appreciably reduced by both remissness in obligations and failure to remember genealogical connections.

This kind of nonunilinear descent is also exemplified by the Maori *hapu*. A person usually affiliates with either of his parents' or his spouse's parents' hapu, but it is also possible to obtain membership in the hapu of a grandparent and even a great-grandparent, provided the genealogical connection is recognized by the hapu in question. Such recognition depends upon the extent to which the claimant has participated in or maintained reciprocal ties with the group. If he has allowed these ties to "grow cold" they lapse, and it is difficult to maintain them with a large number of hapu. Here again potential affiliations are reduced by obligations to participate.

Nonunilinear affiliation is of course not limited to sedentary societies like those just cited. Among the Könkämä Lapps, band membership is determined through either spouse's kin relationships to the pair of male siblings who form the nucleus of the band and by whose name the band is called (Pehrson 1957). A comparable situation probably occurs in nonunilocal bands elsewhere, including those with hunting economies, but we frequently lack sufficient data to determine what the rules of affiliation are.

Several distinct trends are to be noted in the above examples. One is toward an either/or sort of affiliation, whereby an individual is assigned to, or chooses among, limited alternatives and relinquishes all other potential affiliations for himself and his children. Like classic unilinear descent, this is best understood as establishing one right of membership, albeit through the exercise of choice rather than automatic ascription, and at the same time giving up all other such rights, that is, establishing a no-right, in other groups. Contrasted with this is the overlapping kind of membership whereby a person may continue to participate, even though partially, in more than one group. Residence and social participation with a group frequently serve as either contingent or final factors in fixing present affiliation and that of descendants. Nonunilinear affiliation also differs as to whether choice for a married couple includes alternatives through one or both spouses. Possible modes of affiliation may also be narrowed by group agamy and endogamy. Variable as they are, these examples demonstrate the need for classifying such kin groups in a manner that makes them coordinate in most structural respects with unilinear descent groups.

The term "descent group" serves equally well for both unilinear and nonunilinear types, and in accordance with current usage, when they are unilinear they are called sibs or lineages, depending on internal segmentation and genealogical depth. For nonunilinear descent groups the term "sept" is proposed. Though employed by others in various senses, this term is used by Boas (1920:114–115) for the Kwakiutl numaym in an attempt to distinguish it from unilinear kin groups elsewhere on the Northwest Coast. The term "clan"[11] may be used for the localized core of sib and sept plus their inmarrying spouses and other dependents.

The fact that septs are comparable to sibs can be demonstrated by some areal distributions and the evolutionary trends to be inferred from them. The sept can be considered one of the distinguishing traits of social organization of Polynesia, for they are found in Tonga, Samoa, the Societies, the Cook Islands, New Zealand, the Marquesas, Easter Island, and Hawaii. In all these cultures very similar activities are found to be organized by this system. Among the so-called outliers of Polynesia, however, we find certain of these same activities organized by unilinear descent. Tikopia (Firth 1936) organizes some of them by patrilineal descent. Kapingamarangi (Emory 1956) regulates certain of them in part through matrilineal descent, while Ontong Java (Hogbin 1934) organizes by both, that is, by double descent. Pukapuka (Beaglehole 1938), though not strictly an outlier, resembles Ontong Java, and in addition organizes a third set of activities by nonunilinear descent.

A similar areal variation was noted many years ago by Boas on the Northwest Coast of North America, but unlike Polynesia, it cannot be assumed that this differentiation occurred within one genetic group, speaking closely related languages of a single linguistic stock.

[11] This terminology was suggested by Murdock. Cf. his definitions and discussions of "sib" and "clan" 1949, pp. 47–50, 65–78.

Let us now turn to the other major form of bilateral organization, the kindred. Here the means of ascribing and restricting statuses differs radically from that which we have termed the sept. Each person has his own kindred, the personnel and boundaries of which coincide only with those of his siblings, and siblings are members of as many different kindreds as there are kin types in their own (see Murdock 1949:56–58). In making this distinction between kin groups which are identical for siblings only and descent groups whose personnel is the same for all members, Phillpotts (1913:268, 275) used for the former the terms "shifting kindred" and "fluctuating kindred," while more recently Leach (1950:61–62) has suggested "personal kindred." These terms merit serious consideration in this area where terminological confusion has been the rule and not the exception. The term personal kindred will be adopted here, since it most clearly describes the most salient feature of this kind of organization.

One of the most complete descriptions of personal kindreds comes from the Ifugao. Here the kin group, or "family" as Barton[12] has called it, consists of all the descendants of an individual's eight pairs of great-grandparents. It may include as many as two thousand persons, many more than in most of the septs already described. In discussing legal relationships, Barton clearly shows that the only kin types with the same "family" composition are siblings. The extent of one's involvement in legal disputes is a positive function of one's genealogical closeness to the litigants. In reference to property, a rich man who owns much land has a definite obligation to provide land for his less well-situated kindred members, an obligation which decreases as a function of collateral distance. The Kalinga have a similar organization, although some form of sept may also be present in connection with the endogamous tribal districts.[13]

[12] All data on the Ifugao from Barton 1919; 1922; 1930; 1938, pp. 1–19; 1949: passim.
[13] Barton 1949. Goodenough (1955, pp. 75–76, 81) makes nearly the reverse interpretation, claiming the Ifugao have descent groups as land-holding groups, while the Kalinga have only kindreds. Although the present writer feels Goodenough has interpreted incorrectly, the close relationship between large kindreds of this kind and septs will be shown in the paragraphs to follow.

Leach (1950) presents some interesting comparative data on personal kindreds, as defined by marriage regulations, among several peoples of Sarawak. The Semambu Murut prefer marriage with kin who are more distant than fourth cousins, or just within this range, that is, with third cousins, by paying a fine for incest, but marriage with first cousins is absolutely prohibited. The Iban, however, prescribe marriage with second to fifth cousins and prohibit marriage with both first cousins and kin beyond fifth cousins.

The generalized version of Eskimo culture presented by Hoebel (1954:67–99) reveals a personal kindred range for extension of the incest taboo, obligatory action in blood revenge, and other kin-organized statuses which extends only to lineals and siblings. With the contemporary Nunamiut Eskimo of Alaska, Pospisil (1957) reports that the incest taboo is extended only to primary relatives, all other kin being eligible as spouses. Strict obligations to attend life-crisis rites and to extend special hospitality are extended to a wider range of kinsmen, including lineals to great-grandparents and great-grandchildren, first collaterals to siblings' great-grandchildren, second collaterals to children of first cousins, third collaterals to second cousins, and fourth collaterals to siblings of great-grandparents, but never beyond these limits. All relatives outside this scope, even though their relationship is known, are sociologically nonkin.

Clearly, the most variable feature of the personal kindred is its collateral limits. In the same society, moreover, different statuses may be ascribed by different degrees of collateral extension. This can occur in two ways: by a sharp break in status ascriptions across collateral lines (e.g., Iban marriage regulations and the wider extension of obligations in Nunamiut kindreds) or by a gradual transition as collateral distance increases (e.g., Ifugao land distribution and litigations).

The distinction between personal kindreds and descent groups seems clear enough if one recalls their differences in point of reference (an individual or siblingship as contrasted with an ancestor or ancestors), clarity of group boundaries (overlapping and diffuse as contrasted with distinct and discrete), and the presence of some variable degree of collateral limitation in the former and no collateral limitation in the latter. But Leach (1950) gives an example where these differences begin to fade. The Iban longhouse village is composed of a number of apartment groups, all of which are related by consanguineal or affinal ties. Consanguinity is reckoned to include fifth cousins and, at least theoretically, each member of the longhouse community should have a different set of persons in his personal kindred which is calculated to this limit. But consanguine relationships are not accurately calculated to the sixth degree of collaterality, so every member of the longhouse community acts as if he had the same personal kindred. Even though the norms of organization here are not those of a sept, behaviorally and structurally the result is the same.

Collateral limitation may be important, but in a different way, in unilinear descent groups as well. The Garia of New Guinea (Lawrence, 1955), for example, have land-owning patrilineages with considerable genealogical depth. Land may be lent to nonmembers through an affinal link, but after four generations of continuous holding in the same lineage, the jurisdiction over this loaned land passes from the lineage to which it originally belonged to the lineage of the borrowers. These changes are tied in with supporting beliefs about the destiny of the souls of deceased agnatic ancestors.

Commenting on the continuity and corporate function of personal kindred, Goodenough (1955:71) states that, because there is no continuity of membership from one generation to the next, kindreds cannot function as land-owning bodies (see also Murdock 1949:61). This argument follows only if one assumes that ownership of land is an all-or-none kind of relationship. But Hoebel (1954:54–63) and others have clearly demonstrated that ownership, whether by groups or by individuals, can consist of a number of different kinds of rights and limitations which cannot be collected under a single term with any degree of precision. A personal kindred can become a land-owning and land-holding group with continuity, just like a descent group, if the title to the land is vested in a single individual with the limitation that it must be distributed and redistributed among his personal kindred

and cannot be alienated without their consent. A member of this kindred who does not hold the title has the right to claim some land for his use and the power to approve or disapprove its transfer or alienation from the group. If there is a patterned rule of succession to the title, regardless of what form this might be, the system has continuity through time. There will be a genealogical line of title holders, at the end of which is the incumbent's personal kindred. In each generation some genealogically related persons are born outside the collateral range of the kindred and are thereby excluded from it, while those born within this range continue to exercise their rights toward the title holder.

Such a system differs very little from that which occurs in many unilinear systems where land and other valued goods associated with the kin group are held by a title holder or head of that group for distribution and redistribution to members. The nonunilinear version outlined above is not just a hypothetical case, but is exactly what occurs with the Ifugao and Kalinga.[14] In both these societies, primogenitural inheritance keeps lands intact, but each society has a different way of amalgamating lands inherited in other ways. We find related systems in European societies as well. Among the small farmers of County Clare in Ireland (Arensberg and Kimball 1940:61–157), for example, an agnatic line of title holders constitutes the genealogical line of land holders toward whom a small personal kindred have definite obligations, even though they may not be resident on the land. As a consequence of the permanence of the farmstead and the continuity provided by the line of successive title holders, the kin unit itself has a kind of perpetuity. The term suggested for this kind of organization is "stem kindred."

The features that might clearly differentiate the stem kindred from the sept become blurred in some instances, and the Tongan haa provides an excellent example. Each haa is composed of a set of kin who claim consanguine ties through males or females from a common ancestor. It is localized in an unambiguously bounded district, and each haa is headed by a noble in whose title is vested the power to distribute and withhold all

[14] See note 13.

lands within his district. The title holders of all haa are related to each other through an official genealogy of the Polynesian sort that goes back to the mythological past. Since each member of a haa claims to be related to its title holder, although he may not know what the precise relationship is, he can trace his relationship through the latter's genealogy to all title holders of other haa and through them to all members of those haa. This system functions not only in relationship to land, but also determines some everyday kinds of behavior as well. When, for example, a person meets someone from a different haa to whom he cannot trace a direct relationship, their reciprocal behavior is determined by the genealogical relationship of their respective title holders.[15]

Similar stem relationships within septs can be found in other Polynesian societies. Some emphasize an agnatic line of succession; others, like Hawaii, exhibit no sex preference but stress primogeniture alone, while in Samoa the title holders are selected from among the male members of the 'aiga sa so the genealogical relationship between them is obscure. This same kind of stem structure gives both the Iban longhouse community and its constituent bilek a special kind of continuity by way of a line of special status holders which connect the founders with the present-day inhabitants (Freeman 1955: 7–9).

While some of the examples given above were selected to reveal a number of kin group types— sib, sept, personal kindred, and stem kindred— some were also chosen to show how these types are not qualitatively distinct but merge into one another in graduated series. The summary to follow is largely a recapitulation of the features, already discussed, which seem to unite them all. It must be kept in mind that although the unit of analysis is the kin group, the ultimate frame of reference is the society, and that different activities and statuses in the same society are frequently organized by different combinations of features, so that kin groups of several types may occur. Moreover, rarely is an activity or status organized by kin relationships alone, but by kinship in combination with other criteria

<hr/>

[15] All data on Tonga from Gifford 1929.

such as sex, age, maturity, race, religion, and ability. Each of the three features presented below will be defined qualitatively as traits, although they might be ordered into variables.

The first feature is descent, of which the unilinear and nonunilinear subtypes and their measures have already been discussed. The limiting case of nonunilinear descent results in the personal kindred type of kin group, in which any and all means of reckoning relationship are utilized. This is what Parsons (1943:26) has called "multilineal" in reference to the United States personal kindred, and what Fortes (1953: 33) has termed "filiation" in order to contrast it with unilinear descent. However, the term "bilateral descent" seems adequately to describe the symmetrical and nonlinear aspects of this kind of ascription, and since it has been used in this way for many years, there seems no reason to adopt a new term. Where descent is nonunilinear and choice is exercised among a limited number of alternatives, as with the septs described above, then the term "multilinear" would be appropriate and will distinguish this form from both unilinear and bilateral forms.

The second feature, which will be called "jural exclusiveness," refers to whether a status is ascribed by only one of the alternative rules of descent at a time, or is simultaneously ascribable to the same individual by more than one. Put into terms of group affiliation, it refers to whether an individual is permitted to affiliate with only one of the alternative kin groups, relinquishing his claims to all others, or may affiliate with more than one. In the examples above, affiliation in the Mangaian kopu, the Nukuoro te-haka-sa-aluna, and the Lozi mishiku is "exclusive," since there is no overlapping membership. With the Kwakiutl numaym, the Bella Coola minmint, and the Samoan 'aiga sa descent is also multilinear, but individuals are permitted to belong to and participate with more than one group, making affiliation "nonexclusive." Personal kindreds are always nonexclusive, sibs and lineages are always exclusive, while septs may be either. Exclusiveness is specified by Freeman's (1955:7–9) term "utrolateral" (Latin uter-, either of two) which he applies to the Iban bilek, where an individual may have and transmit membership in either his father's or his mother's birth group, but not both. Unfortunately, this term is not quite applicable to instances like the Lozi, where there may be more than two alternative choices. Nonexclusiveness is implied by Firth's (1929: 98–100) term "ambilateral," which he applied to the Maori hapu, but it is not certain that this is exactly what he intended it to mean.

Important details of these two features are often missing from ethnographies reporting them. The potential kinds and number of choices permitted in multilinear descent systems are also frequently omitted, as are discussions of the means by which some of these choices of affiliation in parent's generation are eliminated as possible choices in the children's. Likewise, it is not always clear whether septs are jurally exclusive or nonexclusive, or whether individuals may change affiliation from one group to another during the course of their lives.

The third feature concerns the ascription of statuses collaterally along a type of descent. In sib and sept organization, statuses are ascribed to every eligible person without diminution or limitation, and they are indefinitely extensible to future generations. Since no collateral restrictions apply, this may be called "unrestricted collateral extension." The incest taboo in exogamous descent groups is usually extended in this way, and the same principle may be found in assigning rights to land, ritual obligations, and other activities.

Personal kindreds differ from septs and sibs in this respect by always imposing some degree of collateral limitation on the extension of statuses. In the examples given above, this "collateral restriction," as it will be called, varied from one degree (Nunamiut Eskimo extension of incest) to six degrees (Semambu Murut extension of incest), as measured by the number of ascending generations from Ego to the relative who connects the most removed collateral line. For the sake of clarity, the measure of collateral restriction in personal kindreds should include both the number of ascending generations to the branching of the most distant collateral line as well as the number of descending generations down this and each included line to their limits.

If they were to be expressed in terms of collateral extension, individual ownership of property, occupancy of offices, and possession of titles, together with their associated rules of inheritance and succession, would be instances of maximal collateral restriction. That is, there is no extension of the status along any consanguineal relationship until the occupant of the status is removed; yet ascription, like descent, is by kin relationships.

As noted above, different statuses may be ascribed by different degrees of collateral extension and restriction of bilateral descent (e.g., Iban and Semambu Murut). This is similar in several ways to the internal differentiation of unilinear descent groups. Tiv lineages provide an interesting comparison. As the Bohannans (1953) describe them, each patrilineage has several spans of different degrees of inclusiveness. Each of these spans regulates specific activities which the less inclusive spans do not. These spans, however, are reckoned by agnatic descent from particular ancestors who stand in ascending genealogical relationship to each other, not by a fixed number of ascending generations from an Ego as they are in personal kindreds.

The structural significance of this similarity is that a kind of segmentary organization can be associated with bilateral as well as with unilinear descent where it is very frequently to be found. It was also noted above that septs may have segmentary divisions (e.g., Highland Scottish clan and Samoan 'aiga sa). It is interesting to note again the different means by which this internal differentiation occurs in descent groups and personal kindreds and the way it underscores the different structural characteristics of the two kinds of organization. Descent groups, having a fixed point of origin in some real or hypothetical ancestor, segment by reckoning descent from particular members of the group. Personal kindreds, having no ancestral point of origin, are reckoned bilaterally from an Ego, and since bilateral descent does not exclude consanguines in any way, some degree of collateral restriction must be established in order to form a limited set of kin. Internal differentiation, then, can only take place by a recognition of different degrees of collateral relationships from Ego as the principle of division. When kindreds have the kind of continuity they possess in stem kindreds, we might expect them to differentiate internally on somewhat the same basis that lineages do.

When unilinear and multilinear descent are compared from the point of view of kin-group continuity, some differences are worth noting. As Fortes (1953:27) points out, when a unilinear kin group is faced with extinction, some "fiction" of descent will be resorted to in order to provide a member through whom the group can maintain its continuity (see also Murdock 1949:45). Many societies even formalize and name these emergency fictions. With multilinear descent, and particularly those systems permitting a high degree of choice of affiliation, these emergency measures are built in, so to speak. What Fortes (1953:33–34) has termed "complementary filiation" in unilinear systems—the link between a sibling group and the kin of the parent who does not determine descent—is raised to equal or near-equal importance for affiliation.

When descent is considered from the point of view of a means by which the use of valued resources (e.g., land and spouses) are allocated to members of the society, still other differences between unilinear and multilinear types become apparent. In relatively inflexible unilinear systems, unforeseen events may produce what the society considers to be an inequitable distribution of these resources in relation to the size of the groups. Frequently, there are means by which the surplus of one group is used by and ultimately passes under control of other groups. In effect, a reallocation takes place. The Garia, mentioned above, are an example of this; the transfer for use takes place through complementary filiation, and after four generations of use, title and control of the resources pass to the using lineage. With multilinear descent this kind of readjustment may go on constantly through the exercise of choice in affiliation. When an imbalance occurs, it is corrected by the influence this exerts on affiliation. Instead of reallocating resources to different groups, as above, individuals may be redistributed among the groups.

The important aspects of any multilinear descent system are the patterns of affiliation and the social and ecological factors which influence them. In some like the Mangaian kopu and the Nukuoro te-haka-sa-aluna, the guiding principle seems to be the equal claims of the groups of both parents over the children. In others, like the Lozi mishiku and the Onotoa kainga, membership seems largely influenced by the availability of resources controlled by the group, while affiliation in both Kwakiutl and Bella Coola septs seems best understood in terms of motivations provided by the social status system. The number of societies for which these multilinear groups have been well described are still too few to permit anything but the most superficial kind of comparison, but even if they prove to be rare phenomena, the fact that multilinear descent can and does exist sheds light on some of the structural characteristics of unilinear groups.

Concerning bilateral descent and the resulting personal and stem kindreds, only the obvious is clear—this type of structure occurs where collective and corporate control is absent or minimal. Even though a partial case has been made here for studying these seemingly changing and ephemeral kin groups from the point of view of continuity, that is, as stem kindreds, this may in fact prove to be misleading and unproductive. But it is obvious that we need more detailed analyses of kindred systems and particularly the manner in which different degrees of collateral extension and restriction are used as principles of organization; the ways in which important individuals and the bilateral kin who group around them may constitute the significant kin groups; the function of kindreds as networks which bind other groups together; and as reservoirs of kin from which household groups are increased and sustained.

In framing hypotheses about the evolution of the different kinds of ascription through kinship, the first and third features listed above are of greatest relevance. The first question that arises is, what conditions favor the descent group as opposed to the personal kindred? That is, under what circumstances are bilateral and non-bilateral (unilinear and multilinear) descent most likely to occur? Given this answer, the next questions are, what circumstances favor no degrees of freedom in ascription (unilinear), some degrees of freedom (multilinear), and complete freedom with varying degrees of collateral restriction (bilateral)? Intuitively, the answers seem to lie in the idea that control and regulation are greatest over those items which have the highest value. Thus, when something has high value or is scarce, its scarcity is insured by greater control and fewer degrees of freedom in allocating it, and vice versa. Whether or not this is correct could be determined by testing a number of derived hypotheses dealing with such matters as the limitation of resources, population density, social class, and bride price.

REFERENCES

Adam, Frank, 1952, *The Clans, Septs, and Regiments of the Scottish Highlands*. Fourth edition, revised by Sir Thomas Innes of Learney. Edinburgh: W. and A. K. Johnston.

Arensberg, Conrad M., and Kimball, Solon T., 1940, *Family and Community in Ireland*, Cambridge: Harvard University Press.

Barton, R. F., 1919, "Ifugao Law," University of California Publications in American Archaeology and Ethnology, Vol. 15, No. 1, Berkeley. 1922, "Ifugao Economics," University of California Publications in American Archaeology and Ethnology, Vol. 15, No. 5. Berkeley. 1930, *The Half-way Sun*, New York: Brewer and Warren. 1938, *Philippine Pagans*, London: G. Routledge and Sons. 1949, *The Kalingas*, Chicago: University of Chicago Press.

Beaglehole, Ernest and Pearl, 1938, "Ethnology of Pukapuka," Bernice P. Bishop Museum Bulletin No. 150. Honolulu.

Boas, Franz, 1897, "The Social Organization and the Secret Societies of the Kwakiutl Indians," Report of the U.S. National Museum for 1895. Washington, D.C. 1920, "The Social Organization of the Kwakiutl," *American Anthropologist*, 22, pp. 111–126.

Bohannan, Laura and Paul, 1953, "The Tiv of Central Nigeria," Ethnographic Survey of Africa, part VIII, Daryll Forde (ed.), London: International African Institute.

Buck, Peter H. (Te Rangi Hiroa), 1934, "Mangaian Society," Bernice P. Bishop Museum Bulletin No. 122. Honolulu.

Chinnery, E. W. Pearson, n.d., "Certain Natives of South New Britain and Dampier Straits," Anthropological Report No. 3, Territory of New Guinea. Melbourne.

Drucker, Phillip, 1939, "Rank, Wealth and Kinship in Northwest Coast Society," *American Anthropologist*, 41, pp. 55–65.

Eilers, Anneliese, 1934, Inseln um Ponape. Ergebnisse der südsee-expedition, 1908–1910, II, B, VIII, G. Thilenius (ed.), Hamburg: Friederichsen, De Gruyter and Co.

Ember, Melvin, 1958, "Commercialization and Political Behavior in American Samoa," Unpublished doctoral dissertation, Yale University. New Haven.

Emory, Kenneth Pike, 1956, "Personal Communication."

Firth, Raymond W., 1929, *Primitive Economics of the New Zealand Maori*, New York: E. P. Dutton. 1936, *We, The Tikopia*, London: Allen and Unwin.

Ford, Clellan S., 1941, *Smoke from their Fires*, New Haven: Yale University Press.

Fortes, Meyer, 1953, "The Structure of Unilineal Descent Groups," *American Anthropologist*, 55, pp. 17–41.

Freeman, J. D., 1955, "Iban Agriculture," Colonial Research Studies, No. 18. London, Colonial Office. 1957, "The Family of the Iban of Borneo," Report of the Department of Anthropology and Sociology, Canberra: The Australian National University.

Gifford, Edward Winslow, 1929, "Tongan Society," Bernice P. Bishop Museum Bulletin No. 61. Honolulu.

Gluckman, Max, 1951, "The Lozi of Barotseland in Northwestern Rhodesia," in *Seven Tribes of British Central Africa*, Elizabeth Colson and Max Gluckman (eds.), London: Oxford University Press.

Goodenough, Ward H., 1955, "A Problem in Malayo-Polynesian Social Organization," *American Anthropologist*, 57, pp. 71–83.

Hoebel, E. Adamson, 1954, *The Law of Primitive Man*, Cambridge: Harvard University Press.

Hogbin, Herbert Ian, 1934, *Law and Order in Polynesia*, New York: Harcourt and Brace.

Kubary, J. S., 1900, Beitrag zur kenntnis der Nukuoro- oder Monteverde-Inseln, Karolinen-Archipel. Mitteilungen der Geographischen Gesellschaft in Hamburg, band XVI, pp. 1–67, Hamburg: Friederichsen and Co.

Lawrence, Peter, 1955, "Land Tenure Among the Garia," Australian National University Social Science Monographs No. 4. Canberra, Australian National University.

Leach, E. R., 1950, "Social Science Research in Sarawak," Colonial Research Studies, No. 1. London, Colonial Office.

Linton, Ralph, 1936, *The Study of Man*, New York: Appleton-Century.

Lowie, Robert H., 1948, *Social Organization*, New York: Rinehart and Co.

McIlwraith, T. F., 1948, *The Bella Coola Indians*, 2 vols., Toronto: University of Toronto Press.

Mead, Margaret, 1930, "Social Organization of Manu'a," Bernice P. Bishop Museum Bulletin, No. 76. Honolulu.

Murdock, George Peter, 1949, "Social Structure," New York: Macmillan Co.

Nimuendajú, Curt, 1939, "The Apinayé," Catholic University of America, Anthropological Series, No. 8. Trans. by Robert H. Lowie, Washington, D.C.

Parsons, Talcott, 1943, "The Kinship System of the Contemporary United States," *American Anthropologist*, **45**, pp. 22–38.

Pehrson, Robert N., 1954, "Bilateral Kin Groupings as a Structural Type," *Journal of East Asiatic Studies*, **3**, pp. 199–202. 1957, "The Bilateral Network of Social Relations in Könkämä Lapp District," Indiana University Publications, Slavic and East European Series, Vol. 5. Bloomington.

Phillpotts, B. S., 1913, *Kindred and Clan in the Middle Ages and After*, Cambridge: Cambridge University Press.

Pospisil, Leopold J., 1957, "Unpublished field notes on the Nunamiut Eskimo, Alaska."

Radcliffe Brown, A. R., 1935, "Patrilineal and Matrilineal Succession," *Iowa Law Review*, **20**, pp. 286–303.

Spoehr, Alexander, 1950, "Observations on the Study of Kinship," *American Anthropologist*, **52**, pp. 1–15.

Wagley, Charles and Galvão, Eduardo, 1948, "The Tapirapé," in *Handbook of South American Indians*, Vol. 3, Julian H. Steward (ed.), Bureau of American Ethnology Bulletin, No. 143. Washington, D.C.

5. A Comparative Approach to Incest and Adultery[1]

BY JACK GOODY

IN A RECENT ARTICLE entitled "Changing Emphases in Social Structure" (1955) Murdock maintains that sciences first go through a classificatory stage and subsequently arrive at a second phase in which an attempt is made to analyse the "dynamic processes which give rise to the phenomena thus classified" (p. 361). As far as anthropology is concerned, "the initial classificatory task has by now been substantially accomplished in the field of social structure" (p. 361).

This thesis, which has been propounded on other occasions by other writers, seems to me not only to take a naïve view of scientific discovery, but definitely to mislead those from neighbouring fields of study into thinking that anthropological terms necessarily have some primary referent which is accepted by the large majority of anthropologists. That is by no means the case. In the first place, there is often a considerable measure of overt disagreement. Secondly, even where apparent agreement is found, the ambiguity of the terms themselves may conceal a number of different usages.

Partly this derives from the fact that the continuous analysis in depth of different societies calls for more precise conceptual discriminations than were previously required. And partly too it is related to the fact that the terms often employed by anthropologists are those which we use as members of a particular society to refer to our own institutions. Such concepts may turn out to be quite inappropriate for the purpose of cross-cultural analysis. The English "family" is an obvious case in point. From the sociological point of view, the term has at least four analytically separable meanings. A statement of the kind, "the family is a universal institution among all human societies," is meaningless without further elaboration.

In sum, these concepts cannot be regarded as having been defined once and for all time, leaving anthropologists now free to get on with other types of activity. A refinement of concepts is a product of onward going research; it proceeds hand in hand with it. The depth analysis of societies through long periods of residence by trained anthropologists is a necessary concomitant of the sharpening of concepts for cross-cultural studies.

The particular concept in which I am interested here is that of "incest." I want also to mention the related ones of adultery and fornication, as I shall later be concerned with them as categories of heterosexual offence. The everyday

SOURCE: British Journal of Sociology, *Volume 7 (1956)*, *pp. 286–305. Reprinted by permission of Routledge & Kegan Paul Ltd.*

[1] An earlier version of this paper was read to the Graduate Seminar of the Department of Social Relations, Harvard, in March, 1956.

meanings given by the *Concise Oxford Dictionary* are as follows:

1. Incest   —sexual commerce of near kindred.
2. Adultery   —voluntary sexual intercourse of married person with one of the opposite sex, married (double adultery) or not (single adultery).
3. Fornication—voluntary sexual intercourse between man (sometimes restricted to unmarried man) and unmarried woman.

These particular definitions are by no means standardized. For instance, the *Encyclopædia Britannica* (11th Edition) and *Webster's Dictionary* both define incest as "sexual intercourse between persons so related by kindred and affinity that marriage cannot take place between them," a formula which assumes an identical range in prohibitions on heterosexual intercourse and prohibitions on marriage.

It is these everyday usages which have formed the basis of the anthropological concepts. Malinowski, for example, appeared to treat the incest taboo, the prohibition on sexual intercourse, and exogamy, the prohibition on marriage, as being but two sides of a coin.

Murdock, on the other hand, adheres more closely to the *Concise Oxford Dictionary* when he defines incest and adultery:

When it (heterosexual intercourse) takes place outside of marriage between two persons of whom at least one is married to another person, it is called *adultery*. If its participants are related to one another by a real, assumed, or artificial bond of kinship which is culturally regarded as a bar to sex relations, it is classed as *incest* (1949:261).

Radcliffe-Brown, while retaining the criteria of kinship, offers a more restricted definition of incest. He writes, "Incest is properly speaking the sin or crime of sexual intimacy between immediate relatives within the family, father and daughter, mother and son, brother and sister" (1950:69).

Such extensive controversies have raged around the "incest taboo" that it may perhaps appear impertinent to raise the question whether all these writers are in fact discussing the same range of phenomena or are looking for explanations of the same set of prohibitions. But when we put the definitions of Murdock and Radcliffe-Brown side by side it is obvious that such doubts are not altogether misplaced. It is clear for instance that in terms of Radcliffe-Brown's definition, Murdock's "second factual conclusion" ... "that incest taboos do not apply universally to any relative of opposite sex outside of the nuclear family" (1949:285) is tautologous. Equally, on the basis of Murdock's formula it is difficult to decide whether sexual intimacy with the father's wives other than one's own mother would constitute incest or adultery, particularly in societies like the Tiv or Bedouin where kinship is universal. The difference between the two definitions is this, that though both apparently see the regulations as "grounded in the constitution of the nuclear family" (1949:284), Radcliffe-Brown attempts to limit the application of the term to the elementary family itself, while Murdock prefers to include all kin-based prohibitions, seeing these as "extensions" of the primary taboo. Murdock's emphasis is in line with Malinowski's stress upon the elementary family and with his dogma of "extension of sentiments." Both definitions are clearly based upon the institutions of our own society, where prohibitions on intercourse, like prohibitions on marriage, are bilaterally organized within limited ranges of kin. But are these necessarily adequate for the analysis of non-European societies?

In order to answer this question, let us examine the evidence from two societies characterized by unilineal descent, one by matrilineal, the other patrilineal descent. I have selected for this purpose the Ashanti and Tallensi of the Gold Coast, for which the main sources on incest are Rattray (1929) and Fortes (1936, 1949) respectively. These societies were chosen partly because of the high standard of the reports and partly because of my own familiarity with the area. The Trobriand and the Nuer material will be used as a check upon the results obtained from an analysis of the examples from the Gold Coast. In each case I want to examine both the explicit verbal categories of the actors themselves and the classifications implicit in the system of sanctions. These will be compared with the concepts employed by the observers.[2]

The Matrilineal Case

In his treatment of sexual offences among the Ashanti, Rattray distinguished what he calls sins or tribal offences (*oman akyiwadie*) from household offences (*efiesem*). The former demanded the intervention of the central authority and the execution of the guilty party, although in some instances compensation was allowed. The latter "were settled by the persons directly concerned or were decided by argument before any Elder, without reference to the 'house-father,' who stood entirely aloof" (1929:287). The offences falling under these two categories were discussed separately. I have listed them together in Table 1.

From this table it can be seen that among the Ashanti sexual offences can be categorized in two ways, firstly, according to the different names used by the Ashanti themselves, and, secondly, according to the different sanctions employed. I shall consider first the classification according to the nature of the sanctions.[3]

This reveals three classes of offence. In the first class falls *mogyadie*, intercourse with a woman of the same clan, punishable by death; this includes intercourse with full siblings and maternal half-siblings and with the mother; it excludes intercourse of father with daughter. But there is another type of offence, which though not given the same name, is also punishable by death; this is *atwebenefie* (1), intercourse with a member of the same patrilineal sub-group, which of course includes that between father and daughter. Terminologically this constitutes

a different category, but in respect of the nature of the sanction it must be associated with *mogyadie*. Both are cases of intercourse with members of the same descent group. The terminological distinction indicates that it is intercourse within the matriclan which is the major prohibition here while that within the patrilineal subgroup is subsidiary. This is consistent with the nature of double clanship among the Ashanti.

The second class of offence consists basically of intercourse not with members of the same descent group but with the wives of fellow members, as well as with other classificatory wives. It also includes some prohibitions on intercourse with affines which might tend to confuse the social position of the wife herself. The punishment for this class of offence varies. It is never death, but consists of some variant of the adultery payment.

The third class of sexual offence is with wives of other men, and the sanction here is the simple adultery payment.

---

[2] In the course of this paper I have reconsidered some of the data presented by my teachers, Professor Meyer Fortes and Professor Evans-Pritchard. What may appear as a criticism is in fact a compliment to their work. In the first place, their monographs on the Tallensi and the Nuer remain the most outstanding analyses of the social systems of non-European societies which have been written, and it is because of this fact that I am able to offer such a reinterpretation. In the second place, I am trying to carry their analysis a stage further within the framework of the general approach which they have done so much to develop.

[3] In constructing this table I have followed Rattray's presentation of the offences except in the last category of section B (*atwebenefie* 2). Here is his list for this category (1929, p. 320):

Adultery with
    i a brother's wife
    ii a son's wife
    iii wife's mother
    iv an uncle's wife
    v wife of anyone of same *fekuo* (company)
    vi wife of anyone of same trade or guild
    vii wife of one's own slave
    viii father's wife, other than the adulterer's own mother
    ix wife's sister, married or single.

In all these instances, the punishment is an adultery payment less or more than the standard amount. In addition, an animal has in some cases to be provided for a sacrifice; if a man has committed an offence with his wife's mother he then has to appease his wife with a gift. I have assumed that in i, ii, iv, viii, Rattray was referring to classificatory kin and have therefore reinterpreted the prohibitions in the way shown in the table. It should be added that the wives of fellow company and guild members are called "wife." Apart from affines, this particular category of "vaginas too near" refers to classificatory wives, wives of group members.

Table 1

Heterosexual offences among the Ashanti

Offence		Sanction
Ashanti name	Definition	

Tribal:

	Ashanti name	Definition	Sanction
A i	*mogyadie* "eating up of one's own blood"	SI* with female member of matriclan (*abusua*)	Death for both parties
A ii	*atwebenefie* (1) "vagina near to the dwelling-house"	SI with female of patri-clan (*ntoro*) sub-group	Death or expulsion from matriclan
A iii	*baratwe*	SI with "unclean" woman	Death
A iv	*di obi yere* (1) "eat a man's wife"	(a) SI with chief's wife	Death
		(b) *ahahantwe* (1), SI with unwilling married woman in the bush	Death

Household:

	Ashanti name	Definition	Sanction
B i	*di obi yere* (2)	*ahahantwe* (2), SI in bush with:	
		(a) unmarried woman	Ridicule
		(b) married woman	Adultery payment plus sheep
		(c) own wife	Ridicule
B ii	*di obi yere* (2)	SI of chief with subject's wife	Special adultery payment
B iii	*di obi yere* (2)	SI by master with wife of a slave	Special adultery payment
B iv	*atwebenefie* (2)	SI with wives of matriclan	Special adultery payment
		SI with wives of patriclan sub-group	Special adultery payment
		SI with wives of military company	Special adultery payment
		SI with wives of guild	Special adultery payment
		SI with affines (wife's mother, wife's sister)	Special adultery payment

Household:

	Ashanti name	Definition	Sanction
C	*di obi yere* (3)	Residual—SI with any married woman not falling in any of the above categories	Ordinary adultery payment

* Sexual intercourse. In treating household offences, Rattray explains that "adultery" may include various forms of "intimacy" besides actual intercourse. Since it was not always possible to distinguish from this account where this distinction was relevant, I have included these under the heading of intercourse.

The threefold typology on the basis of sanctions is an indication of the weight placed by the society on these various offences. The first class brings together offences relating to the structure of descent groups, both matrilineal and patrilineal (A i and A ii), offences relating to the hierarchical organization (A iv *a*) and "ritual" offences relating to the cult of the Earth (A iv *b*) and to the fertility of women (A iii).

When we look at the terms used by the Ashanti themselves, we find there is another threefold typology, if we exclude the category *baratwe*, which represents a different method of classifying these offences. Intercourse within the matriclan is sharply differentiated terminologically from intercourse within the patriclan, the latter falling into the same category as intercourse with the *wives* of members of the matriclan and of other social groups. In this way it is assimilated to what I wish to call group-wife offences to distinguish them from intragroup offences. This is clearly related to the overwhelmingly greater importance of the matriclans in the social system. The third category is residual in that it consists essentially in sexual intercourse with people other than the members or wives of members of the descent groups, and of a few other quasi-kin groups such as guilds and military companies. Thus the concepts of the Ashanti themselves concerning heterosexual offences closely reflect the system of social groups. Intercourse with a daughter falls into a different category from intercourse with a sister, although for us both would be classified as "incest."

Now let us turn to Rattray's own use of the terms "incest" and "adultery" to see how he meets this situation. "Incest" he uses simply to translate *mogyadie*, "eating of one's own blood," that is, sexual intercourse with a matriclanswoman. He applies the term to none of the other offences, even those also punishable by death. The term "adultery" he uses to translate all the household offences, "eating a man's wife" (*di obi yere*, 2 and 3) and *atwebenefie* (2)—"a vagina near to the dwelling-house." He also uses it to translate those offences called *di obi yere* (1) which fall under tribal jurisdiction and are therefore punishable by death. This consists of two offences only, intercourse with a chief's wife and

the worst type of sexual sin against the Earth, the rape of a married woman in the bush. His difficulty arises with category A ii, that is *atwebenefie* (1). In his original list of offences, he translates this neutrally as "sexual intercourse with certain individuals other than those related by 'blood' " (p. 304)—that is, females of the same matriclan. On the following pages he writes:

Atwe-bene-fie means literally (having sexual intercourse with) "a vagina that is near to the dwelling-house," and the offence, as the title implies, consisted in committing adultery with the wives of certain persons with whom the existing *ménage* necessarily compelled close social intercourse or constant physical proximity . . . (305).

The term "adultery" has now replaced the neutral circumlocution previously used. However when we examine the list of *atwebenefie* offences we find that those included under "tribal sins" [i.e. *atwebenefie* (1)] are not defined by the affinal relationship to ego. The women are forbidden not because they are someone's wives but because they are female members of the same patrilineal subgroup. For such an offence adultery seems a misleading translation.

The point at issue is this. In English usage the term "adultery" is defined in relation to the marital status of one or both participants and is in effect residual to the category "incest." The term "incest" is defined bilaterally, in keeping with other aspects of the social system. Heterosexual offences among the Ashanti do not fall into these categories, and in trying to translate these simply by the English words "incest" and "adultery" Rattray was faced with an impossible task. The English concept "incest" refers to heterosexual intercourse with persons within a particular range of kin, whether they fall within that range by birth or by marriage. When a male ego marries, the immediate female kin of his wife are assimilated to his own kinship chart by becoming sisters- or mothers-in-law. Intercourse with affines is defined as incestuous and placed in the same conceptual category as intercourse with consanguineous kin.

Thus, whereas the Ashanti differentiate between intragroup offences and group-wife offences, the European system does not have to do this because at marriage the spouses are assimilated, for many social purposes, into each others' natal groups. There is no distinction, in the context of heterosexual offences, between group-member and group-spouse.

This interpretation is strikingly confirmed in another matrilineal case, that of the Trobriands. Malinowski discusses incest in considerable detail in his book *The Sexual Life of Savages* (1932). First let us ask what Malinowski means by incest. "Incest within the family and breach of exogamy," he says, is the meaning of the Trobriand word *suvasova* (p. 389). As the family is bilateral, the term *suvasova* should therefore cover the intercourse of a man with his mother, his sister, or his daughter.

When we look at the Trobriand concepts themselves we find that this is not the meaning of the word *suvasova*. Malinowski himself makes this apparent in another context, although he continues to assume an equivalence.

It must be clearly understood that, although father to daughter incest is regarded as bad, it is not described by the word *suvasova* (clan exogamy or incest), nor does any disease follow upon it; and, as we know, the whole ideology underlying this taboo is different from that of *suvasova* (447).

Suvasova corresponds precisely to the Ashanti concept *mogyadie*. It is the name for what I have called intragroup offences (intercourse or marriage), and has to be distinguished from intercourse with wives of members of the matriclan, such as brother's wife, which to judge from the example Malinowski gives (p. 98) is not heavily sanctioned. The category *suvasova* includes intercourse with the mother, the daughter, and the sister, the latter being considered the most heinous, possibly because this was felt to be the most likely. The worst heterosexual offences in the Trobriands as among the Ashanti, in each case distinguished terminologically, are those committed with members of the same matriclan. Malinowski repeatedly insists that it is the brother-sister prohibition which is the basis of the "incest" taboo in Trobriand society.

The Patrilineal Case

Let us now consider a patrilineal case, the Tallensi. According to Fortes (1949) the Tallensi have no word for incest. There is a term *poγamboon* which might be translated literally "matters concerning women." Fortes himself translates this as "adultery," but on the basis of my own experience among the LoDagaa I would suggest that it covers a wider range of heterosexual offences than is usually indicated by this term.

If the Tallensi have no specific word for incest, what range of phenomena does Fortes include under this term and how does he differentiate this from other types of offence? Looking at his analysis, we find that incest consists of sexual relations within the "expanded family," that is, the family group based upon the inner lineage (1949:111). Thus, in the absence of an indigenous concept, Fortes has introduced what is essentially a bilateral classification, one that includes in the same category offences with a paternal aunt, a sister, or a daughter (intragroup offences) as well as offences with the wife of a father, brother, or a son (group-wife offences). But though he calls both of these offences "incest" he emphasizes that they are differently thought of by the Tallensi, for the first category of offences is merely "disreputable," whereas the latter is viewed with the horror usually taken as being characteristic of incest. Outside the inner (or medial) lineage this dichotomy becomes even more obvious, for a lover relationship with a female lineage member is in fact permitted, whereas intercourse with the *wife* of a lineage or even a clan member is still considered a wrong. Fortes claims that this latter offence is not incest, but "the most reprehensible form of adultery. It does not bear the same moral stigma as the corresponding form of incest, nor does it carry religious penalties for the adulterer" (1949: 116). For Fortes, therefore, incest consists in sexual intercourse with female members of the inner lineage and with the wives of its male members, while adultery consists in intercourse with the wives of male members outside that range as well as with wives of non-clansmen.

There is then no Tallensi term for heterosexual offences other than one for "matters concerning women." Fortes uses the English terms "incest" and "adultery" to divide up this category. The way in which he does so is bilaterally oriented. "Incest" is the offence of sexual intercourse within the "expanded family," "adultery" the offence of sexual intercourse with any married woman outside it.

An alternative method of treating this problem is to infer the implicit classification of offences among the Tallensi from the nature of their reaction to any breach. This in effect is what Fortes does when he insists that "incest" with a sister or daughter falls in a different category of sexual acts than "incest" with a wife of the lineage (1949:114). This standardized procedure for the investigation of moral, ritual, or legal norms gives the following threefold division:

i. sexual intercourse with a member of the same patriclan (up to the inner lineage only).
ii. sexual intercourse with the wife of a member of the same patriclan.
iii. sexual intercourse with the wife of a non-clansman.

I suggest that this classification has more inherent probability for three reasons. Firstly, it appears to fit better with the Tallensi emphasis on unilineal descent. Secondly, it corresponds to the classification I found among the LoDagaa of the same general area who are culturally similar to the Tallensi in very many ways. Thirdly, it is analogous to the classification which we have found among the Ashanti. Thus in both the matrilineal and patrilineal cases prohibitions on sexual intercourse are grouped together depending upon whether they were:

i. with a member of the same descent group (intragroup sexual prohibition).
ii. with the wife of a member (group-wife prohibition).
iii. with another married woman (extragroup prohibition).

I suggest that a similar typology will be found in most societies characterized by unilineal descent, but has been obscured in anthropological reports because of the ethnocentric bias of the observers towards bilateral classifications. It is only possible to rectify this in the case of the Tallensi and Ashanti because of the excellence of the reporting and the fact that the authors have provided us with the terms used by the actors themselves. If we accept these three basic categories for heterosexual prohibitions and offences in societies characterized by unilineal descent groups, it would be reasonable to refer to the last as adultery, or more specifically non-group adultery. But what about the other two types of offence? Which of these should be called "incest"?

The Classification of Heterosexual Offences

The whole lengthy discussion of incest has turned on the supposition that it is a type of illicit sexual intercourse which is characterized by a particular horror. In the Western European system it is true that the whole range of offences included under the category incest is so regarded. But in many other societies, this is not so. Even within the minimal domestic units, heterosexual offences may be differently classified both terminologically and with regard to the organized sanctions with which they are met. Furthermore, they are also distinguished by diffuse sanctions, by the reactions which they arouse in the other members of the community. Among the Tallensi, offences between brother and sister (intragroup offences) are merely "disreputable," while group-wife offences are met with "horror." On the other hand, and this is a point of fundamental theoretical interest, among the Ashanti the reverse is the case. It is the intragroup offences which are dealt with by death, while the group-wife offences are treated as a heightened form of extraclan adultery. I would claim that it is a mistake in either of these societies to class both these types of offences together as "incest," because they are treated in such markedly different ways in terms of the sanctions employed and, among the Ashanti, in terms of the actor categories themselves. Equally it would be difficult to classify either the first or the second types as incest on the basis of the internal reaction to them, as this varies so markedly in the two societies. I suggest that the word incest be retained for the category of offences inside the group and that it be divorced from the criteria of "horror." The group-spouse category should be associated with adultery rather than incest, for at the core of the prohibition lies the fact that the woman is *married* into the group; the taboo depends upon her married status. If she were not

Table 2

Offences that are	Offences with	
	Unmarried person	Married person
Intragroup	Incest	Incestuous adultery
Extragroup	Fornication	i. Spouse of group (group-spouse adultery)
		ii. Other married person (non-group adultery)

married, intercourse with her would be neither incest nor adultery but rather fornication, an act which may not be negatively santioned at all. For the group-wife category I therefore suggest the somewhat clumsy phrase, "group-wife adultery." Let me now schematize the threefold categorization of offences which we found among the Ashanti and the Tallensi. The terminology I suggest seems to me more appropriate for the cross-cultural analysis of heterosexual acts outside marriage (see Table 2).

There are three points about this table which require explanation. First, it is constructed from the point of view of an ego of either sex, whereas previously I have often taken the male ego's vantage point, for example, in speaking of offences with the wife of a group member rather than the spouse of a group member. In certain respects it would have been preferable to have retained the earlier standpoint, for this was not merely a reflection of my own sex role; it corresponds to ethnographic reality. Although in European law adultery is defined as sexual intercourse when one of the partners is married, in most other societies it is only considered adultery when the woman is married. This is the case in Roman law. The reason for this is that in general marriage confers relatively exclusive rights on a man over the sexual services of a woman. It is most unusual to find that the woman acquires similar rights over the male, even in matrilineal societies. However, it seemed preferable to construct the table to take account of this case, rare as it is.

Second, it should be pointed out that in addition to the prohibitions on sexual intercourse which can be discussed in terms of the structure of descent or kin groups, there are also those attached to specific kinship positions. For instance, in English law, it is incestuous adultery to sleep with one's wife's sister. This is also true of

the Nuer and of many other African societies. As Evans-Pritchard points out in this connection, these prohibitions are to be seen as preventing a confusion of kinship statuses, a disruption of the solidarity of the sororal group.

Third, a further variable has been introduced into this table, namely that of marital status. I have already explained why this is essential in considering extragroup offences. But it may also be relevant in the case of intercourse with a fellow-member of the group. For instance, the LoDagaa, of the Northern Territories of the Gold Coast, among whom I worked, and who are in many ways very similar to the Tallensi, regarded intercourse with a clanswoman before her marriage, that is, before her sexuality had been alienated to a member of another clan, as being of very minor importance. But intercourse with the same woman after her marriage, what I have called "incestuous adultery," is more severely treated.

For the comprehensive analysis of heterosexual offences, it is essential to introduce yet a further variable, not shown in the table, that of generation. Social relationships with a member of the same or alternate generation are usually characterized by relative equality, and those between adjacent generations by super- or subordination. This fact is likely to affect the severity with which the offence is treated. It will tend to be more severely treated when the relationship is characterized by authority and especially when the male offender is of junior generation, for example, in the event of intercourse of a man with his father's wife.

The Incidence of Horror

By breaking down the categories of incest and adultery in this manner, it is possible to offer not only a more adequate analysis of heterosexual offences in any one particular society, but also to begin to examine these offences on a cross-cultural basis. I have already called attention to the different incidence of "horror" among the Tallensi and the Ashanti. In the former case it was offences with clan wives which were considered most heinous, whereas among the latter it was with the clan females themselves. The category heavily sanctioned among the Ashanti was relatively lightly treated among the Tallensi and vice versa. Why should the Tallensi represent the "mirror image" of the Ashanti in this respect?

I suggest the following is the explanation of this remarkable reversal. The Tallensi are patrilineal; their classification of offences resembles that of many other patrilineal peoples. The category "wives" is of fundamental importance to the descent group because it is through them that the continuity of the clan is obtained. Hence illegal intercourse with the wife of another member of the group is treated most severely.

The Ashanti are matrilineal. Social reproduction, as distinct from physiological reproduction, is obtained not through wives but through "sisters," the female members of the clan.[4] Hence it is interference with *their* sexuality that constitutes the most heinous heterosexual offence. An interesting aspect of this explanation is that it accounts for the differential treatment of father-daughter and mother-son offences. In neither the patrilineal Tallensi nor in matrilineal Ashanti does the father-daughter relationship fall into the most heinous category, whereas in both societies the mother-son relationship does. In the Tallensi the mother is the closest *wife* of a clansman of *senior* generation, while in the Ashanti she is the closest *female clan member* of *senior* generation. This I suggest forms a more satisfactory explanation of the different treatment of these offences than the usual "biological" one.

To put this difference in another way, in patrilineal societies the rights over a woman which are transferred at marriage include rights to her reproductive capacities as well as rights to her sexual services, whereas in matrilineal societies, it is only the latter which are transferred. Indeed

among the Ashanti, a male only acquires exclusive sexual rights by the payment of a special sum, known as the *tiri-usa*, which is not intrinsic to the "marriage" itself.

The rights over the sexual services of women are customarily vested in one man, except in the rare cases of polyandrous systems. But the degree of this exclusiveness varies. For example, the LoDagaa, like the Tallensi, regard intercourse with the wife of a patriclansman as being the worst form of heterosexual offence. Yet the junior of a pair of male twins, if unmarried, is said to have access to the wife of his elder brother. In this case, the social identification of the siblings is such that it overrules the individualization of rights to the sexual services of the wife. There is always an incipient contradiction in patrilineal societies centering around the fact that although rights to the sexual services of women are in general acquired by individuals, rights to their procreative capacities are to some extent vested in the clan as a whole. An offspring of a particular union is an offspring of the entire clan. This contradiction is differently resolved in various societies. In Brahmin groups, for example, rights over women are so highly individualized that a widowed woman may not marry again. Among the Tallensi a man's exclusive rights in a woman cease at his death, and by the institution of widow inheritance are taken over by another member of the same patriclan. Fraternal polyandry, or polycoity, represents the extreme case of corporate rights over the sexual services of women, at the opposite pole as it were to the individualization of Brahmin society. The problem of plural access is different from, but not unrelated to, that of plural marriage.

The Nuer are an interesting case in this connection, both because of the nature of the material and because of the theoretical position adopted by Evans-Pritchard. Both Evans-Pritchard (1949, 1951) and Howells (1954) speak of the Nuer as having a word for incest, namely *rual*. Evans-Pritchard explains that this term covers offences with clanswomen as well as other kinswomen falling within the range of prohibited degrees of marriage, and further that the prohibition on sexual relationships derives from the prohibition on marriage. But he also adds that the same term is used to designate offences with

---

[4] This formulation was suggested to me in another context by Professor Max Gluckman who told me that it originated with Radcliffe-Brown.

women who are married to kinsmen. Evans-Pritchard brings this within the framework of his explanation of the incest taboo as derived from the rule of exogamy by asserting that such women are "brought within the circle of the incest taboo not so much as wives of kinsmen but as mothers of kinsmen" (1951:44–45). This contention seems somewhat strained. Women married to kinsmen surely fall into the forbidden category by virtue of their marriage and their *potential* child-bearing capacity. The Nuer certainly regard the presence of children as increasing the dangers of incest, but there is no indication in the literature that they look with any approval upon intercourse with the wife of a kinsman who has not yet given birth to children, except in one or two rather special cases (Evans-Pritchard, 1949.97).

Evans-Pritchard then uses incest to translate the Nuer word *rual* and maintains that the Nuer include in this category sexual relations with women falling within the range of prohibited degrees as well as with women married to such kin. If this were the whole situation, then the Nuer would have very similar categories of heterosexual offences to those which exist in our own society. But this does not appear to be altogether the case, for he also writes that "sexual relations with the wives of half-brothers, paternal uncles, and patrilineal cousins of every degree are regarded as being either incestuous peccadillos or not incestuous at all. The wife of a 'bull' is, in a general social sense, the wife of all the 'bulls.' . . . She is our wife" (1951:45). It would appear from this statement that the term *rual* is not generally used for intercourse with the wives of agnates, other than the father, a full brother, or a son. "There is no incest," the Nuer say, "among bulls" (1949:92).

Howell's account confirms this. He includes intercourse with women married to kinsmen in his discussion of adultery rather than under the rules of incest and exogamy, and concludes with the following remark . . . "the act is therefore tantamount to incest (*rual*)" (1954:164). His use of "tantamount" again appears to indicate that the Nuer make a verbal distinction between intercourse with kinswomen ("intragroup offences") which is *rual* and intercourse with the wives of kinsfolk which is "tantamount to *rual*." It

is probable that Howell here means agnates rather than the entire range of kinsfolk, for Evans-Pritchard is quite definite that it is only intercourse with "bulls" that could fall outside the category *rual*, although intercourse with the wives of other kinsfolk is included. The failure to be clear on this matter is yet another example of the way in which reports have been skewed by terminology which reflects the institutions of the society to which the anthropologist belongs rather than those of the society he is analysing. It must be admitted however that in so far as the Nuer classify offences with kinsfolk and the wives of kinsfolk in the same category, their concepts present a closer, albeit deceptive, approximation to our own than is the case with the other societies we have examined.

Let me now turn from the way in which the Nuer classify heterosexual offences terminologically to the sanctions with which a breach of the prohibition is met. The punishment of intercourse with women falling within the prohibited degrees of marriage is left to supernatural forces . . .

there is no question of compensation, and the spiritual contamination which is considered to follow incest (*rual*) and which is manifested in physical disorders (*nueer*), sometimes resulting in death, falls equally on both parties and even upon their relatives (Howell, 1954: 82–83).

The effectiveness of these sanctions varies with the genealogical distance between the two persons involved, for Howell later states that "there is no great condemnation of extramarital intercourse with distant clanswomen" (p. 147).

The statement concerning intercourse with distant clanswomen strongly recalls the Tallensi situation. On the other hand, intercourse within the closer ranges of kin seems more heavily condemned among the Nuer. This is not easy to assess, as both authorities at times omit to state whether their remarks refer to a breach of the prohibition on sexual intercourse or a breach of the rule of exogamy. *Rual* appears to mean both these offences. Indeed it is possibly because of this identification that Evans-Pritchard, like Malinowski, regards incest as being linked so firmly with exogamy.

I now want to deal with the question of intercourse with the wives of kinsmen, or what I have previously referred to as group-wife offences. In a passage quoted above, Evans-Pritchard speaks of intercourse with the wives of agnatic kinsmen as being "incestuous peccadillos or not incestuous at all" (1951:45). It is clear that if we accept the implication that such offences are excluded from the category *rual*, some differentiation in treatment is to be expected. The interesting feature of the Nuer case is that, according to Evans-Pritchard, group-wife offences are relatively lightly treated, a situation quite different from the normative system of the other patrilineal case we have examined, namely the Tallensi. Before discussing a possible explanation of this phenomena, it is necessary to turn to the other authority on the Nuer.

Howell gives some additional information on intercourse with the wives of kinsmen, a subject which, significantly, he treats under the heading adultery rather than incest. I quote in full his main paragraph on this question:

ADULTERY WITH THE WIVES OF KINSMEN. The full rate of compensation is usually demanded unless the husband and the adulterer are on exceptionally good terms in other respects, or their relationship in the kinship structure is sufficiently close to modify feelings of moral indignation on the part of the husband. Although the wives of kinsmen are brought within the sphere of kinship by the process of marriage, and to have relations with the wife of a kinsman is in a sense tantamount to a breach of the rules of exogamy, this is modified by the feeling that a wife, acquired by the transfer of cattle in which other kinsmen have limited rights, is theoretically the wife of all of them. Yet it is not considered correct that two kinsmen should have sexual relations with the same woman at the same period. There is no real conflict in these two concepts, but the attitude behind the payment of *yang kule* includes an idea that sexual relations with the legal wife of another man create an impurity, and that there is greater impurity if two men of the same kinship group have sexual relations with the same woman. It is felt that the wife of a kinsman is in some degree also a kinswoman, especially as a potential mother of kinsmen in the next generation. The act is therefore tantamount to incest (*rual*). (163–164).

It is difficult to compare the statements of the two authorities, for Howell speaks of the "wives of close kinsmen" without indicating whether or not these kinsmen are agnates, while Evans-Pritchard is concerned specifically with these latter. But identity should perhaps be assumed from Howell's use of the phrase "kinship group." In any case the whole tenor of his remarks suggests that Evans-Pritchard's assessment of intercourse with the wives of close kinsmen as "incestuous peccadillos" requires some modification. For although the greater part of the adultery payment may be waived, Howell specifically declares that "adultery is an offence which brings greater spiritual dangers when the husband and the adulterer are kinsmen." From this remark it would seem that Evans-Pritchard has perhaps neglected the spiritual dangers which intercourse with the wives of agnates involves.

Howell accounts for increased spiritual danger as well as the reduced compensation in cases of adultery with a group wife in terms of the conflict between the rule of exogamy and the corporate aspects of marital rights in women. He seems here to be falling into the error, also made by Evans-Pritchard, of confusing intragroup prohibitions (which have a direct relationship with prohibitions on marriage) and group-wife prohibitions (which clearly do not). This confusion, deriving from Western European institutions, makes for some difficulty in interpreting the Nuer data.

Evans-Pritchard uses a similar explanation to account for the comparative leniency with which offences with the wives of agnates are dealt. This he contends can be easily understood by reference to "the importance attached to children by the Nuer." As it stands this explanation is inadequate, in that it could "explain" intercourse not only with the wives of agnates, but also with any married women whatsoever. What Evans-Pritchard means is not the importance attached to children in themselves but the importance attached to children of the lineage, in other words to the continuity of the descent group. This relates to the argument I presented earlier. If we accept Evans-Pritchard's account of intercourse with agnates as a peccadillo, this is clearly a very different situation from the Tallensi one. Another variable is present. This is the extent of the corporate rights over the woman's sexual services. In any society with unilineal descent groups, there must be an incipient conflict between the individualized and corporate aspects of these rights. The Nuer, as distinct from the Brahmin and the Tallensi, tend to extend the corporate aspect to include rights over the woman's sexual services as well as her procreative capacity.

This interpretation receives support from the Nuer version of the common African prohibition on two members of a descent group having intercourse with the same woman. Among the Tallensi and the LoDagaa, this prohibition falls most severely on full siblings. Among the Nuer, however, the corporate character of rights over women receives greater emphasis and the situation is reversed; "it is wrong for two kinsmen to court the same girl, *unless they are members of the same lineage*" (Evans-Pritchard, 1951:45; my italics).

To sum up the Nuer evidence, two points emerge, despite some inconsistencies in the available data. First, there does exist a somewhat similar differentiation of heterosexual offences to the threefold classification which were found in the other descent societies. Whether or not there is any discrimination at the verbal level is not altogether clear, but there appears to be a valid distinction in terms of sanctions brought into play. The three categories are intercourse with the wife of a non-kinsman (simple adultery), intercourse with the wife of a clansman (or rather "bull"), and intercourse with kinswomen and with the wives of kinsmen other than "bulls." The reference group is not merely ego's own patrilineal descent group; it also includes, as far as the last category is concerned, the mother's patriclan and other kin. But at the core of this range of kin lies the descent group. Second, although the evidence regarding the "horror" reaction is not unambiguous, it would seem that intercourse with the wives of patriclansmen is not regarded so severely as among the Tallensi or the LoDagaa. This does not, I think, invalidate the hypothesis that the differential incidence of the horror reaction to intercourse with group members and with group wives among the Tallensi and the Ashanti is related to the nature of the linearity of the major descent groups. What the Nuer material does is to bring out a further variable, namely the degree to which rights over women are vested in the descent group. Put in another way, this factor is the extent to which a distinction is made between rights over the reproductive powers of women and the rights over their sexual services, for where this distinction is emphasized, there appears to be greater individualization of the rights over sexual services.

Explanations of Incest

Once the distinction between intragroup and group-wife sexual offences has been understood the problems of the "explanation" of incest, and of the relationship between incest and exogamy, can be seen in a new light. Explanations of incest fall into three categories. First, there are those framed in terms of the internal relations of the group. These are associated with writers who have concentrated their attention on sexual prohibitions within the elementary family: Freud, Radcliffe-Brown, Malinowski, Brenda Seligman, Murdock, Parsons, and others. Second, there are those framed in terms of the external relations of the group, which are associated principally with Tylor, Fortune, and Lévi-Strauss. In the third category fall the biological, psychological-genetic variety. With this latter I am not concerned here, although I am aware that they find their way into the formulations of some of the writers mentioned above. I take the two sociological hypotheses as my starting point not because I automatically assume that they will serve as complete explanations, but because for heuristic purposes it seems to me desirable to see how far one can get with these before employing theories which from the sociologists' standpoint are residual.

The two sociological theories are normally viewed as alternatives and a considerable literature has accrued as to their relative merits. Brenda Seligman has recently summarized this discussion, herself coming down on the side of internal relations. Her argument is worth presenting not only because it gives some idea of how the discussion has developed but also because it deals fairly with both points of view. She writes:

Dr. R. W. Fortune... considers that the barrier itself is adopted not because of its internal value to the family, but because the external value of the marriage alliance is essential to social structure (1950:313).

She distinguishes two types of incest. "One is the union of parent and child, the other is of siblings of opposite sex" (p. 306). And she maintains that although the marriage alliance might account for the brother-sister taboo, it cannot possibly explain the parent-child prohibition. Therefore, she concludes, it is the internal value of the arrangement which is the most important aspect of incest. "With the prohibition of incest within the elementary family, the foundation of social structure is laid" (p. 307). Thus she succeeds in categorizing heterosexual offences on generation lines and perceives that different explanations might be appropriate to each. However, she fails to dichotomize either in terms of group members and group wives, or in terms of the structure of unilineal descent groups. The reason for this appears to be her commitments to the Malinowskian stress on the elementary family. If this is seen as the primary unit in relation to which the incest taboo functions, then the only possible breakdown of incest is by generation. The point elaborated in this paper is that, in the analysis of descent societies, a further breakdown is necessary, and exists within the actor frame of reference either in the terms used or in the sanctions employed. But the breakdown is made according to whether the prohibition is on intercourse with a group member or with a group wife; and the groups in question are in general based upon unilineal descent. It is from this point of view that explanations of incest and exogamy must be considered.

Incest and exogamy are usually analysed as related prohibitions, the one on intercourse, the other on marriage. For example, Evans-Pritchard in his study of the Nuer maintains that the former is derived from the latter. Malinowski sometimes speaks of incest and exogamy as if they were entirely complementary. This point of view arises from a failure to make the distinction discussed above. For while the rule prohibiting marriage inside the group (exogamy) may be associated with the prohibition on intercourse within the group (intragroup prohibition), it cannot possibly be related, in any direct manner, to the prohibition on intercourse with the wives of the group, for these women must of necessity fall within the general category of permitted spouse. They cannot possibly be excluded by any marriage rule.

Exogamy, then, can only be related to the prohibition on intragroup intercourse. But as Fortes has shown, there need be no complete overlap even here. The Tallensi allow sexual intercourse with distant clansmen where they do not allow marriage. The reason is clear. Marriage affects the alignment of relationships between groups; it has to be publicly validated by overt transactions, and it provides a precedent for similar arrangements in the future. Sexual intercourse in itself does none of this, and therefore when carried on in semisecrecy requires no realignment of social groups. And indeed, as Fortes has also shown, under certain conditions there may be advantages for the individuals concerned if the lover is forbidden as a spouse for then these relationships are necessarily of limited duration. Within groups of more restricted span, however, intercourse between members can render other social relationships difficult. This is especially true where the relationship is characterized by super-subordination, as for example between members of adjacent generations.

Although there is no inevitable overlap between the prohibition of intragroup intercourse and the prohibition of intragroup marriage, there is nevertheless a strong tendency for such an overlap to occur. Exogamy is frequently phrased in terms of kinship: "We cannot marry our 'sisters.' " So is the intragroup sexual taboo: "We cannot sleep with our 'sisters.' " It is true that the classificatory reference of the term "sister" may not be the same in the two cases. This is so with the Tallensi. In the first instance "sister" refers to clan females as a whole, in the second, to those belonging to the inner or medial lineage. But the principle of structural congruence acts in favour of the same referent in both cases. And indeed the prohibition on temporary sexual relations and the prohibitions on semipermanent sexual relations are patently not unrelated.

If therefore the rule of exogamy is to be related to the external value of the marriage alliance, as Fortune and others have suggested, I think correctly, then the intragroup prohibition on intercourse cannot be dissociated from it. The rejection of temporary sexuality within the group is in part a reflection of the rejection of permanent sexuality, and the latter is related to the importance of establishing intergroup relationships by the exchange of rights in women.

Let us now turn 'to the prohibition on intercourse with those who have married members of the descent group. This is spoken of by Seligman, Fortes, and many others as incest. Yet clearly the explanations of Fortune, Lévi-Strauss and others concerning marriage alliances have no bearing at all upon this phenomenon, because it is not intercourse with the women as such which is forbidden, but intercourse with them as wives of group members. Rights over their sexual services have been pre-empted by other males with whom one has prior relationships. These women are not necessarily consanguineal kin at all, with the exception of ego's mother; they are affines. Moreover, when the specific relationship with the member of the descent group ceases, then they may be legitimate sexual partners. In many cases one is in fact obliged to marry them when their husband dies, because of one's relationship with the dead man. Now this type of prohibition has nothing directly to do with marriage alliances, but rather with the other explanation which has been put forward, namely, the necessity of preserving the structure, not merely of the "family," for there would then be no need for a rule of any extensive application, but rather of the descent group; for where rights of sexual access are individualized, conflict over females may be a cause of internecine dispute, and this prohibition renders such disputes less likely. It is indeed closely related to the taboo, found among the Tallensi, and among many other African peoples, against clansmen having sexual relationships with one woman during the same period.

Conclusions

The current sociological explanations of incest are not, then, alternatives. Explanations in terms of external relations are relevant to the prohibitions on intragroup intercourse, while those in terms of internal relations are primarily relevant to the group-wife prohibition, although they also bear upon the intragroup taboo.

Exogamy can be related to the former, but not to the latter.

This paper has attempted to establish a typology of heterosexual prohibitions to facilitate both cross-cultural studies and the depth analysis of particular societies. The typology depends in the first place upon a distinction between women who are considered to belong to the group and women who are married to its male members. In the societies with which the discussion has been mainly concerned, the reference group is the unilineal descent group rather than the elementary family. It is impossible to relate the concepts "incest" and "exogamy" when one term is held to refer to a bilateral group, the family, and the other to a unilineal one, the clan or lineage. It is impossible to account for the different sanctions placed upon these acts among the patrilineal Tallensi and the matrilineal Ashanti unless one introduces the system of descent as a variable. The "grisly horror of incest" is not a universal characteristic of all heterosexual offences with kinswomen and the wives of kinsmen. The reactions to a breach vary within and between societies. This is a fact which psychologists venturing into the cross-cultural field have often forgotten. Indeed, so concerned have they been with their own findings that they have tended, even more than anthropologists, to impose the categories derived from their own institutions upon the other societies with which they have been concerned. This is noticeable even in the type cases which psychologists have taken from classical Greek mythology. The unilineal nature of early Greek society makes it probable that their system of classification was closer to the patrilineal societies of Africa than the bilateral ones of modern Europe.

Like anthropologists, sociologists and psychologists dealing with our own society have patently failed to realize the ethnocentric nature of their categories. They have tended to treat "incest" as an isolate instead of examining the system of prohibitions as a whole in relation to the social structure. Thus there is a quite disproportionate amount of literature devoted to "incest" as compared to "adultery," yet from the standpoint of social problems the latter would seem to deserve the greater attention. However, the lure of the exotic has overcome the attraction of the mundane.

The study of "incest" in any society must be related not merely to the analysis of marriage prohibitions or preferences, but also to "adultery," so that it can be seen within the total constellation of sexual offences within that society. And this can only be done by accepting a breakdown of the monolithic category "incest" into concepts more closely related to the structure of the society in question.

REFERENCES

Evans-Pritchard, E. E., 1949, "Nuer Rules of Exogamy and Incest," in *Social Structure*, M. Fortes (ed.), Oxford. 1951, *Kinship and Marriage Among the Nuer*, Oxford University Press.

Fortes, M., 1936, "Kinship, Incest and Exogamy of the Northern Territories of the Gold Coast," in *Custom is King*, L. H. D. Buxton (ed.), London: Hutchinson. 1949, *The Web of Kinship Among the Tallensi*, Oxford University Press.

Howell, P. P., 1954, *A Manual of Nuer Law*, Oxford University Press.

Malinowski, B., 1932, *The Sexual Life of Savages*, London: Kegan Paul.

Murdock, G. P., 1949, *Social Structure*, New York: MacMillan. 1955, "Changing Emphases in Social Structure," *Southwestern Journal of Anthropology*, **11**, pp. 361–370.

Radcliffe-Brown, A. R., 1950, "Introduction," to *African Systems of Kinship and Marriage*, Oxford University Press.

Rattray, R. F., 1929, *Ashanti Law and Constitution*, Oxford University Press.

Seligman, B., 1950, "Incest and Exogamy: a Reconsideration," *American Anthropologist*, **52**, pp. 305–316.

6. Kinship Laterality and the Emotionally Disturbed Child*

BY BERNARD FARBER

THE ROLE OF KINSHIP in the socialization of children in contemporary American society has not been explored systematically. However, several studies of mental illness have suggested that the kindred does perceptibly affect personality development. This paper is based on an exploratory study of sixteen Champaign-Urbana area families, eight of whom had a child under treatment for a mild personality disturbance at an outpatient psychological clinic. The analysis has not yet been completed, and the discussion represents merely the test of one proposition, namely, that in a bilateral kinship system asymmetry in relations with the husband's as compared with the wife's siblings and cousins tends to affect socialization of children adversely.

The basis for this assertion is discussed in terms of various assumptions relating to (a) the organization of bilateral kinship systems and (b) kinship laterality and the nuclear family.

* An earlier version of this paper was presented at the American Sociological Association 1964 annual meeting, Montreal, Quebec. The study was supported by a grant from the Illinois Department of Mental Health, Psychiatric Training and Research Fund. Cooperation by the University of Illinois Psychological Clinic and the Champaign County Mental Health Clinic in securing subjects is greatly appreciated. Mrs. Marian Penniman supervised the interviewers. Comments by Harry M. Johnson, David Harvey, Efrosini John, and Jerry M. Lewis, University of Illinois, were helpful in revision of the paper.

The Organization of Bilateral Kinship Systems

Assumption 1. Sibling Solidarity. Although sibling solidarity may be important in unilineal kin groups as well, close relationships among siblings seem especially significant for bilateral kinship. It has been suggested that sibling solidarity is the fundamental bond in kinship relations in a bilateral system.[1] Cumming and Schneider have further indicated that emphasis on grouping by age (or on differentiation by generation) in American society facilitates solidarity among siblings.[2] More specifically, this emphasis on sibling solidarity in bilateral kinship relations is reflected in sibling relationships pertaining to parents, in husband-wife interaction, and relationships with siblings-in-law. These relationships are discussed briefly.

One factor in sustaining sibling solidarity is the common relationship with parents. Although ordinarily siblings establish separate residence on marriage, their ties to their family of orientation are not totally severed. Reciprocities established before marriage are to some extent maintained. Family reunions, birthdays, weddings, and other

[1] R. Pehrson, "Bilateral Kin Grouping as a Structural Type," *University of Manila Journal of East Asiatic Studies*, **3** (1954), pp. 199–202; Cited in Elaine Cumming and David M. Schneider, "Sibling Solidarity: A Property of American Kinship," *American Anthropologist*, **63** (June, 1961), pp. 498–507.

[2] Cumming and Schneider, *op. cit.*, p. 498.

events reinforce attachments to the family of orientation. Sometimes business arrangements and assistance services provide additional cement to the sibling bond. Finally, the parents sustain family solidarity by acting as communicators and mediators and as a common focus of interest and concern. As parents grow older, however, their influence on sibling solidarity may change. Especially at the times when elderly parents present problems in management, siblings are expected to collaborate in their solution. As parents die, the siblings provide the only remaining bonds to the family of orientation.

Marriage in contemporary American society also operates to sustain sibling solidarity. In the American kinship system there are no distinctions between children by sex or birth-order. The ideal in child raising is that no child is a "favorite." Under such conditions the preferred relationship among siblings is equalitarian and companionate. Yet these same qualities, equalitarianism and companionship, also characterize the marital relationship in contemporary society. Studies of marital adjustment show that in many respects married couples (apart from sexually relevant activities) act like siblings. Many of the common interests that sustain the marriage are essentially nonsexual. In numerous ways the marriage becomes a quasi-sibling relationship. Insofar as this quasi-sibling relationship is established in marriage, the married couple is incorporated into the husband's and wife's sibling sets. A bilateral sibling group is thereby instituted.

The incorporation of the married couple into a bilateral sibling group implies that there is little differentiation between siblings and siblings-in-law. In the study on kinship relations reported in this paper many repondents gave identical responses to siblings and siblings-in-law in describing feelings of closeness. Goody has pointed out that in bilateral societies brothers-in-law and sisters-in-law are governed by the same incest taboos as brothers and sisters.[3] Thus there is a blending of norms regarded as appropriate for siblings, siblings-in-law, and husband and wife. As the husband and wife are joined in a bilateral sibling group, sibling solidarity becomes intimately connected with marriage and nuclear family relations.

Assumption 2. Rules of Substitution. Various studies have indicated that in American kinship the closer the relatedness among kin, the more intimate the feelings among them.[4] Since interaction with kin ordinarily involves trust and personal concern, priorities in kinship interaction would be positively related to feelings of intimacy. Because the most intimate feelings are generally to be found in the family of orientation, the first priority in kinship interaction would be with members of this family of appropriate sex and generation (i.e., mother, father, brother, sister). The second priority would be given to families linked directly to the family of orientation by a parent or sibling. Members of parents' families of orientation and siblings' families of procreation would be expected to substitute when an immediate-family member of appropriate sex and generation is not available or lacks sufficient personal or financial resources.[5] Cousins, as linked directly to the parents' family of orientation by a consanguine uncle or aunt, can then operate as surrogate siblings. The third order of priority concerns consanguinity. Ordinarily, many loyalties have been developed to expect more of consanguine relatives than of affines. Moreover, consanguinalities cannot be broken by divorce. Except for close relatives, consanguine kin are therefore given priority over affines.

Assumption 3. Interaction and Laterality. Consanguine kinship groups in a unilineal system complement one another by exchange of obligations in marriage, household etiquette pertaining to taboos and respect, observance of one another's territorial rights, and numerous other reciprocities related to domestic life. A consequence of the complementarity in unilineal systems is that corporate groups of families are bound in reciprocal relations by intermarriage of their members. In contrast, a bilateral system generally does not provide a formal arrangement of reciprocities between kin groups. Instead, obligations of the

[3] Jack Goody, "A Comparative Approach to Adultery and Incest," *British Journal of Sociology*, **7** (1956), pp. 286–305.

[4] For example, Lee N. Robins and Miroda Tomanec, "Closeness to Blood Relatives Outside the Immediate Family," *Marriage and Family Living*, **24** (1962), pp. 340–346.

[5] Cumming and Schneider, *op. cit.*, p. 502.

husband's and wife's consanguine kin are defined by the resources of each kindred and the needs of the nuclear family. Laterality in a bilateral system is thereby based more on the nature of specific interpersonal relations than on formal, jural relations. Hence much permissiveness exists in the degree of matrilaterality, patrilaterality, or symmetery in kinship relations in a bilateral system.

Kinship Laterality and the Nuclear Family

This set of assumptions consists of statements about the relationship between kinship laterality and nuclear family relationships in a bilateral system.

Assumption 4. Form of Kinship Influences. The relationship between kinship and the socialization of a child in modern American society is indirect. There is a continual decline in the number of three-generation families sharing a household and a corresponding increase in the number of nuclear families in independent households. Thus relatives cannot be conceived as substitute parents who are actively engaged in the socialization of the children. Instead, the parents ordinarily act as a link between the child and his relatives outside the nuclear family.

Assumption 5. Power and the Person Outside the Kinship Group. Identity and a great amount of contact with one set of kindred rather than the other provides emotional support and reinforcement within the nuclear family for the parent who is a member of that kindred but not for the parent who is an outsider. The sustaining kindred also acts as a reference group for defining problems and appropriate solutions. Therefore the kindred with whom there is a higher involvement and participation would provide one parent with support and sustenance for maintaining a relatively more powerful position in nuclear family relations.[6] When the nuclear family allies itself with one kindred but not the other, the parent who is con-

sidered an outsider is in a markedly weaker power position within the nuclear family. This power differential also suggests than when a spouse is a tyrant an individual may turn for reinforcement to his own kinship group in order to gain power in the marital relationship (and perhaps become a countertyrant). The maintenance of a balance of power would be especially important when equalitarian norms govern husband-wife interaction.

Assumption 6. Asymmetry and Authoritarianism. Various investigations of American families have indicated that there is a strong tendency for power differential and conflict between parents in families whose children develop personality problems.[7] Often coalitions may develop which violate age, sex, or generation norms in family life. Lidz found that the presence of an ineffectual father was related to schizophrenia.[8] Peterson's investigation showed that more parents (especially fathers) of problem children were autocratic than were parents in control groups.[9] Myers and Roberts also reported much authoritarianism in their study of families in which a child had developed mental illness.[10] In contrast, Baldwin and his associates found that democratic relationships were related to effective intellectual functioning.[11]

[6] Goody, *op. cit.;* Bernard Farber, *Family: Organization and Interaction,* San Francisco: Chandler Publishing Company, 1964; see also Dorrian Apple Sweetser, "Asymmetry in Intergenerational Family Relationships," *Social Forces,* **41** (1963), pp. 346–352; and see George Peter Murdock, *Social Structure,* New York: Macmillan, 1949.

[7] A. Farina, "Patterns of Role Dominance and Conflict in Parents of Schizophrenic Patients," *Journal of Abnormal and Social Psychology,* **61** (1960), pp. 31–38; James C. Baxter, Sonya Arthur, Constance Flood, and Betty Hedgepeth, "Conflict Patterns in the Families of Schizophrenics," *Journal of Nervous and Mental Disease,* **135** (1962), pp. 419–424.

[8] Theodore Lidz, Alice Cornelison, Stephen Fleck, and Dorothy Terry, "The Intrafamilial Environment of Schizophrenic Patients: II. Marital Schism and Marital Skew," *American Journal of Psychiatry,* **114** (1957), pp. 241–248.

[9] Donald R. Peterson, Wesley C. Becker, Leo A. Hallmer, Donald J. Shoemaker, and Herbert C. Quay, "Parental Attitudes and Child Adjustment," *Child Development,* **30** (1959), pp. 119–130.

[10] Jerome K. Myers and Bertram H. Roberts, *Family and Class Dynamics in Mental Illness,* New York: Wiley, 1959.

[11] Alfred L. Baldwin, J. Kalhorn, and F. H. Breese, "Patterns of Parent Behavior," *Psychological Monographs,* **58** (1945), No. 268. Uric Bronfenbrenner, "The Effects of Social and Cultural Change on Personality," *Journal of Social Issues,* **17** (1961), pp. 6–18, however, suggests that parents' disciplining of the same-sex child is conducive to the development of initiative and responsibility in children.

Viewed in the context of kinship relationships, the findings of these investigations suggest that the power differential leading to authoritarianism and conflict in the family is based on highly asymmetrical kindred relationships.

Statement of Hypothesis. The specific hypothesis tested was based on the two sets of assumptions just set forth. The first set of assumptions provided a perspective about interaction between kin. Especially relevant for this study were the assumptions that (a) in American society there is much solidarity among siblings (and, by substitution, among cousins), and (b) the bilateral system permits much variation in the symmetry of kinship relations. The second set of assumptions indicated that asymmetry in kinship relations creates a disequilibrium in the balance of power in the husband-wife relationship. This disequilibrium fosters authoritarian interaction and the development of deviant coalitions in the family. The authoritarianism and deviant coalitions, in turn, tend to affect the socialization of children adversely.

To provide empirical support for this line of reasoning, the following hypothesis was tested: families with an emotionally disturbed child exhibit greater matrilateral or patrilateral tendencies in relationships with husbands' and wives' siblings than families in which the children are regarded as normal. Data on closeness to parents were also included in the analysis to determine whether asymmetrical kinship relations with siblings rather than with parents are significant in deviant socialization of children.

Procedure

This section describes the general design of the investigation and the specific procedure for ascertaining degree of integration and collaboration with same-generation kin.

Design of Investigation. Sixteen sets of parents participated in the study.[12] Eight couples were

[12] Data were actually collected for 20 families. However, four cases were not used for the following reasons: two mothers were widows, one family in the comparison group was Negro with a background different from any of the clinic families, and one family did not provide usable responses (e.g., almost all relatives, even if they were hardly known, were rated as very close).

parents of children who were in treatment at an outpatient psychological clinic. No child was diagnosed as schizophrenic: all school-age children were attending their neighborhood schools. The eight clinic families were matched as closely as possible with other families on social characteristics. Variables used in the matching were the following: religious denomination, father's occupation, situs of work (such as, university, air force), urban or rural residence, migration status (e.g., recent migrant versus life-long resident), and approximate number of children. All parents were native-born Caucasians living in the Champaign-Urbana area.

The couples in the clinic group had been married a median of 13 years (range of 7 to 20 years) and the couples in the comparison group had been married a median of 11 years (range of 5 to 21 years). The median age of husbands was 37.5 in the clinic group and 37 in the comparison group. For wives the median age was 34 in the clinic group and 35 in the comparison group. The families in the clinic sample had a total of 25 children and the families with normal children only, a total of 26. In each group there were three professors (roughly matched for academic discipline), one noncommissioned officer, one farmer, and three blue-collar workers. Six of the eight pairs of families were Protestants; the other matched pairs were Roman Catholic and Mormon.

The husbands and wives were separately but generally simultaneously interviewed at home by two interviewers. Social workers and advanced graduate students in sociology were used as interviewers. The information discussed in this paper was part of the data obtained in a series of approximately seven interviews with each family. The total interviewing time for each person was 15–20 hours; the interviews were tape-recorded and later transcribed.

Index of Sibling Solidarity. Sibling solidarity was indicated by feelings of closeness. The question in the interview which evoked an evaluation of each relative was: How close do you feel to ——— now? The parent's responses for his siblings and cousins were analyzed.

In response to the question on closeness, the parents rated each relative in their kindred on a nine-point scale (zero to eight) with verbal descriptions—"not at all" at zero, "somewhat" at four, and "very much" at eight. (A test-retest analysis on a different sample indicates high reliability in ratings in response to this question.)

Variations in the number of siblings and cousins in different kindreds would themselves influence the findings if all of them were included in the analysis. A respondent with eight cousins may feel close to only three of them, whereas a respondent with three cousins may feel close to them all. A mean of the closeness ratings for the eight cousins of the first respondent would probably be smaller than the mean for the three cousins of the second respondent. Yet in terms of *effective* kin (as opposed to nominal kin[13]), there is no difference between the respondents. The strategy adopted in the analysis was to use only a small arbitrary number of kin for each respondent. Three male and three female relatives seemed to be sufficient kin to provide a basis for

[13] R. Firth and J. Djamour, "Kinship in South Borough," in R. Firth (ed.,) *Two Studies of Kinship in London*, London: Athlone Press, 1956.

sibling-group identification and to perform the activities expected of intimate kin. The analysis was thus restricted to only the three male and three female siblings and cousins with the highest ratings on closeness. Because ratings on closeness vary inversely with the distance of relationship between kin, brothers and sisters were always included in the analysis and cousins were used to complete the set of six relatives. Six respondents did not have three male and three female relatives in their own generation of whom they were aware. When this occurred, the missing relatives from the set were given a rating of zero.

The index of solidarity with kin was the mean of the respondent's six highest ratings on closeness with siblings and cousins of appropriate sex.

Findings

The husband's and wive's mean ratings on closeness to their own siblings (and cousins) are presented in Table 1. The husbands in families

Table 1

Mean ratings for feelings of closeness to siblings and cousins by parents of emotionally disturbed child and parents whose children are normal

Family	Mean ratings on closeness		Extent of asymmetry in closeness to kin— ratio of larger mean to smaller: (1)/(2) or (2)/(1)
	Husband (1)	Wife (2)	
Families with Disturbed Child*			
A	2.7	3.8	1.41
B	2.0	7.7	3.84
C	5.2	3.7	1.41
D	5.5	3.0	1.83
E	4.0	5.7	1.43
F	3.0	7.2	2.40
G	2.3	6.0	2.61
H	4.3	1.8	2.39
Grand Mean	3.6	4.9	2.17
Families with Normal Children*			
I	5.0	5.2	1.04
J	2.8	1.5	1.87
K	6.0	5.0	1.20
L	4.5	6.2	1.38
M	3.0	2.5	1.20
N	4.8	5.2	1.11
O	8.0	7.7	1.04
P	2.3	4.0	1.74
Grand Mean	4.6	4.7	1.32

* Families with normal children have been placed in same order as the families with a disturbed child with whom they were matched (i.e., A matched with I; B with J, etc.).

with a disturbed child generally yielded lower mean ratings on closeness than their wives. However, the husbands and wives in normal families tended to be similar in closeness. The difference in symmetry between the clinic and comparison families becomes apparent when a ratio is computed for each couple to show the extent to which the higher mean closeness score is greater than the lower mean score. The greater the ratio, the more asymmetrical the relationships with kin of the couple's own generation. The mean of the ratios for the clinic group is 2.17, whereas the mean for the comparison group is only 1.32. When the matched families are compared (i.e., A with I, B with J, and so on), within each pair, the clinic family invariably reveals greater asymmetry. When the families are treated as unmatched, a Mann-Whitney U test shows a probability of obtaining the distribution of ratios by chance to be .003 (one-tailed; $U = 7$). There is clearly more asymmetry in kinship relations within the same generation for the clinic group.

The major source of asymmetry among the clinic families was revealed when ratings on closeness for siblings and for cousins were analyzed separately. For the clinic group, husbands' ratings for 23 siblings and 19 cousins were included in the analysis and wives' ratings for 24 siblings and 24 cousins were examined. The clinic group husbands' mean rating for siblings was 4.9; the mean rating for siblings by wives was 6.5. However, both husbands and wives in the clinic sample assigned a mean rating of 3.2 to cousins. Thus the asymmetry in same-generated kinship relations for the clinic families can generally be attributed to disparate relations with siblings by husbands and wives. In contrast to the findings on the clinic families, there was little difference between husbands and wives in the comparison-group families on closeness ratings for siblings. The analysis involved a total of 16 siblings and 26 cousins of comparison-group husbands and 19 siblings and 23 cousins of wives. The mean closeness rating for siblings of the comparison-group parents was 6.1 for the husbands and 6.6 for the wives. The mean closeness rating for cousins of the parents in the comparison group was 4.7 for the husbands and 4.3 for the wives. The husbands in

the comparison-families, therefore, generally rated both their siblings and cousins higher than did the clinic-group husbands. Although the mean closeness ratings for siblings were similar for wives in the clinic- and comparison-group samples, the wives in the comparison-group families tended to provide somewhat higher ratings for cousins.

In terms of the verbal designations on the scales used in the interview, the comparison-group couples tended to rate their cousins above the "somewhat-close" designation; the clinic couples generally provided a rating below "somewhat." This difference between samples in rating cousins on closeness resulted in a smaller distinction between siblings and cousins for the comparison group than for the clinic group. The ratio of the mean closeness rating for cousins to the mean rating for siblings was .65 for the clinic husbands and .76 for the comparison-group husbands. The ratio of cousins' to siblings' mean closeness rating was .49 for the clinic wives and .65 for the comparison-group wives. These findings suggest a greater substitutability by cousins for siblings in comparison-group families than in clinic families.

The conception of a bilateral sibling group suggests that not only do both husband and wife maintain approximately equal ties with their own siblings but also that they make little distinction between their own brothers and sisters and those of their spouse. Accordingly, it was anticipated that husbands and wives in the comparison group would reveal a greater similarity in closeness ratings between their own sibling and their siblings-in-law (spouse's brothers and sisters) than would the clinic couples. The ratio of the closeness ratings of own siblings to spouse's siblings (or vice versa) are presented in Table 2. For husbands, the mean for the clinic sample was .38 compared with .62 in the normal-child sample. For wives the means were .40 for the clinic sample and .72 for the comparison sample. In six of the eight pairs for husbands' and wives' responses, the ratios for the comparison group were higher than for the clinic group. Even with these exceptions, the results for both husbands and wives are statistically significant. (For husbands, Wilcoxon matched-pairs, signed-ranks (one-tailed) test, $T = 4$, $p = .025$; for wives,

$T = 3, p < .025$). Thus the ratings on closeness provide additional support for the view that incorporation of the married couples into a bilateral siblings group facilitate effective socialization of children.

In only 4 of the 16 couples participating in the study did both husband and wife have a complete set of parents. Laterality on the basis of feelings of closeness to parents or parental surrogates is shown in Table 3. When a parent was dead or when an individual indicated that he felt closer to an uncle or aunt than to a parent of the same sex, the individual's rating for the uncle or aunt with the highest score was used in the analysis. The assignment of a higher rating on closeness to an aunt or uncle than to a living parent occurred when the parents had been estranged or divorced. In the table the rating on closeness for an aunt or uncle is in parentheses when the parent is deceased. An asterisk indicates that an aunt's or uncle's rating is higher than the

parent's. As in Table 1, the ratios in the table are obtained by dividing the higher rating on closeness (whether it be the husband's or the wife's) by the lower rating on closeness. The table indicates less unilaterality with respect to feelings of closeness to parents than is true of siblings. For the most part there is little difference between the families with disturbed children and families with normal children. With respect to ratings for mothers, the ratios in the clinic families are considerably higher than the comparison families in only two instances. For the data on the fathers there is a slight tendency toward families with normal children to have a higher ratio than families with a disturbed child. Because of the large number of cases in which the father was dead, however, little significance can be attached to this finding. Hence, unilaterality in relations with parents is apparently not so significant as relationships with siblings in fostering emotional disturbance of children.

Table 2

Ratio of mean closeness scores for own siblings and cousins to mean for spouse's siblings and cousins in clinic and comparison-samples

Family	Ratio for husband's ratings	Ratio for wife's ratings
Clinic Sample (with Disturbed Child)		
A	.50	.04
B	.38*	.00
C	.45	.91
D	.31	.61
E	.26	.47
F	.47*	.23
G	.35*	.03
H	.15	.92*
Mean Ratio	.38	.40
Comparison-Sample (with Normal Children)		
I	.16	.71
J	.47	.67
K	.81	1.00
L	.74	.89
M	.84	.38
N	.93	.77
O	.83	.78
P	.14	.58
Mean Rate	.62	.72

* Mean rating for spouse's siblings and cousins greater than mean for own siblings and cousins. Mean for spouse's relatives used as denominator in computing ratio.

Note. On Wilcoxon matched-pairs, ranked-signs test, for husbands, $T = 4$ and $P = .025$ (one-tailed test); for wives, $T = 3$ and $.025 > p > .01$.

Table 3

Ratings for feelings of closeness to own mothers and fathers (or their surrogates) by parents of emotionally disturbed child and parents whose children are normal †

Family	Ratings on mothers			Ratings on fathers		
	Husband	Wife	Extent of asymmetry— ratio of larger rating to smaller	Husband	Wife	Extent of asymmetry— ratio of larger rating to smaller
Families with Disturbed Child						
A	3*	6*	2.00	7	(4)	1.75
B	7	8	1.14	(7)	(8)	1.14
C	8	8	1.00	(–)	8	—
D	(6)	8	1.33	6*	8	1.33
E	8	6	1.33	(8)	7	1.14
F	8	8	1.00	4*	6*	1.50
G	8	8	1.00	8	8	1.00
H	(3)	8	2.67	7	8	1.14
Families with Normal Children						
I	7	7	1.00	7	6*	1.13
J	8	7	1.14	(3)	5	1.67
K	7	7	1.00	7	(5)	1.40
L	7	5	1.40	7	8	1.14
M	(6)	(5)	1.20	7	(4)	1.75
N	8	(6)	1.33	8	(–)	—
O	8	8	1.00	8*	(4)	2.00
P	5	(8)	1.60	(–)	8	—

† Parentheses indicate that this parent is deceased and highest rating for uncle (instead of father) or aunt (instead of mother) is used. The asterisk indicates that the rating for the uncle or aunt is higher than the rating for the parent; accordingly, the table presents the rating for the aunt or uncle. When the parent is deceased and no uncle or aunt is known to the respondent (–) appears in the table.

It can be argued that having an emotionally disturbed child drives the parents more firmly to one set of siblings or the other. If so, the results described may be an artifact of the child's deviance rather than a reflection of kinship relations. To determine the basis for matrilaterality or patrilaterality, the distance of the current residence of the family from the husband's and wife's place of birth was computed. The results are shown in Table 4. Because exactly the same tendencies were found for the clinic and comparison groups, both sets of data are combined in the table. The table indicates that whether the family resides more or less than 100 miles from the wife's birthplace makes little difference in matrilateral or patrilateral tendencies in relations with siblings ($Q = .33$). However, the distance from the husband's place of birth

affects kinship laterality. When the families live more than 100 miles from the husband's birthplace, they tend to be matrilateral; when they live within 100 miles, patrilateral tendencies predominate ($Q = .77$; $p = .07$ on Fisher's exact test).

The findings on distance from the parents' birthplace are consistent with patterns of kinship relations prevalent in middle-class American society.[14] Maintenance of kinship ties is mainly the wife's task. Hence she ordinarily maintains contact and interest, regardless of the distance of residence from kin. For the husband, however, distance is a major factor in his relationships with siblings. When he is geographically close, he need not rely heavily on his spouse

[14] Farber, *op. cit.*, pp. 206–207.

to maintain interest and contact. At a distance, with kinship relations in the hands of the wife, her inclinations would be to maintain ties with her siblings rather than with her husband's.

Because distance from the husband's birthplace appears to be a major factor in laterality in solidary relations with siblings, it seems reasonable to interpret the findings of this study in terms of effects of kinship relations on socialization of the child rather than the reverse.

Conclusion

The findings support the hypothesis that families with an emotionally disturbed child exhibit greater matrilateral or patrilateral tendencies in solidary relationships with the married couple's siblings (and, by substitution, cousins) than do families in which the children are regarded as normal. The results indicated that among comparison-group families there was (a) greater similarity in feelings of closeness by husband and wife to their own siblings and (b) less differentiation in feelings of closeness between siblings and siblings-in-law, and between siblings and cousins. These tendencies imply a greater ability by the parents in the comparison group to incorporate additional

members into their sibling group. The findings on distance also point to asymmetry in kinship relations as a factor in the deviant socialization of the child.

The basis for the asymmetry in kinship relations varied among the families studied. In some families the parent was alienated from his siblings and cousins. Probably this kind of parent has difficulty in maintaining equalitarian relationships with anyone. In other families the parent did not know his relatives well enough to establish solidary relationships, whereas his spouse was highly involved in kinship relations. However, whether alienation or lack of available personnel was responsible, one parent was an outsider in terms of same-generation kinship relations. In either case there was no bilateral sibling group established nor were relationships with cousins sufficiently close to substitute them for estranged or alienated siblings.

The data reported in this paper suggest a problem in the organization of bilateral kinship systems: why is it necessary for the nuclear family to participate about equally with both kindreds? The answer indicated by the findings is: the bilateral system lacks formal reciprocities between corporate kinship groups which would sustain an equilibrium in relationships within a nuclear family if that family affiliated itself with only one of them. Thus in a bilateral system,

Table 4

Distance of current residence from parents' place of birth and comparison of husbands' and wives' mean closeness ratings for own siblings and cousins

Distance	Mean closeness ratings for own siblings and cousins	
	Husband's ratings higher than wife's (patrilaterality)	Wife's ratings higher than husband's (matrilaterality)
Distance from Husband's Birthplace*		
Over 100 miles	2	7
100 miles or less	5	2
Distance from Wife's Birthplace†		
Over 100 miles	2	4
100 miles or less	5	5

* $Q = .77$; Fisher's exact test, one-tailed, $p = .07$.
† $Q = .33$.

when marked tendencies toward asymmetry occur, there are no formal mechanisms for adjusting disequilibrium in power relations in the nuclear family. This disequilibrium would be especially disruptive to family relations when equalitarian norms are supposed to govern husband-wife interaction. The operation of equalitarian norms is inhibited when the married couple does not identify itself as a part of a bilateral sibling group (in which cousins can act as sibling-surrogates). The disequilibrium creates personal problems for family members. These personal problems may result in emotional disturbance in children. Hence in a bilateral system the nuclear family tends to operate effectively in socializing children when solidary relationships with husband's and wife's siblings are symmetrical.

In conclusion, this paper does not suggest that asymmetry in relations with husband's as compared with wife's siblings can be regarded by itself as either necessary or sufficient to explain the presence of emotional disturbance in children. At most, this asymmetry may create or sustain a marital situation which in turn permits the development of pathological family relationships.[15] However, the findings do provide evidence that this asymmetry is highly potent in affecting socialization of children.

[15] Lidz et al., *op. cit.*; Lyman C. Wynne, Irving M. Ryckoff, Juliana Day, and Stanley I. Hirsch, "Pseudo-Mutuality in the Family Relationships of Schizophrenics," *Psychiatry*, 21 (1958), pp. 205–220; Yi-Chuang Lu, "Mother-Child Roles in Schizophrenia," *Psychiatry*, 24 (1961), pp. 133–142, Victor D. Sanua, "Sociocultural Factors in Families of Schizophrenics," *Psychiatry*, 24 (1961), pp. 246–265.

Chapter 3

Open and Closed Families

The distinction between an open group and a closed group has long been useful for describing variation and change in family life. Max Weber defined a relationship as closed when outsiders were excluded, limited, or subjected to particular conditions of participation.[1] Although families are seldom fully open or closed, the distinction is helpful for the analysis of norms and values in family life.

As a closed social group, the family has several characteristics that make it an effective vehicle for carrying on stable social relations. In turn, stable social relations facilitate the transmission of norms and values of family life from one generation to the next.

Robert Redfield chose to define the folk society primarily as an isolated group with no contact at all with outsiders. Certainly the folk society has other attributes, including small size, the presence of an oral tradition, and an economic base sufficient for persistence. Redfield, however, emphasized that the folk society is composed of people who have been isolated from outsiders over numerous generations. Possibly as a consequence of this isolation, all members of the folk society are in intimate contact; members of the society have a strong sense of belonging together; and there is a strong emphasis on tradition, consistency among elements of the culture, and the culture is transmitted from generation to generation without change.[2]

Redfield's discussion implies that nuclear families are open in closed societies. Family interaction in these societies is considered in the public domain. When family relationships are relatively open, the spouse and parent roles extend beyond the nuclear family to other kinship groups in the community. (The spouse and parent roles refer to rights and obligations about authority, family division of labor, child care, and financial support.) In societies characterized by open families the roles of uncle, aunt, grandparent, brother, sister, and cousin embody rights and obligations

---

[1] Max Weber, *The Theory of Social and Economic Organization*, New York: Oxford University Press, 1947, edited by T. Parsons, pp. 139–143.
[2] Robert Redfield, "The Folk Society," *American Journal of Sociology*, **52** (1947), pp. 293–308.

for enacting some spouse-parent roles in families of procreation other than their own. The borderline between an individual's own family of procreation and a kinsman's family of procreation is not well defined.

Societies differ in the extent that they prescribe closed relationships for the nuclear family. When family relationships are closed, a sharp distinction must be made between one's own family and those of kin. There must then be gross differences between spouse-parent roles and uncle, aunt, grandparent, brother, and sister roles. These differences provide a well-defined boundary for the nuclear family.

The variation in closedness in the husband-wife relationship is particularly relevant for mate-lover roles compared with spouse-parent roles. Few societies encourage openness in mate-lover relationships in marriage; nevertheless, in many societies the same person is expected to be simultaneously mate, lover, spouse, and parent. The roles of mate and lover depend on personal attraction and emotion, but social relationships based on personal attraction and emotion are precarious. In contrast to spouse-parent roles, mate and lover relationships are thus unusually vulnerable to openness.

In societies in which nuclear family relationships are expected to be closed, emphasis must be given to the clear definition, distinctiveness, and importance of prescribed spouse-parent roles. Additionally, strong controls must be instituted over mate-lover roles to maintain closed marital relationships. If a closed family is desired, mate selection must emphasize the probable adequacy of the individuals in prescribed spouse and parent roles. Intervention by the parents in mate selection generally occurs on the grounds of apparent adequacy of the prospective son-in-law or daughter-in-law as a spouse or parent (rather than as lover and mate). The failure to emphasize spouse-parent roles in mate selection would interfere with maintaining closed family relationships.

Goode has classified systems of marital selection by extent of parental intervention. At one extreme is child marriage in which the mate selection occurs before love and personal attraction can influence the choice of spouse. At the other extreme is the system of selecting mates through the love and personal attraction of the persons who marry.[3] The marital selection system in contemporary society, based on love and personal attraction, is consistent with tendencies toward a general openness in social relations.

The ideal family in many parts of contemporary society is one with relatively closed relationships: a "togetherness" in household tasks, in leisure, in emotional support, and in decision making. However the incompatibility between permanently closed family relationships and the variation in norms and values in an open society is suggested by Burgess, Locke, and Thomes in their discussion of changes in family life associated with contemporary society. They enumerate four kinds of mobility: residential, personal, vertical, and ideational.[4] Each serves to open social relationships. Residential mobility is a change in location of the domicile that facilitates the creation of new social relationships without necessarily severing completely the old

[3] William J. Goode, "The Theoretical Importance of Love," *American Sociological Review*, **24** (1959), pp. 38–47.
[4] Ernest W. Burgess, Harvey J. Locke, and Mary Margaret Thomes, *The Family from Institution to Companionship*, New York: American Book, 1963.

relationships. Personal mobility is the cyclical movement of individuals either in their daily routine or on occasional trips. An increase in personal mobility makes possible a corresponding increase in the number of social relationships. If there is an average rise in personal mobility, the number of potential social relationships in the group will rise geometrically because of the new combinations of social relationships possible. Vertical mobility is the movement of a person or a family either upward or down- ward in social class position. W. L. Warner and his associates have shown that participation in formal and informal groups in the community (such as cliques, churches, civic organizations, and school activities) is related to social class member- ship.[5] A change in class position leads to the formation of social relationships with other members of the attained social class.

Ideational mobility is the change in ideas and values. Mass communications media introduce individuals to a variety of novel ideas and values. Some of these ideas may conflict with earlier ones and the individuals may eventually form social relationships with persons who support these novel ideas. Contemporary society with its mass communications media, technology of transportation, changes in occupational and educational structure, and residential turnover thus may interfere with a stable conception of parent-spouse roles and with the permanence of mate-lover relationships in the family.

This discussion shows how the openness in social relations in modern society has intruded on family and kinship life. The increased contact with others, amount of freedom and marital choice, and mobility which threaten closed family relations suggested to some sociologists before World War II that the family as a social insti- tution was disintegrating.[6]

However, since World War II evidence has been accumulating that, in reaction to societal openness, individuals have tended to find increased significance in family and kinship relations. Some sociologists have interpreted this reaction as response to a boundary-maintaining system to external threat.[7] Others (notably Schelsky) have viewed it as a means for reconstruction of a stable social order when openness in society has made traditional norms and values inappropriate.

The papers in this chapter indicate how German, Israeli, and Mexican families have responded to this societal openness. The American family is discussed in the next chapter. The response to openness in each society must be placed in the historical setting of its unique family and kinship organization. Yet, in spite of the historical individuality of each society, there is a convergence among societies in the kinds of family and kinship organization that are developing.

Readings on Openness in Family and Kinship

The readings in this chapter examine open and closed family relationships. A major problem in applying the concept of closedness to the family is to specify the

[5] William Lloyd Warner, et al., *Social Class in American*, New York: Harper, 1960.
[6] Pitirim A. Sorokin, *Social and Cultural Dynamics*, New York: Harper, 1937, Vol. 4, p. 776; Carle C. Zimmerman, *The Family and Civilization*, New York: Harper, 1947, p. 796.
[7] Elizabeth Bott, *Family and Social Network*, London: Tavistock Publications, 1957.

particular unit that is closed. In some instances the nuclear family is open and the larger kinship unit such as the lineage is closed. In others the nuclear family is closed and the larger kinship group open.

The paper by Schelsky on the German family suggests that when the community has open social relationships which are highly public the nuclear family tends to become a closed, private group. The condition of post-World War II German society involves simultaneous disillusionment with both the open society and large-scale bureaucracy. This disillusionment drives individuals to the intimacy of the family and places a great strain on family relationships. This strain may eventually overwhelm the family as we know it and stimulate a profound change. Schelsky hypothesizes that this change will result in a reopening or revision of family boundaries.

The paper on the Israeli family, by Talmon-Garber, suggests that buffer-groups may exist that protect the nuclear family from the open society. Thus the collective settlement (i.e., *kibbutz* or *moshav*) enables the nuclear family to operate as an open system even when the society-at-large is characterized by openness. Talmon-Garber regards the *kibbutz* as a relatively closed quasi-kinship group compensating for the dispersion of kin by acting between the family and the society-at-large. In the Israeli cities, however, the isolated refugee families, having no buffer to protect them from the threats and uncertainties of the society, form intensive involvements in the nuclear family. The author indicates that a major task in Israel is to develop ways of disengaging the *kibbutz* nuclear families from the over-all organization of the collective and for extending the participation of "isolated" nuclear families in the cities.

De Hoyos and De Hoyos in their paper on the *Amigo* system and its resulting alienation of the wife in the conjugal Mexican family describe some of the mechanisms and conditions facilitating openness in family life in an urban setting. Their paper indicates that the *Amigo* system is sustained by conflict and dissatisfaction in marriage, the low value placed on marriage by men, control by men of the economic resources, and the high differentiation of male and female roles in marriage. They suggest that, with the growth of the urban middle class in Mexico, both the *Amigo* system and openness in family relations will decline.

7. The German Family and Opposed Developmental Tendencies in Industrial Society

BY HELMUT SCHELSKY

CHANGES IN THE CONTEMPORARY GERMAN family are to be understood in two ways. On the one hand, the changes involve processes associated with the evolving capitalistic-industrial society including the uprooting and mobilization of people and other phenomena induced by industrialization, urbanization, political and social revolution, and deepening economic crises. In this context, the social consequences of being driven from home are parallel to the consequences of various well known events that have occurred since the time of the French Revolution. There has been a continual mixing and dispersion of population. On the other hand, however, the changes also show phenomena in opposition to those developmental tendencies which we have usually regarded as results of industrialization or urbanization or political mass-democracy or the occurrence of great economic crises. In fact, the family manifests *processes of increase in stability* through stress on such things as tradition and on the solidarity and value of the small group. It appears as if the effects on the family of the society uprooted by events within industrial and urban frameworks have, beyond a certain threshold, been transformed into countereffects.

SOURCE: *This is an abbreviated version of pages 347–357 of Schelsky's* Wandlungen der deutschen Familie in der Gegenwart, *Stuttgart: Ferdinand Enke, 1960, relying partly on paraphrase and partly on direct translation. Printed by permission of the author and publisher.*

The two kinds of changes are present simultaneously. The social fate of the refugees, declassed persons, and others is undoubtedly, on the one hand, to be diagnosed as a phenomenon of individuals becoming atoms in a mass, as it were, against a background of disintegration of old social structures and groupings in the entire society. On the other hand, these same elements are involved in the reorganization and stabilization of small-group relationships and have particular bearing on family cohesion.

It is crucial for our discussion that *the relationship between the large-scale abstract orders of society and small primary groups is involved in change.* The recent experience in Germany, especially for refugees and declassed persons, is that governmental and other large organizational structures involved in leadership of the whole society have both demanded a great deal of human beings and have suffered radical collapse. There have been constant disappointments in the overarching systems of political and social order. Personal destinies have been construed as resulting from a deluded trust in the promises and programs of large organizations and their leadership. Now over against these disappointments is the experience that those human relationships which proved to be reliable and unique supports in danger had seemed to play merely a subordinate role in our social structure, a role restricted purely to the private life of the individual. We refer above all to the family in the time of emergency after catastrophe, but also to groups of neighbors, friends, workers, and others. The general social consciousness, disappointed in principle, has turned away from hopes and plans looking for salvation in a reconstruction of society from the ground up, in new orders of state and economy, in new large organizations. It seems most urgent now rather to seek the security of the small world of one's family and occupation. Social concern and deeper human interests begin to shift away from institutions supported on abstract attitudes, big organizations, and collective relations and toward small groups and those personal human relationships that may be encountered in marriage, family, friendship, comradeship, and collegiality.

This, then, suggests once more the character of the second kind of change in the family that has been noted above, a type of change that takes the family outside the framework of certain older realities of capitalistic development. But what this turning away from the abstract orders and large organizations of our bureaucratized society and this turning to primary social modes of conduct and the valuing and stabilization of the latter mean for the future of our social development is quite problematic. One may see therein a renewing return to the origins and sources of our intellectual and social culture. This renewal may be viewed as the beginning of a kind of sociological renaissance without any historical model. In a similar manner, our scientific thought, the political ideas of democracy, even the feeling of freedom of modern man, or our artistic feelings for style once arose in the small, compassable communities of orders, lodges, clubs, scientific and artistic schools and circles, within the boundaries of a small social stratum of those who knew one another personally. However, one may also see in the increased emphasis upon small intimate groups the second phase of a decline in civilization, in which the large-organizational forms of production, politics and administration are beginning to become rigid through their intensifying abstraction, or even incompetent to perform their tasks. In this phase, men are pressed by necessity to find their mainstay in the residues of natural group structure. However, this structure does not have a

genuine chance of development in a society of big industry and thorough bureaucratization. The petrifaction of society into a bureaucratic organizational block and a mosaic of the smallest isolated social cells cannot be arrested through the natural group structure. In the interpretation of these phenomena, optimism and pessimism thus both have broad possibilities.

In a long-range view it seems to us that in this transformed relationship of the family and other small-group structures on the one hand and whole-social organization on the other, two dangerous developments are encountered. We can designate these two developments as the decline of publicness and as the threatening overburdening of intimate groups.

People form themselves and their interests into an Either-Or, between the bureaucratic and authoritarian organization and the familial and other intimate types of group living. With the emergence of a dualism of interests, in principle, between the small-group and big-organization social relationships, the medium of intelligence is contracting. The only remaining choice is between adapting one's intelligence usefully to the bureaucratically directed functionality of the big organizations and withdrawing in isolation into conventicles, intellectual friendship groups, or other groups of smallest scope. With the withdrawal into the small group, any accomplishments that point beyond narrow confines degenerate into a professional activity undertaken simply to take care of the needs of existence.

In these processes of development of "naked bureaucracy" on the one side and of the opposed accentuation and confirmation of isolated small-group interest-complexes on the other, which we can observe in the same measures both in intellectual and cultural life and in economic and occupational life, a social phenomenon, namely, *the public-ness of modern society*, is crumbled and dissolved. We have been all too wont to look upon the existence of publicness as something to be taken for granted; but it is in reality a creation of the social life of the past two hundred years. Publicness arose indeed with the necessary emergence (as modern social structure developed) of the individual out of purely communal-small-group social relationships. It arose out of the individual's self-allocation to a large number of social groupings and interests and his resultant participation in the abstract conflicts of interest and interaction to be found in an entire society organized in many strata. These many-sided claims for social identification and the condition of social conflict involved therein have, however, been increasingly felt as unmeetable and as an oppressive over-burdening of man in modern society. An extraordinarily one-sided development of social interests is in process in the individual, produced as much by the decisiveness with which small-group egoism sets itself off from the total interests of society as by the unrestricted way in which the bureaucracies take hold of and direct the human being who belongs to them. "Publicness" becomes more and more one of the sheer advertisements manipulated by the abstract-bureaucratic organizations themselves—advertisement of their positions, their polemics, their claims. This modern publicness to be sure has a function in the play of tensions between organizations, but scarcely arouses tension in the inner economy of the interests of the individual, whose effort is to flee to the peace and quiet of small horizons. Modern publicness degenerates into a striving for security and unburdening which is as effective in the hardening of the bureaucracies as in the restabilization of the small group.

A second consequence of the direction of social development described, which is fraught with danger in the long run, seems to relate to the re-stabilized intimate group. As our whole-social institutions and organizations can less and less fulfil and meet man's primary psycho-social needs and as gratification of these needs must increasingly be shifted to the small private group, especially the family, the danger grows that in the long run far too large a burden will be imposed on the latter intimate group. This danger increases as the intimate group is already expanded in its functions, its psychological content, and in its condition of having too much demanded of it. In our investigation of the postwar German family, we have already ascertained the occurrence of such things in the families of refugees and declassed persons, especially as regards the role of the wife in those families.

Because the highly specialized division of labor and the discipline and rationalization of the modern conditions of production offered man's psychological and affective life ever less scope in his occupational activity, the family and other intimate groups frequently become the loci for the release of emotional tensions that are created outside these groups but that have to be repressed when they occur. Aggravation (stirred up and "swallowed down" in one's occupational life) and other emotional pressures are unburdened and find outlet in the family and thus "the family becomes the arena in which emotional catharsis occurs" (Harriet R. Mowrer, *Personality Adjustment and Domestic Discord*, New York, 1935, p. 150). This emotionality has already often been stressed as a unique burdening of the family in the modern social constitution. The internal family relationships thus take over the additional task of having to adapt and "ward off" emotional disturbances of the individual's extrafamilial life. Family relationships thereby sometimes accrue the abnormal weight carried by the interaction between psychiatrist and patient. This introduction into the family of tensions that in their origin have nothing to do with the family has undoubtedly led in many cases to the worsening of unfortunate marital and familial relations. On the other hand, there is involved in all this a special opportunity to strengthen the coherence of the bonds among family members. The increase in family coherence occurs insofar as the female head succeeds in creating in domestic life a sympathetic, relaxed, and humanly warm atmosphere in opposition to the emotionally inhibitive objectivity and cold discipline of modern occupational life. (And yet with increasing occupational activity for the woman herself as well as with the overburdening with work of the entire family the opportunity referred to again diminishes, as we have had to point out at various places in our investigation of the present-day German family.)

This emotional overburdening of the family and other intimate groups through modern affect-inhibitive conditions of work nevertheless seems to us relatively insignificant as against other heightened *demands which arise for the intimate groups in the long run. These demands develop out of the turning-back into intimacy those social and intellectual holistic interests of the person that previously were still in the grip of tensions in whole-social organizations.* Although the growing solidarity and firmness of the family reduced the importance of emotional tension, both the family and other kinds of intimate groups will more and more have to fulfil needs relating to value, order and power, demands for intellectual encounter and recognition. Hence, the family becomes involved in the whole arsenal of interests evolved in the sphere of publicness, interests which as such have in no sense been relinquished with the turning away from the public sphere. Thus the family no longer is the place for abreaction but must afford, precisely, the field of encounter and decision for previously extrafamilial social demands and tensions. Because these needs have developed in the conditions of conflict of the public arena, the family (in accordance with its character) will, like other groups, be unable to gratify them suitably. Therefore, it will have to suffer in the situation of over-demand and be a substitute form for the lost public arena until an adaptation of interest structures to the performance-capacity of isolated small-group social setups is attained. Accordingly, in the long run the person-foundation of the family may very well be more strongly threatened and shaken than it has by all previous factors involved in industrial society. The family, by becoming the "world," inevitably loses its separation from the world in which the peculiar intimacy and privacy of the family life in modern times had evolved. Parallel to the decline of publicness there may then be a decline of the intimacy of familial and other private relationships of man; a decline of the intimacy developed in a sense opposed to publicness, a decline of intimacy having its essence in this very opposition. The small-group closeness of family relationships may lose that function of psychological unburdening which it has up to the present performed to a considerable extent in the modern world.

There should be no doubt about the hypothetical character of the lines of development just sketched. A final methodological observation can now be made: in our interpretation of the structural changes of the German family we have believed it necessary to describe two opposing processes. On the one hand, we discussed the developmental traits of deracination, de-institutionalization, and weakening of the stability of the family (all emerging from industrialization, growth of large cities, and bureaucratization). On the other hand, we set beside these traits counter-processes growing out of the social events of the present day—processes of stabilization of the small group, of stress on tradition and authority, of dissolving of that illusion of progress proper to the previous industrial society, and so on. We saw the same polar opposition in the development of the relation of large-scale social organization to small-group at work in all fields of social life. Since the presence and further working out of the older processes neither can nor should be in any way denied, we must understand *the developmental condition of present-day social structure* only as implying *a cross-cutting of opposed directions of social evolution.*

The task of a sociological analysis of the present appears to us to consist precisely in ascertaining this opposed character of social trends and not simplifying them in the sense of a single evolutionary process of going in one line (whether this be optimistically or pessimistically conceived). Thus, the single-line evolutionary hypotheses of family sociology—*Burgess* used the formula "from institution to companionship" (*The Family: From Institution to Companionship,* New York, 1945)—are no longer adequate for the interpretation of the change of present-day family structures. Even a highly differentiated theory of social change that yet somehow remains in the grip of an evolutionary singularism no longer does justice to the changes within present-day society as a whole. Although William F. Ogburn in his theory of social change assumes different rhythms and different standards of social change for different portions of the social system or assumes particularized processes of retardation and restorative phases, nevertheless there remains affirmed in his work the singularistic view of social change as adaptation to the progress of industrial-bureaucratic conditions of production and economy. The question is whether such hypostatization of a material-concrete singularistic denominator of lines of social evolution does not in reality respond more to a metaphysical need for belief than to the requirements of our goals of interpretation in social science. We believe that sociology today is constrained, for the purpose of achieving an evolutionary-historical orientation toward the present world, to work with different theories of social evolution that have an opposed evolutionary meaning. The only alternatives are to simplify dogmatically the realities of the social condition in their fullness and contradictory character or turn to the goals and modes of thought of metaphysics of history. To be effective, *theories of opposed processes* would have to manifest their character as hypotheses more clearly than evolutionary doctrines in social science have hitherto done. Sociology would thus lose, as other empirical sciences have previously done, the feature of naive indentifications of theory and reality that remains attached to it from philosophical speculation. It would, however, thereby become more open in its mode of thought to a future presumably pregnant with many more new realities.

8. Social Change
and Family Structure

BY YONINA TALMON-GARBER

THE PURPOSE OF THIS PAPER is an analysis of the impact of radical and rapid social change on patterns of family organization and on the relationship between the family and the community. We shall be dealing here with three of the types of family found in Israel: (a) the family in collective settlements (Kibbutzim); (b) the family in cooperative settlements (Moshavim) settled by immigrants from Islamic countries; and (c) the family among European refugees in urban centers. We shall focus our analysis on these cases because they represent three analytically distinct modes of interaction between the family and the community. In the Kibbutzim the community reigns supreme and the family is subordinated to it. The traditional family in the Moshavim is kinship centered—the elementary family is subordinated to wider kinship groupings which mediate between it and the community. The isolated refugee family in urban centers is cut off from kin and estranged from the community.

The Family in Collective Settlements[1]

The main features of collective settlements or Kibbutzim[2] are: common ownership of property,

except for a few personal belongings, and communal organization of production and consumption. Members' needs are provided for by communal institutions on an equalitarian basis. All income goes into the common treasury; each member gets only a very small annual allowance for personal expenses. The community is run as a single economic unit and as one household. It is governed by a general assembly, which meets as a rule once a week, by a secretariat, and by various committees. The Kibbutzim are an outgrowth of the revolutionary phase of Jewish immigration to Israel. The ideological urge to migrate to the new country and establish Kibbutzim in it has not affected either whole communities or whole kinship groups—it cut through and disrupted kinship ties. Most

---

[1] This analysis is based on a research project which was carried out in a representative sample of the Kibbutzim affiliated with one of the four federations of Kibbutzim. The project has combined sociological and anthropological field methods. The data obtained from the questionnaires, from various types of interviews and from the analysis of written materials were examined and carefully interpreted by direct observation. R. Bar Yoseph took an active part in the initial planning. A. Etzioni assisted me in direction of the project in its first stage. The other main research assistants were: E. Ron, M. Sarell and J. Sheffer. M. Sarell and E. Cohen took over from A. Etzioni in the second stage. The main research assistants were: U. Avner, B. Bonne, S. Deshen, R. Gutman-Shaku, T. Horowitz, U. Hurwitz, and Z. Stup.

[2] See M. Spiro, *Venture in Utopia, 1956.*

SOURCE: International Social Science Journal, *Volume 14 (1962), pp. 468–487. Reprinted by permission of the author and publisher.*

immigrants during this phase were young and unattached. They came to the country unaccompanied by parents or relatives, having discarded their former way of life and their former social setting. The disposition to establish cohesive communities and relegate the family to a secondary position is closely connected with this process of dissociation from former ties. The cohesion of the new primary relations, developed in the youth movements and later on in the Kibbutzim, replaced the discarded family ties.

Examination of the first stages[3] of the Collective Movement and the first phases of the development of each Kibbutz reveals that there is a certain basic incompatibility between intense collective identification and family solidarity. The members of the Kibbutz agree voluntarily to subordinate their personal interests to the attainment of communal goals and to seek self-expression only through service to their community. The conception of an all-absorbing task dominates their life and defines every aspect of it. The devotion to the realization of communal ideals take precedence over kinship obligations. The intimate person-to-person relations, the intense togetherness, the unity which permeates all contacts, become more significant than family loyalties. The intense collective identification conteracts any tendency to renew contacts with relatives outside the Kibbutzim. Relatives who are not members are by definition outsiders, almost strangers. It is felt that external ties should not be allowed to interfere with internal unity. The formation of families of procreation in the Kibbutzim introduces a new source of conflict, in this case an internal conflict. Deep attachment to the family may weaken the primary group characteristics of the Kibbutz and disrupt its unity. The families may tend to become competing foci of intensive emotional involvement and to infringe upon devotion to the community.

[3] For a similar process, see R. Schlesinger, *The Family in USSR, 1949*; L. A. Coser, "Some Aspects of Soviet Family Policy," *American Journal of Sociology*, Vol. LVI, No. 5, 1953; K. Geiger, "Changing Political Attitude in a Totalitarian Society," *World Politics*, Vol. VIII, 1956; N. S. Timasheff, "The Attempt to Abolish the Family in Russia," in N. W. Bell and E. F. Vogel (eds.), *A Modern Introduction to the Family, 1960*.

From its inception the Collective Movement has realized the danger inherent in external contacts and conflicting loyalties and set out to counteract centrifugal tendencies by a re-definition of the position of the family. The Kibbutzim curtailed family obligations and attachments and took over most of its functions. They have evolved many ingenious devices in order to prevent the consolidation of the family as a distinct and independent unit. Delegation of functions to the Kibbutz is the most important aspect of the "collectivization" of the family during the first phases of the movement. Husband and wife are allotted independent jobs. There is a strict ban on assigning members of the same family to the same place of work. Division of labour in the occupational sphere is based on a denial of sex differentiation. Women participate to a considerable extent in hard productive labour as well as in defence activities. All meals are taken in the common dining hall. Members' needs are provided by communal institutions. Families look after their own rooms but have few other household responsibilities. Thus each mate works in one branch or another and receives his share of the goods and services distributed by the Kibbutz. Interaction between the sexes in the economic sphere occurs on the level of the community as a whole and not directly between mates. There is during this stage a far-reaching limitation of the functions of the family in the sphere of replacement and socialization as well. The birth rate in the Kibbutzim was for a long time below the level of replacement. The Kibbutzim ensured their continuity and growth not so much by natural increase but by means of recruitment of volunteers from external sources.[4] The physical care and rearing of the children were basically the responsibility of the Kibbutz and not so much of their parents. In most Kibbutzim children live apart from their parents. From their birth on they sleep, eat, and later study in special children's houses. Each age group leads its own life and has its autonomous arrangements. Children meet their parents and siblings in off-hours and spend the afternoons and early evenings with them. On Saturdays and holidays they

[4] See Y. Talmon-Garber, "Social Structure and Family Size," *Human Relations*, Vol. XII, No. 2, 1959.

stay with their parents most of the time. In most Kibbutzim parents put their young children to bed every night. There are thus frequent and intensive relations between parents and children. The main socializing agencies are, however, the peer age group and the specialized nurses, instructors, and teachers. The age group is a substitute for the sibling group. It duplicates the structure of the community and mediates between children and adults. Basically the children belong to the community as a whole. The core of internal family activities which looms so large in other types of family has thus diminished considerably. The family has almost ceased to be an autonomous unit from the point of view of division of labour.

Another important aspect of the process is the change in internal family relations. The union between spouses did not require the sanction of the marriage ceremony. A couple who maintained a stable relationship for some time and decided to establish a family applied for a room and started to live together without any formalities or celebrations. The wedding was usually deferred until the birth of children and was performed in order to legitimize them in accordance with the law of the land. Execution of family tasks was based on the tenet of equality of the sexes and husband and wife were in many respects interchangeable. Both conjugal and parent-children relationship were exceedingly non-authoritarian. The dominant pattern of family interaction during this stage is comradeship on equal terms.

A fairly strong antifamilistic bias is clearly manifested in patterns of informal social relations and leisure-time activities. Members spent most of their free time together. They met every evening in the communal dining hall, in the reading room, or on the central lawn and spent their time in committee work and heated discussions. Spontaneous community singing and folk dancing were the main recreational activities. Public opinion discouraged constant joint appearance of the couple in public. Husband and wife who stuck together and were often seen in each other's company were viewed with ridicule. Each member of the family was likely to have friends of his own. There was little regard for the family relationships in work allocation.

Husband and wife were often assigned to jobs with different timetables and consequently did not see much of each other. There was very little coordination of vacations and holidays. Even the weekly day off of the husband and wife often fell on different days. There was hardly any family entertainment or family visiting. Members of the family functioned independently and were pulled in different direction.[5]

It should be noted that while the Kibbutzim limited the functions of the family drastically and emphasized the collective aspect, they did not abolish the family altogether.[6] Even during the earliest phases when the antifamilistic trend was at its strongest the family remained a distinct unit. Although premarital sexual relations were permitted, there was a clear-cut distinction between casual sexual experimentation, love affairs, and the more durable and publicly sanctioned unions. By asking for a room of their own, the couple made public their wish to have permanent relations and eventually have children. Residence in a common bedroom-living room allocated by the Kibbutz conferred legitimacy on the couple. While children did not actually share a common domicile with their parents, they visited their parents' room every day, and it was their home by reference. The family did not relinquish its communal functions completely either. Parents contributed to the economic support of their children indirectly by working jointly rather than separately. Similarly, though educators were the designated representatives of the Kibbutz rather than of the parents, the parents exercised a direct and continuous influence on the trained personnel in charge of their children. Since children's institutions were not segregated from the community either ecologically or socially, parents were able to supervise closely the way their children were raised there. They exercised considerable direct influence on their children during the time they spent together every

[5] For a fuller analysis of the process described here, see Y. Talmon-Garber, "The Family in Collective Settlements," *Transactions of the World Congress of Sociology*, 1957.

[6] See M. Spiro, "Is the Family Universal` The Israeli Case," in Bell and Vogel (eds.), *op. cit.*, pp. 55–64.

day.[7] Although interaction of members of the family with each other was in many cases less frequent than interaction with outsiders, internal ties were more continuous, more meaningful, and more intense. The emotional ties that bound husband and wife and parents and children were much more intimate and more exclusive than their ties with other members of the community. The family combined physical and emotional intimacy and supplied its members' needs for close personal contacts which were partly independent of their position in the community. By providing unconditional love and loyalty, it insulated its members from communal pressures and enhanced their security.

The extreme limitation of familial functions and relations was most pronounced in the initial phases of the development of the collective movement. It is still to be found, though in a less extreme form, in newly-established collectives. The transition from undifferentiated and extremely cohesive communities to more differentiated and less cohesive ones entails a considerable enhancement of the position of the family. The original homogeneity of the initial stage is disrupted by division of labour and by the establishment and growth of families. The community is further differentiated by the crystallization of various groups of settlers that join the core of founders in each community at different stages of its development. The collectives become more tolerant towards differentiation and subdivision and the family is assigned a place among other subgroups.

The appearance of the second generation is of crucial importance in this context because children are the main focus of segregated family life in the Kibbutzim. Marriage does not entail a redefinition of roles and a new division of labour and does not cause a clearly perceptible cleavage between the couple and the rest of the community. The birth of children makes manifest the partial independence of the family. There emerges a core of specific family duties and the continuity of the family is no longer dependent only on the vicissitudes of the love relationship between the spouses. It becomes more safely anchored in their common attachment to their children and their joint responsibilities to them. The birth of children affects the family in yet another way. The appearance of the second generation introduces a gradual shift of emphasis from disruption of intergeneration ties to continuity. Children are expected to settle in the Kibbutzim founded by their parents and continue their life work there. The family of orientation is no longer an external and alien influence. Parents and children are members of the same Kibbutz. They live in close proximity and share, at least to some extent, the same ideals. Identification with one's family may thus reinforce identification with the collective.

The shift of emphasis from discontinuity to continuity in more differentiated and less cohesive collectives is expressed in a partial "emancipation" of the family. The family regains some of its lost functions in the sphere of housekeeping. Most families will have their afternoon tea at home with their children. In some of the Kibbutzim, families will often eat their evening meal at home too. Most families do it only occasionally, as a special treat for the children, but some eat at home regularly almost every evening. Couples spend a considerable part of their personal allowances on their flats. The housing policy of the Kibbutzim has changed considerably. Whereas the houses built during the first phases of the movement were barrack-like and the dwelling unit consisted of only one room, the typical dwelling unit now consists of a semi-detached flat containing one or two rooms, kitchenette and private sanitary facilities. The flat serves in many cases as an important symbol of the togetherness of the family and a physical manifestation of its separateness. Members usually tend their flat with care and have a strong desire to make it as neat and as pleasant as possible.

There is a considerable increase of the family's functions in the sphere of reproduction and socialization. Examination of demographic data indicates a considerable increase in fertility in

[7] See M. Spiro, *Children of the Kibbutz*, 1958; see also R. Bar Yoseph, "The Patterns of Early Socialization in the Collective Settlements in Israel," *Human Relations*, Vol. XII, No. 4, 1959, pp. 345–360; E. E. Irvine, "Observations in the Aims and Methods on Child-Rearing in Communal Settlements in Israel," *Human Relations*, Vol. V, No. 3, 1952, pp. 247–275; A. I. Rabin, "Infants and Children under Conditions of Intermittent Mothering, "*American Journal of Orthopsychiatry*, Vol. 28, No. 3, 1958.

the Kibbutzim. The dwindling of external recruitment sources and the difficulties experienced by the Kibbutzim in absorption of new immigrants have greatly enhanced the importance of natural increase. Emphasis has shifted from recruitment of volunteers from outside to expansion from within. The family is now called upon to help the Kibbutz to ensure its continuity and growth. Parents tend to take a more active part in the socialization of their children. There is much closer cooperation between nurses, instructors, teachers, and parents. Parents help in looking after their young children. They take turns in watching them at night and nurse them when they are ill. They help in the preparation of festivals arranged for the children and attend most of them. There is considerably more parental supervision of the children's behavior, their choice of friends, and their reading habits. Parents try to influence their children's choice of future occupations and insist on their right to be consulted on this matter. Some of the Kibbutzim have introduced a more radical reorganization. Children in these Kibbutzim no longer sleep in the children's houses. They stay with their age groups during the day but return home every afternoon. Duties of child care and socialization have thus partly reverted to the family.

The line dividing internal family activities and external activities has shifted considerably in all spheres except for the occupational sphere. There is considerable pressure to reduce the number of hours that women work in communal enterprises, but only small concessions have been made in this sphere—mothers of babies get more time off from work now and aging women start to work part time earlier than the men. The Kibbutzim put the main emphasis on the occupational role, and it has remained the major focus of activity for both men and women. Yet even in this sphere we witness considerable modifications. There is now a fairly clear-cut sex-role differentiation in work organization. Women are mainly concentrated in occupations more closely allied to traditional housekeeping such as cooking, laundry service, nursing, and teaching.[8]

[8] For a more detailed analysis of the emergence of sex-role differentiation, see Y. Talmon-Garber, *Sex-role Differentiation in an Equalitarian Society*, 1959, mimeographed.

Modification in patterns of internal family relationships is yet another aspect of the process of change. Marriage normally now precedes the establishment of a family. Most couples attach considerable importance to the wedding celebration and want it to be a memorable event. There are many signs of the emergence of a fairly fixed albeit flexible and fluctuating internal division of labour. Husbands help in household duties, but in most families women do most of the work, and it is mainly their responsibility. The husband is regarded as the wife's assistant or temporary stand-in but not as a coworker on equal terms. There is considerable cooperation and interchangeability in the relationship to the children, yet in spite of a considerable blurring of differences between the father role and the mother role, there are some signs of differentiation. The mother is as a rule more concerned with the bodily well-being of the children and takes care of them while they are at home. She has usually more contact with the children's institutions and the school and supervises the upbringing of her children there. There are indications that although the wife has more say in routine matters it is the husband who usually decides on matters of principle.

The tendency towards a more familistic pattern may also be discerned in the subtle transformation of informal relations and leisure-time activities. Free time spent in public has diminished considerably. Members are not as eager as they used to be to participate in public discussions or attend public meetings. Spontaneous dancing and community singing sessions are rare. Members tend to retire to their rooms and to stay at home most of the time. Husband and wife will spend most of their free time together. They usually sit near each other during evening meals and on all public occasions. There is a far better coordination of work schedules as well as of vacations and holidays. Families get special consideration in this respect and are able to spend their free time together. Entertaining and visiting are becoming joint family affairs. It is now considered impolite to invite only one of the spouses. Friends who are not congenial to both husband and wife are gradually dropped. Many families regularly celebrate birthdays and wedding anniversaries and attach considerable importance to such family affairs.

In the sphere of parent-children relations we witness an interesting "dialectical" process. The extreme limitation of the functions of the family in the sphere of maintenance and socialization of its children has not led to disruption of family solidarity. Paradoxically, the curtailment of obligations reinforced rather than weakened parent-children relationship and enhanced the importance of the emotional ties between them. It is mainly within the family that both parents and children have intimate relations unpatterned by their positions in the community and that they are free from routine duties. The child's position outside the family is prescribed only to a small extent. He has to compete with his age peers for a position in his group and for the approval of the adults in charge of it. All children in the same age group have the same claim to attention. It is only in the family that they get love and care which they do not have to share with many others. Insofar as the family has ceased to be the prime socializing agency, it avoids to some extent the inevitable ambivalence towards the agents of socialization. Parents do not have to play the two-sided role of ministering to the children's needs for care and security on the one hand and of thwarting their wishes in various ways on the other. Parents do not carry the main responsibility for disciplining their children and can afford to be permissive. Examination of our material indicates the overall importance of parent-children relationships. The children have come very often to occupy the emotional center of the parents' life. They have become a major preoccupation with most mothers. Young children are deeply dependent and very often overdependent on their parents. The children eventually outgrow this dependence. They become attached to their age mates and drift away to a certain extent from their parents. Parents resent this partial estrangement and will often blame it on the usurpation of communal institutions. Many feel bereaved of function and crave for closer contacts with their children. It is this process which is at the root of recent reorganizations.[9] Parents now

emphasize the unity of the family and encourage closer contacts between all its members. Older children are often entrusted with the care of younger ones and there is a considerable amount of interaction between siblings.

Another outstanding feature of the process of change is the gradual development and renewal of wider kinship ties. As long as the generational structure of the Kibbutz remained truncated, most members did not have any kin besides members of their own elementary family living with them in the same community. A gradual process of change sets in when the children of the founders establish families and the Kibbutz develops into a full-scale three-generational structure. The Kibbutzim have in addition accepted social responsibility for aging or sick parents[10] and transfer many of them to their children in the Kibbutz. Old parents live either in separate blocks of dwellings or in little semi-detached flats adjoining those of their children. Relatives who live in the same community maintain close contacts through frequent visiting and mutual help. There are many indices of the emergence of cohesive kinship groupings. Relatives tend very often to cluster and form united blocks which have a considerable influence on communal affairs. Wider kinship ties serve also as connecting links with the outside world. Members tend to renew their contacts with relatives who live outside the Kibbutz. They will stay with their relatives when they go to town and will invite them to visit them. They accept personal presents from kin and reciprocate by sending farm produce from time to time. The wider kinship category is amorphous and ill defined, but there is quite a strong moral obligation to maintain amicable relations with kin. Kinship ties have thus broken through the self-imposed isolation of the Kibbutzim from outside contacts.

It should be stressed that in spite of the considerable change in the position of the family the Kibbutzim still remain basically nonfamilistic.

[9] See Y. Talmon-Garber, "The Family and Collective Education in the Kibbutz," *Niv-Hekvutsah*, Vol. VIII, No. 1, pp. 2–52 (in Hebrew). See also H. Faigin, "Social Behaviour of Young Children in the Kibbutz," *Journal of Abnormal Social Psychology*, Vol. 56, No. 1,

1958; A. I. Rabin, "Attitudes of Kibbutz Children to Parents and Family," *American Journal of Orthopsychiatry*, Vol. 29, No. 1, 1959.
[10] See Y. Talmon-Garber, "Aging in a Planned Society," *American Journal of Sociology*, Vol. LXVII, No. 3, 1961, pp. 286–295.

The shift from intergenerational discontinuity to continuity attenuates the tension between the family and the Kibbutz, but the basic rivalry is still operative. Insofar as the family accepts the primacy of collective considerations it may become a valuable ally. Inasmuch as it resents a subordinate position and disputes the authority of collective institutions it is still a potential source of conflict and competition.[11] The Kibbutzim make far-reaching demands on their members. The proper functioning of the Kibbutz depends on the wholehearted identification of members with its aims and ideals. The collectives cannot afford to allow the family to become an independent and self-sufficient unit lest it undermine the primacy of collective considerations. They still fear that if the family is given a free hand it will become the main focus of primary relations and kinship ties will become preponderant over the ties between co-members.

The violent antifamilism of the revolutionary phase has abated but all traces of it have not disappeared completely. It is superseded by a moderate collectivism which regards the family as a useful though dangerous ally. The Kibbutzim control and limit the family and employ it for the attainment of collective goals.

The Traditional Family in Cooperative Settlements[12]

The effect of immigration and a new type of community life on the relations between the elementary family and the wider kinship group can be best studied by examination of traditional or semitraditional families in cooperative settlements. We shall deal here mainly with North African Jews who arrived in Israel after the establishment of the State, as there is more reliable and up-to-date information on this group than on any of the others. Moreover, they provide us with the best and clearest example of the transformation taking place in such groups.

Jews in North Africa, before the French occupation, were able to maintain the continuity of their traditional social and cultural structure. In the main, they formed small communities, composed of large patriarchal families of three or four generations. The father directed his married and unmarried sons in work tasks and maintained discipline within a joint residence unit. Kinsmen, in particular patrilineal kin, formed friendship and visiting groups and joined together in cases of conflict and crisis. Males customarily held dominant positions, and female roles were limited to home and family. The synagogue was an important place of male gathering. Allegiance to Jewish ritual and observance centered around the synagogue and the religious schools.

This traditional structure remained more or less intact in the villages and small towns but it has changed considerably in the big urban centers. The French influence and mass migration to the big new cities have greatly undermined this traditional structure. Rapid migration very often splintered the kinship group because kin dispersed throughout different communities. Young men could now enter new occupations and become independent. Upon marriage they tended to sever their close ties with their families of orientation and to establish independent households. Secularization estranged the younger generation from the older one and weakened the allegiance to traditional

[11] On the problems caused by the increased influence of the family on the occupational placement of its children see Y. Talmon-Garber, "Occupational Placement of the Second Generation in Collective Settlements," *Megamoth*, Vol. VIII, 1957, pp. 369 ff. (in Hebrew). See also M. Sarell, "Continuity and Change—The Second Generation in Collective Settlements," *Megamoth*, Vol. XI, 1961, pp. 2–23 (in Hebrew).

[12] Analysis in this section is based on S. N. Eisenstadt, *Absorption of Immigrants*, 1954; C. Frankenstein, *Between Past and Future*, 1956; A. Weingrod, "Change and Continuity in a Moroccan Immigrant Village," *Middle East Journal*, 1960, and *Administered Communities*, 1961, mimeographed; D. Weintraub and M. Lissak, *The Absorption of North African Immigrants in Agricultural Settlements in Israel*, 1959, mimeographed; M. Coles, "Patterns of Cultural Adaptation of Immigrants from the Atlas Mountains," *Megamoth*, Vol. VII, 1956, pp. 345–376 (in Hebrew); O. Shapira, *Social Factors and Economic Development*, 1961, mimeographed (in Hebrew). In addition, we have used extensively reports and memoranda prepared by the sociologists attached to the Settlement Agency. Of special interest are the reports by M. Minkowitz, R. Rahat and O. Shapira.

kinship obligations. In urban sectors of North Africa the traditional structure was undergoing rapid change. There were many manifestations of severe strain in both the nuclear and the extended families. The larger kinship groupings suffered most and were rapidly disintegrating.

Immigration to Israel affected both the traditional and semitraditional sectors. Immigrants from North Africa had, on the whole, a positive identification with Israel, but this identification was a traditional one and differed greatly from the secular-national identification which was dominant in the absorbing society. In the traditional sector immigration was motivated mainly by a deep sense of Jewish solidarity and vague Messianic striving. In the transitional sector the main factor was a search for security and economic advancement. Immigrants from both sectors had little disposition to change. They came to Israel hoping to be able to continue their former way of life undisturbed and unmolested. The adherence to pre-existing patterns of life affected the composition of immigration. Immigration took place in many cases in pre-existing group clusters. Families, neighbourhoods, inhabitants of local areas and even whole communities immigrated together.

Some of the North African immigrants were directed by the settling agency to cooperative settlements. The cooperative settlement or Moshav[13] is based on a semi-independent family working on its family farm. The principles underlying the cooperation of these family units are: public ownership of land and machinery, equality as to size of farm and basic investment, ban on hired labour, mutual aid, and cooperative marketing and purchasing. The cooperative settlement is governed by democratic procedures. Long-term policy is determined at periodic village meetings while daily affairs are entrusted to elected officers, committees and hired experts, and professionals. The cooperative settlements combine a familistic division of labour with mechanized and intensive farming and with centralized and specialized management of cooperative institutions. They emphasize

both autonomy and interdependence. The cooperative settlements which were founded during the pre-State period were formed by volunteer pioneering groups who sought to realize both personal and national ideals. The post-State Moshavim are administered communities planned and managed to a large extent by governmental and semigovernmental agencies. State planners, guided by defence considerations and by a desire to disperse the Israeli population, ordered the construction of 274 cooperative settlements and directed new immigrants to these villages. While some communities become progressively autonomous, many others remain dependent on outside agencies.

The settling agency regarded the traditional kinship-centered social organization of the immigrants as inimical to the development of a modern cooperative village. The planners did not take into consideration the former group composition of the settlers and intentionally disregarded their former attachments and loyalties. The social composition of each village was during the initial phase a matter of organizational decision based on administrative considerations. Kinship groups were dispersed. With the exception of a few relatives and former friends, all the original settlers in the villages were unrelated. Most of the settlers had never met each other before their immigration. Strangers became neighbours and had to cooperate with each other in many vital matters.

It is significant that the traditional kinship structure soon reasserted itself and the composition of most settlements has changed rapidly. Settlers sought out their relatives and encouraged them to settle in the same village. Other settlers left the village and joined their relatives in some other settlement. Kinsmen tended to seek one another out and cluster together. After a considerable reshuffle and change of population, most villages have emerged with two to three major kinship groups. There remains in the villages only a number of smaller kinship groups or of unrelated nuclear (elementary) families. These families try to attach themselves to one of the strong kinship clusters by concluding marriages with them. Some legitimize their connexion with a kinship cluster by fabricating fictitious kinship ties with it. Even

[13] On the structure of the pre-State Moshavim, see Y. Talmon-Garber, "Differentiation in Cooperative Settlements," *British Journal of Sociology*, Vol. III, No. 4, 1952.

purely political allegiances are legitimized in terms of kinship obligations. Kinsmen assist and support each other. In spite of the fact that the Moshav economy is based on the nuclear family and each nuclear family has a separate household, a separate farm, and a separate account, there is intense cooperation between members of the same kinship group. Kinship units are also intervisiting and recreational groups. The nuclear families are subordinated to the kinship groups and the villages have all become kinship dominated.[14]

Reunion of kinsmen occurred more easily and rapidly in traditional families who had maintained their wider kinship ties and had arrived in the country in groups of families and neighbourhood units. However, this process occurred in the semitraditional sectors too. Even relatives who had already been separated in North Africa and had not seen each other for years sought each other out and revived the dormant kinship ties between them. In the unfamiliar and unstructured social setting, kinship ties regained their lost significance and served as a major basis for spontaneous reorganization.[15] As a result of this process, the villages which were at their inception artificial amalgams of unrelated families became communities based on kinship where most elementary families were embedded and controlled by the larger kinship groupings.

Not only was the kinship reconstituted but it also began to assume new functions. The kinship unit has a political significance. Village politics revolve about control of community-wide institutions, and, pre-eminently, control of the central committee. Controlling the central committee involves not only prestige but organizational and financial advantages as well. With control so advantageous, the kin groups became rival factions, each struggling with the other for power. Since membership in the central committee is based upon democratic election, the relative size and internal composition of the kinship units had a direct bearing on their position in the village. The "political history" of each village involves a continuous struggle between the kinship groups, which jockey for control by offering various promises to other families or groups of families. Political alliances are formed and reformed, always with the bigger kinship groups at the center. Politics serve to reinforce the ties between kin. Kinship and the kin group have assumed new, essentially political functions. The relative size of the kinship clusters is of utmost importance in the political struggle yet there are many indications that internal cohesion of the kinship unit is in some cases more important than mere size. It seems that closely knit clusters which unite close relatives are more stable and more powerful than clusters based on more distant and more vague kinship affiliations. Paradoxically, radical modernization has strengthened and revived the kinship dominated traditional order.[16]

The strengthening and reconstitution of the kinship unit has helped the immigrants to adapt to the new settling. The kinship group is a strong cooperative unit. Cooperation within it is legitimized by traditional norms and obligations. It extends to all its members economic assistance and political backing. It creates a basic field of security and continuity. The kinship group mediates between the elementary families and the community and in this way links the old traditional order to the new one. Adaptability to the new setting was found to be highly correlated with kinship solidarity.

[14] We have very little material on internal sex-role differentiation and authority structure of the elementary family and cannot therefore deal with it here.

[15] We have no systematic research on North African immigrants in urban centers. There are, however, many indications that even in an urban setting there is a strong tendency to revitalization of kinship ties and spatial coalescence, Kinsmen serve as important communication outposts and provide the immigrants with badly needed information on jobs, houses and community facilities. They are potential sources of aid and often provide the newcomers with a considerable amount of economic and social support. On the interrelation between migration and kinship ties see E. Litwak, "Geographical Mobility and Family Cohesion," American Sociological Review, 1960, Vol. 25, No. 3, pp. 385–394.

[16] It should be noted that we have completely disregarded internal cleavages based on heterogeneity of country of origin. Some of the Moshavim discussed here have a mixed population, and even in relatively homogeneous Moshavim there are factions based on community of origin. A full analysis of this problem would take us too far afield and we have therefore refrained from dealing with it here.

Yet the growing dominance of the kinship group is fraught with grave danger to the village community. The strong particularistic loyalty to the kinship groups very often destroys the loyalty to the village as a whole. Election of village officers and voting on community issues tend to follow kinship lines. Decisions are not based on any objective criteria. Village officers and committee members function as representatives of their kinship unit and are not much concerned about the interests of the village as a whole. They discriminate, without compunction, against members who are not their relatives and see to it that their kinship unit and its allies get as much of the available facilities and rewards as possible. The nepotism of office holders breeds inefficiency and suspicion. It engenders, in addition, bitter feuds. The villages are often divided into hostile factions which conduct a constant fight against each other. These factions very often reach a deadlock and the management of cooperative institutions on the village level is immobilized for many months. It sometimes becomes necessary to transfer one of the warring factions to another village in order to put an end to a feud which threatens to destroy the village. The solidarity of the kinship group develops at the expense of the solidarity of the village community.

The settling agency was faced with a dilemma. Since radical modernization has strengthened rather than weakened the traditional order, there is now a growing tendency to come to terms with it and initiate gradual and selective change. The planners have come to realize that the kinship groups are vitally important units in the absorption of traditional immigrants and should not be disrupted or suppressed. They therefore accept the kinship groups and only try to restrict them to internal activities by limiting their influence on central cooperative institutions. In some of the villages, there is a growing tendency to replace office holders by hired experts who are unrelated to any kinship unit in the village. They are not involved in the village feuds and are better trained. Consequently, they are more objective and far more efficient. Management is thus partly dissociated from the relations between the kinship units. Cooperative institutions can continue to function even in cases of severe tension.

A certain loosening of the cooperative structure has a beneficial effect in this respect too. Dependence on central institutions enhances the importance of political control of the central committee. Restriction of cooperation to a more limited sphere narrows the area of tension and of competition and diminishes the intensity of conflict. In many cases it has become necessary to enhance the control by external agencies and postpone the initiation of full local self-government until the village becomes an ongoing concern and the settlers have gained some experience in the techniques of communal self-management.

In the long run the future of the villages described here depends on the second generation.[17] The children of the immigrants go to school and join the army. They temporarily leave their village and learn new skills. Their general outlook and their basic value orientation change considerably. In many cases, they develop an aversion to the traditional way of life and tend to ignore, scoff at or openly rebel against it. They feel that their parents are hopelessly dated and out of place and reject them. Conflict between parents and children has a particularly corrosive effect on the traditional order. Reverence for elders and respect of parents are core elements in the traditional value system. The young generation does not have an acknowledged right to independence, and insubordination engenders bitter strife. Since moral precepts and social obligations are to a large extent directly rooted in acceptance of parental authority, deprecation of parents often leads to serious loss of orientation. In many cases, the impinging influences undermine the traditional values and loyalties without replacing

[17] See E. P. Hutchinson, *Immigrants and Their Children*, 1957; also I. Child, *Italians and Americans*, 1949, and O. Handlin, *The Uprooted*, 1954. For analysis of parent-children relationship among Oriental immigrants in Israel, see A. Simon, "Parents and Children among Immigrants from Islamic Countries," *Megamoth*, 1957, pp. 41–55 (in Hebrew), and S. N. Eisenstadt and J. Ben David, "Intergeneration Tensions in Israel," *International Social Science Bulletin*, 1956, pp. 59–75. It should be noted that in some ethnic groups the process of change is much smoother and gradual. See E. Katz and A. Zlotzower, "Ethnic Continuity in an Israeli Town," *Human Relations*, 1961, Vol. 14, No. 4, pp. 293–309.

them effectively with new ones, thus causing confusion and alienation. The hope of an effective and continuous change lies in a system of education and training which orients young people to new values but does not breed estrangement between generations. The second generation is able to transform the traditional order and adapt it to the new social setting only when it retains its basic loyalty to the kinship unit and respects its values.

The Isolated Refugee Family in Urban Centers[18]

This type of family is prevalent mainly among immigrants who came to the country after World War II from countries which were formerly under German occupation. The methodical extermination of Jews in these countries annihilated whole communities. In many flourishing Jewish centers only a few managed to escape, and very few families remained intact. Immigrants of this type were uprooted and isolated. They arrived in the country with few or no relatives. Their former social setting was completely and irrevocably destroyed. They had all undergone severe hardships, and most of them had spent long periods of compulsory collective living in prison camps.

Most immigrants of the type described here were not members of Zionist movements. They had received no preparatory ideological indoctrination and had not undergone vocational training. They were thus unprepared for the difficult conditions of settlement in the new country. Many of them remembered their shattered prewar past with nostalgic yearning and tended to idealize it. Consequently, they had little disposition to change and found it difficult

to adapt themselves to the new setting. They usually had a diffuse positive attitude towards Israel but no strong identification with its aims and values. These immigrants were concerned with their personal problems. They hoped to regain and better their lost status. Their experience of camp life had instilled in them a deep yearning for privacy and undisturbed personal development. This concentration on personal aspirations ran counter to the ideological and collectivist orientations of the absorbing society.

Another important factor which affected the relationship between the immigrants and the absorbing society was the bureaucratization of absorption. The mass immigration was handled by various bureaucratic agencies and not by primary groups of old-timers. During the initial phase of settlement the immigrants had little contacts with old-timers and little opportunity to take the initiative in solving their problems in their own way. They had only a hazy and insufficient knowledge of the aims and norms of the bureaucratic bodies which competed and cooperated in the process of their absorption. They had great difficulty in finding their way in the maze of rules and regulations and resented the impersonal way in which their personal problems were dealt with. They felt confused and alienated.

These immigrants were thus cut off from the community.[19] Their contacts with the institutional framework tended to be formal and specific. As we have already mentioned, they had few relatives and hardly any former friends. The newly acquired contacts with neighbors and

---

[18] Isolated families were found mainly in urban centers. It should be stressed, however, that they were found in rural settlements too. A fuller analysis of isolated families will be found in S. N. Eisenstadt, *Absorption of Immigrants*, 1954. Additional material was obtained from a more recent ecological study of new urban centers in development areas conducted by Professor Eisenstadt and Mr. E. Cohen. I would like to express my gratitude to Mr. E. Cohen, to Mrs. L. Shamgar and Mrs. H. Adoni for placing their material at my disposal and for their useful comments.

[19] It should be noted that cities and towns are not communities in the same sense as the Kibbutz and the Moshav. The Kibbutz and the Moshav are closely knit and cohesive communities which contain the families living in them and mediate between them and the wider social system. The social environment of urban families is best considered not as the local community in which they live but rather as a comparatively loosely knit network of actual social relations which they maintain regardless of whether these relations are confined to the local community or go beyond its boundaries. Yet since we are dealing here mainly with small and medium urban centres in which there is a certain degree of local cohesion and where most significant relationships are confined to the local community, analysis of development of solidarity on the local level is not unwarranted. See E. Bott, *Families and Social Networks*, Chapters III and IV.

work associates revolved around limited interests. In addition, these contacts were of short duration and had not had time to grow into meaningful and mutually binding ties. Consequently, all the wider contacts of immigrants of this type were partial, shallow, and devoid of any deep personal meaning.

The reaction of the immigrants to their alienation and isolation is a wholehearted and very intensive attachment to their elementary family.[20] Since external ties have little significance, the immigrants developed a compensatory involvement with internal family relationships. The family withdraws to its small and isolated private world. The immigrants seek solace and security in the spontaneous and warm intimacy of their family. They defend the independence of their family life in opposition to the constant demands of the absorbing society. In their family they are their own masters and need not constantly accommodate themselves to these demands. They try to insulate the family against outside influences and continue to cultivate their former patterns of life.[21]

The occupational role gains its meaning only in conjunction with the family. Life revolves about the home and the place of work, but the real center of gravity is the home. The occupational role is secondary and derivative and has no meaning in its own right. Instrumental relations developed during work are very often devoid of any expressive significance. The real life goal is the unity, well-being, and economic advancement of the family. The immigrants work indefatigably and persistently as long as it benefits their family, but are unconcerned with purely occupational problems and uninterested in the wider implications of their work.

Isolated families develop only a few significant contacts outside the inner circle of the family. Their informal relations and leisure-time activities are family centered. They refrain from joining voluntary associations and societies. They have a deep distrust of the authorities at any level and hold political parties in cynical contempt. They have no contacts and no identification with established *élites* of any kind. They keep aloof from any political or social activities and are apathetic to the goals of society as a whole.[22]

The crisis of war, mass extermination, and immigration has greatly reinforced the internal solidarity and unity of the nuclear family, but this heightened cohesiveness has developed at the expense of solidarity in wider social groupings. It very often prevents the development of a more comprehensive involvement and identification. It blocks efforts of resocialization since it enables the family to adapt to the new social setting with a bare minimum of conscious reorientation to new goals. The family is able to cling to its initial expectations and role-images, even when these images are incompatible with the new social setting. The isolated family protects the uprooted individual and supports him. It creates a basic field of security and continuity. However, as long as the family remains cut off from the realities of life in the new country and as long as it is unrelated to the wider framework of institutions, associations, and primary groups, it may become a fool's paradise, jealously guarding its fictitious independence against the outside world.

Eventually the self-imposed isolation of this type of family adversely affects its unity. External relations impinge on its internal relations in the form of parents-children conflict. The children gradually adopt the values of the absorbing society. They soon realize that their

---

[20] On a similar development in families of refugees in Germany, see H. Schelsky, *Wandlungen der deutschen Familie in der Gegenwart*, 1954.

[21] We have very little material on internal sex-role differentiation in these families and cannot therefore test E. Bott's hypothesis on the relation between loosely knit networks and cooperation in execution of familial tasks. Our data seem to indicate, however, that the tendency to develop a more joint role relationship is often blocked by a strong defensive attitude towards former patterns of behaviour. These patterns are often ritualized and resist both external and internal pressures towards change.

[22] Since the term "isolated" is often used to describe the position of ordinary families in urban centers, it should be stressed that we do not employ it here in this sense. The urban family is differentiated as a distinct and to some extent autonomous social group but it is not isolated. We use the term "isolated" to describe the refugee family because, unlike the "normal" urban family, it is not embedded in a sustaining network of external relationships and in many cases is at first virtually cut off from relatives, neighbors, friends and colleagues. See E. Bott, *op. cit.*

parents cannot guide them in their efforts to adapt themselves to the new setting and to find their proper place in it. They are torn between gratitude to their parents and disappointment. They develop an ambivalent attitude towards their family and treat it with a mixture of frustrated love and violent hatred. The conflict between parents and children hits the isolated family very hard and destroys its precarious unity and stability. Isolation of the family is thus inimical to its own solidarity as well as to the cohesion of the community.

The main problem which confronts the isolated family from a dynamic point of view is the gradual widening of its horizon of participation and identification beyond its limited confines. Local authorities and community centers have tried to cope with these problems by conducting periodic campaigns among members of isolated families, calling on them to participate in voluntary activities, recruiting them to various associations and nominating them to committees. These efforts of recruiting meet with some success only when concentrated in spheres directly adjoining the family. The best example of such successful extension of spheres of activity are parents' committees in school. "Isolated" parents have the well-being and advancement of their children very much at heart. The children are in fact their main life goal. It is therefore comparatively easy to draw them into voluntary participation in a committee which controls and promotes the local school. By serving on this committee they are able to wield some influence on the education of their children and at the same time gain a better understanding of the norms and aims of the school. They are also better able to understand the problems of their children. They get much closer to their children and at the same time narrow the gap which separates them from the absorbing society. The school may serve as a major link between the isolated family and the wider social setting.

Reorganization of the occupational sphere often serves a similar purpose. Occupational advancement has a direct bearing on the family. It is possible to arouse the interests of the family in the activities of trade unions and professional associations to a certain degree. Organizations dealing with practical issues on the local level may also serve as a starting point for extension of participation. Interest in general ideological and political problems is much more difficult to awaken and most members of isolated families remain politically uncommitted and passive. At first, participation is limited to practical matters which directly concern the family. Gradually, however, the new members of committees regain confidence in themselves and in their fellow members. They learn to take the initiative and plan ahead and accumulate practical experience in dealing with their problems. Since the committees operate on a local basis and involve face-to-face contacts they provide opportunities for getting to know neighbors and making friends. The social environment becomes less menacing, less alien, less confusing, and therefore much more manageable.[23] In many cases, such limited participation becomes a stepping stone to wider participation and to more comprehensive identification.

Conclusion

It was our purpose to examine the impact of radical change on family solidarity and on the position of the family in the community. We have seen that the processes of change entailed in immigration have had a disruptive effect on family cohesion in the case of the Kibbutzim, yet they have greatly enhanced the solidarity and independence of the family in the other two case studies. Internal relations within the elementary family or within the kinship group have become the main source of material assistance and emotional support in these cases. Immigration confronts the family with new problems of adjustment and increases its need for aid. Yet at the same time it cuts it off from its former sources of external support. The family is forced to rely on its internal resources and resort to mutual aid. The absence of competing foci of identification acts in the same way. Inasmuch as members of the family or the kinship unit have fewer comprehensive and significant external ties and loyalties,

---

[23] See E. Litwak, "Voluntary Associations and Neighborhood Cohesion," *American Sociological Review*, Vol. 26, No. 2, 1961, pp. 258–271.

they tend to turn inwards. Intensified cooperation among kin develops also as a compensatory and countervailing mechanism. Intimate face-to-face relations between relatives come to mean so much during the first phases of adjustment because they mitigate the anonymity and the insecurity incurred by immigration. By partly segregating its members, the family protects them from overpowering external pressures and enables them to maintain a partial autonomy. Radical change enhances the importance of familial continuity.

Examination of our case studies indicates that the elementary family, the kinship unit, and the community are in a sense competing foci of identification. Intense involvement with the collective develops at the expense of the solidarity of the family and the kinship unit. The heightened cohesion of the reconstituted traditional kinship group encroaches on the independence of the elementary family and is also inimical to cohesion at the level of community organization. There is an inverse correlation between the intense commitment to the elementary family of the refugees and solidarity in wider social groupings.[24] It should be stressed, however, that while a very intense and comprehensive commitment to any of these units may interfere with and threaten the loyalty to the two others, they are by no means inherently mutually exclusive and incompatible. In the Kibbutzim we witness a transition from intense rivalry to controlled coexistence and coordination. Insofar as the family accepts the primacy of collective considerations, it may become a valuable ally, and

[24] For an analysis which views the elementary family and the kinship group as competing foci of identification, see M. Gluckman, *Custom and Conflict in Africa*, 1955. See also E. Bott, *op. cit.*

identification with it may reinforce the identification with the Kibbutz. A similar transition may be discerned in the Moshavim. Limitation of the functions of the kinship clusters coupled with a concomitant modification of communal organization brings about better coordination and mutual reinforcement rather than opposition. In the case of the refugees we found that participation in voluntary associations serves as a stepping stone to more comprehensive identification. Yet it consolidates the solidarity of the elementary family.

The family in the Kibbutzim and the family among refugees in urban centers develop in opposite directions. In the "collectivized" family we witnessed a partial disengagement and emancipation of the family from the collective. In the "isolated" family we found a process of reengagement and reorientation of the family towards the community. The main problem of the Kibbutzim from a dynamic point of view is how to allow the family units more privacy and more independence without harming the cohesion of the community. The main problem that confronts communities containing a considerable number of "isolated" families is how to preserve the internal solidarity of the elementary families and at the same time find ways and means of extending the range of their participation and identification. The main problem which confronts the Moshavim dealt with here is how to preserve the unity and solidarity of the kinship group and at the same time limit its influence on overall village management. These communities are trying now to introduce a gradual transformation of the traditional kinship-dominated structure by combining continuity and change.

9. The Amigo System
and Alienation of the Wife
in the Conjugal Mexican Family*

BY ARTURO DE HOYOS AND GENEVIEVE DE HOYOS

BOTH SCIENTIFIC AND POPULAR literature on the Mexican family contain disturbing contradictions about the general characteristics of Mexican family life. Some writers have called attention to the closeness of the family ties;[1] to the great respect of Mexican children toward their parents;[2] and to the apparent order and conviviality of Mexican family in general.[3] Other writers, however, have pointed out the extensive family disorganization and trauma which exist in Mexican families, especially in the lower and middle classes.[4]

Careful consideration, however, may show that the contradictions found in the literature are more apparent than real. It is important, of course, to note that many generalizations have been made without either conceptualizing the

* The field work for this study was supported by funds made available to the writers through Dr. Charles P. Loomis, research professor at Michigan State University, by the United States Public Health Service. Dr. Loomis is director of the "Anglo-Latino Relations" Project in the United States-Mexico border. The authors are grateful to Dr. Loomis for this support.

[1] Herbert Cerwin, *These Are the Mexicans*, New York: Reynal and Hitchcock, 1947. This author sees the Mexican family as cohesive (p. 275), and he feels that the Mexican man is monogamous at heart and a solid family man (p. 159). For a similar assertion see R. D. Tuck, *Not with the First*, New York: Harcourt, Brace and Co., 1946. Tuck describes the Mexican family as providing warmth and security through various types of personal relationships, as being a laboratory for the world and a haven from life difficulties, pp. 124–130.

[2] Elizabeth Borton de Trevino, *My Heart Lies South*, New York: Thomas Y. Crowell Co., 1953. The author comments on the great respect shown by children for adults and elders. She also notes that mothers have especially high status and that older people are highly respected and loved.

[3] Cerwin, *op. cit.*, referring to family life, mentions that it is not unusual for ten or fifteen members of one family to sit down regularly for dinner (p. 275). Tuck, *op. cit.*, points out that parental unity in the household is strong especially in the discipline of children (p. 130).

[4] Maria Elvira Bermudez, *La Vida Familiar del Mexicano*, Mexico: Antigua Libreria Robredo, 1955. This author states that respect betweeen husband and wife is not the pattern in the Mexican family (p. 35); that married life is full of arguments, infidelities, and little respect or happiness (p. 43); that this is true for lower and middle-class families; and that the Mexican husband has little interest in the care of the children, his main interest being other women (p. 55). Bermudez concludes that as a consequence, Mexican men are lonely (p. 56). She also points out the husband's constant criticism of the wife for every family mishap and his extreme lack of consideration for her (p. 58). For a similar description of Mexican family life see Oscar Lewis, *The Children of Sanchez*, New York: Random House, 1961. Among a number of social and psychological characteristics of the Mexican family Lewis mentions the following: frequent use of physical violence in training children; wife beating; free unions or consensual marriage; high incidence of abandonment of wife and children; a trend toward mother-centered families and a much greater knowledge of maternal relatives; a strong predisposition to authoritarianism, and on the other hand, paradoxically, an extreme emphasis upon family solidarity—"an ideal only rarely achieved" (p. xxvi).

specific types and dimensions of family inter-action involved or explicitly identifying the factors which appear to be related to both the stability and instability observed in the Mexican family.

The greatest need appears to be for empirical studies directed to the investigation of specific variables and relationships. Studies limited in scope and focused on manageable dimensions of family life would enrich the literature in this field. Especially needed are studies of the relationship between the family system and other social systems in order to understand the reciprocal functions and dysfunctions of the systemic interaction.

The present study was designed to investigate a specific aspect of the husband-wife interaction in the Mexican conjugal family and to relate this interaction to the husband's participation in a specific social system external to the conjugal family. The variables under consideration are the alienation of the wife and the participation of the husband in what is here called the *Amigo* system. The measurement of these two variables is by multiple-item scales constructed for that purpose and described later in this paper.

In an attempt to understand more fully the factors related to the alienation of the wife in the Mexican conjugal system, we became interested in the Amigo system because of its persistence as a social influence even after the male establishes his conjugal family. Assuming the competition between the Amigo system and the conjugal system for scarce resources (such as time, money, or loyalty), we decided to put the matter to an empirical test.

The study is based on the proposition that there is a relationship between the participation of the married Mexican male in his Amigo system and the alienation of his wife. The specific hypothesis, for which some empirical evidence is presented here, is that in those families where the husband is reported to keep close relationship and involvement with his Amigo system, alienation of the wife is present.

Definition of Concepts

The three concepts to be defined are Amigo system, conjugal family, and alienation. These constitute the core of the investigation.

The Amigo System. One of the most significant influences in the socialization of the Mexican male is the informal group of male peers who, in a society of relatively few voluntary formal and informal organizations,[5] constitute for him an important reference group. We call this group the *Amigo system.*

The Amigo system acts as a powerful mechanism of social control which extensively and effectively influences the Mexican male throughout his life. Although there may be some significant class differences in certain dimensions in the nature and extent of this control, the Amigo system appears to be a high status group for males at all socioeconomic levels; therefore it constitutes a universal social phenomenon in Mexican society.

The Amigo system seems to initiate its main social and psychological functions at the onset of adolescence. Beginning in this period, the noninvolvement of the father with his children becomes evident, creating a cleavage that makes communication between father and son almost impossible.[6] The Amigo system then becomes a source of security, social acceptance, and male

[5] The participation in voluntary associations in urban Mexico has been studied by Dotson who reports that 59 per cent of the men and 68 per cent of the women do not report affiliation of any kind. See Floyd Dotson, "Voluntary Associations in a Mexican City," *American Sociological Review,* **18** (August, 1953), pp. 380–386.
[6] Sister Frances Jerome Woods, *Cultural Values of American Ethnic Groups,* New York: Harper and Brothers, 1956. Discussing the culture and family organization of the Mexican group, this author mentions the lack of intimacy between children and father. The mother teaches the children an attitude of paternal respect, which perhaps leads to avoidance of intimacy with the father. The father seldom carries an infant in his arms and rarely plays with his children. In his presence, the children are usually obedient, subdued, and inhibited. The children respect the father for his position in the family rather than for any personal quality he may have; and his anger is greatly feared (p. 286). See also Oscar Lewis, *Five Families,* New York: Basic Books, Inc., 1959. Lewis makes reference to the phenomenon of the "absent father" in the Mexican home not only physically, through death and desertion, but also psychologically because of his authoritarian way of relating to the family. The children develop great closeness to their mother (p. 18).

identification for the young Mexican male. It is the Amigo system that encourages the youth's independence, his aggressiveness, his impulsive behavior, and other related characteristics.[7]

As he matures, the young Mexican male is introduced by his Amigo system to a number of role expectations that every *macho*, or real he-man, must know. Concern and attitudes toward sex, women, work, money, friends, and authority are acquired, developed, and reinforced in the informal interaction within the Amigo system.

The Amigo system is committed to *machismo*. The machismo complex, as a cultural value, is transmitted to the young Mexican male by his Amigo system through a number of informal *rites de passage*.[8] The set of values and attitudes thus acquired becomes the basis for the young man's self-image as a *macho*, a carefree, undomesticated, romantic Don Juan who is supposed to disregard and devaluate any types of domestic responsibilities, especially those consisting of the practical aspects of daily home life.[9] Machismo emphasizes independence, impulsivity, physical strength as the "natural" way of settling disagreements, roughness as the best way to relate to women, and force as the best way to relate to the weak or to subordinates.

The loyalties that develop between *amigos* are often considered more binding than those of kinship. The best example of this is the phenomenon of the *amigo intimo*, who, as part of the Amigo system, usually becomes "more than a brother." The rules which control the social relationship between *amigos intimos* are at the highest level of cultural valuation and are themselves enforced by an effective system of positive and negative sanctions.[10]

In some ways, the Amigo system in Mexican society may be viewed as usurping some of the socialization functions usually ascribed to the family of orientation. On the other hand, it apparently also fills a void in the social structure, a void partly caused by the noninvolvement of the father with his children. However, a description of the overall functions of the Amigo system and the extent to which these are functional or dysfunctional for the adjustment of the individual to all other institutional structures and cultural imperatives are problems which fall outside the scope of the present study.

The complete description and functional analysis of the phenomenon of the Amigo system remains a worthy subject for empirical investigation. At this time we are concerned, first, with its conceptualization as an actual interaction system of importance to the Mexican male, and second, with studying some aspects of its functional relationship to the conjugal family system.

The Conjugal Family. In the present study we limit the application of this concept to the roles of husband and wife.

Alienation. This concept, which constitutes the dependent variable in the present study, is limited here to the condition experienced by the wife in the conjugal family in which "*la soledad de dos en compania*"[11] is evident. This phrase expresses both the idea of isolation of two while in mutual company, and "accompanied loneliness." This type of isolation is different, therefore, from that used by Seeman and others as one of the meanings of alienation.[12]

---

[7] Oscar Lewis, *The Children of Sanchez.* Here Manuel describes explicitly the daily influence his *Amigos* have on him; how he is introduced to premarital sexual relations at an early age and to gambling; and how he is induced to prove his manliness by fighting. In one incident described, his *Amigos* ridiculed him and forced him to give up a good and stable job.

[8] Street fighting is probably the most important. In *The Children of Sanchez*, Roberto relates how he was accepted as a member of the group. He had to fight every one in the group including the main "gallo" or leader. In turn, he later had to perform the role of "tester" for new potential members.

[9] According to Bermudez, *op. cit.*, the general attitude of the Mexican male is that "anything which signifies sentimentality, harmony, prudence, elegance, or beauty, is unworthy of a true man." This generalization may be more typical of the lower class male (p. 51).

[10] There are no secrets among *amigos intimos*. There is no limit to the expression of loyalty. A man who might fear legal action on the part of a pregnant girl may ask his *amigo intimo* to get involved with the girl so as to put the paternity of the child in doubt and thus avoid responsibility. See *The Children of Sanchez*, p. 42.

[11] Bermudez, *op. cit.*, p. 56.

[12] Melvin Seeman, "On the Meaning of Alienation," *American Sociological Review*, **24** (December, 1959), pp. 783–791. See also John P. Clark, "Measuring Alienation within a Social System," *American*

By alienation, then, we refer to a type of cleavage or apartness in the Mexican conjugal relationship. It is applied especially to the wife because, as the other role incumbent in the conjugal system, it is she who faces the competition of the Amigo system. The alienated wife is physically a member of the conjugal family, but she does not experience fully the cohesion which that membership might lead the average wife to expect.

Although further study may be necessary to fully conceptualize this phenomenon, we are at this time satisfied to identify it as a type of alienation, and to define it operationally by the scale we have used to measure it.

Interrelationship of the Amigo and Conjugal Family Systems

As stated before, the Amigo system tends to persist in influencing the Mexican male even after his marriage. This persistence appears to be at the base of conflict with the conjugal family, at least in those areas of social interaction where the role of the husband is involved. The husband, being an incumbent in both systems, is thrust in a conflicting role in the two systems. The wife, however, being the only other role incumbent in the conjugal system (as defined in this study), becomes wholly dependent on the husband for the integral maintenance of the conjugal system. When conflict between the systems develops, even though both mates suffer the consequences of the conflict, it is the wife who becomes alienated as an incumbent in the family system.

Sociological Review, **26** (October, 1961), pp. 753–758. It should be pointed out that in our use of the concept alienation we do not imply any individual maladjustment of the wife; rather, we refer strictly to her alienation *as a member of the conjugal system*. Nor do we imply that her alienation is in reference to other groups such as the extended family, the church, or even informal neighborhood groups. Whether she has access to other supporting groups or not becomes, of course, an important factor affecting her perception of alienation within the conjugal system as well as a consequence of it. However, although important and obviously relevant, these considerations remain empirical questions beyond the scope of the present study.

Considering the interrelationship between the two systems we can identify at least four different factors which are the basis of the possible conflict: (1) allocation of scarce resources, (2) conflicting value orientations, (3) relative low status of marriage in the culture, and (4) differential status of male and female in the culture.

1. ALLOCATION OF SCARCE RESOURCES. When an individual maintains membership in more than one social system, he faces a problem of allocation of relevant resources. As soon as the Mexican male marries, a portion of his time, loyalty, money, and services are claimed by his conjugal system. To what extent a conflict in the allocation of the scarce resources develops depends on a number of factors. Some of these are the following: the relative prestige of the man's premarital status in his Amigo system (whether it was high or low); his emotional investment in the Amigo system (whether intense or not); the type of support from his family of orientation (whether in favor of his marriage or not); the number of memberships in other organizations (whether few or many); the personality characteristics of his wife (for example, whether dominating or passive); and the relative emotional involvement of the man in the marriage. To be sure, the outcome of the allocation of scarce resources depends on a multiplicity of factors, but the fact remains that the allocation must be made, and both systems can seldom be equally satisfied.

2. CONFLICTING VALUE ORIENTATIONS. With respect to certain basic attitudes and cultural values, the Amigo system and the conjugal family appear to be mutually exclusive. This is perhaps one of the most serious difficulties facing the Mexican male in his accommodation to the demands of familial life (whether or not he gives up his membership in the Amigo system). If he withdraws from the Amigo system, the problem of accommodation is of course lessened to some extent.

As stated before, the Amigo system socializes the young Mexican male to a number of attitudes and role expectations which are highly valued, especially in the young, single male subculture. When he enters marriage, however, the Mexican male is suddenly faced with an entirely new set of role expectations. The demands of his new roles not only include a number of practical considerations for most of which he has had little (if any) training; but most of these new expectations are based on attitudes and values which are in almost direct conflict with the self-image which has been organized and developed in his youth.

Perhaps no greater discrepancy exists between two roles in the entire social structure than that between the role of the single man and that of the married man in the Mexican culture. The more the socialization of the Mexican male has been influenced by the Amigo system with its particular emphasis on *machismo*, the greater his difficulty in establishing functional relationships in his conjugal family. In essence, to be sure, this conflict in role expectations and in value-orientation constitutes the well known phenomenon of role discontinuity in the socialization process which exists also in other cultures.[13] However, the Mexican case is characterized by at least two other factors which contribute to the severity of the role discontinuity. These are the relative low status of marriage as an institution and the differential ascribed status of the sexes in the conjugal system.

3. LOW STATUS OF MARRIAGE IN THE CULTURE. The entrance of the Mexican male into the conjugal system constitutes for him, in some ways, a sacrifice in status. From his socially meaningful and culturally valued position as an unmarried male, and in particular as a member of his Amigo system, the Mexican male senses a lowered social prestige as he enters marriage. Although there may be other factors related to this feeling of loss of social prestige, one of the most obvious ones is the cultural devaluation of the role of the married man vis-à-vis the bachelor. In several important aspects, marriage as an institution has not been ascribed high prestige in Mexican society and culture.[14] The popular prestige of

marriage is even lower than its ideal cultural prestige. This may explain partly why many Mexican males regard their entrance into marriage as a questionable step forward in the social validation of the individual. They do not feel *socially* rewarded even when, at the *personal* level, marriage may be sufficiently rewarding.[15] The popular attitude is that the married man becomes a "zero to the left" as a Spanish saying goes. From the point of view of his Amigo system, the member who marries "loses his independence." All this, of course, is in direct contrast to the social prestige which his Amigo system as a reference group has provided for him through the years.

4. DIFFERENTIAL STATUS OF THE SEXES IN THE CONJUGAL SYSTEM. By cultural ascription the female has a lower status than the male in Mexican society.[16] This situation is not necessarily modified in the conjugal family. The difficulties faced by the Mexican male in the process of accommodation from the role expectations of his Amigo system to those of the conjugal family (that is, his conflicting demands for the allocation of scarce resources, the conflicting value-orientations, and the relative loss

---

man's frequent involvement with other women as his way to tolerate the "horrible load of marriage." The full consideration of this point falls outside the scope of the present study, but support for the claim that marriage has low prestige in the culture is not lacking in the literature, and it appears to be somewhat related to the religious values of the society. Celibacy, for example, is regarded as superior to parenthood. By many, becoming a priest or a nun is culturally regarded as infinitely superior to marrying and raising a family. From many points of view, marriage and sex are regarded, at best, as necessary evils.

[15] Bermudez, *op. cit.*, pp. 34–36.

[16] Ibid., p. 53. See also Cerwin, *op. cit.*, p. 154, Tuck, *op. cit.*, pp. 88, 115, 123. Daughters, sisters, wives, and women in general have traditionally had lower social status than their role reciprocals in Spanish-American society. Many observers have wondered why Mexican women, especially wives, are often conspicuous for their absence in public social functions. It is never clear to these observers whether Mexican men are ashamed of their women; or think that their women hinder them socially; or feel their women would be out of place. The differential status of the sexes is manifest in every aspect of social interaction, and it permeates completely the institutional structure of the society.

---

[13] Ruth Benedict, "Continuities and Discontinuities in Cultural Conditioning," *Readings in Sociology*, edited by E. Schuler et al., New York: Thomas Y. Crowell Co., 1960, pp. 166–175. Originally published in *Psychiatry*, Vol. 1 (1938), pp. 161–167.

[14] Cerwin, *op. cit.*, pp. 154–155. It is reported here that men fear marriage, especially religious marriage, because they feel it is the woman's tool to "imprison" them. Another author, Bermudez, *op. cit.*, p. 55, sees

of prestige as he enters marriage), are compounded further by this differential status of the sexes.

As mentioned before, the Mexican male on entering marriage is faced with a problem of deciding whether or not to abandon his Amigo system. At this crucial period in the marriage, his wife (because of her low status) is hardly in a position to grant him any support which may be socially meaningful to him. Moreover, his wife depends entirely on him for her present and future social status. Considering this, it is understandable why the husband may perceive a "status vacuum" which encourages him to continue his participation in the Amigo system after marriage. This perception thus provides a basis for conflict between the Amigo and conjugal family systems.

One might even say that one of the functions of the Amigo system is to provide the male with a positive self-image and social prestige in a culture in which not only marriage, the family, and woman (by their low prestige), but also institutional structures such as the church, the economic system, or the political system often fail to provide the individual with sufficient opportunities for self and social validation.[17]

Probably the wife resents most acutely the competition of the Amigo system at the beginning of the marriage. Perhaps at that time too the most telling competition between the two systems takes place. This competition may occur overtly or covertly, and the extent to which the wife and husband are consciously aware of the struggle may vary.

From the status point of view, the Amigo system presents the greatest challenge to the conjugal system probably just before and just after marriage. This is especially true among those couples where the wife expects and perhaps even demands all the manifestations of loyalty from a husband who has strong commitments to his Amigo system. To many a husband the trauma may be as genuine even when not fully understood. It is not necessary for the individual to be consciously aware of the struggle between the two systems to suffer its consequences.

This transition from a higher prestige to a lower prestige system and from close relationship with social equals in one system to close relationship with a socially inferior mate in the other system presents a dilemma to the Mexican male. This dilemma, which must be solved as the man desperately struggles for social identity, consists of the challenge to reconcile his identification with, and membership within, two social systems with essentially conflicting value-orientations, with mutually exclusive role-expectations, and also with differential rewards.

In this dilemma three alternatives are open to the married man: (1) he may continue his active participation in the Amigo system to the eventual detriment of his relationship in the conjugal system; (2) he may develop a strong conjugal orientation and, thus, eventually give up membership in the Amigo system; or, (3) he may attempt to achieve a working compromise between (1) and (2) which, depending on a variety of factors, may or may not develop into a satisfactory arrangement.[18]

Taking into consideration all the factors discussed above, it becomes obvious that an infinite number of types and degrees of accommodation is possible. However, it seems highly probable that alienation of the wife is related to the relative importance of the Amigo system within the social universe of the Mexican married male. Our hypothesis suggests that the relationship of the variables is positive, and an empirical test of this hypothesis is presented in this paper.

Study Design

Site. Field work was conducted in Ciudad

[17] The current changes in the social and economic structure encouraged by the increasing political stability and emphasis on everything "Mexican and the Mexicans" is likely to affect directly many of these traditional attitudes and values. See Manuel German Parra, *La Industrialization de Mexico*, Mexico: Imprenta Universitaria, 1954., G. W. Hewes, "Mexicans in Search of the 'Mexican'," *The American Journal of Economics and Sociology*, XIII, 2 (January, 1954), pp. 209–223, also the entire series of volumes on "Mexico y lo Mexicano" published by *Antigua Libreria Robredo*, Mexico, D.F.

[18] The factors related to the selection of one of these alternatives is the subject of another study which is under preparation. At this time we are concerned merely with the fact that these alternatives are available.

Juarez, Mexico, a rapidly growing border city. In 1930, the city population was a mere 30,000; in 1960, the population was over 350,000.[19]

Ciudad Juarez is the major port of entry on the United States-Mexican border. It is a city of small businesses, many of which depend on tourist trade. The city has numerous local, state, and federal employees and contains an army post, a brick and several furniture factories, many small industries, and a large brewery with a substantial payroll. About 15,000 men and women who live in Ciudad Juarez are employed full-time in El Paso, Texas, the twin border city. To serve the 40,000 children in school, there are 1237 teachers paid by the city, state, and federal governments. The slow but steady growth of a strong, dynamic, and influential middle class can be observed in Ciudad Juarez, even though, as it is true for the entire Republic of Mexico, a significant reduction of the lower strata through industrialization and education advance is yet to come.[20]

Sample. The data were obtained from personal interviews with 101 married women. Common-law marriages were included. The writers spent nearly six weeks on the research site and, with a prepared schedule, interviewed the subjects in their own homes.[21] The subjects constitute a cluster sample selected through a multistage sampling procedure from neighborhood to city block and then to household as the ultimate unit.[22]

The subjects ranged in age from 18 to 67, with a median age of 34.3 years. The range in the length of marriage was from 1 to 52 years with a median of 13.2. Most of the women (91 per cent) reported they had married only once, 7 per cent reported no children. Two per cent reported from 13 to 15 children. However, the median number of children from the sample was 4.38. Education achievement ranged from zero to ten years of school, with a median of 4.5 years.

A little over one fourth of the women in the sample were employed outside their home. Only 15 per cent were working full time, and 13 per cent reported part-time employment. The religious preference of 91 per cent was the

[19] This is the figure from the 1960 census which was available to the writers only in its prepublication form, as the official publication was not yet available. All census information was obtained through the courtesy of Attorney C. Moreno Reza, whose office was the official headquarters for the Federal Census of the city and municipio. Grateful acknowledgement is hereby extended.

The most important factor in this fast population growth is migration from the interior. During the last few years a large number of migrants have come to Juarez, hoping to cross over to the United States to work. It is estimated that about 90 per cent of these migrants stay in the city after realizing that their immigration to the United States is impossible. They are unable or unwilling to return South. Most of these migrants are poorly prepared to make a living in an urban environment and have created enormously complex social and economic problems for the city. The housing problem is especially acute and *paracaidismo* (squatting) has become a major social problem in Juarez in the last ten years. Literally thousands of families have taken over private and public lands in the outskirts of the city and there now exist large areas or neighborhoods of makeshift, provisional, and even permanent dwellings which lack the most essential utilities, facilities, and services. Paracaidismo increases daily.

[20] Julio Duran Ochoa, *Poblacion*, Mexico: Fondo de Cultura Economica, 1955. See also M. G. Parra, *op. cit.*, Chapter 7.

[21] Rapport was excellent in the great majority of the interviews. There were only two refusals. Entry was achieved by candidly stating that, as a married couple, the writers were studying the family and wanted to know the opinions of families in the area with respect to family life. The wives were usually eager to speak and many volunteered much information. Some became so involved that they even asked for advice about specific family problems. In one case, a "wife" asked the writers to convince her husband to marry her.

[22] The natural areas and neighborhoods were identified and delineated by an actual reconnaissance of the city, using a city map and other sketch maps constructed on the spot for the purpose. When the several stages of the sampling procedure were completed, a total of 150 households had been selected. A daily quota of interviews was imposed in order to complete the field work within the six-week deadline; but realities limited the original goal, and the sample was reduced. While the multiplication of "call-backs" became a factor, an important reason for the failure to achieve the original goal was the number of lengthy interviews obtained from many of the subjects. Other time-consuming circumstances were also involved. All the wives in 101 households and 49 of the husbands were interviewed, as the latter were physically less accessible. The analysis of the data from husbands is to be reported elsewhere.

Catholic faith; various Protestant denominations were represented among the other 9 per cent. Of the total sample, 69 per cent went to church at least once a month. Only 15 per cent reported social club membership and/or participation.

Home ownership was reported by 50 per cent of the sample. However, most of the houses were small (45 per cent with two or less rooms) and had limited facilities. Inside plumbing was reported in 49 per cent of the homes; 22 per cent of the sample obtained water from an outside faucet which was shared with neighbors; and 29 per cent had to buy their water from ambulant commercial carriers.[23] Electricity was observed in 73 per cent of the homes; electric refrigerators were present in 45 per cent of the homes; 26 per cent of the sample reported different types of ice box. No facilities for food preservations were reported by 29 per cent of the sample. As a contrast, 74 per cent had radios and 46 per cent television sets.[24] Only 29 per cent of the families owned a car or truck.

Construction of Scales. Previous to the field work, the writers perused the literature and compiled a list of approximately three hundred items thought relevant to the problem. From these items, 46 were ultimately selected for inclusion in a schedule, and subjects were asked to respond affirmatively or negatively to them. The two scales used in the present study were part of that schedule. Data on control variables and other usual background information were obtained with another schedule, which included open-ended questions.

Measuring the Husband's Participation in the Amigo System. Five items which were scattered throughout the schedule were combined into an index of husband's participation in the Amigo system. The items are a combination of feelings on the part of the wife and of her "objective" reports of the husband's behavior.

If we paraphrase the statements, from their original in Spanish, the five items (with their respective weights to obtain a composite score) were:

1. Husband spends money in ways which do not benefit the family.   Yes (1)   No (0)
2. Husband goes out by himself (without family) too often.   Yes (1)   No (0)
3. Husband prefers to use his leisure time with his friends rather than with wife and children.   Yes (1)   No (0)
4. Husband spends too much money with his friends.   Yes (1)   No (0)
5. Husband spends nights away from home for other than work reasons.   Yes (1)   No (0)

The item-total score correlation coefficients are .68, .63, .74, .60, .69. The coefficient of reproducibility, using the Guttman scale analysis, is .93. These figures provide at least some indication of internal consistency and unidimensionality.

Operationally, a high score indicates high participation in the Amigo system. When certain aspects of data analysis required the index to be dichotomized, a score of three or more was considered as an indication of sustained participation.

Measuring the Alienation of the Wife. Six items which were also scattered throughout the schedule were combined into an index of alienation of the wife. In terms of content, the items are statements that refer to problems the wife might experience in the conjugal relationship. Existence of these problems is taken as an indication of her alienation. Operationally, a high score in the scale indicates high degree of alienation.

Paraphrased from their original in Spanish, the items (with their respective weights) were:

1. I often have to seek emotional support outside my marriage.   Yes (1)   No (0)
2. My husband does not tell me how much he earns.   True (1)   False (0)
3. On family money matters, my husband does not ask my opinion.   True (1)   False (0)
4. My husband makes plans for the future without asking for my opinion.   True (1)   False (0)

[23] Most of these dwellings were occupied by squatters.
[24] All T.V. programs originate in U.S. stations. Most are in English, but the few in Spanish are obviously designed and directed to the Spanish-speaking population on both sides of the border which constitutes a significant market for U.S. goods and services.

5. My husband does not talk over his personal problems with me. True (1) False (0)
6. I can always talk over my personal problems with my husband. Yes (0) No (1)

Item-total correlation coefficients are respectively .51, .51, .55, .61, .33, .57, .69. The coefficient of reproducibility is .90.

Findings

The central point in the analysis of the data was to determine the relationship between the husband's participation in the Amigo system and the wife's alienation. However, as the analysis proceeded, certain questions about prevalence suggested the investigation of differentials between the subgroups which would result from the application of control factors. Questions of relationship and questions of prevalence, therefore, constitute a two-dimensional point of view in the analysis of the data.

The first dimension in the analysis concerns questions of relationship between the two variables as measured by the scales. The analysis here is focused on the problems of existence, degree, and direction of the relationship between the participation of the husband in the Amigo system and the alienation of the wife. Correlation analysis, for the total sample first, then for the subgroups, was the technique applied in this part of the analysis. A Z-test of statistical significance indicated whether the null hypothesis of no association was tenable. The criterion for statistical significance was .05.

The second dimension in the analysis concerns questions of prevalence. The analysis here is focused on the description of differentials in the persistence of the Amigo system first for the total sample and then within the subgroups resulting from the control of relevant factors.

Questions of Relationship

The basic question in this part of the analysis is suggested by the hypothesis which the present research is testing: Is there a significant relationship between the participation of the husband in the Amigo system and the alienation of the wife in the conjugal Mexican family? A correlation of the variables, as measured by the two scales, produced a coefficient which is statistically significant ($r = .70; P < .01$). This finding tells us that the greater the husband's participation in the Amigo system, the more the wife is alienated.

The correlation analysis of the data was further refined by controlling for social class, education of wife, length of marriage, and number of children.*

Social class. The sample was divided into two classes, the lower class ($N = 56$) and the middle class ($N = 45$).[25] The latter group included a small number of upper-middle-class subjects. The correlation coefficient for the lower class was .50 and for the middle class was .63. Controlling for social class, the data show that among conjugal families in both classes, the relationship between the variables exists and is positive and statistically significant. However, the difference in magnitude between the correlations suggests that women of the middle class are more likely to be alienated by their husband's involvement in the Amigo system than are women of the lower class. It may also indicate a greater tolerance or greater passivity in the lower-class woman.[26]

Education of Wife. Since the measurement of social class did not include education, we thought it desirable to control for this factor. The relevant question here would be: is there a difference in the magnitude of the relationship of the variables when the wife's education varies?

---

* These factors were treated as control factors only and not as alternative independent variables as in an analysis of covariance. Our major interest was in the relationship of the two variables; controlling for relevant factors was only to sharpen the analysis in order to develop more precise empirical hypotheses for further study.

[25] The sample was stratified into two classes on the basis of the revised form of Sewell's socioeconomic scale. See John C. Bercher and Emmit F. Sharp, "A Modification of Sewell's Socioeconomic Scale," *Technical Bulletin Number T–46*, (September, 1952), Oklahoma Agricultural and Mechanical College, Stillwater, Oklahoma. A six-point scale rating the overall quality of the subject's dwellings was also used. The correlation coefficient between the two scales was .82.

[26] Bermudez, *op. cit.*, p. 35.

In terms of education of the wife, the sample was divided into those having six years of schooling or less ($N = 82$) and those with seven years of schooling and over ($N = 19$). The correlation between the two variables for the first group was .55, and for the second .67. This difference in the magnitude of the association follows the trend detected through the control for social class. The higher the education of the wife, the more likely that she feels alienated. Apparently education sharpens sensitivity, or perhaps higher education makes the wife less passive about the competition she might perceive in the Amigo system.

Length of Marriage. Is the association of variables affected by the number of years the couples have been married? To answer this question, couples married four years or less ($N = 18$) were compared to those married five years and over ($N = 83$). The correlation coefficient for the younger couples was .76, and for the older couples .55. As with the other findings, we can only speculate as to the possible meaning of these differences. The fact that the wives in the younger families are more likely to be alienated may indicate an increasing rebellion on the part of the modern Mexican wife. On the other hand, it is possible that this difference only signifies the dynamic struggle for marital adjustment which generally characterizes the first years of married life. It is not known, of course, to what extent the apparently lower association of the variables in the older families reflects selective factors in the survival of marriages (for example: the personality of the wife, compromises achieved to minimize the competition of two systems).

Number of Children. The size of the family was thought to be another relevant factor which might affect the relationship of the two variables. Do wives with few children react to the competition of the Amigo system in the same way as do wives with many children? Couples with three or fewer children ($N = 46$) were compared to couples with four or more children ($N = 55$). The correlation coefficient for the small families was .46 and for the larger families .61. In terms of our measure of alienation it appears that the Amigo system is somewhat more dysfunctional

in the larger families. In a culture where children are still considered assets, especially to the mother, the wife's emotional and economic dependence on the husband may deteriorate as children become sources of gratification.

Question of Prevalence

The first question to consider here is: to what extent is the Amigo system prevalent among conjugal Mexican families as represented by our sample?

A score of three points or more in the Amigo scale was taken as an indication of participation by the husband. The actual distribution was as follows:

	Distribution
All those scoring five points	15
All those scoring four points	7
All those scoring three points	12
All those scoring two points	8
All those scoring one point	15
All those scoring zero	45
	———
	101

Using the score of three as the cutting point for participants and nonparticipants, as reported by the wives, it can be seen that 34 husbands, or one in every three, participate in the Amigo system.

As shown in the analysis of relationship, some important trends appeared when control factors were applied and the analysis was done by subgroups.

Social Class. Is the Amigo system as prevalent among the conjugal families of the lower class as it is among the middle-class families? The data show that 24 per cent of the husbands of the middle class participate in the Amigo system whereas 41 per cent of the lower-class husbands are reported as participants.

This finding suggests that the Amigo system might be common to all social strata in the Mexican society. Of course, this is not to imply that the patterns of interaction, attitudes, and over-all functions of the system in general are identical among diverse subcultural groups. The existence, extent, and nature of these differences remain open empirical questions at this time.

Education of Husband. The factor considered relevant here was the education of the husband, since the phenomenon studied—the Amigo system—was one in which he was the participant. The general question was: is participation in the Amigo system equally prevalent among husbands with different educational achievement? Husbands with six or less years of schooling were compared to those having seven years or more of schooling. The data show that 24 per cent of the husbands with higher education and 36 per cent of those with lower education participate in the Amigo system. This finding may indicate a trend which, if true, may have important implications in view of the current educational changes going on in Mexico.

Age of Husband. The general question here was: do husbands of different ages participate in the Amigo system to the same extent? Husbands under 36 and husbands 36 years or over were compared. The data show that 38 per cent for the younger group and 31 per cent for the older group are reported as participants.

Length of Marriage. The number of years a couple had been married was related to the husband's tendency to participate in the Amigo system. Couples married four years or less were compared to those married five years or longer. Of the older couples, 34 per cent were found to be involved in the Amigo system compared with 33 per cent of the younger couples.

It appears, then, that length of marriage does not generally affect the involvement of the husband with his Amigo system; involvement in the Amigo system may be a stable life-long adjustment for the male.

These last two factors, age of husband and length of marriage, present some problems of sampling that are difficult to solve. The higher probability for divorce and separation during the early years of marriage affects the results based on length of marriage. On the other hand, the higher mortality rates of the older group influence the analysis of data by age. For these and other reasons, these findings must be regarded as tentative.

Number of Children. Do husbands with small families participate in the Amigo system as much as husbands with large families? To answer this question families with three or fewer children were compared to families with four or more children.

The data show that 22 per cent of the husbands with the small families and 44 per cent of those with larger families were involved in the Amigo system. This difference may be related to the husband's need to escape responsibility and/or to the failure of the wife (because of the large family) to be a companion to her husband. At any rate, if this finding is representative, many male children in the society go through the socialization process with little chance of establishing an indentification with their father as a full-time role incumbent in the conjugal system.

Summary and Discussion

The purpose of the present study has been: (1) to conceptualize the phenomenon of the Amigo system in the Mexican society; (2) to demonstrate empirically the functional relationship of such system to a specific aspect of instability in the Mexican conjugal family, the alienation of the wife, and (3) to describe the prevalence of some characteristics of conjugal families in which the Amigo system is found to persist.

The findings of the study are:

1. For the whole sample, there is a statistically significant, positive association between the husband's participation in the Amigo system and the alienation of the wife.

2. For selected subgroups, controlling for one variable at a time, the relationship between the two variables is found to be stronger among wives of the middle class, wives with higher education, wives married fewer years, and wives with more children.

3. In terms of prevalence, husband's participation in the Amigo system tends to be higher among males of the lower class, males with a lower education, males under 36 years of age, and males with larger families. Among the subgroups differentiated by length of marriage, the participation of the husband in the Amigo system was almost identical.

We have found that the prevalence of the Amigo system extends to 33 per cent of the families in our sample. Even assuming that this is the present pattern for the population, we have no way of knowing whether the current trend is toward an increase or decrease in prevalence. The little we have learned about the system, however, has provided us with some guidelines on the basis of which tentative hypotheses about its persistence can be advanced.

First of all, the data indicate that when social class is taken into consideration, the Amigo system is less conspicuous among the middle class. Second, it appears safe for us to assume that the middle class and the level of education in Mexican society are likely to increase rather than decrease. On the basis of this assumption and the data on social class, it is our hypothesis that the Amigo system eventually will decrease in prestige because of its inability to compete successfully with other social systems, especially the family, for the scarce resources which seem to be vital for its survival. Specifically, our hypothesis is that the wife will tend to increase her ability to compete successfully for the time and the loyalty of the husband, time and loyalty being only two of the scarce resources for which the two systems compete. In other words, in the struggle for survival between the two systems, we see the Amigo system as the expendable one. This point may be clarified further by considering it more specifically.

A sociological theory[27] suggests that all social systems must solve four basic problems in order to survive. These are (1) adaptation, (2) goal achievement, (3) integration, and (4) latency or pattern maintenance. Our discussion is not intended to be a description of how these problems are being solved by the Amigo system at present. More data than we now have are required for such an undertaking. At this time we can only tentatively suggest whether the system is likely to solve these problems in the future and survive, or whether external social realities are likely to force its extinction.

Adaptation. All systems must accommodate to reality demands of the environment. That is, if a

[27] Talcott Parsons, *Structure and Process in Modern Societies*, Glencoe, Ill.: Free Press, 1960, pp. 16–96.

system is to survive, it must allocate resources to adapt to changes in the external social situation. The survival of the Amigo system in the past might have been related, as we have suggested, to the lack of prestige of the conjugal system and especially to the relatively low social status of the wife and also, perhaps, to her attitudinal conditioning from infancy to accept (apparently with resignation), the "evilness of man." It can be expected, however, that as the social relationship between the sexes changes, in part, because of the increased education of the woman, the Amigo system will have to face a major problem of adaptation. A socially and economically more independent wife is likely to demand not only greater loyalty, but also more of her husband's time. The persistence of the Amigo system will depend on the type of adaptation it makes to these and related changes in the general society. Our hypothesis is that, since these changes affect the very core of the Amigo system, its viability is likely to be undermined.

A corollary to this hypothesis is that before the struggle between the conjugal and the Amigo systems is resolved, a social price will most probably be paid by society. Indeed, this struggle is already under way. The observations of the writers indicate that in those conjugal families where the wife has a higher education, the tension and conflict in the conjugal relationship tends to increase. The forces for the emancipation of the woman will put the Amigo system under constantly increasing pressure. If and when it is able to solve the problem of allocation of resources, this adaptation is likely to involve quite radical changes in its structural and functional characteristics.

Goal Achievement. All systems must develop mechanisms, as well as mobilize resources, to attain their goals or objectives. Now, as stated before, the complete delineation of the overall goals of the Amigo system are a matter for empirical research. However, it seems that at least one of its basic goals is simply expressive interaction. That is, a great portion of the social interaction between Amigos is an end in itself rather than being instrumental for the achievement of other goals. Of course, the basic facility, or resource, for the achievement of this goal is time; and in the culture where the Amigo system has flourished, time has been readily available.

As we consider the survival of the Amigo system from the point of view of its needs to solve the problem of goal achievement, it can be hypothesized that its implementation of mechanisms for the achievement of the goal of expressive interaction may become more difficult as time, in itself, acquires greater value as a means to achieve other goals in an increasingly mechanized society. From this point of view, the solution of the problem of goal achievement becomes directly related to the solution of the problem of adaptation. The capacity of the Amigo system to adapt to changing social structural reality and to develop mechanisms to achieve its redefined or new goals will determine its persistence.

Integration. The problem of integration demands the internal harmony of the units of a system. As is true with any other social system, the persistence of the Amigo system will depend on its ability to avoid conflict between its values, norms, beliefs, and role-expectations at the same time that it attempts to solve the problem of adaptation to social and cultural changes of external systems. It can be hypothesized, for example, that the value of *machismo* will diminish in importance if the values which support the social and educational independence of the woman become actually internalized and institutionalized in Mexican society. We suggest that these values and those of *machismo* present a major problem of integration. The beliefs, norms, and role-expectations which complement these two sets of values are almost mutually exclusive. It is perhaps relevant to mention at this point that some of the values opposing the Amigo system are manifesting themselves in new legislation for the protection of mother and child and also in the enforceable social demand for the reduction of common-law marriages.[28] From this point of view, then, the solution of the problem of integration by the Amigo system will also constitute another necessary aspect of the adaptive process.

[28] A recent Social Security Law in Mexico demands that a couple be married by civil law before they can be eligible for any family benefits. Another law, though not yet widely enforced, makes it possible for the wife to sue for divorce on the grounds of adultery.

Latency or Pattern Maintenance. To survive, all systems must develop mechanisms to maintain their values, organizational characteristics, and identity as distinctive entities over time. If the Amigo system were to solve the problem of latency, then, by definition, its problems of adaptation would disappear and the problems of goal achievement and integration would be reduced to strictly known elements and functions. Recent changes in Mexican society impede the solution of the latency problem by the Amigo system. As stated before, in its competition with other social systems (including the conjugal family), it is the Amigo system which appears as expendable.

As far as can be determined by the limited data available, the problem of pattern maintenance of the Amigo system has been solved in the past, at least partially, by the mechanisms of the "vicious" circle. As mentioned before, the Mexican family is often characterized by the physical and/or emotional absence of the father. It is perhaps related to this fact that the young male's participation in the Amigo system becomes institutionalized, since the system provides some support in the socialization of the young man. When the young man continues his participation in the system even after his marriage, the pattern of the absent father is repeated, thus contributing to the need in the next generation of males to seek male identification outside the home.

Our suggestion that this pattern maintenance process will eventually be broken is based on the Gemeinschaft-Gesellschaft general theory of social change.[29] When Gesellschaft forms of social organization make their appearance in a given society, the Gemeinschaft forms tend to decline, albeit after a period of some undetermined amount of social disruption. As contractual forms of social facilitation become institutionalized, the informal ways of facilitation, such as those that characterized the Amigo system, tend to decline in value. In the Mexican economic system, the trend is to modify the widespread philosophy among employers of

[29] For the latest treatment of these theoretical concepts see Charles P. Loomis, *Social Systems, Essays on their Persistence and Change*, New Jersey: D. Van Nostrand Co., 1960.

nonresponsibility for (and noninvolvement in) the personal and family adjustment of the worker outside of the job. As interest by employers in the workers' family life increases, then the informal facilitation and mutual aid and protection, such as might be found in an Amigo system, can be expected to decline in importance. Also, from another point of view, as the economic system increases its power in the society, it may demand greater social stability on the part of the worker, particularly family stability. Directly, or indirectly, this may discourage the type of association or interaction which appears to be a paramount value in the Amigo system.

As the Mexican society becomes increasingly industrialized, more formal organizations may develop to take over some of the functions of informal groups. Along with these and other changes in the economic, social, and political structures, a lower birth rate can also be expected. We suggest that these factors might eventually be associated with greater prestige for the conjugal system, especially with higher social status, for the wife who thus may find herself in a more strategic position to demand greater involvement of the husband in the conjugal family system. These changes may eventually break up the vicious-circle phenomenon in the pattern maintenance of the Amigo system since the more the Mexican male fulfills the father role, the less his children will seek male identification outside the family.

Chapter 4

Family and Kinship
in Contemporary Society

This chapter describes the general character of family and kinship in contemporary industrial society. It provides a background for the subsequent chapters on courtship, family development, the organization of the nuclear family, and socialization of children. First, two views of the contemporary family are discussed. Then the role of kinship in pluralistic societies is described. Finally, trends that have influenced kinship organization in the United States are indicated briefly.

Isolated Families and Kinship Groups

Many sociologists regard the contemporary family as becoming increasingly specialized in its functions. The family in a primarily agricultural society was the locus for a variety of activities related to religion, protection, education, and leisure.[1] With urbanization these activities were delegated to other institutions, and the family has concentrated on affectional relationships, socialization of children, and reproduction.

According to these sociologists, specialization has resulted in the rejection of many traditional ties that might impede the adaptation of family members to modern industrial society, and the kinship group has consequently declined as a political and economic force. Family or kinship control is no longer involved in the ownership of facilities for production, and the locus of power has shifted to government. A relatively independent nuclear family is considered more consistent with the high social and residential mobility that characterizes modern society.[2]

Although many sociologists emphasize the independence of the nuclear family in contemporary industrial societies, others focus on the persistence of kinship structures

---

[1] William F. Ogburn and Meyer F. Nimkoff, *Technology and the Changing Family*, New York: Houghton Mifflin, 1955.
[2] Talcott Parsons and Robert F. Bales, *Family, Socialization and Interaction Process*, Glencoe: Free Press, 1955.

117

in these societies. Both groups agree that empirically these kinship structures exist in modern urban life. The major disagreement between the two views is over the significance of these structures. Those sociologists who emphasize the independence of the nuclear family suggest that the extended family ordinarily does not play a significant role in the destiny of the individual. They contend that the economic and political requirements of contemporary society are constituted to make the extended family inconsequential. They consider that the extended family persists only because of sentimental or other nonrational factors and regard the kinship group as superfluous to the characterization of the modern family.

Those sociologists who emphasize the persistence of kinship structures in contemporary societies stress the role of the family in the continuity of the social order. Because of its genetic character and composition, the family tends to be a conservative institution. The parents and grandparents attempt to socialize the children according to norms and values they regard as necessary and proper. Thus, the family tends to be an instrument for maintaining patterns of social life from one generation to the next.[3]

The modern family is in a state of tension between tendencies toward adaptation and tendencies toward the maintenance of traditional patterns of social organization. It is under stress to adapt to the political and economic order. At the same time the kinship groups operate to sustain traditional patterns of organization. Extensive control by the kinship group over financial and personal resources for the welfare of individual members facilitates the maintenance of traditional patterns. If the kinship group were deprived of all control over the individual nuclear family, stabilization of the social order would be impeded. In contemporary American society a major problem in the organization of family life can be stated as follows: how can the stabilization of patterns of social order be maintained when major control of financial and personal resources has passed to other institutions? Note that the problem is not one of maintaining a particular marriage or of maximizing personal adjustment in an uncertain changing society. Rather, the problem is of continued control by stable kinship units when their economic and political bases for this control are minimized.

There appear to be two consequences of the existence of viable kinship groups in modern societies. First, if we assume that civilization is constantly transformed by the development of inventions, there must be an agency that inhibits change so that sufficient time elapses to observe the effect of the invention on the social order. Without this conservative pressure continuity of the social order would be impeded. There is no other institution in modern society that is so heavily committed to tradition as the kinship group. Yet not all forms of kinship may be appropriate to modern industrial society. If the kinship group were organized unilaterally rather than bilaterally, its emphasis on lineage tradition might pervade the political and economic order. Specific individuals acting as lineage heads would provide pervasive control over kin. In bilateral kinship, however, the husband's and wife's kin are treated alike and emphasis is more on affiliation than descent. These characteristics

[3] For a discussion of the role of the family in the orderly replacement of one generation by the next, see Bernard Farber, *Family: Organization and Interaction*, San Francisco: Chandler, 1964.

impede centralization of authority in the kindred and minimize control over political and economic activities of relatives. Bilateral kinship is appropriate to modern society precisely because it lacks the mechanisms for pervasive control over kin but does not ignore entirely descent and the maintenance of tradition.[4]

A second basis for the persistence of the kinship groups in contemporary society, according to those sociologists who regard the kindred as an important aspect of organization, is the role of the kindred (the bilateral group of relatives) in promoting the welfare of the members of individual families. The kindred promotes welfare in its families in a variety of activities. It rewards adherence to traditional ceremonies and rituals by gifts and congratulatory rewards. Members of the kindred sponsor other members in economic activities and perform special favors to promote their economic welfare. In time of emergency, the kindred provides the source of aid and personal service as well as sympathy. Since these activities cannot be easily relegated in any institutionalized way to another recognizable group, many sociologists regard the persistence of the kindred as a reflection of its operation as a unit influencing the personal destiny of its members.

Family and Kinship in a Pluralistic Society

Kornhauser has suggested a distinction between mass society and pluralistic society.[5] His distinction is concerned mainly with the organization of the political institutions in modern society. Kornhauser postulates the existence of intermediate groups between the small primary group relationships (such as the family) and government (especially the national government) in pluralistic societies. These intermediate groups are the publics emerging from the special interests of various sectors of the population. These collectivities then apply pressure on government in the formation and execution of policy. Mass society, however, is characterized by the absence of intermediate groups between the small intimate groups and government.

Miller and Swanson have made a distinction between the entreprenurial and bureaucratic families.[6] The entreprenurial family presumably emerged as a response to the growth of individualism in a competitive society. It exists in the equivalent of the mass society when there is no recognizable relationship between one nuclear family and the next. Reliance or dependence on others is considered a necessary evil for the entreprenurial family. The bureaucratic family, however, presupposes large-scale economic organizations and produces individuals who cooperate well in these organizations. In William H. Whyte's book about the organization man and his family,[7] much of his description concerns not only the type of family life dictated by policies of large-scale organizations, but also informal organizations and associations which have evolved in middle-class suburbs. Thus Whyte describes the rise of quasi-kindreds in congeries of families of organization men. These quasi-kindreds as well as paternalistic corporations emerge as domestic special-interest groups.

[4] *Ibid.*
[5] William Kornhauser, *The Politics of Mass Society*, Glencoe: Free Press, 1959.
[6] Daniel R. Miller and Guy E. Swanson, *The Changing American Parent*, New York: Wiley, 1958. See Miller and Swanson paper in Chapter 9 of this volume.
[7] William H. Whyte, *The Organization Man*, New York: Simon and Schuster, 1956.

The Burgess view of the family is consistent with the concept of mass society as described by Kornhauser and the entreprenurial family as described by Miller and Swanson. Burgess calls the highly specialized, independent nuclear family the companionship family.[8] This family is held together mainly by bonds of affection rather than by external forces. It is relatively free to change its position in the social organization of the community and to move from one community to another.

In contrast to the mass-society view is the conception of the kinship group as an intermediate group comparable to a voluntary association or a special-interest group. In the pluralistic-society view the kindred is an interest group. As such, it may operate in competition with voluntary associations, economic-interest groups, and government agencies. The kindred's persistence in contemporary society suggests that it continues to operate as the bilateral equivalent of the lineage segment discussed in Chapter 2, Kinship and Family.

Trends Influencing Family and Kinship

Most major sociologists who emphasize the independence of the American nuclear family (that is, mass organization) developed their conceptions prior to World War II.[9] Assuming the accuracy of their description of the prewar family as a unit increasingly independent from its kindred, we ask whether a shift occurred in the character of family life following the depression of the 1930's and World War II. This shift may represent an increase in the tendency of kinship groups to further family interests in the society.

Four possibilities exist with respect to the relationship between social trends in American society and the character of family and kinship. First, there can be a continuation of past trends in society and family. Second, although trends in society may continue, their effect on family relations may be reversed after a certain point is reached, the relationship thus being curvilinear. Third, social trends may change and produce corresponding changes in family and kinship. Fourth, social trends may produce changes that do not affect the family. Because of difficulties in finding supporting evidence, the fourth possible relationship (change in social trends but none in family) is not discussed here.

Continuation of Trends. Certain long-term social trends appear to facilitate the continued independence of the nuclear family from kindred. There is a steady high rate of social and especially residential mobility in the population.[10] This fluidity hinders the maintenance of an intimate relationship between family and kindred. Moreover, the rural-farm population, traditionally more stable than the urban population, has continued to decline in number.[11] This decline is consistent with the continued trend

---

[8] Ernest W. Burgess, Harvey J. Locke, and Mary Margaret Thomes, *The Family from Institution to Companionship*, New York: American Book, 1963.

[9] *Ibid.;* Parsons and Bales, *loc. cit.;* Kingsley Davis, *Human Society*, New York: Macmillan, 1949.

[10] U.S. Census Bureau, Current Population Reports, Population Characteristics, Series P-20, No. 113, 1962; Murray Gendell and Hans L. Zetterberg, *A Sociological Almanac for the United States*, New York; Scribners, 1964, Tables 4.53, 4.55, and 5.53.

[11] Gendell and Zetterberg, *op. cit.*, Table 4.53.

toward family mobility. Similarly, the decline of an independent middle class and the rise of a salaried middle class has meant a continued increase in mobility and a decrease in the role of family property in holding the kindred together. These trends signify the continuing tendency toward a mass type of organization among families in the society.

Curvilinear Relationship. Various social trends may have at one time facilitated the breakdown of kinship relations. However, as these trends have continued, their effect on family and kinship seems to have changed. For example, the continued decline in age at marriage may have a curvilinear effect on family and kinship relations. Since 1890 the median age at first marriage for both men and women (but especially for men) has been declining.[12] Before the postwar era, this decline in age at marriage may have symbolized an increasing tendency for independence. However, when marriages occur before the young couple is financially independent or occupationally secure, the effect may be to maintain ties with kindred. Similarly, the trend towards increased employment of married women may affect relationships between family and kindred curvilinearly.[13] The relative economic independence of women may free them from controls by the kindred, and being away from home may reduce the frequency of contacts with kindred (especially with the wife's mother). However, as married women with children enter the labor market in increasing numbers, they must rely on grandmothers and other relatives to assist in the care of the children and for household services. Thus even a continuation of those trends that heralded the decline of kinship in the first part of the twentieth century may eventually foster the development of kinship structures that protect the nuclear family.

Changes in Social Trends. Various trends, developed since the 1930's have changed the character of family and kinship. Before the depression there was a continual decline in the number of children per family. However, the birth rate twenty years after World War II is still relatively inflated.[14] High birth rates would operate indirectly to strengthen kinship ties through a greater demand for both financial and service assistance and ceremonials connected with birth, religious status of children, and marriage. Similarly, divorce rates are relatively high compared with prewar rates.[15] Divorced persons tend to rely on kin for emotional support and financial and service assistance from the time of alienation from the spouse to the time of remarriage.

These birth and divorce rates are undoubtedly affected by the affluence of the American society as well as by changes in governmental policy between 1930 and the present. Affluence and government policies have affected family life in many ways. For example, before the 1930 depression and World War II, no explicit policy sustained full employment. High income levels and an enormous consumer debt have raised the standard of living in American families and have increased the resources available for the assistance of kindred.[16] Moreover, governmental welfare services to

[12] *Ibid.,* Table 1.62.
[13] *Ibid.,* Table 4.51.
[14] *Ibid.,* Table 1.70.
[15] *Ibid.,* Tables 1.63 and 1.65.
[16] *Ibid.,* Table 4.72.

the nonindigent have increased. The social security program and the national programs on health have indirectly sustained family and kinship values by increasing longevity, health, and available financial resources. These increases have affected kinship relations at various stages of the family life cycle. For example, the elderly can maintain an indulgent role with children and grandchildren over a longer period. Married children need not fear that their aging parents will be financially or personally dependent on them. These changes in the economic system and government policy have facilitated a pluralistic (rather than mass) organization in family life.

Readings on Contemporary Family and Kinship

The first paper in this section is by Sussman and Burchinal. It provides a general discussion of nuclear family theory and its deficiencies as well as a summary of major findings about the social activities and services performed by the kin network. This paper emphasizes the role of kindred in the performance of activities benefiting relatives in an urban setting; it thus describes the kinship group as an intermediate unit between the large society and the small nuclear family.

In the second paper Robins and Tomanec set forth factors which influence interaction among kin in an urban setting, including respondent's age, marital status, religion, and ethnic background. Their study also focuses on factors in the kinship structure affecting interaction. They found that maternal relatives were closer than paternal relatives and females closer than males. Presumably, as cousins married they tended to lose contact. Looking at the assignment of priorities in kinship role in a bilateral system, it is noteworthy that when an individual has few siblings his relationships to kin outside the nuclear family tend to be closer.

The third paper, by Cumming and Schneider, emphasizes the integrative role of the sibling relationship. They suggest that in adulthood similarity in age acts to sustain solidary bonds between siblings. Their findings also indicate the importance of the substitutability of different relatives in kinship roles in a bilateral system. Cumming and Schneider regard sex and generation as the major criteria for choosing substitutes in kinship roles when siblings or parents are not available.

In the final paper Irish reviews past research on sibling interaction and indicates directions for future investigation. Both the Cumming and Schneider paper and the report on kinship and socialization by Farber in the chapter on Kinship and Family emphasize the significance of sibling relationships for contemporary kinship organization. Irish suggests that factors in sibling interaction also affect kinship relations as the siblings mature. Hence to understand the character of kinship organization in contemporary society it is necessary to investigate influences on sibling interaction.

10. Kin Family Network: Unheralded Structure in Current Conceptualizations of Family Functioning*

BY MARVIN B. SUSSMAN AND LEE G. BURCHINAL

MOST AMERICANS REJECT THE NOTION that receiving aid from their kin is a good thing. The proper ideological stance is that the individual and his family should fend for themselves. The family in this instance is nuclear in structure and consists of husband and wife and children. Further investigation would probably reveal that most of these rejectors are receiving or have received financial and other types of aid from their kin long after the time they were supposed to be on their own. After marriage many are involved within a network of mutual assistance with kin, especially with parents. Moreover, one would find that independence of the nuclear family of procreation is being maintained. When independence is threatened, it is probably owing to other causes. The rejection of the idea of receiving aid from kin and actually being helped by them is another case of discrepancy between belief and practice.

Discrepancies between belief and practice of "ideal" and "real" behavior are common in our society. In family sociology the reason is "academic cultural lag," the lag between apparently antiquated family theory and empirical reality. The theory stresses the social isolation and social mobility of the nuclear family, while findings from empirical studies reveal an existing and functioning extended kin-family system closely integrated within a network of relationships and mutual assistance along bilateral kinship lines and encompassing several generations.[1]

The major purpose of this paper is to reduce the lag between family theory and research in so far as it concerns the functioning of the American kin-family network and its matrix of help and service among kin members. The procedure is to review relevant theory and conclusions derived from research on kin-family networks completed by sociologists and anthropologists. Appropriate modifications of existing theory which posits the notion of the isolated nuclear family are then suggested.[2]

[1] The authors adopt Eugene Litwak's interpretation of the modified extended family. It is one that "does not require geographical propinquity, occupational nepotism, or integration, and there are no strict authority relations, but equalitarian ones." See "Geographical Mobility and Extended Family Cohesion," *American Sociological Review*, **25** (June, 1960), p. 385. The components of the system are neolocal nuclear families in a bilateral or generational relationship. This system is referred to as the "Kin Family Network."

[2] The implications of parental support to the married child's family for the functioning of the American Family System is discussed in another paper. The major question is whether parental aid affects the independence of the married child's family. "Parental Aid to Married Children: Implications for Family Functioning" in *Marriage and Family Living*, November, 1962.

SOURCE: Marriage and Family Living, *Volume 24* (*August, 1962*), *pp. 231–240. Reprinted by permission of National Council on Family Relations.*

* Graduate School, Western Reserve University, and published as Journal Paper No. J–4197 of the Iowa Agricultural and Home Economics Experiment Station, Ames, Iowa, Project No. 1370.

Nuclear Family Theory

Durkheim, Simmel, Toennies, and Mannheim have stressed that the family in urban society is a relatively isolated unit. Social differentiation in complex societies requires of its members a readiness to move, to move to where there are needs for workers and where there are opportunities for better jobs.

American social theorists such as Linton,[3] Wirth,[4] and Parsons,[5] support this position. Parsons suggests that the isolated nuclear family system consisting of husband and wife and offspring living independent from their families of orientation is ideally suited to the demands of occupational and geographical mobility which are inherent in modern industrial society. Major obligations, interactions, and nurturance behavior occur within the nuclear family. Although bonds exist between the nuclear family and other consanguineous relatives and affinals of the kin group, these lack significance for the maintenance of the individual conjugal family.

Family sociologists generally accept the isolated nuclear theory as promulgated above. They report the changes in the structure and functions of the American family system which have occurred as the system has adapted to the demands of a developing industrial society. There is general agreement that the basic functions reserved for the family are procreation, status placement, biological and emotional maintenance, and socialization.[6] However, these functions are generally analyzed in the context of the "isolated" nuclear family. The functions of intergenerational and bilateral kin-family networks regarding the processes of biological and emotional maintenance or socialization are given little attention by theorists or analysts. The conclusion reached is that demands associated with occupational and geographical mobility have brought about a family pattern in urban areas consisting of relatively isolated nuclear family units which operate without much support from the kinship system.

The textbooks are written by family sociologists. Few among them, either texts on the sociology of the family or those written for marriage and family preparation courses, give theoretical or empirical treatment to the maintenance of the family system by the mutual assistance activities of the kin group. Among the texts examined, only one considers in any detail financial arrangements among kin members.[7] One result of the review of basic family and preparation for marriage texts regarding current knowledge of the functioning of the kin network and its matrix of help and service is that the theory of the isolated nuclear family prevails.

Discussion of the Theoretical Argument

The lack of research until the 1950's and the almost complete omission of the topic, kin-family network and its matrix of help and services, in family texts are closely related. If the generalized description of the American family system as atomistic and nuclear were valid, there would be very little exchange of financial help or services within the kin-family network. Parental support of married children or exchange of services and other forms of help among kin members would be comparatively rare and hence, unimportant.[8] Research would be unnecessary and discussion of the subject, except

[3] Ralph Linton, "The Natural History of the Family," in Ruth N. Anshen, *The Family: Its Function and Destiny*, (New York: Harpers, 1959), pp. 45–46.

[4] Louis Wirth, "Urbanism As a Way of Life," *American Journal of Sociology*, **44** (July, 1938), pp. 1–24.

[5] All by the same author, see Talcott Parsons, "The Kinship System of the Contemporary United States," *American Anthropologist*, **45** (January–March, 1943), pp. 22–38; "Revised Analytical Approach to the Theory of Social Stratification," in R. Bendix and S. M. Lipset (eds.), *Class, Status, and Power*, Glencoe, Illinois: Free Press, 1953, p. 166 ff.; "The Social Structure of the Family," in Ruth Anshen, *op. cit.*, p. 263 ff.; Parsons and Robert F. Bales, *Family, Socialization and Process*, Glencoe, Illinois: Free Press, 1955, pp. 3–33.

[6] Compare Robert F. Winch, *The Modern Family*, New York: Holt, 1952, and William J. Goode, "The Sociology of the Family," in Robert K. Merton,

Leonard Broom and Leonard S. Cottrell, Jr. (eds.), *Sociology Today*, New York: Basic Books, 1959, pp. 178–196.

[7] Evelyn M. Duvall, *Family Development*, Chicago: Lippincott, 1957, pp. 129–133, 206–210.

[8] See Reuben Hill, *Families Under Stress*, New York: Harpers, 1949.

in crisis situations, could be safely omitted from textbook discussions. However, accepting this theory as essentially valid without considerable empirical substantiation has contributed to errors in descriptions of kin-family networks and aid patterns among families. A new empiricism emerging in the late 1940's questioned the persistence of the isolated nuclear family notion and presented evidence to support the viability of kin-family network in industrial society.

The ideal description of the isolated nuclear character of the American family system cannot be applied equally to all segments of American society. Regional, racial, ethnic, and rural and urban, as well as socioeconomic status differences in modified extended relations and family continuity patterns are known to exist. Family continuity and inheritance patterns of families in several social strata have been described.[9] Among upper-class families direct, substantial, and continuous financial support flows from the parents, uncles, aunts, and grandparents to the children both before and after marriage. Only by receiving substantial kin support can the young high-status groom and his bride begin and sustain their family life at the financial and social level which is shared by their parents, other relatives, and their friends. This support frequently includes obtaining a position for the husband in his or his in-law family's economic enterprise.

Members of lower-class kin groups generally have few financial resources with which to assist married children. Among certain European ethnic groups some effort is made to assist the young couple at marriage; the notion of a dowry still persists. Generally, however, there is little knowledge, tradition, or tangible forms of assistance transmitted to children which directly aids children in establishing or enhancing their socioeconomic status.[10] Kin support in this class most frequently takes the form of providing

services and sharing what financial resources are available at the time of crises or of exchanging nonmonetary forms of aid. Marginal financial resources and the impact of unemployment hits all kin members alike.[11]

The description of the isolated, nuclear American family system, if valid, is most suited to the white, urban, middle-class segment of American society.[12] Presumably, the leisure time of the members of these families is absorbed in the activities of secondary, special interest social groups. Since urban, lower-class family members participate less than middle-class family members in voluntary organizations, it is believed that social activities of adult lower-class family members are restricted to informal visiting patterns. Visiting with relatives would be a significant proportion of all of their social relations. However, prevailing sociological theory suggests that the disparities between an extended kin-family system and the requirements of a mobile labor force and intergenerational family discontinuities generated by social mobility should be reflected in the lack of continuity among lower-class families as well as among middle-class families.

The degree to which urban lower or middle-class families function as relatively isolated from their extended kin-family systems is critical for all subsequent discussions of the question of kinship network and its matrix of help and service. Unless there is a reasonable frequent occurrence of primary group interaction among kin members, very likely there will be an insignificant help pattern.

The emphasis on the atomistic character of urban families has contributed to incorrect assumptions concerning interaction within the kinship matrix. It has led family sociologists to assume incorrectly that assistance among kin

---

[9] W. Lloyd Warner and Paul S. Lunt, *The Social Life in a Modern Community*, New Haven, Connecticut: Yale University Press, 1941. See also Cavan, *The American Family*, op. cit., pp. 119–187, for a review of other studies of social status differentials in family behavior.

[10] R. E. L. Faris, "Interactions of Generations and Family Stability," *American Sociological Review*, **12** (April, 1947), pp. 159–164.

[11] Ruth S. Cavan, "Unemployment-Crisis of the Common Man," *Marriage and Family Living*, **21** (May, 1959), pp. 139–146.

[12] Someone has facetiously suggested the samples of white, urban, middle-class Protestant respondents be labeled as WUMP samples. If family sociologists continue to draw samples principally from this segment of our social structure or wish to limit generalizations to this segment, there would be more than a facetious basis for arguing for the merit of the convenient shorthand expression represented by WUMP.

members was comparatively rarely sought or offered. A reconsideration of these assumptions is necessary. The bases of reconsideration are logical constructs and empirical realities set forth in the following data.

Family Networks and Mutual Aid: Conceptualization and Research

A theory is here considered to be composed of logically interrelated propositions which explain phenomena. Concepts are elements of a theory, defining what is to be observed. Concepts by themselves cannot be construed as a theory. They require integration into a logical scheme to become a theory.

The existence of a modified extended family with its intricate network of mutual aid in lieu of the isolated nuclear family notion is probably more of a conceptualization than a theory. However, it approaches the state of being a theory since it is not an isolated concept but is integrated with other propositions concerned with the maintenance over time of the family and other social systems of the society.

Family networks and their patterns of mutual aid are organized into a structure identified as a "modified extended family" adapted to contemporary urban and industrial society.[13] This structure is composed of nuclear families bound together by affectional ties and by choice. Geographical propinquity, involvement of the family in the occupational placement, and advancement of its members, direct intervention into the process of achieving social status by members of nuclear family units, and a rigid hierarchical authority structure are unrequired and largely absent. The modified extended family functions indirectly rather than directly to facilitate the achievement and mobility drives of component families and individual members. Its tasks complement those of other social systems. By achieving integration with other social systems, concerned with the general goals of maintenance and accomplishment of these systems, the

extended family network cannot be considered as an isolated or idiosyncratic concept. Its elements require organization as logically interrelated propositions and whereupon it should emerge as a theory replacing the prevalent one of the isolated nuclear family.

Our concepts die hard, and one way to speed their demise is to examine the evidence supporting the new ones. Evidence and measurement are difficult terms to define. When do you have evidence and when have you achieved a measurement? The reader will have to judge. The approach here is to examine the writings and research emerging from several disciplines. In some cases the work is focused on testing hypotheses or describing relationships relevant to the new conceptualization. In others, the discussions and findings emerge incidentally to the major purpose of the study. There are cases of serendipity. They occur more frequently than one would expect and add to the uncertainty of the notion of the isolated nuclear family.

One assumption of the isolated nuclear family conceptualization is that the small nuclear family came into existence in Western Europe and the United States as a consequence of the urban-industrial revolution. Furthermore its small size is ideally suited for meeting requirements of an industrial society for a mobile workforce. The effect of the urban-industrial revolution is to produce a small sized family unit to replace the large rural one. This assumption can be challenged. A study of different societies reveals that industrialization and urbanization can occur with or without the small nuclear family.[14]

If household size reflects in any way the structure and characteristics of the joint extended family in India, then little changes have occurred in this system during the period of industrialization in India from 1911 to 1951.[15]

The uprooting of the rural family, the weakening of family ties, and the reshaping of the rural family form into a nuclear type as a consequence of the industrial revolution are disclaimed

---

[13] Eugene Litwak, *op. cit.*, p. 355. See also by the same author, "Occupational Mobility and Extended Family Cohesion," *American Sociological Review*, **25** (February, 1960), p. 10.

[14] Sidney M. Greenfield, "Industrialization and the Family in Sociological Theory," *American Journal of Sociology*, **67** (November, 1961), pp. 312–322.

[15] Henry Orenstein, "The Recent History of the Extended Family in India," *Social Problems*, **8** (Spring, 1961), pp. 341–350.

for one Swiss town in a recent investigation. On the contrary, many fringe rural families were stabilized and further strengthened in their kin ties from earning supplementary income in nearby factories. Able-bodied members obtained work nearby and no longer had to leave the family unit in search of work. Families which moved closer to their place of employment were accommodated in row houses; these units facilitated the living together of large family groups.[16] These findings question the impact of industrialization upon the structure and functioning of the pre-industrial family.

It is difficult to determine if the conditions of living during the transition from a rural to an industrial society ended the dominance of the classical extended family and replaced it with a modified kin form, or if it was replaced by the nuclear one. The question is whether the modified extended family has existed since industrialization occurred; is it a recent phenomenon or an emergent urban familism, a departure from the traditional nuclear form; or is it nonexistent? The evidence to support either of these positions is inconclusive. It remains however that the family network described variously as "an emergent urban familism" or "modified extended family" exists and functions in the modern community.

The family network and its functions of mutual aid has implications for the functioning of other social systems. With the growth of large metropolitan areas and concomitant occupational specialization, there is less need for the individual to leave the village, town, city, or suburb of the urban complex in order to find work according to his training. Large urban areas supply all kinds of specialized educational and occupational training. The individual can remain in the midst of his kin group, work at his speciality, and be the recipient of the advantages or disadvantages preferred by the kin family network. If individuals are intricately involved within a kin-family network, will they be influenced by kin leaders and be less amenable to influence by outsiders; will they seek basic gratifications in kin relationships in lieu of the work place or the neighborhood; will they

modify drastically current patterns of spending leisure time thus affecting current leisure forms and social systems?[17]

Empirical evidence from studies by investigations in a variety of disciplines substantiate the notion that the extended kin family carries on multitudinous activities that have implications for the functioning of other social systems of the society. The major activities linking the network are mutual aid and social activities among kin related families. Significant data have been accumulated on the mutual aid network between parents and their married child's family in a number of separate and independent investigations.[18,19,20] The conclusions are:

1. Help patterns take many forms, including the exchange of services, gifts, advice, and financial assistance. Financial aid patterns may be direct as in the case of the young married couples Burchinal interviewed; or indirect and subtle, such as the wide range of help patterns observed by Sussman, Sharp, and Axelrod.

[16] Rudolph Braun, *Industrialisierung Volksleben*, Erbenback-Zierrich: Reutsch, 1960.

[17] A. O. Haller raises interesting questions on the significance of an emerging urban familism. See "The Urban Family," *American Journal of Sociology*, **66** (May, 1961), pp. 621–622.

[18] Marvin B. Sussman, "The Help Pattern in the Middle Class Family," *American Sociological Review*, **18** (February, 1953), pp. 22–28. For related analyses by the same author see, "Parental Participation in Mate Selection and Its Effect Upon Family Continuity," *Social Forces*, **32** (October, 1953), p. 76–81; "Family Continuity: Selective Factors Which Affect Relationships Between Families at Generational Levels," *Marriage and Family Living*, **16** (May, 1954), pp. 112–120; "Activity Patterns of Post Parental Couples and Their Relationship to Family Continuity," *Marriage and Family Living*, **27** (November, 1955), pp. 338–341; "The Isolated Nuclear Family: Fact or Fiction," *Social Problems*, **6** (Spring, 1959), pp. 333–340; "Intergenerational Family Relationships and Social Role Changes in Middle Age," *Journal of Gerontology*, **15** (January, 1960), pp. 71–75.

[19] Harry Sharp and Morris Axelrod, "Mutual Aid Among Relatives in an Urban Population," in Ronald Freedman and associates (eds.), *Principles of Sociology*, New York: Holt, 1956, pp. 433–439.

[20] Lee G. Burchinal, "Comparisons of Factors Related to Adjustment in Pregnancy-Provoked and Non-Pregnancy-Provoked Youthful Marriages," *Midwest Sociologist*, **21** (July, 1959), pp. 92–96; also by the same author, "How Successful Are School-Age Marriages," *Iowa Farm Science*, **13** (March, 1959), pp. 7–10.

Table 1

Direction of service network of respondent's family and related kin by major forms of help

Major forms of help and service	Direction of service network				
	Between respondent's family and related kin per cent*	From respondents to parents per cent*	From respondents to siblings per cent*	From parents to respondents per cent*	From siblings to respondents per cent*
Any Form of Help	93.3	56.3	47.6	79.6	44.8
Help During Illness	76.0	47.0	42.0	46.4	39.0
Financial Aid	53.0	14.6	10.3	46.8	6.4
Care of Children	46.8	4.0	29.5	20.5	10.8
Advice (Personal and Business)	31.0	2.0	3.0	26.5	4.5
Valuable Gifts	22.0	3.4	2.3	17.6	3.4

* Totals do not add up to 100 per cent because many families received more than one form of help of service. Marvin B. Sussman, "The Isolated Nuclear Family: Fact or Fiction," *Social Problems*, **6** (Spring, 1959), 338.

2. Such help patterns are probably more widespread in the middle- and working-class families and are more integral a feature of family relationships than has been appreciated by students of family behavior. Very few families included in available studies reported neither giving nor receiving aid from relatives. However, these relationships until recently have not been the subject of extensive research.

3. The exchange of aid among families flows in several directions, from parents to children and vice versa, among siblings, and less frequently, from more distant relatives. However, financial assistance generally appears to flow from parents to children.

4. Although there may be a difference in the absolute amount of financial aid received by families of middle and working-class status, there are insignificant differences in the proportion of families in these two strata who report receiving, giving, or exchanging economic assistance in some form.

5. Financial aid is received most commonly during the early years of married life. Parents are probably more likely to support financially "approved" than "disapproved" ones, such as elopements, interfaith, and interracial marriages. Support can be disguised in the form of substantial sums of money or valuable gifts given at the time of marriage, at the time of the birth of children, and continuing gifts at Christmas, anniversaries, or birthdays. High rates of parental support are probably associated with marriages of children while they are still in dependency status; those among high school or college students are examples.

6. Research data are inadequate for assessing the effects of parental aid on family continuity and the marital relations of the couple receiving aid. Few studies report associations between the form and amount of aid given with the parents' motivations for providing aid. Additional studies on these points are necessary before the implications of aid to married children can be better known.[21]

Social activities are principal functions of the kin-family network. The major forms are interfamily visitation, participation together in recreational activities, and ceremonial behavior significant to family unity. Major research findings are:

1. Disintegration of the extended family in urban areas because of lack of contact is unsupported and often the contrary situation is found. The difficulty in developing satisfactory

[21] Further analyses on the implications of parental aid to married children are found in a paper, "Parental Aid to Married Children: Implications for Family Functioning," in *Marriage and Family Living*, November, 1962.

primary relationships outside of the family in urban areas makes the extended family *more important* to the individual.[22]

2. Extended family get-togethers and joint recreational activities with kin dominate the leisure time pursuits of urban working class members.[23]

3. Kinship visiting is a primary activity of urban dwelling and outranks visitation patterns found for friends, neighbors, or co-workers.[24, 25, 26, 27, 28]

4. Among urban middle classes there is an almost universal desire to have interaction with extended kin, but distance among independent nuclear related units is a limiting factor.[29]

5. The family network extends between generational ties of conjugal units. Some structures are identified as sibling bonds,[30] "occasional kin groups"[31] family circles, and cousin clubs.[32] These structures perform important recreational, ceremonial, mutual aid, and often economic functions.

Services performed regularly throughout the year or on occasions are additional functions of the family network. The findings from empirical studies are:

1. Shopping, escorting, care of children, advice giving and counselling, cooperating with social agencies on counselling and welfare problems of family members, are types of day-to-day activities performed by members of the kin network.[33, 34]

2. Services to old persons such as physical care, providing shelter, escorting, shopping, performing household tasks, sharing of leisure time, and so on are expected and practiced roles of children and other kin members. These acts of filial and kin responsibility are performed voluntarily without law or compulsion.[35, 36, 37, 38, 39, 40, 41, 42]

[22] William H. Key, "Rural-Urban Differences and the Family," *Sociological Quarterly*, 2 (January, 1961), pp. 49–56.

[23] F. Dotson, "Patterns of Voluntary Association Among Urban Working Class Families," *American Sociological Review*, 16 (October, 1951), pp. 689–693.

[24] Morris Axelrod, "Urban Structure and Social Participation," *American Sociological Review*, 21 (February, 1956), pp. 13–18.

[25] Scott Greer, "Urbanism Reconsidered," *American Sociological Review*, 21 (February, 1956), pp. 22–25.

[26] Wendell Bell and M. D. Boat, "Urban Neighborhoods and Informal Social Relations," *American Journal of Sociology*, 43 (January, 1957), pp. 381–398.

[27] Marvin B. Sussman and R. Clyde White, *Hough: A Study of Social Life and Change* (Cleveland: Western Reserve University Press, 1959).

[28] Paul J. Reiss, "The Extended Kinship System of the Urban Middle Class" (Unpublished Ph.D. Dissertation, Harvard University, 1959).

[29] E. Franklin Frazier, "The Impact of Urban Civilization Upon Negro Family Life," in P. K. Hatt and A. J. Reiss, Jr. (eds.), *Cities and Society*, Glencoe: Illinois, Free Press, 1957, rev. ed., pp. 495–496.

[30] Elaine Cumming and David M. Schneider, "Sibling Solidarity: A Property of American Kinship," *American Anthropologist*, 63 (June, 1961), pp. 498–507.

[31] Millicent Ayoub, "American Child and his Relatives: Kindred in Southwest Ohio," project supported by the Public Health Service, 1961, Dr. Ayoub in continuing her studies under the subtitle, "The Nature of Sibling Bond." She examines the solidarity or lack of it between siblings in four focal subsystems and at different stages of the life cycle.

[32] William E. Mitchell, "Descent Groups Among New York City Jews," *The Jewish Journal of Sociology*, 3 (1961), pp. 121–128; "Lineality and Laterability in Urban Jewish Ambilineages," read at the 60th Annual Meeting of the American Anthropological Association in Philadelphia, Pa., November 16, 1961; and William E. Mitchell and Hope J. Leichter, "Urban Ambilineages and Social Mobility," unpublished paper based on research from the project, "Studies in Family Interaction," sponsored jointly by the Jewish Family Service of New York and the Russell Sage Foundation.

[33] Sussman, *op. cit.*, "The Help Pattern in the Middle Class Family."

[34] Hope J. Leichter, "Kinship and Casework," paper read at the meetings of the Groves Conference, Chapel Hill, North Carolina, 1959; "Life Cycle Changes and Temporal Sequence in a Bilateral Kinship System," read at the annual meetings of the American Anthropological Association, 1958; Washington, D.C. "Normative Intervention in an Urban Bilateral Kinship System," paper read at the meetings of the American Anthropological Association, 1959.

[35] John Kosa, Leo D. Rachiele and Cyril O. Schommer, S. J., "Sharing the Home with Relatives," *Marriage and Family Living*, 22 (May, 1960), pp. 129–131.

[36] Alvin L. Schorr, *Filial Responsibility in a Modern American Family*, Washington, D.C.; Social Security Administration, U.S. Department of Health, Education and Welfare, 1960, pp. 11–18.

[37] Peter Townsend, *The Family Life of Older People: An Inquiry in East London*, London: Routledge and Kegan Paul, 1957.

3. Families or individual members on the move are serviced by units of the family network. Services range from supplying motel-type accommodations for vacationing kin passing through town, to scouting for homes and jobs for kin, and in providing supportive functions during the period of in-migration and transition from rural to the urban pattern of living.[43, 44, 45, 46, 47]

4. Services on occasions would include those performed at weddings or during periods of crisis, death, accident, disaster, and personal trouble of family members. A sense of moral obligation to give service or acknowledgement of one's kin appropriate to the occasion is found among kin members. The turning to kin when in trouble before using other agencies estab-

lished for such purposes is the mode rather than the exception.[48, 49, 50, 51]

5. General supportive behavior from members of the kin-family network facilitates achievement and maintenance of family and community status.[52] Supportive behavior of kin appears to be instrumental in affecting fertility rates among component family members.[53]

A convergence of many of these findings occurs in the work of Eugene Litwak. In an extensive study of a middle-class population Litwak tests several hypotheses on the functional properties of the isolated nuclear family

[38] Michael Young and Peter Willmott, *Kinship and Family in East London*, Glencoe, Illinois: Free Press, 1957.

[39] Elizabeth Bott, *Family and Social Network*, London: Tavistock Publications, Ltd., 1957.

[40] See *Adjustment in Retirement*, by Gordon F. Streib and Wayne E. Thompson, *Journal of Social Issues*, 14 (1958). Streib and Thompson have done the most creative thinking and analysis of data on these points. Streib's paper "Family Patterns in Retirement," pp. 46–60 in this issue is most pertinent.

[41] Ethel Shanas, "Older People and Their Families," paper given at the meetings of the American Sociological Association, September, 1961. A more complete report is in *Family Relationships of Older People*, Health Information Foundation, 1961.

[42] The best treatment of uses of leisure during the later years of life is found in Robert W. Kleemeier (ed.), *Aging and Leisure*, New York: Oxford University Press, 1961. See particularly the chapters by Wilensky, Streib and Thompson.

[43] M. B. Sussman and R. C. White, *op. cit., Hough: A Study of Social Life and Change.*

[44] C. Wright Mills, Clarence Senior and Rose K. Goldsen, *Puerto Rican Journey*, New York: Harper Bros., 1950, pp. 51–55.

[45] James S. Brown, Harry K. Schwarzweller, and Joseph J. Mangalam, "Kentucky Mountain Migration and the Stem Family: An American Variation on a Theme by LePlay," paper given at the meetings of the American Sociological Association, September 1, 1961.

[46] Peter H. Rossi, *Why Families Move*, Glencoe, Illinois: Free Press, 1955, pp. 37–38.

[47] Earl L. Koos, *Families in Trouble*, New York: Columbia University Press, 1946.

[48] Sussman, *op. cit.*, "Family Continuity: Selective Factors Which Affect Relationships Between Families at Generational Levels."

[49] Seymour S. Bellin, *Family and Kinship in Later Years*, N.Y. State Dept. of Mental Hygiene, Mental Health Research Unit Publication, 1960.

[50] Sharp and Axelrod, *op. cit., Mutual Aid Among Relatives.*

[51] Enrico L. Quarantelli, "A Note on the Protective Function of the Family in Disaster," *Marriage and Family Living*, 22 (August, 1960), pp. 263–264.

[52] Bernard Barber, "Family Status, Local-Community Status, and Social Stratification: Three Types of Social Ranking," *Pacific Sociological Review*, Vol. 4, No. 1 (Spring, 1961), pp. 3–10. In this paper Barber challenges the current conceptualization of social class for designating an individual's position, and power within a community. He differentiates social class position, family status and local-community statuses into three types of social ranking. Each one has its own structure and functions; each allocates position, power and prestige; and each has its own range of variation. The family kin network and support received from it determines family status. President Kennedy's family and its extended-family relations illustrates the point of this thesis.

[53] David Goldberg, "Some Recent Developments in Fertility Research," Reprint No. 7, *Demographic and Economic Change in Developed Countries*, Princeton University Press, 1960. Recent fertility research has focused upon the relationship of family organization to differential fertility since variations in family planning and family size cannot be explained by differences in socioeconomic status. One variable of family organization is the family kin network. Goldberg observes, "—and incidentally one which may ultimately prove fruitful in cross-cultural studies, is a consideration of the relative benevolence of the environment in defraying the economic and social costs of having children. Here it is hypothesized that the greater the amount of help available from one's community or kinship system the weaker the desire to prevent or postpone pregnancy." *Ibid.*, p. 9.

for an industrial society: (a) occupational mobility is antithetical to extended family relations; (b) extended family relations are impossible because of geographical mobility. His findings summarized briefly are (1) The extended kin family as a structure exists in modern urban society at least among middle-class families: (2) Extended family relations are possible in urban industrial society; (3) Geographical propinquity is an unnecessary condition for these relationships; (4) Occupational mobility is unhindered by the activities of the extended family, such activities as advice, financial assistance, temporary housing, and the like provide aid during such movement; and (5) The classical extended family of rural society or its ethnic counterpart are unsuited for modern society, the isolated nuclear family is not the most functional type, the most functional being a modified extended kin family.[54]

Conclusions

There exists an American kin-family system with complicated matrices of aid and service activities which link together the component units into a functioning network. The network identified by Litwak as extended family relations is composed of nuclear units related by blood and affinal ties. Relations extend along generational lines and bilaterally where structures take the form of sibling bonds and ambilineages, that is, the family circle or cousin club.

As a consequence of limited historical work and particularistic developments in theory and research in sociology there is uncertainty concerning the impact of industrialization upon the structure and function of the pre-industrial family. Was the extended classical type found in rural society replaced by a nuclear one, or did it evolve into the modified kin form described in this paper? It is suggested that the notion of the isolated nuclear family stems from theories and

research on immigrant groups coming into the city to work during the period of urbanization in Western society.[55] Anomie in family behavior resulted from individual and institutional failure to make appropriate adjustments required by this migration. The coldness and indifference of the workplace and the city as a steel and concrete bastion contributed to a feeling of aloneness and isolation. The basic concern of the immigrant was survival in an unknown man-made jungle. Survival was related to dependence upon small family units. These could make quicker and more complete adjustments to the new ways of urban life. The ethos of a competitive and expanding industrial society supported the flexibility of movement now possible by an atomistic unit. Every man is for himself, every man should be unencumbered by ties that will hinder his economic or social progress, and every man should seize opportunities to better himself. One assumption of this position is that early urban man had little time for concern or activity with kinsmen. A more logical assumption is that isolation, a depressive workplace, and uncertainty produced greater reliance upon kin. Once new immigrants became established in the city they served as informants, innkeepers, and providers for later kin arrivals.[56] Once these followers arrived the kin-family network then functioned most effectively to protect and acculturate their members into urban ways.

Major activities of this network are that members give to each other financial aid and good of value, and a wide range of services at specific times and under certain conditions. The aid and service provided within the network supplement rather than displace the basic activities of nuclear family units. Kinship behavior assists more than negates the achievement of status and occupational advance of component families and their members.

[55] Key, *op. cit.*, "Rural-Urban Differences and the Family," p. 56; Sussman, *op. cit.*, "The Isolated Nuclear Family: Fact or Fiction," p. 340.

[56] Key discusses this point in his paper "Rural-Urban Differences and the Family," *op. cit.* From studies on immigration to the United States and geographical movement of families within the country one concludes that family members perform invasion of scout roles and then attract other kin into their communities and neighborhoods.

[54] Eugene Litwak, "The Use of Extended Family Groups in the Achievement of Social Goals: Some Policy Implications," *Social Problems,* **7** (Winter, 1959–60), pp. 177–187; *op. cit.*, "Occupational Mobility and Extended Family Cohesion"; *op. cit.*, "Geographical Mobility and Family Cohesion."

The main flow of financial aid is along generational lines, from parents to young married children and from middle-aged parents to aged parents. Such aid is not restricted to emergencies, but may be given at various occasions such as support for education, to start a family, at time of marriage, to begin a career, and the like.

The network is used among middle-class families as a principal source of aid and service when member families or individuals are in personal difficulty, in times of disaster and crisis, and on ceremonial occasions. There are some indications that established working-class families are following the same pattern. Some situations cannot be handled by the nuclear unit alone, for example, destruction of the family home by a tornado; while other situations involve more than one nuclear family or individual member, for example, the death of an aging parent. In such situations these are mutual expectations of going to the aid of kin. Aid is sought from the most immediate kin chiefly along sibling or generational lines. Then it is followed by help from more distant kin.

In many instances everyday or weekly activities link together the members of the kin family network. Joint participation in leisure time activities are possible because of reduction of the work week. Visiting among kin is facilitated by high speed highways and other conveyances of a modern transportation system. Constant communication among kin members is possible by the widespread adoption on all class levels of the telephone as a household necessity.[57, 58]

[57] Several empirical studies are currently in progress on the extensity of kin family network functions in metropolitan areas. Robert W. Habenstein and Alan D. Coult are conducting one in Kansas City on "The Functions of Extended Kinship in an Urban Milieu." "The purpose of this research is to discover, describe, and analyse the social correlates and functions of extended kinship in representative samples of blue collar and white collar socio-economic classes in Kansas City." p. 1, Research Proposal, July 1, 1961.
[58] A second study is being undertaken by Marvin B. Sussman and Sherwood B. Slater in Cleveland, Ohio. "The objectives of the Cleveland Study are to investigate the working and middle-class families; to compare the kinship networks of 'illness' and 'non-illness' families; to estimate the normative form of kinship networks for social class and family life cycle stages to variations in normative patterns," p. 1, research plan, September 27, 1961.

The feasibility of the kin network in modern society is due to the existence of modern communication and transportation systems which facilitate interaction among members; a bureaucratic industrial structure suited to modern, society which removes the responsibility for job placement from the network will still permit the network to concentrate on activities intended to aid the social and economic achievement of network members;[59, 60] and expansion of metropolitan areas in which individuals can obtain educational, occupational and status objectives without leaving their kin area. Kin members can live some distance from each other within the metropolitan area and still have relationships within the network. Nuclear units function autonomously. Decisions on what and when to act are responsibilities of the nuclear family. Influence may be exerted by the kin group upon the nuclear units so that the latter may make the "right" decision. However the kin group seldom directs the decision or action of the nuclear family in a given situation. Immunity from such control is guaranteed by legal and cultural norms which reaffirm the right and accountability of the nuclear family in such situations. The role of the family kin network is supportive rather than coercive in its relationship with the nuclear family.

Understanding of the family as a functioning social system interrelated with other social systems in society is possible *only by rejection of the isolated nuclear family concept.* Accepting the isolated nuclear family as the most functional type today has led to erroneous conclusions concerning the goals and functions of these other social systems. In social service fields, for

[59] One investigation being conducted by John Bennett is concerned with the variations in business operations due to kinship behavior. Business organization practice according to current theory operates with bureaucratic, universalistic, and impartial norms. Bennett is investigating the compatability and conflict between these bureaucratic norms and those which characterize the kinship network, particularistic behavior for idiosyncratic situations. "Kinship in American Business Organization," meetings of the Central States Anthropological Society, May, 1961.
[60] William Mitchell, "Lineality and Laterality in Urban Jewish Ambilineages," *op. cit.*, finds some integration of kinship and business activity. There is a tendency to "Throw business to kin members."

instance, institutions establish goals and programs concerned with caring for individuals and families who are unable to fend for themselves. Institutions assume that the family unit is a small and isolated unit easily injured and upset by the many problems it faces in contemporary society. The therapeutic approach is to treat the individual or at best the members of the nuclear family. The kin network is overlooked. Often nuclear families respond hesitantly to the overtures of these institutions; the nuclear unit prefers to find solutions to its problems within the family-kin network. When such solutions are impossible then the specialized service institution may be used. How the operations of the family-kin network affect the functioning of other social systems is yet to be established. Their positive or negative effects are unknown. Some beginning research on this problem is now underway.[61]

[61] Hope J. Leichter, *op. cit.*, see footnote 34.

11. Closeness to Blood Relatives Outside the Immediate Family

BY LEE N. ROBINS AND MIRODA TOMANEC

CONSIDERABLE INTEREST HAS BEEN SHOWN in recent years in testing Parsons' statement that the contemporary middle-class American urban family is characterized by an "almost symmetrical onion-type structure" which results in "the structural isolation of the individual conjugal family."[1] His observation that both affect and obligations are concentrated mainly within the nuclear family does not, of course, deny that there are also bonds, albeit weaker than in some other societies, between the members of the nuclear family and other consanguineal relatives. Many studies[2] have presented evidence that such bonds exist, but few have presented evidence concerning the conditions under which bonds to consanguineal relatives in the larger family are maintained, attempted to test the extent to which the ideally symmetrical pattern with respect to line of descent is observed in practice, or sought to specify the norms governing the selection among the available relatives of those with whom to maintain reciprocal performance of services and demonstrations of concern and affection.

Studies which have presented evidence that the nature of relationships with relatives vary under certain conditions include Litwak's study of young American mothers in Buffalo,[3] Willmott and Young's study of slum and suburban London communities,[4] and Schneider and Homan's study of the kinship terminology employed by Harvard students.[5] These studies

SOURCE: Marriage and Family Living, *Volume 24* (*November, 1962*), *pp. 340–346. Reprinted by permission of National Council on Family Relations.*

[1] Talcott Parsons, "The Social Structure of the Family," in Ruth N. Anshen (ed.), *The Family: Its Function and Destiny*, New York: Harper, 1959, p. 250.
[2] Marvin B. Sussman, "The Help Pattern in the Middle Class Family," *American Sociological Review*, **18** (February, 1953), pp. 22–28; and "The Isolated Nuclear Family: Fact or Fiction," *Social Problems*, **6** (Spring, 1956), pp. 333–340; W. Bell and M. D. Boat, "Urban Neighborhoods and Informal Social Relations," *American Journal of Sociology*, **62** (January, 1957), pp. 391–398; Scott Greer, "Urbanism Reconsidered," *American Sociological Review*, **21** (February, 1956), pp. 19–25; Morris Axelrod, "Urban Structure and Social Participation," *American Sociological Review*, **21** (February, 1956), pp. 13–18; Floyd Dotson, "Patterns of Voluntary Association Among Urban Working-Class Families," *American Sociological Review*, **16** (October, 1951), pp. 689–693.

[3] Eugene Litwak, "Occupational Mobility and Extended Family Cohesion," and "Geographic Mobility and Extended Family Cohesion," *American Sociological Review*, **25** (February and June, 1960), pp. 9–21 and 385–394.
[4] Michael Young and Peter Willmott, *Family and Kinship in East London*, London: Routledge and Kegan Paul, 1957; Peter Willmott and Michael Young, *Family and Class in a London Suburb*, London: Routledge and Kegan Paul, 1960. See particularly Chapter IX in the former and Chapter VII in the latter volume.
[5] David M. Schneider and George C. Homans, "Kinship Terminology and the American Kinship System," *American Anthropologist*, **57** (December, 1955), p. 1199.

have considered the role of geographic separation, occupational mobility, and line of descent in determining relationships with relatives outside the nuclear family. Both Litwak's study and Willmott and Young's found middle-class family ties less affected by geographic separation than lower-class family ties. Willmott and Young found that social mobility on the part of the nuclear family interfered with maintaining close relationships, although the difference was found only among male informants and was perceived more by families whose status was lower than their relatives than by families whose status was higher. Litwak found that upwardly mobile families had *more* contact with relatives than the class from which they had risen, but less than the class to which they moved. Maternal relatives were found to be closer than paternal by both Willmott and Young (as reflected in visiting patterns of both slum and suburban families) and Schneider and Homans (as reflected by the use of informal terms of address to aunts and uncles).

The current study was designed to test the hypothesis that the American family, ideally symmetrical, in practice emphasizes relationships with maternal relatives. To test this hypothesis it was necessary to control on variables other than line of descent which previous investigations indicated might influence the selection of relatives with whom one interacts. Therefore, our study can also be viewed to some extent as a replication of previous studies of the effect of geographic distance, social status, and kinship role on closeness of relatives. However, in the interest of evaluating relationships with the maternal versus the paternal line as a whole, it extends its investigation to kinship roles other than those of Ego's parents and siblings, which formed the basis of Litwak's and Willmott and Young's studies, and to other forms of interaction in addition to visiting, financial aid, and terms of address, which have been the central interests of previous studies.

Methods

The present study should be viewed as a pilot attempt to develop promising hypotheses, since it suffers from serious limitations in selection of a sample. In the interest of collecting a fairly sizeable set of interviews to work with, careful sampling was neglected. The interviews were collected by students in a junior-senior level course in *Marriage and the Family*. The class developed a standardized questionnaire and standard kinship chart notations which permitted collection of information about relationships between informants and every secondary and tertiary consanguineal relative in Ego's own generation and in the first and second ascendent generations (i.e., all grandparents, parents' siblings, first cousins, and grandparents' siblings) who had survived at least until Ego reached the age of five years. (Information about affinal relatives was also collected but will not be discussed in the present paper.) Each student was asked to interview three informants between the ages of eighteen and forty-five, but was not required to meet other sampling specifications. Interviews took about three hours to complete, varying in length with the size of the family and Ego's fund of information. One hundred and sixty-two informants were interviewed. Of these, interviews with 22 were not adequately recorded and were dropped from the study, leaving interviews with 140 informants, who reported on their relationships with a total of 2,609 consanguineal relatives—388 grandparents, 690 aunts and uncles, 1,073 first cousins, and 458 great aunts and uncles. The mean number of relatives per informant was 18.6, with a range of 3 to 70.

The questionnaire was designed to obtain a measure of closeness of interaction between Ego and relatives on the paternal and maternal side and to control on variables other than line of descent which might influence this interaction. Our measure of closeness of interaction is the number of avenues used for communication, performance of services, and fulfillment of obligations between Ego and his relatives. We intentionally omitted measures of affection and respect not expressed by concrete acts; nor did we distinguish between acts grudgingly and willingly performed, since we wanted to measure the extent to which kinship roles were fulfilled, not personal preference or sentiment. Frequency with which a given avenue had been used was not taken into account because of the difficulty in obtaining reliable estimates of frequency. Acts which we agreed on as indicators of closeness included: Ego's knowing the relatives' address, visiting the relative, spending nights in his home, the relative's having lived in Ego's home, mutual financial aid, mutual care and supervision of each other or each other's children, mutual attentions when sick, participation in family ceremonies and exchanges of presents, communication by telephone and letter, inheritance of names and property, and use of informal terms of address. Questions were also asked which permitted evaluation of the informant's and his relative's opportunity to perform these acts— including their relative ages, whether they had ever lived in the same town, whether either had children, whether the relative had died, and if so, his and Ego's age at his death. Each act was scored as present, absent despite having the opportunity to perform the act, or no opportunity. Opportunities for financial aid from a relative were not considered to exist, for instance, if the relative was not yet self-supporting; opportunities for visiting a relative were not considered to exist if the relative lived in Ego's home; opportunities to have someone in the family named for the relative were not considered to exist if the relative was still alive in a Jewish family, or younger than the existing offspring, and so on. Closeness between Ego and his relative was scored as the per cent of positive acts by Ego and his relative based on the total number of acts for which the opportunity existed. Closeness scores were grouped in 15 per cent intervals.

For each informant's family, a "family closeness" score was computed by finding the median of the closeness scores for all his reported relatives. Those whose family median fell at 45 per cent or higher were considered members of "close" families; the remainder were considered members of "distant" families. Each relative of each Ego was considered "close" to Ego if his score fell in an interval higher than that in which the median for Ego's particular family fell.

Control variables were included to test three hypotheses which grew out of the studies of others referred to above: (1) that rate of interaction would vary with the kinship role of the person with whom Ego was interacting; (2) that nuclear families rather than individuals feel obligations toward a given relative, which leads to the corollary that the share of obligation falling upon a single Ego will be larger as the number of members of his nuclear family is smaller; (3) that rate of interaction with relatives, like the rate of interaction with nonrelatives, is influenced by homologies of status and location between Ego and his relative. To ascertain the relative's kinship role, each relative was placed on a kinship chart. Number of siblings were used to measure the size of Ego's nuclear family. To test homologies of status and location, for Ego and each relative, sex, age, his own and breadwinner's occupation, education, marital and parental status, religion, ethnic background, and the length of time they had lived in the same town or within 50 miles of each other were asked.

The Sample

Since students were not required to meet sampling quotas, they tended to choose informants who were readily accessible—largely their fellow students at a midwestern, private, coeducational university. Students accounted for 74 per cent of all informants. Inevitably then, the sample of informants was also young (80 per cent under 25), white (99 per cent), unmarried (76 per cent), and had white collar breadwinners (79 per cent). Forty-five per cent of the informants were male and 55 per cent female.

Findings

A. Family Size. The number of consanguineal relatives was not found to be related to how close the family was. About half of both large (20 or more relatives) and small families (19 or fewer) had an average closeness score of 45 per cent or higher.

B. Characteristics of Ego Related to Family Closeness. When Ego was young, single, or without children if married,[6] he was likely to be close

[6] This difference between married Egos with and without children was below statistical significance. However, computation of the contingency coefficient ($C = .22$) indicated that this difference accounted for a significant proportion of the variance. The small X^2 apparently results from the small number of married Egos in the sample.

Table 1

Characteristics of ego related to family closeness

| | Per cent with: | | |
	Distant family (mdn. closeness < 45 per cent)	Close family (mdn. closeness = 45 per cent +)	Number
Age of Ego*			
Under 25	45	55	111
25 or above	79	21	28
Marital Status*			
Single	44	56	107
Married	79	21	33
Having Children			
Has Children	89	11	19
Married, no children	64	36	14
Number of Siblings			
Zero to two	47	53	90
Three or more	70	30	27
Religion			
Protestant	56	44	89
Catholic	57	43	21
Jewish*	32	68	25
Ethnic Background*			
Old Amer., Brit., Irish	61	39	64
Other European	42	58	71

* Statistically significant.

N's vary as a result of omitting cases where the relevant characteristic of Ego was not reported.

to his relatives (Table 1). If he was the only child or had only one or two siblings, he appeared somewhat more likely to be close to his relatives than if he was one of a large nuclear family, but differences were slightly below significance ($p < .10$). If he and his family were Jewish, he was likely to be close to the extended family, and if his family was of European extraction other than from the British Isles, he was likely to be close to the extended family.

Whether Ego was male or female, whether he had or had not attended college, whether his breadwinner was a blue or white collar worker were not related to his closeness to his family.

C. Characteristics of Relatives with Whom Ego Has Close Contact. To distinguish the characteristics of relatives with whom Ego has relatively close contact, families were grouped by their median closeness scores. Relatives falling at the median or below for their particular families were compared with relatives closer to Ego than the median for their family.

By far the most striking determinant of closeness was the kinship role occupied by the relative. Ego was closer to his grandparents than to other consanguineal relatives, followed next by aunts and uncles, then cousins, with great aunts and uncles very rarely among the relatives to whom he was closer than average (Table 2).

Table 2

Kinship role and closeness

| | Per cent | | |
	Equal to or more distant from ego than family mdn.	Closer to ego than the family mdn.	Number
Grandparents*	47	53	358
Aunts and uncles	60	40	690
Cousins	64	36	1,073
Great-aunts and uncles†	88	12	458

* Significantly *closer* than every other kinship role at the .001 level.

† Significantly *more distant* than every other kinship role at the .001 level.

Since kinship roles were so important, it was necessary to control on kinship role when seeking other determinants. Within kinship roles, maternal relatives were found to be closer than paternal relatives, female relatives closer than male relatives, relatives who have lived in the same town with Ego closer than those who have only lived away, and those single closer than those married (Table 3). These differences were found to be statistically significant within all kinship roles except between maternal and paternal great aunts and uncles, between the sexes for grandparents and great-aunts and uncles, between single and married aunts and

Table 3

Characteristics of relatives related to closeness to ego for each kinship role

| | Per cent closer to ego than family median | | | | | | | |
| | Grandparents | | Aunts and uncles | | Cousins | | Great-aunts and uncles | |
	Per cent	N	Per cent	N	Per cent	N	Per cent	N
Line of Descent†								
Maternal	61*	185	48*	322	43*	519	9	223
Paternal	45	203	33	368	30	553	14	236
Sex†								
Male	49	184	34*	345	31*	588	8	207
Female	56	204	46	340	42	465	14	251
Marital Status†								
Single	—	—	47	74	42*	649	24*	66
Ever Married	53	388	41	585	30	396	12	322
Location†								
Lived in Ego's Town	62*	260	45*	426	43*	621	16	198
Never lived in Ego's town	39	104	35	236	30	410	11	191
History of Divorce								
Divorced	45	22	48	65	26	19	6	18
Married, no divorce	57	334	40	520	43	377	12	304

* Statistically significant.

† For sum of partial chi squares, $df = 4$, $p < .001$.

N's vary as a result of omitting cases where the relevant information about the relative was not obtained.

uncles, and between great-aunts and uncles who did and did not live in Ego's town. The non-significant differences were in the same direction as the significant ones except in the case of maternal versus paternal great-aunts and uncles. There was a slight tendency for Ego to be less close to relatives who had been divorced than to those who had not, but the differences were below significance. Only among aunts and uncles was the proportion of distant relatives among the divorced not higher than the proportion among the married relatives who had not been divorced.

The social status of the relative, measured either by his own education or his breadwinner's occupation, was not significantly related to closeness.

Discussion

That Ego is close to his grandparents and distant from his great aunts and uncles seems so expected a finding that it hardly warrants comment. However, this finding could have been anticipated not only on the basis of our common experiences in our culture but also as a corollary of Parsons' description of the American kinship structure. In his well-known diagram of this structure,[7] grandparents, aunts, and uncles fall within the "outer circle," whereas cousins, great-aunts, and great-uncles fall beyond it. The "outer circle" includes all relatives who are within the nuclear families of members of Ego's nuclear family. If we accept Parsons' statement that one's loyalty to one's own nuclear family is the primary obligation, we would expect that the resulting close association of Ego with his parents is likely to involve his second closest association with those relatives to whom the parents feel *their* primary obligation, the parents' nuclear families, which include Ego's grandparents, aunts, and uncles. This finding substantiated our hypothesis that kinship role

[7] T. Parsons, *op. cit.*, p. 243.

would be an important variable on which to control.

Our findings also tend to support our hypothesis that the rate of fulfillment of obligations outside the nuclear family increases as the nuclear family is smaller, though differences are much less impressive than differences resulting from kinship role. But other findings of this study suggest that the reason for increased activity by members of small nuclear families may not be simply the parceling out of obligations among fewer people, as we had supposed. A more general explanation seems to be that Ego has a relatively constant amount of time and effort to devote to interaction with relatives, and that his primary obligations are to members of his nuclear family. Whatever enlarges the nuclear family, whether it is the presence of many siblings in Ego's family of orientation or Ego's entering a new nuclear family through marriage or expanding it through childbirth, reduces the amount of time and effort available to expend on relatives outside the nuclear family. When Ego has few siblings or has not yet entered into marriage, his relationships to his relatives outside the nuclear family are closer. As he marries, and particularly as he has children of his own, his relationships with his secondary relatives diminish. These findings support Parsons' observation that "ego by his marriage is drastically segregated from his family of orientation and other relatives."[8] The demands of the nuclear family of the relatives with whom Ego has contact similarly appears to determine the closeness of his relationship to them. His greater closeness to grandparents than to aunts and uncles (although both are members of his parents' nuclear families) can be explained by the fact that the families of procreation of his aunts and uncles do not include members of Ego's nuclear family, while the families of procreation of his grandparents do. Marriage then segregates the aunts and uncles from him, but not the grandparents. Similarly his distance from his great aunts and uncles can be explained by the extent to which their family activities are concentrated on the family group in which they act as parents and grandparents. Where more distant relatives, both great aunts and uncles

[8] *Ibid.*, p. 252.

and cousins, have not entered into families of procreation, and therefore do not have parental and grandparental roles to fulfill, Ego was found to be closer to them. Townsend, in his study of old people in a London slum,[9] similarly found that siblings tended to drift apart after the death of the parents unless one or both of the siblings were unmarried. It is particularly interesting that the Jewish family, which is commonly believed to be close to its extended family (and was found to be so in this study), has the lowest average number of offspring of the three large religious groups in America. It would be worth exploring to what extent the cohesion of the extended Jewish family can be explained by the smallness of the nuclear family.

Our third hypothesis, that homologies of status and location would be important was only partially confirmed. Geographic location, even for these predominantly middle-class families, appeared to be an important determinant. Within each kinship role, relatives in the same town are closer to Ego than those who live elsewhere. Although this finding appears not to support the findings of Litwak and Willmott and Young concerning middle-class families, we should point out that our finding is highly dependent on our definition of who has the opportunity for performing acts designated as indicating closeness. Whereas one clearly does not write letters or travel to visit a relative if one lives in the same town, or telephone frequently if one lives at a distance, there remain other acts such as attending family ceremonies and notifying of family occasions, which, although not impossible for relatives who live out of town, are clearly more convenient for those relatives who are geographically near. It seems highly probable that the convenience with which acts are performed will be a factor in their performance. We do not know from our data whether geographic distance also makes relatives *feel* subjectively less close.[10]

[9] Peter Townsend, *The Family Life of Old People*, London: Routledge and Kegan Paul, 1957, pp. 100 ff.
[10] Sussman's paper, "Family Continuity: Selective Factors which Affect Relationship between Families at Generation Levels," *Marriage and Family Living*, **16** (May, 1954), pp. 112–120, suggests that geographic distance diminishes acts of closeness where family relationships are harmonious, but increases them

Homologies of status do not appear to be very important in determining relationships with relatives. From the point of view of age and marital status, Egos most resembled their cousins, but cousins were less close to them than grandparents and aunts and uncles. To the extent that Ego's marital status resembled that of most of his older relatives—that is, as he married and had children, his closeness to them declined rather than increased. Although Egos were almost all college students, they did not choose among their relatives on the basis of the relatives' education. Although they came largely from families supported by white collar breadwinners and had every expectation of themselves holding high status occupations, they showed no preference for white collar over blue collar relatives. Our data, therefore, failed to support these findings of Willmott and Young that relationships outside the nuclear family are weaker if one nuclear family is more upwardly mobile than another as well as the finding of Litwak that family visiting increases with Ego's status. Studies of Axelrod, Bell and Boat, and Sussman (see footnote 2), like ours, found no important differences between the closeness to secondary relatives based on the status either of Ego or of his relatives. These points in particular need retesting in a sample which has a broader economic base and which is representative of the family types and the social strata existing in the general population. It is quite possible that our student informants discriminate among their relatives less on the basis of occupation and education than they will after they are setting their social status through their own or their husband's job and after their involvement in their future families of procreation forces them to choose among available relatives in whom to invest their more limited remaining energies.

Homologies of religion and ethnicity could not be tested in this study because we are dealing with consanguineal relatives only, who with very rare exceptions shared Ego's religious and ethnic identification. However, we have also collected information about relationships between Ego and the spouses of these relatives. Analysis of Egos relationships with affinal relatives may show that for affinal relatives, status similarities have more importance than for his relationship with consanguineal relatives. Affinal relatives in this respect may hold a middle position between consanguineal relatives, whose kinship role is the chief determinant of interaction, and friends and potential marriage partners, where status similarities have been reported to be very important determinants of relationships.

This study points to the central role that middle-class women play in maintaining relationships with relatives. Female relatives tend to be closer to Ego than male relatives, and relatives to whom he is related through his mother tend to be closer than those to whom he is related through his father. The greater closeness to female relatives can probably be explained by the fact that women tend to act as the representative of the nuclear family in fulfilling obligations to relatives. Therefore, any given Ego is more likely to have had contact with his female than with his male relatives. The central role of the woman in performing duties imposed by kinship apparently also provides opportunities for her to show preference for the maternal side of the family despite the normative pattern of treating maternal and paternal relatives equally. In those activities with relatives which are not clearly obligatory, a woman is able to express her preference for her own blood relatives, and in doing so increase their contact with her children as compared with her husband's relatives' contact. This tendency to emphasize the maternal line is recognized by the informants themselves, who when asked to which side they felt closer, named the mother's family in 60 per cent of the cases, the father's family in only 31 per cent, and could not choose between them in 9 per cent. We have, therefore, supported our initial hypothesis that in practice the American family emphasizes relationships with maternal over paternal relatives.

If our explanation for how this occurs is correct, that is, if it in fact depends on the central role of women in carrying out kinship obligations, future studies of the patterns or interaction with relatives outside the nuclear family

---

where relationships are strained. If we assume that most relationships between relatives tend toward the harmonious, his paper would support our findings that even for middle-class families, geographic distance is negatively associated with closeness.

should take into account the hierarchy of demands on women created by obligations to spouse, children, siblings, and parents. The smaller nuclear family in the middle class, and its subsequent decreased demands on the housewife's time, may explain Litwak's finding that there is more contact between housewives and their relatives as their social status increases.[11] His study might show that the middle class is

no more likely to maintain ties with relatives than lower-class families when family size is controlled. But further research will be necessary, and in particular, studies permitting adequate representation of all social classes and ethnic groups, if we wish to specify more precisely the conditions under which closeness and distance in relationships with the extended family occur.

---

[11] Jerzy Berent in "Fertility and Social Mobility," *Population Studies*, **5** (March, 1952), pp. 244–260 has shown that the number of offspring in upwardly mobile families falls between the number in the class from which they came and the class to which they rise. Therefore, Litwak's upwardly mobile families probably had smaller families than the lower class and larger than the upper. Since his upwardly mobile families had a medium amount of contact with relatives, this would be consistent with our finding that family size is negatively associated with contact with relatives.

12. Sibling Solidarity: A Property of American Kinship*

BY ELAINE CUMMING AND DAVID M. SCHNEIDER

AMERICAN KINSHIP HAS BEEN DESCRIBED most fully in those aspects in which it differs from other social institutions. The nuclear family stands out from the occupational world like a figure on a ground. The specific technical competence required in the occupational world contrasts sharply with the requirements of familial loyalty and devotion to parents, siblings, and children[1] (Parsons 1943).

Although American kinship is sharply differentiated from other social institutions, both empirical and theoretical considerations suggest significant points of continuity and consistency between kinship and other parts of the social system (Schneider and Homans 1955).

We will describe here findings which draw attention to a feature of American kinship which shows this consistency with other features of the American social system and which has not yet been adequately described. This feature is a solidarity among siblings[2] (Pehrson 1954:199–202) which we believe to be a special case of the generational solidarity which is a feature of American life[3] (Codere 1955).

This is an age-graded society. We make a distinction between a nursery-school child and a kindergarten child, and both differ from a school-aged child. We have "preteens" and "teens" and subdebs and debutantes, and young married couples. At this point, we seem to relax our efforts, only to begin again with middle age, late middle age, older people, and finally old age.[4] This rather fine age-grading probably has two important sources; it is generated by the equalitarian ideology which renders us less comfortable with vertical relationships than with horizontal ones, and second, by an industrialized society of refined technology in which it is important

SOURCE: American Anthropologist, *Volume 63 (June, 1961), pp. 498–507. Reprinted by permission of the authors and American Anthropological Association.*

* Our thanks are due to David S. Newell, who did much of the interviewing for this study and made many helpful suggestions. Mary Lou Parlagreco and Roxane Cohen assisted with the often tedious job of analyzing the genealogical material described herein. Both of them contributed ideas to the analysis.

[1] For the classical description of the structure of American kinship, see Parsons (1943).

[2] Pehrson (1954) has suggested that sibling solidarity is the "fundamental kinship bond" of bilateral systems, of which the American kinship system is, of course, a particular instance.

[3] Codere has described a sibling solidarity among Vassar students, but she interprets this in terms of the strength of nuclear-family bonds. We wish, rather, to draw attention to its relationship to the generational solidarity of the larger society.

[4] Inquiry among colleagues reveals that the ages associated with these various age-graded terms are well known to everyone. Among the dozen people asked to name the age which each term suggested to them there was tight concurrence. Furthermore, there was almost no overlapping between one age grade and the next.

both to keep the young out of many key roles until they know enough to fill them and to remove the old before what they know is obsolete.

We are familiar with the structural evidence of age-grading. For example, there are the adolescent gangs and cliques (Whyte 1955) and in the middle class, there are women's clubs. In working and lower-class societies, there are important men's groupings. We will present here preliminary evidence that solidarity among siblings is the counterpart in the kinship structure of this tendency to horizontal solidarity, and we will trace out some functional implications of this feature.

The Study

Two hundred and twenty adults between the ages of 50 and 80 have given information regarding their kindred.[5] They form a stratified random sample of the residents in this age group of the metropolitan area of Kansas City. From this panel, 15 were chosen as reasonably representative, their genealogies were recorded, and they were interviewed intensively about kinship. There were 6 general areas of inquiry: (1) patterns of sociability with kindred; (2) patterns of mutual aid in crisis; (3) power, authority, and influence in the kinship system; (4) solidary groupings within the kinship system; (5) coresidential patterns; and (6) the history of the marriage and nuclear family. From the formulations developed by studying this group, we developed 4 hypotheses which were testable on data available for the total population.

Emergent Patterns

The salient feature of the 15 intensive interviews is the importance placed on the nuclear family. There was a good deal of well-formed

[5] These respondents were being studied primarily for the purpose of developing a theory of aging. They were members of a panel selected for the Kansas City Study of Adult Life, a project of the University of Chicago. The Principal Investigator was William E. Henry; the study was financed by the National Institute of Mental Health.

opinion about its boundaries. All agreed that to include non-nuclear kin in the household is an error, especially if these extra members mean that 3 generations are present under the same roof. Although 14 of these 15 people have lived in extended families, and for an average of 5 years, they almost all claimed "exceptional circumstances." All expressed the hope never to have to live with their children, although some thought it might happen if luck deserted them. In Levy's terms (Levy n.d.) the ideal American family is a nuclear family, but the real American family is often an extended one. When the ideal is abandoned, our respondents feel vertical extension to be worse than horizontal.

Within the nuclear group itself, the mother is an important figure. All 15 respondents said that they were closer to their mothers than to their fathers. Mothers were described as instrumental leaders also. Only 4 people reported that their fathers had handled the money in their homes, and of these, 3 felt that he did it inadequately. We felt at the time, during the interviews, that this emphasis upon the superiority of the mother in both instrumental and expressive roles was primarily the expression of an ideal. Furthermore, this focus seemed not to be on mother exclusively, as in the English case (Young 1957), but rather upon women in general. Wives, mothers, and sisters are all focal figures in American family life. We might temporarily call this gynefocality.

Within the nuclear family the parent-child bond was manifestly strong, with the sibling bond running it a close second. The spouse bond, on the other hand, seemed surprisingly little emphasized among these middle-aged and older respondents. In particular, the sister-sister bond seemed to override it among the women.

A second important pattern emerging from these interviews was the large number of kin recognized[6] (Litwak 1960). The range is between 34 and 280, and the median is 151. This number includes the in-marrying affinals of the respondent's consanguineal kin, but not the spouse's kin. However, all but 2 of these 15 people recognized

[6] There have been several recent suggestions that the "isolation" of the nuclear family has been exaggerated, see for example the several publications of the Detroit Area Studies and more recently Litwak (1960).

Table 1

Knowledge of the names of kin by type of relationship

Class of kin*	Number having this class available	Per cent knowing the names of more than half recognized in the class
Nuclear Family	14	100
Secondary Ascending (aunts, uncles, grandparents)	14	100
Tertiary Collaterals (first cousins)	13	100
Quaternary Ascending (parents' first cousins)	10	90
Quinternary Collaterals (third cousins)	8	75
Tertiary Descendants (great-grandchildren and cousins of grandchildren)	10	70
Tertiary Ascendants (great-grandparents and great-aunts and uncles)	13	69
Quaternary Descendants (cousins' children)	12	33
Quinternary and Sexternary Ascendants and Descendants	11	29

* Primary kin can be described by one word: mother, brother, daughter, and so forth. Secondary kin require two words, mother's brother, and so forth; tertiaries, three words, and so on. This nomenclature exactly reflects degree of consanguinity.

their spouse's kin; these numbers represent for most people only half of the actual pool of kindred. When we examine the number of kin for whom names are known, we find that the number shrinks to about one-half. Among kin for whom names are known, there is an emphasis on collaterals rather than ascendants or descendants. In Table 1 we show the order in which for various classes of kin more than half of the number recognized are known by name.

The first-cousin relationship is roughly as intimate (in terms of knowing the names of cousins) as that of uncles and aunts. Parents' cousins, a class of people to whom the respondent is linked through the close parental bond, are almost as well known. On the other hand, the respondent's own cousins' children, who stand in just as close a consanguineal relationship as parents' cousins, are known by name only one-third as often. The collateral relationship consistently appears in the table ahead of where it would be expected in terms of its consanguineal closeness alone.

A third pattern among the 15 respondents was the granting of relatively equal status to all those kin who are not either in the nuclear family or immediately available geographically. No class of kindred are specially favored for interaction.

There appears to be a selection of people who live close by on the grounds of personal compatibility, although in some cases this seems less apparent because *all* kin are described as close. Kindred who are geographically distant are in an available pool; intimacy will come with opportunity. This is in a sense, an equalitarian attitude toward kin. With such an attitude, which does not prescribe any set modes of deference between people of different generations, the naturally equalitarian relationship with collaterals would probably be more comfortable and appropriate and, therefore, perhaps selected where there was a choice[7] (Firth 1956).

A fourth pattern is the predominant style of interaction among kin. We found some reluctance among our respondents to discuss instrumental activities or mutual aid and an eagerness to discuss socio-emotional and ritual activities.[8] In all 15 cases, initial questioning about financial

[7] This is in marked contrast to Firth's description of London kinship with its concentric circles of kindred moving from intimacy through peripherality and on to recognition alone.

[8] It should be noted here that these respondents were well known to us; their reticence could not have been owing to shyness—several had endured ten to twenty prior hours of interviewing. All were friendly and open in the interviews.

aid among kinsmen elicited the belief that borrowing and lending among kindred was a mistake. Further questioning, however, revealed that such mutual aid had, in fact, taken place recently among 6 of the 15. Even exchange of service is discussed reluctantly. Kinship appears to include friendliness, rite of passage, family reunions, and sociability, but ideally it does not include service or financial help, although this may, through bad fortune, be necessary. This type of sociable relationship is characteristic of those freely choosing each other's company, of peers, and in general of those related through horizontal ties.

The final pattern, and possibly the most important one, is a shift in solidarity through time. After each interview, we made a note of the predominant *motif* of the interview. Sibling solidarity stood out very forcibly from all other themes, and in the case of the older respondents, it seemed stronger than nuclear family solidarity. However, when we examined the history of the marriage and nuclear family, it became clear that this was, in part, a characteristic of the stage of family development for people of this age.

These respondents appear to have had a childhood solidarity with their parents, especially the mother, which persisted even after marriage, until the bond with children replaced it. However, during childhood and adolescence, the solidarity among siblings[9] (Garigue 1956), and sometimes cousins, appears second only to the mother-child bond. At about the time the children leave home, the parents of these respondents are most likely to become a problem of management. The sibling bond may be reinvoked initially to manage a crisis, but ultimately it may act as a fundamental axis of socio-emotional interaction. It appears that for most people the sibling ties are mediated through women who, in the absence of siblings of their own, become solidary with the siblings of their spouses. This generational solidarity seems to be a very important relational tie of the last 20 or 30 years of life.

[9] Our sample shows, as we have mentioned, primarily a sister-sister solidarity. Men tend to get assimilated to solidarities of sisters, and sister-in-law, in contrast to the brother-brother-in-law solidarity of the French Canadians, for example.

We will now turn to our total sample of 220 people in order to discover whether the information bearing on kinship supports this patterning.

When we asked our respondents which of their kindred, other than those living in the house with them, they felt closest to (intimate kin), they named 88 per cent of their living children, 74 per cent of their sibs, and 63 per cent of their parents. When we asked whom they felt close to, but not quite so close to (peripheral kin), the remainder of the children and siblings were added, but none of the unchosen parents. This failure probably represents strain between certain respondents and their parents-in-law. Combining intimate and peripheral choices, we find that 25 per cent of the group chose cousins, 10 per cent chose grandchildren, and 25 per cent chose the children of siblings. Six per cent chose parents-in-law, and all of these were men choosing their mothers-in-law. Less than 5 per cent chose children-in-law; again, this probably reflects strain between the spouse bond and the tight parent-child bond. Forty per cent of the group chose sibs-in-law. These choices seem to suggest a perception of solidarity with siblings second only to the solidarity parents perceive between themselves and their own children, but stronger than that which they perceive between themselves and their parents.

This solidarity becomes more obvious when we look at who is chosen as intimate or peripheral by those respondents who lack parents, siblings, or children. Table 2 shows the classes of people "substituted" in these cases, as well as those added by persons with a full inner circle of kin. A "substitute" is any class of kinsman, affinal or consanguineal, of the same generation as the kinsman being substituted for, except that grandchildren are included with nephews and nieces as substitute children. By the same token, aunts and uncles are substitute parents and cousins are substitute siblings.

Looking at Table 2, we see a marked pattern in the choice of "substitutes" and "additions." Choosing members of the ascending generation is associated strongly with having parents geographically available. This no doubt reflects attrition of the ascending generation, but may also arise because of associations with these

Table 2

Substitutes for and additions to primary kin

	Number interviewed	Per cent choosing substitutes and additions whether or not these are geographically available*
Total	220	
Class of Kin Alive but Geographically Unavailable:		
Parents	25	84
Siblings	126	55
Children	28	46
Class of Kin Available:*		
Parents	18	94
Siblings	60	38
Children	132	28
Class of Kin Lacking Entirely:		
Parents	177	22
Siblings	34	64
Children	60	55

* Close enough to visit and return home in one day.

ascendants which are mediated through the parents. That is, while they still have parents, the respondents choose their parents' collaterals. However, among those without children there appears to be a genuine substitution. Respondents without any children choose the most descendants, those with geographically unavailable children choose the next most, and those with available children choose the fewest. The choice of sibling substitutes follows the same pattern but is even more marked. Two-thirds of those without siblings choose other collaterals, and more than half with unavailable siblings do so. Over a third with available siblings choose supplementary collaterals.

The choices of sibling substitutes are all about 10 per cent higher than those of children substitutes and this difference is significant. Furthermore, the universe of collaterals is restricted to one generation even though there are often two generations of descendants available. This suggests that the difference between choices of children and sibling substitutes might be greater than it appears.

When we look at Table 3 we see that there is an overall tendency for the respondent to choose "substitutes" for the class of kin he does not have, but again the tendency to add collaterals to the intimate group is stronger than the tendency to add descendants. This suggests that, although the parent-to-child bond is the "strongest," the sibling bond is the more widespread. If the former is lacking, it may or may not be substituted for; if the latter is lacking it is very likely to be substituted for. We do not, of course, know the content of these relationships. It may well be that for this age group the parent-to-child bond is *primarily* affection, the child-to-parent *primarily* obligation, and the sibling bond *primarily* sociability. Because they may not be comparable, we cannot really use these indices to decide that one solidarity is "stronger" than another.

Our next test is concerned with the role of friendship. It is commonly observed that friendship is a substitute for kinship, and in this study we have examined the respondents' descriptions of their friends in terms of their

Table 3

Substitutes for, and additions to, intimate kin, by availability of siblings and children

	Number interviewed	Per cent choosing			
		Collaterals	Descendants	Both	Neither
Totals	220	72	39	42	67
Class of Kin alive:					
Siblings and children	135	30.3	14.9	18.5	36.3
Siblings only	51	29.4	27.4	22.3	20.9
Children only	25	44.0	16.0	8.0	32.0
Neither	9	55.6	11.1	33.3	0

similarity to and differences from kinship. Generally speaking, we have assigned descriptions of diffuse qualities to the kinship category and descriptions of specific activities to the non-kinship categories. Examples of the former are: "she's my old friend and would do anything for me," or, "he is a nice likeable man"; and examples of the latter are: "we play bridge together," or, "we go fishing together." All coding has been done blind for the kinship variables.

We find in Table 4 that those who have no siblings at all are significantly more inclined toward a "kinship" style of description of their friends than those who do have siblings, whether or not they have parents or children available. It is of interest, too, that asked to give descriptions of their "best friends" 13 per cent included their siblings.

In all of these data there are some differences between men and women, as we have indicated by singling out the sister-sister bond for comment. However, the overall findings are true for both sexes to a greater or less degree, except where the contrary is explicitly mentioned.

Finally, we turn to two data which are available through our study of morale among this group of aging people (Cumming, Henry 1961). Among men, morale is higher when there are siblings available nearby. Among women the situation is more complicated. By and large, the highest morale is enjoyed by widows, the lowest by older married women. (Recall that the sample is from 50 to 80 years of age.) Among the married women, the presence of siblings ameliorates low morale.[10]

The difference in the death rate between men and women results in many more women than men being widowed; there are 8 years of married life remaining to the average married couple after the last child leaves home before women can expect to be widowed. However, widowhood gives a woman a whole new membership group,

[10] For a description of the instrument of measurement used see Cumming, Dean, and Newell (1958).

Table 4

Diffuse descriptions of friends by presence of siblings

	Number interviewed	Per cent giving		
		The most diffuse descriptions	Less diffuse or specific descriptions	No answer
Totals	220	117	88	15
With siblings	180	49.5	43.5	7.0
Without siblings	34	73.5	20.6	5.9

that of other widows, and a clique of widows is almost the prototype of the solidary horizontal relationship. Women whose husbands survive find themselves in an increasingly limited group of peers, and if they do not have siblings they may be quite isolated. Although it is possible to include a husband in a social system composed of kin, it is impossible to include him in one composed of widows. A society of widows can, therefore, be looked upon as a substitute for a society of siblings, and, importantly, both can be looked upon as special cases of the general horizontal solidarity in the total society.[11]

Discussion

Vertical and horizontal solidarities differ from one another in a very important way, and the difference resembles that which Durkheim describes as organic and mechanical. In organic solidarity, with its division of labor and mutual dependency, there is dissimilarity of the units, a high degree of mutual obligation, and a restricted degree of choice. In mechanical solidarity, the units are solidary, not because of mutual dependence, but because of mutual resemblance. By the same token the units are interchangeable, bonds are more easily broken, and choice among the units is more flexible. In a society in which industrialization demands a good deal of organic solidarity in the occupational world but in which freedom of choice is highly valued, it is perhaps not surprising that the less demanding collateral bonds are emphasized, and that, within them, the mutual dependency of mutual aid is ideally absent, and sociability is predominant.

[11] Our findings lead to important questions about the different function of marriage for men and for women after children leave home and if and when sex becomes irrelevant. Unfortunately, we cannot pursue these questions here.

It is reasonable to think of husband-wife solidarity as shifting through time. During child raising, a maximum of mutual dependency occurs, but after retirement and the departure of children the bond between spouses, from this point of view, resembles the bond between siblings.

Horizontal solidarity with collateral kin can be thought of as an integral part of a social sytem which requires a high level of coordination and mutual dependency but which, at the same time, values a high level of autonomy, freedom of choice, and equalitarianism.

REFERENCES

Codere, Helen, 1955, "A Genealogical Study of Kinship in the United States," *Psychiatry*, **18**, pp. 65–80.

Cumming, Elaine, Lois R. Dean, and D. S. Newell, 1958, "What is Morale, A Case History of the Validity Problem," *Human Organization*, **17**, p. 2.

Cumming, Elaine and William E. Henry, 1961, *Growing Old, The Process of Disengagement*, (Chap. 7). New York: Basic Books.

Firth, Raymond, 1956, *Two Studies of Kinship in London*, London: The Athlone Press.

Garigue, P., 1956, "French Canadian Kinship and Urban Life," *American Anthropologist*, **58**, pp. 1090–1101.

Levy, Marion, n.d., "Some Aspects of the Analysis of Family Structure." (Unpublished manuscript.)

Litwak, Eugene, 1960, "Occupational Mobility and Extended Family Cohesion," *American Sociological Review*, **25**, pp. 9–21.

Parsons, Talcott, 1943, "The Kinship System in the Contemporary United States," *American Anthropologist*, **45**, pp. 22–38.

Pehrson, R., 1954, "Bilateral kin grouping as a structural type," *University of Manila Journal of East Asiatic Studies*, **3**, pp. 199–202.

Schneider, D. M. and G. C. Homans, 1955, "Kinship terminology and the American kinship system," *American Anthropologist*, **57**, pp. 1194–1208.

Whyte, W. F., 1955, *Street Corner Society*, Chicago: University of Chicago Press.

Young, M. and P. Willmott, 1957, *Family and Kinship in East London*, Glencoe: The Free Press.

13. Sibling Interaction: A Neglected Aspect in Family Life Research*

BY DONALD P. IRISH

ABSTRACT

Although considerable significance has been attributed to sibling relations by behavioral scientists, little empirical research has been conducted regarding the interaction of siblings with each other. Several factors account for the paucity of such research. Social problems involving children have focused attention on the adult-child dimension. Freudian thought has stressed the regimes of infancy, not socializing influences during childhood and youth. Occupational pressures upon family sociologists have prompted an emphasis on dating, courtship, and marital interaction. The attenuation of kinship and certain methodological problems have made study difficult. Nonetheless, research is needed concerning this neglected aspect of family life.

Inattention to Sibling Interaction

One of the earliest and most productive of the orientations still current in research is the theoretical approach in which the family is considered as a "unity of interacting personalities." Within that framework, there are several sets of structural relationships about which sociological

SOURCE: Social Forces, *Volume 42 (March, 1964)*, *pp. 279–288. Reprinted with permission of the University of North Carolina Press.*

* This exposition was prepared as a basis for analysis of data for a project supported by PHS research grant M-2045, from the National Institute of Mental Health, and was directed by Charles E. Bowerman.

research concerning life in the nuclear family can be organized: interactions between adult members, between parents and children, and among children.

The relationships laterally between husbands and wives—the parent generation—have primarily occupied those family sociologists who for several decades have been most engrossed with the processes of mate-selection, marital adjustment and interaction, prediction studies of marital success, parenthood, and related matters.

Vertical connections between parents and children—intergenerational influences—have been investigated extensively by psychologists as well as sociologists. Among the concerns that have occupied numerous researchers interested in these vertical dimensions of family life have been the effects of differential child-training practices of parents on the development of designated personality traits in their children, parent-child interactions and adjustment, comparisons of the belief and behavior patterns of the elder and younger generations, the attainment of appropriate sex roles by the children with parents as models, and the achievement of various developmental tasks. These aspects are introduced with the advent of child-rearing.

The interactions between and among children in the home—the horizontal relationships within the younger generation itself—seem to have been given relatively little heed. An examination of the research literature for the decades since

World War I provides very few examples of empirical studies focused primarily on sibling relations. The many investigations of ordinal position have usually examined the parent-child nexus—the variations in parental treatment of children because of their position in the birth order and the effects of such divergencies in child-rearing patterns and parental attitudes on the development of the children's personalities.[1] The multifarious discussions and studies of "sibling rivalry" likewise have tended to consider the relations of siblings to each other mainly in terms of the vertical dimension—the competition of children in the family for the love, attention, and favor of one or both parents.[2]

Among sociologists and social psychologists, Bossard and Boll contended that the security of children has been treated as if based almost exclusively on (1) the adequacy of parent-child (and often just mother-child) relationships and (2) the interactions with peers outside the home. They point out that

the role of siblings has been considered chiefly in the light of "displacement" and "rivalry." It is rarely that one finds any but the negative aspects of sibling relationships, and warnings how to deal with them.[3]

Furthermore, they assert that, while the contributions of peer groups to the socialization and psychic security of children have been recognized,

The differences in social situations obtaining as between a non-family and a family group have not

been so appreciated . . . having come into prominence in an era of the small family system, the peer group has meant, exclusively, non-family peers.[4]

Some of the relationships existing among siblings in diverse cultures have been described by ethnologists interested in socialization and personality development, kinship patterns, family life as a cultural complex, and related aspects. As summarized by Murdock, in many societies:

Siblings are . . . bound to one another through the care and help given by an elder to a younger, through cooperation in childhood games which imitate the activities of adults, and through mutual economic assistance as they grow older. Thus, through reciprocal material services sons and daughters are bound to fathers and mothers and to one another. . . .[5]

For the most part, however, inquiry into the meaning siblings have for each other, and their interactions within the nuclear family, have not been the focus of attention in anthropological research.[6]

Numerous investigations of "individual psychology" have been conducted, using sibling

[1] Already, thirty years ago, Jones was able to list almost 100 research articles on order of birth and its relation to other traits in individuals. See H. E. Jones, "Order of Birth," in C. Murchison (ed.), *Handbook of Child Psychology*, Worcester, Mass.: Clark University Press, 1933. Also, Leonard Carmichael (ed.), *Manual of Child Psychology*, New York: John Wiley and Sons, 1954, second edition.

[2] For example, David M. Levy, "Hostility Patterns in Sibling Rivalry Experiments," *American Journal of Orthopsychiatry*, **6** (April, 1936), pp. 183–257; *Studies in Sibling Rivalry*, Monograph No. 2, published by American Orthopsychiatry Association, 1937; and his "Sibling Rivalry Studies in Children of Primitive Groups," *American Journal of Orthopsychiatry*, **9** (January, 1939), pp. 205–214.

[3] James H. S. Bossard and Eleanor Boll, "Security in the Large Family," *Mental Hygiene*, **38** (October, 1954), p. 532.

[4] *Ibid.*, pp. 553–534.

[5] George Peter Murdock, *Social Structure*, New York: The Macmillan Company, 1949, p. 9.

[6] The culture-personality specialists have examined extensively the consequences for basic personality structure of the child-rearing patterns prevalent in numerous societies, with some attention to birth order and sex roles. Anthropologists also have studied the socialization of children through age and sex-graded friendship and ritual groups. Some have explored the relationships between siblings in the small nuclear families of hunting bands in the simplest societies. Others have presented and explained the customary avoidance of preferential, joking, or respect relationships among them. Many have reported about the custodial supervision of younger children by their older brothers and sisters.

It is recognized that, among many preliterate groups and some civilized societies, the frequency of polygamous marriage arrangements, often further complicated by the levirate or sororate, joint residence patterns, the commonality of adoption, and other influences, modify the intensity and extensity of sibling interactions and probably minimize their significance. It is perhaps in the simplest hunting and gathering cultures, most of all in those in which the nuclear family may be isolated to itself for a considerable portion of each year, that sibling relationships are of greatest importance, relatively.

position, number, and differentiation by sex as independent variables to examine the influence that particular sibship configurations may have upon the personality characteristics and competencies that persons manifest later during their life span. Krout long ago felt that "virtually every problem of socio-psychological importance has been studied" in terms of birth order.[7] Most of these inquiries, however, have focused merely on the relation of a structural sib-*position* to particular personality *traits*, as presumed end-products. Generally, they have failed to elucidate the intervening interactions among sibling roles.

Thus far, it would appear that very little empirical research has been conducted in any of these related fields regarding the interaction of siblings with each other either within the family setting during the years of childhood and youth when they reside together, or later among them when they have become adults.

The Significance Attributed to Sibling Relations

While the bonds between parent(s) and child(ren) are customarily strong within our nuclear-family system, the ties between and among siblings will in most homes generally also be close, being second in strength only to the former. Pehrson has suggested that "sibling solidarity" may be the "fundamental kinship bond" within bilateral systems, of which our own society is one illustration.[8] Cumming and Schneider found that some persons, particularly during certain phases of the life cycle, find sibling ties to be more meaningful than their spouse-bonds.[9] During childhood and adolescence the degree of affection between siblings, and

sometimes toward cousins, may be second only to the mother-child ties.[10]

Within the immediate family, siblings constitute an important sub-"we-group" for research analysis. They comprise a significant portion of the family group structure distinct from other combinations that may be isolated for investigation. Three decades ago, Chapin recognized that both a manifest and latent structural pattern may be discerned in family interaction. The manifest factors—parent pattern, number of siblings, sex and age distribution of the children, and guests in the home, among others—have been given most attention. However, as Chapin pointed out:

> The latent structural pattern is of a subtler nature. It is revealed in the separate member roles and in the pattern of equilibrium of the whole family group. It has to be inferred from the common reciprocating attitudes of the individual members of the family group. . . . The manifest structure of the sibling group may determine the latent structure of the member role.[11]

Shortly thereafter, Sletto stated that differences in children's personality traits might be attributed to the divergent roles which they play in "intrasibship interaction," patterns associated with the sibling position of the children, as well as to the dissimilar treatments by the parents.[12] Siblings, Krout has pointed out, "create an ever-changing milieu in the family." A sibling "is not a silent witness of a drama in which the parent and another child participates."[13]

Toman likewise has recognized the influence of interactions among siblings as important supplements to the parent-child relationships.

[7] M. H. Krout, "Typical Behavior Patterns in Twenty-six Ordinal Positions," *Journal of Genetic Psychology*, **55** (1939), p. 5.

[8] R. Pehrson, "Bilateral Kin Grouping as a Structural Type," University of Manila *Journal of East Asiatic Studies*, **3** (1954), pp. 199–202; and also Helen Codere, "A Genealogical Study of Kinship in the United States," *Psychiatry*, **18** (February, 1955), pp. 65–79.

[9] Elaine Cumming and David M. Schneider, "Sibling Solidarity: A Property of American Kinship," *American Anthropologist*, 63 (June, 1961), pp. 498–507.

[10] P. Garigue, "French Canadian Kinship and Urban Life," *American Anthropologist*, **58** (1956), pp. 1090–1101. For a cogent, succinct delineation of American kinship structure, see Talcott Parsons, "The Kinship System in the Contemporary United States," *American Anthropologist*, **45** (January–March, 1943), pp. 22–28.

[11] F. Stuart Chapin, "The Experimental Approach: The Advantages of Experimental Sociology in the Study of Family Group Patterns," *Social Forces*, **11** (December, 1932), p. 204. See Katherine Lumpkin, *Family Life: A Study in Member Roles* (manuscript, 1931) for one example of an analysis of member roles.

[12] Raymond F. Sletto, "Sibling Position and Juvenile Delinquency," *American Journal of Sociology*, **39** (March, 1934), pp. 657–669.

[13] Krout, *op. cit.*, p. 4.

He has contended that a person can be characterized appropriately

in terms of the people who have been living with him longest, most intimately, and most regularly, and by incidental losses of such people—i.e., primarily his parents and siblings.[14]

This psychoanalyst recently set forth in exposition a schema for examining family constellations, using eight basic types of sibling positions in both the child and parent generations.[15]

Sibling relationships can perform a number of functions. Brothers and/or sisters spend many hours together and share a wide range of activities.[16] Such contacts within the nuclear family tend to be intimate and inclusive in character, and to constitute primary groups characterized by frankness, informality, cohesiveness, intensity, and extensity. Interaction with siblings functions as one avenue for the socialization of children. It helps bring them into social reality, gives them experience in resolving interpersonal conflicts, introduces them to the rights of others, and provides a "school of mirrors." On occasion, siblings may act as substitutes for parents. They may turn to each other when sufficient attention or understanding is not shown by an indifferent, harried, or uncomprehending parent. Sometimes siblings are more effective teachers than adults, particularly if youthful skills are involved. Siblings may often understand childhood problems and new situations better, in some ways, than do the parents they share. They are associates that can contribute importantly to emotional security; and, ordinarily, it is pleasant and helpful for children to have other children as companions. Siblings

may serve as role models for one another; particularly may the younger observe the older siblings of the same sex. They can serve as challengers and stimulators. Finally, in the creation of a "sense of family," a psychological unity of members who perform the essential and peripheral tasks of habitation together, each person develops his niche in the total structure. The larger the family, the greater the number, variety, and degree of specializations that may develop in these roles.[17]

Of course, sibling associations can also be dysfunctional in their consequences. They may engender so much security and cohesiveness within the group that a member comes to feel insecure or "homesick" when away from it. Frequently, particularly in the larger families, the presence of many siblings may considerably increase the difficulty of the life struggle. Some siblings, we recognize, become bullies of the smaller and younger; while in other circumstances the latter may be coddled. The talents of some children in the family may be sacrificed to the needs or desires of others. Jealousy and rivalry may disrupt cordial relations and hinder the attainment of adequate personal and social adjustments both within and outside the family. Results such as these also require investigation in the study of the meaning of sibship.

Research Studies of Sibling Interaction

Sears has highlighted the two divergent but supplementary approaches to family study—the sociological and the psychological.[18] The former focuses on the family group, or portion of it, as a unit, recognizing that such entities have some properties that differentiate them from others—diverse structures of internal relationships, specified by roles, and contrasting status relations with others. The latter accepts the individual as focal and recognizes the family as a

[14] Walter Toman, "Family Constellation as a Basic Personality Determinant," *Journal of Individual Psychology*, **15** (November, 1959), p. 199.
[15] Walter Toman, *Family Constellation*, New York: Springer Publishing Company, Inc., 1961. In addition, he developed some "formulas of family constellation," suggesting how certain sibling relationships might be algebraically represented and quantified.
[16] A number of publications have been prepared for parents, teachers, and children to guide them in sibling relationships. For example, Edith G. Neisser, *Brothers and Sisters*, New York: Harper and Brothers, 1951; Frances Ullman, *Getting Along with Brothers and Sisters*, Chicago: Science Research Associates, 1950; and *Life with Brothers and Sisters*, Chicago: Science Research Associates, 1952.

[17] James H. S. Bossard and Eleanor S. Boll, *The Sociology of Child Development*, New York: Harper and Brothers, 1960, third edition, Chapter 5: "Interaction between Siblings," pp. 89–111; and in their "Security in the Large Family," *op. cit.*, pp. 529–544.
[18] Robert R. Sears, "Ordinal Position in the Family as a Psychological Variable," *American Sociological Review*, **15** (June, 1950), pp. 397–401.

social structure in which the individual is enmeshed and with which he interacts. The family functions as an environment for life and learning. The contributions of several investigators who have focused most sharply on *sibling interaction* will be reviewed.

Krout began by accepting the proposition that "the attempt to explain behavior in terms of non-psychological factors such as birth order is thoroughly futile." He classified siblings by "ordinal *positions*" rather than by mere birth order, desiring thereby to "emphasize psychological position in the family, resulting from certain types of social constellations." Utilizing birth intervals, family size, sex of subject, and sex of sibling preceding and following, he delineated 26 such sibship positions, 13 for each sex. His 1093 subjects all lived with two parents in 432 family groups, and a college student was at least one subject in each home. The questionnaire used in the research secured a complete roster of family members and contained 24 statements concerning intrafamily relations. From these data Krout derived a number of statistical relationships between personality traits and ordinal position.[19]

In a suggestive study, Paulette Cahn explored the use of a sociometric approach to sibling research. She found that preferences of siblings were most often directed to the youngest, except among children reared in institutions. Also, the strongest affective attitudes developed between siblings of corresponding sex.[20]

Davis and Northway observed five pairs of siblings during a period of five years. They hypothesized that "each child uses his sibling as a means of his own self-definition." In observing their differences, siblings may strengthen their relationships while yet each one can enhance his own individuality. The researchers' data supported their contention, and they were able to interpret the everyday behavior of the siblings in terms of the hypothesis.[21]

The most frequent contributor to the socio-psychological literature of statistical research concerned with sibling relationships appears to be Helen Koch. Her major research interest in this regard has been the effect on the personalities of children of various family constellation factors: sex of child, sex of sibling, ordinal position of child in sibship, and differences in age between subjects and their siblings. Her 498 subjects, half boys and half girls, averaged about six years of age, were enrolled in public and private Chicago schools, constituted the children in white, two-child families, were free from any known mental or physical disabilities, and resided in every case with both natural parents, who were native born. She divided her group into three sib-spacing levels; and each level was, in turn, divided into eight possible sibling patternings. Fels Child Behavior Rating Scales, the California Behavior Inventory for Nursery School Children, Children's Apperception Test (CAT), teachers' ratings, and interviews provided the data for the total inquiry. Her extensive findings have been published in numerous separate articles[22] and

[19] M. H. Krout, *op. cit.*, pp. 3–30.

[20] Paulette Cahn, "Experimentations Sociometriques Appliquees au Groupe Fraternal," (Sociometric Experiments on Groups of Siblings) *Cahiers International Sociologie*, **12** (1952), pp. 169–173; and in *Sociometry*, **15** (1952), pp. 306–310.

[21] Carroll Davis and Mary L. Northway, "Siblings—Rivalry or Relationship " *Bulletin of the Institute for Child Study*, **19**, 3 (Toronto, 1957), pp. 10–13.

[22] Helen L. Koch, "The Relationship of Primary Mental Abilities' in Five and Six-Year Olds to Sex of Child and Characteristics of His Sibling," *Child Development*, **25** (1954), pp. 209–223; "The Relation of Certain Family Constellation Characteristics and the Attitudes of Children toward Adults," *Child Development*, **26** (1955), pp. 13–40; "Some Personality Correlates of Sex, Sibling Position, and Sex of Sibling among Five and Six-Year-Old Children," *Genetic Psychology Monographs*, **52** (1955), pp. 3–50; "Attitudes of Young Children Toward Their Peers as Related to Certain Characteristics of Their Siblings," *Psychological Monographs*, **70** (1956), No. 426, 41 pages; "Sissiness and Tomboyishness in Relation to Sibling Characteristics," *Journal of Genetic Psychology*, **88** (1956), pp. 231–244; "Some Emotional Attitudes of the Young Child in Relation to Characteristics of His Sibling," *Child Development*, **27** (December, 1956), pp. 393–426; "Sibling Influence on Children's Speech," *Journal of Speech Disorders*, **21** (1956), pp. 322–328; "Children's Work Attitudes and Sibling Characteristics," *Child Development*, **27** (1956), pp. 289–310; "The Relation in Young Children between Characteristics of Their Playmates and Certain Attributes of Their Siblings," *Child Development*, **28** (1957), pp. 175–202; and "Der Einfluss der Geschwister auf die Persönlichkeitsentwicklung jungerer Knaben," (The Influence of Siblings on the Personality Development of Younger Boys), *Jb. Psychol. Psychother.*, **5** (1958), pp. 211–225.

have been even further analyzed by others.[23] The congruence of her findings in many regards led her to believe that the effects of sibling interactions were effectively being probed. She, more than many others, has studied personality traits within the context of sibling relationships and roles.

Brim has suggested three propositions regarding the development of sex roles, which he based on Koch's evidence:

One would predict that cross-sex, as compared with same-sex, siblings would possess more traits appropriate to the cross-sex role.

. . . one would predict that this effect would be more noticeable for the younger, as compared with the older, sibling in that the latter is more powerful and is more able to differentiate his own from his sibling's role.

. . . on the assumption that siblings close in age interact more than those not close in age, one would predict that this effect would be more noticeable for the siblings who are closest together in age.[24]

He found that the data supported the first two hypotheses, but provided little evidence for the third. He suggested that more varied configurations would develop in families with more than two children. For example, in a four-child setting, with a 3 to 1 sex split, the parents might be relatively more influential in helping the one to find his role. In a two-by-two division, cross-sex interaction among siblings might be relatively minimized.

Several investigators have stimulated interest in sibling interactions through their concern for the "large family" as a social structure. Ellis and Beechley utilized data from 1000 child guidance case histories to study the characteristics of individuals from "large families" (seven or more children) compared with those from "medium" (two to six children) and "small," one-child families.[25] Their subjects, of course, were not a representative sample of all children in the area but included those involved in adoption procedures and those with behavior, emotional, or other problems. They did produce evidence that family size may be an important variable in mental hygiene.

Bossard and Boll have discussed the contrasts between large and small families most.[26] In a first report, based upon a study of 25 large families of diverse background and involving 222 children, Bossard and Sanger introduced the concept of the "interacting size of the family."[27] There, they contended that almost every facet of family life tends to be different in the large family and that a quite different type of personality is fostered. In such a family, the group rather than the individual tends to be stressed. The larger the family becomes, the more internal organization develops, and dominance of some one or two persons appears. The large family typically involves greater specialization and multiplicity of roles and functions—greater complexity. Children in a large family system discipline each other, adjustments being made relatively more often to intra-family peers.

The study was expanded to include 879 children living in 100 large families of diverse background and having six or more living children. The information was secured over a six-year period from persons within the families through the use of questionnaires, nondirective interviews, and written family-life documents. One of the queries reported in the 1955 publication concerned the specialization of sibling roles as seen by the other sibling respondents—descriptions of brothers and sisters as fully as

---

[23] Orville G. Brim, Jr., "Family Structure and Sex Role Learning by Children: A Further Analysis of Helen Koch's Data," *Sociometry*, **21** (March, 1958), pp. 1–16.

[24] *Ibid.*, pp. 4–5.

[25] Albert Ellis and Robert M. Beechley, "A Comparison of Child Guidance Clinic Patients Coming from Large, Medium, and Small Families," *Journal of Genetic Psychology*, **79** (September, 1951), pp. 131–144.

[26] James H. S. Bossard and Eleanor S. Boll, "Security in the Large Family," *op. cit.*, pp. 529–544; "Personality Types in the Large Family," *Child Development*, **26** (March, 1955), pp. 71–78; "Adjustment of Siblings in Large Families," *American Journal of Psychiatry*, **112** (1956), pp. 889–892; and *The Large Family System*, Philadelphia: University of Pennsylvania Press, 1956.

[27] James H. S. Bossard and Winogene Sanger, "The Large Family System—A Research Report," *American Sociological Review*, **17** (February, 1952), pp. 3–9. Also Chapter 3: "Families by Size," pp. 47–67 in *The Sociology of Child Development*, *op. cit.*; and James H. S. Bossard, "Large and Small Families—A Study in Contrasts," *The Journal* of the American Society of Chartered Life Underwriters (Summer, 1959), pp. 221–241.

possible as personality types, Distilled from these data were eight general, composite types of personality roles, not all of which would be found in each family. Bossard and Boll point out that there are only a limited number of role choices available to a sibling, even in a large family. They suggest that each child tends to develop his or her role on the basis of, and in relation to, the roles which have already been preempted by others in the family.

An earlier study by Nye had indicated that adolescents from small families showed better relations with parents than did those from larger families.[28] Hawkes, Burchinal, and Gardner investigated the matter of adjustment further,[29] utilizing data from 256 fifth-grade children from rural areas and small towns in four Midwestern states, all of whom lived with both parents and had at least one sibling. These authors found, also, that children from the smaller families had more favorable relations to parents *and* to siblings than did those from larger families. Their data did not corroborate the notion that the large family atmosphere is more favorable to personality adjustment. However, the small number of respondents precluded the application of controls for socioeconomic class and other important variables.

Only recently, have family sociologists begun to focus their research interests directly and with more emphasis upon sibling interaction. From an area sample of households in Cleveland, Sussman secured information concerning the interactions among the adult siblings and between parents and their mature children for the nuclear families selected. He examined the functions of ceremonial occasions, interfamily visitations, and help and services exchanged. That study is a precursor for a longitudinal study of urban family networks, "an investigation of the quantity and type of aid exchanged in connection with the movements of the immediate family through the

life cycle."[30] Sussman believes that the notion of the atomized and isolated nuclear family is not being confirmed by empirical research findings.

In a somewhat similar study of randomly selected middle-class Boston families, Reiss also manifested interest in "the factors related to the frequency of interaction with extended kin and attitudes about the frequency of interaction."[31] He found that "females are in contact with relatives more than males, but males are in contact with in-laws more than are females." Further, he asserts:

As a consequence of this slight matrilineal tendency, interaction in those sibling relationships involving two sisters, or a brother and a sister, would be more frequent than that of two brothers. Paradoxically, . . . the families of siblings with least contact with each other are those of two brothers, the only ones with the same last name— a residue of our now defunct patrilineal tradition.[32]

Farber has presented interesting insights into the meaning that normal and retarded siblings can have for one another. In a monograph, he reported that normal girls who interacted frequently with retarded siblings were more often rated by their mothers as possessing more neurotic or negative traits than did other girls who did not have as frequent contact with the retarded child.[33] In a second report, he examined the "life goals" of 83 boys and girls, age 10–16, who lived with a retarded sibling.[34] He found that both boys and girls who interacted daily with such handicapped brothers and sisters showed less interest in goals related to success in personal relations.

[28] F. Ivan Nye, "Adolescent-Parent Adjustment: Age, Sex, Sibling Number, Broken Homes, and Employed Mother as Variables," *Marriage and Family Living*, **14** (November, 1952), p. 328.

[29] Glenn R. Hawkes, Lee Burchinal, and Bruce Gardner, "Size of Family and Adjustments of Children," *Marriage and Family Living*, **20** (February, 1958), pp. 65–68.

[30] Marvin B. Sussman, "The Isolated Nuclear Family: Fact or Fiction," *Social Problems*, **6** (Spring, 1959), pp. 333–340.

[31] Paul J. Reiss, "The Extended Kinship System: Correlates of and Attitudes on Frequency of Interaction," *Marriage and Family Living*, **24** (November, 1962), pp. 333–339.

[32] *Ibid.*, p. 334.

[33] Bernard Farber, "Family Organization and Crisis: Maintenance of Integration in Families with a Severely Mentally Retarded Child," *Monographs of the Society for Research in Child Development*, **25** (1960), No. 1 (Serial No. 75).

[34] Bernard Farber and William C. Jenné, "Interaction with Retarded Siblings and Life Goals of Children," *Marriage and Family Living*, **25** (February, 1963), pp. 96–98.

Both boys and girls who had sustained interaction with their retarded siblings ranked devotion to a worthwhile cause and making a contribution to mankind as high. Perhaps feeling that they are serving a welfare function in the family provides the frequent interactors with motivation to achieve in a welfare profession.[35]

His inquiry concluded with the suggestion that continual interaction with retarded siblings often may come to be considered as a duty by the normal children, and "in the performance of this duty, the normal sibling internalizes welfare norms and turns his life career toward the improvement of mankind or at least toward the achievement of goals which will require much dedication and sacrifice."

A perusal of the literature has not revealed any empirical study of sibling relations among and between stepchildren and the other children of "reconstituted" families. In the studies reviewed, stepchildren and those with half-sibling relations have almost always been excluded.

Factors Impeding Sibling Research

Thus far, social scientists have rarely attempted to conduct statistical studies to explore the significance that brothers and sisters have for each other. Why have there been so few investigations that would provide a "child's eye-view" of peer experiences within the family? Several influences operating together may account for the paucity of such research.

Parental Responsibility. In a society that traditionally has held parents responsible for the behavior, as well as the care and nurture, of their children, many of the concerns of the larger society for the health, education, and welfare of the younger generation tend to fix attention primarily upon the parent-child dimension. The dominance of adults and the dependence of children foster an adult-directed orientation. The social problems surrounding juvenile delinquency, school maladjustments, and infant and child health usually highlight the "vertical" adult or parent-child dimension.[36]

Freudian Thought. The initial impact and continued stress of Freudian thought upon family sociology have brought emphasis almost exclusively upon the importance for personality development of the regimes of the infancy period. Thereby, the significance of socialization influences later in childhood, youth, and adulthood—among them, interaction with siblings—has been minimized or even ignored. When Freudians have considered sibling interaction, "rivalry" was the relationship primarily or almost exclusively studied. In the psychoanalytic discussions of sex-role achievement and of the resolution of the Oedipal and other complexes, the parent-child affectional bonds or sex linkages are featured, with little attention paid to the part siblings can play in role-performance learning, knowledge dissemination, satisfaction of emotional needs, and other aspects of socialization.

Occupational Pressures. Family sociologists themselves have had certain types of problems both pressed upon, and open to, them because of the occupational roles in which they have been employed—usually as college teachers, sometimes as marriage counselors. The strong, immediate, and personal interests of students in dating, courtship, and mate-selection, and the imperious desires of husbands and wives for successful marital adjustment, brought principal attention of the occupation to *adult* perspectives. It would appear that marriage and family texts and marriage guidance manuals give little attention to the influence that siblings have upon each other. When children are considered at all, the materials in use would lead one to conclude that parents rear their children one at a time—or in separate compartments!

---

[35] *Ibid.*, p. 97.
[36] Those specialists who deal with these problems on a case-by-case basis have related to the *individual* children in therapy but have not often had the inclination, time, or competence to conduct research concerning *sibling groups* and their influence on the lives of such children, beyond a case study approach.

The specialists that have been professionally most concerned with youth in "the group," either as a functioning entity or a structure, have been the practitioners within agencies, the social group workers, or the researchers interested in sociometric. However, in either field, they have almost exclusively focused upon nonfamily peers, whether in "natural" gangs or in "fabricated" residential, class, or activity groups.

Primacy and Generality. It is understandable that the life stages which occur earlier and in the greatest proportion of instances within family cycles have received major attention. After all, the interaction of spouses can be studied whether or not the couple has children; and parent-child relations can be examined with regard to one or several youngsters. Siblings, as a family subgroup, are not universal to all households. And while the new experiences brought by the advent of a first child provide great challenges for adult adjustment and require major changes in the allocation of time and endeavor, from primarily adult relationships to heavily parent-child pursuits, the arrival of each additional child alters the established pattern less drastically.

Practical Problems. A number of practical problems present themselves to any who wish to study sibling interaction directly and statistically. Efforts to examine the effects of and changes in sibling interaction through time, as a function of age distribution and in varied social situations, would present extremely complex methodological problems. As an ideal design extended longitudinal research would be required. The inclusion of all children within families of a given sample would require the use of data collection techniques and an orientation of content that are appropriate to the diversity of response levels that are to be found among children of a wide age span. The very youngest cannot themselves talk or write but can be only communicated about. Except for relatively small families in the "middle-range" of the cycle, some siblings will not yet have been born, while others will have left home and would be difficult to question directly.

Furthermore, a very considerable number of child subjects from a large number of families would be required for statistical studies of all but the smallest families. Also, the increasing prevalence of remarriages involving children introduces complicating subgroups among them —the relations between step, half, and full siblings. Too, as *sibling groups*, children are not as physically accessible or as socially amenable to study as they are as *separate individuals* enrolled in public school or college classrooms or as *members of gangs* or other age and sex-graded

peer groups. Moreover, in any given interacting sibling cluster, but a few individuals comprise the group. Finally, with the increased participation of mothers in the working force and their delegation of child care to age-graded nurseries and kindergartens, siblings become separated at earlier ages and in greater numbers than ever before. (The effect which such institutionalization of child care has upon sibling ties in childhood and later life warrants study.)

Attenuation of Kinship. Extended kinship ties are recognized and stressed in typical folk societies, with the consequent privileges and responsibilities involving a wide variety of relatives. In modern, urban societies, the nuclear family of orientation and, after marriage, one's own nuclear family of procreation, are the two small centers of kinship that function as the principal sources of emotional satisfaction and areas of responsibility within the family and kin group. How much of the mutual affection, associations, and shared values of the family in which persons grow up carry over into the sibling relations within adult life? Although there has been some research interest in the relation of adult children to their aging parents, the strength, continuity, and nature of ties among adult siblings in our society have been given almost no attention. Sometimes the retention of contacts between aging parent(s) and their adult child(ren)—the intergenerational vertical dimension—serves to stimulate continuing lateral relationships among the now-independent adult siblings. Yet among certain segments of our society, the maintenance of separate households, mobility and impersonality of a mass society, and relative solitariness have submerged or attenuated even those kinship bonds, making direct research contacts often difficult.

Age of Researchers. Although it is neither required, nor feasible, that one must *be* a child to study children, the interplay of youngsters within the home may have been neglected, in part and inadvertently, because of the age differential between scholars and their young subjects. Aspects of childlife that seem insignificant to adults may loom as prominent features for children, and conversely.

If the younger generation were to conduct inquiries concerning family life, their perception of the members' roles would likely be quite different. The museum examples of household rooms, constructed to fit the eye-level perspective of young children, suggest how a "view from below" might considerably alter the assessment of the relative importance of parental, sibling, and peer influences. The parent generation cannot help but be somewhat "adultomorphic" in its perceptions, forgetting the important roles that siblings played in their own childhood.

Sex of Researchers. Finally, traditional sex roles have militated against research regarding siblings. In our society children are cared for predominantly by women—whether they be mothers, activity club leaders, grammar school instructors, or Sunday School teachers—whereas trained research investigators have generally been men. Those who have been most intimately associated with children have usually not been those who have been analytical in their concerns. The child psychologists have more frequently combined these interests and talents than have the family sociologists. Admittedly, it is difficult and unusual to embody strong nurturing and research roles simultaneously in the same persons. However, the specialization of the sexes has resulted in few persons of either sex securing facility with both child-serving and knowledge-building activities. Thus far, those who have been most aware of sibling interaction have tended not to be those who would be prone to study it, and vice versa.

Conclusions

A more adequate understanding of the socialization processes within childhood requires research concerning sibling interaction. The influences of brothers and/or sisters upon each other during adolescence need recognition and examination as significant factors both for personality development and social control. And in a civilization wherein numerous societal mechanisms have replaced earlier kin functions, the importance that continuation of family sentiments and contacts may have for the lives of adult and aged "children" might be profitably studied.

Chapter 5

Courtship and Availability for Marriage

This chapter discusses the relationship between courtship practices and marital norms. Social relations between a pair of individuals cannot be expected to change abruptly merely because legal or religious authority has defined that relationship as a marriage. Moreover, unmarried individuals generally continue to use the same courtship practices even when they change partners. There appears to be a continuity established in the formation of cross-sex social relations associated with courtship and later with marriage.

In those societies in which adult males and females spend most of their leisure time as well as work time in same-sex groups, premarital relationships between the sexes are marked by formality, and steps are taken to prevent intimacy in courtship. This situation occurs frequently in unilineal (especially patrilineal) societies. For example, in Latin countries the chaperone system has been developed to restrict intimacy between young men and women. In the old Chinese extended-family system, strong ties were required between agnatic relatives (i.e., members of the male line), and a son's wife was more involved with her mother-in-law and fellow sisters-in-law, who were outside the agnatic group, than with her husband. Indeed, the choice of marriage partners by parents rather than by the participants requires a separation of males and females before marriage. If premarital etiquette between the sexes is perpetuated throughout the life cycle, considerable formality and separateness in the husband-wife relationship may be expected. This lack of intimacy operates to prevent conflict in relationships in which sustained interaction between kinship groups is desired.

Demands for continuity and orderly replacement of family and values from one generation to the next in unilineal kinship systems require careful selection of mates to fill parent-spouse roles. If the individual who marries into the lineage does not conform to traditional family practices, he may disrupt the entire system of property ownership, inheritance, status structure, and personal identification which justify continued existence of the lineage. It is important therefore for particular members of the lineage to supervise selection of mates and to enforce conformity to existing practices. The individual's competence as a mate-lover has no significance for the continuity of the lineage, for these roles refer to a personal relationship and do not affect the lineage. A primary responsibility of the lineage-official (e.g., the maternal uncle in a matrilineage; the patriarch in a patrilineage) is to supervise conformity to spouse-parent roles rather than to mate-lover roles. Lineage continuity thus requires certain kin to participate in mate selection, using criteria for spouse-parent roles and assigning less importance to mate-lover roles.

Although mate-lover roles are considered less important than spouse-parent roles in unilineal societies, they are nevertheless included in the set of marital roles. Because of this inclusion, only persons who are eligible to assume spouse-parent roles with one another can be lovers or mates either inside or outside of marriage. For persons ineligible to marry to have sexual intercourse would violate the set of marital roles in the society and threaten the existence of the lineage. (See Goody paper in Chapter 2.)

The role of the "lineage" changes in bilateral kinship systems with regard to formation and continued existence of a particular nuclear family. First, although membership in a unilineal group is defined by a single direct ancestor in each generation, "lineage" membership in bilateral kinship doubles with each generation of ancestors. This situation precludes the restriction of goods, real estate, personnel, or rituals as the inheritance property of an identifiable lineage. There is little motivation for close supervision of marriage and nuclear-family relations using criteria of parent-spouse adequacy. Second, if both the husband's and wife's kin have the same rights and obligations (as suggested in Chapter 4), no specific relative can be expected to supervise the marital or nuclear-family relationships of an individual. Moreover, because there is no lineage property (even if there were a responsible relative), the relative cannot invoke sanctions concerning an individual's rights to this property. Hence motivation for lineage maintenance is inhibited, and lineage supervision of marriage and nuclear-family relations cannot be maintained effectively in a bilateral kinship system.

Without regulation of marital and nuclear-family practices by lineages, emphasis on traditional parent-spouse roles in the family declines. Rigorous conformity to these roles is not required in bilateral kinship nor is marriage to persons with similar conceptions of parent-spouse roles necessary. Restrictions on cultural or ethnic group membership for eligible mates tend to disappear.

As the importance of the parent-spouse roles declines in bilateral kinship, the mate-lover roles increase in relative significance. The mate-lover roles become the primary basis for marriage, and the spouse-parent roles become the means for maintaining them. Greater emphasis on mate-lover roles implies less emphasis on sustaining patterns of norms and values over generations. The stress is on the more immediate gains and accommodations in a personal relationship. Consequently, courtship and marital relations must involve the attunement of the boy and girl to their common needs and interests as well as the development of skills that will enable them to disengage from one another when their interests and needs change.

Because the primary criterion for establishing a marriage is adequate performance of the mate-lover roles, as long as an individual is able to fulfill these roles, he is eligible for marriage or remarriage. There is no necessity to maintain a marriage for lineage reasons, and an individual is free to form a new marriage at will. He thus becomes permanently available for marriage regardless of his current marital status.[1]

Of course, continuity in society would be impossible if permanent availability operated without restriction. This restriction is found in the conservative nature of the family and kinship. The kinship system acts to de-emphasize the mate-lover roles in mate selection and also provides support during periods of marital stress and crisis.

Emphasis on the mate-lover roles in marriage in a bilateral kinship requires a courtship system that prepares the youth of the society for this kind of marital relationship. In contemporary society premarital male-female relationships are often fragile. They emphasize marital selection for mate-lover roles rather than parent-spouse roles. The current practice is for young individuals to experience a series of relationships defined as "going steady." The study by Burgess and Wallin of 1,000 engaged couples indicated that many of the couples had been previously engaged.[2] About one fourth of the men and one third of the women reported former engagements. In addition, about 15 per cent of the couples in the study subsequently broke their engagements.[3] According to Burgess and Wallin, the reasons for broken engagements can be classified into five categories: (a) slight emotional attachment, (b) extended separation of the couple, (c) parental opposition, (d) differences in cultural norms and values, and (e) personality problems. The comparable fragility of marital relationships is indicated by the current high divorce rate in the United States.

Courtship relationships are not only fragile, they also tend to be intimate. This intimacy is reflected in affectional and sexual interaction. The extent of premarital intercourse with potential marriage partners has been increasing steadily,[4] just as there has been a rise in the illegitimate birth rate.[5] The continuity of this trend towards the development of fragile and intimate nonmarital cross-sex relations after marriage is also indicated by the reported increase in adultery.

The norm of going steady or becoming engaged a number of times has important implications for courtship and marriage. For example, the termination of each steady relationship requires skill in breaking off and in initiating a new relationship. In his article on "cooling out the mark" Goffman has suggested that male-female relationships involve not only courting to develop a relationship but also decourting to break off the relationship. He suggests that skills are developed in decourting as well as in courting.[6] More generally, societies in which permanent availability predominates show the following trends: (a) increase in expected remarriage during the course of a

[1] Permanent availability for marriage is discussed more fully in Bernard Farber, *Family: Organization and Interaction*, San Francisco: Chandler, 1964, esp. Chapter 4, "A Conceptual Model of the Contemporary Family," pp. 103–133.

[2] Ernest W. Burgess and Paul Wallin, *Engagement and Marriage*, New York: Lippincott, 1953.

[3] *Ibid.*, p. 273.

[4] Ira L. Reiss, "The Double Standard in Premarital Sexual Intercourse," *Social Forces*, **34** (1956), pp. 224–230; Alfred C. Kinsey, et al., *Sexual Behavior in the Human Female*, Philadelphia: Saunders, 1953.

[5] U.S. Department of Health, Education and Welfare, *Vital Statistics of the United States: 1959*, Volume I, p. 3–29.

[6] Erving Goffman, "On Cooling the Mark Out: Some Aspects of Adaptation to Failure," in Arnold M. Rose (ed.), *Human Behavior and Social Processes*, Boston: Houghton Mifflin, 1962, pp. 482–505.

lifetime, (b) decline in premarital chastity as a value, (c) lessened effect of children as a deterrent to divorce,[7] and (d) increased emphasis on maintaining personal attractiveness even after marriage.[8]

The concept of permanent availability assumes that both divorce and marriage have ambivalent connotations in a society. Otherwise, the sequence of marriage-divorce-remarriage could not occur. If the divorced state (in which the person engages in active courtship) were always valued over marriage, no one would ever marry or remarry. Similarly, if the married state were always valued over divorce, no marriages would be dissolved. However, if both divorce and marriage have ambivalent meanings, the individual can alternate in choosing one or the other in appropriate situations. Divorce in general must be regarded as undesirable because it interferes with efforts to maintain marital integration and with tendencies toward orderly replacement of family values in the succeeding generation. However, in specific instances in which marital integration is lacking, the marriage becomes a situation of forced participation and divorce is then desirable. This ambivalent view permits both a positive valuation of marriage and the permanent availability of adult members of the society for future courtship and remarriage.

Readings on Courtship and Availability for Marriage

Patterns in courtship and divorce are understood as integral aspects of patterns of family life when they are discussed in relation to lineage and family role. In his paper on courtship in modern Ghana, Omari indicates how the courtship process has been modified as emphasis on lineage and traditional family forms has declined.

In the second paper Heer shows how changing ideas about religion have influenced marital practices in Canada. Over a period of thirty-five years there has been an increasing amount of religious intermarriage. The rate probably reflects a reduction in authoritarianism within family life, a trend that may also be related to norms regarding divorce. There is a tendency for persons who intermarry to have a higher divorce rate than those who marry within their own religion.[9] Moreover, children of parents who have intermarried are more likely to marry a person of a different religion than are those whose parents married within their own religious group.[10] The decline of religious endogamy can thus be regarded as a part of the general trend in family life toward mate selection on the basis of mate-lover rather than parent-spouse roles. This trend is consistent with bilateral kinship systems and permanent availability for marriage.

[7] The number of families with children involved in divorce has increased steadily. In 1953, about 45.5 per cent of divorces granted involved families with children. The percentage grew to 50.9 in 1957 and to 60.3 in 1961. U.S. Public Health Service, *Vital Statistics of the United States*, 1961, Volume III, p. 3–14.

[8] See Farber, *op. cit.*, pp. 113–120.

[9] Lee G. Burchinal and Loren E. Chancellor, "Survival Rates Among Types of Religiously Homogamous and Interreligious Marriage, Iowa, 1953–1959," *Social Forces*, **41** (1963), pp. 353–362; Judson T. Landis, "Marriages of Mixed and Non-Mixed Religious Faith," *American Sociological Review*, **14** (1949), pp. 401–407. See also Jerold Heiss, "Interfaith Marriage and Marital Outcome," *Marriage and Family Living*, **23** (1961), pp. 228–233.

[10] Milton L. Barron, *People Who Intermarry*, Syracuse: Syracuse University Press, 1946.

The paper by Lowrie indicates how far the courtship career of individuals in the United States has become a series of "steady" relationships with intervening periods of "playing the field." His study indicates that a norm of "going steady" has developed among young adolescents. Lowrie points out the social conditions which influence courtship careers.

The fourth paper in this chapter, by Michal McCall, discusses various changes in courtship and marriage interaction over the last several generations. She describes courtship as a bargaining process and suggests that the system of permanent availability eliminates the need for separate bargains concerning eligibility for marriage, conditions for maintaining the courtship, and conditions for entering marriage. To the extent that traditional restrictions on social status, religion, ethnic-group membership, and race decline as criteria for establishing eligibility for marriage, bargaining over these characteristics becomes unnecessary. Under conditions of permanent availability, courtship differs from marriage mainly in degree of involvement or temporal closeness rather than in kinds of norms governing the relationship. Because the difference is primarily quantitative rather than qualitative, there need be no separate bargains over conditions for maintaining the courtship as opposed to conditions for marriage.

The paper by Goode presents data from his study of 425 Detroit women in their twenties and thirties who, in 1948, had been divorced less than 26 months. Although these results reflect the situation existing shortly after World War II, they indicate the kinds of practices and resources prevalent in modern urban society for maintaining a system of divorce and remarriage.

14. Role Expectation in the Courtship Situation in Ghana

BY T. PETER OMARI

THE QUESTION OF WHO MARRIES WHOM and the basis for selection have been of sustained interest to sociologists interested in the scientific study of the family. Theories have centered around two types of explanations—homogamy and heterogamy. One stresses that like seeks like; the other, that opposites attract. From the work of Hollingshead[1] and Reeves[2] we can predict that men are more likely to marry women similar to themselves with respect to race, religion, ethnic grouping, social class, and age group than they are to marry women who differ from themselves in these social characteristics. But from the work of Koller[3] and others who have studied the relation between mate-selection and propinquity, we can say there is some evidence, too, to support the view that men will tend to marry women who live near them rather than those whose residences are remote.

Of more recent vintage is Robert Winch's theory of complementary needs[4] which is further amplified upon by Thomas and Virginia Ktsanes in their article, "The Theory of Complementary Needs in Mate-Selection."[5] This theory states that "in mate-selection each individual seeks within his or her field of eligibles for that person who gives the greatest promise of providing him or her with maximum need gratification." In other words, personality needs of marriage partners tend to be complementary rather than necessarily similar.

It is often a valid criticism of many research findings in sociology that these are Western oriented and that replication in non-Western societies is a desirable goal.[6] In this respect this article is intended to make a modest contribution. It is not an attempt to prove or disprove Winch's theory nor is it intended to test the hypothesis. In a society in which individual choice of mate in

SOURCE: Social Forces, *Volume 27 (1962), pp. 245–250. Reprinted with permission of the University of North Carolina Press.*

[1] August B. Hollingshead, "Cultural Factors in the Selection of Mates," *American Sociological Review*, **15** (1950), pp. 619–627.

[2] R. J. R. Kennedy, "Single and Triple Melting-Pot? Inter-Marriage Trends in New Haven, 1870–1950," *American Journal of Sociology*, **58** (July, 1952), pp. 56–59, (September, 1952), p. 201.

[3] M. R. Koller, "Residential and Occupational Propinquity," *American Sociological Review*, **13** (October, 1948), pp. 613–616.

[4] See Robert F. Winch, *The Modern Family*, New York: Holt, Rinehart, and Winston, 1952, pp. 209–213.

[5] In Robert F. Winch and Robert McGinnis, *Marriage and the Family*, New York: Holt, Rinehart, and Winston, 1953, pp. 435–453.

[6] See Robert M. Marsh, "Training For Comparative Research in Sociology," *American Sociological Review*, **27** (1962), pp. 147–149 in which report he concludes, "Ideally, if sociology is truly 'the science of society,' then the best studies in any given subfield (e.g. stratification, formal organization) should as likely be based upon data from other major societies as upon U.S. data."

Table 1

Distribution of sample of students, by sex and by age

Sex	Total		17–20		21–24		25–28		29 or more	
	No.	Per cent	No.	Per cent	No.	Per cent	No.	Per cent	No.	Per cent
Total	292	100	86	29	140	48	47	16	19	7
Male	142	100	36	25	59	42	30	21	17	12
Female	150	100	50	35	81	54	17	1	2	—

the marital situation has been negligible and discouraged, the first attempt should be directed toward an examination of the trend toward individual choice. Properly, therefore, this paper is directed at an examination of the extent to which young people in Ghana are aware of future needs in their selection of a marital partner. Propinquity is here seen not as a complete theory of mate selection on the Ghanaian scene, but as an aspect of the need for belonging and perhaps as an indication of the extent to which individuals are still willing to submit to long established traditions. The whole theory of complementary needs, as well as associated theories of mate selection, presupposes that there is a rational basis for marital selection and that the individual is the final judge of whom he or she will marry. We shall not be testing sharply defined hypotheses in this paper: my role at the moment is one of exploration.

Source of Data. This is the second report on a study designed to gain insight into the trend of change in the marital institution in Ghana.[7] It is based upon interviews with 142 male and 150 female secondary school and Teacher Training College students who were in their final year of studies and who represent a cross-section of the "emancipated"[8] youth of Ghana. The inter-

[7] See T. Peter Omari, "Changing Attitudes of Students in West African Society Toward Marriage and Family Relationships," *The British Journal of Sociology*, XI (September, 1960), 197–210.

[8] For a definition of the "emancipated Ghanaian" see T. Peter Omari, *Marriage Guidance for Young Ghanaians*, Edinburgh: Thomas Nelson and Sons, Ltd., 1962, p. 5. "This is the individual who because of his education, cultural background and interests, has come face-to-face with the problem of reconciling traditional practices with Western institutions. It is

viewing itself was done in 1957. The sample falls within the age-group, 17–31, the mode being between 21 and 24. It will be noted also (see Table 1) that the male students are much older, on the average, than the female students, about a quarter of the males being twenty-five or over, whereas less than 2 per cent of the females were in this age group.

The traditional Ghanaian family structure has not permitted individual choice in the selection of a mate. Since the parents of the young adolescent have sought a partner for him or for her, personal tastes have been irrelevant for the success of a marriage. With increasing facilities for education, through such mass media as the cinema, foreign magazines, books, and the local press, as well as the local women's organizations, a new awareness is being created which promises to have profound repercussions on the traditional method of mate selection. The "emancipated" Ghanaian's attitude is considered to be expressed by the results of this study.

Modern Trends in Courtship

From the moment the young Ghanaian enters secondary school, a profound change comes over him. He is not yet an "intellectual" but he knows he is going to become one and feels he cannot "go native" in many ways. For example

this type of individual who would wish to court or be courted, question parental interference in the choice of a mate, be married, for instance, by the civil Marriage Ordinance, maintain a conjugal family, go to night clubs and dances or to the cinema for entertainment. It is also he who is apt to disregard or pay little attention to established traditional practices."

he considers himself adult and wishes to be allowed a certain amount of independent action in many things not the least of which is in inter-sex relations. He likes to have his own room when he returns home on vacation—a situation not easily reconcilable with the fact that his parents may be poor and cannot oblige him with such a luxury. He likes to have the freedom of entertaining friends of the opposite sex and must do so under various guises if an open avenue is not available to him. The farm is most unsuitable for his new status; the cinemas and the night clubs are a more favorable haunt and offer an opportunity for social and cultural expression. If he lives in the capital city, Accra, he probably goes to the *Metropole*—a night club for young-sters—every other Friday. That he may come from a rural town is no hindrance to the acqui-sition of these pleasures nowadays since cinemas and night clubs are to be found in the most re-mote areas of the country. Parental supervision is generally limited to expressions of disapproval. A university education, of course, serves to con-firm much of his secondary school notions of himself, his relationship with his family and his friends. Many college students have returned to their villages to live in public resthouses rather than share the uncomfortable but familiar crowded bed of the family house.

At secondary school, if he happens to be in a boarding school, his contacts with members of the opposite sex are limited. But if he had not had one before, and he is in a mixed boarding school, he begins to be preoccupied with the acquisition of a girl friend and the girl also ac-quires a boy friend or, at least, learns how to do

so. Since secondary school is generally away from the home town and from parental control, the young boy or girl often gets his or her first opportunity there of meeting other young people from different parts of the country and of making his own assessment of their relative suitability as marital partners independent of parental pres-sures or traditional ethnocentricism.

Traditional attitudes and parental preach-ments about marriage within the tribal group begin to run counter to the liberal education at these institutions. Very often the mere novelty of befriending a boy or girl from a different tribal group has had a great deal of appeal for many more so than any desire to follow through with the friendship into marriage. But the ex-perience is often the beginning of much parent-youth conflict in mate-selection in Ghana. This type of conflict, at this time, is more personal than social in that it is largely confined to the occasional student who wishes to take his newly acquired sense of liberalism too far, in the eyes of parents.

Significance of Propinquity, Ethnicity and School subculture

Quite a number of the students in the sample, 35 per cent had friends from the same town as themselves while the friends of an additional 32 per cent were from the same state or tribal group (see Table 2). Only 33 per cent of the students in the sample had friends from other than the same state or tribe (17 per cent had met friends at school, and 16 per cent elsewhere

Table 2

Students' response to where boy or girl friends come from, by age

Age	Where boy or girl friends come from									
	Total		Same town		Same state or tribe		Met at school		Other	
	No.	Per cent	No.	Per cent	No.	Per cent	No.	Per cent	No.	Per cent
Total	292	100	102	35	94	32	50	17	46	16
17–20	86	100	31	36	16	19	19	22	20	23
21–24	140	100	53	38	45	32	25	18	17	12
25 & over	66	100	18	27	33	50	5	9	9	14

χ^2: 21.09, 6 *d.f.*, $P < .01$; The same is not correlated with sex.

but not of the same tribe or state). This of course does not mean that the distributions at the time of marriage would follow a similar pattern. For example only 40 per cent of the sample students who had friends at the time of the study (32 per cent of the total) had any intention of marrying their current friends. The remainder stated they were sure of getting married to someone else (6 per cent), or were uncertain as to whether they would marry their friends or some other person they had yet to meet (54 per cent).

The fact that only 19 per cent between seventeen and twenty years say "same state or tribe" while 36 per cent say "same town" is significant; also that 50 per cent of the "25 and over" age group say "same state or tribe" while only 27 per cent of this age group respond to the "same town" category is also significant. Comparison between the two columns, "same state or tribe" and "met at school," also yields significant results (see Table 2).

Many adolescent love affairs in the secondary schools and the Training Colleges are carried out in secrecy but generally openly at home during vacations. At this time the girl begins to read as much as possible about love and sex, and the boy acquires much of his knowledge through discussions with other boys and through experimentation. H. Rider Haggard is easily the favorite intellectual fare for both sexes at this age even as after boarding school days.

Increasing Role of Love Affairs among Adolescents. Many young people in Ghana are actively taking the initiative in various fields of endeavor. Not the least of these enterprising realms is that of love. The tendency for the freely chosen mate is definitely on the increase. One of the reasons may be due to the inceasing role of the young in economic matters and increase in level of education, as well as the increasing role of the youth in the political field. A combination of these factors has produced the young Ghanaian who is as independent in his thinking as in occupational and economic pursuits. Not only does he like to give his name to his children, but the young Ghanaian husband also wants to look after his own children rather than to entrust their upbringing to the uncle or some other member of the family as tradition has generally demanded

in the past among the majority of the people. The Ghanaian woman is no less independent than the male. As the author has noted in a previous article, "those who have observed the active role of women in their social, political and economic development can appreciate the fact that as go the women, so goes Ghana."[9] This holds true in the realm of adolescent love.

Consistent with traditional expectations, men take the initiative in the acquisition of "friends." Traditionally, the woman who played an active role in the courtship situation was considered "cheap," and is still considered so in traditional society. But the young adolescent woman is increasingly becoming active in this sphere. Even though there is a significant relationship between sex and whether or not the young person would take the initiative in love affairs (see Table 4), the number of women who would take the initiative (in response to the statement "if I saw a person I wanted to marry or with whom I came to fall in love, and if he/she did not make any effort to attract my attention") is socially significant (20 per cent) in view of the fact that a decade or two ago this same question might not have elicited any response in the affirmative at all. And it is not known whether the 26 per cent of the women who would "wait for awhile" before deciding, would take the initiative or not (it can safely be assumed in view of certain other data revealed through this study, that in these matters, the young Ghanaian woman is likely to take an active measure when actually presented with the situation, rather than a passive one). In any event, only 54 per cent of the women definitely stated they would not do anything at all in such a situation.

Parental Role in the Courtship Situation. The average young Ghanaian does not feel his parents should interfere unduly when it comes to his choice of a courtship or dating partner—even when it comes to the choice of a marriage partner. Asked what they would do if their parents objected to their choice of marital partners, 41 per cent of the sample said they would obey their parents but as many as 24 per cent stated that they would disobey them, and 31 per cent were undecided. The women were more inclined

[9] *Ibid.*, p. 208.

to be obedient in this respect than the men ($P < .001$). Eighty-four per cent of those who said they would obey were also those of the sample with "friends" at the time of the study, while those who never had a "friend" before and those who "once had 'friends' but not at the time of the study" together constituted 52 per cent of the group which said they would disobey their parents ($P < .001$). Over half of the men (56 per cent) and an almost equally high proportion of women (54 per cent) either said they would disobey or were uncertain.

Instead of accepting the idea of marriage being negotiated by parents on behalf of their children, there is now a strong tendency for young people themselves to wish to go through this procedure unaided. This has been accelerated by the fact that young people can now go out on dates and enter into courtships with or without parental knowledge and consent. Dating is not courtship; but the system of dating generally leads to the emancipation of the young from parental control of the process of mate selection. Likewise, courtship does not always result in marriage but it is nevertheless the basic step in the selection of a mate in "emancipated" societies. It is therefore significant for our analysis that 83 per cent of the sample who had ever had boy or girl friends acquired them by their own efforts and without assistance from any source. This is in comparison with only 6 per cent and 10 per cent whose friends had been arranged for them by their parents and "others" respectively. Twice as many females as males said they would let parents or someone else pick their friends for them.

Not only has parental influence been undermined in this respect, but the men would go further and disregard much of the traditional family ties—extended family relationships—in favor of a much stronger tie with the wife. A conjugal family with less interference from relatives is a much desired goal for many of the male students. Asked about the truth of the statement, "In a crisis most brothers or sisters would take sides with their sisters or brothers against their wives or husbands" (a statement which was intended to reveal their own biases and sentiments on the subject), 41 per cent of the men as compared with 50 per cent of the women said

they would. Fifty-nine per cent of the men and 44 per cent of the women would rather stick by their wives and husbands respectively, against their kinsfolk.

Enters Cupid. One of the benefits of the traditional system of courtship through intermediaries was that it relieved anxiety on the part of the young suitor. Parents and friends did the "shopping around" and selected a good prospective bride for a dutiful son. Marriage and sex were utilitarian devices for the perpetuation of the family and a means toward economic emancipation. The traditional husband found himself with a wife. According to one very elderly man, "My mother said the homeliest women were the most hardworking and helpful and made the best wives. So she looked around and found me a woman no other man would care to seduce; and that is my wife over there. I must say that she worked very hard for me and enabled me to acquire much of the wealth I have today." Such a fatalistic attitude is almost entirely lacking among the youth of Ghana today. Letters like the one produced below, are frequently found in the local papers and attest to the direction of change in this respect:[10]

I love a young man. He also wants me to be married to him. He earns a good salary, has a car and can provide a home. He says he loves me, and he certainly behaves as such because he never looks at any other girl. When I was in the hospital he visited me many times until my discharge.

But all the same, I feel there is something missing. He never says sweet things to me and does not like discussing love affairs with me. This upsets me. Do you think our marriage will be a happy one?

Whereas in grandfather's time he was lucky if he was permitted any opinion as to whom he would rather marry, today young men and women in Ghana not only want to arrogate to themselves the sole prerogative of this choice but are inclined not to welcome even parental advice on the subject. Grandmother, of course, had nothing to say about these things. She did not

[10] From the author's collection of letters sent for solution in the various publications in West Africa. This one first appeared in the *Sunday Mirror* of Accra, and has been reproduced in the author's *Marriage Guidance for Young Ghanaians, op. cit.,* p. 14.

know anything about "love," and never expected her husband to say sweet things to her. She knew she had to get along with the man—for her own happiness, and for the happiness of her family, which had taken "head money" on her. Above all, she was grateful to the man and served him for the care he took of her and *her* children (the children are traditionally not the man's in matrilineal society). "Love" then was a post-factum development, not a prior perceptive experience as must be the case today.

But the ephemeral paraphenalia of courtship seem to be an obvious requirement for marriage these days. When individual choice of marriage partner supersedes parental choice, immature considerations come to the fore. This is necessarily so since the adolescent mind is relatively immature and is easily distracted by events of the moment and the trivialities of youth. Love, as vaguely as they may define it, comes to play an ever increasing part in the courtship situation. An examination of these practices therefore becomes of great significance to those who wish to fully understand the changes taking place.

Of our sample, not very many had any clear-cut idea as to what he or she meant by the word, love. (As a matter of fact who is so erudite as to know?) But almost everyone seemed to have some idea about it. Eighty per cent of the sample said that when it came to marrying, "love" would be a most important factor in their choice of a mate. The girls were more concerned with the phenomenon of "love" than the men, however ($P < .01$), but age has a low-level correlation with this phenomenon also ($P < .05$).

The Kissing Game. With the introduction of love into the courtship process, marriage partners in Ghana are being chosen not only from the utilitarian point of view but for the personal happiness response. Marriage is getting away from being a union between families as was the case before. The period of courtship is not being used only for discriminative selection of a marriage partner but also for ego-involvement. Among the activities indulged in is "kissing" (a very unorthodox practice on the African scene). Kissing (on the lips) is a relatively new innovation in the courtship situation in Ghana and is only prevalent in the present generation. The head-mistress of a girls' secondary school who was expected to be up to date on such matters said in 1956, "Why waste your time asking questions about kissing from these girls? Kissing may be practiced in America but here in this country it is unknown. We don't kiss. Most of us don't even know about it or don't like it. It is unhygienic."

Of the sample under discussion, three-fourths reported that they "had kissed or had been kissed before." Only one-fourth reported no previous experience with it. The girls have had more experience with kissing than the men ($P < .01$). The students who "have" or "have had" boy or girl friends at the time of the study were more likely to have kissed before (78 per cent as compared with only 43 per cent of those who had never had boy or girl friends; $P < .01$). (See also Table 3 below.) Although only 32 per cent of the total sample professed to have learned to kiss from books, 57 per cent who "had never

Table 3

Mode of experience with kissing by sex of students

Sex	Total		Books		Cinema		Female friend		Male friend	
	No.	Per cent	No.	Per cent	No.	Per cent	No.	Per cent	No.	Per cent
Total	292	100	94	32	88	30	65	22	45	16
Male	142	100	38	27	54	38	43	30	7	5
Female	150	100	56	37	34	23	22	15	38	25

The relationship between sex and mode of acquiring experience with kissing is statistically significant: $\chi^2 = 35.20$: $P < .01$.

had a boy or girl friend" said they learned from this source.

It may be asked (from a glimpse of Table 3) in what way do girls teach other girls to kiss. Does this indicate homosexualism among the 20 per cent who acquired their knowledge from members of the same sex? We cannot say that this is any indication of homosexual tendencies any more than we can impute similar motives to boys dancing with other boys, or girls dancing with other girls—a scene to be found everywhere in Ghana, sometimes even in the night clubs and social centers. On the other hand teaching how to kiss could be on the verbal level only; as it probably is in the case of most men in this category. But it does point to a practice among all-female schools and even among the female students of mixed boarding schools, in which the more senior female students take "lovers" or what they call "*me* my dear" from among the junior female students of the same sex.

In some of the more established girls' secondary schools in Ghana, as even in Nigeria and in other West African countries, it is an internally accepted practice for a senior girl to have a "my dear." The junior "my dear" is supposed to

(and generally does) provide the senior one with the services of a lover short of the sex act itself. These include washing of clothing, making of the bed, running errands, making "love" to and sharing bed with her when the senior partner wants the junior one to do so. If this practice is not to be called homosexualism it is only because this is essentially an adolescent subculture of the boarding school which is most often done in fun. Affection for the girl "lover" is easily and readily transferred to men when school is in recess and at the end of boarding school days.

The Love Object and Role Expectation. If the young Ghanaian is to enter into marriage without any assistance from relatives as to whom he or she could marry, is he generally aware of what marital needs are, and what does he look for in a prospective partner? It is true that a large proportion of young people claim to wish to be in love before they marry. Is love expressed in terms of something concrete through expectations, is this state of euphoria confined to the courtship days, or is it carried through into marriage? In other words when it comes to getting married

Table 4

Rank order of desirable characteristics of a mate: sample secondary school students in Ghana*

The men wanted their wives to be:			The women wanted their husbands to be:
Educated, intelligent	1	1	Of dependable character, polite
Hardworking, ambitious	2	2	Kind, understanding
Obedient, patient, humble	3	3	Sociable, of cheerful disposition
Beautiful, good looking	4	4	Educated, intelligent
Sociable, of cheerful personality	5	5	Faithful, constant, trustworthy
Of dependable character, polite	6	6	Obedient, patient, humble
Very fond of children or family	7	7	Very fond of children or family
Kind, understanding	8	8	Moderate drinker or smoker†
Faithful, constant, trustworthy	9	9	Religious, Christian
In love with me, affectionate	10	10	In love with me, affectionate
Clean, neat, healthy	11	11	Handsome, good looking
Of good standing	12	12	Hardworking, responsible
Religious, Christian	13	13	Clean, neat, healthy
Thrifty, economical	14	14	Thrifty, economical
Rich, having good financial prospects	15	15	Of good standing
		16	Rich, having good financial prospects
		17	Courageous, brave†
		18	From same town†

* This table appears on p. 121 of *Marriage Guidance for Young Ghanaians.*
† Variable only of significance to the women.

Table 5

Preferred educational standard of spouse by sex of students

Sex	Total		College University		Secondary high school		Std. 7 Grade 8		Immaterial	
	No.	Per cent	No.	Per cent	No.	Per cent	No.	Per cent	No.	Per cent
Total	292	100	103	35	104	36	67	23	18	6
Male	142	100	26	18	40	28	65	46	11	8
Female	150	100	77	51	64	43	2	1	7	5

$\chi^2 = 90.80$, d.f., 3, $P < .001$.

what do most young people look for; is this desire consistent with reality?

To get at an understanding of these questions, the sample students were presented with the following statement: "The man/woman I marry must have the following desirable characteristics (make the list in order of importance)." Each student was given a maximum of five contributions ranked from 1 to 5. Table 4 is a summary of responses to this statement.

Table 4 indicates a divergence of interest along sex lines. There is a tendency on the part of the men to wish for and to admire the educated woman cut to fit the pattern of a traditional hardworking housewife.

Education. In the first place the men want the wife to be educated. This may be expected, since an educated husband would normally wish, as a mate, a woman who complements him on the cultural level. It is noteworthy that the women ranked education fourth on the list. Is it because the women do not admire or place in esteem an educated husband? Such a conclusion would be inaccurate since in the Ghanaian society education holds the key to the "good life"—high occupational status, high social class position, and the possession of modern comforts of life such as a car, refrigerator, bungalows, and credit facilities and so forth. It is more likely that since educated women are at a premium (as evidenced by the fact that the men place this factor uppermost on their list) these women are first and foremost concerned with the personal characteristics of their prospective spouses.

When presented with the following statement: I would like my future wife or husband to have at least college or university education; secondary or high school education; standard 7 or form 4 education; or less; however, the response appears contradictory to the position of education on the order of Table 4 (see Table 5).

We can interpret this discrepancy to mean that even though men desire the educated woman as a marriage partner, most of the men were nevertheless aware that unless they themselves are able to get a degree their chances of marrying a college-educated woman are practically nil. As a matter of fact very few degree-holding males in Ghana can hope to marry girls of similar qualification since there just aren't many such women about. Rather, a secondary school (high school) or Teacher Training College male graduate can aspire to marrying a secondary school female graduate or one with lower educational status.

The responses of Table 5 may be considered as exemplifying a high degree of practicality on the part of the male students. One might also interpret the responses to mean that while a man wants a woman with an education he prefers one without too much education. An educated man may well prefer the company of a learned scholar but not a learned wife. On the other hand, the female students of the secondary school and Teacher Training Colleges can afford to hitch their wagons to the stars because they know they are at a premium. Hence their responses here indicate a high degree of awareness that they can practically ingratiate themselves into the good graces of the educated male elite in Ghana for the purpose of marriage.

The responses of Table 4 do not rule out the possibility that the secret desires of many a young emancipated Ghanaian would be to marry an educated (in its relative sense) woman whereas the female might care more for the personal qualities that go to make a successful husband among a class of educated eligible males.

Economic Considerations and Mate Selection. The first six items of Table 4 seem to indicate the status quo of the woman: her passive role in the courtship situation. Not being the active member, she seems to be content to be married to a man who is dependable in character, polite, kind, understanding, cheerful, faithful, patient. Economic considerations appear to mean less to her than such items as education, love for children, affection, and good looks. A hardworking and responsible man comes 12th, as does a thrifty, economical man (14th) or a rich man or one with good financial prospects (16th). As a matter of fact, the men rank "rich, good financial prospect" last. But this may be expected because the man is supposed to be the provider—the breadwinner. But when the women rank such a seemingly important item at the bottom of the list, some explanation is called for.

One such explanation may be sought in the fact that the women place education high up on their list—fourth. As had been indicated in the above section, education holds the key to the good life in Ghana. And if Dr. Nkrumah's cardinal preachment may be paraphrased,[11] an enterprising young Ghanaian woman should seek first an educated husband and all other material things will be in sight. Then, also, this may be related to the fact that hard work is rated 12th. It cannot be contended that educated Ghanaians are the hardest working element in the world. The woman must therefore have a very good understanding of the Ghanaian male indeed, in first of all seeking for herself a considerate man who is educated, who likes to have children, and would show her some love and affection—not necessarily hardworking, thrifty, rich, or of good financial prospects.

[11] According to Dr. Nkrumah, "Seek ye first the political kingdom, and all other things shall be added unto you."

Love in the Courtship Process. It has been said at one point in this article that "love" is a preoccupation of the emancipated Ghanaian adolescent. How does he see this phenomenon in comparison with other desires in marriage? It is very interesting to note that both boys and girls rate "love for children or family" seventh, and "love for me" tenth. What does this signify? First of all, we can assume that love for children overrides personal love or affection; secondly, that this is the kind of "love" most profoundly understood—more so than what is generally considered to be "love" in the Western world. This is made more meaningful when it is considered that 30 per cent of the sample (74 per cent of them, men) indicated that they would either leave their spouses or they would lose their love for them if they were unable to give them children. What they seem to be saying is, "love alone without other things is not highly desired, and other things express love."

Love, in the final analysis, must be expressed in terms of something concrete if it is to have any meaning at all. If this is expressed as a factor of ego's "needs" then we may assume here that the various variables preceding the 10th item which is "love for me" constitute the need disposition of ego. We further assume that any combination of items 1 through 9 would be looked for in a prospective partner by the Ghanaian adolescent in this educational category; that the presence of a majority of these traits would make the heart throb.

Conclusion

It can safely be concluded, on the basis of an analysis of our data, that the educated young Ghanaian has a fairly clear notion as to his or her wishes and "needs" in the courtship situation. Furthermore these "needs" or role expectations are articulated. The courtship process, though partly freed from parental dominance, is nevertheless attended by rational, rather than purely emotional or sentimental, considerations. These considerations are necessarily culture-bound and do not appear to be entirely free of traditional role expectations in the marital situation.

Winch's theory of complementary needs is on the personal and psychic levels as opposed to the mass needs of a group in a homogamous situation. The data with which we are concerned at the moment deal with the "needs" of a group, but taken at the psychic level.[12] In other words it is hypothesized that the subject, while answering the question as to what he or she considers most desirable in a mate, is indicating a complementary "need" and not a homogamous one. Until this is rigorously tested we cannot be sure of the extent to which this statement is true of married couples in Ghana—especially since people do not always marry the ideal mate. Nevertheless it is significant for further research to attempt to see in what ways the need dispositions of the boys in our sample complement or are similar to those of the girls.

An examination of Table 4 shows that with the exception of three items, namely, "love for

[12] See Robert F. Winch, "The Theory of Complementary Needs in Mate Selection: Final Results on the Test of the General Hypothesis," *American Sociological Review*, **20**, No. 5, pp. 552 ff.

children," "love for me," and "thrifty or economical," the "needs" variables are on different planes. It can further be observed that the divergencies are quite far apart, the extreme of such cases being "hardworking," "good looks," "kindness," and "religiosity." With a gap this great, adjustment in marriage would seem to be complicated.

We cannot at this stage postulate these as "motivational categories," and we are on shaky ground to call these variables "needs." Nevertheless, it is quite clear that the men and the women represented by this sample do not look for the same thing in a mate even though both groups may safely be considered homogamous with respect to education, social and cultural background, and economic interests (or intentions). Whether verbal responses to a question such as was posed to them is significant for eventual choice of a mate is a subject for further research. On the basis of these findings, a hypothesis in the direction of complementariness in choice of mate among the young of Ghana seems appropriate.

15. The Trend of Interfaith Marriages in Canada: 1922–1957[*]

BY DAVID M. HEER

POPULAR LITERATURE HAS FREQUENTLY discussed a purported trend toward increased interfaith marriages in the United States. Scholarly writers citing this trend have frequently documented their statement with a reference to the work of John L. Thomas, S.J. Thomas studied mixed marriages that had been sanctioned by the Roman Catholic Church in several dioceses throughout this country and found "a gradual but more or less constant increase from 1910 to the present." However, he modestly concluded that "because intermarriage rates vary so much in different sections of the country, one could venture no generalization on such an inadequate basis."[1]

In truth, because there have never been pertinent statistics in the United States, there is no factual basis for determining the existence of a nationwide trend toward increasing interfaith marriage in this country. For only two States, Iowa and Indiana, are there official statistics on the incidence of interfaith marriage. But no long-term trend can be deduced even for these

States, since the Iowa marriage license has noted the religion of bride and groom only since 1953, and the Indiana license only since 1959.[2]

By contrast, the vital statistics published by the Dominion Bureau of Statistics in Canada provide an annual series of statistics on the religion of bridegroom cross-classified by religion of bride back to 1921.[3] This information is currently available concerning the entire nation and for each province. The present research was conducted under the premise that a study of Canadian statistics would not only be of interest in its own right but might also prove useful in analyzing the trend in the United States. Specifically, it was believed that if a uniform trend in the proportion of interfaith marriages could be found among the provinces in Canada, despite their differing social conditions, such a trend would provide additional grounds for presuming a similar trend in the United States.

In this study an interfaith marriage is defined as one in which the religion reported by one spouse at the time of marriage differs from that reported by the other. It should be emphasized that alternative definitions of interfaith

---

SOURCE: American Sociological Review, *Volume 27* (*1962*), *pp. 245–250. Reprinted by permission from author and American Sociological Association.*

[*] Revision of a paper read at the Annual Meeting of the Population Association of America, Washington, D.C., May 6–7, 1960.

[1] John L. Thomas, S.J., "The Factor of Religion in the Selection of Marriage Mates," *American Sociological Review*, **16** (August, 1951), pp. 487–491.

[2] For a statement of the findings concerning interfaith marriages in Iowa, see Loren E. Chancellor and Thomas P. Monahan, "Religious Preference and Inter-Religious Mixtures in Marriages and Divorces in Iowa," *American Journal of Sociology*, **61** (November, 1955), pp. 233–239.

[3] See Dominion Bureau of Statistics, *Vital Statistics* (an annual publication), Ottawa.

marriage might yield trends unlike that discussed here.[4]

Analysis has been confined to Protestants, Catholics, and Jews. "Catholic" as defined here combines the reported categories of Roman Catholic and Greek (Byzantine Rite) Catholic. "Protestant" is defined as all religions except those categorized as Roman Catholic, Greek Catholic, Jewish, Eastern Orthodox, Oriental religions, other religions, nonreligious denominations, and unknown.

Table 1 shows the proportion of all Protestants, Catholics, and Jews in Canada and in each Canadian province who have married outside their respective faiths. To show the trend over time, statistics are included for 1922 (where available),[5] 1927, 1932, 1937, 1942, 1947, 1952,

and 1957. The direction and regularity of the trend in Canada and in each province during each of these years is measured by a rank-order coefficient, Kendall's *Tau*.[6]

Looking in Table 1 at the proportion of interfaith marriages in Canada as a whole, we see an almost steady rise from 5.8 per cent in 1927 to 11.5 per cent in 1957. For Canada, Kendall's *Tau* has a value of .90. Although the provinces vary considerably in their proportions of interfaith marriage, in each, the direction of the movement is positive. The increase in proportion of interfaith marriages shows great regularity in all provinces except Quebec. In that province the value of *Tau* is only .49, whereas in the other provinces the range in the value of *Tau* is from .79 to 1.00.

[4] One alternative definition would regard a marriage as an interfaith marriage if the two partners were reared in different religions. Other definitions would treat a marriage as interfaith if at a given time after the marriage the religion of husband and wife were to differ.

[5] No data are available for Quebec in 1922 because Quebec was not then part of the marriage registration area. Data concerning Catholics in 1922 are not available for the provinces of Manitoba, Saskatchewan, and Alberta, since in the 1922 statistics data for the Eastern Orthodox and the Greek (Byzantine Rite) Catholic denominations were combined under the category "Greek Churches." For those provinces where in 1927 the Greek Catholics formed less than 5 per cent of the total number of Catholic brides and

grooms, i.e., in Prince Edward Island, Nova Scotia, New Brunswick, Ontario, and British Columbia, estimates for Catholics in 1922 were made from the 1922 data on Roman Catholics, the 1927 data concerning Greek Catholics, and the 1922 data for "Greek Churches."

[6] The value of *Tau* ranges from minus one, when the rank order of one series is completely opposite from that of the other, to a value of plus one when the rank order of the first series is completely congruent with that of the other. Its value is a function of the minimum number of interchanges between neighbors which is required to transform one ranking into another. For further details, see Maurice G. Kendall, *Rank Correlation Methods*, London: Charles Griffith & Company, Limited, 1948.

Table 1

Proportion of all brides and grooms of Protestant, Catholic, or Jewish religion marrying spouse of different faith, for Canada and each province, 1922 to 1957

Area	1922	1927	1932	1937	1942	1947	1952	1957	Value of Kendall's *Tau*
Canada	—	5.8	7.6	7.3	9.3	9.9	10.9	11.5	+ .90
Newfoundland	—	—	—	—	—	—	11.9	12.0	+1.00
Prince Edward Island	3.1	3.8	5.3	6.7	7.5	6.5	8.7	7.5	+ .79
Nova Scotia	8.1	7.8	9.4	8.6	11.0	11.6	12.2	12.4	+ .86
New Brunswick	4.9	5.0	6.1	5.5	7.8	8.1	9.7	9.4	+ .86
Quebec	—	2.6	3.6	2.7	3.9	3.3	3.6	3.7	+ .49
Ontario	5.4	6.1	7.0	7.9	10.4	11.9	13.1	13.8	+1.00
Manitoba	—	6.9	9.6	10.5	12.6	14.7	15.3	16.9	+1.00
Saskatchewan	—	7.6	9.4	10.8	12.0	12.6	13.6	16.4	+1.00
Alberta	—	9.9	11.3	13.3	14.6	14.2	15.9	16.8	+ .90
British Columbia	8.7	9.9	10.7	10.6	12.9	14.4	16.3	17.2	+ .93

A "dash" indicates data not available.

We may also examine interfaith marriages within each of the three major religious groups —Protestant, Catholic, and Jewish. These trends, for Canada and for each province, are presented in Table 2. For Canada as a whole, we see the same general trend for each of these three groups considered separately as when we look at them combined. For Protestants the rank-order consistency is perfect, and for Catholics very high (.88). For Jews the consistency is considerably less (*Tau* equals .62), but the positive direction is maintained. Among Protestants, the proportion of brides and grooms marrying outside their faith increased from 5.0 per cent in 1927 to 11.6 per cent in 1957; among Catholics, from 7.2 per cent in 1927 to 11.5 per cent in 1957; and among Jews, from 3.0 per cent in 1927 to 6.8 per cent in 1957. Thus, from 1927 to 1957 the percentage increase in the proportion of partners to interfaith marriages was greatest among Protestants (132 per cent), slightly less among Jews (126 per cent), and least among Catholics (60 per cent).

For Protestants the direction of the trend is positive, and its consistency is extremely high, for each province except Newfoundland, where only two observations are available. Although the direction for Catholics is always positive, the consistency of the trend in each province is substantially less than for Protestants. The trend toward increasing interfaith marriage in Quebec in particular is very slight, and the value of *Tau* is only .21. However, only 1.5 to 2.2 per cent of the Catholics in Quebec married persons of other religions throughout the thirty year period. The trend by province among Jews is shown only for those three provinces where during the years covered in this study there were, on the average, at least 100 Jewish brides, and grooms. In these three provinces—Quebec, Ontario, and Manitoba—the trend toward increasing intermarriage is more consistent than for Jews in Canada as a whole.

The trend toward increased proportions of persons marrying outside their own faith is thus seen to be quite general in Canada, extending in varying degree to all provinces and to all three religious groups. We shall now consider some of the circumstances which may have caused this increase. One of the factors mentioned most often to explain varying proportions of interfaith marriage is that of religious distribution, that is, the proportion of the total population which identifies itself with each religious group. The smaller the religious group relative to other groups, the larger the proportion in that group who marry outside the group. Thomas shows the importance of this factor in comparing the intermarriage rates for Catholics in various dioceses in the United States.[7] Locke, Sabagh, and Thomes show that for each of the Canadian provinces in 1954 there was a perfect rank-order correlation between the percentage of Catholic brides and grooms having interfaith marriages and the percentage of the total population of each province that was Catholic.[8] Glick has shown that for the United States the factor of religious distribution helps to explain the fact that there is a higher proportion of interfaith marriage among couples where at least one spouse is Catholic than among couples where at least one spouse is Protestant.[9]

Let us now consider the religious composition of brides and grooms in Canada and in each Canadian province. The data from the vital statistics records indicate that in every province the proportion of all brides and grooms who are Catholic is increasing and the proportion who are Protestant decreasing (except in Newfoundland, where we have only two observations). The trend in the Jewish proportion is somewhat unstable but in recent years has declined.[10] If the religious distribution factor alone were operative, we should expect the proportion of Catholic

[7] Thomas, *op. cit.*
[8] Harvey J. Locke, Georges Sabagh, and Mary Margaret Thomes, "Interfaith Marriages," *Social Problems*, 4 (April, 1957), pp. 329–333.
[9] Glick studied differences in religion between husbands and wives who had been married for varying periods. See Paul C. Glick, "Intermarriage and Fertility Patterns Among Persons in Major Religious Groups," *Eugenics Quarterly*, 7 (March, 1960), pp. 31–38.
[10] The religious composition of brides and grooms in the United States has probably shown a less pronounced pattern of change than in Canada. See the distribution of the United States population by religious preference and age in U.S. Bureau of the Census, "Religion Reported by the Civilian Population of the United States: March 1957," *Current Population Reports*, Series P–20, No. 79, February 2, 1958.

Table 2

Proportion of Protestant, Catholic, and Jewish brides and grooms marrying spouse of different faith, for Canada and each province, 1922 to 1957

Area	1922	1927	1932	1937	1942	1947	1952	1957	Value of Kendall's *Tau*
Canada									
Protestant	—	5.0	6.7	6.8	8.2	9.1	10.5	11.6	+1.00
Catholic	—	7.2	9.4	8.1	11.1	11.1	11.4	11.5	+ .88
Jewish*	—	3.0	2.8	2.7	4.9	4.4	5.9	6.8	+ .62
Newfoundland									
Protestant	—	—	—	—	—	—	9.1	9.1	0.00
Catholic	—	—	—	—	—	—	16.8	18.0	+1.00
Prince Edward Island									
Protestant	2.5	3.2	4.4	5.2	6.6	5.8	7.6	6.8	+ .93
Catholic	4.4	4.9	7.1	9.7	8.6	7.4	10.1	8.4	+ .71
Nova Scotia									
Protestant	5.9	5.4	7.0	6.6	8.1	8.6	9.2	9.6	+ .86
Catholic	14.3	14.3	15.0	13.0	16.7	18.1	18.0	17.7	+ .55
New Brunswick									
Protestant	3.9	4.2	5.3	5.4	7.2	7.6	9.7	9.7	+ .98
Catholic	6.8	6.4	7.3	5.7	8.5	8.8	9.8	9.0	+ .65
Quebec									
Protestant	—	9.9	12.0	12.0	16.3	16.2	17.8	20.6	+ .88
Catholic	—	1.5	2.2	1.5	2.2	1.8	2.0	2.0	+ .21
Jewish	—	2.0	1.9	2.1	2.6	3.2	2.8	3.7	+ .81
Ontario									
Protestant	3.5	4.0	5.6	5.5	7.1	8.3	9.8	10.8	+ .93
Catholic	14.1	14.7	18.0	16.3	22.3	23.0	20.5	19.9	+ .57
Jewish	2.6	2.9	2.2	2.4	4.9	3.3	6.4	8.0	+ .64
Manitoba									
Protestant	4.3	4.7	7.2	7.8	8.8	10.4	11.1	13.0	+1.00
Catholic	—	14.0	15.4	17.9	23.8	27.3	25.6	25.8	+ .81
Jewish	1.8	2.5	4.9	2.7	4.9	4.0	6.1	5.3	+ .69
Saskatchewan									
Protestant	4.9	5.2	6.9	8.0	8.2	9.0	10.4	13.2	+1.00
Catholic	—	15.4	15.7	17.7	23.3	22.1	20.4	22.4	+ .62
Alberta									
Protestant	6.4	6.9	8.1	9.1	9.4	9.5	11.3	12.3	+1.00
Catholic	—	20.4	20.7	27.7	33.5	31.8	29.1	18.4	+ .43
British Columbia									
Protestant	5.0	6.0	7.0	6.6	7.8	9.8	10.4	11.5	+ .93
Catholic	32.1	37.5	32.2	37.3	45.3	47.0	42.5	39.0	+ .50

* Data for Jewish brides and grooms shown only for those provinces where there were, on the average, at least 100.

A "dash" indicates data not available.

brides and grooms marrying outside their faith to decrease. We conclude, therefore, that factors other than religious distribution have operated to increase the proportion of Catholics marrying outside their faith. Conversely, if the religious distribution factor alone were operative, the decrease in the proportion of brides and grooms who are Protestant would cause an increase in the proportion of Protestants marrying outside their faith. Thus, at least some of the observed increase in interfaith marriage among Protestants is accounted for by the factor of religious distribution. Similarly, at least some of the increase in interfaith marriage among Jews may be accounted for by this factor.

Insofar as the religious distribution factor operates, its operation is completely mechanical: increased availability of marriage partners of differing religion and decreased availability of partners of the same religion cause interfaith marriage to increase, and vice-versa. If religious distribution were the only factor affecting interfaith marriage, the proportion of grooms of a given religion marrying outside their own faith would be identical to the proportion of all brides who were not of that faith. If the religious distribution factor were to have no effect, there could be no interfaith marriage at all.

Let us now consider the ratio of the actual proportion of grooms (or brides) entering interfaith marriages and the proportion who would marry outside their faith if the religious distribution factor alone were operative and brides (or grooms) were selected without regard to religion. It can be seen that, regardless of the actual religious distribution, this ratio is constant if the factors other than religious distribution which inhibit interfaith marriage remain constant, that this ratio increases when the strength of the other inhibiting factors diminishes, and that it decreases when the strength of the other inhibiting factors increases. Thus, we may attempt to determine whether interfaith marriages among the three major religious groups increase in each Canadian province when the religious distribution factor is held constant.

This has been done in Table 3. To simplify the computation, we have taken the ratio of the proportion of brides and grooms of the given religious group in each province marrying outside their faith to the proportion of all brides and grooms of other faiths in that province.[11]

For Protestants, holding constant in this fashion the effect of changes in religious distribution, a trend toward increased interfaith marriage is found in each province. The trend is highly consistent in every province except British Columbia, where the value of *Tau* is only .50. For Catholics also, the trend is positive in every province and is quite consistent except in Alberta, where the value of *Tau* is .52, and in British Columbia, where the value of *Tau* is .57. Among Jews the direction of the trend is positive and also reasonably consistent in each of the three provinces for which data are shown. It may be noted, incidentally, that in all cases the value of the ratio for Jewish brides and grooms is considerably lower than the value of the corresponding ratio for Protestants or Catholics.

We have now shown that the religious distribution within each province cannot entirely account for the increase in interfaith marriage among either Protestants, Catholics, or Jews in Canada. To what additional factors may this increase be due? Our curiosity leads us to inquire whether the reason may not be a change of societal attitude toward interfaith marriage. Militating against the validity of such a conclusion is the fact that several factors unrelated to societal attitudes may also help to explain the results presented in Table 3.

It must first of all be conceded that the exact effect of the religious distribution factor has not been precisely measured. No account has been taken of the fact that there are variations in different parts of a province in the proportion of brides and grooms within each religious group and that the proportion for each part of

---

[11] To be precise, one should compute the ratio separately for brides and grooms and sum the weighted results. Thus, one should compute the ratio of the proportion of grooms of a given religion marrying outside their faith to the proportion of brides of different faith, multiply this ratio by the proportion of grooms among the total brides and grooms of the religious group, and add to it the ratio of the proportion of brides of the given religion marrying outside their faith to the proportion of grooms of different faith multiplied by the proportion of brides among the total brides and grooms of the religious group. However, the differences between the two methods of computation are minuscule.

Table 3

Ratio of actual to "expected" proportion of brides and grooms with interfaith marriage by major religious group, each Canadian province, 1922 to 1957

Area	1922	1927	1932	1937	1942	1947	1952	1957	Value of Kendall's Tau
Newfoundland									
Protestant	—	—	—	—	—	—	.259	.272	+1.00
Catholic	—	—	—	—	—	—	.257	.269	+1.00
Prince Edward Island									
Protestant	.060	.084	.127	.151	.151	.132	.178	.155	+ .76
Catholic	.068	.079	.108	.146	.152	.132	.176	.149	+ .71
Nova Scotia									
Protestant	.201	.199	.228	.204	.246	.267	.272	.274	+ .79
Catholic	.195	.195	.213	.190	.246	.265	.270	.271	+ .73
New Brunswick									
Protestant	.111	.112	.130	.115	.157	.167	.148	.192	+ .86
Catholic	.104	.101	.122	.106	.155	.160	.189	.179	+ .79
Quebec									
Protestant	—	.144	.140	.135	.185	.180	.197	.225	+ .81
Catholic	—	.096	.115	.106	.147	.138	.159	.171	+ .81
Jewish	—	.020	.020	.022	.027	.033	.029	.038	+ .88
Ontario									
Protestant	.167	.175	.216	.207	.267	.294	.287	.294	+ .84
Catholic	.173	.183	.230	.211	.292	.307	.295	.297	+ .79
Jewish	.026	.030	.023	.025	.050	.034	.065	.081	+ .64
Manitoba									
Protestant	.152	.164	.197	.227	.282	.330	.322	.362	+ .93
Catholic	—	.182	.217	.249	.321	.369	.359	.372	+ .91
Jewish	.019	.026	.051	.028	.051	.041	.062	.054	+ .69
Saskatchewan									
Protestant	.185	.182	.201	.237	.287	.293	.294	.346	+ .93
Catholic	—	.199	.215	.241	.307	.299	.293	.334	+ .71
Alberta									
Protestant	.241	.256	.266	.319	.375	.354	.367	.384	+ .86
Catholic	—	.258	.271	.348	.421	.402	.384	.389	+ .52
British Columbia									
Protestant	.352	.392	.389	.382	.481	.576	.493	.464	+ .50
Catholic	.364	.424	.374	.426	.521	.546	.515	.486	+ .57

A "dash" indicates data not available.

the province may change with time. Thus in New Brunswick the Catholics are found primarily in the northern part of the province and the Protestants in the south. Holding constant the religious composition of the province, one would expect an increase in interfaith marriage if Catholics were to spread south and Protestants to the north. To hold constant more completely the religious distribution factor, one would need statistics on religion of groom by religion of bride for each county.

In addition to religious distribution, other adventitious factors unrelated to societal attitudes may affect the trend in the proportion who marry outside their faith. Thomas has mentioned two such factors.[12] The first of these relates to the association of religious with ethnic differences. This association affects the interfaith marriage rate because of the tendency for members of ethnic groups to marry among themselves regardless of religion. When members of one religion are predominantly members of a particular ethnic group while members of a second religion are predominantly members of a second ethnic group, ethnic ties reinforce religious ties to militate against a high proportion of persons marrying outside their faith. Thomas states that under these conditions, a decrease in ingroup feeling among ethnic groups leads to a diminution of the hindrance which such groups present to interfaith marriage.[13] The second factor mentioned by Thomas is the association of

religious difference with social-class difference. In this case the distance between social classes provides an impediment to interfaith marriage, and this impediment would be lessened if the association between religious and social-class differences were to be reduced.

It is possible that both of the factors mentioned by Thomas have been operative in Canada and that the nation has experienced diminutions of ingroup solidarity among the predominantly Catholic group of French origin and the predominantly Protestant group of British origin as well as lessening of association between religious and social-class differences. If so, these factors may help to account for the increase in interfaith marriage in Canada.

Thus the data at hand do not permit one to answer conclusively whether or not societal attitudes in Canada toward interfaith marriage have changed. However, the plausibility of this hypothesis has been somewhat enhanced by the finding that the proportion of brides and grooms of each religion marrying outside their faith increased even after the religious distribution within each province was held constant.[14]

Generalizations about trends in Canada are not necessarily applicable to the United States, but, in this instance, we believe that the uniformities discovered among the Canadian provinces lend further support to the hypothesis that there has been an increase in interfaith marriage in the United States. We think that changes in religious composition do not provide the only explanation. However, conclusive evidence of the validity of this hypothesis awaits further research.

---

[12] Thomas, *op. cit.*

[13] We might also expect that changes in the coincidence of religious and ethnic groupings would result in an inverse change in the proportion of interfaith marriages. However, the relevance of this factor to the increase of interfaith marriage in Canada is uncertain. Data are not available concerning the religion of Canadian brides and grooms cross-classified by national origin, and the available census data for the total population during the period 1921–1951 do not indicate any substantial lessening of the coincidence of religious and ethnic groupings.

[14] If attitudes in Canada concerning interfaith marriage have in fact become increasingly tolerant, this phenomenon may be partially due to the change in religious distribution. If we assume that frequently violated norms cannot be maintained, the more frequent incidence of interfaith marriages caused by changes in religious distribution would tend to weaken the norms themselves.

16. Early and Late Dating: Some Conditions Associated with Them*

BY SAMUEL H. LOWRIE

WHAT ARE THE IMPLICATIONS of beginning to date early in comparison with waiting late to date? Opinions differ widely.

Some hold that dating is a preliminary phase of intersex association among persons who are aware of the fact that they are too young to marry.[1] These writers usually regard dating practices as an unfortunate development of this century, and conclude with Margaret Mead that "the more successfully adolescents deal with . . . dating, the less prepared they are to meet . . . sex adjustments after marriage."[2] In sharp contrast are those who conceive the dating process to be a more or less spontaneous development whereby young people gain experience, develop discriminating understanding of associates, and thereby become more capable of selecting mates with judgment.[3]

To the first group, dating is logically disadvantageous at any age. Among those who regard dating as educational, there is difference of opinion about when it should begin, and what the relative merits are of initiating it at an early or at a late age. Some think youngsters are fortunate if they become absorbed in projects and put off dating until they are relatively near the age of marriage. Others are so positive about the merits of learning through association across sex lines, that they are anxious to see adolescents begin dating associations early. Failure to date until the end of high school is therefore looked upon as an individual as well as a social handicap.

In reality, few have investigated the objective facts to determine the home conditions associated with early dating or analyzed the behavior patterns of either early or late dating. Necessarily, a first effort can do little beyond scratching the surface; still if it is found that measurable differences in family and social patterns exist between early and late daters, further inquiry may be expected to delineate more fully the nature and significance of these differences.

For a number of years, the writer has been studying dating behavior among high school and college students, publishing in 1952 an article showing that among five thousand students the

SOURCE: Marriage and Family Living, *Volume 23* (1961), *pp. 284–291. Reprinted by permission from author and National Council on Family Relations.

* The writer gratefully acknowledges three grants-in-aid from Bowling Green State University in partial support of this inquiry.

[1] Willard Waller, *The Family, A Dynamic Interpretation*, New York: The Cordon Company, 1938, is the most widely quoted statement of this view.
[2] Margaret Mead, *Male and Female*, New York: William Morrow and Company, 1949, p. 295.
[3] Samuel H. Lowrie, *American Sociological Review*, Vol. 16, No. 3, pp. 334–340, June, 1951, gives a statement of this view. Actually, variations of the view are implicit or explicit in a great number of the discussions of dating in articles and texts on marriage relationships over the last twenty-five years.

initial age of dating varied with the age of those furnishing information but was practically the same for boys and girls. More recently, dating has been investigated in the high schools of three cities of approximately one hundred thousand population, located in distinctive sections of the country: Ohio, Texas, and California.[4] The purpose is to check the 1952 findings, to obtain a broader base for inference, and to get some indication as to variations in different parts of the country. In each of the three cities the evidence supports the earlier conclusions. Indeed it goes beyond the earlier findings and shows that respondent age is such a large and constant influence that both it and sex must be controlled if reliable conclusions are to be obtained as to the age dating begins.

The purpose of the present article is (1) to analyze some of the characteristics of those who start dating early in comparison with those who begin late, and (2) insofar as the data in hand permit, to determine some of the differences in dating practices between those who begin dating early and those who begin late.

The method of investigation involved gaining the cooperation of the school authorities in each city and getting home room teachers to distribute and collect responses to a questionnaire as a part of the regular school work in the two (in South the three) upper classes of the high schools of the three cities. Such a procedure led to a minimum of interference with class activity, because the questionnaire was normally completed in ten minutes. A brief explanation at the head of the questionnaire was intended to arouse the interest of the students and impress on them that responses would aid in a scientific attempt to find some of the conditions and facts associated with dating. Teachers were asked to report whether students appeared interested and seemed to fill out the forms with sincerity. Their statements were practically unanimous—many of them expressing surprise—that the students were so careful and painstaking in their replies. Returns varied between 72 and 97 per cent of the students enrolled in the classes surveyed in the three cities.

[4] The cities will be referred to as North, South, and West to indicate their location. However, no one of the three is necessarily representative or typical of the region in which it is located.

The chief determinant of the proportion of returns was the efficiency of distribution and collection of forms to home rooms, a condition related to the number of schools in the cities and to the interest of administrators in the inquiry. Teachers agreed that few students who were given the opportunity failed to respond. Whatever selection may have occurred, therefore, was accidental rather than conscious, the result of the mechanical processes of data collection. In the nature of the case a small fraction of the responses had to be discarded as incomplete or inconsistent, a smaller proportion as facetious.

On the whole it appears likely that the returns are a rough approximation of the school and age groups covered.

It was a part of the plan of study that data were to be used only where there were adequate numbers of each sex from each age classification to permit control both by sex and age. In consequence, those over and under age were as a rule not included since numbers were too small to permit control. Further, inquiry was focused on those who were distinctly American, on the assumption that dating is peculiarly characteristic of this country. As a result, in the two situations where there were concentrations of ethnic groups that might be expected to differ from predominantly American behavior, the groups were not included because numbers were inadequate to permit separate ethnic classification with control by sex and age. Thus data were not gathered from a segregated Negro high school in South; and those gathered in a low-status school, divided more or less equally between two distinct minorities in West, were discarded. In addition, since interest was on immediate dating behavior, the few students who were married, practically all of them girls, were not included in analysis.

The purpose of these restrictions was to concentrate in each community on students who were in normal day-to-day association with those of the same age of the opposite sex. Logically, it would have been desirable to restrict inquiry to the distinctly assimilated Americans and to have excluded the children, if not the grandchildren, of immigrants. However, two communities would not permit questions as to race or ethnic origin. As a result, except for the concentrations previously mentioned, members of ethnic and racial minorities were not identified, and were necessarily included in considerable numbers, particularly in North and West. It would have been enlightening to study the dating behavior of minorities had it been possible to identify them in sufficient numbers to permit adequate controls. In this study, whatever influence they have is merged with that of the assimilated majority and is not identifiable except by parental language, as will be shown in the subsequent discussion.

Some Factors Affecting the Age Dating Begins

Besides sex and respondent age, there are other influences that may be associated with the age of initial dating. Among these are, first, rural in contrast to urban conditions of living; and, second, the effect of conditions in large metropolitan areas in comparison with those in moderate-size cities. Neither of these could be checked with the material gathered in the regional cities on which this study is focused. From the communities surveyed, evidence was sought concerning five possible influences that may be related to dating age; parental home language (degree of assimilation of American culture), parental education, size of family, socioeconomic status, and region of the country. The evidence concerning four of the factors is summarized in Table 1; regional differences will be considered later.

Table 1 shows that, especially among girls, linguistic background in the home appears to be definitely related to the age dating begins. The question used in this classification was introduced because there was objection to asking students their ethnic origin. The makeshift was to ask whether a foreign language was spoken in the childhood home of either parent. Responses to such an inquiry were probably not as accurate as those that pertained to the individual experience of the respondents. Nevertheless, the question brought out distinct differences according to age of initial dating. The essential conclusion is that children, particularly girls, from English-speaking homes begin to date earlier than those where a foreign language had been used in the preceding generation; that is,

Table 1

Critical ratios of differences between mean ages of initial dating with variations in specified conditions*

	Respondent Age†	No. of cases	Boys			No. of cases	Girls		
			North CR	West CR	South CR		North CR	West CR	South CR
Parental Home Language:	16	502	—	—	—	755	−2.97	−1.60	−1.63
English vs. Foreign	17	899	−1.70	−2.23	−1.92	1090	−3.49	−1.97	—
	18	560	−1.23	—	−1.09	593	−4.05	−2.95	−3.90
Parental Education: High	16	499	−1.10	—	2.24	751	3.17	1.82	1.53
School of Less vs. Any	17	898	1.87	1.24	2.24	1085	3.38	2.30	1.97
College Training	18	553	—	4.03	2.08	519	4.15	1.24	—
Size of Family: One or	16	504	1.11	—	−1.37	749	−1.11	—	−2.54
two Children vs. Three	17	900	−1.30	—	—	1084	−3.01	—	−2.11
or More	18	565	—	−1.53	—	518	−3.10	—	−2.02
Socio-economic Status:	16	145	—	—	—	238	−1.33	—	—
High vs. Low Status	17	335	−2.24	—	—	434	−3.21	—	—
	18	205	−1.55	—	—	179	−3.44	—	—

* Critical ratios are not given if less than 1.00. A negative sign indicates that the second condition is larger than the first.

† Respondent ages in South 15, 16, and 17.

children from distinctly American homes begin dating earlier than those from homes of parents less completely assimilated. Such a finding is logical when it is recognized that dating is distinctly American. Further, it is reasonable to suppose that differences between boys in dating behavior will be less marked than differences among girls in homes that are not thoroughly assimilated. In other words, recent immigrants are more likely to be strict in their control of daughters than of sons.

Parental education seems to be a factor also, particularly among girls, in the age dating begins. The direction of variation is consistent, except among boys of 16 and 18 in North. The differences in age of initial dating are significantly large in five out of the nine classifications of girls and among all classifications of boys in South, and of boys of 18 in West. A tentative conclusion, therefore, is that, especially among girls, the higher the level of parental education, the younger the age dating begins.

Possibly, also the size of the family from which students come—those from homes with one or two children in comparison with those with three or more—affects the age of initial dating, at least of girls. While the direction of variation tends to be the same for both sexes, only among girls of North and South are differences significant statistically. To the extent that such incomplete evidence can be taken as suggestive of a tendency, girls in small families tend to begin to date at earlier ages than those from families of three or more children.

Socioeconomic status may possibly affect dating age. Logically, it might be expected to do so because the three preceding factors are generally associated with social and economic position. Unfortunately, the data concerning social and economic status are very inadequate, limited to one city only. Even here the evidence is based on the local report of informed individuals of the status of the neighborhoods in which high schools are located. In this city, North, in spite of such a loose and dubious base of differentiation, the data indicate a tendency among those in middle and upper class neighborhoods to begin dating earlier than those from lower status areas. The direction of variation is consistent for both sexes, but differences are

significant in only three of the six classifications. As with the preceding factors, differences are more pronounced among girls than among boys.

Thus the strength of the evidence varies with the four conditions discussed in the preceding paragraphs. Nevertheless, the interdependence of the factors, the consistency of the evidence in direction, and the strength of the evidence in the first two conditions suggest that further inquiry is likely to support the hypothesis that these influences are all associated with variation in the age dating begins.

It has been mentioned that no one of the three samples can be shown to be fully representative of the classes of the schools furnishing returns, much less of all those of dating age in the cities involved. Nor can it be maintained that the cities studied were necessarily typical of the regions in which they are located, though initially it was hoped they might be. At best the returns are only rough approximations of dating practices of specific school classes of specific cities in different sections of the nation. In spite of the inadequacies in sampling, there is considerable probability that the data obtained point in the direction that acceptable sampling will show. Until further and more reliable evidence is available, there is then a strong presumption that reality is being approximated.

A further difficulty arises in considering differences between the cities, differences suggestive of regional variations. The analysis thus far has been of relationships found in each sample; no attention has been given to differences between samples. Measurement of these differences is complicated by the fact that age groups in South are not exactly the same as those in the other two cities, a fact not so far mentioned.

An explanation for this unforeseen condition lies in two incidents. First, six years before the gathering of data in South, the conditions of admission to the public schools in the city were modified, and most students were accelerated a half year.[5] Second, data were obtained in South in November, and in North and West in late spring. Since in South, as in most schools, the age of admission is related to opening in September, students responding in this area were six

[5] Letter from the principal, June 12, 1957.

or seven months younger than if they had responded in the last months of the school year. The net effect of these two conditions is that students in South were at the time of responding younger than those in corresponding grades at the time of investigation in North and West. To complicate the situation further is the probability that dating practices are related in some degree to the grade level of students in school.

No method of correction for these divergencies can be fully satisfactory. Therefore, three different methods of comparison were used. First, students in South were considered a year older than they reported, as 16, 17 and 18, and the chi-square test was applied to each class of each sex of the three samples. By this process the samples were found to differ at less than the one per cent level in each of the six sex-age classifications. Second, students in the South reporting ages 16 and 17 were compared with those of these ages in the other two areas. Again differences were at less than the one per cent level in each of the four sex-age classifications. Third, comparisons were made between South and each of the other cities, both considering students in South a year older than reported and also considering them the ages they reported. By both methods, differences were in every classification below the one per cent level. Beyond question, South differs statistically from the other two samples, unless the divergencies in age invalidate the results. Further, comparisons between North and West reveal differences below the five per cent level of significance in at least two of the age groups of each sex.

In descriptive terms the three samples differ in the age dating begins; especially is South different from the others in that dating of each sex begins early, earlier than in either of the other samples. In North, in comparison with West, boys begin to date earlier, girls later.

While regional representativeness of the samples cannot be demonstrated, the sharpness of differences found suggests the likelihood of regional distinctiveness.

In summary, then, besides sex and respondent age, the two factors held constant in all comparisons, several other factors seem to affect the age dating begins. The evidence supports the following hypothetical conclusions:

1. Children, especially girls, of the more thoroughly assimilated part of the population begin dating as a rule earlier than those of more recent foreign origin.

2. Similarly, daughters of parents with at least some college training tend to begin to date at earlier ages than those of parents who have a high school education or less.

3. Also, children, especially daughters, who come from small families tend to begin dating earlier than those from large families.

4. Apparently students from homes of higher economic and social status tend to initiate dating at earlier ages than those from lower status homes.

5. The age of dating seemingly varies from region to region; particularly does dating in South begin earlier than in either of the other areas.

6. The preceding conclusions emphasize the apparent fact that the age of dating of girls is affected by changed conditions more readily than that of boys.

Some Behavioral Traits Found to Vary with Dating Age

The behavior of individuals who have begun to date appears to be related to the age at which they began the process.

First is dating frequency. For simplicity, discussion is of those who began to date at the age of 13 or less, in comparison with those who began at 14 or over. Except for minor irregularities, the evidence is equally clear if arranged by the specific year at which dating began.

Without exception, the average frequency of dating of those who began dating at 13 or less was greater than that of those who began at 14 or more. In other words, the evidence supports the conclusion that the earlier dating begins the more frequently individuals tend to participate in the progress, but the strength of the evidence varies by region. In West and South, differences are significant in a majoriy of age classifications, while in the North they are significant at the five per cent level in only two of the six sex-age classifications. Particularly different are girls; in North none of the age groups shows significant

Table 2

Mean age of initial dating by sex, age, level, and region

Region, sex, and age	Number of cases	Level of dating				CR*
		No date last month	Playing field		Now going steady	
			Never gone steady	Gone steady		
		(1)	(2)	(3)	(4)	
NORTH						
Boys						
16	142	14.6	14.5	13.9	14.8	2.76
17	321	15.2	14.5	14.4	14.5	1.64
18	201	15.2	15.1	14.4	14.8	2.90
Girls						
16	232	15.0	15.1	14.4	14.3	4.40
17	433	15.4	15.0	14.6	14.7	3.13
18	175	16.6	15.8	15.1	15.2	3.30
WEST						
Boys						
16	215	14.7	15.1	14.2	14.4	4.53
17	356	15.3	15.3	14.4	14.8	5.79
18	201	15.6	15.8	14.7	15.1	4.39
Girls						
16	291	14.8	14.9	14.3	14.2	3.73
17	396	15.4	15.4	14.3	14.5	7.12
18	147	15.5	15.8	14.2	15.1	4.61
SOUTH						
Boys						
15	127	13.9	14.0	13.4	13.3	3.21
16	188	14.5	14.5	13.5	13.6	5.78
17	148	15.1	15.0	13.6	14.1	6.23
Girls						
15	193	14.1	14.2	13.6	13.6	4.32
16	237	14.7	14.7	14.0	13.9	5.29
17	186	14.6	14.7	14.1	14.2	2.57

* Critical ratio between columns (1) and (2) combined in comparison with column (3). Means carried to hundredths in calculating critical ratios.

differences, while in each of the other regions significant differences are found at all ages. In spite of these irregularities, the evidence points to the conclusion that the earlier dating begins, the more frequently it tends to occur.

Another condition that is definitely related to the age dating begins is the level of the process. Responses permit the classification of those who had dated under four headings or levels: (1) those who had dated, but not during the month preceding the inquiry; (2) those who were playing the field and had never gone steady; (3) those

who were playing the field, but had at some previous time gone steady; and (4) those who were going steady. In this order from least to most involvement, variation in the age of dating might logically be expected either to rise or fall progressively. The data are presented in Table 2.

Examination of this table shows that the large differentiating factor is whether individuals have or have not gone steady—columns 1 and 2 in contrast to 3 and 4. Differences between these combinations are characteristically large and significant. Clearly those who have gone or are now going steady began dating much earlier than those who have never gone steady.

The unexpected finding from this table is the break in the direction of variation; those who are playing the field now, but have previously gone steady, began as a rule to date at younger ages than those now going steady. Such an anomalous variation in the age of beginning to date among those going steady suggests that the ages of beginning to date and of going steady are related, but not in the same way in all cases.

Examination of such a relationship is not simple. In the first place, it should be remembered that consideration is necessarily limited to those who have gone steady, roughly three-quarters of the boys and less than half of the girls. In the second place, presentation of the ages at which individuals begin two types of behavior is complex. The method used was to calculate the mean age of beginning to go steady for an age class of beginning to date, and then subtract the midpoint of the dating class from the calculated mean of beginning to go steady. For example, in North, boys of 16 who began to date at 12 or younger had begun to go steady on the average at the age of 15.1 years. Subtracting the midpoint of the dating group, 12.5 years, from this mean gives 2.6 years, the mean period those who began to date at 12 had waited before they began to go steady. Corresponding calculations were made for each age class of those beginning to date from 12 or less up to 16 or more. Then, to determine significance of differences, comparisons were made between those who began to date at 13 or less in comparison with those who began at 14 or more. In this calculation the original mean ages of going steady were used. Since the data are invariably consistent in direction and highly significant in every classification, the data are for want of space not presented in tabular form.

The consistency of relationships between the age of dating and that of going steady is unusual. With great regularity, the earlier the age at which dating begins the longer the delay in beginning to go steady. Thus for boys of 17 in North, the delay decreases regularly from 2.5 years when dating started at 12 or younger to 0.4 year when dating began at 16 or older. Variation is regular for each age group of each sex. In addition, a minor point is that in each sex with each increase in respondent age, the delay in going steady becomes greater. Further, in all age and sex classes in all three regional samples, differences between the age of beginning to date and the mean age of initially going steady are significantly greater among those who began to date at 13 or younger than among those who began at 14 or older. Beyond any question, in these samples the younger respondents were when they began to date the longer the delay in beginning to go steady.

For the sake of clarity attention needs to be called to the fact that this finding does not mean that those who date early start going steady at later ages than those who begin late. Actually, the reverse is true. What it does mean is that early daters have had much more experience in dating when they begin to go steady. To take a specific example, boys of North of 17 who began to date at 12 or younger, began to go steady at 15.0 years, while those who began to date at 16 or older initiated going steady at 16.9 years. Thus, those who began dating early also began going steady early. On the other hand, to follow the same example, boys of 17 in North who began dating at 12 or younger had had 2.5 years of experience in dating before they began going steady, while those who began at 16 or older had dated only 0.4 year before they started going steady.

The inference from such evidence is that those who begin to date at a relatively early age play the field for a long time and become acquainted with a number of members of the opposite sex before they initiate going steady. The fact that those now playing the field began to go steady at younger ages than those now going steady is important. It implies that those who begin to date early begin to go steady at a comparatively early age also. However, they revert to playing the field in considerable proportions. Apparently then, beginning to date at an early age tends to be associated with dating a variety of individuals, with going steady after considerable experience in dating, and with breaking off and returning to playing the field. In contrast, beginning to date at a relatively late age usually involves beginning to go steady without dating long, presumably with few individuals, and by implication becoming emotionally involved.

Further, the evidence shows rather convincingly that those who have never gone steady begin to date quite late (compare columns 1 and 2 of Table 2 with column 3). Presumably they will behave like those now going steady, a group that also began to date late; and they will likewise rush into going steady quickly with little dating experience. If going steady is assumed to imply greater emotional involvement, late daters may therefore be expected to become highly emotional without much dating experience. Logically, they may likewise be expected to rush into marriage relatively quickly with limited dating acquaintance with members of the opposite sex. If experience in paired association with the opposite sex means increased ability to judge associates, the evidence suggests that late daters are likely to rush into marriage with persons they have dated for a short period, with persons they do not know well enough to judge or size up as mates. Unfortunately, very limited data have been gathered concerning the relationship between the ages of beginning to date and of beginning to go steady, and the quickness with which marriage occurs.[6] In the nature of the case such

evidence could not be obtained in these three samples of high school students. Actually, the proportion of students who were married was very small. With numbers too small to give reliable results, the married were excluded from analysis.

From the evidence concerning behavioral differences with variations in the age of initial dating, four tentative conclusions may be drawn:

1. The earlier dating begins, the more frequently it tends to occur.

2. The age dating begins varies among students according to previous dating experience: that is, those playing the field who have previously gone steady began dating early; those who have never gone steady and those now going steady began dating relatively late.

3. Attempts to explain the irregularities involved in the age dating begins and the level of its occurrence led to the finding that the earlier dating begins the longer the delay in beginning to go steady; or conversely, the later dating begins the more quickly going steady is started.

4. While early dating and early going steady are inter-related, early dating tends to go with relatively broad and lengthy experience in paired sex association before going steady is initiated; or conversely, late dating tends to go with a relatively short period of dating before going steady begins—that is, with comparatively little experience in intersex association before going steady starts.

---

[6] Lee G. Burchinal, *Marriage and Family Living*, **20** (November, 1959), pp. 378–384, presents evidence concerning sixty girls who married while in high school. By matching these with a corresponding number of unmarried girls he shows that the married began to date and to go steady earlier than the unmarried, the reverse of that hypothesized above. Of course, further research is needed to determine actual relationships, but the samples studied offer a plausible explanation of the differences in findings. Burchinal is not sure that high school girls who marry differ from average, but he does show that in his sample they are of low socio-economic status. Further, roughly two-fifths of them were pregnant at the time of marriage, a condition that obviously did not characterize the girls who did not marry. Rather generally those who marry while in high school are supposed to be atypical in still other respects. If they are not representative, the sixty girls with whom they were matched may likewise be presumed to vary from the typical. In contrast, the regional data used in this article approximate representativeness of the school population in the three cities surveyed. Is it possible that in Burchinal's study both the married and the unmarried, being selected on the same basis except for marital state, are exceptional in their dating habits? Just why, if they are, is a matter of speculation. One of many possibilities is the large proportion of rural girls in his study in contrast to the fact that in this

present study all the girls are urban. Another possibility is the age of the males with whom at least the married girls in Burchinal's sample consorted, a point he does not consider. However, he himself points out, *Iowa Farm Science*, **12** (June, 1958), p. 13, that in school age marriages in Iowa, in 1956, "as the bride's age decreased, the difference between her age and that of her husband increased. For 18-year-old brides, for instance, the groom-bride age difference was 3.1 years; for 16-year-old brides and their husbands, 4 years; for 14-year-old brides and their husbands, 5 years." The same point is shown for the United States registration area in 1953, in Paul C. Glick, *American Families*, John Wiley, New York, 1957, pp. 122–126.

In view of these and other possibilities, more definite evidence is needed before undisputed conclusions can be drawn concerning the relation between the age of initial dating and that of marriage.

Conclusions

From the conclusions in the preceding pages, those concerning the conditions associated with early and late dating, and those just reached concerning the age of dating and subsequent behavior, two distinctive patterns emerge. In the nature of the case, these represent tendencies to be found more generally at the extremes. On the one hand is the first pattern, made up of those who are thoroughly American, above average in education, with small families, and of relatively higher social and economic status. Children of this group tend to date early and comparatively frequently; and after considerable experience in dating they tend to go steady relatively early, but revert fairly quickly to playing the field. Indeed, of all those surveyed in the three samples, this group playing the field includes over half of those who have ever gone steady.

The second pattern is made up of the opposite extreme: those of more recent foreign origin, of lower education, of large families, and of lower socio-economic status. Children of these families tend to begin to date late, and to begin going steady relatively quickly without much experience in dating. Further, data not presented show the differences in the age of individuals paired in dating are consistently large both among those of lower status and among those of lower parental education, both on first and last dates, and that these differences are significant among girls in over half the age classes. Unfortunately, these data were not classified by the age dating began.

To the extent that these two patterns of conditions and modes of behavior are substantiated by further inquiry and by evidence concerning the age of marriage, there will begin to appear objective bases of inferences concerning the effects of variations in the age of dating. This study offers hypotheses as to what relationships may be found. These hypotheses need to be tested and extended, to discover their bearing on the age of marriage.

17. Courtship as Social Exchange: Some Historical Comparisons*

BY MICHAL M. McCALL

ONE SIGNAL CONTRIBUTION of Willard Waller's classic treatise on the family[1] was his analysis of courtship conduct as bargaining and/or exploitative behavior. His use of an exchange framework was dictated by the more or less practical reason that ordinary individuals recognized bargaining at work in the courtship process and modified their behavior accordingly.

When one marries, he makes a number of different bargains. Everyone knows this and this knowledge affects the sentiment of love and the process of falling in love.[2]

Today it is perhaps not so true that "everyone knows this." The courtship bargaining and exploitation that Waller saw and explained theoretically are no longer so widely recognized in the society as being operant. In this sense, Waller's analysis has become a bit dated, and the theory of courtship as exchange and bargaining is therefore in some danger of being discredited. In the hope of averting this possibility, the present paper undertakes an analysis of historical changes in American courtship practices to highlight the changing types of bargaining embodied in these practices.

It should be noted that Waller did recognize that there had been changes in the process of courtship bargaining. However, he failed to account for these changes or to incorporate them into his general model. Furthermore, Waller failed to make consistent use of the exchange framework in his discussion of courtship. That is, he had much more to say about courtship than one would suppose from a look at his rather sketchy discussion of courtship as bargaining. In fact, he was more interested in *exploitation* than in honest bargaining and used the discussion of courtship bargaining almost as a stepping-stone toward that topic.

... (T)here is a powerful impulsion toward getting something for nothing, and bargaining tends to go over by imperceptible stages into exploitation.
... Within the courtship group, the exploitative attitude spreads like a disease. So it is that disillusioned adolescents learn the jungle law: exploit or be exploited.[3]

This interest in exploitation is at least in part a result of Waller's historical setting, as we shall see.

The very sparseness of Waller's discussion of bargaining is itself related to his place in time. Writing as he did in a transitional phase of courtship practices, he could not see clearly what was muddied by transition. Hence, his understanding of courtship and bargaining was restricted, as he himself recognized:

* This investigation was supported (in part) by a Public Health Service fellowship 1-fl-MH-25, 958-01 from the National Institute of Mental Health.
[1] Willard Waller, *The Family: A Dynamic Interpretation*, New York: The Cordon Company, 1938, Ch. 10 ("Bargaining and Exploitative Attitudes").
[2] *Ibid.*, p. 239.

[3] *Ibid.*, pp. 239, 250.

In modern society, groups are confused, and cultural imperatives are in conflict, and therefore the nature of the bargaining process is more complex and its outlines are confused.[4]

Despite its weaknesses, however, Waller's was an important discussion of courtship bargaining. He pointed out that "two kinds of bargains (are) struck in the courtship process"— those which have to do with the conditions of association in courtship, and those which have to do with marriage. Waller further implied the existence of another and logically prior class of bargains, those which determine the eligibles for a given person, that is, delimit the field within which the bargaining *per se* will take place.[5] By the bargains which determine the conditions for association, Waller meant such decisions as who was to be the dominant (i.e., least interested) member of the pair and whether there would be sexual intimacy (or how much). As for the final bargain,

The traits which determine whether one will win, place, or show in the marriage competition are such things as family background, economic power, education, and personal qualities such as age, beauty, and sexual attractiveness.[6]

Although it will turn out that even the number of bargains which must be struck in any courtship is to some extent historically relative, Waller's three bargains provide an important organizing principle and, accordingly, can profitably be used to analyze the changing modes of courtship behavior. We will refer to the bargains as: (1) bargains that determine who is eligible to court whom, (2) bargains that determine how courtship will proceed, and (3) bargains that determine who will marry whom. That is, we will discuss them in their chronological order in the courtship process, within each historical period.

Before proceeding to such an analysis, however, it will be necessary to indicate the major outlines of social exchange theory and to examine certain broad changes which have been, and are, taking place in American courtship practices.

Exchange and Bargaining in Social Behavior

The notion of *exchange* as an overarching fact of human behavior is one useful framework in which to view such behavior. Blau defines this sort of "exchange behavior" as

limited to actions that are contingent on rewarding reactions from others that cease when expected reactions are not forthcoming.[7]

That is, man is seen as choosing those social associations or relationships which are rewarding to him and as continuing in such relationships only so long as these remain rewarding. Likewise, the person is seen as providing rewards to the other party (or parties) to the relationship in exchange for those he has received from them. Rewards of this sort are as varied as are an individuals' wants, including money, social approval, power, commitment, prestige, aid, love, and so forth.

To the extent an individual has no viable alternatives to the present relationship as a source of such rewards, the other person is said to possess *power* over him. This other person, being less dependent upon the relationship as a source of rewards is the person who (in Waller's terms) is "least interested" in the continuation of the relationship.

Bargaining, as distinguished from simple exchange, implies a certain purposive awareness of the exchange of rewards. Individuals bargain about whether they will reward one another, in what ways, under what conditions, and to what degree. In this sense, then, exchange behavior may occur even though bargaining does not. Bargaining entails some knowledge of other sources of reward and an ability to draw on these alternative sources (or to threaten to do so), as well as a sense of how much one can reasonably expect to get in social exchange of a given variety.

[4] *Ibid.*, p. 240.

[5] In fact, although Waller merely implied the first type of bargain, concerning the eligibles, in his enumeration of courtship bargain, specifically naming only the second and third types, he discussed in the text only the first and second of these. Such is a further source of confusion and incompleteness in the Waller discussion of courtship as bargaining.

[6] *Ibid.*, p. 240.

[7] Peter M. Blau, *Exchange and Power in Social Life*, New York: Wiley, 1964, p. 6.

A View of Contemporary Mate-Selection

Bernard Farber has recently advanced an explanation of changing courtship practices and of marriage in the United States based upon what he calls the "permanent availability model" of marriage;[8] that is, Farber proposes that in some sense all adult persons are permanently available to contract a marriage, even if they happen to be married already. (This model might better have been called the "universal availability model," since Farber means to include complete availability across persons as well as through time.) However, Farber's provocative model fails to provide an explanation of why an individual might remain loyal to his partner in a single marriage relationship or, conversely, might choose to make himself available for other marriages. An exchange theory of courtship, on the other hand, would provide just such an explanation, as will be detailed below. First, we must examine more closely Farber's views of contemporary trends in American marriage and courtship practices.

In this view, these practices are no longer kin-controlled, because of increases in societal complexity and of changes in residence patterns (especially the rural-urban shift). With the consequent losses of power and importance, the kin group no longer delimits the relationships among persons. This means that, as fewer people are "related," more people are eligible as possible mates, including members of religious, ethnic, and social status groups other than one's own. Simultaneously with this broadening of availability, there has been a change toward *permanent* availability through time. Divorce has lost its social stigma in most cases, making both divorce and remarriage more common. Because virginity as a condition for remarriage is obviously impossible, it is less important even for first marriages; that which is impossible for *every* marriage is less important for *any* marriage. Furthermore, the realization that there can be divorce and remarriage has meant that young marriages are more likely than formerly in the middle classes, since one needn't wait to marry until one is most desirable economically and

socially and since an unsuccessful first marriage needn't prohibit a remarriage. Finally, the prevalence of divorce and remarriage means that individuals are permanently available, even when already married to someone else; they have only to terminate that relationship to begin another. Since marriages need not last a lifetime, "complementarity of personality" and of needs is no longer at a premium as it was when a couple had to face many crises together, hence needed between them the widest possible range of psychological strengths. Rather, there is today an emphasis upon likeness of personality and of interests, values, and needs, insuring greater compatibility; after all, if a crisis does arise, the couple need not stay together.

Exchange notions are implied here, although Farber does not develop them. If a person has no other choice of relationship than the one he is already in, he must continue in it even though it is no longer rewarding (and may be positively taxing). If, however, he does have other choices, he need not continue in the less rewarding one.[9] He is free to begin again even though the second relationship may turn out to be no more rewarding than was the first one. In that case, the whole process may be repeated, hence, the pattern of multiple divorce and remarriage.

Farber points out that there is also an emerging *courtship* pattern congruent with this model of permanent availability for marriage. This courtship pattern, which he calls the "series of involvements" pattern, is to be differentiated from the older "ever-narrowing field" pattern discussed by Burgess and Locke.[10]

(These authors) described the stages of courtship in American society as: Dating, keeping company, going steady, a private understanding

---

[8] Bernard Farber, *Family: Organization and Interaction*, San Francisco: Chandler, 1964, Chs. 4–5.

[9] This may be the sense in which the husband is no longer so powerful in the American family. When neither partner had much choice, a woman, being tied to the home, had even less, both because she met fewer people and because a divorced woman bore greater stigma than did a divorced man. Today, however, women work outside the home and are no longer under any greater onus than are their ex-husbands. In this sense, there is greater equality, and less power, in the marriage; both parties are equally independent of the relationship.

[10] Ernest W. Burgess and Harvey J. Locke, *The Family from Institution to Companionship*, New York: American Book Co., 1953.

between the man and woman to be married, and engagement.[11]

Today all this has changed, even the terms; as Farber points out: "keeping company" is no longer in the courtship vocabulary. As for "going steady," it has come to mean "merely . . . the person with whom the individual is currently involved." In short,

. . . the system of mate selection of the 1920's and 1930's, in which there was a continual narrowing of the field of prospective spouses, has given way to a series of personal involvements. One of these involvements eventuates in marriage."[12]

Farber might almost have called this model of courtship the "continual series of involvements" model or even the "permanent availability for involvements" model, so well does the courtship arrangement fit the marriage system. Young people are involved with one partner at a time, in various degrees of intimacy. One such involvement "eventuates in marriage." This marriage itself is subject to change, however, and the mates may become involved with other persons. In other words, marriage is merely a more total type of involvement which may end quite as lesser involvements do, leaving the individuals free for new involvements, whether of the marriage type or some other.

The term "involvement" itself points up an apparent contradiction which Farber's analysis of the changed pattern reveals. Along *with* the permanent availability norms and the consequent lack of exclusiveness (which Farber points out in the going-steady phase but which is true as well of all involvements), there is simultaneously an increased emphasis on *total commitment* (including sexual) and deep involvement of both partners. This paradox results from the lack of structural constraints implied by the notion of permanent and universal availability, and the consequent needs for *interpersonal* constraints. In the old days merely breaking an engagement was often grounds for legal action; today one enters and leaves "involvements," including marriage, much more easily, whenever one is "dissatisfied" or "incompatible."

This is related to the dropping of still another

[11] Farber, *op. cit.*, p. 160.
[12] *Ibid.*, p. 161.

of the old terms, not mentioned by Farber. Today no one (except perhaps clandestine lovers) has *private* agreements. Emphasis is rather upon *public* commitments, once again as a means of social control where few such plans exist. Indeed, "dating" has, to a considerable extent, been replaced, both as behavior and term. Today young people are "going with" other people, not merely dating them. The new term (and behavior) implies greater involvement than does mere dating.

This account of Farber's views is less than complete but will serve to delimit one endpoint of the continuum of changing courtship patterns that will be elaborated in the following sections.

Three Historical Patterns of Courtship

The courtship patterns under consideration here may be divided into three broad types, each roughly associated with a specific historical period: the traditional, the intermediary, and the contemporary. These patterns are analytic abstractions from concrete courtship behaviors, of course, and therefore cannot be construed as the moulds into which all matings in a given period were deliberately cast by the participants. The patterns do seem, however, to have been characteristic of most matings among individuals not located at the extremes of the socio-economic scale. The feature of these three patterns of primary interest to the present paper is that each pattern (or period) involved highly distinctive types of courtship bargains.

So different have these bargains been, in fact, that to speak of "courtship" rather than the more general phenomenon of "mate-selection" ought actually to limit us to the second of our three historical periods. That we do typically speak of "courtship" is related to the fact that our knowledge of American mate-selection is largely based on a picture that may no longer be valid. This picture, here called the intermediary pattern, has dominated American culture since its beginnings, and it is this mode that Waller described. Thus, it turns out that it is only to this period that Waller's three bargains actually apply directly. They do not apply precisely to the traditional and contemporary patterns.

Exchange and Bargaining in the Traditional Pattern. The traditional pattern of mate selection was characterized by bargaining between kin groups or the parents of two young persons. Eligibility was not *bargained* about; instead, exchange terms were set in much the same way that prices in American stores are set. Goods are marked with a price, and the buyer can either pay the price or he must shop elsewhere. Analogously, the kin group decided[13] in which market they would shop, on the basis of the prices charged there and the quality of the merchandise. That is, they decided who the eligibles were, knowing full well the prices they would have to pay and the kind of mate they would be getting.

Furthermore, because the very act of inclusion in the group of eligibles meant full consideration as a marriage partner, there was only one actual bargain struck—the marriage bargain itself. There was no bargain about the conditions of association in courtship, because *there was no courtship.* Rather, one's kin bargained with the kin of a young member of the opposite sex concerning the terms of marriage. With regard to this third (marriage) bargain, the traditional pattern represented bargaining par excellence.

This bargain, often called the "arranged marriage," is described by Zelditch:

Arranged marriage is found where the consequences of marriage concern whole groups of kinsmen. Kinsmen usually have three kinds of interest in a marriage. The marriage is often conceived as an alliance between two kinship groups, not simply the relation of the two partners to the marriage, and the group is anxious to select allies carefully. Significant economic interests are usually involved, both in the exchange of goods that accompanies the marriage and in the effect of marriage on the dispersal or concentration of inherited property, wealth, and resources. When the kinship unit as a whole is the unit of the stratification system, so that a "peer marriage" lowers the social rank of the whole group, the kinsmen are concerned to protect the family name.[14]

Thus, in the traditional pattern there is no courtship between individuals, nor is there even any bargaining between kin groups except at the level of the marriage bargain itself, where this bargaining is most explicit indeed.

As mentioned, this pattern has never been characteristic of American mate selection. It is instead an ideal-typical picture of the early European system and of the systems of many primitive societies. It does not apply to the American case because, as Zelditch points out, it occurs only where marriage is a kin affair, and the kindred has never been as powerful or important here as it is elsewhere. An unusually high degree of mobility has always characterized American society. The first settlers came unaccompanied by their entire kin. Unattached males, or in some cases nuclear families, came, but whole clans, tribes, or even complete extended families were unlikely to come at once. Therefore, there was not the rigid control by the kin group which is so characteristic of mate-selection in the traditional mode. Furthermore, the valuables which were bargained about in those more stable societies in which the traditional pattern occurred were fluid in the United States. One could, at that time, have land almost for the asking, so that the protection of family holdings was less important. Social status, too, was won and lost almost daily. Finally, there has been in the United States an important cultural value stressing the freedom of the individual to make his own decisions, a freedom that would be contradicted by the kin-control characteristic of the traditional pattern of mate selection.

Nonetheless, the American mating game did not present a sudden and sharp break with the traditional pattern. Rather, it has throughout its history exemplified the intermediary pattern, which at first tended toward the traditional and has gradually come to resemble the contemporary mode described by Farber.

Exchange and Bargaining in the Intermediary Pattern. This pattern was "intermediary" in the

---

[13] Of course, this "decision" was never literally a decision. Rather, such things were "decided by" one's place in the social stratification system. A middle-class college girl today knows few construction workers or Boston Brahmins; accordingly, she chooses a mate from among upper-lower to lower-upper-class men. Similarly, in the traditional pattern, a young prince of France knew precious few commoners, and the ones he did know were of the highest classes.

[14] Morris Zelditch, Jr., "Family, Marriage, and Kinship," Ch. 18 in R. E. L. Faris (ed.), *Handbook of Modern Sociology*, Chicago: Rand McNally, 1964. Quotation from pp. 686–687.

sense that the kin group did not have complete authority in mate selection, but neither was it powerless. The young people themselves were highly involved in the selection process (here properly called "courtship"), but their parents were also. Love was the ideal and was properly encouraged, but restrictions on falling in love remained:

In Western countries, and especially in America, it is assumed that men and women marry because they are in love. There is a broadly based mythology about the character of love as a violent, irresistable emotion that strikes where it will, a mystery that is the goal of most young people and often of the not-so-young as well. As soon as one investigates, however, which people actually marry each other, one finds that the lightning shaft of cupid seems to be guided rather stringently within very definite channels of class, income, education, racial and religious background. If one investigates a little further into the behavior that is engaged prior to marriage under the rather misleading euphemism of "courtship," one finds channels of interaction that are often rigid to the point of ritual. . . . In other words, when certain conditions are met or have been constructed, one allows oneself "to fall in love."[15]

It is this intermediary mode, the mode we know the most about, to which we may properly apply the term "courtship" and upon which most theories of mate-selection are based. It was this pattern Waller tried to describe, albeit in its transition to the contemporary pattern, thus producing the "confusion" of which Waller complained. In this intermediary pattern, the three bargains Waller described can indeed be seen.

The first of these, the bargaining over eligibility, was clearly a true bargain in this pattern. Eligibility was decided (but not set) on the basis of one's economic and social position. This meant that the primary bases were still in the positions of the parents, but it was no longer so much a matter of keeping the family lands intact as of marrying one of equal or slightly higher "station" in life. The young person had not only family position and his promise of a portion of his father's wealth or business to bargain with, but also his own level and place of education (where one went to school was socially highly important), his occupation, and his own social position.

All this may sound much like the traditional pattern, but the important thing is that here there was true *bargaining* about eligibility (not mere exchange). That is, one could *raise or lower* one's chances of being considered eligible by those whom one, in turn, considered eligible and desirable; this could be done by increasing one's education, by "hard work," and even by a display of great personal charm.

This becomes clear if we return to Burgess and Locke's depiction of the courtship sequence. Waller's first bargain was a bargain about with whom one would begin the sequence. Not all of one's acquaintances were considered eligible in this sense; not all of one's classmates or neighbor's nor even all of one's boyhood or girlhood chums were eligible as suitors. Conversely, a young person whose parents were quite low in the stratification system of status and class might yet be considered eligible, perhaps on the basis of exceptional charm or drive or intelligence. Burgess and Locke's phrase, "to be accepted as a suitor," exemplifies the first bargain in this pattern.

Once accepted as suitor (i.e., once the first bargain has been satisfactorily carried off), Waller's second type of bargain became important in the sequence; suitors began to bargain over the conditions of association in the courtship process. Of primary importance here is that a young woman might begin the sequence with several suitors in the field (and likewise the young man might court several women, although this was not similarly stressed in the folk culture) and that the young people themselves carried on this bargaining.

Individuals did not form exclusive attachments (at least until the latest stages of the courtship process), but rather bargained with several others and narrowed the field of suitors by successively dropping the least favorable bargains. This type of bargaining, where commitment must be allocated among several role relationships in an attempt to maximize reward and minimize loss, has been fruitfully analyzed by Goode.[16] The point was to keep several alters as bargaining partners and to allocate and reallocate commitments among them through bargaining.

[15] Peter L. Berger, *Invitation to Sociology*, New York: Doubleday Anchor, 1963, pp. 35–36.

[16] William J. Goode, "A Theory of Role Strain," *American Sociological Review*, 1960, **25**, pp. 483–496.

(This is clearly seen in the picture of behavior at the social dance; a young woman judged the success of her evening by the number of young men who signed her card and danced with her.)

The individuals involved undoubtedly did not perceive this bargaining as being concerned with "commitment." They were interested in finding their "one true love," the "person I was meant for." But one way, perhaps the most important way, of determining which person one was meant for, was on the basis of which person seemed to love one the most (i.e., who was most commited to one, and most willing to admit such commitment). In large part, "being meant for one another" came down to complementarity of personality and of needs, as discussed above. As mentioned there, this complementarity was an important resource for marriage under the societal conditions of this historical period.

As the "ever-narrowing field" model suggests, bargains were attempted and judged favorable or not, and were dropped or continued accordingly. However, at some point in the courtship sequence, two individuals had progressively narrowed the field until only they were left as suitors. Up to this point, the bargaining had been taking place between and among individuals in the field. That is, the young woman, while she bargained with each of her suitors, also played them off against one another, allocating and reallocating her commitment. It was during this process that her sense of what she was worth as a product and her knowledge of what was generally available on the market had been established. Then, when the sole remaining couple turned inward, as it were, and bargained exclusively with one another, they were thus quite aware of market conditions and could drive a vigorous bargain.

This turning inwardly typically occurred at the stage of engagement, after the couple had already progressed through dating, keeping company, and going steady. The "private understanding" discussed by Burgess and Locke was a sort of intervening, transitional phase during which both persons had fairly clearly decided that the field was narrowed to the other alone, but during which one could still legitimately and without social pressure resume one's bargaining with someone else, too. In any case, the great length of the courtship period was functional in just this fashion. It was intended as a period in which individuals made sure that they were meant for each other, because there could be no turning back (divorce) after marriage.

Thus, we have in a sense already described the third (marriage) bargain as well. The persons bargained until they struck the most favorable bargain, as suggested, and then they made a contract: the marriage contract. The person tried to find the *one* other who was meant for him (who most loved him, who he most loved, and who was most complementary to him), and then formed a permanent contract of exchange. This contract was a bargain to end any further cross-sex bargaining.

Thus, in the intermediary pattern, there were three true bargains struck in what we can properly call a courtship process. Furthermore, both the young people themselves and the parents of both parties participated in the bargaining. The parents' role was largely implicit, setting the market to a considerable extent by their place in the stratification system. However, they did participate more actively at certain points of the process too. This courtship pattern dictated that the young man ask the girls' father and then, with his consent, propose marriage to the girl. This meant that, although his main bargaining was done with the young lady herself, he was obliged to bargain with her parents as well. Not the least of his selling points was an economic one, as is seen in the famous question, "Young man, are you able to support my daughter in the manner to which she has become accustomed?" The role of the boy's parents was also largely economic; if they disapproved of the young woman of his choice, they might cut him off from a share of an inheritance or, in those days of father-and-son businesses, might even put him out of work. That the young woman bargained with the boy's parents is seen in the practice of "taking her home to meet his mother."

Under the impetus of the two World Wars and all of the social changes they wrought, including the increase in urbanization and residential mobility mentioned above, this intermediary courtship pattern eventually broke down. The change was gradual. Waller recognized its beginnings at the time he wrote, and it has probably not been completed even yet. However, we must deal with a different ideal-typical model of mate-selection when discussing the contemporary period.

Exchange and Bargaining in the Contemporary Pattern. As Farber points out, the kin group has lost much of its power as an agent in mate-selection. The contemporary arrangement includes a joint decision of the two young adults and a subsequent announcement by them to both sets of parents that they will be married and when (or that they *were* married, and when). Thus, from a traditional arrangement in which only the kin groups participated, to an intermediary one in which both sets of parents participated along with the two young people, we have come to an arrangement which does not include the participation of either set of parents as active bargaining agents.[17]

This arrangement does not include all three of Waller's bargains: as in the case of the traditional arrangement, there is only one genuine bargain struck. As Farber's concept of permanent (or universal) availability suggests, there is no bargaining over eligibility, the first of Waller's three bargains. In the contemporary pattern, every person with whom the individual comes in contact is eligible as a possible mate, regardless of marital status, religion, ethnicity, or social class.[18]

The one bargain which *does* take place in this contemporary pattern is the second of Waller's bargains, that dealing with "conditions of association in courtship." However, even this bargain is quite different from its counterpart in the intermediary pattern.

As Farber points out, there is no longer a belief in the inevitability of one's mate. If a person can be married more than once and involved any number of times, it is not possible that there is one and only one person "meant for him." Rather, we may say, there is an emphasis upon the uniqueness of *each* of his successive relationships, in Simmel's sense of "uniqueness."[19] That which the individuals are bargaining about is still commitment to the relationship and to the mate, but an individual is expected to become commited *each* time he becomes involved. The emphasis is upon intimacy or exclusiveness of involvement at any time. Thus, the couple "turns inward" from the beginning in this mode. If this is true, how can there *be* any bargaining, since bargaining requires the presence of an alternative relationship? The nature of the mate-selection process supplies the alternative: each person is free to leave any involvement (including marriage) at any time. The whole pattern is *set up* to give individuals training and experience in "getting along with others" in intimate relationships. Because there is no longer a belief in the "one and only," there is no longer an emphasis upon complementarity; the involvement (including marriage involvements) need not last through crises, and consequently the emphasis is now upon likeness and compatibility and (in the case of differences) upon toleration.

It is obvious that today's mate-selection is no longer a period of determining the best bargain and sealing that bargain in marriage. Rather, today this "courtship" period is one of training in bargaining. In other words, "courtship" teaches the individual how to bargain—how to form, maintain, and leave relationships. The emphasis in modern life is on keeping up one's bargaining skills, for one never entirely leaves the market. This, as Farber points out, helps explain the mania for "youthfulness" and "glamor" in contemporary American culture. Marriage may occur at any time in one's life, so one must make an effort to remain desirable and must polish up his skill in striking a good bargain.

In this sense, involvements (including the marriage involvement) are not contracts but restrictive trade agreements. The two individuals agree to exchange only with one another, at least

---

[17] Of course, once again, the position of the parents in the stratification system determines to a large extent where the person will stand in that system and, thus, what kinds of people he will meet, as well as his mode of bargaining.

[18] It is important to note that we say "everyone a person comes in contact with," and not merely everyone. This suggests, once again, that one's social position limits the number and variety of individuals considered as possible mates. A college girl is more likely to marry a college boy, because she knows many college boys but very few high school dropouts.

[19] Georg Simmel, *The Sociology of Georg Simmel* (trans. Kurt H. Wolff), New York: Free Press, 1950, pp. 118–144.

until such time as the balance of trade becomes unfavorable in terms of broader market considerations. They agree to exchange exclusively for so long as the rewards in *this* involvement exceed the costs of continuing it in the face of chances for other rewards elsewhere. The individual, by forming numerous such exclusive and reciprocal trade agreements at various times, gets some idea of his overall worth as a product and of the market conditions, as well as learning bargaining skills, as mentioned above.

Finally, there is no real third (marriage) bargain under this arrangement. Given that marriage is merely one kind (though perhaps a more stable and lasting kind) of involvement, there can be no marriage bargain apart from the second type of bargain. That is, the "conditions for association in *marriage*" are no different in kind than the "conditions for association in courtship."

Changes in Sexual Bargaining and Exploitation

The sense of change in the American patterns of mate selection may become still stronger if we examine more closely certain aspects of the intermediary pattern, as this pattern grew out of the traditional pattern and then as it approached the shape of the contemporary pattern. The most profitable focus for this examination is the second of Waller's bargains, concerning conditions of association in courtship. With both the intermediary and contemporary patterns, when indeed there was association between the individuals before marriage, these individuals were bargaining over commitment, as we have seen, and the type of commitment has already been shown to have differed characteristically between the intermediary and contemporary patterns. The differences become even sharper, however, if we look at one specific kind of commitment (perhaps the most important kind), namely, sexual intimacies of various degrees.

During the traditional period, and in the first stages of the intermediary, premarital sexual behavior was not involved in the second bargain. Rather, it was involved in the first bargain about eligibility for marriage. In this arrangement, women engaged in "price-fixing" about sexual intimacy. There was a strict dichotomy between "good women" (those who did not engage in sexual behavior) and "bad women" (those who did). Since only the good women were eligible as marriage partners (except in the lowest socioeconomic classes), the young man had either to pay the price in this first bargain (i.e., accept the condition that the girl didn't do such things) or fail to make a purchase at all; there was no haggling about it.

In the later phases of the intermediary pattern, however, this had changed somewhat. Premarital sex was no longer subsumed by the first bargain, and its possibility had become one of the matters which the individuals bargained about in concluding the bargaining about conditions of association in courtship. Women were still engaged in "price-fixing," but the price was now not so rigidly fixed. Some good women could be induced to lower their price, and hence haggling became worthwhile. For a good woman to permit any serious premarital sexual behavior, however, indicated two things: (1) that she was deeply committed to the relationship, and (2) that the young man was being rewarded for his own deep commitment. One only made a *sexual* commitment once—to the "one and only"—and to do so was tantamount to marriage. This is related to the emphasis on virginity at the time of marriage in this pattern. One was a virgin until one met one's true love, and then one married him and submitted. If one submitted *first*, then marriage was a foregone conclusion.

There might, however, be slip-ups in this process. Young women might commit themselves thus to several men, or, more likely, a young man might indicate deep commitment to (and be thus rewarded by) several young women. As a consequence, while a woman might or might not indulge, her popularity depended upon the fact that she did not.

The interest of girls in protecting the value of sexual favors against depreciation gives rise to social pressures among girls not to grant these favors readily. Coleman's study of high schools shows that these pressures tend to take the form of making a girl's social standing contingent on her reputation in regard to her sexual behavior with boys.[20]

[20] Blau, *op. cit.*, pp. 80–81.

Slip-ups did occur, and it was to slip-ups of the second type mentioned above that Waller referred with his concept of exploitation. As we have seen, exploitation was Waller's chief concern about courtship as bargaining. Having defined exploitation as the witholding of something which is supposed to be given in return for that which one is receiving, he went on to point out that the most common kind of exploitation was sexual exploitation. The gold digger among women and the cad among men, both promised something but failed to meet the terms of exchange; the gold digger offered sexual favors in return for costly attention, and the cad promised marriage in return for sexual favors, but neither delivered.

It is important to realize that exploitation of this kind could occur only in a period during which sexual favors were problematic (i.e., when a person might or might not indulge) and in a time when the granting of them represented deep commitment, with concomitant and legitimate expectations of a permanent relationship. When the young son of a royal house forced sexual attentions upon some slave girl or peasant's daughter, he could not be called a cad; he was not exploiting the girl, since she had no legitimate expectations of anything further. She could not expect that he would marry her, and so his failure to do so in return for her favors was not exploitation. (If, on the other hand, he did promise something else, such as economic recompense or a chance to be his mistress, and failed to keep his promise, he might certainly be considered a cad.) This is true because in the traditional pattern, as mentioned, sexual behavior was not problematic; rather, it was involved in the delimitation of eligibles. Any woman who "did" was automatically ineligible for marriage (although she might be eligible to become a mistress or a paid prostitute).[21]

[21] If we follow out our analogy about the way in which eligibility was set under the traditional arrangements whereby deciding which market one would shop in was analogous to deciding which persons were eligible and where this choice of markets was based on their price and quality of goods, we might say that while a young man bought his suit at Brooks Brothers (that is, chose his wife in an elite group of eligibles), he might shop for underwear at Sears (that is, have a mistress from a lower class or patronize a prostitute).

Likewise, sexual exploitation of this sort is not associated with the contemporary pattern. Today, total commitment is expected in every involvement, whether marriage or otherwise. This total commitment includes sexual commitment. As Farber points out, a young woman is not expected to be a virgin at the time of her first marriage (since she could hardly be expected to be a virgin at the time of any subsequent marriages). The person with whom one enters a marriage involvement is no more the "one and only" than is the person with whom one enters *any* involvement (each involvement partner is the one-and-only for the time being, as indicated by the emphasis upon intimacy and exclusiveness), and it little matters whether the previous involvement of a nonvirgin was a marriage or another kind of involvement.

That which does, however, mark the marriage involvement as different from others is the decision to have children. Farber explains that while this decision does not necessarily imply a permanent commitment (as witnessed by the prevalent belief that divorce is better for children than keeping together an unhappy family), it does imply at least a relatively long term one. Parents expect that they will remain together to rear the offspring and furthermore recognize a permanent link between them in the form of shared parenthood. In addition, insofar as the norm remains one of child rearing under the auspices of "holy matrimony," parenthood sets the marital involvement apart from others.

Thus, exploitation today refers to the impregnation of the woman in an involvement. If a woman becomes pregnant and the man refuses to marry her, he is considered a cad. There is a legitimate expectation that marriage follows impregnation in this pattern, just as the intermediary pattern included a legitimate expectation that marriage followed sexual intimacy. Of course, there were also "shotgun weddings" in the intermediary pattern, but this was because sexual behavior and impregnation were practically coterminous. Today, sexual intimacy need not imply pregnancy, and herein lies the difference between the two patterns. Today sexual behavior is only an involvement; children constitute (marriage) commitment. In fact, an individual may decide not to have children with a specific marital partner, often giving as a reason the fact that the marriage is unstable or that he or she is not fully committed.

Thus Waller's preoccupation with sexual exploitation marks him, once again, as a product of the intermediary period. One gets a definite sense of this (as well as of the breakdown of the "ever-narrowing field" type of courtship in favor of the "series of involvement" type) in the following quotation:

> According to the moral standards which are still formally in force, courtship is a process in which every step is a commitment of the whole person, and the whole process of interaction moves rapidly toward total involvement and total commitment in marriage. . . . We now face a situation in which these meanings have disappeared and one person seeks to derive thrills from the person or the body of another without any involvement of his own personality.[22]

[22] Waller, *op. cit.*, p. 244.

Summary

An historical analysis of American courtship practices has shown three differing types of bargaining embodied in these practices. The traditional pattern has never been characteristic of American mate-selection but is important for an understanding of the other two types.

The intermediary pattern, which is the only one truly meriting the name of "courtship," has been the basis for most sociological theories of mate-selection. However, it is no longer fully characteristic of our society. A shift in mate-selection practices has included a transition to a third, contemporary pattern. Because this third type of bargaining is perhaps dominant today, it has been suggested here that our theories of mate-selection must change to match these changes in actual behavior.

18. Steady Dating, Imminent Marriage, and Remarriage

BY WILLIAM J. GOODE

IN THE VOCABULARY of contemporary American courtship, the stage or status of "steady date" has a different meaning for different social circles and strata, and even for different age groups. These varying meanings need not be discussed here. What is significant is that in our family system we enter marriage typically through courtship, and that therefore a marriage is more likely to grow out of a steady dating relationship than out of an ordinary dating relationship; and much more likely than out of no dating relationship at all. If the normal progression for the unmarried is from dating to steady dating to being engaged, and thus to being married, with each such activity or phase acting as a selective process for the succeeding phase, then we must take steady dating more seriously than general dating, and more seriously than even frequent dating.

On the other hand, precisely because these occur in sequence, grow from the same sets of social relationships, and are affected by the same factors, we need not reproduce for *steady* dating all the tables that merely parallel our findings for dating in general. Although certain factors are associated with general dating that are not associated with steady dating, we have found almost *no* items that run in a *contrary* direction. We shall be able to point to only few factors that

facilitate or increase frequency of dating, but hinder or reduce steady dating. Since it is through general dating that people in our society move toward steady dating (and remarriage), factors with a contrary effect at these two consecutive phases should be rare.

For the older or the once married, steady dating is doubtless more closely associated with marriage than for those who are younger or never married. Steady dating in later adolescence is a common pattern, but its social definition points to various types of mutual exploration, with no commitment on either side to an eventual marriage. Two adolescents who are "going steady"[1] are protected from further commitments by this social definition.[2]

By contrast, there is some feeling in most circles that when the couple is older, neither party to a steady dating relationship "has the right" to hold the other in exclusive possession, unless there is some possibility of eventual marriage. The social definitions are, then, that the older or the once married do not have an infinitely wide number of potential marriage

[1] We use the phrases, "going steady," or "dating steady" as acceptable American idiom.
[2] Parents of adolescents who are going steady do recognize, however, the statistically greater likelihood of still more intimacy, or even marriage, growing out of such a relationship, and consider general dating permissible at an earlier age than steady dating; or forbid steady dating with partners whom the adolescent is allowed to date generally.

SOURCE: *Reprinted with permission of The Free Press from* After Divorce, *by William J. Goode. Copyright 1956 by The Free Press, a Corporation.*

201

partners, or time to find them. Therefore, they should not stay, or hold others, in a steady dating relationship if there is no chance at all of marriage. A basic assumption of our society is, as we have analyzed previously, that almost all *will* get married, and that almost all *should* get married. Thus, relationships are disapproved that hinder adults from entering the statuses, and thereby the role obligations, that are prescribed for them.

For these reasons, we treat both steady dating and remarriage in this chapter, locating some of the factors that appear to be associated with these steps toward resuming the previous status of "married mother." Here, we look at the 303 divorcees who had not yet remarried by the time of the interview.

Let us first state the obvious, that frequency of dating is associated with steady dating: 68 per cent of the frequent daters (more than once weekly at the time of interview) are steady daters, while 38 per cent of the medium daters (once weekly to once a month), and only 5 per cent of the infrequent daters are also steady daters. It is useful to state the obvious, since the obvious is not always correct.

However, the proportion of steady daters might not increase much over time, for over time we also *lose* the steady daters into the remarried group. Thus the proportion of steady daters *cannot* increase indefinitely.

Now, the proportion dating steady does increase somewhat with time since separation, from 30 per cent of those separated 0–1 year, to 49 per cent of those separated 3 years and over. However, time since separation does not measure whether they *could* have remarried. Some had separated two or three years before the decree. From such segments, then, we would not lose the remarried, and thus the proportion could increase. By contrast, when we arrange our divorces into Time Groups (since divorce) the proportion of steady daters among all divorcees does not change systematically: they form 27 per cent of Time Group I, and 23 per cent of Group IV.

Those who were not daters become daters. These become frequent and then steady daters, and then remarry. Thus, the *number* of steady daters drops, but so does the numerical base. When we eliminate the remarried, we find that

the steady daters form 29 per cent of the not remarried in Group I, and increase to 49 per cent in Group IV. In Time Group IV, there are 51 divorcees who have not remarried; 25 of these are steady daters, 10 are dating without being steady daters, and 16 are not dating. Thus, the ratio of steady daters to ordinary daters rises over these Time Groups. By Group IV, the steady daters are two and one-half times as many as the ordinary daters. With reference to the larger institutional processes, we call attention to the fact that 76 per cent *of the divorcees who obtained their decrees 26 months before the interview were either remarried or were going steady by the time of the interview.*

Steady Dating and Other Close Relationships

Although Protestants form a slightly higher proportion of steady daters than do Catholics, the difference is small. No apparent relationship seems to exist between (1) the divorcees's education and steady dating, although we saw that there was such a relationship between dating frequency and education. We shall treat this factor once more when we speak of remarriage. (2) Women who had been married to middle-class husbands are less likely to be dating steady at the time of interview than wives of husbands from either upper or lower occupations (33 per cent versus 38 per cent and 42 per cent), but this relationship is unimportant. There is no apparent relationship between (3) the length of the marriage and the movement into steady dating: 41 per cent of the women who had been married 15 years or more were going steady at the time of the interview, but 40 per cent of those who had been married less than 5 years were also going steady. Of the themes of conflict, only (4) that of Triangle seems to have a substantial effect, in that a lower percentage of these wives are going steady. (5) Age has a complex relationship with steady dating, as it does with dating frequency. Of course, the younger are more likely to be steady daters than the older ex-wives. But the difference is largely to be found between those who are *less* than 25 years of age and *all others* (48 per cent are steady daters, while of the other age groups 34–36 per cent are steady daters). The young seem not to move into re-marriage swiftly. They date heavily and steadily first. However, we should look at steady dating along with other related patterns. We asked these unmarried divorcees whether there was some-one among their close men friends whom they would *consider* marrying, and we also asked whether there was a *fair chance* that this marriage might take place. Let us, then, compare the differences in these answers by reference to their age distribution. (See table below.)

First of all, we see that it is among the youngest age group that the highest frequency of steady dating is to be found, and once more we note that there are few differences among the remaining age groups. With reference to the *existence of potential spouses* among the close friends of the divorcee, however, these relationships change interestingly. For all age brackets except the age bracket 30–34 years, a higher percentage has a potential spouse among the very close friends than has a steady date. Loosely put, more women have their eyes on a potential spouse than have their hands on a steady date. Or, not all have as their steady date the person whom they would consider an eligible spouse.

Whether the age group 30–34 years is really different, we cannot say. The difference is not great and is not statistically significant. We sup-pose that whether such a potential spouse is to be found among a woman's very close friends depends upon two main factors: (a) the *numbers* of men she is acquainted with, and whom she

would consider her "very close men friends," and (b) her standards for a spouse. We have speculated that in the age bracket 30–34 years these women have not yet lowered their stan-dards for a spouse, but their circle of close men friends is smaller than when the women were younger. Consequently the proportion with a potential spouse in mind is smaller than in the other age brackets. By contrast, the age group 35 years and over may have a *smaller* circle of close men friends, but here we believe that their standards for a spouse have lowered to corres-pond to the objective social situation.

Looking at the table again, we notice that it is in the younger age brackets that the greatest optimism is to be found: as high a percentage believe that there is a *fair chance* of a marriage taking place as are dating steady (48–48 per cent), and this figure is only slightly lower than the proportion who state that among their close men friends there is someone that they might *consider* marrying. On the other hand, the other age groups seem less optimistic or more realistic. The only difference of significance, however, is found between those who are 30 years and over and those who are under 30 years of age.

There are actually no adequate data for the national population with respect to the effect of children upon the remarriage of divorcees. In this study we cannot, of course, compare the da-ting and remarriage of divorcees without children as against those with children, since all of our respondents did have one or more children. The slight relationship between number of children

Steady dating, existence of eligible spouse, and judgment that the marriage may take place—by age of respondent (not remarried)

Age	Dating steady per cent	Consider marrying someone among close men friends per cent	Fair chance of this marriage taking place per cent	Base
20–24 years	48	52	48	52
25–29 years	36	42	34	102
30–34 years	36	35	24	84
35 years and over	34	39	25	65
Totals	38	41	32	303

and the patterns now under consideration would seem to be the following: (1) There is a slightly higher proportion dating steady among those who have *one* child than among those who have *more* than one child. (2) The proportion dating steady among those who have three children and over is very slightly *higher* than among those who have only two children. This relationship is not significant. (3) Those who have the greatest number of children are slightly more inclined to consider marriage to someone of their close men friends. However, the difference is small and insignificant. (4) Of the proportion of those who say there *is* a fair chance that the marriage might take place, the frequency is *higher* for those with only *one* child, but only *slightly* lower for those who have *two* or more children. Even if these relationships do hold, they are in part spurious, since number of children is also a function of age of the spouse; and these relationships have already been outlined in that connection. Perhaps the most important conclusion is simply this: *among divorced mothers, the number of children* seems to have almost *no significant effect* on the activities leading to remarriage. This tentative conclusion will *not* be entirely borne out for those who *actually remarry*, as we shall see later.

Indeed, we can summarize our findings by stating that in general the same factors are at work here as in frequency of dating. We cannot locate important factors that move some daters, but not others, into steady dating. This is partly a result of our failure to develop any adequate theory on this point, and to build our theoretical expectations into our interview. On the other hand, we are not certain that there are any *major* differences to be found. That is, (1) almost all daters become steady daters eventually; (2) the factors that lead to steady dating earlier rather than later are the same that lead to frequent dating, but (3) these are fine, cumulative differences rather than major ones. We can distinguish somewhat the factors that lead to early rather than late remarriage, but these items are useful only for major actional differences, while between dating and steady dating the change of difference is not major. Thus, we record what slight differences the apparently relevant factors seem to make, but their combined effect does not seem to be great.

We did find an interesting, puzzling, and complex set of relationships that seem to suggest that the factors of trauma and first suggestion of divorce may have a reversed effect for steady dating, as against dating frequency and remarriage. We shall not present the data or the complexities here, but only the problem. In general, when the husband first suggested the divorce there was higher trauma, and when there was mutual suggestion there was lower trauma. And when there was higher trauma, in general there was a lower dating frequency. But the high trauma respondents are more likely to remarry early, while the effect of trauma upon steady dating is inconsistent when we hold first suggestion constant. Moreover, when we hold trauma constant, there is a consistent relationship between who first suggested the divorce, and both dating and remarriage: mutual suggestion is most positive in its effect, husband suggestion is least, and wife suggestion falls between. But this effect is reversed for steady dating. Factors such as age introduce further complexities. We mention these complexities, without presenting them or interpreting them, only because they suggest at least the possibility that the phase of steady dating deserves more serious study. At the present time, we are inclined to dismiss this notion, and to view the interesting consistencies in some of our tables as no more than statistical accidents. At best, without a true panel study we cannot measure the movement into and out of steady dating.

We have already made some mention of the relationship of steady dating, thinking of someone in the group as a possible spouse, and judging that a marriage with him might take place, when we discussed the influence of age on steady dating. Let us look once more at these judgments.

There are many possibilities of error. The divorcee might not at first take her steady date seriously as a possible spouse, but afterwards be forced by lack of real choice to accept him as a husband. Moreover, any divorcee might be too optimistic or pessimistic regarding the "fair chance" that such a marriage might take place.

Yet it is clear that our respondents differentiated between these two judgments, as we noted in considering age. Considering a man as a possible spouse is different from asserting that there is a fair chance that the marriage would occur. Of the total number of unmarried respondents, 38 per cent were dating steady, while 41 per cent said that among their very close men friends there was someone whom they might consider marrying. However, only 32 per cent of these respondents stated that there was a *fair chance* of this marriage taking place.

The attitudes of friends and family toward the divorce are part of the divorcee's background experience by this time, but we suppose that these attitudes would affect remarriage through the help they give the divorcee in meeting people generally and eligible men in particular. The effect of those attitudes upon the patterns now under consideration is very little, after so many intervening experiences, but it is visible and rather consistent. The percentage of (1) steady daters, (2) women who know someone among their close friends whom they might consider marrying, and (3) women who think there is a fair chance that this marriage might occur, is slightly *lower* for (1) divorcees whose family or friends *disapproved* the divorce originally, than for (2) those whose family or friends *approved or felt indifferent* toward the divorce: e.g., 30 per cent of those with family disapproval were steady daters, versus 40 per cent of those whose families were approving or indifferent; 35 per cent versus 37–43 per cent for considering marriage; 23 per cent versus 35 per cent for fair chance the marriage might take place.

Of course, the movement of divorcees from nondating to dating, and thence to steady dating and the consideration of marriage, is a continual sieving and seeping process, so that from each time grouping we are always losing those whose dating relationship becomes a remarriage. Thus, slightly under *one-third* of the divorcees in Time Group I (2 months since divorce) were dating steadily; only slightly more knew someone within their circle of close men friends whom they would consider marrying; and slightly more than one-fourth thought there was a fair chance this marriage would occur. By Time Group IV (26 months after decree) one-half of those not remarried were steady daters, and at least knew someone who could be thought of as a marital

candidate; and almost the same proportion thought there was a fair chance this marriage might occur. Moreover, there is a Q of .90 between steady dating and considering someone as a possible spouse, among all Time Groups.

Thus it is that about three-fourths of all our urban, divorced mothers who had divorced 26 months prior to the interview had either remarried, or seemed to be well on the way to a remarriage.

Here, as with dating frequency, it is important to have a circle of friends, and to have opportunities for meeting people. (1) 32 per cent of those who do not have friends and are not finding friends are going steady, as against 40 per cent of those who already have such a circle. About the same difference exists between these two categories with reference to whether there is someone these divorcees would consider marrying. The percentages drop somewhat for the more serious question as to whether there was a fair chance the marriage might occur, and the difference is unimportant (28 per cent versus 32 per cent).

Similarly, when we look at opportunities for meeting people, the main differences are between those who have *no* such opportunities, and those who do have such opportunities. Whether these are few, many, or some is of little significance. About one-fourth of those with no opportunities for meeting people are steady daters and consider someone within their close circle of men friends as a possible spouse (as against two-fifths of those with some such opportunities); and 22 per cent of those with *no* opportunities think that there is a fair chance the marriage might take place, as against 30–34 per cent of those with *some* opportunities.

Help from Friends and Family

We have pointed out that although most divorcees do not receive help from family and friends in meeting eligible mates, this help is fruitful. Of those who obtained help from *both* family and friends, 50 per cent were going steady. Forty-seven per cent who got help from the family but *not* from friends, were going steady, as against 38 per cent of those who got

Steps toward remarriage, by frequency of dating

Frequency of dating	Steady dating per cent	Considering marriage per cent	Fair chance of marriage per cent	None of these per cent	Base
More than once weekly	68	64	53	24	105
1/wk. to 2/month	38	44	32	49	103
Almost never	5	13	7	85	95

help from friends but not from the family. Thirty-four per cent of the not remarried who got help from *neither* were going steady.

Now, it is clear that help from both is most fruitful, and there is evidence that help from the family alone is more useful than that from friends alone (47 per cent versus 38 per cent). We would suppose, then, that this documents the thesis that the family has a more continuing commitment to the divorcee's life and happiness, and thus the help they give is more effective because more continuous. The help of friends was more useful for dating frequency.

However, we also asked whether among their close men friends there was someone these divorcees would consider marrying. Then we find that the above ranking is *reversed* (except of course for those who got help from neither friends nor family). That is, 37 per cent of those who obtained help from family *and* friends knew a man they would consider marrying, 41 per cent of those who got help from family but *not* friends, and 52 per cent of those who got help from friends *alone*. (Thirty-six per cent of those receiving help from neither knew someone they would consider marrying.)

If we understand these apparent patterns, the help from the family *is* more effective in providing a partner, one who is eligible enough to be a steady date. On the other hand, the peer group is more effective than the family in producing men with whom the *divorcee* would consider marriage, for they know men who are more desirable as potential spouses. To the extent that the peer group does share values, tastes, and activities, an unattached male who is brought in to meet the divorcee will be closer to an acceptable mate. The family, by contrast, will begin from a slightly different set of values, because removed by one generation, and might be more

inclined to introduce a "safe" rather than desirable potential mate, an escort rather than a date. Moreover, the same result may occur when both family and friends combine forces, for then they are likely to be in interaction with one another. In this case, their effectiveness is no better than when there is no help from either.

It is almost by definition that those with a high dating frequency are more likely to be steady daters. However, it is worth documenting that it is *also* among the high frequency daters that we find a higher proportion of women actually considering marriage, or judging a hypothetical marriage to have a fair chance of taking place. This relationship is shown in the above table.

Emotional Ties with the Ex-Husband

Since we have moved from background factors to items of more immediate importance, let us consider one more such item, the emotional involvement of the ex-wife with the ex-husband. We shall look at this item independently in a later section, but it is useful now to see how similar is its effect upon these steps toward marriage, compared with its effect on dating frequency.

There are several points worth bringing out in the succeeding table: (1) Again we see that those who express antagonistic *or* loving attitudes toward the former husband show (a) the lowest frequency of steady dating, (b) the lowest frequency of potential spouses among their close men friends, and (c) the lowest frequency of claiming that there is a fair chance the marriage might actually take place. (2) With reference to those who might consider marrying, we note that among those who have antagonistic feelings

Proportion dating steady, considering marriage, or claiming that a marriage has a fair chance of occurring, by affect toward ex-husband

Affect toward ex-husband	Dating steady per cent	Consider marrying someone among close men friends per cent	Fair chance of marriage taking place per cent	Base
Friendly	48	49	40	85
Indifferent	42	45	36	93
In Love	30	35	15	40
Negative	26	31	26	85

toward their husbands the proportion who would consider marrying one of their close men friends is *lower* than the corresponding frequency among those who are in love with their former husbands. (3) Once more, however, women who claim a positive but not loving feeling for their former spouses are those most likely to claim that a potential spouse is to be found among their close men friends. On the other hand, (4) the proportions reporting there was a fair chance that such a marriage might occur were almost the same as those going steady, for all groups *except those in love with their former husbands.* Only 15 per cent of this last group stated that there was a fair chance of the marriage taking place, while 30 per cent of them were going steady. In none of the other categories is the difference so great. Thus, these comparisons reflect the readiness for and movement toward remarriage on the part of these divorcees.

Remarriage

Let us continue to follow this movement toward remarriage. We have attempted to outline some of the social activities of the divorced mother after her divorce, and have paid some attention to the dating and courtship patterns which lead to a new marriage. We have sketched in some detail the processes which lead to this reassumption of an old status, that of married mother. We have not, of course, assumed that the marriage ends all problems, and in our

chapter on relations with the ex-husband we shall show that not even all of the remarried women have assimilated the divorce experience completely. Nevertheless, as we commented earlier, entering new social activities and new roles may be seen as both an *index* of and a *stimulus* to the social and emotional readjustment of the divorcee. It is an index in that she will ordinarily find these new activities difficult if she is not ready for them in some fashion; and it is a stimulus in that the new roles demand different activities and attitudes from her, and those who associate with her in these new roles come increasingly to ignore the old set of relationships and to emphasize the new ones.

This is particularly true, of course, for the social role of "new wife." With respect to this new status, there are two main sets of facts which we wish to present: (1) We would like to continue to show which divorcees are more likely to remarry within the short 26 months' period of adjustment under our eyes; and elsewhere, (2) we want to ascertain just how these wives feel about their new marriages.

The Chances of Remarriage. Now, the chances of ultimate remarriage are high for the total population of female and male divorcees. We have fairly good knowledge about the proportion in each age and sex category which will *ultimately* remarry—for example, about 94 per cent of all women divorced at age 30 will remarry—but we do not have adequate data on the remarriage of mothers versus nonmothers, Catholics versus Protestants, those with more education versus those with less, etc. That is, we suspect there may be much greater chances of ultimate remarriage for some strata and groups than others, but we have no firm knowledge about these differences. Moreover, and perhaps of greater importance for comparisons of social structures, we do not know much about the differential *rates* of remarriage. That is, even if it is true that Catholics ultimately remarry in as high a *proportion* as Protestants, perhaps they take *longer* to get remarried. Or, even if most divorcees age 38 and under will *eventually* marry, perhaps those 38 and under who were also in love with another person prior to the divorce will get remarried at a faster rate during the first few years after the divorce, than those not in love.

Answers to these two questions—the chances of *ultimate* remarriage for various categories of the divorced, and the *rate* of remarriage year by year, for those categories—can not be obtained from our study. Much larger samples are needed, and the period for recording the information must, of course, extend over many years. Indeed, we shall get these answers, when we finally get them, only from official records. Meanwhile, we shall interpret briefly the suggestive results from our small sample, with its short time span after the divorce.

Differentiating Factors in Remarriage. These data on remarriage point to the following conclusion. Most of the differentiating factors we have already located also have an effect upon remarriage, as they do on dating frequency and steady dating. These factors include such status items as race, religion, education, age (but not rural-urban background), as well as items more immediately from the postdivorce experience, such as trauma, the remarriage of the ex-husband, or activities at separation. However, two qualifications should be added to these statements: (a) Many of these differentiating factors, such as "attitudes of friends toward the divorce," begin to lose much of their effect by Time Group IV. (b) Certain other differentiating factors, such as religion, continue to have an effect through Group IV, but the differential remains about the same. Indeed, we can say that *almost no factor has a cumulatively differentiating effect, and almost all these women seem to be moving toward marriage.*

The structural factors that lead to this consequence have already been discussed. Referring to our comments on accounting models for analyzing decisions, we see that most of our sample would have a strong set of predispositions or values in favor of marriage. If this statement seems paradoxical to some, we must remember that our divorcees did, after all, marry, and they were mothers. It is of course true that some mothers have no great interest in marriage as a life pattern, but it is at least safe to claim that among all women who get married, those who have children are on the average more committed to home and marriage than those who do not have children; and the claim is even safer if we compare them with women who do not even marry once. Aside from these *predisposing factors*, we have analyzed both theoretically and by reference to our field data the pressures which would lead these young, divorced mothers to enter marriage again. Consequently, almost all of them do move in that direction.

As we would expect from our previous data on dating frequency, Negroes appear to move toward remarriage somewhat more rapidly than Whites. By 26 months after the divorce, however, the differences are of no importance, for 59 per cent of the Negroes in Group IV have remarried, as against 53 per cent of the Whites (in Group III, the percentages were 48 per cent versus 37 per cent). Thus, although the one segment starts more rapidly to move back into new marriages, the differences gradually diminish. By contrast, the differential between Protestant and Catholic divorcees remains much the same throughout the time groups, with the percentage of Protestants remarrying always somewhat higher: 17 per cent versus 13 per cent in Group II, 41 per cent versus 35 per cent in Group III (14 months after the divorce) and 59 per cent versus 49 per cent in Group IV.[3]

We have seen that although those with some college education do seem to find circles of friends, opportunities to meet people, and even dates, more than women with lesser education, there were no educational differences of note

[3] To save tedium for those disliking arithmetic, the Catholic proportion in these three groups is the following fraction of the Protestant: .76, .85, .83.

between those going steady and those not going steady. Indeed, we would expect that the apparent social advantage enjoyed by the women with more education might be more than wiped out, as we move closer to marriage itself, since it is doubtless still true that women who go to college have less probability of ultimately getting married than those who do not go to college. Just what these probabilities are at present, cannot be easily ascertained. We usually calculate the percentage of college women 45 years old and over who have ever married, but this only gives the probabilities for a generation earlier. In 1940, 6 out of 10 women college graduates of this age had married, compared with 9 out of 10 for general female population.[4] These 1940 women had, of course, graduated 25 years earlier, while the chances of marriage for women graduates, or women with some college education, have apparently risen substantially.[5] Of course, men college graduates have greater chances of marriage than the general male population.

On the other hand, we do not know what are the chances of *remarriage* for *mothers* who have had some college education. We are here willing to be statistically incautious, by predicting what will be found when we do know: that even though these women have been married, a lower proportion will ultimately remarry than of mothers who have had only some high school or have completed high school education. Through our first two time groups (2 months and 8 months after the divorce), the women with some or a completed college education marry less than other educational strata. This difference is entirely erased by 14 months after the divorce, when 50 per cent of the college women have remarried, as against 30 per cent of the women with a completed high school education, 43 per cent of those with some high school, and 37 per cent of those with only grammar school education. By Time Group IV, however, the two high-school categories have moved ahead of the college category slightly, while among the

college women there are *still* only 50 per cent remarried. The grammar-school women remain behind all the rest (39 per cent), but they continue to enter marriage. All that we see is that they move into marriage more slowly than the other classes. Since, by contrast, the percentage married does not change for the *college* women, we are now going beyond our data to suggest that their chances of ultimate remarriage are not as great as those of high-school mothers. We believe that this is due mainly to two structural elements in their mate selection problem: (a) generally, their choice is narrower than that of other women, since they wish and expect to find a mate with equal or greater education; and (b) at their age levels there are proportionately fewer men "between marriages" simply because marriages are more stable in the higher educational strata. Marital dissolutions from either death or divorce are lower in rate, while some 60 per cent of the spouses of all these women will be found among the once married.[6]

Remarriage is affected by age, as were dating frequency and steady dating. However, once again the greater step that is remarriage affects the changes over time. Both the youngest (20–24 years) and the oldest (35 years and over) age groups are slower to re-enter marriage immediately after the divorce than the middle age brackets. However, by 14 months the youngest class has moved ahead of all the rest, while the oldest divorcees continue to lag behind. By 26 months after the divorce, the percentage remarried was as follows:

Time Group IV

Age	Per cent remarried	Base
20–24 years	80	10
25–29 years	56	36
30–34 years	50	38
35 years and over	46	26
	$N = 110$	

[4] F. Lawrence Babcock, *The U.S. College Graduate*, New York: Macmillan, 1941, Table 2, p. 62.
[5] See Ernest Havemann and Patricia S. West, *They Went to College*, New York: Harcourt, Brace, 1952, Ch. 5.

[6] Glick, "Remarriages...," *op. cit.*, p. 728. In contrast with wife's *education* is remarriage by ex-husband's *occupation*: by Time Group IV, 57 per cent of the *lowers* had remarried, 48 per cent of the middle occupations, 40 per cent of the upper-stratum wives.

We guess that the youngest divorcees simply avoided remarriage for a while, in order to enjoy themselves a bit, since their dating frequency was so high. We expect the oldest to remarry more slowly if at all, since the ultimate proportion remarried among those over 35 years old *is* lower than among women who are younger, for the national population of the divorced.

A parallel but puzzling comparison may be found by looking at the *duration of marriage.* This is to some degree an overlapping comparison, since, in general, those who have had a short marriage are also more likely to be younger. However, we have seen before that the effects of these two factors are not always the same. Once again, the rate of remarriage is less in the first period after the divorce for those who have had a short marriage (0–4 years) than for those who have had slightly longer marriage. Similarly, those who have been married 15 years or more also fail to begin marrying during the first two time periods. Important differences between these different lengths of marriage do not begin showing up until 26 months after the divorces, and then the relationship is not a simple one. Those who were married 5–9 years have a *higher* proportion married in the 26-month period (61 per cent), while the women married 10–14 years and 15 years and over show a lower proportion remarrying (47 per cent and 48 per cent); but those married 0–4 years *fall in between* (54 per cent). The failure of those with short marriages to remarry quickly is caused by factors that we do not understand adequately, although various *ad hoc* hypotheses are possible.

The Effect of Children upon Remarriage. We have already hinted that the relationship between the number of children and the movement toward remarriage is complex. In the light of the data already presented, it is interesting to learn that those with *more* children seem to remarry *faster* than do those with fewer children. Let us look at this fact more closely.

It will be remembered that the highest frequency of dating at the time of our interview is to be found among those who dated during the separation period, while the lowest was found among those who "did nothing at all," or took part in church activities to fill the gap caused by the marital breakup. Slightly less than half of the women reported that they gave more attention to their children at that time, and these women were dating *less* frequently at the time of the interview (33 per cent dated more than once weekly) than any other women except those who did nothing or who took part in church activities.

Women who had more children were less likely to date frequently than those who had fewer children (41 per cent of those with one child dated more than once weekly; 34 per cent of those with two children; 19 per cent of those with three or more children). Moreover, to move to steady dating, those who gave more attention to their children during separation are less likely to be dating steady than any other class at the time of interview. Twenty-eight per cent of these mothers who paid more attention to their children have steady dates, but 35–38 per cent of those who gave more attention to church activities, went about with their girl friends, went to movies alone, or did nothing, had steady dates. And 50–52 per cent of those who took a part in club activities or dated, were going steady by the time of the interview. Thus, it would appear that the mothers who gave more attention to their children would fail to get married.

Next, those with *more* children were more likely to give *more* attention to their children at the time of the marital breakup. Thirty-three per cent of those with one child, 45 per cent of those with two children, and 54 per cent of those with three or more children gave more attention to their offspring. In addition, to make the picture darker still, it is the older mothers of course who have more children: none of those 20–24 years of age had 3 or more children; 13 per cent of those 25–29; 26 per cent of those 30–34; and 30 per cent of those 35 years of age and over. And the older women are less likely to find ultimately a new mate.

These facts seem interrelated, and point to a rather simple set of processes. That is, the most effective way for a divorcee to remarry, it would appear, is to take part in all those activities which lead away from the home or female associations, and toward men. By dating frequently, she increases the chances of going steady and of remarrying. So far, we seem to be merely documenting the commonsense expectation, that those divorcees who are young and are not burdened by many children, will date frequently and those who date frequently will have a high likelihood of getting remarried promptly. These expectations are indeed borne out.

On the other hand, when we moved to steady dating and the number of children, we found this relationship somewhat ambiguous. Although those with *one* child were more likely to be dating steady than those with more than one child, it was also true that those with three or more children were *more* likely to be dating steady than those with two children. This fact might be a statistical accident, or might suggest there is no relationship between the number of children and remarriage itself. However, we also found that those with *more* children are *more* likely to be remarried soon: By Time Group IV, 45 per cent of those with one child had married; 57 per cent of those with two children had married; and 61 per cent of those with three or more children had married. True enough, those with three or more children had not married at all in the first few months after the divorce, but in the three succeeding time groups those with three or more children ranked either first (II, IV), or were only four percentage points behind first rank in proportion remarried (III).

These facts would suggest that women with many children are more "efficient" in their remarriage activities than those with fewer children. That is, those with more children apparently date less, but get more husbands from those dates, than those with fewer children. Indeed, we are tempted into guessing that there are two main roads toward remarriage, one of which lies through an active participation in dating, and the other through a continued dedication to the home. Or, one way of attracting a new husband is following the model of the never married, in being attractive as a sex and love partner. The other way is not usually open to the never married, that of being an attractive mother and homemaker. For we no longer find the dim picture that was apparent in the dating process. There, it was apparent that the women who went out and met men were destined for early marriage. By contrast, there were women who stayed at home, and dated little, and who therefore seemed headed for a late remarriage, or none. Burdened by many children, they seemed to have little chance of competing with their sisters in divorce.

True enough, those who *had* dated during the separation do marry most rapidly. By Time Group IV, 63 per cent of them have remarried, and they had maintained this lead at each previous time group. However, 60 per cent of the women who had paid more attention to their children at that time have *also* remarried by Time Group IV. No other class of separation activities is as likely as these to be associated with early remarriage. And, as we noted, those with more children were more likely to be remarried by Time Group IV.

In retrospect, it is easy to take these two patterns for granted. It is somewhat more difficult to have predicted them in advance. As we have already noted, divorcees most often select the once-married as partners in a new marriage. The dates of our divorced mothers are older, and most of them have a real interest in home and family life; else they would not be dating mothers. Without denying or lessening the importance of the usual female attributes of graciousness, prettiness, and so on, in attracting husbands, we must keep in mind that men are like women in also weighing a prospective spouse by the standards of homemaking. Also, among the pretty tableaux, or theatrical scenes, that a woman can create is that of the loving mother surrounded by happy children in a pleasant home. Although there is smiling in our day at the old saw, "The way to a man's heart is through his stomach," this proposition when sufficiently broadened is doubtless true (as it is also true for women). Perhaps in our time men find the choice difficult between the gay charm of the popular girl and the quieter charm of the homemaker. Certainly the latter dates less often. However, her commitment to marriage doubtless causes these dates to be more productive. Thus—to take a highly special but pertinent datum—the proportion of women who ultimately marry is almost as high among the college graduates of, say, the Cornell School of Home Economics as it is among the population at large. (As of January, 1955, 85 per cent of all their living graduates had married, and 60 per cent of those graduated less than 5 years previously had married.)[6a] We shall not sketch this kind of courtship process, since it is observable to all. What is striking is that, even among our divorcees, the women who apparently wanted to spend more time with their children, and who were burdened (or blessed) with more children, had less opportunity to date as often as other divorcees, but managed to choose as dates those men who were more inclined to marry. Phrasing it pragmatically, they wasted less time with men who were not serious.

Remarriage and Adjustment to Separation. In general, those who took longer between first serious consideration of the divorce and filing the suit were more likely to remarry early. This we would expect, since this longer period of time allows the divorcee to find a new social role, and thus a new definition of herself. The relationship is fairly consistent in each Time Group, although small. By Group IV (26 months after the divorce), 42 per cent of those who took 0–4 months for these steps had married, and 53 per cent of those who took 5–12 months; while 45 per cent of those who took over one year but less than two had remarried, and 63 per cent of those who took two years and over. Thus, the difference is really between this last class and all others.

We have already presented sufficient evidence that the length of this period is important in readjustment, by showing its relationship to dating and other activities. It might be worth while to indicate once more that the underlying factor is the actual adjustment, rather than a mechanical transition from, say, consideration to filing, or marriage to final divorce. We can, for example, find out whether there are any differences in the remarriage of those who felt most *loneliness* at different periods, since this experience would seem to be connected with understanding that the marriage has ended. We find, in conformity with our previous data, that those in Group IV who said their period of greatest loneliness was at the *time of the interview*

had the lowest proportion of the remarried (43 per cent). It might be thought that those who claimed they were never at all lonely might be the most adjusted, and thus might be quickest to move toward remarriage. This is not true. Those (a) who never felt lonely, (b) who felt most lonely at the first filing, and (c) who felt most lonely at the final decision were all remarried in Group IV in about the same proportion: 51 per cent, 50 per cent, and 54 per cent. But those who felt most lonely at either of the two *genuine finalities*, (1) the social finality of final separation or (2) the legal finality of the decree, were more likely to remarry soon. Fifty-nine per cent of these two groups had remarried by 26 months after the divorce. This is in part a psychodynamic process, of course, in that the loneliness, however painful, seems to be a response to a full recognition that the marriage has really ended. This means that a change in role definition is possible and likely.

We have followed in some detail the continuing influence of first initiation of the divorce on postdivorce activities. We would expect, because this factor has an effect upon entering new social relations, that remarriage might also be affected by it. When the husband suggested the divorce first, remarriage is delayed, and even 26 months after the divorce the difference is still observable. When there was mutual suggestion, remarriage by 14 months is slightly greater than when the wife suggested first; but drops slightly behind by 26 months after divorce.

Percentage remarried, 14 and 26 months after divorce, by who first suggested the divorce

	Time groups	
Who first suggested divorce	III 14 months after divorce per cent	IV 26 months after divorce per cent
Husband	30	31
Mutual	50	58
Wife	41	64

Since we have already discussed this factor, we need not comment further, except to emphasize how long after the divorce these conflict patterns affect the behavior of the divorcee.

[6a] Personal letter from Esther H. Stocks, Placement Director, Secretary of the College.

Percentage remarried, within time groups, by whether woman admits she was in love with another man before divorce

Were you in love with another man before the divorce?	I Divorced 2 months per cent	II Divorced 8 months per cent	III Divorced 14 months per cent	IV Divorced 26 months per cent
Yes	12	44	71	81
No	4	12	34	49

With reference to the attitudes of friends toward the divorce, their effect on remarriage is the same as that upon dating behavior. That is, the lowest percentage is found among those whose friends *disapproved* the divorce (46 per cent remarried 26 months after the divorce), and the highest among those whose friends were *indifferent* (56 per cent remarried), with those whose friends approved the divorce falling between (53 per cent). However, the differences are unimportant, as they are for the attitudes of *family* toward the divorce.

Emotional Ties and Remarriage. Of course, if the woman admitted that she was in love with another man prior to the divorce, her movement toward remarriage was much more rapid than if she was not in love with another. The difference begins 2 months after the divorce, and continues to be high.

We believe that these women would not, in general, have admitted that they were in love with another prior to the divorce unless the relationship was a fairly serious one. However, it is clear that there was some attrition and disenchantment in this postdivorce period. We suppose that many of these women did not marry the man they were in love with before, since so many failed to marry soon after the divorce became final. On the other hand, having been in love with another man prior to the divorce is an index of her emotional *readiness* to think in terms of future relationships, and of her ability to free herself emotionally from her former husband. Consequently, even 26 months after the divorce, the percentage remarried among those who *had* been in love is much higher than among other ex-wives.

In the following chapter, we shall explore at greater length the various aspects of the wife's continuing emotional involvement with the former husband. By way of anticipation, however, we might see now the relationship between *his* remarrying and *her* remarrying. If, as we have implied at several points in our analysis, their attitudes toward one another are to some degree parallel, then (1) there should be a strong association between the two separate movements toward remarriage. On the other hand, (2) this relationship should *diminish* over time, as each assumes independent social roles within his or her own group.

This is indeed what we do find. In the succeeding table, we present this association, and again note that the women who say that they do not know whether their husbands have remarried seem to be like those who say that he *has* remarried. We have assumed that these men have gone off to assume independent lives (and thus their ex-wives have, too).

Thus we see that by 14 months after the divorce (Group III), there is practically no association at all between his remarrying and her remarrying, even though the percentage of the remarried among *both* ex-husbands and ex-wives continues to rise together.

We would expect a similar relationship to hold between (a) dating at the time of separation, and (b) later remarriage. That is, those who began to date at the end of their divorce conflict have already begun to establish new social relationships with other men, and we expect them to move more rapidly than other women toward remarriage. On the other hand, these other women also begin to date, so that the *difference* between these two segments should *decrease*

Relationship between her remarrying and his remarrying, over time

Time Groups	She has remarried	He has Remarried				
		Yes per cent	No per cent	Not known per cent	Totals per cent	
I						
Q = .88*	Yes	33	50	17	100	(6)
	No	4	86	10	100	(108)
II						
Q = .43	Yes	21	43	36	100	(14)
	No	13	65	22	100	(77)
III						
Q = −.13	Yes	28	51	21	100	(43)
	No	36	51	13	100	(67)
IV						
Q = .16	Yes	58	29	14	101	(59)
	No	51	35	14	100	(51)

* Q measures the association between the two "yes" responses.

over time. Thus, at 2 months after the divorce, the proportion remarried of those who had dated toward the end of their marriage is six times as large as that of women who had not dated (12 per cent and 2 per cent). By Time Group II (8 months after divorce), this proportion is twice as large (23 per cent and 12 per cent). By 14 months after divorce, the ratio decreases to one and one-half times (53 per cent and 34 per cent), and by 26 months after divorce it is only one and one-third times larger (63 per cent and 48 per cent). By that time those who had not begun to date early have nearly caught up with the average. Thus, the initial advantage of the early daters does decrease over time. We have already discussed the other main differentiating separation activity, devoting more attention to the children. Among the remaining items, there is little differential importance for remarriage. Perhaps the sole fact of significance is that, although those who at the separation filled their social gap with church activities were most likely to date infrequently, they remarry about as rapidly as those who went to movies alone, or who took part in women's clubs, and more rapidly than those who did

nothing at all. Thus, their apparent initial disadvantage in the competition for new husbands was lessened considerably when we turn from mere frequency of dating to remarriage itself.

Summary

To a cynic in a mass society such as ours, many of the rewarding activities involving other people seem at times to take on the structural character of a slot machine: the payoff function is very low. All of us attempt many things and fail in many of them. Statistically speaking, far more of us aspire to than achieve posts, positions, honors, and possibly even pleasures that our society offers. Maintaining this situation, the cynic might claim, are two further circumstances: (a) We have no choice. We must play. (b) If we do not put any coins in any given slot machine, we have no chance at all of getting anything out of that one.

It is true, then, that for both women and men the chance of a love relationship or a marriage growing out of any given date will be low. Those who are bitter about the impersonal patterns of contemporary urban life, who complain of the commercial character of dating, who bewail the lack of a deep relationship between men and women even in the dating process, may have some ethical basis for their objections to the courtship and mating customs of our time.

On the other hand, if one does not date at all in this society, the chances of marriage at all become very low. As against the cynic's disappointment, there is optimism in this: we thus expose ourselves to the chances of good events as well. Those who risk nothing in this process will ordinarily gain nothing. It is true that most of those who try for a given job will fail to receive that job. On the other hand, almost all of those who do not try at all will fail to receive it. Moreover, as we have shown in our lengthy analyses of the interaction of status, situation, motivation, behavior, and the actions of others, the steps from the bitterness of marital conflict to a new marriage do not occur at random. Those who *try* to move again toward marriage appear to *move* most definitely. Those who wish to marry, expose themselves most often to the chance. Moreover, although our society imposes few if any obligations upon friends or family to help the divorcee, many do so nevertheless. Not even the divorcee is alone. Finally, the total effect of the larger institutional pressures as we analyzed them earlier, and of the more immediate temptations and actions of dates, friends, co-workers, and families, appears to lead to the remarriage of almost all divorcees. Few can resist these complex adjustmental factors.

Chapter 6

Trends in Nuclear Family Relationships

Chapter 5 emphasized similarities between courtship interaction and marital relationships. This chapter examines changes in marital interaction and parent-child relationships over the family life cycle.

Marital Interaction

The introductiory statement to Chapter 1 indicated that sociologists who define the family in terms of interaction have attempted to predict marital success from the premarital characteristics of the husband and wife. In their research they have generally defined success as "happiness" or "adjustment."[1] They have rarely applied the concept of integration explicitly. However, criteria such as personal adjustment or happiness are undoubtedly highly associated with integration. For example, in the Burgess and Cottrell index of marital adjustment, the score is determined to a great extent by the ability of the couple to agree on a number of potential issues in family life.[2]

The studies predicting marital success implicitly assume stability in marital relations throughout the marriage. However (as Pineo's investigation indicates), because couples generally marry at a time when their relationship is most integrated, it is possible that this integration declines over the years. Indeed, the concept of permanent availability suggests that (a) interests change during the marriage, (b) involvement in the particular mate-lover relationship is erratic, and (c) marital integration tends to decrease over time. Presumably, in a society in which marriage is established on the basis of mate-lover roles and common concerns, the lower the integration, the greater the tendency for the couple to emphasize views consistent with permanent availability.

[1] Various criteria for marital success are described in Ernest W. Burgess, Harvey J. Locke, and Mary Margaret Thomes, *The Family from Institution to Companionship*, New York: American Book, 1963.
[2] Ernest W. Burgess and Leonard S. Cottrell, Jr., *Predicting Success or Failure in Marriage*, New York: Prentice-Hall, 1939.

The assertion is frequently made that married couples develop new interests over time and in this way compensate for the loss of romantic attachment. Some of the findings in marital prediction studies support this contention. For example, Burgess and Wallin found that a favorable attitude toward children and a desire to have several children are effective predictors of high marital adjustment.[3] Sharing outside interests after marriage is also related to high marital adjustment.[4] In Chapter 10 of this book, the suggestion is made that certain strategies of family organization can maintain high integration. These strategies involve specific values in family life: the welfare of the children, the home, or the parents' relationship to the community.

As the selections in the chapter on solidarity in the nuclear family will indicate, however, there are many interests and commitments that compete with those in the nuclear family. The husband and wife continually encounter conflicting demands and temptations. With the passage of time, unless common interests in children, leisure-time activities, or a home are developed, husband-wife commitments may decline.

Parent-Child Relationships

Integration in parent-child relationships tends to develop in a curvilinear manner.[5] An adolescent and young adult must become independent of his family of orientation to establish his own family of procreation. Accordingly, adolescence is a time when the individual acts more independently of his parents, possibly even becoming antagonistic to them. This increased independence enables him to devote his energies and resources to the formation of his own family of procreation. As his family is established and children are born, the individual's relationship with his own family of orientation can be re-established. Although the relationship between in-laws and their newly married children may prove threatening to a marriage based primarily on mate-lover roles, the relationship with grandchildren is generally nonthreatening and is frequently characterized by indulgence.

Parenthood and grandparenthood, being consistent with the continuation of tradition, reinforce familial interests. The adult's family of orientation may provide assistance and emotional support if problems arise. Additionally, with the emergence of uncle and aunt roles, sibling rivalry is subdued and solidary relationships with brothers and sisters can be maintained.

As in unilineal systems, the children serve to integrate kinship units potentially in conflict. This integration is accomplished in unilineal kinship through the children's dual loyalty to the lineage of descent and to the lineage of affiliation. In bilateral kinship the children are constrained to treat their mother's and father's relatives alike. Consequently they are encouraged to be equally loyal to both sets of kin. To maintain this equal loyalty, the parents and other relatives must avoid situations that might

---

[3] Ernest W. Burgess and Paul Wallin, *Engagement and Marriage*, Philadelphia: Lippincott, 1953.
[4] See Burgess, Locke, and Thomes, *op. cit.*, pp. 547–569, for list of specific predictive items related to marital adjustment.
[5] See Bernard Farber, *Family: Organization and Interaction*, San Francisco: Chandler, 1964.

induce the children to disparage one set of kin or to take sides in a family conflict. Thus in both unilineal and bilateral kinship the presence of children generally reduces conflict between kin groups.

Although the birth of children facilitates the re-establishment of cordial relationships between the family of orientation and the family of procreation, the parents may still emphasize mate-lover roles in marriage. In spite of the over-all stabilizing effect of parenthood on family relations, the marital relationship continues to be vulnerable to dissolution, and the parents remain available as potential spouses in a new marriage.

Readings on Trends in Nuclear Family Relationships

Two kinds of trends are discussed in the readings: (a) the trend in husband-wife relationships and (b) the trend in relationships with members of families of orientation.

Studies of marital prediction have been moderately successful in predicting adjustment in marriage from premarital information about the couple. Statistically, between 15 and 25 per cent of the variance in marital adjustment scores is explained by premarital influences.[6] In their paper Litwak, Count, and Haydon attempt to determine the extent that creativity in interpersonal relations can account for errors in marital prediction. Although their study indicates that creativity did account for much of the marital adjustment, they are unable to determine whether this creativity has been developed in the course of the marriage or had been present prior to it.

The second paper, by Pineo, is on disenchantment in the later years of marriage. Pineo suggests that as the marriage progresses the initial integration with respect to common interests and agreement on values tends to decline. The couple gains less satisfaction from the marriage and the extent of companionship diminishes. Incidentally, Cumming, Dean, Newell, and McCaffery suggest that disengagement continues into old age. They indicate that older persons prepare for widowhood by disengaging from interaction with the spouse but that they may again remarry after widowhood.[7] Their analysis supports the interpretation that the American marriage system is becoming one in which all individuals are permanently available for another marriage, regardless of current marital status.

The third paper, by Sussman and Burchinal, points out the relationship between financial assistance and integration between the person's family of procreation and his family of orientation. These authors suggest that during the years when the married children become established and themselves become parents the flow of aid is from their own parents to them. Apparently the parents take the initiative for integration, and in striving for independence the children may even be reluctant to accept this bid. As their parents become older, the flow of financial aid may be reversed. Regardless of the direction of flow, however, the maintenance of financial aid indicates a continual integration between families. The continual extended-family integration contrasts with the disenchantment in marriage described by Pineo.

---

[6] Clifford Kirkpatrick, *The Family as Process and Institution*, New York: Ronald Press, 1963, pp. 394–398.
[7] Elaine Cumming, Lois R. Dean, David S. Newell and, Isabel McCaffrey, "Disengagement— A Tentative Theory of Aging," *Sociometry*, **23** (1960), pp. 23–35.

19. Group Structure and Interpersonal Creativity as Factors which Reduce Errors in the Prediction of Marital Adjustment[*]

BY EUGENE LITWAK, GLORIA COUNT,
AND EDWARD M. HAYDON

INVENTIVENESS IN ROLE-TAKING has become sociologically more relevant as it has become increasingly clear that contemporary urban society may be characterized by permanent and rapid change. This has been noticeable to sociologists who have attempted to investigate ongoing relations over long-time periods. In this respect the field of family sociology has been in the forefront. The need to deal systematically with the problem of interpersonal inventiveness or creativity arose in this field as a consequence of the empirical attempts to account for family survival during major social changes such as wars and depressions.[1]

The purpose of this paper is to reexamine, in the light of interpersonal creativity, the predictions made by Burgess and Wallin twenty years ago as to the current marital adjustment of their respondents. Burgess and Wallin pointed out that their predictions would suffer because they had no way of measuring the spouses' interpersonal creativity—the capacity for developing new and effective means for carrying on their roles.[2] This paper will demonstrate that if indeed they had taken into account both interpersonal creativity and the structure of the marital relation, errors in their predictions could have been reduced by as much as 61 per cent.

Group Structure and the Measurement of Interpersonal Creativity

Before exploring this point, however, it is necessary to say something about the structure

SOURCE: Social Forces, *Volume 38 (1960), pp. 308–315. Reprinted with permission of the University of North Carolina Press.*

* This study was supported by funds provided jointly by the Family Study Center at the University of Chicago and the study, Middle Years of Marriage, financed by the Rockefeller Foundation. Ernest W. Burgess provided considerable aid in the analysis and carrying out of the research. However, the positions taken in this paper do not necessarily reflect his views.
[1] Robert C. Angell, *The Family Encounters the Depression*, New York: Scribner's Sons, 1936; Ruth S. Cavan, The Restudy of the Documents Analyzed by Angell in *The Family Encounters the Depression* (unpublished); Reuben Hill, *Families Under Stress: Adjustment to the Crises of War, Separation and Reunion*, New York: Harper & Brothers, 1949, p. 132 ff. Terms such as adaptability and flexibility are used interchangeably with creativity in this paper. Since these works were written, writers such as Burgess and

Wallin and Foote and Cottrell have suggested that a major institutional crisis only highlights what is characteristic of everyday life in contemporary urban society—the need to deal with change. Ernest W. Burgess and Paul Wallin, *Engagement and Marriage*, New York: J. B. Lippincott Co., 1953, p. 620 ff. Nelson N. Foote and Leonard S. Cottrell, Jr., *Identity and Interpersonal Competence: A New Direction in Family Research*, Chicago: The University of Chicago Press, 1955.
[2] Behavior which is new but not effective may be moronic and is eliminated from consideration by this definition. Behavior which is effective but not new is also eliminated.

of the family and the measurement of interpersonal creativity. Under traditional investigations it was more or less assumed that creativity on the part of either husband or wife would be equally meaningful to marital adjustment. Operationally this has meant that creativity or flexibility of scores of husbands and wives are averaged together to arrive at a family score. Under such an assumption the husband who makes a creative innovation in housework or the wife who makes a creative innovation in the occupational world will both increase the adjustment of their marriage. Creativity is assumed to operate independently of family structure. Stated less dogmatically, a simple additive theory of structure is assumed.[3]

In contrast to this point of view, another position maintaining that any measure of interpersonal creativity must take into account the structure of the group will be advanced. It is only when creativity takes place within the overall structure that it is likely to lead to marital adjustment. More specifically, it may be argued, following Parsons' analysis, that the roles of husbands and wives follow a sex-linked division of labor. The wife takes the internal-expressive roles and the husband takes the external-instrumental ones.[4] The expressive-internal role is characterized by the wife's providing emotional support within the confines of the family while the instrumental-external roles are typified by the husband earning a living or dealing with strangers outside the family. Since these role divisions, according to Parsons, are firmly rooted in the industrial structure, it is unlikely that they can be changed unless one is ready to give up industrial urban society with its higher standards of living and its equality of opportunity.

If it is granted that industrial society will remain and that Parsons' analysis is valid, it would then be argued that marriages are most likely to be successful when the husband displays creativity in the instrumental and external

family matters while the wife does so in the internal-expressive areas.[5] If either spouse becomes creative in the other's area, it may lead to a lack of adjustment in marriage. This means that creativity measures should explicitly take into account group structure. Where one is concerned with external-instrumental areas of life it may be more important to know the amount of creativity the husband and wife have vis-à-vis each other than the absolute sum of their creativity. Operationally this means that the investigator might want to divide the husband's creativity score by the wife's rather than average them both together. Measures which are explicitly formulated on the basis of group structure will be called relational measures while other types will be designated individual ones.

Hypotheses to be Tested

The present study seeks to test relationships between interpersonal creativity and current and

[3] For some illustrations of additive structures see Eugene Litwak, "Group Pressure and Family Breakup: A Study of German Communities," *The American Journal of Sociology*, LXI (January, 1956), pp. 345–347.

[4] Talcott Parsons and Robert F. Bales, *Family, Socialization and Interaction Process*, Glencoe, Ill.: The Free Press, 1955, pp. 22–26.

[5] The position taken in this paper is that Parsons' analysis is only partially correct. He is right in pointing out that a sex-linked division of labor is typical of such middle-class groups as the respondents in this study. However, he is incorrect in assuming that this is an inevitable family structure given the demands of industrialization. For an opposing point of view see Eugene Litwak, Primary Group Instruments of Social Control in an Industrial Society (unpublished Ph.D. dissertation, Columbia University, 1958), p. 175 ff. This in turn highlights one of the limitations of the present definition of interpersonal creativity. It refers to the person's ability to carry out a role—the role is given in a situation. A different type of flexibility or creativity may be thought of as a group flexibility which more directly relates to changes in roles rather than a means for carrying out a given role. There are certain properties of groups which encourage innovation regardless of the level of interpersonal creativity among the individuals. For instance, a husband and wife relation which is institutionally defined as equalitarian and which does not have a sex-linked division of labor permits each member of the marital dyad greater freedom in deciding which role he or she will undertake than a husband and wife relation which is institutionally differentiated along sex lines. The capacity for developing innovation can be increased by either developing interpersonal creativity or group flexibility. For an exploration of how group flexibility operates see Eugene Litwak, "The Use of Extended Family Groups in the Achievement of Social Goals," *Social Problems*, **7** (1959–1960), pp. 177–187.

predicted marital adjustment scores using two different assumptions regarding family structure. The first assumption is that group structure plays a small role as far as the effects of interpersonal creativity are concerned, while the second assumption is that there is a sex-linked division of labor which specifies the conditions under which interpersonal creativity will operate to produce adjustment.

So that these various hypotheses and dependent variables may be clearly understood they have been schematized in Figure 1.

Research Design

To test these hypotheses the following steps were taken:

1. The first 83 couples (166 people) of the third panel of the Burgess and Wallin study were given, in addition to their regular interview, a role-playing test of creativity. These are the same people who were interviewed twenty years ago when they were engaged and again three years after their marriage. At the time of their first interview they were high school and college students in their early twenties or late teens. They are now middle-aged and members of the middle and upper middle classes.[6]

Two types of creativity scores were computed for the family. First, an individual measure was

[6] Burgess and Wallin, op. cit., p. 620. More specifically the respondents referred to in this paper are couples still living in Chicago who have not divorced, separated, and where no death has occurred among one of the spouses.

Hypotheses tested assuming that family structure does not affect interpersonal creativity	Hypotheses tested assuming that family structure (sex-linked division of labor) is significant and that the test situation involves external-instrumental relations	Null hypotheses
1. Creativity is positively correlated with marital adjustment.	3. If the husband is more creative than his wife both will be better adjusted, and where he is less creative both will have a poorer adjustment.	5. Creativity is not related to marital adjustment.
2. Two situations will account for the majority of errors in marital prediction of adjustment: (1) Where Burgess and Wallin predicted marital adjustment would be high for couples who were not creative and (2) Where Burgess and Wallin predicted poor marital adjustment for couples who were creative.	4. Two situations will account for the majority of errors in marital prediction of adjustment: (1) Where Burgess and Wallin predicted good marital adjustment but the husband had less external creativity than the wife and (2) Where Burgess and Wallin predicted poor marital adjustment but the husband had greater creativity than the wife.	6. Creativity is not associated with errors in marital predictions.

Figure 1. Hypotheses to be Tested in this Study

compiled for husband and wife. On the assumption that group structure was unimportant their creativity scores were added together to provide a total score. Secondly, a relational measure of creativity was computed by dividing the wife's creativity score into the husband's. This was an index of the relative dominance of husband's creativity over that of the wife's.

2. As part of their regular interview each respondent was given a 20-item marital adjustment test.[7] Separate scores were compiled for husband and wife.

3. For each respondent there were available the marital predictions made by Burgess and Wallin twenty years ago when the respondents were engaged.[8]

4. By comparing 1 and 2 above, it could be seen how individual and relational measures of creativity are associated with marital adjustment (Hypotheses 1, 3, and 5 above).

5. By comparing 1, 2, and 3 it was determined how individual and relational measures of creativity are associated with errors in prediction (Hypotheses 2, 4, and 6 above).

Thus far in the discussion interpersonal creativity has been defined only conceptually—the ability to develop new and effective means for carrying out one's roles. At this point, the role-playing test used to operationalize this definition will be described. A more detailed operational description of the test is given in the appendix.[9] The procedure for the role-playing test is to assign the husband and wife a task which they agree to do. At the same time the scene is so structured that the tester can control interpersonally the subject's success in achieving his goal. The tester in turn allows the subject to be successful only when the subject utilizes an extremely novel approach.

[7] Burgess and Wallin, *op. cit.*, pp. 483–500. Exact items will be furnished on request.
[8] Burgess and Wallin, *op. cit.*, p. 507 ff.
[9] The test was designed by Howard Stanton and Eugene Litwak and is briefly reported in "Toward the Development of a Short Form of Interpersonal Competence," *American Sociological Review* (December, 1955), p. 672. Because the test is of such importance to the design of the present study it has been reported in some detail in the methodological note.

Findings Relevant to the Traditional Creativity Hypothesis

According to the traditional hypothesis presented by past investigators there should be a positive relation between individual measures of creativity and marital adjustment. The sum of the husband's and wife's creativity should correlate with either the husband's or the wife's marital adjustment. Table 1 indicates that our data do not support this hypothesis. The relation

Table 1

Creativity and marital adjustment

	Husbands[a]		Wives[b]	
	Good marital adjustment[c]	Poor marital adjustment	Good marital adjustment	Poor marital adjustment
High[d] creativity	29	25	29	31
Low creativity	12	16	14	09

[a] For the husband $Q = .22$, χ^2 not sig., $N = 82$.
[b] For the wife $Q = -.25$, χ^2 not sig., $N = 83$.
[c] Variables in this and succeeding tables have been dichotomized by taking the median value as the cutting point.
[d] The creativity scores for the boss and cousin scene have been combined by placing all those who score above the median in either one or both scenes in the high group.

is low and scattered. There is a small[10] nonsignificant positive relation ($Q = .22$) between creativity and the man's adjustment as well as a small nonsignificant negative relation between

[10] Chi square test was used to measure statistical significance. Measures of association are Yule's coefficient of Association "Q." For some of the underlying implications of the "Q" see Leo Goodman and William H. Kruskal, "Measures of Association for Cross Classifications," *Journal of the American Statistical Association*, **49** (1954), p. 747 ff.

It is especially important to note that because of the *ex post facto* analysis in which variables were tabulated to maximize association with the dependent variable the use of statistical tests in the present inquiry must be treated with caution.

the wife's adjustment and the creativity score ($Q = -.25$). In short, the first hypothesis has not been confirmed. If the second hypothesis dealing with errors in prediction is examined it can be seen that the same low and scattered results emerge. According to Hypothesis 2 there are two situations in which errors should occur with greater frequency than in any other situations. These are: (1) where Burgess and Wallin predicted a good marital adjustment and the couple was not creative and (2) where Burgess and Wallin predicted a poor marital adjustment and the couple was creative. Table 2 shows that

13 per cent more errors[11] occurred in predicting the husband's adjustment in these two situations than in any others. This figure is low but in the direction anticipated by the hypothesis. Paradoxically enough these two situations contained 10 per cent fewer errors than any others in the prediction of the wife's adjustment. This is in the opposite direction from what would have been anticipated by the hypothesis. In short, the evidence is scattered and not significant.

Findings Relevant to the Modified Creativity Hypothesis

The question which now remains to be settled is whether the null hypothesis or the hypothesis embodied in the relational definition of creativity is appropriate. Table 3 shows that where creativity is measured in terms of the man's relation to his wife (does he have more or less)

Table 2

Relation of creativity to errors[a] in prediction

	Proportion of errors in the prediction for men	Proportion of errors in the prediction for women
Predictions made by Burgess and Wallin are consistent with creativity scores[b]	33 (33)[c]	39 (40)
Predictions made by Burgess and Wallin are inconsistent with creativity scores[b]	46 (48)	29 (42)
Extent to which the differences between Row I and II go in the direction predicted	13[d]	−10[d]

[a] The errors are defined as the number of times good marital adjustment was predicted when in fact it was poor or the number of times low marital adjustment was predicted when in fact it was high.

[b] Consistency between prediction and creativity is defined as being the state where creativity and prediction are both high or both low.

[c] Numbers in parentheses indicate the absolute numbers upon which the proportion is computed.

[d] Not significant for men or women.

[11] To test the proposition a one-tail normal approximation of the binomial distribution was used. The null hypothesis was that for any given row in the table below there was an equal probability of a person's falling in the well adjusted as opposed to the poorly adjusted group.

	Good marital adjustment	Good marital adjustment	Total
High Creativity Prediction of Good Adjustment	P_1		N_1
High Creativity Prediction of Poor Adjustment		P_2	
Low Creativity Prediction of Good Adjustment	P_3		N_3
Low Creativity Prediction of Poor Adjustment		P_4	

The null hypothesis would be suspect if the following held:

$$\frac{P_1 + P_4 - P_2 - P_3}{\sigma P_1 + \sigma P_2 + \sigma P_3 + \sigma P_4} = Z \geq 1.282$$

The same test was used for Table 4 below. This formula also included the Yates corrections for small samples.

Hypothesis 3 tends to be confirmed. Using the relational measure rather than the individual measure increases the positive association between creativity and the man's marital adjustment from $Q = .22$ to $Q = .65$. For the women the jump in association is equally dramatic going from $Q = -.25$ to $Q = .43$. In short, Hypothesis 3 which states that marital adjustment will be greater for both husband and wife where the husband has more creativity than the wife in the external-instrumental areas of life seems to be confirmed.

Table 3

Relational creativity by marital adjustment

	Good marital adjustment	Poor marital adjustment
Husband[a]		
Husband has higher creativity than his wife in one or both scenes	36	23
Husband has lower creativity than his wife in both scenes	06	18
Wife[b]		
Husband has higher creativity than his wife in one or both scenes	33	26
Husband has lower creativity than his wife in both scenes	08	16

[a] For the husband $Q = .65$, χ^2 sig. at $.01$, $N = 83$.

[b] For the wife $Q = .43$, χ^2 sig. at $.10$, $N = 83$.

Furthermore, it should be emphasized that this relational measure of creativity seems to relate very strongly to the errors in predictions made by Burgess and Wallin as specified in Hypothesis 4. Table 4 reveals that in situations in which (1) Burgess and Wallin predicted a good marital adjustment but the husband in fact was less creative than the wife or (2) where

Table 4

Relational creativity by errors in prediction

	Proportion of errors in the prediction for men	Proportion of errors in the prediction for women
Husband's greater creativity is consistent with prediction of marital adjustment[a]	19 (36)	27 (44)
Husband's greater creativity is not consistent with prediction of marital adjustment[a]	51 (46)	44 (39)
Extent to which differences in Row I and II go in the direction predicted	33[b]	17[b]

[a] Consistency is defined as that situation where high marital adjustment was predicted and the husband had more creativity than the wife or where low marital adjustment was predicted and the husband had less creativity than his wife.

[b] Significant at .025 for men and .09 for women.

Burgess and Wallin predicted a poor marital adjustment and the husband was more creative than the wife, there were 33 per cent more errors in the prediction of the man's marital adjustment than in any other situation. There were 17 per cent more errors in predicting the wife's marital adjustment. Using the relational definition of creativity permitted the investigators to explain errors in prediction, 23 per cent more successfully among the husbands and 27 per cent more successfully among the wives than the non-relational definition. Stated somewhat differently, of the 165 predictions made, 60 (36 per cent) were in error, and of these, 41 (61 per cent) could be accounted for by the attribute of interpersonal creativity as specified in Hypothesis 4.

More broadly, the foregoing analysis suggests that in order to assess the effects of interpersonal abilities in the marriage situation, the measure should reflect the structure of the group. It is only in a special type of structure (additive structure) or in situations where structure is unimportant that the investigator can safely use individual measures or the average of several individual scores to index the interpersonal ability.

Discussion and some Major Limitations of Present Study

The present study has some major limitations which should be made explicit so that the possible avenues of research may be profitably followed if data presented are to be confirmed. One major limitation of the present study is that the creativity tests were given *ex post facto*. For a definitive confirmation of Hypothesis 4, the tests should have been given twenty years ago when the original predictions were made. The present findings would certainly suggest that such an endeavor is well worth-while in future longitudinal studies.

A second major problem is the validity of the test. Though the test seems reasonable enough to the investigators it should be validated in a more rigorous manner against some known criterion group. Initial correlations with criteria groups are encouraging.[12] It should be made clear in this regard that the test does not simply measure the volume of verbal behavior. The design of the test prevents this. In order for the respondent to display creativity in the second of two scenes used to measure creativity he or she must be silent. Therefore a high score for this scene is not necessarily correlated with much verbal interaction. It should also be pointed out that this scene is related to marital adjustment in the same degree as the other scene which encourages a great deal of verbal interaction.

Reliability of the test must also be explored and some initial findings have already been reported.[13] What is most reassuring in this regard is that the present findings on Hypothesis 3 were duplicated in an independent group of 10 couples (20 people) in a pretest.

A third major problem is the assumption that the test situation involved the respondents in an

instrumental-external relation. It was only by using such an assumption that the theoretical explanation for the findings could be presented. There is no reason why this assumption should not be empirically investigated in future research. This means that future research design should explicitly seek to test interpersonal creativity in two situations: those involving internal-expressive roles and those involving external-instrumental roles. Four interrelated hypotheses should be tested in such a situation. These have been presented schematically in Table 5. It can be seen that the maximum marital adjustment should occur where the husband has lower expressive-internal creativity than his wife but higher instrumental-external creativity.

Table 5

Ways in which types of interpersonal creativity interact with roles of husband and wife to produce dyadic integration

	External-instrumental creativity	
	Husband has more	Husband has less
Internal-expressive creativity		
Husband has more	Moderate integration	Very low integration
Husband has less	Very high integration	Low integration

Conclusion

From a theoretical point of view it was argued that relational measures of interpersonal abilities which explicitly take into account the structure of the family were better than those which ignored group structure. It was then demonstrated that errors in the Burgess and Wallin marital adjustment predictions could be accounted for in 61 per cent of the cases by relational measures of interpersonal creativity. If these findings are given support by future research it would signify that the approach herein described allows for considerable illumination of one of the key theoretical and practical

[12] Howard Stanton, Kurt W. Back, and Eugene Litwak, "Role-Playing in Survey Research," *The American Journal of Sociology*, LXII (September, 1956), 176.
[13] *Ibid.*, p. 175.

problems of our time—the ability to develop new and effective ways for carrying out social roles.

Methodological Note

The Stanton-Litwak creativity test has not been described in detail. It is, however, central to the argument advanced. Therefore, a more detailed presentation is called for. As mentioned above the test consists of two role-playing scenes.[14] In the first scene the husband and wife were asked to take the role of a husband and wife who were entertaining a bashful young cousin just in from the country. Their task in the scene was to make the cousin feel at home. The husband and wife were further instructed to try as many things as they could think of to make the cousin feel at home.

There were three people in the scene—the tester, the husband, and the wife. The tester played the role of the bashful cousin. He classified all interactions of the respondents into one of four categories: (1) appeals for help, e.g., won't you help me do the dishes? (2) offers of help, e.g., we are going to take you to a show; (3) questioning behavior, e.g., how are your mother and father? (4) rejecting behavior, e.g., sorry, have too much work so can't spend much time with you. In this particular scene where the husband's and wife's remarks fell into the first category the tester responded by saying how much he felt at home. As the remarks approached the fourth category the tester responded by indicating how ill at ease he felt and that he should perhaps leave. For each of the four categories of the respondent's behavior the tester had a pre-arranged and semi-standardized set of responses.

While the interaction between the husband, the wife, and tester proceeded, a second interviewer acted as an observer. He recorded all new

statements by the husband and wife separately, using the same four categories. Since these recordings were made along a time dimension the entire sequence of husband and wife interactions is preserved. At the end of eight minutes the observer informs the tester who then terminates the scene. It is important to note that there is an infinite number of things the respondent can ask the tester to do even when he grasps the correct approach—the appeal behavior, e.g., wash dishes, help with the children, shop at the store, etc.

The measure of creativity is a product of the number of new interactions of the respondents (an index of novelty) and the extent to which the response approaches category one, "appeals for help" (a measure of their effectiveness). The respondents' task is to make the tester feel at home. The tester feels at home when they appeal for his help. Thus, the extent to which the respondents appeal for help is a measure of their effectiveness.

By definition, the efficiency of the test to determine creativity is improved if the solution used by the tester is somewhat unusual. Thus in the present inquiry it is thought that asking a bashful cousin for help in order to make him feel at home is not the usual mode of interaction. There is some evidence that this assumption was true among our respondents. In no case did the respondents commence a scene with this solution. The three prevalent solutions used were: (1) the cousin was asked about near relatives; (2) he was asked if he or she would like to meet friends of own age; and (3) the cousin was asked if he or she would like to see the sights.

To guarantee further the novelty of the solution other scenes can be used which require entirely different solutions. In the present inquiry a second scene was used. The respondents were assigned the task of keeping an employer with a job opening near them and away from competitors during the course of a party. The husband and wife played the roles of a husband and wife in this situation and the tester played the role of the employer. The tester as employer reacted favorably to the couple the less they spoke to him and acted unfavorably the more they demanded a response from him. Thus if they were perfectly quiet he

---

[14] For a general approach to interpersonal creativity including attention to other components see Edwin Piper and Joseph Zygmunt (Family Study Center, University of Chicago). Their work is to appear in a publication in Interpersonal Competence (Russell Sage Foundation). They were extremely helpful in criticizing the present test procedures.

would tell them how highly he thought of the husband's work; on the other hand if they attempted to make him talk by asking about his family, the business, or flattering him, he acted as if he were unhappy. Again it was assumed that the customary mode of interaction in such a situation is not to be silent. This scene was scored in the same way as the first with one or two elaborations for coding meaningful silences.

In the first scene the effective response was to appeal for help while in the second scene the effective response was to be silent. It is assumed that the truly creative person can do both while the uncreative person, although he might use one as a customary mode of interaction, is unlikely to use both. As many different scenes with as many different solutions can be used as the investigator feels are necessary.

The successful adoption of a role requires other elements of competence—empathy, autonomy, judgment—aside from creativity. In order to isolate out creativity, the test attempts to minimize the effects of these other elements.

First, the subject is explicitly told to try as many different things as he can and that some will work better than others. In the case of the boss scene he is even told what behavior of the boss indicates a favorable response. During the course of the scene the respondent is given increasingly obvious cues. All of these factors tend to minimize his need of empathy. In order to minimize autonomy the task assigned is one which is acceptable to the respondent. It is true that the boss scene seems threatening for the man and therefore tends to be a test of his autonomy. To reduce the influence of autonomy the subjects are told beforehand that the boss might be unpleasant but they are to ignore it and stick to the task. This seems to minimize their feeling of threat. Finally, since there is one unambiguous task and the subject knows what it is there is very little call for judgment. In short, the subject is more or less reduced to deciding whether he will use a novel solution or insist on traditional ones despite their obvious lack of relevance.

20. Disenchantment in the Later Years of Marriage*

BY PETER C. PINEO

SINCE THE TIME OF Ernest W. Burgess's 1927 article "The Romantic Impulse and Family Disorganization"[1] there has been an interest in family research in the process of disenchantment in marriage. Willard Waller, in *The Family, A Dynamic Interpretation*,[2] discusses the probable consequences of idealization in mate selection, emphasizing disillusionment and the growth of conflict. Recently Charles Hobart has presented empirical information showing disenchantment effects in the early years of marriage. In independent articles and with Clifford Kirkpatrick he has shown that an index of disagreement,

which measures the accuracy of one spouse's estimate of the other's response to a series of questions, shows a phase movement during courtship.[3] The married phase typically shows more disagreement than the previous ones. For men, at least, there is a slight association between increases in such disagreement and the extent of premarital romanticising.

E. E. LeMasters, in another recent article in the *Midwest Sociologist*, discusses disenchantment as an aspect of divorce.[4] Among his thirty divorced couples he reports a tendency to a nonspecific disappointment in the spouse and in marriage as a cause of divorce.

LeMaster's work is concerned with disenchantment effects beyond the period of early marriage. That there is disenchantment after the marriage has endured for several years has not been shown in empirical work previously, to our knowledge. In part this is because for such a study longitudinal data are ideal and data of this kind are relatively scarce. But also the

SOURCE: Marriage and Family Living, *Volume 23 (February, 1961), pp. 3–11. Reprinted by permission of National Council on Family Relations.*

* Paper read at the Eastern Canadian Sociological Conference (on Kinship and the Family) sponsored by the Department of Sociology, McMaster University, Hamilton, Ontario, February, 1960.

Data are from the Burgess-Wallin longitudinal study of marriage; analysis was performed while the author was Assistant Director, United States Public Health Service National Institutes of Health Research Grant M–2159, at the Family Study Center, University of Chicago. Collection of data was made under grants-in-aid by the Rockefeller Foundation and the Grant Foundation by E. W. Burgess and associates.

[1] Ernest W. Burgess, "The Romantic Impulse and Family Disorganization," *Survey*, **57** (December, 1926), pp. 290–295.
[2] Willard W. Waller and Reuben Hill, *The Family: A Dynamic Interpretation*, New York: Dryden Press, 1951, pp. 253–256.

[3] Charles W. Hobart, "Disillusionment in Marriage, and Romanticism," *Marriage and Family Living*, **20** (May, 1958), pp. 156–162. Clifford Kirkpatrick and Charles Hobart, "Disagreement, Disagreement Estimate and Non-Empathetic Imputations for Intimacy Groups Varying from Favorite Date to Married," *American Sociological Review*, **19** (February, 1954), pp. 10–19.
[4] E. E. LeMasters, "Holy Deadlock: A Study of Unsuccessful Marriages," *Midwest Sociologist*, **21** (July, 1959), pp. 86–91.

emphasis on romanticism in mate selection as the source of disenchantment may have dissuaded researchers from searching for effects well into the marriage.

In 1954, Burgess and his associates began a third wave of interviewing of the 1000 couples he and Paul Wallin had investigated for their verification study of the Burgess-Cottrell prediction instruments. The results of the initial interviewing and the first follow-up had previously been discussed in *Engagement and Marriage* by Burgess and Wallin.[5] The third interviewing, called the Middle Years of Marriage Study, was accomplished when the couples had been married up to 20 years. This paper is a report of some of the changes which occurred to the marriages between the early and middle years periods.

Four processes appear to dominate the data:

1. There is a general drop in marital satisfaction and adjustment, which we conceptualize as a process of disenchantment.

2. There is a loss of certain intimacy. Confiding, kissing, and reciprocal settlement of disagreements become less frequent; more individuals report loneliness. This loss of intimacy appears to be an aspect of disenchantment.

3. Personal adjustment and reports of personality characteristics are relatively unaffected by the process of disenchantment or loss of intimacy.

4. Certain forms of marital interaction are found to change as the frequency of sexual intercourse diminishes and the amount of sharing of activities drops, without any major link to disenchantment.

The evidence is presented in Table 1, below. As certain of the indices in the table are unfamiliar a few comments on their performance are required. None of the new indices have been made with sufficient precision or have been tested enough to be considered more than short-term analytical devices, however.[6]

---

[5] Ernest W. Burgess and Paul Wallin, *Engagement and Marriage*, Philadelphia: J. B. Lippincott Co., 1953.
[6] The construction of the Marital Adjustment score is reviewed in *Engagement and Marriage* as is that of Love, Permanence, Consensus, Own Happiness and Sexual Adjustment indices. The Dominance score is

Characteristics of the Indices Included in Table 1

The scores classified as indices of marital satisfaction are highly intercorrelated and may all be said to measure a generalized marital adjustment or satisfaction. The marriage complaints score is based upon a long check list of possible complaints about the spouse on the marriage. Because the complaints cover many areas of marital life this index tends to be another, weaker measure of general adjustment.

Under the heading of "Indices of Marital Type" are listed five indices which measure something besides generalized adjustment, and for which no desirable and undesirable ends to the continuum each represents can immediately be named. Within any time period none is related to marital adjustment above the .40 level (Pearsonian correlation coefficient). While the median correlation of the satisfaction indices with marital adjustment is around .67, the median association with marital adjustment of the indices of marital type is around .22.

The index of Traditionalism consists of five, equally-weighted questions concerning attitudes toward strong discipline of the child, independence for the wife, authority for the husband, sexual activity prior to marriage, and the sexual education of children. The total is felt to measure acceptance of "traditional" (i.e., patriarchal, restrictive) rules of marital behavior. The index has a positive association with marital adjustment, suggesting that within this cohort the traditional marriage was somewhat more satisfying for both husbands and wives than the non-traditional.

The scoring of "Sharing of Interests and Activities" comes from a long list of leisure activities which the respondents were asked to

---

discussed in Yi-Chuang Lu, "Marital Roles and Marital Adjustments," *Sociology and Social Research*, **36** (July, 1952), pp. 365–368. The Index of Personal Growth is discussed in Robert A. Dentler and Peter C. Pineo, "Marriage Adjustment, Sexual Adjustment and Personal Growth of Husbands: A Panel Study," *Marriage and Family Living*, **22** (February, 1960), pp. 45–48. The Thurstone Neurotic Inventory is discussed in *Engagement and Marriage* and elsewhere. Scoring instructions for the other nine indices may be obtained by writing to the author.

Table 1

Standardized mean gain from early to middle years of marriage for eighteen indices of marital satisfaction, marital type, and personal characteristics (N = 400)

Indices	Gain from early to middle years	
	Husbands	Wives
A. Marital Satisfaction		
Marital adjustment	−4.63*	−5.42*
Love	−2.01*	−2.87*
Permanence	−2.12*	−2.64*
Consensus	−2.26*	−2.37*
Marriage complaints (absence of)	−1.59	−2.09*
Own happiness	−1.13	−1.42
Sexual adjustment	−1.14	− .93
B. Marital Type		
Sharing of interests and activities	−3.84*	−4.56*
Frequency of sexual intercourse	−2.31*	−2.13*
Traditionalism	−1.86	−1.76
Attitudes to having children	− .04	− .72
Dominance	.79	− .26
C. Personal Characteristics		
Idealization of mate's personality	− .60	− .67
Personal growth gains due to marriage	− .16	− .36
Non-neuroticism or autonomy	− .24	− .12
Rating of own personality traits	−1.07	− .34
Rating of mate's personality traits	.34	−1.31
Number of felt personality needs	1.45	1.25

* Statistically significant changes at the .05 level of confidence or better; the standardized gains are numerically equivalent to z-scores between actual mean change and hypothesized no mean change.

$$\text{Gain} = \frac{\Sigma D}{\sqrt{\frac{\Sigma D^2 - \Sigma D)^2}{N-1}}}, \text{ where } D = \text{time period two score} - \text{time period one score}$$

check as either engaged in alone, engaged in with the mate, or not engaged in. The score is the ratio of number of activities shared to the total number of activities undertaken. The lists were slightly revised in the middle years schedule and this may have contributed to the great drop shown in Table 1. Other information (see Table 2) indicates that the drop must largely be real, however.

Three of the indices of personal characteristics derive from a single battery of questions. This is a list of ten personality traits, such as stubbornness or sense of humor. The respondent is asked to report, on a scale ranging from "very much so" to "not at all," how much both he and his mate, separately, possess each characteristic. The Rating of Own Personality is formed by equal-weighting of the self-reports on all ten traits; the Rating of Mate's Personality is scored identically except that it is formed of the individual's rating of his mate rather than of himself.

For the Idealization of Mate index, which is perhaps misnamed, only five wholly negative traits are used. "Not at all" as a response is given the highest score and all items are weighted equally in the total. Only the rating of the mate is used.

The Personality Needs index comes from a check list of felt needs, such as needs for "someone who can give me self-confidence," "someone who makes me feel I count for something," "someone who sympathizes," etc. The respondents were asked to check any needs they felt they had, whether they were satisfied by the mate or not. The score is simply the number of such needs checked. It tends to be a measure of dependency, and in a cross-sectional analysis marital adjustment is found to be higher where the wife feels such needs and the husband does not.

The ratings of personality traits, the neurotic inventory and the personal growth index are associated cross-sectionally from .30 to .55 with marital adjustment. On the whole the indices of personal characteristics associate more strongly with marital adjustment than do the indices of marital type, but less strongly than do the indices of marital satisfaction.

Evidence of Disenchantment

In Table 1 the standardized gains from the early to the middle years of marriage on these 18 indices of marital satisfaction, marital type, and personal adjustment are presented. Four hundred couples for whom schedules have been collected in both time periods are included. The standard error used in the standardization was calculated directly from the arithmetic differences between the middle years and the early years index scores.

Chance expectation would be that the "gains" would be found to fluctuate around zero.[7] In fact, however, virtually all are negative and 13 of the 36 show statistically significant drops.

[7] In part, the 400 couples are not equivalent representatives of the two time periods. They are *all* who were contacted in the middle years, but only 400 of the 666 who were contacted in the early years. Put another way, all the 400 of the early years were to have at least 15 more years of married life; some of the 400 in the middle years may become divorced tomorrow. Investigation shows virtually no difference between, for example, the marital adjustment scores of the 400 used and the 266 unused from the early years. The differences cannot explain the observed losses between the time periods.

The drop in the marital adjustment score is roughly five standard deviations of the mean for both husbands and wives. On virtually all scores there was typically a move to the less desirable end of the continuum, as indicated by the negative signs.

The drops are particularly great and systematic within the category of indices of marital satisfaction. We conceptualize this process of dropping satisfaction as one of "disenchantment." The term "loss of satisfaction" is insufficient to express the fact that this is a process which appears to be generally an inescapable consequence of the passage of time in a marriage. In its recent usage the term "disenchantment" or its equivalent "disillusionment" has been used to refer to such a process without its origin necessarily having been in lack of realism or over-romanticising in courtship. It must feel much like the classic disenchantment process to the individuals involved, even if its origin is different. Terms such as "disinvolvement," "individualization," "alienation," or "deterioration" have even stronger specific meanings than do "disenchantment" and so are less adequate to describe the general process.

There are two definite indications that the loss in satisfaction is a general process, rather than several independent changes.

1. On the seven satisfaction indices, losses by husbands tend to associate with the losses by their wives. The median correlation between husbands' and wives' changes on these indices is approximately .30. This approaches the static husband-wife correlations for the same scores which range around a median of .42.

2. The change on any one score correlates with changes on the others. For example, just as the static scores on the indices tend to associate highly with the static marital adjustment score, so the changes on the indices associate with the changes on the marital adjustment score. The median correlation of change on the scores with change on the marital adjustment index is .41 for men. This approaches the median static correlation between the scores and marital adjustment of .68.

In an analysis of changes in marital satisfaction a general factor of reducing adjustment may be expected, just as an analysis by factor

Table 2

Percentage dropping in desirability of response to questions forming the marital adjustment score for groups showing least and most disenchantment between early and middle years ($N = 400$) (Husbands only)

Content of item by area of marital adjustment	Percentage changing to a less desirable response among:		Contribution to drop in total score (Phi-coefficient)
	Least disenchanted	Most disenchanted	
Consensus (amount of agreement) on			
Finances	18	51	.37
Recreation	10	45	.43
Religious matters	13	41	.35
Demonstration of affection	16	61	.48
Friends	17	42	.31
Table manners	13	39	.33
Conventionality	13	46	.39
Philosophy of life	13	52	.44
Ways of dealing with your families	13	47	.40
Intimate relations	21	58	.40
Satisfaction with marriage			
Would you marry the same person again?	1	43	.70
Do you ever regret your marriage?	3	50	.66
Number of things spouse does not like	13	47	.39
Number of things annoying about marriage	9	38	.39
Common interests and activities			
Spouse and self agree in leisure preferences	12	17	.10
Spouse and self share outside activities	58	86	.34
Adaptability			
Do you confide in your spouse?	2	36	.59
Do you settle disagreements by give and take?	4	26	.42
Demonstration of affection			
How often do you kiss your spouse?	1	34	.65
Absence of feelings of unhappiness or loneliness			
Do you often feel lonesome?	5	24	.38
Are you usually even-tempered?	5	13	.23
Do you often feel just miserable?	3	12	.29
Does some particular useless thought bother you?	6	14	.21
Are you usually in good spirits?	3	11	.29
Do you often experience periods of loneliness?	4	16	.32
Are you in general self-confident?	4	12	.25

Note: "Least disenchanted" are the top 27 per cent of the 400 husbands when they are ranked from low to high by amount of loss in marital adjustment, "Most disenchanted" are the bottom 27 per cent. The selection of 27 per cent is arbitrary.

methods of cross-sectional data would tend to show a general factor of adjustment.[8]

Theory of Disenchantment

That there is a short-term disenchantment effect which derives from romanticism in mate selection seems likely. Essentially any misperception or misinformation in the selection process must bring about some reality shocks. But there are also aspects to the selection of a mate which cannot possibly be known to the individuals at the time of marriage. Insofar as personality changes and changes in environment must occur as time goes on, perfect mating could only occur with some element of luck. No couples during courtship could adequately forecast subsequent invalidism or chronic illness, for example.

We feel it is the unforeseen changes in situation, personality, or behavior, which contribute most to the disenchantment occurring after five years of marriage. The effects of exaggerated idealization of the mate or of intense romanticising probably are felt in the earlier years. Because the changes producing later disenchantment could not have been foretold, it is misleading to speak of "lack of realism" as the cause of later disenchantment.

Why is it that the unforeseen changes result in loss of marital satisfaction? Why do they not as frequently result in increases? The answer to these questions lies in the fact that mating occurs by personal choice. It is moreover, a decision which may be deferred, even permanently. If mating were by random pairing, as many gains in the "fit" between husband and wife would occur as losses. But marriage by personal choice implies that a marrying group, at the time of marriage, has a self-contrived high degree of fit between the individuals involved. Individuals do not marry unless, to some extent, they feel they have more basis for union than would have occurred if their mating were determined by chance. The fit between the two is maximized before marriage will occur, as is the satisfaction such "fit" brings about. Subse-

quently a regression effect occurs. The deviant characteristics which provided the grounds upon which the marriage was contracted begin to be lost, as later changes tend toward the population mean and the couples become more and more like ones who married at random rather than by choice. Couples, for example, who might marry because of identical religious attitudes could only retain or lose this characteristic; they could not become more identical.

Similar disenchantment effects may be expected in other social situations. Friendships are formed by choice and on the basis of perceived valuable characteristics. Change will reduce the fit between friends, but friendships can be terminated so that the process probably does not frequently move to completion. Individuals also choose occupations somewhat on the perception of a degree of fit between their own personal characteristics and the role demands of the job. Here the commitment is often irreversible, as in marriage, so that the process of progressive loss of fit may move toward completion. Marriages are formed of individuals, while jobs involve an individual and an institution so that there is a lack of symmetry in the source of professional disenchantment which undoubtedly makes it differ from marital disenchantment.[9]

Simply put, we argue that the grounds upon which one decides to marry deteriorate; the fit between two individuals which leads them to marry reduces with time. There is nothing in this argument which makes it necessary that satisfaction also reduce with time, however. The loss of fit could occur without reverberations in the amount of satisfaction, but our empirical finding is that satisfaction does progressively reduce as time passes. This suggests that the grounds upon which these couples married were sufficiently in phase with the actual experience of being married to maximize satisfaction at the beginning and to produce its gradual and progressive loss as the marriage wore on.

---

[8] The assumption that marital adjustment is a "general factor" has not been proven at this time.

[9] The "cynicism" which develops among medical students as reported in Howard S. Becker, "Interviewing Medical Students," *American Journal of Sociology*, **62** (September, 1956), pp. 199–201 does not appear as such in our data and may be a special result of the case in which an individual and collectivity are involved rather than two individuals.

In any situation, such as marriage, in which individuals have made a major, irreversible decision to accept a long term commitment and where the data upon which they decide are not or cannot be perfect, some process of disenchantment is to be expected. When fit and satisfaction are maximized at the point of accepting the commitment, they must, on the average, subsequently reduce.

Other Changes in Marriage

Beyond this tendency to loss of marital adjustment there are secondary processes which may be recognized in Table 1. Particularly great losses are shown in the area of "sharing of interests and activities." The losses here exceed those of any of the general indices with the exception of the marital adjustment score, and the drop is not highly correlated ($r = .24$) with the drop in marital adjustment. There is apparently a secondary process with some independence.

One explanation for the loss may be derived from our knowledge of courtship practices. During courtship the sharing of leisure activities is emphasized precisely because other sorts of intimacy are disallowed. Domestic and sexual involvement enter largely after marriage and may automatically result in less emphasis on the sharing of leisure. The term "disengagement" may be an appropriate name for this process. The degree of disengagement is not highly related to the degree of disenchantment.

This explanation should, however, predict that the changes in sharing leisure would occur in the early years of marriage. The change noted here occurs after three to five years of marriage. It is more probable that it is the child-rearing duties rather than the sharing of a household which produces the change. Although 30 per cent of the couples had children by the early years of marriage, none had been parents long nor were the families large.

Other secondary changes may be noted. The frequency of sexual intercourse drops without as much reduction in sexual adjustment. Particularly for the women the process of reduced sexual activity can occur without producing more dissatisfaction.

A paradox exists in the contrasting changes in "dominance" and in "traditionalism." On the one hand the couples have typically moved to a position of less traditionalism, but at the same time the amount of dominance by the husband and submission by the wife has increased. While the husbands are actually becoming more authoritarian, both husbands and wives are stating more and more that this is not the ideal. One variable which associates with marital dominance in a manner paralleling these changes is income. High income families tend to show above-average dominance by the husband and submissiveness by the wife. The high degree of occupational success which has characterized the couples in this panel may have produced the shift to greater husband dominance. At the same time these high income couples are found to give more support to the presumably emergent, liberal norms of marital organization. Acceptance of the liberal ideal and actual changes in behavior appear not to be directly related in this case.

The small magnitude of the drop in attitudes to having children is unexpected, considering that to a large extent the task of having children has been completed by these couples. Their children are now entering their 'teens. That the couples still report interest in children may reflect that the task was rewarding beyond expectation.

Within the area of personal adjustment and personality characteristics the changes are unexpected. Quite highly associated with marital adjustment and other indices of marital satisfaction within any time period, the indices demonstrate an unanticipated independence in the change analysis. They have the following characteristics:

1. Within any time period they tend to associate with marital adjustment between .30 and .50, with the exception of the personality needs index.

2. Change on these indices also tends to associate with change on marital adjustment with, of course, the correlations being reduced, but ranging from .10 to .30, again with the exception of the personality needs.

3. Their central tendencies, however, are not sufficiently different between time periods to achieve a statistically significant drop.

Although personal adjustment and personality characteristics are influenced by disenchantment there appears to be sufficient compensation coming from other, unrelated factors to cancel out the effect when the whole cohort is considered. It appears, for example, from the Idealization of Mate scores, that any devaluation of the mate as an individual which may be a by-product of disenchantment with the marriage is compensated by other factors.

The absence of drop in personal adjustment suggests that the loss of marital satisfaction is properly considered an aspect of disenchantment in the marriage rather than part of a process of aging of the individual. Moreover it indicates, insofar as some of the scores deal with ratings of the spouse, that the drop in satisfaction is largely concerned with the fact of being married, not with esteem for the spouse as a person.

The changes in the number of felt personality needs present problems of interpretation. Both husbands and wives show an increase in number of needs, which we would interpret as an increase in dependency. Because dependency in the wife relates positively to marital adjustment this implies some gains in adjustment. But dependency in the husband relates negatively to marital adjustment so that losses of adjustment are equally likely. Moreover, how an increase of dependency fits into a general picture of reduced satisfaction with the marriage but stable personal adjustment remains a problem.

Why is it that the Idealization of Mate index shows virtually the same amount of drop for men and women, while the ratings of personality traits, which are partly formed of the same questions, show a larger drop for men, whether reported by themselves or their wives, and almost no change for women? The difference must lie with the four traits which are excluded from the Idealization score, specifically, the traits of "assumes responsibility willingly," "sense of duty," "sense of humor," and "likes belonging to organizations." Husbands tend to lose these traits while wives must gain on them sufficiently to off-set the general tendency to increased possession of the undesirable traits.

The mean scores indicate that three of these four traits are "masculine," which is to say men generally have higher scores on them than do women. The concept of homogenization of the sexes could then explain the change, as men lose and women gain on the more masculine characteristics. Separate analysis of the changes in ratings of each trait would be a worthwhile topic for further investigation.

The Loss of Marital Adjustment

The marital adjustment score shows appreciably more drop from the early to the middle years of marriage than does any other score. Why is this drop so great? Is the score simply a keener measure of disenchantment, or is there extraneous information included which is magnifying the effect through including secondary processes in the change?

To help answer these questions we have made an item analysis of the score to determine the contribution made by each of the 26 items to the observed total drop in the score. For the two extreme groups, those who have actually gained in adjustment and those who became most disenchanted, we have presented, in Table 2, the percentage which changed to a less desirable response for each item. Only the husbands' responses are presented. Using standard tables for estimating correlation from the tails of a distribution,[10] we calculated phi-coefficients which estimate each question's contribution to the observed drop. No correction for spurious correlation was made.

The percentages in Table 2 are in themselves of interest. For example, it may be noted that the largest percentage drops occur for the item concerning the sharing of outside activities. This adds weight to the earlier finding that there is a change in this area. Furthermore the phi-coefficient for this item is below the median (.34) indicating that this loss of shared activities is a process relatively independent of disenchantment. It may be noted also that there are relatively few drops among either those of high or low disenchantment in the area of personal adjustment, which is titled "absence of feelings of unhappiness or loneliness." These questions

[10] Helen M. Walker and Joseph Lev, *Statistical Inference*, New York: Henry Holt and Co., 1953, pp. 472–473.

come from the Thurstone Neurotic Inventory. Again there is confirmation of the earlier finding of only minimal losses in this area.

Initially we had expected that it was the inclusion of items dealing with the sharing of interests and activities which had magnified the drop in the marital adjustment score, but these questions do not contribute highly to the drop. Instead, the largest contributions come from two questions: Do you ever regret your marriage? and Would you marry the same person again? This finding underlines the extent to which it is a generalized feeling of disenchantment which has been measured.

The second largest contributions come from the questions dealing with the extent of intimate interaction. Practices of kissing, confiding, and reciprocity in the settlement of disagreements are typically lost by those who lose marital adjustment between the two time periods. And, from the other point of view, loneliness grows. Of the seven items designed to measure absence of feelings of unhappiness and loneliness, the two dealing specifically with loneliness make the largest contribution to the drop in total score. Among the ten items forming the consensus battery, it is the loss of agreement on "affection," although not "intimate relations," which makes the highest contribution.

Can it be the two questions dealing with satisfaction which explain the major drop on this score? We do not think so, largely because it is general questions of this sort which form almost all of the other indices of marital satisfaction and none of them dropped even three standard deviations. And from another point of view the items contributing at about the level of the 10 consensus items are probably not sufficiently important to explain the magnified drop. The consensus index is largely formed from these 10 items, and it, by itself, showed a drop of only 2.26 standard deviations for men and 2.37 for women. It is apparently those questions contributing an amount falling between the consensus group and the satisfaction group which make the difference. These are: confiding, settlement of disagreements, frequency of kissing and agreement on affection.

In a factor analysis of the marital adjustment score made recently, Harvey J. Locke isolated five factors and named them companionship, agreement, affectional intimacy, masculine interpretation, and euphoria or halo effect.[11] Inspection of his rotated factor matrix shows that of these five factors the one which most includes and is heavily loaded on both satisfaction and intimacy is that of "euphoria." The congruency between the loadings on "euphoria" and the correlation coefficients in Table 2 is impressive. On the other hand, companionship, masculine interpretation, and to some extent affectional intimacy have loadings on the sharing of activities, which our analysis indicates his independency of the sort of adjustment which we find drops extensively as the marriage progresses. Agreement, or consensus, is not the major source of drop in the marital adjustment score.

Our own analysis is not adequate to settle the questions of whether the items dealing with intimacy are introducing a second element into the measured drop in adjustment. But when the results of this research are coupled with those of Locke's it seems most probable that it is "euphoria," which Locke describes as the set in the individual to "react to these questions with great enthusiasm and perceive all marital relationships as perfect,"[12] which forms the core of the disenchantment process. We feel that, somewhat by chance, the marital adjustment score has hit to the root of the disenchantment process, both through its inclusion of items relating to intimacy and loneliness and its direct questioning on the issue of regrets and feelings of a poor matching in the marriage.

One argument which might suggest the contrary would emphasize that the amount of confiding, of kissing and/or mutual give and take in settlement of disagreement would tend to characterize the newly wed and quickly diminish from that initial high point. But in fact these elements are not found to disappear shortly after marriage. Even in Locke's group, where the mean age was 33 years, 86 per cent reported kissing "every day," 73 per cent reported settlement of disagreements by give and take, and 88

[11] Harvey J. Locke and Robert C. Williamson, "Marital Adjustment: A Factor Analysis Study," *American Sociological Review*, **23** (October, 1958), pp. 562–569.

[12] *Ibid.*, p. 568.

per cent said they would certainly marry the same person again. Table 2 underlines this point. The items which contribute most to the total drop are those in which the "enchanted" actually showed no drop. Loss of confiding is far from the general condition; among those who did not become disenchanted, only 2 per cent showed any drop. Those items which contributed most highly to the drop in adjustment are the ones on which husbands tend to drop very little whether they become disenchanted or not.

Although the reverse argument seems plausible, the fact is that those patterns of behavior which would seem most appropriate to the newly married are not readily given up. Their loss, in fact, is accompanied by the growth of real regrets and dissatisfactions in the marriage and is a core part of the process of disenchantment.

Disenchantment in the Early Years of Marriage

Charles Hobart and others have found signs of disenchantment in the early years of marriage, and the generally accepted link between romanticism and early disenchantment implies, as Waller suggests, that this should be a time of major reality shocks. Our data so far have demonstrated the existence of loss of adjustment and satisfaction between the early and middle years of marriage. Is there evidence of a similar process in the earliest years?

Changes on certain single questions indicate that there is disenchantment in the earliest years. For example, two thirds of the individuals who changed increased, rather than decreased, the number of criticisms of the mate they offered in response to an open-ended question included in both the engagement and early marriage schedules.

The engagement and early marriage adjustment scores cannot be used to answer the question, however, because they are not exactly comparable. On the average the 510 husbands in the panel scored 7.9 points higher on the marital adjustment score than on engagement adjustment and their wives scored 9.2 points

higher. This amount of "gain" (from 148.2 to 156.1 for men and 149.0 to 158.2 for women) must represent a real loss in amount of adjustment.

The interesting feature of these scores, then, is the fact that the men have apparently suffered more disenchantment in the earliest years than have the women. This is in sharp contrast to Table 1, where the losses in adjustment from early marriage to the middle years were almost invariably larger for wives than husbands. At engagement the adjustment scores of the men and women are approximately equal; subsequently the men become disenchanted more quickly than the women so that by the time of early marriage their adjustment scores are typically lower than their wives'. Between early marriage and the middle years the trend reverses, so that by the middle years the adjustment scores of the husbands and wives are again equal (147.6 for husbands; 147.5 for wives).

Why do husbands experience disenchantment earlier than their wives? There is some evidence, in Hobart's work, that they may have romanticised more than the women. We would also suggest that the occupational commitment may operate as a "reality drag," quickly reducing the euphoria of the early years. The comparable event for women is perhaps the birth of a child.

The finding of differing rates of disenchantment for men and women at various points in the marriage history suggests, however, that had we contacted the couples more frequently an even more complex picture of the disenchantment process might have been found.

Disenchantment and Divorce

For the majority of divorces we have information at only the engagement period so that no measure of disenchantment for these "early divorces" is possible. This is because the majority of divorces occur in the first few years of marriage. But for 34 late-divorcing couples, however, we have early marriage schedules so that both engagement and early marriage adjustment scores are available. For the divorcing men, the mean engagement adjustment score was 151.5 and the mean early marriage adjustment was 147.1. For the women the equivalent scores were 144.1 and 144.7. These may be compared to the scores given above for 510 couples who are still married. The following differences between the married and divorced may be noted:

1. The divorced men have initially higher rather than lower adjustment than the married men. They are typified by a great drop rather than by an initially low score. Among these late divorces it is the magnitude and speed of their disenchantment which most fully characterize the husbands.

2. The divorced women begin with below average adjustment and although their losses are greater than the married women their initially low adjustment is also a factor in divorce. One of the clear elements contributing to the divorces in this panel is that the women tended to have definite doubts during the engagement period but did not act upon these doubts until after the marriage had occurred. The men, more typically, broke the engagement if they had doubts. In the few cases where men married despite severe doubts they did not frequently divorce.

The later divorces in this panel typically occurred when the wife experienced aggravation of doubts which she had held for some time while the man suddenly lost his above-average degree of contentment. If prior appearance of a characteristic in time indicates casual priority, the women's dissatisfaction is a more basic cause of divorce than the men's. This generalization, again, only applies to the late divorces.

Summary and Discussion

Data from the Burgess-Wallin longitudinal study of marriage indicate that a process of gradually reducing marital satisfaction of euphoria typically characterizes the marriages studied. It is further found that this loss of marital adjustment is not accompanied by equal loss of personal adjustment. Finally, different rates of disenchantment are found to characterize those who have remained married and those who subsequently divorced.

Viewing marriages in a processual sense, in which change is emphasized, offers a fruitful addition to the static view, which regards marital adjustment, for example, as a contemporary configuration of a limited number of attitudes and background factors.

21. Parental Aid to Married Children: Implications for Family Functioning*

BY MARVIN B. SUSSMAN AND LEE G. BURCHINAL

THIS IS A SECOND and comparison paper on the continuance and functioning of a kin family network in contemporary industrial society.[1] The concept of the kin network is proposed as a replacement for the one which posits that a nuclear family unit is most suited functionally for the exigencies of modern life. The kin family network is composed of nuclear families bound together by affectional ties and choice. Unrequired for the maintenance of the network are geographical propinquity, neolocal residence, occupational nepotism, intervention in occupational and social mobility efforts, or a rigid hierarchical authority structure.[2] Members and nuclear families of the network volunteer to help rather than to direct such activities. They perform supportive rather than coercive roles.

The lifelines of the network are help and service exchanged among members of nuclear families related by blood and affinal ties. Help, service, and social interaction characterize the activities of this interdependent kin family system indentified as the kin family network.

Help and service among kin members take many forms. The principal form of help among parents and their married offspring is financial aid. One purpose of this paper is to examine how much aid binds together nuclear related families along generational lines. A second purpose is to discuss the implications of financial aid for the independence of nuclear units within the network.

In this paper the term parental aid for married children is limited to financial assistance which may be in the form of cash, gifts, or services. The financial nexus is used since it is a measurable quantity. It is recognized that parents and the kinship system generally provide social and emotional support for the marriages of the younger generation. Furthermore, support of children is characteristic of parental roles related to preparing and assisting youth for dating, courtship, and eventual mate selection. Nevertheless, the limited definition of parental aid

SOURCE: Marriage and Family Living, *Volume 24* (*November, 1962), pp. 320–332. Reprinted by permission of National Council on Family Relations.*

* Graduate School, Western Reserve University, and published as Journal Paper No. J4248 of the Iowa Agricultural and Home Economics Experiment Station, Ames, Iowa, Project No. 1370.

[1] The first paper is Marvin B. Sussman and Lee Burchinal, "Kin Family Network: Unheralded Structure in Current Conceptualizations of Family Functioning," *Marriage and Family Living*, **24**, No. 3 (August, 1962), pp. 231–240.
[2] Eugene Litwak provides a sound empirical basis for this position. See "Geographical Mobility and Extended Family Cohesion," *American Sociological Review*, **25** (June, 1960), pp. 385–394; "Occupational Mobility and Extended Family Cohesion," *American Sociological Review*, **25** (February, 1960), pp. 9–21, and "The Use of Extended Family Groups in the Achievement of Social Goals: Some Policy Implications," *Social Problems*, **7** (Winter, 1959–60), pp. 177–87.

(financial) is used at the point of marriage of the child and the establishment of a separate household apart from parents. Financial aid, when given by parents to the married child, provides one efficacious test of the theory of the isolated nuclear family and of the alternative proposal of the viability of the kin family network in modern urban society.

Research Findings

Before 1950 only a few studies dealt specifically with this subject. Thorpe reports data for money management practices of a sample of married students at a Midwestern university in 1946–1947, but data on parental aid are unreported.[3] One finding from a study of the effect of campus marriages upon participation in college life was that 13 per cent of a random sample of married students at Iowa State University in 1956 reported financial help from parents, whereas, this was reported by 60 per cent in two journalistic descriptions of parental subsidies for married college students.[4] Marriages involving 110 students at Antioch College were described in *The Ladies' Home Journal* story. Interview data were used to support the generalization that threats to withdraw support from the college-level children if they were going to marry seldom led to the desired effect. The support was withdrawn only in isolated cases where parents refused the final emancipation of their children. Among these college marriages, parental support was substantially accelerated at the birth of the baby. However, lavish aid was rejected by the student. As much as possible, the married students desired to finance their own marriages.[5] Christopherson and his associates report on

contributions of parental families to the monthly income of college student families. Thirty-eight per cent of the student families receive some subsidy. The subsidies ranged from 5 to 80 per cent of their total money income.[6]

Additional studies on family continuity and help patterns among intergenerational families emerged during the 1950's. Several groups of families were studied by Sussman in New Haven and Cleveland.[7] Data for the New Haven families were based on interviews with 97 families who had 195 married children living away from home. In 154 of these cases (79 per cent) parents had established a pattern of giving moderate help and services to their married children's family. Direct financial assistance for larger expenditures such as the purchase of a home, loans, or gifts of money, or less direct assistance as in providing gifts such as furniture, household equipment and providing services including baby care, gardening, or provisions for inexpensive vacations were combined in the 79 per cent estimate. Unfortunately, questions on the specific amounts of financial aid given by parents to their married children were not asked in the original project. More recent and more detailed analyses of the original data show that in 136 of the 195 cases, parents gave direct financial assistance at the child's marriage to cover major expenses or purchases incurred during the first year of marriage. Monies given were to cover a number of situations: cost of the

[3] Alice G. Thorpe, "How Married Students Manage," *Marriage and Family Living*, **13** (Summer, 1951), pp. 104–105, 130.

[4] Everett M. Rogers, "The Effect of Campus Marriages on Participation in College Life," *College and University*, **34** (Winter, 1958), p. 195.

[5] Profile on Youth, Subsidized Marriages," *Ladies' Home Journal*, **66** (December, 1949), pp. 58, 193–196; and J. L. Herman, "Should Parents Finance Youthful Marriages " *Cosmopolitan*, **139** (October, 1955), pp. 82–85.

[6] Victor A. Christopherson, Joseph S. Vandiver, and Marie N. Krueger, "The Married College Student," 1955, *Marriage and Family Living*, **22** (May, 1960), pp. 122–128.

[7] Marvin B. Sussman, "The Help Pattern in the Middle-Class Family," *American Sociological Review*, **18** (February, 1953), pp. 22–28. For related analyses by the same author see, "Parental Participation in Mate Selection and Its Effect Upon Family Continuity," *Social Forces*, **32** (October, 1953), pp. 76–81; "Family Continuity: Selective Factors Which Affect Relationships Between Families at Generational Levels," *Marriage and Family Living*, **16** (May, 1954), pp. 112–120; "Activity Patterns of Post Parental Couples and Their Relationship to Family Continuity," *Marriage and Family Living*, **27** (November, 1955), pp. 338–341; "The Isolated Nuclear Family: Fact or Fiction," *Social Problems*, **6** (Spring, 1959), pp. 333–340; "Intergenerational Family Relationships and Social Role Changes in Middle Age," *Journal of Gerontology*, **15** (January, 1960), pp. 71–75.

Table 1

Direction of service network of respondent's family and related kin by major forms of help

Major forms of help and service	Between respondent's family and related kin per cent*	From respondents to parents per cent*	From respondents to siblings per cent*	From parents to respondents per cent*	From siblings to respondents per cent†
Any Form of Help	93.3	56.3	47.6	79.6	44.8
Help During Illness	76.0	47.0	42.0	46.4	39.0
Financial Aid	53.0	14.6	10.3	46.8	6.4
Care of Children	46.8	4.0	29.5	20.5	10.8
Advice (Personal and Business)	31.0	2.0	3.0	26.5	4.5
Valuable Gifts	22.0	3.4	2.3	17.6	3.4

* Totals do not add up to 100 per cent because many families received more than one form of help or service.

† Marvin B. Sussman, "The Isolated Nuclear Family: Fact or Fiction," *Social Problems*, **6** (Spring, 1959), p. 338.

honeymoon trip, purchase of an automobile, down payment on a home, "to go into business," or to begin a savings program. The specific amounts are unavailable, but it was clear that in 35 cases, money was given to meet more than one major expense or purchase.

After the initial financial gift at marriage few children received money regularly. Financial giving was limited to emergencies, for celebrations such as birthdays or anniversaries, or for grandchildren. These patterns permit extension of aid yet prevent usurpation or provider roles in the newly formed child's family.

Another form of financial aid is low cost or no interest loans by parents to the young married couple. The amount of these loans are unknown but 82 of the 97 parental families reported providing a "sizeable" loan to married children to help them with a major purchase or undertaking.

Additional data on help patterns within the kinship matrix are provided from another Cleveland sample of families. An adult member of 27 working-class and 53 middle-class households was interviewed. In terms of the wide range of help items described from the New Haven study, all of the middle-class and 92 per cent of the working-class families were actively involved in a network of inter-family help by either giving or receiving one or more items of assistance within a one-month period prior to the interview.[8] Percentages for various types of aid; "any form of help," "help during illness," "financial assistance," "care of the children," "advice (personal and business)," and "valuable gifts" among family members of the kinship network are reported in Table 1.

In the context of the present discussion, the service network which included "from parents to respondents" is of particular interest. The percentages of respondents who indicated they received any of these forms of help from parents are 80, 46, 47, 20, 26 and 18, respectively, for types of aid just described. The two items of particular interest are: receive financial aid, 47 per cent; and received valuable gifts, 18 per cent. It is necessary to point out limitations of the data. The form, extensiveness or continuity of the assistance is unreported. An expensive gift at marriage or occasional valuable gifts are considerably different from regular contributions to the family income. Middle-class families gave or received financial assistance to relatives more frequently than the working-class families;

[8] Sussman, "The Isolated Nuclear Family," *op. cit.*, p. 335.

although a nonsignificant difference was found for financial aid given by the parents to the child. Exchanges of help during illness were similar among families in the two social strata. Middle—more than working—class families exchanged advice (personal and business), provided for care of children and gave valuable gifts to one another.

Data from still another study in Cleveland based upon interviews with 401 households in a transitional area revealed an intricate matrix of inter-family activities which included the exchange of advice, financial assistance and various services. Among the families interviewed, relatives were second only to banks as sources of financial aid and second only to clergymen for assistance in times of personal trouble. When first, second, and third sources of assistance were combined, relatives were most frequently sought for assistance.[9]

The extensive nature of mutual aid relationships among related nuclear families has also been observed for urban families in Detroit. About 70 per cent of the 723 wives interviewed indicated they both gave and received some kind of help from relatives outside of their immediate household.[10] The specific type of help under consideration, financial aid, was twice as likely to come from parents as from siblings. This is expected since more parents are in a position to provide financial assistance to married children than are married siblings who are frequently in similar stages of family development. There was an inverse relationship between the age of the wife, taken as an index of the family life cycle, and receiving financial help. Fifty-three per cent of the wives who were 29 or younger reported receiving financial assistance; 36 per cent of the wives in the 30–34 year range did so; 18 per cent of the 45–49 year old wives and 20 per cent of the wives who were 60 or older reported financial assistance from relatives. Financial aid given by families to other relatives showed little

relationship to age of wife; about 30 per cent of all families reported giving financial assistance.

It is reasonable to expect considerable parental support extended to children involved in young marriages. Parental aid was more frequent among marriages involving brides of high school ages when the brides were premaritally pregnant (P).[11] Among 22 married couples involving a premaritally pregnant bride who was of high school age, the weekly median family income was $51.20 compared to $61.60 for 35 couples where the bride was of high school age but not pregnant at the time of marriage (NP). Obviously both groups are on weak economic grounds. Parental aid appeared to be the major source of financial assistance. This aid took three forms: (1) providing housing and sharing meals or groceries; (2) providing a sizeable portion of the family income of the young couples; and (3) providing all of these forms of assistance.

Only 14 per cent of the couples in the P group has always maintained a separate residence since the time of their marriage compared to 46 per cent of the couples in the NP group. The difference is statistically significant. Approximately 32 per cent of the Pregnant and 26 per cent of the Non Pregnant couples had always lived with one of the families of orientation. An additional 55 per cent of the former (P) and 29 per cent of the latter (NP) couples lived at one time or another with in-law families prior to or after having their own place of residence. The economic dependency of the young couples also was indicated by the fact that only 18 per cent of the P couples and 49 per cent of the NP couples had lived entirely on their own incomes. The difference is statistically significant. An additional 18 per cent of the couples in the P group received help only when they were getting started after marriage, 59 had been or were receiving continuous help from their families and five per cent involved in cases where the wife lived at home at no expense while her

[9] Marvin B. Sussman and R. Clyde White, *Hough: A Study of Social Life and Change*, Cleveland: Western Reserve University Press, 1959, pp. 72–76.
[10] Harry Sharp and Morris Axelrod, "Mutual Aid Among Relatives in an Urban Population," in Ronald Freedman, et al. (eds.), *Principles of Sociology*, New York: Holt, 1956, pp. 433–439.

[11] Lee G. Burchinal, "Comparisons of Factors Related to Adjustment in Pregnancy-Provoked and Non-Pregnancy-Provoked Youthful Marriages," *Midwest Sociologist*, 21 (July, 1959), pp. 92, 96; also by the same author, "How Successful are School-Age Marriages" *Iowa Farm Science*, 13 (March, 1959), pp. 7–10.

husband was in the service. The economically dependent couples in the NP group included nine per cent who received help immediately after their marriages only; 11 per cent who had been and were receiving continuous help; and 31 per cent where the wives lived at home while their husbands were in the service.

The Economic and Social Matrix of Financial Aid

Changes in family income since 1930 permit parents to provide financial support to their married children. Real incomes for working- and middle-class families have risen steadily since the depression. It is now possible for middle-class and working-class parents to provide some form of financial support, valuable gifts, interest free loans, contributions to down payments, or substantial gifts of money to their married children. In an affluent society, a considerable proportion of the family's income in the middle years of life can be devoted to a variety of ends which reflect the values and special interests of the parents rather than being dictated by requirements of biological necessity.

American males reach their peak of income close to the point in life when the expenses of their families are rapidly declining. Peak earning for nonfarm male heads are reported for ages 45 to 64. Family expenses are generally declining in these years because the education of children is near completion or already completed and children have established their separate residences. It is estimated that the last child marries when the median age of the father is about 50.3 years and that of the mother 47.6 years.[12] Frequently among both lower- and higher-class families the house is paid for and other major expenditures are at a minimum.

The increases in employment of wives heightens the family income during these later middle years. In March, 1960, approximately 35 per cent of all wives with husbands present and having no children under 18 were in the labor

force. This figure had increased from 28 per cent in April, 1948. In March, 1960, approximately 39 per cent of all wives with husbands present and having children between 6 to 17 years of age were in the labor force. The comparable figure in April, 1948, was 26 per cent.[13]

Retirement programs, both public and private, developed since the enactment of the Social Security Act in the early 1930's help relieve parents of the apprehension of limited resources in their retirement years. Obviously the provisions of retirement are unequal for all segments of the population and are probably more appropriate to the middle- and upper-class parents to play Santa Claus with their money.

A final economic condition, inheritance tax laws, makes it prudent to transfer accumulated wealth to relatives at regular intervals before the death of the aging parents rather than in lump sums after their death. As middle-class families accumulate wealth in the form of real estate, insurance policies, and investments of various sorts, provisions for the orderly transfer of wealth to children and grandchildren are becoming increasingly common. This is a downward diffusion of an upper-class norm.

Whether parents will use their "unencumbered" income to give financial aid to children is another question. Middle- and working-class parents are caught in a set of countervailing values. Long established custom requires that the young married couple is provided with some assistance in "setting-up housekeeping." In rural areas during earlier periods, family, kinship, and sometimes community cooperation was used to clear land and build buildings for a newly married couple. Some equipment, stock or other capital items were provided by the families of the young bride and groom. Farming is still largely a hereditary occupation. Even where contractural arrangements are made to transfer farm property and equipment from father to son or son-in-law, frequently lower

---

[12] Paul G. Glick, *American Families*, New York: Wiley, 1957, see pages 54, 67–68, 72–73, and 98, for data on family life cycle points and incomes of American families.

[13] The 1948 data were taken from "Working Mothers in the United States," Note No. 32–1958, October 1, U.S. Department of Health, Education and Welfare, unpublished manuscript; the 1960 data were taken from Special Labor Report, No. 13, "Marital and Family Characteristics of Workers," U.S. Department of Labor, Bureau of Labor Statistics, April, 1961, Table G. p. A–13.

value estimates are made than commercial transactions with nonrelatives would permit; frequently interest-free arrangements are agreed upon, or some proportion of the property is provided as a gift and the rest purchased under fairly generous terms.[14] Many of these features are generic to the transfer of family owned and managed business operation in the urban society.

With the development of bureaucratic occupational roles in the urban setting, the only forms of parental support to married children which generally can occur are those of providing services or financial support as expressed in giving valuable gifts, direct grants of money, transfer of investments, trust funds, and titles to property. Expressions of financial assistance at the time of marriage is congruent with the earlier practices supported in rural society. Continuing financial assistance after marriage in any substantial form, whether direct or subtle, may be contrary to the norm that the young husband should be able to provide entirely by his own efforts for the proper support of his wife and family. Financial help in rural families was and still can be disguised in the form of donations of labor, loans of equipment, of joint ownership of stock or equipment, most of which is paid for by the father, whereas among urban families help is less easily disguised. Disguised is probably an improper description for the farm situation because the son who receives generous treatment in terms of inheritance or contractual agreements generally has contributed years of labor, skill, and management which have increased the value of the farm firm he is now receiving. There is a real question however, whether the financial autonomy norm has a sufficiently high saliency to preclude acceptance of parental assistance after marriage by young, urban, middle-, or working-class married couples.

Numerous social developments have contributed to a weakening of this norm. Young couples today exhibit a much more casual attitude toward economic readiness for marriage. Approximately 20 per cent of the college under-

graduate students in the United States are married. Marriage rates are considerably greater among graduate or professional students. Even if the most extreme concessions are made, these couples by their marriage decisions, have rejected the norm of a reasonably assured financial status before marriage and reasonable assurance of complete fiscal autonomy and responsibility after marriage. In effect, these young couples indicate faith in their resources, those of their parents, and the economic system in which they participate. Furthermore, the increase in employment of wives indicates that many young husbands apparently maintain their status when there is a second family wage earner.

Over the past 50 years the increasing length of time during which parents have assumed financial responsibilities for their children has been an inducement to continue parental support for married children. Parental responsibility until the eighth grade gave way to the norm of "seeing the children through high school"; and currently this norm is being replaced by the expectation that middle-class parents should try, if at all possible, to provide for the college education of their children.[15] Support of children who marry while in college may cause some misgivings among parents, but in most cases parents continue their financial support.[16] Even among non-college married couples the long period of parental support prior to marriage is conducive to a mutual set of expectations which permits parental contributions to the income or level of living of married children. The child is viewed by the parent as an object of consumption. His economic contribution to the family generally is nil. In turn, the child can easily

[15] For instance, among students at the three state supported institutions of higher education of Iowa, approximately 43 per cent of their expenses were paid by parents or guardians. The extent of parental support ranged from 26 to 62 per cent among students in various colleges or departments. *Iowa State University Faculty Newsletter*, Iowa State University, Ames, Iowa, Vol. 5, No. 31, April 24, 1959, p. 3.

[16] *Ladies' Home Journal, op. cit.,* The article reports that about one-half of the parents of the married students received the news of marriage as a "severe blow"; only one-fifth of the parents received the news with "equanimity"; yet parental support was seldom withdrawn.

[14] Roger W. Strohbehn and John F. Timmons, "Changing Paths to Farm Ownership," *Iowa Farm Science,* **14** (March, 1960), pp. 465–466.

accept this perception of himself. In middle-class and frequently in working-class families, his role as the recipient of goods and services is deeply entrenched. Given this mutually compatible definition of the consumption role of children, even into early adulthood, aid could be extended to the post-marital period quite easily. The increased frequency of youthful marriages, frequently combined with student roles, further contributes to this possibility.

The assumption of grandparent roles extends further the pattern of financial giving. Helping grandchildren carries less threat to the provider role of the son or son-in-law. Grandparents can provide the "extras" of the good life to the new family while demanding the right to fulfill a kinsman's obligation. This notion is expressed by grandparents as "you should not deprive me of the joy of making my grandchild and myself happy."

Attitudes Concerning Financial Aid

The results of several attitude studies support the view of neolocal family financial independence and autonomy. Ninety-four per cent of the 260 married couples interviewed at Washington State University in 1946 by Cushing stated parental aid is unexpected and 96 per cent did not expect to inherit anything. However, these couples had a relatively high economic status both at the time of their marriages and at the time of the interviews.[17]

A study of 285 college married couples at the University of Maryland in 1950, showed that only eight per cent of the couples approved of help from the wife's parents, 12 per cent approved of help from the husband's parents, 16 per cent approved of help from any source, and 19 per cent approved of help from the government other than the G.I. Bill. Fifty-six per cent of the couples disapproved of help from any source, yet 90 per cent of the couples were receiving support on the G.I. Bill.[18]

Financial aid to parents is the other facet of the help pattern. Dinkel's college and young married adult respondents reported that they are reluctant to support aged parents when other institutional sources of aid are available. In times of parental need the obligation is assumed more unwillingly by the members of the middle than the lower classes.[19]

Sussman found that 96 per cent of parents interviewed in the New Haven study stated that they would "never accept financial aid from their children." This expressed attitude is contrary to actual behavior. The attitudes of parents and children are idealized representations required to support the notion that children reaching maturity are on their own.

Alvin L. Schorr has evaluated succinctly the current practice of filial responsibility in the United States and the relationship of it to current social security programs. He is concerned principally with how children assist aged parents. However, he concludes, "Two key points are implicit in the material. . . . First is the reciprocal nature of filial relations. In the net, parents may give more to adult children in cash, though less in living together. . . . The other key point is the spontaneous nature of filial relations. What children and their parents give to each other has little connection with law or compulsion. The money contribution, which is the only gift that can actually be compelled *from children to parents*, is a relatively unimportant pattern. Helping each other with chores, which cannot be compelled, is the dominant pattern."[20]

These attitudes data testify to the strength of the post-marital financial autonomy norm. However, while the norm of post-marital financial independence persists, it is probably eroded by social changes which are conducive to aid patterns among generationally linked nuclear families, some of which may be significant

[17] H. M. Cushing, "Economic Status of Married College Students," *Journal of Home Economics*, **40** (January, 1948), pp. 25–26.

[18] William F. Kenkel, "A Sociological Study of Married Student Veterans at the University of Maryland." Unpublished M.A. thesis, University of Maryland Library, College Park, Maryland, 1950, pp. 56–75.

[19] Robert M. Dinkel, "Parental-Child Conflict in Minnesota Families," *American Sociological Review*, **8** (August, 1943), pp. 412–419; and "Attitudes of Children Toward Supporting Aged Parents," *American Sociological Review*, **9** (August, 1944), pp. 370–379.

[20] Alvin L. Schorr, "Filial Responsibility in the Modern American Family," Washington, D.C.; Social Security Administration, U.S. Department of Health, Education, and Welfare, 1960, pp. 11–18.

contributions to the younger family's level of living or the maintenance of aged parents during the latter's retirement.

Parental Aid Model

A diagrammatic model of parental support to married children is suggested from the present discussion.[21] The model is composed of variables affecting patterns of parental support. Also considered are the implications for recipients of aid and the consequences of aid for the individual, family, and society.

Five general familial variables have been delineated as affecting the offering, acceptance, or rejection of parental aid. These include the values of the family of orientation, the position of the family in the social structure, the economic level of the family, its family structure, and the pattern of relationships within the structure.

The types of parent-child economic support are classified into three major categories: goods, money, and services. Family emergencies or crises may result in multiple types of aids such as care of stricken family members and cash to pay for medical services. The major types of economic aid exchanges are enumerated but the list is not intended to be exhaustive.

The family system is influenced by other systems found within the society. Social systems such as the economic, the religious, and the educational can either support or constrain parents in offering and children in accepting economic aid. Four societal factors support or constrain parental aid: the economic well being of people within the society; the demographic characteristics influencing the organization of the family; its structure shaped by organizational patterns of the larger society; and the family's value system which incorporates the dominant values of the society.

[21] The authors are indebted to Murray A. Strauss who constructed the original model from which this one is derived. The model is an outgrowth of discussions in the seminar, "Parental Aid to Married Children: Implications for Family Independence," held at the 1960 Groves Conference on Marriage and the Family, Columbus, Ohio, April 4–6, 1960. Marvin B. Sussman served as chairman, Lee G. Burchinal presented the foundation paper, and Murray A. Strauss served as recorder.

Twelve intervening variables may affect the giving and receiving of parental aid. These include the amount of aid given in a particular situation; expectations concerning aid and the basis for giving and receiving; the particular stage in the family cycle (requirements during the early years of childbearing are different from the later years when children are being sent to college); the occasion and technique used in giving aid without usurpation of provider roles; the expected return of parents; the residential location of the two sets of households; the social status of the family within the community and expectations concerning this status; the married child's image of the in-laws as helping or interfering persons; and generalized attitudes learned from interaction with in-laws, varied information sources and peer group experience.

Consequences of parental aid to married children are viewed in three areas, consequences for the family, consequences for the individual personality, and consequences for the general society.

Aid may affect husband-wife marital relationships in strengthening or weakening marital relationships and in determining the allocation of power within the newly organized family. It may affect intergenerational relationships and strengthen parental authority in such areas as occupational choice, mobility of children, and in mate selection. Aid may be related also to family size, the pattern of adjustment in old age, and the rate of divorce particularly among younger married persons.

Parental aid given to children may affect the development of dependence, the motivation to achieve, increased personal anxiety, increased feelings of security, and emancipation from mundane routines with freedom to concentrate on developments of skills and abilities and cultural interests. Opposite conditions may also prevail.

The general consequences for the society may be to reduce or further geographical or occupational mobility of families while maintaining a neolocal nuclear family system within a network of kin relationships. There are further consequences for population growth, economic and occupational striving of persons within the society, the cultural development of individuals, and current ideological systems.

The model is offered as a tool in the conceptualization and development of appropriate designs for the study of parental aid.

Theoretical Implications of Parental Support for Married Children

Variables Related to Parental Aid. Precise data are needed on a number of variables related to the form and amount of support, attitudes, and motivations toward giving and receiving aid, and the relations of each complex of variables to the effects of the exchange of aid and services. Social status levels and family resources of the parents and the second generation families must be controlled in such research. Careful attention should be given to the definition and measurement of the parental assistance variable.

Conceptualizing the Parental Assistance Variable. The types of economic support given to married children and the occasion and frequency of giving need elaboration in order to conceptualize the basic parental aid variable. Typologies of parental and married child exchanges of assistance, with net balances, need to be devised. In studying parental aid to young married couples, Burchinal classified parental aid as being supplied only immediately following the marriage, continuously or as having been generally absent. This typology requires expansion to include types of contributions or assistance from parents to children, goods, money, or services, the returns of children to parents, and the net balance within some time period with recognition of the continuity of the type and amount of aid.[22]

Conversion of types of aid into dollar values may permit exact determinations of amount of all types of aid and the net balance of aid exchange patterns between parents and married child. Jean Warren, Marjorie Knoll and some of their students at Cornell University have completed pioneering work in this area. Recently A. B. Clark in a study of two samples of families (107 and 77) established the feasibility of this approach. She converted economic contribution of goods and services given by parents to

married children into dollar values for given periods.[23] This approach is promising in obtaining specific information on the amount of aid in relations to actual income of the families within an intergenerational family network.

A further problem in defining the basic variable, parental assistance, involves the time dimension. Aid given at different times has different consequences. Aid given at the time of marriage will produce frequently different effects on the relationships between the husband and wife and among various affinal relationships than a similar amount of aid provided for other purposes over a number of years.

Research with married college students offers excellent opportunities to delineate specific variables affecting parental aid patterns. However, major research based on general population samples would be preferable in order to establish adequate generalizations.[24] Specification of other variables rooted in the complex of relations among husbands and wives in the younger generation families and each of the in-law families is beyond the scope of the present discussion. The assessment of the current situation may lead to theoretical specification and elaboration and to ultimate empirical testing.[25]

Parental Aid and Family Fertility. The availability of financial aid from parents and other supports obtained from friends and kin may affect size of the family. In a recent review of studies on fertility the author concludes that researchers to date have failed to consider the family as a social system with complex roles, tasks, and goals which together affect attitudes

---

[22] Burchinal, *Midwest Sociologist, op. cit.*

[23] Marjorie Knoll, *Economic Contributions and Receipts of Household Members*, Ithaca: Cornell University; Memoir 350; October, 1957; and A. B. Clark, "Economic Contributions Parents made to Children," Department of Home Economics, Cornell University, mimeographed abstract of a thesis.

[24] Cf. Judson T. Landis, "Values and Limitations of Family Research Using Student Subjects," *Marriage and Family Living*, **19** (February, 1957), pp. 100–105, and Manford Kuhn, discussion following the paper by Landis, *op. cit.*, p. 106.

[25] For an excellent starting point see, Mirra Komarovsky, "Functional Analysis of Sex Roles," *American Sociological Review*, **15** (August, 1950), pp. 508–516, and by the same author, "Continuities in Family Research: A Case Study," *American Journal of Sociology*, **62** (July, 1956), pp. 42–47.

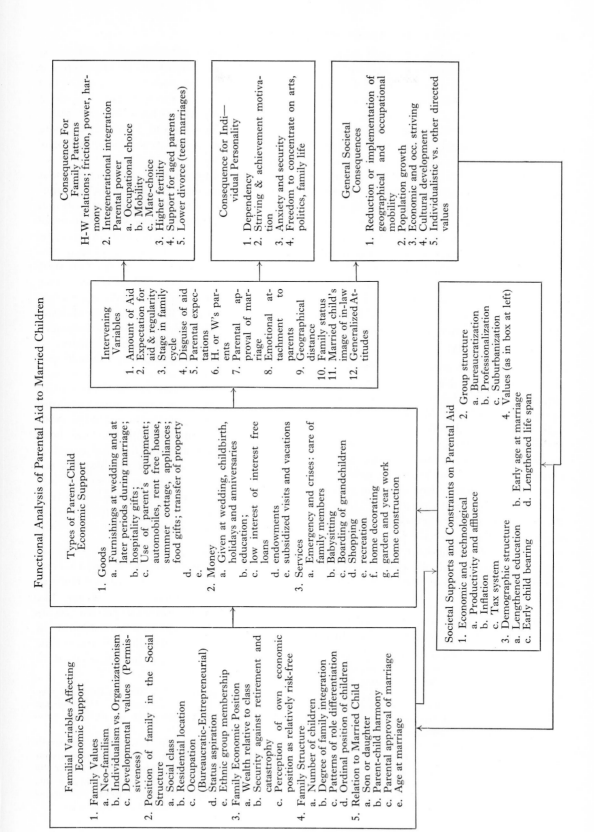

Functional Analysis of Parental Aid to Married Children

and behavior concerning fertility.[26] Different factors affect the decision to increase the size of the family at different stages in the family building process. In the Princeton study, the important factors affecting the decision to add another member are home-centered leisure and inter-family relationships of the young married couple in which the young wife had one or no children.[27] For the young marrieds, income of the husband correlated negatively and education not at all with the decision to increase the size of the family. Among couples with three or more children the decision to enlarge the family is related positively both to income and education.

It should be hypothesized further that the greater the amount of parental aid the larger the size of the young couple's family. The activities of the kin family network and role of parental aid are among the more exciting developments in theories of fertility.

Parental Aid and Social Class Theories. One social class theorist has argued succinctly that the conventional assignment of high social class to individuals who are highly educated and in high occupational classifications is erroneous.[28] He suggests that there are three types of social ranking: social status, family status, and local-community status. Family connections are far more important determinants of status positions than are recognized currently, either in theoretical formulations or classificatory systems of social class. The effects of parental aid to the achievement of maintenance of status within varied systems is a promising area of research relative to reformulation of current social class theories.

Parental Aid and the Security Function of the Family. The extended family functions to pro-

tect its kin in times of disaster and crisis. Quarantelli has reviewed over fifty different reports of disasters and summarizes, "The extended family is the major source to which disaster victims turned to help—and the smaller the scope of the community disaster the more probable is the kin group the major source of help."[29]

Quarantelli's brief review is unspecific about types and inter-family patterns of aid. Presumably parents and married children have reciprocal aid patterns. Disaster removes the traditional restraints concerning the giving of aid. It can be hypothesized that parents are more likely to give financial rehabilitation aid and relief to their children than to receive financial assistance from them. Moreover, parents who are victims of disasters are more likely than their children to rehabilitate themselves without the assistance of kin, friends, and formal welfare agencies.

The significance of the findings from disaster studies goes beyond the implications of parental aid among generational families. Quarantelli succinctly summarizes this point. "Disaster studies lend little support to the general proposition that the protective function has been basically relinquished and that the extended family is of little importance in mass societies. The kin group is the preferred, sought, and major source of short and long run help in time of such crises. In this sense at least the protective function is clearly still a major function of the extended family."[30]

Parental Aid and Retirement. Parental aid and the kin network are being studied in relation to social and economic adjustment in old age. The establishment of a retirement pattern has its roots in the aid and kin arrangements made in the middle years.[31] Explanations of leisure time pursuits of older persons include analysis of

[26] David Goldberg, "Some Recent Developments in Fertility Research," Reprint No. 7 *Demographic and Economic Change in Developed Countries*, Princeton University Press, 1960, pp. 8–9.

[27] *Ibid.*, The Princeton study is concerned with the social and psychological factors presumed to affect fertility behavior. The sample consists of 1,165 two parity native-white women living in the seven largest metropolitan areas in the United States.

[28] Bernard Barber, "Family Status, Local-Community Status, and Social Stratification: Three Types of Social Ranking," *Pacific Sociological Review*, Vol. 4, No. 1 (Spring, 1961), pp. 3–10.

[29] Enrico L. Quarantelli, "A Note on the Protective Function of the Family in Disasters," *Marriage and Family Living*, **22** (August, 1960), pp. 263–264.

[30] *Ibid.*, p. 264.

[31] See *Adjustment in Retirement*, Gordon F. Streib and Wayne E. Thompson, (eds.), *Journal of Social Issues*, **14**, 1958. Streib and Thompson have done the most creative thinking and analysis of data on this point. Streib's paper, "Family Patterns in Retirement," pp. 46–60 in this issue is most pertinent.

inter-family aid and kin networks.[32] Studies of housing for older people cannot ignore the aid variable. Shanas reports on the important functions of children and relatives in meeting financial and health needs of older persons.[33] In three large national samples an average 58 per cent believe that government should have principal responsibility for the support of aged persons while 36 per cent believe children or relatives should have this responsibility. In health crises involving older people, financial responsibility for it should be taken by public welfare or governmental agencies according to 57 per cent of the respondents of two samples; 37 per cent believe children should handle this problem. The norm of government responsibility is dominant in so far as individual beliefs are concerned but by no means universal. Children and relatives still have important roles in the care of aged parents.

Study after study on retirement indicates the lack of repudiation of the elderly by children. Whether this is because of cultural norms of filial responsibility inculcated in early childhood or due to reciprocity of assistance patterns developed during the leavestaking period is uncertain. Until more specific studies on this point are made, it is hypothesized that social and economic adjustment in the later years is functionally related to parental aid patterns established at an earlier stage of the family life cycle. Parents who develop an effective aid pattern with their children create a set of expectations for reciprocation in kind during their retirement.

Parental Aid and Family Life Education. Present research supports the description of the modified extended family system in urban as well as rural communities. This has implications

for the teaching of family life in the schools. Although conceptualizations and methodologies have lacked precision, there appears to be widespread economic aid patterns, chiefly from parents to married children among related nuclear families. It is the responsibility of family life specialists to study and interpret various patterns of parental aid to married children. *A priori* normative standards condoning or condemning parental aid *per se* must be supplanted with an orientation which helps parents assess the effects of aid given married children, both for the children and for themselves. Ways need to be found to acquaint parents and children with the characteristics of hazardous or destructive effects of aid. Also, family specialists must help prepare parents to provide aid in constructive ways and for the young married couples to receive aid in a constructive manner which contributes to their own welfare and to the welfare of the parents offering aid. If the general economic and societal conditions were correctly described in this discussion, giving and receiving aid among related families will become increasingly important topics in family life education.

Appraisal of Practical Implications of Parental Aid. A careful appraisal of the question of parental support to married children by family specialists is needed. Lack of empirical data and lack of familiarity with existing research encourages uncritical judgments concerning imputed effects of such aid. Some specialists believe that complete economic autonomy and responsibility of nuclear families are necessary for well functioning in our society. To them, parental aid is potentially destructive to family independence, conducive to in-law difficulties, and suggestive of husband-wife disagreements. Aid from the husband's family is less likely to create dissension because the husband's status as provider is less threatened than if comparable aid is provided by the wife's family. In either case, aid is viewed as having a detrimental influence on the relations within the younger generational family and between this family and the two in-law families.

Undoubtedly some forms and quantities of assistance in the presence of certain types of husband-wife and affinal relations will produce

[32] The best treatment of uses of leisure during the later years of life is found in Robert W. Kleemeier (ed.), *Aging and Leisure*, New York: Oxford University Press, 1961. See particularly the chapters by Wilensky, Streib and Thompson.

[33] Ethel Shanas, "Older People and Their Families," paper given at the meetings of the American Sociological Association, September 2, 1961. Professor Shanas presented data on three national samples; $N = 1734$, $N = 1405$, and $N = 2567$. A more complete report is found in *Family Relationships of Older People*, Health Information Foundation, 1961.

detrimental results. Situations where disagreements exist between husbands and wives in the younger families over the need of help; attitudes toward receiving aid and from whom; or where parents feel compelled to provide assistance, but do so with reluctance because of original objections to the marital choice; current money management practices, and other situations are probably fraught with potentially hazardous consequences. Only systematic research will determine specifically the consequences of aid to children.

A contrary view is that parental aid is one means of establishing and maintaining family continuity. It provides more benefits to both families than possible disadvantages. Parental aid contributes to greater family interdependence, greater family stability, and increased long-term personal satisfactions than is possible by preservation of strict financial independence of the younger generation family.

Parental aid may contribute directly to marital stability. It assists the young couple in maintaining a given level of living, thus removing one of the possible sources of conflict, financial deprivation, while permitting young couples to focus on their marital relationships. Numerous variables are involved in the attachment and dependence of each spouse of the younger generation to his or her parents; for instance, the degree of acceptance of each spouse of his in-laws and spousal perceptions of the in-laws' acceptance of themselves. These must be considered in evaluating effects of aid even within a favorable social context for receiving such aid.

Despite the lack of specific information about the relations among the variables, nevertheless, it is postulated that financial aid from parents has a definite positive value to all persons involved when the level of living aspirations of the younger couple exceed their current level of living and when the parents of husband/or wife are aware of this aspiration and provide support which makes it possible for the children's aspirations to be more nearly realized. Sussman found that about 70 per cent of his 97 middle-class New Haven parents said they give sufficient aid to their married children to help maintain or raise the status position of their children. As an example, one wife remarked: "My husband feels they ought to have a good start and not to struggle like we had to."[34] It would be valuable to have the responses of the recipients of the aid to a series of questions regarding need of aid, type and amount of aid received, and perceptions of the effects of the aid on their marital relationship. Further research along this line must include sampling of both parents and their married children.

Obviously most of the New Haven parents felt a definite sense of gratification in assisting their children attain or maintain a level of living beyond that which the children could attain by their own means. When aid of this sort is expressed as a demonstration of continuing affectional relations, mutual satisfactions and positive results are likely forthcoming. Parental aid is one way parents can demonstrate continuing interest in and approval of the marriages of their children. In turn the older parents, frequently grandparents as well, receive the satisfaction of continuing to help their children and the pleasures of continuing companionship with their children and grandchildren. Although the American population is highly mobile, increased leisure time and available resources for long distance travel will likely increase parental visits to the homes of married children. Anecdotal evidence suggests that "hospitality" gifts such as a new living room rug, living room or dining room furniture, or expensive clothes for the children are valuable contributions to the young family's level of living.

It is probable that aid from parents of this kind are found among families with a high degree of family continuity, homogamous marriages, parental approval of marriage partners, and where a developmental child rearing philosophy has prevailed.[35] These families begin with considerable interpersonal and at least adequate material resources. Aid patterns probably do not pose a threat to the independence or stability of most of these families. Parental aid provides a means of increasing inter-family continuity which may serve to strengthen the family life of the younger and parental families.

[34] Sussman, "The Help Pattern," *op. cit.*, p. 27.
[35] See the publications by Sussman cited in footnote 7.

Many of the younger families have two wage earners. Is there any need for parental assistance? Need is always relative to aspirational levels. In general, American couples "demand" a high level of living early in married life replete with acquistion of the goods and services associated with the conspicuous consumption patterns of modern living. These are the years when family costs increase due to family expansion. Few young families have sufficient means to enjoy all the goods and services they "need" or desire. Parental aid is one means of attaining or approximating more closely the desired level of living.

The status of the husband as provider for the family can be maintained even though parental aid is received. One reason is that among middle- and working-class families parental aid rarely is related to job procurement or advancement. While parental aid is instrumental in providing for the educational requirements necessary for many middle-class occupational roles, the social status of the husband is chiefly determined by his occupational achievement for which he alone is generally responsible. In the present industrial setting, occupational achievement for men from middle- and working-class family backgrounds is by merit. Professionalization of occupational roles has led to more objective measurement of merit and evaluation in terms of occupational achievement and less reliance on family background or the present social status of one's parents.

In this occupational status-role complex, significant extended family aid can occur in non-occupational areas.[36] Family aid during these circumstances is not visible to neighbors, friends, or co-workers. The accouterments of the household can be acquired early in marriage from the husband's income, the liberal use of credit, the combined incomes of the husband and wife, and parental assistance. Neighbors, friends, and co-workers are unable to judge how much of the hard goods is given by parents. Children can maintain a level of living commensurate with their occupational status and even above it. The maxim that success breeds success is appropriate

in this instance. The young family that has the material equipment demonstrates occupational achievement. The fine home, the cars in the garage, the nursery school for the kids, and the manicured lawn all signify that the husband has met the expectations of success in his occupational role. He is to be rewarded with additional promotions. Parental aid may be the hidden sponsor in the successful occupational movement of the young husband.

Summary

1. Financial aid exchanged between parents and their married children is one of the activities which binds together nuclear units of the kin family network along generational lines.

2. During the early years of the child's marriage the flow of aid is from parents to children. As children become middle-aged the stream of aid may be reversed, children now help their aged parents. Middle-class, middle-aged children may be giving subsidies to young married children and aged parents at the same time. A frequent pattern of aid is to turn to the needs of aging and often ailing parents after children have been aided in beginning their marriages and careers. This pattern is more a function of high income of parents and the age of members of nuclear linked units than preference to help a child over a parent. Most of these parents in their forties and fifties have completed their child rearing chores and often their acts of subsidy to married children. Their income may continue to rise or at least it remains the same. With lessened financial obligations they are now in a position to assist aged parents in their sixties and seventies with financial aid and to provide for the latter's physical care if necessary.

3. The conclusions from empirical studies are that parental aid, for the most part,
  (a) is given voluntarily and is based on feelings and sentiments held by parents towards their children and vice versa rather than upon legal and cultural norms;
  (b) is intended to assist rather than to direct achievement of occupational goals of family members receiving aid;

<hr>

[36] Cf. Litwak, "Occupational Mobility and Extended Family Cohesion," *op. cit.*, p. 11, and his discussion of nepotism.

(c) is available for an increasing number of families because of higher per capita income during the past twenty years, increased earning power over a longer life span, widespread adoption of retirement programs, restrictive inheritance tax laws, and new norms for a post-parental period in which there are emerging and identifiable grandparent roles; and

(d) has weakened the financial autonomy norm of the nuclear family unit without replacing it. There are some grounds for expecting changes in the nuclear, basically financially autonomous American family structure.

4. A diagrammatic model is presented for researchers to use in the study of parental aid to married children. It contains variables affecting patterns of support and implications of giving and receiving support. The model should facilitate the development and conceptualization of appropriate designs for the study of parental aid.

5. Several theoretical implications of parental support for married children are presented:

(a) The parental aid variable requires careful definition, conceptualization and control of intervening variables such as family resources, social status levels, duration of pattern, etc. in future research on general population samples.

(b) Typologies of exchanges of aid with net balances need to be devised. A conversion index is required for determining the cash value of all types of aid given and received. The use of this cash nexus permits more specific measurement of the effects of independent upon dependent variables, e.g., amount of aid given to the maintenance of the financial autonomy norm.

(c) Parental aid is a variable effecting family size, family continuity over time, family status, family behavior in times of disaster, and retirement patterns.

(d) Family life education programs require review in light of the viability of a functioning kin family network in contemporary society. Aid patterns are the life lines of the network. These need study and interpretation for their positive and negative effect upon participants.

Chapter 7

The Nuclear Family:
Tradition Maintenance
and Contingency Management

This chapter devotes attention to the internal processes in the nuclear family and concentrates on the ways in which families are organized to maintain tradition and to meet contingencies.

Tradition maintenance in families often is associated with the types of organization characterized by a central family authority. Moreover, this family authority must be constituted to persist over generations. The preceding chapters have suggested that in most societies the foci of authority in the family and kinship groups are becoming more diffuse, whereas authority in economic institutions and government is becoming more centralized. Under these conditions the maintenance of traditional patterns of family life becomes difficult.

Eisenstadt has emphasized that societies characterized by traditional practices show a strong bond between generations.[1] The intergenerational bonds between parents and children and between grandparents and their grandchildren sustain the authority of the older generation. Societies oriented toward change show primary cohesiveness among age-graded groups. Several papers in this volume (for example, Farber, Irish, Cumming and Schneider) have suggested that sibling bonds play a significant role in American kinship relations.

Under unilineal kinship, mating systems emphasize spouse-parent rights and obligations. Since child rearing is one of the main activities in family life that contribute to tradition maintenance, sentimental ties between parents and their children must exist for effective socialization. Individuals are selected for marriage in unilineal systems on the basis of their membership in lineages holding similar spouse-parent conceptions. Conflict between husband-wife obligations and parent-child obligations (insofar as it affects the continuity of the lineage) is thus reduced.

Tension, however, exists in bilateral kinship between husband-wife and parent-child bonds. In bilateral kinship, as suggested in the chapter on Courtship and Availability for Marriage, the marital relationship is based primarily on mate-lover

---

[1] S. N. Eisenstadt, *From Generation to Generation*, New York: Free Press, 1956.

roles and only secondarily on spouse-parent roles. The conflict generated by the incompatible demands of the mate-lover and the spouse-parent roles creates tension between generations and interferes with tradition maintenance. Emphasis on the mate-lover role minimizes the importance of traditional family division of labor and child-rearing practices in contemporary society. However, under certain conditions described by the readings in this chapter, spouse-parent roles and traditional maintenance may be stressed.

Readings on Tradition Maintenance and Contingency Management

The readings in this chapter emphasize conditions in contemporary society that facilitate tradition maintenance. By implication, opposite conditions represent mobilization for change in family norms and values.

The paper by Edward M. Saveth indicates how patriarchal family organization, inheritance practices, and maintenance of a particular life style sustain family tradition from one generation to the next. His paper shows how patrilineal organization permits the integrity of family property in a society of entrepreneurs. Saveth points out how the symbols of family permanance emerge and also suggests that not all members of the lineage need be identified by these symbols. Instead, a small number of individuals may sustain the family identity over generations. Under contemporary conditions, although the major symbols of lineage may become invisible, the lineage as a reference group may remain important to many people.

The second paper, by Aldous and Hill, describes sex-role factors which facilitate the continuity of patterns in family organization from one generation to the next. Their finding is that "same-sex" lineages (parent and adult-child of the same sex) promote continuity to a greater extent than do "cross-sex" lineages. Possibly, cross-sex family interaction is erotically tinged, and an avoidance relationship is encouraged between fathers and adult daughters and between mothers and adult sons. This avoidance may inhibit continuity in cross-sex lineages.

Melvin Kohn reports the results of his investigation of child-rearing techniques in different social classes. He finds that middle-class parents want to produce self-reliant children and that their socialization practices emphasize internalization of norms. This self-reliance facilitates the development of means for contingency management. On the other hand, working-class parents are more concerned with conformity, and their socialization practices involve more authoritarian practices. Presumably this authoritarianism facilitates maintenance of tradition.

Specific kinds of family ideology not only influence the continuity of certain norms and values but also maintain their potency through the development of authoritarian personality attributes. In the final paper Elder examines correlates of autocratic family ideology in the United States, Great Britain, West German, Mexico, and Italy. He reports that autocratic family ideology is related to social class, parent-child relations, education, migration, and work settings in each country. Family ideology is associated with political and economic views for middle-class men. For these men, tradition maintenance in family life is strongly connected with conservatism in other institutions.

22. The American Patrician Class: A Field of Research*

BY EDWARD N. SAVETH

"HISTORY RECEIVES ITS VOCABULARY, for the most part, from the very subject matter of its study," remarked the late Marc Bloch. The vocabulary, he added, lacked unity.[1] The word class, for example, had one meaning for John Adams at the end of the eighteenth century and another for his great-grandsons, Henry and Brooks, at the end of the nineteenth. John Adams preferred "rank" to class. He thought of himself as belonging to the "middle rank of people in society" and spoke of a patrician "rank" which "exists in every nation under the sun and will exist forever."[2] Thomas Jefferson noted the existence of "a Patrician order" in Virginia.[3] Jefferson's and Adams' use of "rank" and "order" sustains Professor Briggs' view that prior to the Industrial Revolution the word class was "used in its neutral, 'classifying' sense, and its place supplied by the 'ranks,' 'orders' and 'degrees' of a more finely graded hierarchy of great subtlety and discrimination."[4]

Following the Industrial Revolution, class became increasingly identified with conflict, a category for "the analysis of the dynamics of social conflict and its structural roots." Recently, the tendency has been to treat class as two analytically separable elements: class stratification harking back to the eighteenth-century conception of rank and, secondly, class action or conflict.[5]

Since history assigns many meanings to class, definition is the better part of historical wisdom. Class theory, however, includes many definitions and the result, as Bloch observed, is to leave "every man for himself."[6] The historian, therefore, tends to write about class in the hope that the outline of what he is discussing will flow from the narrative.[7] This approach avoids the bias inherent in schematization. To write about class without struggling with definition, however, can lead to mistaken analyses of the relationship between class and political action, the kind of analytical errors for which Charles A.

SOURCE: American Quarterly, *Volume 15* (*Summer Supplement, 1963*), *pp. 235–252.*

* This article is the result of a grant from the American Philosophical Society.

[1] *The Historian's Craft*, New York, 1953, p. 158.
[2] Quoted in Zoltan Haraszti, *John Adams and the Prophets of Progress*, Cambridge, 1952, p. 248.
[3] "Autobiography," *The Life and Selected Writings of Thomas Jefferson*, Adrienne Koch and Walter Peden (eds.), New York, 1944, p. 38.
[4] Asa Briggs, "The Language of Class in Early Nineteenth-Century England," in *Essays in Labor History*, A. Briggs and J. Saville (eds.), London, 1960; Ralf Dahrendorf, *Class and Class Conflict in Industrial Society*, Stanford, 1959, pp. 3–7.
[5] *Ibid.*, pp. 76, 153.
[6] *The Historian's Craft*, p. 176. For the multiple definitions of class see Leonard Reissman, *Class in American Society*, Glencoe, Ill., 1960, *passim;* Joseph Kahl, *The American Class Structure*, New York, 1957.
[7] Rowland Berthoff, "The Working Class," in *The Reconstruction of American History*, John Higham (ed.), New York, 1962.

Beard and Howard K. Beale have been taken to task.[8] What is required is interplay between class theory and the actual situation, with the concept refined by the process.

Professor Robert A. Dahl's statement concerning the concept of power is also true of class. "We are not likely to produce—certainly not for some considerable time to come—anything like a consistent, coherent 'Theory. . . .' We are much more likely to produce a variety of theories of limited scope, each of which employs some definition . . . that is useful in the context of the particular piece of research or theory but different in important respects from the definitions of other studies."[9]

An important clue to definition is Schumpeter's statement, echoed by Parsons, that "the family, and not the physical person, is the true unit of class theory."[10] This definition is applicable particularly to the patrician family that "has been established for at least one, and preferably two or three generations, as members of the upper class,"[11] that has a long tradition of literacy and a "moving sense of the overlap of history."[12]

Schumpeter's approach to class may be less meaningful when applied to the lower classes who have a shorter tradition of literacy, less of what Max Weber called "prestige of descent," and less of a sense of history and precedent. Only relatively recently have the Alfred Kazins and the James Baldwins been telling us how it really was in Brooklyn and Harlem.

Patrician personal literature—memoirs, autobiographies, letters, diaries, and similar memorabilia—are plentiful throughout most of our history. On the other hand, family history which derives from these sources and which could

advance us along the road to class definition, is an under-developed aspect of American historiography.

There are several reasons for this. If it is true, as many European observers noted, that the family unit was weaker here than in Europe, then the role played by family was less likely to impress itself upon the historian's consciousness.[13] Stress which American culture has placed upon the individual may have caused the historian to minimize or take for granted the extent to which family is important in providing means of access to education; to social, economic, and political opportunity; to marriage; and to the various forms of status.[14]

Second, there is a tendency for the achieving individual to complicate further the historian's problem by minimizing, in public statements, the role of ancestry. Theodore Roosevelt, according to Howard K. Beale, consistently understated the wealth and accomplishment of his ancestors.[15] Indeed, in a society devoted to egalitarianism, pride of ancestry becomes for the patrician politician an aspect of covert culture that finds expression in privately printed and in manuscript genealogies; in personal and private papers; and in membership in ancestral and patriotic societies.[16]

[13] Michael Chevalier, *Society, Manners and Politics in the United States*, edited with an introduction by John William Ward, New York, 1961, p. 398; G. W. Pierson, *Tocqueville and Beaumont in America*, New York, 1938, p. 603.
[14] Oscar Handlin, "A Note on Social Mobility and the Recruitment of Entrepreneurs in the United States," *Explorations in Entrepreneurial History*, (Winter Supplement, 1956), pp. 1–5; Bernard Bailyn, *New England Merchants in the Seventeenth Century*, Cambridge, 1955, pp. 87–91, 135–158; John A. Munroe, *Federalist Delaware, 1775–1815*, New Brunswick, 1954, p. 199.
[15] "Theodore Roosevelt's Ancestry, A Study in Heredity," *New York Genealogical and Biographical Record*, LXXV (1954), pp. 196–205.
[16] "By covert culture we refer to traits of culture rarely acknowledged by those who possess them." B. Bowron, L. M. Marx, and A. Rose, "Literature and Covert Culture," *American Quarterly*, IX (Winter, 1957), p. 377.

An example of the private satisfactions of genealogy is offered by the late Myron C. Taylor who took great pride in his descent from a vigorous personality named Captain John Underhill, a pioneer settler of Oyster Bay in the early seventeenth century. So

[8] Lee Benson, *Turner and Beard*, Glencoe, Ill., 1960, pp. 108, 111; Robert P. Sharkey, *Money, Class and Party*, Baltimore, 1959, p. 293.
[9] "The Concept of Power," *Behavioral Science*, III, July, 1957, 201–215.
[10] Joseph Schumpeter, *Imperialism and Social Classes*, New York, 1951, p. 148; Talcott Parsons, "Social Classes and Class Conflict in the Light of Recent Sociological Theory," in *Essays in Sociological Theory*, Glencoe, Ill., 1954, p. 328.
[11] Kahl, *The American Class Structure*, p. 189.
[12] Francis Biddle, *A Casual Past*, New York, 1961, p. 17.

Third, historians have tended to regard the field of family history as allied to genealogy. Those genealogists who interpret the concern of genealogy as limited to date of birth, date of death, and the tracing of family relationship, deny the association.[17] On the other hand, most of the family history that has been written by genealogists is, by the standards of professional historiography, not a little amateurish and antiquarian. We have not as yet developed in American a Horace Round or an Anthony Richard Wagner, capable of blending successfully genealogy and history.[18] Lester J. Cappon concluded that the volumes which line the shelves of American genealogical societies, with their overtones of filiopietism, family pleading, and amateurism are not likely to interest greatly the professional historian.[19]

In all fairness, however, no estimate has been made of this data provided the right questions are asked of it. The field of local history, for example, is a comparable intellectual desert, but Elkins and McKitrick have used the data of local history very effectively in seeking a new meaning for the Turner thesis. So have Curti

and his associates.[20] Genealogy has the potential of a valuable tool for social analysis, as Joseph Schumpeter indicated decades ago.[21]

As a problem in historiography, family history is complicated by its not inconsiderable sprawl. In the preface of *The Cokers of Carolina A Social Biography of a Family*, George Lee Simpson Jr. described both an "inherent problem" and an "inherent unfairness" in writing the history of a family over four generations. Caleb and Hannah Coker and their ten children, Simpson continued, have hundreds of descendants. "Clearly it is impossible to write in a single coherent volume of all those people who, whether they bore the Coker name or not, are members of the family."

Simpson concentrated on those "who bore the name of Coker and who identified themselves with the location where the family achieved recognition." He further limited himself to those Cokers who, "in the public eye and by common agreement," have been a part of a notable achievement, either as individuals or as a part of a persisting family unit bearing the name Coker.[22] Accordingly, it is the achieving individuals within the achieving family who become family history.

Bernard Bailyn is also troubled by the sprawl of family history and its nature "apart from the total of the unrelated careers of a number of people who happened to have the name. . . . In what way, that is, did the family have meaning in itself? What historical importance is there to the fact that these individuals, as opposed to any others, find places on the vast genealogical chart the author furnishes us within his text? What, in other words, can be said about the family as such that illuminates the lives of its members and the evolution of American society?" Bailyn suggests pruning the family tree except for those elements that determine the family life style, that contribute to comprehension of its "permanent identity," that establish the core of its

---

devoted was Mr. Taylor to this ancestor that he sponsored and financed a four-volume genealogy of his Underhill ancestors. (J. C. Frost, *Underhill Genealogy* [New York, 1932]). He was also the prime mover of the Underhill Society, composed of the descendants of Captain John Underhill, *New York Genealogical and Biographical Record*, XC, 92.

[17] Introductory "Note" to Kenneth E. Hasbrouck and Ruth P. Neidgerd, *The Deyo (Deyoe) Family* (1958). See the review of this volume by A. D. Keator in the *New York Genealogical and Biographical Record* (October, 1959).

[18] Anthony R. Wagner, *English Genealogy*, London, 1960, pp. 178–205, 304–354.

[19] Lester J. Cappon, "Genealogy, Handmaid of History," *Special Publications of the National Genealogical Society*, XVII, pp. 3, 8. Some idea of the scope of genealogical literature, indexed as to family, may be obtained from Freeman Rider (ed.), *The American Genealogical Index* (Middletown, Conn., 1942–1952) and *The American Genealogical-Biographical Index to American Genealogical, Biographical and Local History Materials*, (Middletown, Conn., 1952- date. See also Cappon, "Bibliography of American Genealogical Periodicals," *Bulletin of the New York Public Library*, LXVI (January, 1962), pp. 63–66; Cappon, *American Genealogical Periodicals A Bibliography* . . . New York, 1962.

[20] Merle Curti et al., *The Making of An American Community A Case Study of Democracy in a Frontier County* (Stanford, 1959), pp. 1–11; Stanley Elkins and Eric McKitrick, "A Meaning for Turner's Frontier," *Political Science Quarterly*, LXIX (September, 1954), p. 349.

[21] *Imperialism and Social Classes*, p. 169.

[22] Chapel Hill, N. C., 1956, preface and author's note.

"inner continuity," that are the "symbols of family permanence within the flux of births and deaths and passing careers."[23]

Family style, however, does not go on forever. Brooks and Henry Adams believed that three generations was the limit of familial adjustment and that, in the case of the Adams family, the world was too much for the fourth generation.[24] Alphonso Taft, father of William Howard and grandfather of Robert A. Taft, reminded a gathering of approximately one thousand Tafts who collected at Uxbridge, Massachusetts on August 12, 1874 that "brilliant political careers have not been characteristic of the Tafts in the past." He added, however, it was not safe to say what the future held in store because even as there was a tide in the affairs of men, there was a tide as well in the destinies of families.[25] The tide took its time in the case of the Tafts as it did with the Churchills who, like the Cecils (disguised as Salisburys, Cranbornes, and Balfours), for centuries accomplished nothing except to remain on their estates.[26]

Insofar as a component of definition of the patrician class is the patrician family, a "working model" of the patrician family, both in its internal structure and external relations, is needed. Professor Bridenbaugh has identified the history of the American family as a priority in American historiography[27] and the following variables have been suggested as foundation for such a history: the family's "internal structure (the inter-related roles of father, son, daughter, mother, uncle, and other kin), its relationship to the culture and society of which it is a part (the effects of industrialism, urban living, wider educational opportunities, the 'emancipation' of women, and similar elements), and the processes through which changes in internal structure

are affected by, and in turn affect, its external relationships."[28]

To this list of variables should be added, in the case of the patrician family, the figure of the patriarch whose role, Talcott Parsons[29] and Daniel Bell[30] suggest, is conditioned by different stages in the evolution of capitalism. The patriarchal family is strongest under the conditions of agrarian, mercantile, and the early stages of industrial capitalism—all of which rely heavily upon family capital and family management. The position of the patriarch as head of family is strengthened by his role as chief of enterprise.

From patrician personal literature centered upon the middle decades of the nineteenth century, it is possible to limn the patriarch as a real type.[31] The patriarch makes his fortune and then establishes roots in the community. He

[23] "The Beekmans of New York: Trade, Politics and Families," *William and Mary Quarterly*, XIV (October, 1957), pp. 605–606; *Idem*, XI (January, 1954), pp. 98–104.

[24] *The Degradation of the Democratic Dogma*, New York, 1949, p. 93.

[25] Henry F. Pringle, *The Life and Times of William Howard Taft*, New York, 1939, I, 19.

[26] Peter de Mendelssohn, *The Age of Churchill*, New York, 1961, p. 56.

[27] "The Great Mutation," *American Historical Review*, LXVIII (January, 1963), p. 323.

[28] *The Social Sciences in Historical Study*, Bulletin 64 of the Social Science Research Council, New York, 1954, p. 96.

[29] "The Kinship System of the Contemporary United States," *Essays in Sociological Theory*, p. 185.

[30] "The Break-Up of Family Capitalism," *Partisan Review*, XXIV (Spring, 1957), pp. 317–320.

[31] The real type differs from the ideal type construct of Max Weber. Writing of the ideal type as "formed by the one-sided accentuation of one or more points of view and by the synthesis of a great many diffuse, discrete, more or less present, and occasionally absent *concrete individual* phenomena, which are arranged according to these one-sidedly emphasized viewpoints into a unified *analytical* construct," Weber seems to be outlining the process whereby fictional types are created. (My position on Weber follows closely that of Gabriel Kolko, "A Critique of Max Weber's Philosophy of History," *Ethics*, LXX [1959], pp. 21–36; "Max Weber on America: Theory and Evidence," *History and Theory* [1961], p. 243.)

Not that fiction and aesthetics are without value for social science research, as Karl Deutsch has indicated. The semi-fiction of the ideal type meets and resembles the semi-reality of the fictional image of the patrician drawn by such careful hands as Marquand, Wharton, Holmes Sr., Auchincloss, Glasgow, and Faulkner. ("Summary statement on Results of the Conference on the Social Sciences in Historical Study," [mimeo, June 20–22, 1957], p. 19; A. Arnold, "Why Structure in Fiction: A Note to Social Scientists," *American Quarterly*, X [Fall, 1958], p. 135.) See also the interesting statement by A. J. Toynbee, "History, Science and Fiction," *The Philosophy of History in Our Time*, Hans Meyerhoff (ed.), New York, 1959, pp. 117–118.

builds a big house—big enough, as the first Nicholas Longworth explained, to accommodate "all the Longworths in the nation."[32] Master of the big house, the patriarch tended to be jealous of his brood and of his authority. The patriarch is the first Wade Hampton writing to an acquaintance: "I thank you for your friendly effort to procure me a landed estate for my Sons in the Western Country but must decline it for the present. . . . I do not wish my children at too great a distance from me."[33] The patriarch is James Lides, the South Carolina planter, who permitted his daughter to marry Caleb Coker, the rising young businessman from Society Hill, only after Coker promised that he would not take her West.[34] In the West, the hold of the patriarch did not loosen. Lawson Clay, trained in the law, wanted to move away from Huntsville, Alabama, "to some place where my services professional would be required" but he could not "gain the consent of any member of the family." The latter, said Lawson, "wish me to return to Huntsville and finish an existence, miserable in dependence and satiety." Despite efforts to be "on 'my own hook' unpropped by father," Lawson stayed on in the latter's large

household which included many relatives in addition to the nuclear family.[35]

In Cincinnati, noted Clara Longworth de Chambrun, "a model son-in-law, according to the Longworth pattern, [was] content to spend more time in Ohio than in New York, and one who showed an affectionate veneration for his wife's parents. . . ." It was, she continued, a curious "clan" life, as it was lived under their father's roof. "He had invented an extremely simple plan in regard to accounts and allowances, 'hating to be pestered for money,' as he said. Daily, a liberal sum was placed in the open drawer of his desk, accompanied by the verbal recommendation: 'let every one take what he wants or what he needs, and don't bother me.' "[36]

A great deal more research is needed to establish the patriarch as a real type on a less tentative basis than the above, which is more outline than definitive portrayal. Even more uncertain is the status of the patriarch under the later stages of industrial and on into the era of finance and managerial capitalism. It is apparent that the business fate of the Coker family of South Carolina was typical of many other families as the needs of enterprise for money and managerial skill transcended what the family could provide. The result was separation between family structure and business. When Charles Coker died in 1931, the board of directors of the family-founded Sonoco enterprises was composed entirely of members of the Coker family. A quarter of a century later, nonfamily outnumbered family board members, two to one.[37]

What happens to the patriarchal status under industrial, finance, and managerial capitalism is better established in theory than in fact. Talcott Parsons,[38] A. A. Berle,[39] and Daniel Bell[40] have

[32] Clara Longworth de Chambrun, *The Making of Nicholas Longworth*, London, 1933, pp. 46–47. Other references to the big house in patrician personal literature include Julia Davis, *Family Vista*, New York, 1958, p. 9; Elting E. Morison, *Turmoil and Tradition*, Boston, 1960, p. 11; E. S. Ives and H. Dolson, *My Brother Adlai*, New York, 1956, p. 22; Herman Hagedorn, *The Roosevelt Family of Sagamore Hill*, New York, 1954, pp. 38–40; W. E. Smith, *The Francis Preston Blair Family in Politics*, New York, 1933, I, p. 186; Eleanor Roosevelt, *This is My Story*, New York, 1939, pp. 117–123.

The big house and its significance is discussed in Edward C. Kirkland, *Dream and Thought in the Business Community*, Ithaca, N.Y., 1956, pp. 29–40 and by E. L. Godkin, "The Expenditures of Rich Men," *Scribner's Magazine*, XX (October, 1896), p. 495.

[33] *Family Letters of the Three Wade Hamptons*, Charles E. Cauthen (ed.), Columbia, S.C., 1953, p. 14. The letter is dated February 6, 1811.

[34] *Planters and Business Men The Guignard Family of South Carolina 1795–1930*, Arney R. Childs (ed.), Columbia, S.C., 1957, pp. 17, 38–39; *The Lides Go South . . . And West, The Record of a Planter Migration in 1835*, Fletcher M. Green (ed.), Columbia, S.C., 1952, p. v.

[35] Ruth K. Nuermberg, *The Clays of Alabama*, Lexington, Ky., 1958, pp. 77–78, 85, 93, 103; Allen Tate, "A Southern Mode of the Imagination," *Studies in American Culture*, J. J. Kwiat and M. C. Turpie (eds.), Minneapolis, 1960, p. 104.

[36] Chambrun, *The Making of Nicholas Longworth*, p. 47.

[37] Simpson, *The Cokers of Carolina . . .*, p. 291.

[38] "The Kinship System of the Contemporary United States," p. 185.

[39] *Power Without Property*, New York, 1959, p. 74.

[40] "The Break-Up of Family Capitalism," pp. 317–320.

discussed the waning of family capitalism and Bell, particularly, has emphasized the relationship between this phenomenon and the weakening of family structure. However, additional research is needed to determine the extent to which multi-millionaire oilman, J. Paul Getty is a representative mid-twentieth-century patriarch. He was divorced five times; his four sons by different wives are all but lost in the structure of the far-flung Getty business empire. Said one of the half brothers, "we don't keep up. Years and years go by when I see none of them, although recently we have been meeting about twice a year—once at the annual meeting of the family trust."[41]

While the Getty family pattern appears to sustain the thesis that the weakening of family structure is a concomitant of giant enterprise to which family is only remotely related, the Kennedy family experience demonstrates that there are factors beyond business which serve as basis for family cohesion.[42]

The patriarchal role may have altered since John Hay married Clara Stone in 1874 and Amasa, Hay's rich and patriarchal father-in-law, gave Hay a fine residence in Cleveland and a place in the business.[43] It seems logical to assume that there has been a change in the patriarchal role. But so little is known about the process of transformation that it is hard to say what it was, how it came about if, in fact, it has come about. Is Joseph P. Kennedy less of a patriarch than was Nicholas Longworth? What of the continuation of family influence in large, publicly-owned corporations such as Du Pont? What of managerial dynasties or continuities like the Sarnoffs in Radio Corporation of America?[44]

There is every indication that there are additional variables, beyond the economic factors stressed by Parsons and Bell, which condition family structure. The scope of these, however, is not likely to be revealed prior to intensive research into family history.[45] Only a history of the American family could comprehend these variables and provide basis for an accurate typology of the patriarch at various stages in American history as well as a contribution to class theory.

Family history is particularly relevant to that aspect of class which Max Weber called the "life-style." An important component of the latter is an inherited pattern of family culture—a rare emphasis in historiography and an important one that finds expression in Elting E. Morison's biography of Henry L. Stimson.[46] The current social science emphasis upon "achievement"[47] has no counterpart in historical studies of families which have been prominent in successive generations. Most family histories,

[41] Ralph Hewins, *The Richest American*, New York, 1960, pp. 17, 20, 39, 391–392, 395.

[42] "How Joe Kennedy Made His Millions," *Life*, January 25, 1963.

[43] Tyler Dennett, *John Hay*, New York, 1933, p. 101.

[44] Osborn Elliott, *Men at the Top*, New York, 1959, pp. 37, 67–68. For executive continuity along family lines in Russia see David Granick, *The Red Executive*, New York, 1960, p. 53.

[45] Closest to such an account is A. W. Calhoun, *A Social History of the American Family*, 3 vols.; Cleveland, 1917–19. This is more than a half-century old and inadequate on many levels.

Without such a history, the tendency is to flounder in controversy that cannot be readily resolved. Witness the current sociological dispute over whether the American family is characteristically "extended" or characteristically "nuclear." Ruth Cavan, *The American Family*, New York, 1959, pp. 119–147; A. B. Hollingshead, "Class and Kinship in a Middle Western Community," *American Sociological Review*, XIV (1949), pp. 469–475; John Sirjamaki, *The American Family*, Cambridge, 1959, pp. 141–143; Eugene Litwak, "Occupational Mobility and Extended Family Cohesion," *American Sociological Review*, XXV (February, 1960), pp. 9–21; "The Use of Extended Family Groups in the Achievement of Social Goals: Some Policy Implications," *Social Problems*, VII (Winter, 1959–60), pp. 177–187; Marvin B. Sussman, "The Isolated Nuclear Family: Fact or Fiction," *Social Problems*, VI (Spring, 1959).

Theoretical studies of the American family, not solidly grounded in history, have caused Richard Titmuss to exclaim: "much of the nonsense that is written in the subject [of family structure] today requires challenging." Especially, he added, "the theoretical studies of family emanating from the United States." Preface to Michael Young and Peter Willmott, *Family and Kinship in East London*, Glencoe, Ill., 1957.

There is an echo of this controversy in historical literature, Bernard Bailyn, *Education in the Forming of American Society . . .*, Chapel Hill, N.C., 1960, p. 250.

[46] *Turmoil and Tradition*, Boston, 1960.

[47] See especially David C. McClelland, *The Achieving Society*, Princeton, 1961.

those that are something more than puffed-up genealogical trees, revolve around the records of a business enterprise and the enterprise rather than family structure, or the aptitude that made possible the continuity of the enterprise, is stressed.[48] We have had political dynasties, now as in the past, but histories of political families such as W. E. Smith's *Francis Preston Blair Family in Politics* are by no means plentiful. Still more uncommon is the tracing of professional or artistic talent over the generations.

The facts of material inheritance, to say nothing of their implication for family culture, are barely known. In England, the continuity of aristocracy has been ascribed less to family feeling and blood ties than to the perpetuation of "the family estate, which provided the family not only with its revenue and residence, but with its sense of identity from generation to generation. . . ."[49] In America, inheritance was of no less significance. Professor Habakkuk has indicated that the role of inheritance has been little studied in this country. He ascribed this to the absence of a backlog of materials.[50] Perhaps a more accurate statement of the problem in its American context is not the lack of materials—but that the materials have been neither systematized nor used widely in historical and sociological treatises.[51] Legal history has failed to "tell of the shaping force exercised by law from outside it, by what people wanted, by the functional needs of other institutions, and by the

mindless weight of circumstances."[52] The reverse is also true. So admirable a study as Edmund S. Morgan's *The Puritan Family* places slight stress upon legal factors and inheritance.[53]

Primogeniture, an aspect of inheritance with manifold implications for family structure, lacks a full-scale treatment. Joel Barlow asserted that "the simple destruction of these two laws, of *entailment* and *primogeniture*, if you add to them the *freedom* of the press, will ensure the continuance of liberty in any country where it is once established."[54] However, the last significant study of primogeniture and entail was by Richard B. Morris more than thirty years ago.[55] At about the same time Charles R. Keim wrote of the "Influence of Primogeniture and Entail in the Development of Virginia."[56] More recently, knowledge of entail in Virginia has been extended by brief treatment in an article by Dr. Bailyn.[57] However, so significant an observation as that by Professor Morris that on the eve of the American Revolution there was a revival of entail in Massachusetts, has not been followed up.[58] It would be interesting to examine the background against which Thomas Cheseborough, in 1756, advised Ezra Stiles, perhaps facetiously and perhaps not, never to divide or alienate any land or other estate but leave it to the eldest son: "'tis not good to be upon a Level or under the Foot of every Scoundrel." This scheme was to be kept quiet even as others were to be encouraged "to Divide their Estate."[59]

---

[48] See, for example, William J. Parish, *The Charles Ilfeld Company*, Cambridge, 1961, and other volumes of the Harvard Studies in Business History.

[49] Lewis B. Namier, *England in the Age of the American Revolution*, London, 1930, pp. 22–23; H. J. Habakkuk, *The European Nobility in the Eighteenth Century*, A. Goodwin (ed.), London, 1953, p. 2.

[50] "Family Structure and Economic Change in Nineteenth-Century Europe," *Journal of Economic History*, XV (1955), pp. 1, 4.

[51] There is, for example, ample material in the debates of the various state legislatures and the proceedings of the state constitutional conventions.

Wills, as sources of insight into family structure and also into family relationships, have been much neglected. There was a time when the making of a will was not the cut-and-dried procedure that the legal profession has made of it. Wills were more personal documents than they now are; individuals not only disposed of property but told why they acted as they did and it is the whys which are of interest to

the student of family history. Eugene E. Prussing, *The Estate of George Washington Deceased*, Boston, 1927, p. 3. Washington declared that in the construction of his will, "it will readily be perceived that no professional character has been consulted, or has had any agency."

[52] James W. Hurst, *Law and Social Process in United States History*, Ann Arbor, 1960, p. 10.

[53] (Boston, 1944).

[54] *Advice to the Privileged Orders . . .*, p. 29.

[55] "Primogeniture and Entailed Estates in America," *Columbia Law Review*, 1928.

[56] Unpublished doctor's thesis, University of Chicago, 1927.

[57] "Politics and Social Structure in Virginia," *Seventeenth Century America*, James M. Smith (ed.), Chapel Hill, 1959, pp. 110–111.

[58] *Studies in the History of American Law*, New York, 1930.

[59] Carl Bridenbaugh, *Cities in Revolt*, New York, 1955, p. 138.

It is well known that in the last two decades of the eighteenth century, state legislation was enacted prohibiting entail and primogeniture. However, only in Virginia has the background of the legislation been explored.[60] Certain questions remain unanswered. Did legislation by the various states against primogeniture and entail apply only to cases of intestacy? What legal sanctions were there against individuals who wanted to concentrate the bulk of their property as a legacy to a single heir? What were the popular sanctions against such practices and how did they evolve?[61] What of the beneficiaries of partible inheritance who elected to leave an estate undivided that it might function better as an economic unit?[62]

Inheritance is an important factor determining family position within a class over the generations. Movement into and out of the patrician class has been more observed than analyzed largely because the elements that determine the patrician life style are difficult to isolate.[63] Using methods of genealogy and family history, it is possible to trace the status of individual families over successive generations. However, what did Schumpeter mean when he spoke of "the mobility of a whole social class?" Schumpeter himself insisted that any estimate of class mobility would be less "science" than "party slogan." He then went on to frame, virtually without proof, his own account of the ascendancy of European families as "uniformly along the lines of the American saying: 'Three generations from shirtsleeves to shirtsleeves.' "[64]

The "American saying" was a "slogan" put forth by Oliver Wendell Holmes Sr. who, in 1861, spoke of three generations as marking the duration of powerful New England families.[65] There remains a continuing tendency on the part of historians to write of mobility in terms of "slogans."[66]

Difficulties with respect to the ascertainment of "whole class" mobility[67] return the analyst to the individual family,[68] "the relative position of families within a class," and the discovery of what there is about family "life" and "spirit" which causes one family to adjust and go forward and another to decline.[69] In many respects, a model for this kind of investigation is William T. Whitney's account of the rivalry between the Derby and Crowninshield families for priority in Salem.[70] Yet, generalization about the movement of a "whole class" on the basis of what is known about a few families, involves a problem in sampling no easier to resolve in the case of the American patriciate than with respect to the status of the English gentry in the seventeenth century.[71]

---

[60] Bailyn, "Politics and Social Structure in Virginia," pp. 110–111.

[61] Sigmund Diamond, *The Reputation of the American Businessman*, Cambridge, 1955.

[62] R. Richard Wohl, "Three Generations of Business Enterprise in a Midwestern City: The McGees of Kansas City," *Journal of Economic History*, XVI (December, 1956), pp. 514–528.

[63] G. W. Pierson, *Tocqueville and Beaumont in America*, pp. 117, 368, 603; *Journey to England and Ireland*, J. P. Mayer (ed.), New Haven, 1958, p. 70.

[64] *Imperialism and Social Classes*, p. 169. Schumpeter's conclusion as to the mobility of the European aristocracy, that the class could be likened to a "bus whose passengers are always changing," avails us little because there is almost no society without some mobility. The problem is not whether there is mobility, but its extent and rate; the relationship of

mobility rates to time and place; whether the passengers change more rapidly in America than in Europe and in one period of history rather than another; and, finally, the circumstances of the change.

[65] *Elsie Venner*, Boston, 1861, pp. 1–2.

[66] Professor Richard B. Morris, referring to mobility in colonial America, affirmed the applicability of "the expression from shirtsleeves to shirtsleeves in three generations." "Class Struggle and the American Revolution," *William and Mary Quarterly*, XIX (January, 1962), p. 27. N.S.B. Grass peaks vaguely of the "chronic tendency of mercantile families to dry up." *Business and Capitalism*, New York, 1946, p. 162.

[67] Certain problems involved in historians' concern with mobility are noted by Oscar Handlin, "Ethnic Factors in Social Mobility," *Explorations in Entrepreneurial History*, IX (October, 1956), pp. 1–7; *Class, Status and Power*, R. Bendix and S. M. Lipset (eds.), pp. 5–6; Oscar and Mary Handlin, *The Dimensions of Liberty*, Cambridge, 1961, pp. 133–154.

[68] Catherine S. Crary, "The Humble Immigrant and the American Dream, 1746–1776," *Mississippi Valley Historical Review*, (June, 1959).

[69] Schumpeter, *Imperialism and Social Classes*, pp. 140, 149, 166, 169.

[70] William T. Whitney, Jr., "The Crowninshields of Salem 1800–1808," *Essex Institute Historical Collections*, (April and June, 1958).

[71] H. R. Trevor-Roper, "The Gentry 1540–1640," *The Economic History Review Supplements*, n.d., Cambridge, pp. 6, 31 and *passim*; Alan Simpson, *The Wealth of the Gentry 1540–1660*, Chicago, 1961, p. 21.

Virtually all that is known about class is on the local and community levels, the domain of the community sociologists. Professor W. L. Warner and his associates identified a patrician class in Newburyport which was described as an "upper-upper class" within a pattern of stratification which included five other classes. The upper-upper class was identified as a precipitate of the economic activities of previous generations and prevailed in the older sections of the country, along the Atlantic seaboard and in the South.[72]

To mention the Warner system of community stratification is to invite a large body of criticism of it by historians and sociologists.[73] The historian sees the Warner approach as lacking in depth and rarely transcending what the late C. Wright Mills described as "that dull pudding called sketching in the historical background."[74] One of the best of the community studies is Robert A. Dahl's account of New Haven, a chapter of which deals with the period 1784–1842 when "public office was almost the exclusive prerogative of the patrician families." Yet, in his discussion Dahl shows scant awareness of newer understandings by historians of the nature of power in colonial America and its relationship to class structure and "patrician control."[75]

Understanding of the patrician class could be increased by integrating community sociology and local history. Eric Lampard has pointed to the need for a blend of historical and social science techniques within an ecological framework.[76] Studies by Merle Curti and his associates and by Stanley Elkins and Eric McKitrick working together have advanced local history beyond mere narrative to engage it with such questions as mobility, social role, decision-making, group formation, and elite function.[77] The effect of this kind of an approach is not only to contribute a time dimension to community sociology, but to endow class with historical continuity.[78]

While discussions and analyses of class enter into numerous community studies, on the national level class is virtually undefined.[79] Efforts to depict a national elite by Mills[80] and Hunter[81] have met with sharp critical attack. Equally vulnerable is the attempt by E. Digby Baltzell to go beyond his rather good study of the Philadelphia upper class and in the direction of identifying a "national aristocracy." According to Baltzell, the communications revolution, the nationalization of business, and the attendance by scions of prominent families at far-from-home New England boarding schools and

[72] W. L. Warner, et al., *Social Class in America*, Chicago, 1949, pp. 16–17.

[73] See especially the criticisms by Ruth R. Kornhauser, "The Warner Approach to Social Stratification," in *Class, Status and Power*, Bendix and Lipset (eds.); Harold W. Pfautz and Otis D. Duncan, "A Critical Evaluation of Warner's Work in Community Stratification," *American Sociological Review*, XV (April, 1950), pp. 205–215; Oscar Handlin, *New England Quarterly*, XV (1942), 554; XVIII (1945), p. 523; *Journal of Economic History*, VII (1947).

[74] C. Wright Mills, *The Sociological Imagination*, New York, 1959, p. 154.

[75] *Who Governs? Democracy and Power in an American City*, New Haven, 1961, p. 11. The book contains no reference to important historical studies such as Leonard W. Labaree, *Conservatism in Early American History*, New York, 1948, and M. M. Klein, "Democracy and Politics in Colonial New York," *New York History*, XL (July, 1959), pp. 221–246, that could have contributed depth to the earlier chapters. For additional references that could have improved Dr. Dahl's understanding of power and its exercise in the colonial period see Bernard Bailyn, "Political Experi-

ence and Enlightenment Ideas in Eighteenth-Century America," *American Historical Review*, LXVII (January, 1962), p. 341, n2. See also Roger Champagne, "Family Politics versus Constitutional Principles: The New York Assembly Election of 1768 and 1769," *William and Mary Quarterly*, XX (January, 1963), pp. 57–79.

[76] Eric E. Lampard, "American Historians and the Study of Urbanization," *American Historical Review*, LXVII (October, 1961), pp. 49–61.

[77] "A Meaning for Turner's Frontier," *Political Science Quarterly*, LXIX.

[78] "Local History Contributions and Techniques in the Study of Two Colonial Cities," *Bulletin of the American Association for State and Local History*, II (February, 1959), esp. the comment by Bayrd Still, pp. 246–250, which has important bearing upon the integration of local history and community sociology. See also Philip D. Jordan's survey, *The Nature and Practice of State and Local History*, Washington, 1958.

[79] Heinz Eulau, *Class and Party in the Eisenhower Years*, Glencoe, Ill., 1962, p. 19; Reissman, *Class in American Society*, pp. 203–205.

[80] *The Power Elite*, New York, 1956.

[81] *Top Leadership U.S.A.*, Chapel Hill, N.C., 1959.

Ivy League colleges where they allegedly meet marriage partners of the same life style but from different communities, has disrupted the local roots of aristocracy.[82] Unfortunately, however competent Mr. Baltzell's treatment of the Philadelphia scene, his assumptions nationally are unproven. They seem particularly vulnerable in the light of changes that have taken place in the admissions policies of the Ivy League colleges.[83]

With the patrician class difficult to define and identify nationally, the kind of research problem formulated by Dr. Pumphrey with reference to England has no American counterpart. Pumphrey sought to determine the extent to which industrialists penetrated the British peerage.[84] This problem, if it could be stated in terms of the American scene, would shed light upon mobility between old families and new wealth. But what is the American equivalent of an English peer?

The late Marc Bloch defined nobility as a class having legal status with its social privileges and hereditary succession receiving legal recognition.[85] However, at the time when the legal privileges of the nobility of most European nations were being defined constitutionally, the United States Constitution banned the class altogether.[86] Not only is there no American establishment to sustain the American patriciate, but there is also no vestigial establishment which would give this class even a derivative basis.[87]

A third aspect of class, not unrelated to its economic basis and to the expression of a particular life style, is the political: "class oriented toward acquisition of 'social' power . . . toward influencing a communal action. . . ."[88] Among the concerns of research into the political role of the patriciate is the extent to which inherited ideas of responsibility and service, of what Edmund Burke called the gentle uses of power, developed in the course of centuries by the English aristocracy and the American patriciate, are incorporated into political action.[89] There is also the question, posed by Professor Hesseltine, as to the extent to which a political tradition is class-oriented and how much of it is diffused across class lines.[90]

Implied in political action is the concept of power. Social scientists disagree as to whether power in American society is concentrated in an elite or diffused throughout the structure of society.[91] Historians have expressed different

---

[82] E. Digby Baltzell, *Philadelphia Gentleman*, Glencoe, Ill., 1958, p. 21.

[83] Lawrence Bloomgarden, "Our New Elite Colleges," *Commentary*, (February, 1960).

[84] "The Introduction of Industrialists into the British Peerage: A Study in Adaptation of a Social Institution," *American Historical Review* (October, 1959), pp. 1–16.

[85] *Feudal Society*, pp. 283–285.

[86] R. R. Palmer, *The Age of the Democratic Revolution*, Princeton, 1959, pp. 508–517.

[87] Not that an establishment or even a vestigial establishment is an infallible guide. Compilations such as Burke's *Peerage* and the *Almanach Da Gotha* and its successor, the *Genealogisches Handbuch Des Adels*, are by no means decisive in establishing antiquity and continuity in family lines. (Wagner, *op. cit.*, p. 84). Even so, they are rough indices of class belonging which, with all their faults, are probably more useful as a finder for European aristocracy than is the *Social Register* for the American patriciate. (My observations

as to the *Social Register* are based on a conversation with Norton Mezvinsky who is preparing a study of Boston and New York aristocracy between 1875 and 1925. He has compared *Register* data with other materials and places less reliance upon the *Register* than does Baltzell.)

[88] H. H. Gerth and C. Wright Mills, *From Max Weber*, New York, 1958, pp. 180–195; Kahl, *American Class Structure*, p. 16.

[89] Arthur B. Ferguson, *The Indian Summer of English Chivalry*, Durham, N.C., 1960, pp. 119–120, 182; Lewis Namier, *The Structure of Politics at the Accession of George III*, London, 1957, p. 10; Frank Freidel, "The Education of Franklin Delano Roosevelt," *Harvard Educational Review*, XXXX (Spring, 1961), pp. 158–167.

[90] William B. Hesseltine, "Four American Traditions," *Journal of Southern History*, XXVII (February, 1961), p. 4.

[91] Robert A. Dahl, "A Critique of the Ruling Elite Model," *American Political Science Review*, LII (1958). The literature on the nature of community power is a large one. The extent to which power is concentrated or diffused has been shown to be much influenced by the researcher's procedure. (R. E. Wolfinger, "Reputation and Reality in the Study of 'Community Power,'" *American Sociological Review*, XXV [October, 1960], pp. 636–644; David B. Truman, "Theory and Research on Metropolitan Political Leadership: Report on a Conference," *Items, Social Science Research Council*, March 1961, p. 3).

Using one type of research design, Floyd Hunter developed an elitist conception of power. Other viewpoints concerning the nature and exercise of power in colonial society. Becker,[92] Sydnor[93] and Labaree[94] see power as concentrated in an elite composed of the great colonial families whose political actions were said to be expressive of a unified class interest. Another point of view regards interest group rather than class as the focus of power.[95] Interest group, in so far as it transcends class lines and is a basis of divergence within the class framework, encourages a conception of power that is more fragmented than concentrated. Dr. Klein's account of family politics in colonial New York, for example, is of alliances cemented and broken; of shifting configurations of power within the framework of the patrician stratum.[96] The class concept, having become operational in terms of interest and conflict, breaks up into tangents of individual and family action.

How is group interest ascertained? Charles A. Beard's use of the technique of economic biography is generally credited with having established the rudiments of career line analysis. This is, essentially, a biographical approach to history in which certain questions are posed with reference to the individuals involved in a particular group. The answers are the basis upon which individuals are grouped and group attributes are correlated with political action so that a relationship between them becomes apparent.[97] I use correlate rather than cause because career line analysis, since it cannot comprehend all possible variables as well as for other reasons, has methodological limitations restricting it as a form of proof to correlation rather than cause.[98] How causation itself can be established is far from clear.[99]

Use of the technique of career line analysis by David Donald, Richard Hofstadter, Alfred D. Chandler Jr., George E. Mowry, Ari Hoogenboom, among others, has illumined aspects of patrician political behavior.[100] However, career line analysis, correlating biographical factors with political action, does not explain how one leads to the other. One explanation of patrician political behavior is in terms of reference group theory which "aims to systematize the determinants and consequences of those processes of evaluation and self-appraisal in which the individual takes the values or standards of other individuals and groups as a comparative frame of reference."[101]

Using reference group theory as an explanation of motivation Professor Donald and Professor Hofstadter asserted that a certain

approaches to power, like that employed by Dahl in his study of New Haven, see power as more diffused than concentrated with the balance likely to shift with the issue being decided. N. W. Polsby, "The Sociology of Community Power: A Reassessment," *Social Forces*, XXVII (March, 1959), pp. 232–236.

[92] *The History of Political Parties in the Province of New York, 1760–1776*, Madison, Wis., 1909.

[93] *Gentlemen Freeholders*, Williamsburg, Va., 1952.

[94] *Conservatism in Early American History*, New York, 1948, pp. 1–31.

[95] See, for example, Robert P. Sharkey, *Money, Class and Party*, Baltimore, 1959, pp. 290–311; Forrest McDonald, *We The People*, Chicago, 1958, pp. 358–399.

[96] Klein, *New York History*, XL, p. 240; Champagne, "Family Politics. . . ."

[97] J. E. Neale, "The Biographical Approach to History," *History*, New Series, XXXVI (October, 1951), pp. 193–203.

[98] Herbert Butterfield, "George III and the Namier School," *Encounter*, 1957, pp. 70–76; *George III and the Historians*, New York, 1959; Lee Benson, *Turner and Beard*, pp. 159, 195.

[99] The difficulties involved in establishing cause are dealt with by Sidney Hook in *Theory and Practice in Historical Study*, New York, 1946, pp. 110–115. Among the better more recent accounts is Cushing Strout's in *History and Theory*, I (1961), pp. 175–185.

[100] David Donald, "Toward a Reconsideration of the Abolitionists," in *Lincoln Reconsidered: Essays on the Civil War*, New York, 1956; Richard Hofstadter, *The Age of Reform*, New York, 1960; Alfred D. Chandler, Jr., "The Origins of Progressive Leadership," in Elting E. Morison (ed.), *The Letters of Theodore Roosevelt*, Cambridge, 1954, VIII, appendix III, 1462–65; George E. Mowry, *The California Progressives*, Berkeley and Los Angeles, 1951, pp. 86–104; Ari Hoogenboom, *Outlawing the Spoils. A History of the Civil Service Reform Movement*, Urbana, Ill., 1961, pp. 190–197; Gerald W. McFarland, "The New York Mugwumps of 1884: A Profile," *Political Science Quarterly*, LXXVIII (March, 1963), pp. 40–65. Critiques of this method include R. A. Skotheim, "A Note on Historical Method . . .," *Journal of Southern History*, XXV (1959), pp. 356–365; Richard B. Sherman, "The Status Revolution and Massachusetts Progressive Leadership," *Political Science Quarterly*, LXXVIII (March, 1963), pp. 59–65.

[101] Robert K. Merton, *Social Theory and Social Structure*, Glencoe, Ill., 1957, pp. 50–51.

amount of anxiety over status with reference to competing groups in the population led men of old family background into the abolitionist and, at a later date, into reformist political movements in an effort to recoup lost power and prestige. Recently, the reference group concept has been amplified to include not only a contemporary competing group but individuals and groups in the past, such as ancestry, for example, whose achievement must be equaled or exceeded.[102]

My own researches into the history of the American patriciate tend to support Herbert H. Hyman's conception of the role of ancestry as reference group, apparent particularly in the careers of Henry Cabot Lodge, Theodore Roosevelt, Henry Adams, Brooks Adams, and Charles Francis Adams Jr.[103]

Other explanations are advanced of patrician political behavior. Dr. Berthoff accounted for the prominence of the man of family in contemporary American political life in terms of the reintegration of "society somewhat as it was before 1815" in which the "Roosevelts, Tafts and Rockefellers [he might have added Kennedy, Morgenthau, Steers, Stevenson, Wallace, Wadsworth, Scranton, Plimpton, Dilworth, Byrd, Saltonstall, and Stimson) not only accept responsibility of their class to lead the common voter but are in turn accepted by him, it is evident that we once again have an established upper class with privileges and duties roughly equivalent to those of the eighteenth-century gentry." Thus far in my own researches I have found little to sustain this aspect of Mr. Berthoff's "conservative hypothesis."[104]

Nor would I agree with Mr. Lipset's attempt to compress the patrician political tradition within the framework of the Republican party.[105]

This thesis would be reasonable, if not altogether valid, applied to the politics of the 1890s when Republicanism qua Republicanism had a real meaning for Roosevelt, Lodge, and the neo-Federalists. However, C. Vann Woodward has shown that even during this period the Virginia Populists were inclined to entrust leadership of their movement of Virginia's old families.[106]

There is no simple definition of the patrician class. It is possible, however, to present a model of what such definition involves. The model includes family history with stress upon the factors, material and cultural, which make for family continuity; the structuring of real types of the patrician family centered in factors related to the family's internal structure and external relationships. The development in history of these attributes contributes to a general description of the patrician class as "rank."

To comprehend class as cause involves awareness of group structure and component factors. The latter enter into career line analysis and, when correlated with action, contribute to ascertaining the group interest. Reference group theory, advanced as suggestive of motive underlying the expression of patrician group interest, has been attacked sharply in recent years and it is my impression that the assumptions of reference group theory, even as modified by Dr. Hyman, have marked limitations as explanation of patrician political behavior.

Even career line analysis, which takes less for granted about motivation than does reference group theory, is a device that must be used discreetly and with reference to the reservations expressed in Mr. Butterfield's critique of Sir Lewis Namier.[107] That is to say, there is more to history than its relationship with theory which has been stressed in this article. Theory and analysis are subsumed by the flow of historical narrative and this includes unique factors, which may be alien to an analytical framework but are very much part of the history of the American patrician class.

[102] Herbert H. Hyman, "Reflections on Reference Groups," *Public Opinion Quarterly* (Fall, 1960), pp. 383–396.

[103] Edward N. Saveth, "Henry Adams: Waning of America's Patriciate," *Commentary*, October, 1957.

[104] Rowland Berthoff, "The American Social Order: A Conservative Hypothesis," *The American Historical Review*, LXV (April, 1960), p. 511.

[105] Seymour M. Lipset, *Political Man*, New York, 1959, p. 301.

[106] C. Vann Woodward, "Populist Heritage and the Intellectual," *American Scholar*, XXIX (Winter, 1959), p. 70.

[107] *George III and the Historians, passim.*

23. Social Cohesion, Lineage Type, and Intergenerational Transmission*

BY JOAN ALDOUS AND REUBEN HILL

ABSTRACT

A theory is presented that cultural transmission through the family is greater in same-sex than cross-sex lineages due to the greater social cohesiveness of the former. The theory is further specified as to which normative areas will show the most intergenerational continuity in all-male or all-female lineages. The theory is examined in the light of data obtained from a sample of three-generation families composed of grandparents, parents and married children. The findings offer support for several aspects of the theory.

Continuity from generation to generation is essential for the maintenance of group life. Simmel wrote that the preservation of the "unitary self of the group" is made possible by the "physiological coherence of successive generations."[1] The process of transition whereby older members of society disappear and are replaced by persons of the next generation is a gradual one. There is ample opportunity for the initiated to introduce the young into the ways of society. Thus the group maintains its identity despite the continuing change in its membership.[2]

Karl Mannheim was concerned with the specific continuities that linked successive generations and their consequences for the young. The "basic inventory of group life"—traditional beliefs and behaviors that constitute the cultural heritage—which the previous generation passes on gives the recipient the resources that will enable him to function satisfactorily in new situations.[3] At the same time the "social remembering" resulting from use of the inventory insures the continuance of society.[4] There are no sharp breaks between the generations. Simmel and Mannheim, therefore, saw the intergenerational continuities that make possible an enduring society as dependent upon the socialization of each generation by its predecessors.

Faris went beyond Simmel and Mannheim to examine one of the agencies of socialization. He focused on the family as the "central mechanism for the transmission of culture,"[5] and discussed

SOURCE: Social Forces, *Volume 43 (May, 1965), pp. 471–482. Reprinted with permission of the University of North Carolina Press.*

* Revision of a paper read at the annual meeting of the American Sociological Association, August, 1963. The research was carried out while the senior author was holding a Predoctoral Research Fellowship from the National Institute of Mental Health.

[1] George Simmel, "The Persistence of Social Groups," *American Journal of Sociology*, 3 (March, 1898), p. 669.

[2] *Ibid.*, p. 670.

[3] Karl Mannheim, "The Problem of Generations," in Paul Kecskemeti (ed.), *Essays on the Sociology of Knowledge*, Oxford: Oxford University Press, 1952, p. 299.

[4] *Ibid.*, p. 294.

[5] Robert E. L. Faris, "Interaction of Generations and Family Stability," *American Sociological Review*, 12 (April, 1947), p. 159.

the intangible elements of capital which the family passed on to its descendants. Prior to the twentieth century, for example, family apprenticeship was the surest means for acquiring the techniques of such occupations as farming, carpentering, plumbing, and printing. Even today occupations exist that require "tricks of the trade" rarely imparted with the formal job skills. Other forms of folk wisdom which family elders present in daily life give the members of the younger generation concrete demonstrations of how to conduct social relations. The young learn criteria of mate selection, methods for maintaining the authority necessary to rear children, and techniques for encouraging group unity.[6]

Despite general agreement that socialization of the members of the new generation is one of the primary functions of the family, there has been little theory or research tracing intergenerational continuities through the family. Studies in three research areas have shed some light, but none is concerned with more than a limited aspect of the problem.

The first body of research can be quickly dismissed as inadequate. It consists of the "genealogical" studies of families tracing their successes and vicissitudes over the generations. Some are concerned with famous families like the Livingstons of New York State[7] or the regionally prominent Cokers of South Carolina.[8] In others, such as the intriguingly titled, "Five Generations of a Begging Family,"[9] the family lines studied were obviously selected for reasons other than that of social prestige. The idiographic nature of all this research, however, restricts its usefulness to providing hypotheses for later studies of much broader scope.

Occupation is one content area in which there have been a number of investigations of intergenerational transmission. Sociologists have used occupational inheritance as an indicator of changes· in social stratification, a problem that has long concerned them. In the mid-twenties Sorokin provided an empirical foundation for his pioneering work on social mobility with a series of questionnaire studies of occupational inheritance over four generations. He discovered that father-son occupational continuity in his sample of University of Minnesota students and Minneapolis businessmen had decreased as one went from the era of the great-grandfathers to the era of the respondents.[10]

Almost 20 years later, Rogoff, using more sophisticated analytical techniques in Marion County, Indiana, obtained somewhat similar results. She compared trends in father-son occupational inheritance for the two periods, 1905–1912 and 1938–1941. From information supplied by sons on marriage application forms, she found that only in the unskilled, protective services, and farming classifications was occupational transmission higher in the more recent period.[11]

Other local studies have been done by Davidson and Anderson[12] as well as by Bendix, Lipset, and Malm;[13] but they present father-son occupational data for only one period. This was also true of the nationwide inquiries conducted by Centers[14] and by the staff of the National Opinion Research Center.[15] Moreover, all of

[6] Ibid., p. 161.

[7] Patricia J. Gordon, "The Livingstons of New York: Kinship and Class," unpublished Ph.D. dissertation, Columbia University, 1959.

[8] George L. Simpson, Jr., The Cokers of Carolina: A Social Biography of a Family, Chapel Hill: University of North Carolina Press, 1956.

[9] Harlan W. Gilmore, "Five Generations of a Begging Family," American Journal of Sociology, 37 (March, 1932), pp. 768–774. See also David L. Hatch and Mary G. Hatch, "An Unhappy Family: Some Observations on the Relationship Between the Calvinist Ethic and Interpersonal Relations Over Four Generations." Marriage and Family Living, 24 (August, 1962), pp. 213–223.

[10] Pitirim Sorokin, Social Mobility, New York: Harper & Bros., 1927, p. 421.

[11] Natalie Rogoff, Recent Trends in Occupational Mobility, Glencoe, Illinois: The Free Press, 1953, p. 57. Table 11.

[12] Percy E. Davidson and H. Dewey Anderson, Occupational Mobility in an American Community, Stanford: Stanford University Press, 1937.

[13] Reinhard Bendix, Seymour M. Lipset, and Theodore Malm, "Social Origins and Occupational Career Patterns," Industrial and Labor Relations Review, 7 (January, 1954), pp. 241–261.

[14] Richard Centers, "Occupational Mobility of Urban Occupational Strata," American Sociological Review, 13 (April, 1948), pp. 197–203.

[15] National Opinion Research Center, "Jobs and Occupations: A Popular Evaluation," in Reinhard Bendix and Seymour M. Lipset (eds.), Class, Status and Power, Glencoe, Illinois: The Free Press, 1953, pp. 424–425.

these studies depended upon respondents' reports of their fathers' occupations. In the case of Sorokin's work, the individual's memory was plumbed as far back as three generations. The problem of faulty recall has been compounded by the ambiguities introduced by individual job changes over the father's occupational career. The occupation that the respondent reported for his father could have been any one of the following: the father's current position, the job held by the father when the son was last at home, the occupation held during the father's career of highest prestige, or the job held for the longest period of time. These deficiencies in the data render suspect many of the generalizations about occupational transmission made to date.

There is a fairly sizable amount of psychological research concerned with intra-family resemblances in personality characteristics. The requisite data are usually obtained separately from individuals. Weltman and Remmers, for example, asked teachers, high school students, and their parents in Midwest small towns and rural areas to fill out political attitude questionnaires. Correlations between parents and their children ranged from .87 for the mother-daughter comparison to .80 on mother-son and father-daughter comparisons. The teacher-pupil correlation was .65 on the same attitude measure.[16] This particular research was methodologically superior to some others of its type which present no data to show whether or not intra-family resemblances are greater than those occurring in non-familial interpersonal comparisons. Like others in this area, however, the Weltman and Remmers study is limited to comparisons between two generations.

The present research is designed to meet some of the shortcomings of the previous studies. It focuses on continuities over three generations, a period long enough for intergenerational similarities to take on the characteristics of a family heritage. The current study also represents an attempt to close the gap between the many speculative discussions and the empirical research that has characterized the work to date. On the one hand, generational theorists have focused primarily on the necessity for cultural transmission through the family and have provided little assistance for research workers interested in the content of what was transmitted. On the other hand, empirical studies have been primarily descriptive in nature whether concerned with family histories, similarities in attitudes or occupational inheritance.

Search for Theory

In attempting to account for the similarities linking the various generations of a family, the concept of social cohesion is essential. Without strong social bonds between parents and children, competing influences outside the family will prevail. The younger generation will squander its normative heritage instead of preserving the family's cultural estate to pass on to its children. But what are the factors making for social cohesion? According to Durkheim, social cohesion depends upon the degree of interaction among persons. "The integration of a social aggregate can only reflect the intensity of the collective life circulating in it. It is more unified and powerful the more active and constant is the intercourse among its members."[17] Thus to translate Durkheim with respect to our problem, the more numerous the activities and interests shared by the generations, the stronger the bonds linking them. This linkage of the generations will result in more elements of the cultural heritage being transmitted through the family line. Where cohesiveness is lacking in the family group, there will be barriers to interaction between parents and children. The individual will be less committed to family ways and will be more likely to acquire the ways of outsiders, thus minimizing or preventing intergenerational continuity altogether.

Given the sex structure of the American family and its bilateral nature, some relationships will show more cohesiveness than others.

[16] Naomi Weltman and H. Remmers, "Attitude Inter-Relationships of Youth, Their Parents and Their Teachers," *Journal of Social Psychology*, **26** (August, 1947), p. 65.

[17] Emile Durkheim, *Suicide: A Study in Sociology*, John A. Spaulding and George Simpson (trans.), Glencoe, Illinois: The Free Press, 1951, p. 202.

Whether or not the parent and child are of the same sex has a differential effect on social cohesion. There is a tendency in our society for mothers to take primary responsibility for rearing daughters and fathers to be concerned with sons. As a result, there are often more contacts as well as greater intimacy and understanding between mother and daughter and father and son than between mother and son and father and daughter. If this is the case, same-sex parent-child systems should have tighter social bonds and show more cultural transmission than cross-sex lines.[18] Similarly, where three generation lineages are involved, a grandmother-mother-daughter lineage or a grandfather-father-son lineage will show more continuity than cross-sex combinations such as grandmother-mother-son or grandfather-father-daughter lineages.[19]

Taking the mother-daughter system first, the mother by virtue of her caretaker role is in an advantageous position to fulfill the daughter's dependency needs in such a way that the latter internalizes the mother's values and behavior patterns. The mother also provides a model for sex-appropriate behavior. Even when the daughter grows older, the mother continues to serve as an important source of information and a visible exemplar of appropriate behavior. As

Young and Willmott pointed out in explaining the closeness of the mother-daughter ties among families of East London, the daughter plans to follow or is presently performing the same home centered roles as her mother. They, therefore, have a host of expressive interests in common.[20] Thus the bonds uniting mother and daughter over time continue strong, and the cultural transmission from mother to daughter is highly durable. The daughter, in turn, is in the same advantageous position to pass the same family values on to her daughter in the third generation.

In contrast, the linkages between father and daughter are fewer. Initially, the father has little responsibility for the care of the child, so the little girl is less dependent upon him. Although the father can reward the child for feminine behavior, he can serve his daughter neither as a model nor as an authority on sex-appropriate behavior. As a result, there is not the same solidarity in the father-daughter relationship making for intergenerational continuities in behavior as in the mother-daughter system.

Similarly, the all-male line contains cohesive relationships based on the father-son system that are absent in the mother-son linkage. The mother, it is true, as primary provider for the physical maintenance of the young boy establishes dependency needs in him which she can manipulate to encourage the behaviors she approves. But the boy must look to the father as his sex model, and this modeling assumes increasing importance as the boy approaches manhood. The mother can provide rewards for proper male behavior, but because of her sex, she is less effective than her husband in setting standards. In addition, father and son possess the instrumental interests and values that come from participating in the world of work even if they happen to be in different occupations. Thus father and son share a number of interests, and these bonds encourage intergenerational continuity from father to son over mother-son linkages.

The normative content of the cultural heritage, however, also plays a part in the ability of the family of procreation to perpetuate its values

[18] Joan Aldous, *Family Continuity Patterns Over Three Generations: Content, Degree of Transmission and Consequences*, unpublished Ph.D. dissertation, University of Minnesota, 1963, pp. 106–116. Additional factors which might be hypothesized as affecting family cohesiveness are social class, place of residence, and religious affiliation. The sample was too heavily middle class and urban to permit an examination of variations in the first two factors. As for religious affiliation, the hypothesized greater cohesiveness among Catholic families due to the Church's emphasis on family unity showed up only in greater intergenerational continuities on variables of central importance to Catholic doctrine in the area of family.
[19] For a lucid discussion of Freud's changing views of identification, see Urie Bronfenbrenner, "Freudian Theories of Identification and Their Derivation," *Child Development*, **31** (March, 1960), pp. 15–40. Sigmund Freud, of course, emphasized the importance of the cross-sex parent to the child, particularly prior to the Oedipal (Electra) period. He theorized, however, that after this crisis period the child identified with the parent of the same sex and internalized this parent's moral standards to form his superego.

[20] Michael Young and Peter Willmott, *Family and Kinship in East London*, Glencoe, Illinois: The Free Press, 1957, p. 157.

in the next generation. Regardless of the sex structure of the lineage, the family has more control over the transmission of some norms than others. It has the greatest ability to insure continuity among its descendents for attitudes supported by organizational affiliations. The child acquires the organizational commitments embodying family attitudes while still young. To take religious affiliation as an indicator of religious commitment, for example, the family is relatively powerful, compared with other agencies in insuring the transmission of religious identity. In the interest of preserving religious continuity, the parents can begin early in seeing that the child attends the church of their choice.

Less subject to transmission is a second set of norms having to do with role allocation in the division of duties between husband and wife. As Davis noted, each new family of procreation represents not the renaissance of one family of orientation but the coming together of the off-spring of two families of orientation.[21] The new union brings together persons from varying backgrounds whose values and ways of action do not always coincide. These differences cause strain which must be reduced in some way, particularly in such areas as task specialization on which the day-to-day functioning of the household depends. Either one partner will have to give up his values and behavior patterns and internalize the other's role expectations, or both must modify their values to establish a relation at variance with their families of orientation. In any case, the difference in backgrounds may cause discontinuity in husband-wife interaction patterns from one generation to the next.

A third set of norms which depend upon individual ability or are strongly affected by extra-familial forces will be even more difficult for families to transmit unchanged. Occupation and amount of education are variables that reflect broad social changes over the generations. In the first case technological developments have created new jobs and wiped out old ones. The country's occupational structure has changed, with clerical and professional workers increasing in numbers and unskilled laborers declining.

Professional workers made up only 4.4 per cent of the labor force in 1910, but this figure had changed to 11.1 per cent in 1959. Clerical employees more than doubled their numbers in the same interval, changing from 10.2 to 20.6 per cent of the gainfully employed. The unskilled, however, dropped from 36 per cent of the labor force in 1910 to 22.2 per cent in 1959. The most drastic change in proportion involved farmers, who in 1910 constituted 16.8 per cent of those working, but by 1959 had dropped to 4.8 per cent—about as scarce as the 1910 professional.[22] These broad changes in the demand for labor have operated to discourage continuity in occupations from parent to child. There are fewer jobs involving farming or unskilled labor available today for the children's generation to fill than there were in past generations.

Along with the shift in the occupational distribution has gone a steady increase in the educational requirements and attainments of the population. In the period 1924 to 1932 the educational average for all adult males was completion of the eighth grade. This had increased to 10.3 years by 1960.[23] Correspondingly, one youth in eight graduates from college today but in 1900 the proportion was one in sixty.[24] Thus social trends make it unlikely that there will be

[22] The 1910 figures for occupations other than farming come from Edward Gross, *Work and Society*, New York: Thomas Y. Crowell Co., 1958, p. 61, Table 1. The 1910 farming percentages come from *Ibid.*, p. 63, Table 2. The 1959 figures are from U.S. Bureau of the Census, *Current Population Report: Labor Force*, Series P–57, No. 202 (May, 1959), p. 16. In comparing the 1910 percentages with those of 1959, two things must be noted. First, the 1910 figures include all the "gainfully employed," i.e., any worker was included in a given occupational category if he reported it as his regular occupation whether or not he was currently employed. Beginning in 1940, the Census, using the "labor force" concept, counted only those individuals actually working during the week the census is taken or actively seeking work. Gross, *op. cit.*, p. 60. Second, the jobs included in the categories have changed slightly over the years as new occupations have appeared and others have gone the way of the hitching post fabricator.

[23] Thomas P. O'Donovan, "Intergenerational Educational Mobility," *Sociology and Social Research*, **47** (October, 1962), p. 62, Table 1.

[24] Dael Wolfle, *America's Resources of Specialized Talent*, New York: Harper & Bros., 1954, p. 24.

[21] Kingsley Davis, *Human Society*, New York: The Macmillan Co., 1947, p. 396.

much family continuity in absolute years of education completed over the generations.[25]

Crosscutting the content dimension of family norms is the expressive-instrumental division which interacts with the family sex structure to produce greater continuity in some inter-generational lineages than others. The parental division of labor in socializing the next generation modifies the structural effects of same-sex lineages. Mothers have the role of culture bearers for religious and other expressive attitudes consistent with the focus of the maternal role on interpersonal relations within the family. For this reason continuity in such attitudes whether reflected in organizational memberships or not will be found in all female or predominantly female descent groups. In like manner parts of the culture having to do with achievement within the broader community fall within the father's sphere of responsibility. He has most to do with the transmission of education and occupational goals. Thus instrumental patterns will show higher continuity through all-male or predominantly male lines.[26]

To summarize our theory of the family as an agency of cultural transmission, we hypothesize more intergenerational continuity in same-sex family lineages than cross-sex lineages because of the greater parent-child cohesiveness of the former. At the same time, we specify that, regardless of lineage, intergenerational continuity will be greater for those portions of the family heritage involving affiliative variables, followed next by marital interaction patterns,

with achievement variables last. We also specify that there will be interactional effects between instrumental and expressive elements of the cultural heritage and lineage type.

Research Design

We have examined these several hypotheses in the light of empirical evidence we collected from a sample unique in the literature. Unlike previous intergenerational research, our sample allowed a three-generation focus with data provided by the adult members of each generation. We were not dependent upon our respondents for reports of the characteristics of their predecessors, nor were we limited to an examination of parent-child similarities. We could look for intergenerational continuities extending over three generations. The sample consisted of 88 white lineages composed of the families of grandparents, parents, and married children living within 100 miles of Minneapolis-St. Paul. The families were obtained from a series of area probability samples drawn from the metropolitan area by the research department of the Minneapolis *Star and Tribune* and the University of Minnesota School of Journalism. It required a fairly long period of time and sustained effort to obtain such an unusual sample. For six months before beginning the study, all persons contacted by the interviewers for the Minnesota Poll and the Minnesota Homemakers Survey were asked whether they were members of three-generation families, and whether or not the vertical kin with whom they were linked lived within 100 miles of the Twin Cities. All persons whose claims were verified were included in the study along with the families of the other two generations, whether grandparents, parents, or married children, provided both spouses in each generation were present. Extrapolating from the number of three-generation families obtained from the two area probability samples to the general Twin Cities population, it appears that intact three-generation families where both spouses in each generation are present constitute a bare three per cent of the population. Each generational unit constituted an independently housed nuclear family

---

[25] Factors other than historical trends also can operate to discourage continuity in occupation and education. The person marrying into the lineage who comes from a higher class background may deliberately discourage continuity in education and occupation for his or her children as compared with the spouse's attainments in these areas. Thus, a British study showed that working class parents more often preferred to send their children to grammar school rather than to secondary modern or technical schools when the wives had worked in nonmanual occupations. F. M. Martin, "An Inquiry into Parent's Preference in Secondary Education," in D. V. Glass (ed.), *Social Mobility in Britain*, London: Routledge & Kegan Paul, 1954, p. 169.

[26] Cases where the male's instrumental competence is challenged by his wife's higher class status are in exception.

Table 1

A comparison of the composition of the three-generation sample and of the population of the standard metropolitan statistical area for Minneapolis-St. Paul, 1959[a]

	Three-generation sample		Standard-metropolitan statistical area
	f	per cent	per cent
Age of Male			
Under 20	3	1.1	40.7[b]
21–30	71	26.9	12.6
31–40	16	6.1	13.6
41–50	37	14.0	11.5
51–60	42	15.9	9.2
61–70	19	7.2	7.2
71–80	55	20.8	3.9
80 and over	21	8.0	1.1
Occupation of Male			
Professional, Technical	16	10.1	14.6[c]
Mgrs., Officials, and Prop.	34	21.5	12.6
Clerical and Kindred	9	5.7	10.0
Sales	12	7.6	9.4
Craftsmen, Foremen	35	22.2	21.3
Operatives and Service except Household Workers	38	24.1	24.7
Farmers	10	6.3	1.1
Laborers	4	2.5	6.2
Residential Mobility			
Same House as in 1955	139	63.8	48.0[d]
Different House, Same County	62	28.4	30.8
Different House and County, Same State	14	6.4	10.8
Different House, County, and State	3	1.4	8.1
Residence in 1955 not Reported	—	—	1.5
Education (25 years and older)			
No school	15	3.3	.7[e]
1–6	78	17.2	5.9
7–8	121	26.7	23.8
9–11	65	14.3	17.0
12	119	26.2	30.0
13 or pver	56	12.3	22.6
Income			
Under 2000	22	10.2	5.6[f]
2000–3999	41	19.1	10.4
4000–5999	71	33.0	22.3
6000–7999	43	20.0	26.0
8000–9999	13	6.1	16.0
10,000 and over	25	11.6	19.8

[a] The *N*'s on the various comparisons differ with the proportion of individuals in the sample falling into the particular categories.

Table 1 *continued*

Religious Affiliation	Sample St. Paul		Population St. Paul[g]	Sample Minneapolis		Population Minneapolis[g]
	f	per cent	per cent	f	per cent	per cent
Roman Catholic	64	61.5	45.0	51	40.1	33.3
Protestant	40	38.5	50.0	71	55.9	66.6

[b] U.S. Bureau of the Census, U.S. Census of Population: 1960, *General Population Characteristics, Minnesota*, Final Report PC (1)-25B (Washington, D.C.: U.S. Government Printing Office, 1961), p. 54, Table 20.

[c] U.S. Bureau of the Census, U.S. Census of Population: 1960, *General Social and Economic Characteristics, Minnesota*, Final Report PC (1)-25c (Washington, D.C.: U.S. Government Printing Office, 1961), p. 237, Table 74.

[d] *Ibid.*, Table 72, p. 227.

[e] Census, General Social and Economic Characteristics, *op. cit.*, p. 232, Table 73.

[f] *Ibid.*, p. 247, Table 76.

[g] Minneapolis and St. Paul Council of Churches. The St. Paul Catholic Chancery gives different percentages for Catholics, as follows; St. Paul, 41 per cent; Minneapolis, 26 per cent.

linked vertically to two other nuclear families. The data, therefore, were obtained from 264 married couples.

The sample because of its special character differs in certain major respects from the population living in the Minneapolis-St. Paul Standard Metropolitan Statistical Area (Table 1). The inclusion of the grandparent generation skews the sample to the older ages with a consequent lower average income and educational attainment than is found in the SMSA population. The presence of three generations of the same family living in the area means that the respondents have also been less mobile geographically. There is also an overrepresentation of persons claiming affiliation with the Roman Catholic faith. Though differing from the general population, the sample is representative of the universe of intergenerationally linked families living within the same metropolitan area. Data from the sample, moreover, can provide some indication of the lineage theory's worth, as well as the different ability of families to transmit various elements of the cultural heritage.

To examine the hypothesized differential effect on intergenerational continuity of same-sex as opposed to cross-sex parent-child systems, we traced the gender of the individuals linking each three-generation descent group. We developed four lineage types to accentuate same and cross-sex ties between generations. These are as follows: Type I. grandfather-father-son; Type II. grandmother-mother-daughter; Type III. grandfather-father-daughter; Type IV. grandmother-mother-son.[27]

The 32 pure matrilineages greatly outnumber the 15 pure patrilineages. (Table 2). The cross-sex lineages are almost equal in size. Using the chi-square goodness of fit test, assuming equal probabilities of occurrence of the four types, the difference from the actual distribution approaches the significance level of .05. The disproportion in size between the female descent groups and the male descent groups is large enough to suggest a greater holding power for daughters than sons and a greater geographical

[27] Where it is possible in the analyses that follow, we have compared individuals in the second generation with the cross-sex as well as the same-sex parent and presented the results. For these comparisons we have the additional lineage types of grandmother-father-son; grandfather-mother-daughter; grandmother-father-daughter; and grandfather-mother-son. Unfortunately, we could not examine all the hypothetically possible combinations among the three generations. We possessed data from the grandparents on either the maternal or paternal side of our children's parents but not from both. Thus we could trace continuities over three generations only through the specific father or mother whose parents were included in the sample.

Table 2

Distribution of three-generation families by constructed lineage types

			Number	Per cent
Type I	Grandfather-father-son	(Pure patrilineage)	15	17
Type II	Grandmother-mother-daughter	(Pure matrilineage)	32	36
Type III	Grandfather-father-daughter	(Cross-sex lineage)	21	24
Type IV	Grandmother-mother-son	(Cross-sex lineage)	20	23
TOTAL			88	100

$\chi^2 = 6.999$
$P < .10$

mobility for sons than for daughters.[28] Aside from size, the four lineage groups did not vary in gross characteristics, having approximately the same Protestant-Catholic, socioeconomic, and age distributions.

We have drawn upon a number of different family patterns to serve as indicators of inter-generational continuity. The variable to represent the affiliation portion of the family cultural heritage is *religious affiliation*. For husband-wife interaction patterns we have data from the wives in each generation on the degree of *role specialization* in household tasks maintained by the marital partners. They reported the number of taks performed exclusively by one spouse as compared with the number both spouses performed interchangeably. The extent to which role specialization involved each partner's doing only those tasks traditionally associated with his or her sex provided a second variable, *role conventionalization*, in the marital interaction area. For example, we considered mowing the lawn to be as conventional a task for husbands as straightening the living room in preparation for company was for wives. For the

achievement segment of the family culture, we chose *occupation* and *education* as indicators of family continuity. The occupation to which each male generational representative had devoted the major portion of his work career was the one selected for classification, using the *Alphabetical Index of Occupations and Industries*.[29]

In calculating intergenerational continuity in education we allowed for the general upgrading of the population in amount of schooling over the last half century. Rather than looking at the absolute amount of schooling the members of a descent group had completed, we determined the individual's achievement relative to the others in the sample of the same generation and sex.[30] By dividing into terciles the frequency distribution of years of education for each sex within a generation, we could then see whether there was transmission of a high, middle, or low position from generation to generation.

We will relate lineage type to the extent of intergenerational continuity on the affiliative, marital interaction and achievement variables by showing the per cent of descent groups where each generation scored in the same classification

---

[28] Even taking into account the unbalanced sex ratio in the Standard Metropolitan Statistical Area of the Minneapolis-St. Paul of 873 in the 15 to 19 year age group and 788 in the 20–24 age group—the two age groups where the third generation members cluster—does not explain the ratio of over twice as many all-female as all-male lines. For the 25 to the 29 year age group in which very few of our respondents fell, the sex ratio is 975. See U.S. Bureau of the Census, U.S. Census of Population: 1960. *General Population Characteristics, Minnesota.* Final Report PC (1)-25B, Washington, D.C.: U.S. Government Printing Office, 1961, p. 54, Table 20.

[29] U.S. Bureau of the Census, 1960 Census of Population, *Alphabetical Index of Occupations and Industries*, rev. ed.; Washington, D.C.: U.S. Government Printing Office, 1960. Restricting the data to male occupations precluded our testing the hypothesized interaction effect of male lineages and instrumental norms on intergenerational continuity. The small number of women in the first two generations with work experience early in their lives, made analysis of intergenerational occupational continuity impracticable.

[30] The differential educational achievements of the two sexes led us to control for sex as well as generation.

Table 3

A comparison of the extent of intergenerational continuity by same-sex and cross-sex lineage types for seven selected variables

Class of Variable	Type I	Type II	Type III	Type IV	
	Grand-father-father-son	Grand-mother-mother-daughter	Grand-father-father-daughter	Grand-mother mother-son	All lineages
	Per cent continuity 3 generations $N = 15$	Per cent continuity 3 generations $N = 32$	Per cent contintuity 3 generations $N = 21$	Per cent continuity 3 generations $N = 20$	Per cent continuity 3 generations
Affiliation					
Religious Affiliation	53 (8)	69 (22)	62 (13)	65 (13)	64 (56)
Marital Interaction					
Role Task Specialization[a]	29 (4)	38 (12)	28 (5)	40 (8)	34 (29)
Role Task Conventionality[b]	31 (4)	25 (8)	11 (2)	25 (5)	23 (19)
Achievement					
Occupation, Husband	47 (7)	25 (8)	38 (8)	25 (5)	32 (28)
Educational Level	20 (3)	12 (4)	38 (8)	15 (3)	20 (18)

[a] There were 14 cases in the Type I lineage and 18 in the Type III lineage for this variable.

[b] There were 13 case in the Type I lineage and 18 in the Type III lineage for this variable.

category on the variable in question.[31] Because of the size and special characteristics of our sample we are not using statistical analyses in the presentation of our findings. Until the hypotheses can be tested with larger samples, the cumulative trend of the findings is more suggestive of our theory's plausibility, we believe, than conclusions based on statistical tests.

Findings

The result of the tests of our major hypotheses have been incorporated in Table 3, which cross-classifies the degree of intergenerational continuity on indicators of several cultural norms by lineage type. Let us examine each of the hypotheses in the light of the data.

[31] We are using percentages to enable the reader more easily to compare proportions across the various lineage types. For a complete description of the indexes used to determine the degree of intergenerational continuity, see Aldous, *op. cit.*, Appendix A.

Transmissibility of Norms. Examination of the extreme right hand column of Table 3 shows that there does appear to be a marked variation in the inherent transmissibility of various elements of the cultural heritage through the families. There is a fairly large range in the degree of intergenerational continuity given the limited sample size for the five variables traced over three generations. We hypothesized earlier that the rank order in continuity of norms would be highest for religious affiliation, next highest for marital interaction norms, followed in turn by the achievement norms of occupation and education. Occupation is out of the hypothesized order, falling slightly below one of the marital interaction variables, role task specialization. This higher continuity than expected may be accounted for by occupational endogamy. The data show that women tend to marry men from the same occupational level as their father.[32]

[32] See among others, Thomas C. Hunt, "Occupational Selection and Marital Status," *American Sociological Review*, 5 (August, 1940), pp. 495–504; and A. Philip Sundal and Thomas C. McCormick,

The remaining variables fall in the hypothesized order. We conclude, therefore, that the variability in continuity due to the properties of the norms being transmitted needs to be taken into account in future studies of intergenerational transmission. A good theory covering intergenerational continuities must encompass not only the greater cohesiveness of particular lineages, but also take into account the particular aspects of the cultural heritage which are to be transmitted.

Social Cohesiveness and Same-Sex Lineages. Continuity on the highly transmissible norm of religious affiliation does appear to be consistent with the social cohesiveness hypothesis though the differences are small. It is necessary, however, to introduce specification along the expressive-instrumental dimension, to account for the order in which the lineage types fall. The all-female lineages are highest (69 per cent continuity), the predominantly female lineages of grandmother-mother-son (Type IV) second, demonstrating the mother's major role in the transmission of this expressive norm. The predominantly male lineages of grandfather-father-daughter (Type III) and the all-male lineages are lowest.

The important part played by the mother in the transmission of religious affiliation is further documented by an analysis of the few interfaith marriages in the sample. There were ten couples in the grandparent generation where the spouses did not share the same religion. For the initial analysis we traced religious membership through the grandparent of the same sex as the individual in the next generation. We substituted grandmothers for grandfathers in the all-male descent groups making grandmother-father-son lines. This resulted in an increase in religious continuity from 53 to 63 per cent (eight to ten descent groups). The changing of all-female lines to grandfather-mother-daughter descent groups resulted in a slight drop of one case in continuity (69 to 66 per cent).[33] These results

are generally consistent with the contention that women are keepers of the religious heritage in our society.

We find some further evidence in line with the hypothesis of greater social cohesion in same-sex lineages in the findings from one of the two marital interaction variables though again the differences are not large. On role task conventionality the all-male descent type showed the most continuity, followed by the all-female type. The results were more equivocal on the role task specialization variable. Here the cross-sex grandmother-mother-grandson descent groups (Type IV) had the most continuity, but they were closely followed by the all-female lines. Next came the all-male groups, and the grandfather-father-daughter lines (Type III) were last. These findings suggest that mothers have more to do with transmitting patterns of role allocation on household tasks to both sons and daughters than do fathers. The reason may lie in the wife's primary responsibility for housekeeping. Children see her taking the initiative in setting the pattern of doing tasks alone on the one hand, or asking for assistance from her husband on the other and model their behavior accordingly.

The findings on the occupational variable are also consistent with the cohesiveness hypothesis. Almost half of the families in the all-male descent groups displayed occupational continuity, as did 38 per cent in the Type III grandfather-father-daughter lines. This was true of only a fourth of the families in both the all-female lines and the Type IV grandmother-mother-son lineage type. These same findings also provide empirical evidence in support of an initial assumption in continuity research: namely, that familial transmission and not social trends account for generational similarities.[34] Only in the three-generation or two-generation male lines was intergenerational transmission in the family of orientation pos-

"Age at Marriage and Mate Selection, Madison, Wisconsin, 1937–1943," *American Sociological Review*, 16 (February, 1951), pp. 37–48.

[33] When grandmothers replaced grandfathers in the grandfather-father-married daughter lines, there was a drop in continuity of one case, making a change of

62 to 57 per cent. Substitution of grandfathers for grandmothers in the grandmother-mother-married son families resulted in no change.

[34] For further evidence that the continuity descent groups display is due to familial transmission and not due to social trends external to the family, see Aldous, *op. cit.*, pp. 83–88.

sible, and it was in precisely these lines that there was the most occupational inheritance. The men in the female lineage types had married into the descent groups and had but an in-law relation to each other.

Although educational level showed the lowest continuity of the five variables examined, it does provide us with an opportunity to test the hypothesized interaction of all-male or predominantly male lineage types and continuity on instrumental norms. The findings shown in Table 3 though based upon small differences suggest the reasonableness of the hypothesis that continuity will be highest for this instrumental norm in all-male or predominantly male lineages. The most continuity is in the predominantly male lineage Type III, with families of all-male lineages second and the Type IV predominantly female lineages lowest in continuity.

We performed this original analysis by tracing education through the grandparent of the same sex as the individual in the next generation. For a second analysis we substituted the cross-sex grandparent's educational level. The amount of continuity dropped slightly when the grandmother's education was substituted for the grandfather's in the all-male lineage and in the predominantly male lineage. The continuity in the all-female lineages increased slightly when the grandfather's education was substituted for the grandmother's.[35] Thus, though the subsitution in each lineage type of the cross-sex grandparent's educational level made only slight differences, these differences were consistent with the hypothesized relations between male lineage and continuity on this instrumental norm.[36]

To summarize the results of our several analyses in Table 3, the hypothesis of differential transmissibility of norms and the hypothesis of greater cohesiveness in lineages based on same-sex linkages received some affirmative support. The trend of the limited data were in the hypothesized direction for occupation and role conventionality though the differences were not large. The predicted interaction effect between all-females and the predominantly female lineages and continuity on expressive norms and all or predominantly male lineages and continuity on instrumental norms also appeared. Continuity in the expressive norm of religious affiliation was greatest in the female lineages. The predominantly male and all-male lineages showed the greatest continuity on the instrumental norms of occupational and educational achievements.

Conclusion

The study has demonstrated that it is possible to develop a theory of the family as an agency of intergenerational continuity which lends itself to operational specification and testing with empirical data. The study has gone beyond the speculative essays on the importance of continuity from generation to generation and the assertion that the family is the crucial agency of socialization. It has documented empirically by means of data from a unique, difficult to obtain three-generation sample, the lineage structures, and the cultural norms where the family is operative in joining the generations. The findings from the present limited sample, though involving only small percentage differences, suggest that the inherent transmissibility of the various norms in the cultural heritage may have more to do with the extent of intergenerational continuity than the degree of grandparent-parent-child cohesiveness arising from the family's lineal sex structure.

[35] The change to the cross-sex grandparent in the all-male, the predominantly male and all-female lineages affected one case in each instance. There was no difference in the amount of continuity in the grandmother-mother-son descent group when the grandfather's educational attainment was used instead of the grandmother's.

[36] One further analysis utilizing educational data was undertaken. There were three cases in both the grandparents' and the parents' generations where men had married women with at least three more years of education than their husbands. Using this educational superiority as a rough indicator of status differences, we found in each generation that two of

the three men had sons with higher educational attainments but with the same occupational level as their fathers. Thus the wife's superior status appeared to affect only her son's years of schooling. If we had possessed data on either the job backgrounds of the women who married into all-male descent groups or the occupational levels of their fathers, these data might have proved more relevant than husband-wife educational discrepancy for detecting a maternal influence on occupational discontinuity.

24. Social Class and Parent-Child Relationships: An Interpretation

BY MELVIN L. KOHN

ABSTRACT

The argument of this analysis is that class differences in parent-child relationships are a product of differences in parental values (with middle-class parents' values centering on self-direction and working-class parents' values on conformity to external proscriptions); these differences in values, in turn, stem from differences in the conditions of life of the various social classes (particularly occupational conditions—middle-class occupations requiring a greater degree of self-direction, working-class occupations, in larger measure, requiring that one follow explicit rules set down by someone in authority). Values, thus, form a bridge between social structure and behavior.

This essay is an attempt to interpret, from a sociological perspective, the effects of social class upon parent-child relationships. Many past discussions of the problem seem somehow to lack this perspective, even though the problem is one of profound importance for sociology. Because most investigators have approached the problem from an interest in psychodynamics, rather than social structure, they have largely limited their attention to a few specific techniques used by mothers in the rearing of infants and very young children. They have discovered, *inter alia*, that social class has a decided bearing on which techniques parents use. But, since they

have come at the problem from this perspective, their interest in social class has not gone beyond its effects for this very limited aspect of parent-child relationships.

The present analysis conceives the problem of social class and parent-child relationships as an instance of the more general problem of the effects of social structure upon behavior. It starts with the assumption that social class has proved to be so useful a concept because it refers to more than simply educational level, or occupation, or any of the large number of correlated variables. It is so useful because it captures the reality that the intricate interplay of all these variables creates different basic conditions of life at different levels of the social order. Members of different social classes, by virtue of enjoying (or suffering) different conditions of life, come to see the world differently—to develop different conceptions of social reality, different aspirations and hopes and fears, different conceptions of the desirable.

The last is particularly important for present purposes, for from people's conceptions of the desirable—and particularly from their conceptions of what characteristics are desirable in children—one can discern their objectives in child-rearing. Thus, conceptions of the desirable—that is, values[1]—become the key concept

SOURCE: American Journal of Sociology, *Volume 68* (*January, 1963*), *pp. 471–480. Reprinted by permission of University of Chicago Press (Copyright 1963).*

[1] "A value is a conception, explicit or implicit, distinctive of an individual or characteristic of a group, of the desirable which influences the selection from

for this analysis, the bridge between position in the larger social structure, and the behavior of the individual. The intent of the analysis is to trace the effects of social class position on parental values and the effects of values on behavior.

Since this approach differs from analyses focused on social class differences in the use of particular child-rearing techniques, it will be necessary to re-examine earlier formulations from the present perspective. Then three questions will be discussed, bringing into consideration the limited available data that are relevant: What differences are there in the values held by parents of different social classes? What is there about the conditions of life distinctive of these classes that might explain the differences in their values? What consequences do these differences in values have for parents' relationships with their children?

Social Class

Social classes will be defined as aggregates of individuals who occupy broadly similar positions in the scale of prestige.[2] In dealing with the research literature, we shall treat occupational position (or occupational position as weighted somewhat by education) as a serviceable index of social class for urban American society. And we shall adopt the model of social stratification implicit in most research, that of four relatively discrete classes: a "lower class" of unskilled manual workers, a "working class" of manual workers in semiskilled and skilled occupations, a "middle class" of white-collar workers and professionals, and an "elite," differentiated from the middle class not so much in terms of occupation as of wealth and lineage.

Almost all the empirical evidence, including that from our own research, stems from broad comparisons of the middle and working class. Thus we shall have little to say about the extremes of the class distribution. Furthermore, we shall have to act as if the middle and working classes were each homogeneous. They are not, even in terms of status considerations alone. There is evidence, for example, that within each broad social class, variations in parents' values quite regularly parallel gradations of social status. Moreover, the classes are heterogeneous with respect to other factors that affect parents' values, such as religion and ethnicity. But even when all such considerations are taken into account, the empirical evidence clearly shows that being on one side or the other of the line that divides manual from non-manual workers has profound consequences for how one rears one's children.[3]

Stability and Change

Any analysis of the effects of social class upon parent-child relationships should start with Urie Bronfenbrenner's analytic review of the studies that had been conducted in this country during the twenty-five years up to 1958.[4] From the seemingly contradictory findings of a number of studies, Bronfenbrenner discerned not chaos but orderly change: there have been changes in the child-training techniques employed by middle-class parents in the past

[3] These, and other assertions of fact not referred to published sources, are based on research my colleagues and I have conducted. For the design of this research and the principal substantive findings see my "Social Class and Parental Values," *American Journal of Sociology*, LXIV (January, 1959), pp. 337–351; my "Social Class and the Exercise of Parental Authority," *American Sociological Review*, XXIV (June, 1959), pp. 352–366; and with Eleanor E. Carroll, "Social Class and the Allocation of Parental Responsibilities," *Sociometry*, XXIII (December, 1960), pp. 372–392. I should like to express my appreciation to my principal collaborators in this research, John A. Clausen and Eleanor E. Carroll.

[4] Urie Bronfenbrenner, "Socialization and Social Class through Time and Space," in Eleanor E. Maccoby, Theodore M. Newcomb, and Eugene L. Hartley (eds.), *Readings in Social Psychology*, New York: Henry Holt & Co., 1958.

available modes, means, and ends of action," (Clyde Kluckhohn, "Values and Value Orientations," in Talcott Parsons and Edward A. Shils (eds.), *Toward A General Theory of Action*, Cambridge, Mass.: Harvard University Press, 1951, p. 395). See also the discussion of values in Robin M. Williams, Jr., *American Society: A Sociological Interpretation*, New York: Alfred A. Knopf, Inc., 1951, chap. xi, and his discussion of social class and culture on p. 101.

[2] Williams, *op. cit.*, p. 89.

quarter-century; similar changes have been taking place in the working class, but working-class parents have consistently lagged behind by a few years; thus, while middle-class parents of twenty-five years ago were more "restrictive" than were working-class parents, today the middle-class parents are more "permissive"; and the gap between the classes seems to be narrowing.

It must be noted that these conclusions are limited by the questions Bronfenbrenner's predecessors asked in their research. The studies deal largely with a few particular techniques of child-rearing, especially those involved in caring for infants and very young children, and say very little about parents' over-all relationships with their children, particularly as the children grow older. There is clear evidence that the past quarter-century has seen change, even faddism, with respect to the use of breast-feeding or bottle-feeding, scheduling or not scheduling, spanking or isolating. But when we generalize from these specifics to talk of a change from "restrictive" to "permissive" practices—or, worse yet, of a change from "restrictive" to "permissive" parent-child relationships—we impute to them a far greater importance than they probably have, either to parents or to children.[5]

There is no evidence that recent faddism in child-training techniques is symptomatic of profound changes in the relations of parents to children in either social class. In fact, as Bronfenbrenner notes, what little evidence we do have points in the opposite direction: the over-all quality of parent-child relationships does not seem to have changed substantially in either class.[6] In all probability, parents have changed techniques in service of much the same

values, and the changes have been quite specific. These changes must be explained, but the enduring characteristics are probably even more important.

Why the changes? Bronfenbrenner's interpretation is ingenuously simple. He notes that the changes in techniques employed by middle-class parents have closely paralleled those advocated by presumed experts, and he concludes that middle-class parents have changed their practices *because* they are responsive to changes in what the experts tell them is right and proper. Working-class parents, being less educated and thus less directly responsive to the media of communication, followed behind only later.[7]

Bronfenbrenner is almost undoubtedly right in asserting that middle-class parents have followed the drift of presumably expert opinion. But why have they done so? It is not sufficient to assume that the explanation lies in their greater degree of education. This might explain why middle-class parents are substantially more likely than are working-class parents to *read* books and articles on child-rearing, as we know they do.[8] But they need not *follow* the experts' advice. We know from various studies of the mass media that people generally search for confirmation of their existing beliefs and practices and tend to ignore what contradicts them.

From all the evidence at our disposal, it looks as if middle-class parents not only read what the experts have to say but also search out a wide variety of other sources of information and advice: they are far more likely than are working-class parents to discuss child-rearing with friends and neighbors, to consult physicians on these matters, to attend Parent-Teacher Association meetings, to discuss the child's behavior

---

[5] Furthermore, these concepts employ *a priori* judgments about which the various investigators have disagreed radically. See, e.g., Robert R. Sears, Eleanor E. Maccoby, and Harry Levin, *Patterns of Child Rearing*, Evanston, Ill.: Row, Peterson & Co., 1957, pp. 444–447, and Richard A. Littman, Robert C. A. Moore, and John Pierce-Jones, "Social Class Differences in Child Rearing: A Third Community for Comparison with Chicago and Newton," *American Sociological Review*, XXII (December, 1957), pp. 694–704, esp. p. 703.

[6] Bronfenbrenner, *op. cit.*, pp. 420–422 and 425.

[7] Bronfenbrenner gives clearest expression to this interpretation, but it has been adopted by others, too. See, e.g., Martha Sturm White, "Social Class, Child-Rearing Practices, and Child Behavior," *American Sociological Review*, XXII (December, 1957), pp. 704–712.

[8] This was noted by John E. Anderson in the first major study of social class and family relationships ever conducted, and has repeatedly been confirmed (*The Young Child in the Home: A Survey of Three Thousand American Families*, New York: Appleton-Century, 1936).

with his teacher. Middle-class parents seem to regard child-rearing as more problematic than do working-class parents. This can hardly be a matter of education alone. It must be rooted more deeply in the conditions of life of the two social classes.

Everything about working-class parents' lives—their comparative lack of education, the nature of their jobs, their greater attachment to the extended family—conduces to their retaining familiar methods.[9] Furthermore, even should they be receptive to change, they are less likely than are middle-class parents to find the experts' writings appropriate to their wants, for the experts predicate their advice on middle-class values. Everything about middle-class parents' lives, on the other hand, conduces to their looking for new methods to achieve their goals. They look to the experts, to other sources of relevant information, and to each other not for new values but for more serviceable techniques.[10] And within the limits of our present scanty knowledge about means-ends relationships in child-rearing, the experts have provided practical and useful advice. It is not that educated parents slavishly follow the experts but that the experts have provided what the parents have sought.

To look at the question this way is to put it in a quite different perspective: the focus becomes not specific techniques nor changes in the use of specific techniques but parental values.

[9] The differences between middle- and working-class conditions of life will be discussed more fully later in this paper.

[10] Certainly middle-class parents do not get their values from the experts. In our research, we compared the values of parents who say they read Spock, Gesell, or other books on child-rearing, to those who read only magazine and newspaper articles, and those who say they read nothing at all on the subject. In the middle class, these three groups have substantially the same values. In the working class, the story is different. Few working-class parents claim to read books or even articles on child-rearing. Those few who do have values much more akin to those of the middle class. But these are atypical working-class parents who are very anxious to attain middle-class status. One suspects that for them the experts provide a sort of handbook to the middle class; even for them, it is unlikely that the values come out of Spock and Gesell.

Values of Middle- and Working-Class Parents

Of the entire range of values one might examine, it seems particularly strategic to focus on parents' conceptions of what characteristics would be most desirable for boys or girls the age of their own children. From this one can hope to discern the parents' goals in rearing their children. It must be assumed, however, that a parent will choose one characteristic as more desirable than another only if he considers it to be both important, in the sense that failure to develop this characteristic would affect the child adversely, and problematic, in the sense that it is neither to be taken for granted that the child will develop that characteristic nor impossible for him to do so. In interpreting parents' value choices, we must keep in mind that their choices reflect not simply their goals but the goals whose achievement they regard as problematic.

Few studies, even in recent years, have directly investigated the relationship of social class to parental values. Fortunately, however, the results of these few are in essential agreement. The earliest study was Evelyn Millis Duvall's pioneering inquiry of 1946.[11] Duvall characterized working-class (and lower middle-class) parental values as "traditional"—they want their children to be neat and clean, to obey and respect adults, to please adults. In contrast to this emphasis on how the child comports himself, middle-class parental values are more "developmental"—they want their children to be eager to learn, to love and confide in the parents, to be happy, to share and cooperate, to be healthy and well.

Duvall's traditional-developmental dichotomy does not describe the difference between middle- and working-class parental values quite exactly, but it does point to the essence of the difference: working-class parents want the child to conform to externally imposed standards, while middle-class parents are far more attentive to his internal dynamics.

The few relevant findings of subsequent studies are entirely consistent with this basic

[11] "Conceptions of Parenthood," *American Journal of Sociology*, LII (November, 1946), pp. 193–203.

point, especially in the repeated indications that working-class parents put far greater stress on obedience to parental commands than do middle-class parents.[12] Our own research, conducted in 1956–1957,' provides the evidence most directly comparable to Duvall's.[13] We, too, found that working-class parents value obedience, neatness, and cleanliness more highly than do middle-class parents, and that middle-class parents in turn value curiosity, happiness, consideration, and—most importantly—self-control more highly than do working-class parents. We further found that there are characteristic clusters of value choice in the two social classes: working-class parental values center on conformity to external proscriptions, middle-class parental values on *self*-direction. To working-class parents, it is the overt act that matters: the child should not transgress externally imposed rules; to middle-class parents, it is the child's motives and feelings that matter: the child should govern himself.

In fairness, it should be noted that middle- and working-class parents share many core values. Both, for example, value honesty very highly—although, characteristically, "honesty" has rather different connotations in the two social classes, implying "trustworthiness" for the working-class and "truthfulness" for the middle-class. The common theme, of course, is that parents of both social classes value a decent respect for the rights of others; middle- and working-class values are but variations on this common theme. The reason for emphasizing the variations rather than the common theme is that they seem to have far-ranging consequences for parents' relationships with their children and thus ought to be taken seriously.

It would be good if there were more evidence about parental values—data from other studies, in other locales, and especially, data derived from more than one mode of inquiry. But, what evidence we do have is consistent, so that there

is at least some basis for believing it is reliable. Furthermore, there is evidence that the value choices made by parents in these inquiries are not simply a reflection of their assessments of their own children's deficiencies or excellences. Thus, we may take the findings of these studies as providing a limited, but probably valid, picture of the parents' generalized conceptions of what behavior would be desirable in their preadolescent children.

Explaining Class Differences in Parental Values

That middle-class parents are more likely to espouse some values, and working-class parents other values, must be a function of differences in their conditions of life. In the present state of our knowledge, it is difficult to disentangle the interacting variables with a sufficient degree of exactness to ascertain which conditions of life are crucial to the differences in values. Nevertheless, it is necessary to examine the principal components of class differences in life conditions to see what each may contribute.

The logical place to begin is with occupational differences, for these are certainly pre-eminently important, not only in defining social classes in urban, industrialized society, but also in determining much else about people's life conditions.[14] There are at least three respects in which middle-class occupations typically differ from working-class occupations, above and beyond their obvious status-linked differences in security, stability of income, and general social prestige. One is that middle-class occupations deal more with the manipulation of interpersonal relations, ideas, and symbols, while working-class occupations deal more with the manipulation of things. The second is that middle-class occupations are more subject to self-direction, while working-class occupations are more subject to standardization and direct supervision. The third is that getting ahead in

[12] Alex Inkeles has shown that this is true not only for the United States but for a number of other industrialized societies as well ("Industrial Man: The Relation of Status to Experience, Perception, and Value," *American Journal of Sociology*, LXVI [July, 1960], pp. 20–21 and Table 9.)

[13] "Social Class and Parental Values," *op. cit.*

[14] For a thoughtful discussion of the influence of occupational role on parental values see David F. Aberle and Kaspar D. Naegele, "Middle Class Fathers' Occupational Role and Attitudes Toward Children," *American Journal of Orthopsychiatry*, XXII (April, 1952), pp. 366–378.

middle-class occupations is more dependent upon one's own actions, while in working-class occupations it is more dependent upon collective action, particularly in unionized industries. From these differences, one can sketch differences in the characteristics that make for getting along, and getting ahead, in middle- and working-class occupations. Middle-class occupations require a greater degree of self-direction; working-class occupations, in larger measure, require that one follow explicit rules set down by someone in authority.

Obviously, these differences parallel the differences we have found between the two social classes in the characteristics valued by parents for children. At minimum, one can conclude that there is a congruence between occupational requirements and parental values. It is, moreover, a reasonable supposition, although not a necessary conclusion, that middle- and working-class parents value different characteristics in children *because* of these differences in their occupational circumstances. This supposition does not necessarily assume that parents consciously train their children to meet future occupational requirements; it may simply be that their own occupational experiences have significantly affected parents' conceptions of what is desirable behavior, on or off the job, for adults or for children.[15]

---

[15] Two objections might be raised here. (1) Occupational experiences may not be important for a mother's values, however crucial they are for her husband's, if she has had little or no work experience. But even those mothers who have had little or no occupational experience know something of occupational life from their husbands and others, and live in a culture in which occupation and career permeate all of life. (2) Parental values may be built not so much out of their own experiences as out of their expectations of the child's future experiences. This might seem particularly plausible in explaining working-class values, for their high valuation of such stereotypically *middle-class* characteristics as obedience, neatness, and cleanliness might imply that they are training their children for a middle-class life they expect the children to achieve. Few working-class parents, however, do expect (or even want) their children to go on to college and the middle-class jobs for which a college education is required. (This is shown in Herbert H. Hyman, "The Value Systems of Different Classes: A Social Psychological Contribution to the Analysis of Stratification," in Reinhard Bendix and

These differences in occupational circumstances are probably basic to the differences we have found between middle- and working-class parental values, but taken alone they do not sufficiently explain them. Parents need not accord pre-eminent importance to occupational requirements in their judgments of what is most desirable. For a sufficient explanation of class differences in values, it is necessary to recognize that other differences in middle- and working-class conditions of life reinforce the differences in occupational circumstances at every turn.

Educational differences, for example, above and beyond their importance as determinants of occupation, probably contribute independently to the differences in middle- and working-class parental values. At minimum, middle-class parents' greater attention to the child's internal dynamics is facilitated by their learned ability to deal with the subjective and the ideational. Furthermore, differences in levels and stability of income undoubtedly contribute to class differences in parental values. That middle-class parents still have somewhat higher levels of income, and much greater stability of income, makes them able to take for granted the respectability that is still problematic for working-class parents. They can afford to concentrate, instead, on motives and feelings—which, in the circumstances of their lives, are more important.

These considerations suggest that the differences between middle- and working-class parental values are probably a function of the entire complex of differences in life conditions characteristic of the two social classes. Consider, for example, the working-class situation. With the end of mass immigration, there has emerged a stable working class, largely derived from the manpower of rural areas, uninterested in mobility into the middle class, but very much interested in security, respectability, and the enjoyment of a decent standard of living.[16] This

---

Seymour Martin Lipset [eds.], *Class, Status and Power: A Reader in Social Stratification*, Glencoe, Ill.: Free Press, 1953, and confirmed in unpublished data from our own research.)

[16] See, e.g., S. M. Miller and Frank Riessman, "The Working Class Subculture: A New View," *Social Problems*, IX (Summer, 1961), pp. 86–97.

working class has come to enjoy a standard of living formerly reserved for the middle class, but has not chosen a middle-class style of life. In effect, the working class has striven for, and partially achieved, an American dream distinctly different from the dream of success and achievement. In an affluent society, it is possible for the worker to be the traditionalist—politically, economically, and, most relevant here, in his values for his children.[17] Working-class parents want their children to conform to external authority because the parents themselves are willing to accord respect to authority, in return for security and respectability. Their conservatism in child-rearing is part of a more general conservatism and traditionalism.

Middle-class parental values are a product of a quite different set of conditions. Much of what the working class values, they can take for granted. Instead, they can—and must—instil in their children a degree of self-direction that would be less appropriate to the conditions of life of the working class.[18] Certainly, there is substantial truth in the characterization of the

middle-class way of life as one of great conformity. What must be noted here, however, is that *relative to* the working class, middle-class conditions of life require a more substantial degree of independence of action. Furthermore, the higher levels of education enjoyed by the middle class make possible a degree of internal scrutiny difficult to achieve without the skills in dealing with the abstract that college training sometimes provides. Finally, the economic security of most middle-class occupations, the level of income they provide, the status they confer, allow one to focus his attention on the subjective and the ideational. Middle-class conditions of life both allow and demand a greater degree of self-direction than do those of the working class.

Consequences of Class Differences in Parents' Values

What consequences do the differences between middle- and working-class parents' values have for the ways they raise their children?

Much of the research on techniques of infant- and child-training is of little relevance here. For example, with regard to parents' preferred techniques for disciplining children, a question of major interest to many investigators, Bronfenbrenner summarizes past studies as follows: "In matters of discipline, working-class parents are consistently more likely to employ physical punishment, while middle-class families rely more on reasoning, isolation, appeals to guilt, and other methods involving the threat of loss of love,"[19] This, if still true,[20] is consistent with middle-class parents' greater attentiveness to the child's internal dynamics, working-class parents' greater concern about the overt act. For present purposes, however, the crucial question is not *which* disciplinary method parents prefer, but when and why they use one or another method of discipline.

The most directly relevant available data are on the conditions under which middle- and working-class parents use physical punishment.

[17] Relevant here is Seymour Martin Lipset's somewhat disillusioned "Democracy and Working-Class Authoritarianism," *American Sociological Review,* XXIV (August, 1959), pp. 482–501.

[18] It has been argued that as larger and larger proportions of the middle class have become imbedded in a bureaucratic way of life—in distinction to the entrepreneurial way of life of a bygone day—it has become more appropriate to raise children to be accommodative than to be self-reliant. But this point of view is a misreading of the conditions of life faced by the middle-class inhabitants of the bureaucratic world. Their jobs require at least as great a degree of self-reliance as do entrepreneurial enterprises. We tend to forget, nowadays, just how little the small- or medium-sized entrepreneur controlled the conditions of his own existence and just how much he was subjected to the petty authority of those on whose pleasure depended the survival of his enterprise. And we fail to recognize the degree to which monolithic-seeming bureaucracies allow free play for—in fact, require—individual enterprise of new sorts: in the creation of ideas, the building of empires, the competition for advancement.

At any rate, our data show no substantial differences between the values of parents from bureaucratic and enterpreneurial occupational worlds, in either social class. But see Daniel R. Miller and Guy E. Swanson, *The Changing American Parent: A Study in the Detroit Area,* New York: John Wiley & Sons, 1958.

[19] Bronfenbrenner, *op. cit.,* p. 424.
[20] Later studies, including our own, do not show this difference.

Working-class parents are apt to resort to physical punishment when the direct and immediate consequences of their children's disobedient acts are most extreme, and to refrain from punishing when this might provoke an even greater disturbance.[21] Thus, they will punish a child for wild play when the furniture is damaged or the noise level becomes intolerable, but ignore the same actions when the direct and immediate consequences are not so extreme. Middle-class parents, on the other hand, seem to punish or refrain from punishing on the basis of their interpretation of the child's intent in acting as he does. Thus, they will punish a furious outburst when the context is such that they interpret it to be a loss of self-control, but will ignore an equally extreme outburst when the context is such that they interpret it to be merely an emotional release.

It is understandable that working-class parents react to the consequences rather than to the intent of their children's actions: the important thing is that the child not transgress externally imposed rules. Correspondingly, if middle-class parents are instead concerned about the child's motives and feelings, they can and must look beyond the overt act to why the child acts as he does. It would seem that middle- and working-class values direct parents to see their children's misbehavior in quite different ways, so that misbehavior which prompts middle-class parents to action does not seem as important to working-class parents, and vice versa.[22] Obviously, parents' values are not the only things that enter into their use of physical punishment. But unless one assumes a complete lack of goal-directedness in parental behavior, he would have to grant that parents' values direct their attention to some facets of their own and their children's behavior, and divert it from other facets.

The consequences of class differences in parental values extend far beyond differences in disciplinary practices. From a knowledge of their values for their children, one would expect middle-class parents to feel a greater obligation to be *supportive* of the children, if only because of their sensitivity to the children's internal dynamics. Working-class values, with their emphasis upon conformity to external rules, should lead to greater emphasis upon the parents' obligation to impose constraints.[23] And this, according to Bronfenbrenner, is precisely what has been shown in those few studies that have concerned themselves with the over-all relationship of parents to child: "Over the entire twenty-five year period studied, parent-child relationships in the middle-class are consistently reported as more acceptant and equalitarian, while those in the working-class are oriented toward maintaining order and obedience."[24]

This conclusion is based primarily on studies of *mother*-child relationships in middle- and working-class families. Class differences in parental values have further ramifications for the father's role.[25] Mothers in each class would have their husbands play a role facilitative of the child's development of the characteristics valued in that class: Middle-class mothers want their husbands to be supportive of the children (especially of sons), with their responsibility for imposing constraints being of decidedly secondary importance; working-class mothers look to their husbands to be considerably more directive—support is accorded far less importance and constraint far more. Most middle-class fathers agree with their wives and play a role close to what their wives would have them play.

[21] "Social Class and the Exercise of Parental Authority," *op. cit.*

[22] This is not to say that the methods used by parents of either social class are necessarily the most efficacious for achievement of their goals.

[23] The justification for treating support and constraint as the two major dimensions of parent-child relationships lies in the theoretical argument of Talcott Parsons and Robert F. Bales, *Family, Socialization and Interaction Process*, Glencoe, Ill.: Free Press, 1955, esp. p. 45, and the empirical argument of Earl S. Schaefer, "A Circumplex Model for Maternal Behavior," *Journal of Abnormal and Social Psychology*, LIX (September, 1959), pp. 226–234.

[24] Bronfenbrenner, *op. cit.*, p. 425.

[25] From the very limited evidence available at the time of his review, Bronfenbrenner tentatively concluded: "though the middle-class father typically has a warmer relationship with the child, he is also likely to have more authority and status in family affairs" (*ibid.*, p. 422). The discussion here is based largely on subsequent research, esp. "Social Class and the Allocation of Parental Responsibilities," *op cit.*

Many working-class fathers, on the other hand, do not. It is not that they see the constraining role as less important than do their wives, but that many of them see no reason why they should have to shoulder the responsibility. From their point of view, the important thing is that the child be taught what limits he must not transgress. It does not much matter who does the teaching, and since mother has primary responsibility for child care, the job should be hers.

The net consequence is a quite different division of parental responsibilities in the two social classes. In middle-class families, mother's and father's roles usually are not sharply differentiated. What differentiation exists is largely a matter of each parent taking special responsibility for being supportive of children of the parent's own sex. In working-class families, mother's and father's roles are more sharply differentiated, with mother almost always being the more supportive parent. In some working-class families, mother specializes in support, father in constraint; in others, perhaps in most, mother raises the children, father provides the wherewithal.[26]

Thus, the differences in middle- and working-class parents' values have wide ramifications for their relationships with their children and with each other. Of course, many class differences in parent-child relationships are not directly attributable to differences in values; undoubtedly the very differences in their conditions of life that make for differences in parental values reinforce, at every juncture, parents' characteristic ways of relating to their children. But one could not account for these consistent differences in parent-child relationships in the two social classes without reference to the differences in parents' avowed values.

Conclusion

This paper serves to show how complex and demanding are the problems of interpreting the effects of social structure on behavior. Our inquiries habitually stop at the point of demonstrating that social position correlates with something, when we should want to pursue the question, "Why?" What are the processes by which position in social structure molds behavior? The present analysis has dealt with this question in one specific form: Why does social class matter for parents' relationships with their children? There is every reason to believe that the problems encountered in trying to deal with that question would recur in any analysis of the effects of social structure on behavior.

In this analysis, the concept of "values" has been used as the principal bridge from social position to behavior. The analysis has endeavored to show that middle-class parental values differ from those of working-class parents; that these differences are rooted in basic differences between middle- and working-class conditions of life; and that the differences between middle- and working-class parental values have important consequences for their relationships with their children. The interpretive model, in essence, is: social class—conditions of life—values—behavior.

The specifics of the present characterization of parental values may prove to be inexact; the discussion of the ways in which social class position affects values in undoubtedly partial; and the tracing of the consequences of differences in values for differences in parent-child relationships is certainly tentative and incomplete. I trust, however, that the perspective will prove to be valid and that this formulation will stimulate other investigators to deal more directly with the processes whereby social structure affects behavior.

[26] Fragmentary data suggest sharp class differences in the husband-wife relationship that complements the differences in the division of parental responsibilities discussed above. For example, virtually no working-class wife reports that she and her husband ever go out on an evening or weekend without the children. And few working-class fathers do much to relieve their wives of the burden of caring for the children all the time. By and large, working-class fathers seem to lead a largely separated social life from that of their wives; the wife has full-time responsibility for the children, while the husband is free to go his own way.

25. Role Relations, Sociocultural Environments, and Autocratic Family Ideology*

BY GLEN H. ELDER, JR.

The formation and reinforcement of autocratic ideology about the participation of youth in family decision-making are investigated in a secondary analysis of data from five nations which vary widely in cultural and institutional support for this belief: the U.S., Great Britain, West Germany, Mexico, and Italy. Parent-youth relations, education, residential patterns, and work settings were found to be related to autocratic ideology in each nation. Examination of autocratic and democratic family orientations in relation to ideological perspectives in other areas—politics, intergroup relations, education, and economics—indicated substantial consistency only among middle-class men.

Adherence to autocratic ideology in adult life results in part from childhood socialization and supportive cultural patterns.[1] Parental domination is a prevalent antecedent of autocratic ideology among adults concerning the degree of

autonomy considered appropriate for youth.[2] Education during the adolescent years also influences ideological orientations; autocratic views in child rearing are inversely related to level of education.[3] Among adults, changes in residence and conditions in the work setting may either modify or reinforce autocratic ideas acquired during years of dependency.[4]

The relation of these experiences to an autocratic position on the participation of youth in family decision-making is assessed in this paper in five nations which differ markedly in cultural

SOURCE: Sociometry, *Volume 28 (June, 1965), pp. 173–196. Reprinted by permission of the author and American Sociological Association.*

* I am indebted to John Clausen and M. Brewster Smith for comments and suggestions on aspects of the manuscript and the analysis, and gratefully acknowledge research support from the Institute of International Studies and the Computer Center at Berkeley.

[1] Daniel J. Levinson, "Idea Systems in the Individual and in Society," in George K. Zollschan and Walter Hirsch (ed.), *Explorations in Social Change*, Boston: Houghton-Mifflin Co., 1964.

[2] Hazel L. Ingersoll, "A Study of the Transmission of Authority Patterns in the Family," *Genetic Psychology Monographs*, **38** (1948), pp. 225–302; E. Bjorklund and J. Israel, *The Authoritarian Ideology of Upbringing*, Uppsala, Sweden, 1957; Richard H. Willis, "Political and Child-Rearing Attitudes in Sweden," *Journal of Abnormal and Social Psychology*, **53** (July, 1956), pp. 74–77; Leone Kell and Joan Aldous, "Trends in Child Care Over Three Generations," *Marriage and Family Living*, **22** (May, 1960), pp. 176–177; and Gerald R. Leslie and Kathryn P. Johnsen, "Changed Perceptions of the Maternal Role," *American Sociological Review*, **28** (December, 1963), pp. 919–928.

[3] For an extensive list of sources see Leslie and Johnsen, *op. cit.*

[4] On the relation of occupational role and work setting to the attitudes, values, and behavior of fathers in the family see Donald G. McKinley, *Social Class and Family Life*, New York: The Free Press of Glencoe, 1964; and Martin Gold, *Status Forces in Delinquent Boys*, Ann Arbor, Michigan: Institute for Social Research, 1963.

support for autocratic ideology in the family: the United States, Great Britain, West Germany, Italy, and Mexico.[5] The analysis uses data which were originally collected from approximately 1,000 persons in each nation for a study of political behavior.[6] We shall also investigate the extent to which an autocratic orientation in this area of family life is related to similar orientations in other content domains among respondents in each nation. Available evidence indicates that a person who is autocratic in family ideology is likely to be similarly inclined in intergroup relations and in politics.[7]

[5] Family ideology, constitutes "a *rationale* that serves to justify, interpret and integrate" norms, social patterns, and processes in the family; see Levinson, *op. cit.*, p. 306. Child-rearing and family ideology have been conceptualized along a variety of dimensions: traditional-modern, strict-permissive, and democratic-autocratic. Each of these conceptual dimensions indicate a continuum running from large power and status differences and a unilateral flow of communication between parent and child, at one extreme, to minimal power and status differences at the other. A general ideological orientation in the family, whether autocratic or democratic, tends to be a composite of ideas regarding different behavioral areas. And these ideas may not be consistently autocratic or democratic. Leslie and Johnsen, *op. cit.*, found considerable variation in American maternal role concepts and performance across three behavioral areas: aggression toward mother, self-direction, and sex behavior.

[6] These samples were obtained in 1959 and 1960 by Gabriel Almond and Sydney Verba for a study of political behavior in these five countries. See, *The Civic Culture*, Princeton: Princeton University Press, 1963. I am indebted to the Data Library of the Survey Research Center at Berkeley for the opportunity to conduct this secondary analysis. The United States sample used in the present study does not include Negroes.

Though the samples in each of the five countries are stratified, multi-stage, probability samples, the institutes that designed and executed the surveys differed in the techniques employed and in field experiences. Each sample was originally intended to be a representative cross section of the national population, yet this objective was not achieved in Mexico. In the other four nations, only a rough approximation was obtained. Due to cost and technical difficulties, the Mexican sample was drawn from an urban population of persons living in urban places of 10,000 or more in size. Furthermore, it was necessary to weigh the interviews in Mexico City by a factor of 2.5 in order to make this urban stratum of the sample equivalent to its proportion in the national population. These conditions, as well as the high mortality rate in obtaining interviews at assigned

Autocratic ideology refers in this analysis to the belief that youth of 16 should not participate in family decision-making.[8] The index used reflects autocratic and democratic orientations toward the position of youth in the family based on conceptions of age and status differences between youth and parents. One aspect of the democratic family which distinguishes it from an autocratic family is the greater inclusion of children in family decision-making and consideration of their ideas and opinions. An autocratic orientation is illustrated in Herbert Gans' description of an adult-centered ideology among second-generation Italian parents in the West End of Boston. Children "are raised in a household that is run to satisfy adult wishes first."[9] The distance between the parents' and child's

addresses (40 per cent), seriously weaken any cross-national comparison between Mexico and the other four nations. Exclusion of the rural population tends to yield, in effect, an underestimation of the actual differences between Mexico and the other nations. One indication of the quality of the other four samples is shown by the noncompletion rate in interviewing: Germany, 26 per cent; Italy, 28 per cent; Great Britain, 41 per cent; and the U.S., 17 per cent.

[7] See Levinson, *op. cit.*, p. 301.

[8] Ideally, a composite index of the amount of involvement and responsibility of youth in making decisions in a set of areas would have been desirable to measure ideology regarding the participation of youth in family decision-making. In the absence of such specific indicators, a general index of the amount of responsibility and involvement in decision-making which is viewed as appropriate for 16 year olds is used. The item used is, "In general, how much voice do you think children of 16 should have in family decisions "—*Democratic ideology*, "Great deal" and "Some"; *Autocratic ideology*, "Little" and "None"; "Other" and "Don't know" responses were not scored. Though one item may be highly unstable, the association of this item with other items measuring democratic and autocratic orientations (see Table 8) and with background variables yield consistent relations and results which parallel findings reported in other studies. Internal analysis of the data constitutes a critical test of the validity and usefulness of any indicator. A cross-national analysis based on a single item index of adolescent independence in job choice is reported in Robert J. Smith, Charles E. Ramsey, and Gelia Castillo, "Parental Authority and Job Choice: Sex Differences in Three Cultures," *The American Journal of Sociology*, **69** (September, 1963), pp. 143–149.

[9] Herbert J. Gans, *The Urban Villagers*, New York: The Free Press, 1926, p. 56.

world in these families appears in clear detail in patterns of age-segregation and in the passivity of children when in the presence of adults. Similarly, in the Mexican village of Tepoztlan, "children are brought up to obey their elders and to submit to the will of their mother and father as long as they live under the parents' roof. From infancy on, they are encouraged to be passive and unobtrusive; older children are expected to be self-controlled and helpful."[10]

The five nations represent a wide range of sociocultural contexts and of ideological variation. Over the past three decades, democratic family ideology seems most widespread in the United States and Great Britain, and is least prevalent in Italy and Mexico. The spread of this ideology is possibly linked with changes in family patterns. Goode notes that "the modern doctrine that members of the nuclear family should love one another, that permissive love is 'psychologically healthful' for the child, has given ideological support to the normal pressures of children toward greater choice in all matters and to the greater opportunity to be free economically at an early age."[11]

Four interrelated factors, we suggest, account in large measure for a decline in, and the relative prevalence of, autocratic family ideology in the five nations: (1) a decline or absence of cultural and institutional support, (2) increasing urbanization and industrialization, (3) an elevation in median educational attainment, and (4) the exposure of the national population to democratizing child-rearing literature.[12] Rural residence and low education are particularly related to intolerance and to acceptance of traditional authority patterns.[13] If a numerical

index of each of these factors were constructed, it would show conditions in the United States to be most favorable to both a low prevalence and a decline in this ideology with Britain and West Germany next in order. Italy and Mexico, on the other hand, would rank lowest.[14]

Data on the attitudes, ideology, and practices of American parents suggest that permissive and democratic ideology have become more widespread most noticeably in the middle-class over the last 30 years.[15] A recent comparison of 265 college-educated American mothers and grandmothers on desirability of self-direction on the part of children indicated a trend toward greater tolerance for the child in making his own decisions.[16] Also, in a study of Vassar alumnae, about one-third of the class of 1904 disagreed with the statement, "obedience and respect for authority are the most important virtues that children learn" in contrast to 77 per cent of women in classes 1940–1943.[17] Similar downward trends across age groups were obtained by Stouffer in a national sample of Americans.[18]

In a sample of German adults, nearly two-thirds agreed that children should have their own views, suitable for their own world, which should be respected and not corrected by the person who rears them.[19] This statement does not refer to the inclusion of youth in family decision-making. Yet the data suggest that autocratic family ideology is less common among

1955; Robin M. Williams, Jr., *Strangers Next Door*, New York: Prentice-Hall, 1964; James G. Martin, *The Tolerant Personality*, Detroit, Michigan: Wayne State University Press, 1964; and Seymour M. Lipset, "Working-Class Authoritarianism," in *Political Man*, New York: Doubleday & Co., 1960, Chapter 4.

[14] On national variations in education and in economic development, see Frederick Harbison and Charles A. Myers, *Education, Manpower, and Economic Growth: Strategies of Human Resource Development*, New York: McGraw-Hill Co., 1964.

[15] See Martha Wolfenstein, "The Emergence of Fun Morality," *The Journal of Social Issues*, 7 (1951), pp. 15–25, and Leslie and Johnsen, *op. cit.*

[16] Leslie and Johnsen, *op. cit.*

[17] Mervin B. Freedman, "Changes in Six Decades of Some Attitudes in Values Held by Educated Women," *Journal of Social Issues*, 17 (1961), No. 1, pp. 19–28.

[18] Stouffer, *op. cit.*

[19] Cited in Goode, *op. cit.*, p. 78. See also Rene König, "Family and Authority: The German Father in 1955," *Sociological Review*, 5 (July, 1957), pp. 107–127.

[10] Oscar Lewis, *Tepoztlan: Village in Mexico*, New York: Rinehart, Holt, and Winston, 1960, p. 59.

[11] William J. Goode, *World Revolution and Family Patterns*, New York: The Free Press of Glencoe, 1963, p. 77.

[12] See Goode, *op. cit.*, and Urie Bronfenbrenner, "Socialization and Social Class Through Time and Space," in Eleanor E. Maccoby, Theodore M. Newcomb, and Eugene L. Hartley (eds.), *Readings in Social Psychology*, New York: Henry Holt & Company, 1958.

[13] On intolerance towards others, see Samuel G. Stouffer, *Communism, Conformity and Civil Liberties*, Garden City, New York: Doubleday & Co., Inc.,

post- than prewar generations of German parents.

In Italy and Mexico, the father-centered authoritarian family and male-oriented, traditional cultural patterns generally persist. Wives are subservient to their husbands, and children are subordinate to both.[20] The Mexican-American male, Madsen observes "is entitled to unquestioning obedience from his wife and children. He is above criticism due to his 'superior' male strength and intelligence."[21]

The effects of these national variations on hypothesized relations within nations are most likely to be evident in Italy and Mexico, the two nations in which autocratic family ideology seems most prevalent. Due to supportive cultural and institutional patterns, differences in role relations and in status changes are apt to account for appreciably less variation in autocratic ideology in these two countries. Specific hypotheses on the formation and support of autocratic ideology and on the relation of this perspective to similar views in other domains within these contexts are presented below.

Hypotheses

1. The Acquisition and Reinforcement of Autocratic Ideology. We hypothesize that parent-youth relations, educational attainment, residential change, and occupational role and work setting are related to adherence to autocratic ideology. Research and theory relevant to the effects of each of these independent variables are discussed briefly in relation to the following hypotheses.

a. PARENT-YOUTH RELATIONS. In the family, children learn how to relate to others through interaction with their parents, and orientations acquired during these years are frequently carried over into adult life. Thus, we find that the child-rearing practices of mothers who are themselves from strict homes are more likely to be autocratic than those of mothers from any other type of home.[22] Aggressive tendencies may also result from authoritarian up-bringing since autocratic parents are frequently punitive and coercive.[23] Later in life these tendencies may find expression in relations with subordinates such as children. Data presented in *The Authoritarian Personality* and in subsequent studies also show a moderate relationship between dominant parents and an autocratic view toward children in adulthood.[24] According to these data, *adults who report authoritarian parents should be most inclined to advocate the exclusion of youth from family decision-making.*[25]

b. EDUCATIONAL ATTAINMENT. In accordance with a large number of studies which have found autocratic family ideology and child-rearing practices to be inversely related to parental education, we hypothesize that *persons in each nation will be most likely to be autocratic in ideology if they have not attended secondary*

---

[20] See, for instance, Oscar Lewis, *op. cit.*; Charles J. Erasmus, *Man Takes Control*, Minneapolis, Minnesota: University of Minnesota Press, 1961; Edward C. Banfield, *The Moral Basis of a Backward Society*, New York: The Free Press of Glencoe, 1958; and Luigi Barzini, *The Italians*, New York: Atheneum, 1964.

[21] William Madsen, *The Mexican-Americans of South Texas*, New York: Holt, Rinehart, and Winston, 1964, p. 48.

[22] Leslie and Johnsen, *op. cit.*, p. 928.

[23] Martin Gold, "Suicide, Homicide, and the Socialization of Aggression," *The American Journal of Sociology*, 56 (May, 1958), pp. 651–661.

[24] See Theodore W. Adorno et al., *The Authoritarian Personality*, New York: Harper & Row, 1950; Willis, *op. cit.*; and Ingersoll, *op. cit.*

[25] An index of parent-youth relations was constructed from the following two items, with scores ranging from 0 to 4. "As you were growing up, let's say when you were around 16, how much influence do you remember having in family decisions affecting yourself " (2, much influence; 1, some; 0, none at all; other and don't know responses not scored); "At around the same time, if a decision were made that you didn't like, did you feel *free* to complain, did you feel a little *uneasy* about complaining, or was it *better not* to complain " (2, felt *free;* 1, felt a little *uneasy;* 0, it was *better not* to complain; other and don't know responses were not scored). Gamma coefficients based on total samples in each nation show these items to be highly related: U.S., .61; Italy, .63; West Germany, .65; Great Britain, .56; and Mexico, .46. For the purposes of the following analysis, we shall consider scores 3 and 4 as an indication of *democratic* parent-child relations, and 0 and 2 as indicating an *authoritarian* pattern.

school.[26] This relation may be modified substantially by the degree to which autocratic ideology receives cultural and institutional support—i.e., Italy versus the United States.[27]

c. PLACE OF RESIDENCE AND MIGRATION. Adults who have remained in rural areas and those rural-born persons who now live in urban communities should be most and least inclined to adhere to an autocratic perspective since father-centered, authoritarian families are generally more common in rural than urban areas.[28] Data which partially support this expectation are provided by Bronfenbrenner in a re-analysis of Miller and Swanson's Detroit data: mothers with a rural background were likely to adhere to more restrictive techniques of socialization than mothers of urban background who were comparable in social class status.[29]

A rural-born adult who moves to an urban community is likely to be confronted with a set of child-rearing and family practices which are foreign to his past experiences and acquired perspectives. For some newcomers the experience may create confusion and be unsettling as shown in the feelings and responses of European immigrants in New York City.[30] Seeing children question parents and assert independence might support the rationale for autocratic policy in child rearing. On the other hand, newcomers might adopt the more democratic views prevalent in the community. Both of these responses are plausible alternatives, yet it seems most probable that adoption of a democratic perspective would be more common among second-generation, urban residents. Newcomers to urban areas, on the other hand, *should be more inclined to rely upon self-other orientations acquired through socialization in rural areas.* Of the rural-born living in urban places, this should be most true of those who experienced authoritarian control in their families of orientation and who did not reach secondary school.

d. OCCUPATIONAL ROLE AND WORK SETTING. The work experiences of men significantly affect their behavior in the family and their attitudes toward children. Dissatisfaction on the job is associated with conflict in the home,[31] and a low, subordinate occupational status has been found to be linked with paternal coerciveness in rearing sons.[32] *Thus, autocratic family ideology is most likely among men who occupy low-status work roles, and among those who experience coercion by supervisors in the work setting.*

Moving from the unskilled to professional workers, many of the conditions which support democratic, humanistic values increase in frequency and strength. High-status occupations require more years of formal education, are more rewarding from a monetary standpoint, and require ambition, self-reliance, judgment, and drive. Advocacy of the exclusion of youth from the decision-making process in the family seems neither compatible with the greater potential satisfactions derivable from professional

[26] For a listing of studies, see Leslie and Johnsen, *op. cit.*; see also, Marvin Zuckerman and Mary Oltean, "Some Relationships Between Maternal Attitude Factors and Authoritarianism Personality Needs, Psychopathology and Self-Acceptance," *Child Development*, **30** (March, 1959), pp. 27–36; and Melvin L. Kohn, "Social Class and the Exercise of Parental Authority," *American Sociological Review*, **24** (June, 1959), pp. 352– 366.

[27] Educational attainment is measured by the question, "How far did you get with your education " The responses ranged from no education to various types of higher education. For an index of high educational attainment (a level which is achieved by appreciable members of persons in each of the five countries), it was decided to use the proportion who said they reached secondary school. The phrasing of the question does not necessarily imply completion of this level of education. The item measuring the education of Italian respondents distinguished between junior and senior high school within the secondary level. For these respondents, the per cent reaching junior high school was used as the index of achievement with the result that the percentage of Italian respondents reaching secondary school is slightly inflated. The proportion who reached twelve years of education was used as the index in the United States, since it seems to be similar in level of achievement to reaching secondary school in the other four nations.

[28] See Glen H. Elder, Jr., "Achievement Orientations and Career Patterns of Rural Youth," *Sociology of Education*, **37** (Fall, 1963), pp. 30–58.

[29] Bronfenbrenner, *op. cit.*, p. 441.

[30] Oscar Handlin, *The Uprooted*, New York: Little Brown, 1951.

[31] O. A. Oeser and S. A. Hammond, *Social Structure and Personality in a City*, London: Routledge & Kegan Paul, 1954, p. 248.

[32] McKinley, *op. cit.*, and Gold, *op. cit.*

and white collar work, nor with personal qualities stressed in these work settings. A partial test of these observations was made by Inkeles in a secondary analysis of child-rearing values in eleven nations.[33] Inkeles assumed that "traditional, restrictive, cautious, conventional values are much stronger among manual workers, whereas the belief in effort, striving, energetic mastery, and the sacrifice necessary to those ends is much stronger among the middle-class."[34] Of the values presented, manual workers were least likely to choose ambition in six of the countries and most likely to indicate obedience in eight nations. The consistency of these results in encouraging, although percentage differences were relatively small.

Two types of worker-supervisor relationships, benevolent and coercive, should produce quite different attitudes and ideas about controlling youth. In benevolent relationships, the worker can express his views and make complaints, while workers under coercive management are not allowed to discuss problems and air complaints. Hostility and resentment stirred by coercive management may heighten the receptivity of workers to autocratic dogma regarding subordinates.[35] Under such conditions, differences in age and wisdom may be emphasized in adult-youth relations.

2. Autocratic and Democratic Family Ideology in Relation to Orientations in Other Ideological Domains. Data indicate that individuals who are autocratic in one ideological domain are inclined to hold autocratic orientations in other areas.[36] These domains include the family, polity, education, intergroup relations, religion, and the economy. Willis, in a Swedish sample of 73 men and 71 women, ages 18 and over, obtained a correlation of .43 between a scale measuring

acceptance of authoritarian political policies and a thirteen-item index measuring demands for obedience from children.[37] Both of these ideological orientations were moderately related to authoritarian upbringing (.25 for political and .28 for child-rearing ideology). Ethnocentrism has been shown in numerous studies to be related to autocratic family and child-rearing ideology.[38] In the domain of economic life, pessimism regarding social advancement and the future is moderately associated with autocratic, intolerant beliefs.[39]

Correlations across ideological domains obtained in a number of studies are not particularly strong, ranging from .3 to .8.[40] Both personality and environmental factors may account for this variation. Levinson suggests that it is partly "a reflection of deeper-lying contradictions of personality," and partly an indication of "contradictory ideological demands and opportunities in the social milieu."[41] It seems probable that ideological consistency is apt to be greatest under conditions which minimize the influence of relevant environmental factors on the expression of personal orientations. Middle-class status seems likely to index such a condition for individuals who adhere to an autocratic family ideology. Structural support for autocratic thinking is least likely to be experienced in the middle-class, yet when this orientation does occur, it should be largely a function of personality, and thus should be more likely to be expressed in a variety of social and political areas. *Democratic and autocratic views in family ideology should be more strongly related to similar types of orientation in other domains among middle- than working-class persons.* In other words, autocrats and democrats in family ideology who are working class in status should be less likely to differ in their views in other domains.

Before examining data relevant to these hypotheses we shall first assess the actual prevalence and possible decline in autocratic ideology in each of the five nations.

[33] Alex Inkeles, "Industrial Man: The Relation of Status to Experience, Perception, and Value," *American Journal of Sociology*, **66** (July, 1960), p. 22, Table 9.
[34] *Ibid.*, p. 21.
[35] Hamblin found punitive supervision to be related to high turnover, tension, and aggressive feelings among workers in a concrete-products company; see Robert L. Hamblin, "Punitive and Non-punitive Supervision," *Social Problems*, **11** (Spring, 1964), pp. 345–359.
[36] Levinson, *op. cit.*, p. 301.
[37] Willis, *op. cit.*
[38] Adorno et al., *The Authoritarian Personality*, *op. cit.*, and Williams, *op. cit.*
[39] Martin, *op. cit.*
[40] Levinson, *op. cit.*
[41] *Ibid.*, p. 306.

Table 1

Percentage autocratic in family ideology by age and nation

Nation	Age (and year of birth)						
	18–25 (1934–41)	26–30 (1929–34)	31–35 (1924–29)	36–40 (1919–24)	41–50 (1909–19)	51–60 (1900–09)	61 + (Before 1900)
United States	$10^{(100)}$	$10^{(72)}$	$14^{(79)}$	$13^{(86)}$	$16^{(153)}$	$25^{(138)}$	$31^{(208)}$
Great Britain	$31^{(81)}$	$29^{(93)}$	$35^{(111)}$	$32^{(136)}$	$25^{(188)}$	$52^{(169)}$	$58^{(159)}$
West Germany	$24^{(107)}$	$40^{(76)}$	$45^{(91)}$	$39^{(102)}$	$44^{(158)}$	$44^{(171)}$	$58^{(165)}$
Italy	$58^{(156)}$	$69^{(107)}$	$70^{(100)}$	$64^{(106)}$	$71^{(178)}$	$83^{(156)}$	$74^{(113)}$
Mexico	$53^{(229)}$	$44^{(208)}$	$43^{(170)}$	$45^{(167)}$	$44^{(209)}$	$54^{(165)}$	$66^{(97)}$

Note: Total *N*'s per cell are given in parentheses.

Prevalence and Change in Autocratic Ideology

Secular change in the prevalence of autocratic ideology is shown in Table 1 across seven age groups ranging from respondents (18–25 years of age) who were born just prior to or during the early part of World War II to those (61 years of age and older) who were born before 1900.

National differences in the spread and decline of autocratic ideology are generally similar to those we have described. Moving from older to younger respondents, the percentage against adolescent involvement in family decision-making declines appreciably for the United States, Great Britain, and West Germany. Little consistent change is evident in Italy and Mexico. Autocratic ideology is least extensive in the United States and is most prevalent in Italy. Great Britain and West Germany are in between these two extremes, although percentage differences between the two are not sufficiently consistent to indicate meaningful national differences. No appreciable variations by sex were obtained.

In the United States and Great Britain, the greatest percentage decrease occurs among those who were adolescents during the late 1920's and early 1930's; thereafter, little consistent change is evident. Technological and mass communication innovations following World War I may have contributed to this decline. The sharpest declines in Germany and Italy appear among persons who were adolescents during the two world wars. Among Germans and Italians whose adolescence post-dates World War II, the results seem to reflect the impetus given democratization in all sectors of national life since the war. These changes have been most noted in the German family.[42] In Mexico, an autocratic perspective is least common among those born between the Revolution of 1910 and 1935; this curvilinear pattern appears to parallel the high rate of social and economic change which occurred in rural areas as part of agrarian reform.[43] Equalitarianism, as part of the revolutionary spirit of these reform years, may have inculcated generations born in this period with a more democratic ideology regarding parent-youth relations. It is also likely that social change resulted in an entrenchment of traditional beliefs for some. For instance, the distribution of land to peasants and collectivization during the years of agrarian reform in Mexico may have had quite different effects on the rural family system and on traditional beliefs. These possibilities merely suggest that the relation between social-structural change and ideological change is complex, and requires a more detailed empirical assessment.

National differences in the pervasiveness of autocratic ideology (shown in Table 1) correspond to differences inferred from area studies and other materials. Secular trends in ideology

[42] König, *op. cit.*
[43] Oscar Lewis, *Five Families*, New York: Basic Books, 1958, p. 17.

Table 2

Percentage autocratic in family ideology by type of parent-youth relation, age and nation

Nation	Type of parent-youth relations	Age and birth group cohorts		
		18–30 (1929–41)	31–50 (1909–29)	51 + (Before 1909)
United States	Authoritarian	13[45]	24[131]	40[194]
	Democratic	9[128]	16[169]	14[152]
Great Britain	Authoritarian	48[54]	45[164]	75[227]
	Democratic	22[120]	21[261]	35[141]
West Germany	Authoritarian	44[75]	56[212]	67[243]
	Democratic	26[114]	23[154]	23[105]
Italy	Authoritarian	67[146]	71[246]	86[184]
	Democratic	57[116]	65[138]	65[85]
Mexico	Authoritarian	53[309]	54[372]	63[184]
	Democratic	39[129]	22[174]	40[78]

in each nation also parallel known differences among these nations and vary meaningfully in relation to their social, economic, and demographic histories. Yet these results are subject to a number of methodological problems. Since we do not have measurements on adult-child pairs, we lack a base from which to assess degree of change. Furthermore, we compared the prevalence of autocratic ideology across age groups at a point in time rather than across time periods among persons of the same age: as a result, the findings obtained may be a function of age differences rather than of social, economic, and ideological conditions during periods of this century. Several aspects of the data suggest that the trends obtained are a result, to a significant extent, of conditions during the childhood and adolescence of the respondents. First, the trends vary in expected fashion in relation to events such as world wars and social upheavals. In addition, the percentage urban-born and reaching secondary school—factors which we have suggested partially account for change toward more liberal ideology—tend to increase from the oldest to the youngest age groups in the three nations which show substantial change. Finally, if age is the main factor, a decline in ideology should be fairly similar in each nation. This pattern, of course, does not hold for Mexico and Italy. Yet, even with this supporting evidence, weaknesses in the data require that these results be considered as tentative.

The Formation and Support of Autocratic Ideology

Parent-Youth Relations. Data from other studies indicate that the strictest adults in both ideology and in practices are those who were themselves reared by domineering parents. Since the spread of equalitarianism resulting from other changes in society tends to enhance the probability of movement away from an extreme ideological position, the most pronounced decline in autocratic ideology across age groups should be evident among authoritarian-reared respondents.

Table 2 supports our expectations. Autocratic ideology is more widespread among persons within each age group who described relations with their own parents during adolescence as authoritarian. All fifteen comparisons produce differences in the expected direction (an average difference of 22 per cent). A decline in this perspective is primarily evident among those who described their parents as authoritarian. Of the persons with authoritarian parents in each nation, we find that autocratic ideology occurs most frequently among those born before 1910 and least among those born after 1929. Much less change is shown for democratically-reared persons in the three birth cohorts. If national comparisons are made among persons reporting similar adolescent role patterns, differences between nations remain large and of the same order as those shown in Table 1.

Table 3

Percentage autocratic in family ideology in relation to level of educational attainment in the United States, Great Britain, and Italy with age controlled

Nation	Level of education	Percentage autocratic by age groups			Average percentage differences
		18–30	31–50	51+	
United States	Primary	12(41)	21(137)	33(242)	9.7
	Secondary	9(132)	10(180)	18(104)	
West Germany	Primary	39(105)	46(299)	56(305)	20.3
	Secondary	16(43)	27(66)	37(41)	
Italy	Primary	70(150)	71(267)	80(209)	9.3
	Secondary	52(111)	64(117)	77(60)	

Although measures of permissive ideology and parent-youth relations were not available in the data, it seems likely that a number of adults who were reared in this manner by their parents would be inclined to move away from this extreme position in family ideology. Leslie and Johnsen found that a number of the American mothers who were permissively-reared with respect to self-direction moved toward a more moderate position in their own ideas and practices.[44] Movement away from parental patterns thus appears most likely among adults who experienced extremes in power relations in their families of orientation. In such cases change can occur in only one direction.

Educational Attainment. It was hypothesized that autocratic ideology would be most common among persons who had not attended secondary school. The paucity of rural-born British respondents and Mexicans with a secondary education required exclusion of these two nations from the analyses on educational attainment and residential patterns.

Persons who have attained secondary school are less likely to adhere to autocratic ideology than those with a primary education in each of the three age groups (Table 3). Absolute percentage differences between the old and young age groups indicate that the decline in autocratic ideology is greatest among persons who reached secondary school in West Germany and Italy.

The association is relatively weak among Americans. The low prevalence of autocratic ideology in the United States and the index of educational attainment, which is least satisfactory for indicating differences in the United States, may partially account for this result. As indicated earlier, surveys in the United States tend to show greater change toward democratic and permissive ideas in the middle- than in the working-class.[45] The equally small relation between education and ideology in Italy may be due to the countervailing influence of socio-cultural patterns.

In each of the three nations, persons adhering to an autocratic ideology are most likely to have been born early in the 20th century, to have been reared by authoritarian parents and to have gone no further than primary school in their formal education. Thus, the greatest contrasts in adherence to this normative belief should be indicated by contrasts in age, parent-youth relations, and education.

In Table 4 the highest and lowest prevalence of autocratic ideology in each nation tend to appear in these extreme subgroups (percentage differences of 30 for the United States and Italy, and 47 for West Germany). The new generation of adults who attended secondary school or were reared by democratic parents are least likely to have autocratic views. Yet, even in this subgroup, Italians are nearly seven times as likely as Americans to be autocratic. The

---

[44] Leslie and Johnsen, *op. cit.*, p. 927.

[45] *Ibid.*

Table 4

Percentage autocratic in family ideology by parent-youth relations, educational attainment, and age: United States, West Germany, and Italy*

Nation	Type of parent-youth relations	Level of educational attainment	Percentage autocratic by age groups		
			18–30	31–50	50+
United States	Authoritarian	Primary	11 [18]	30 [61]	38 [142]
		Secondary	15 [27]	15 [68]	27 [45]
	Democratic	Primary	14 [24]	13 [62]	22 [82]
		Secondary	8 [108]	8 [106]	9 [57]
West Germany	Authoritarian	Primary	46 [66]	53 [174]	65 [188]
		Secondary	20 [11]	50 [23]	47 [20]
	Democratic	Primary	29 [73]	29 [94]	26 [71]
		Secondary	18 [38]	17 [42]	12 [17]
Italy	Authoritarian	Primary	70 [86]	66 [161]	83 [121]
		Secondary	52 [46]	68 [60]	82 [27]
	Democratic	Primary	64 [46]	73 [73]	63 [51]
		Secondary	53 [64]	62 [50]	73 [27]

* Since the overall pattern of differences is of primary interest in this table, percentages based on fewer than 20 cases are shown.

greater cultural and institutional support for autocratic family ideology in Italy is the most likely explanation for this pronounced difference. It is also possible that the meaning of the item differs between these nations. Adolescent involvement in family decision-making may represent a substantially different type of behavior in an extended family than in an urban nuclear family unit. Nevertheless, the national differences obtained do appear to correspond to inferences based on ethnographic reports.

Another indication of the socialization orientation of the home and its effect on the formation of ideology is provided by religious affiliation. Comparison of Protestant and Catholic respondents in the United States with education controlled, shows that Catholics are more likely to be autocratic, both on the primary (24 versus 18 per cent) and secondary level (15 versus 8 per cent). Among West Germans, a similar difference was obtained for persons who failed to enter secondary school. The number of Catholics in the British sample were too few to permit analysis.

Residential Patterns. Autocratic ideology, we reasoned, should be most wide-spread in the rural-to-urban group among authoritarian-reared persons with a primary education.[46] The lowest prevalence over all migration patterns should be characteristic of democratically-reared persons in the urban-urban subgroup who reached secondary school.

The above expectations are only partially realized in the above analysis (depletion of cases made an analysis of German cases impractical). Overall, autocratic ideology is most widespread among authoritarian-reared persons with a primary education who moved from a rural to an urban community. These respondents stand out from all other persons in the rural-urban subgroup. On the other hand, the lowest prevalence of this belief is not clearly specified by any of the migration patterns.

[46] Rural residence is indicated by communities of 5,000 or less, and urban places are those larger in size. Rural-urban is thus a residential move to communities above 5,000 in size. The relatively small size of the rural to urban flow in West Germany and Italy necessitated a crude breakdown of this kind.

Table 5

Percentage autocratic in family ideology by educational attainment, residential patterns, and parent-youth relations in the United States and Italy: Persons 18–50 years old   •

Nation	Type of parent-youth relations	Level of educational attainment	Residential patterns		
			Rural to rural	Rural to urban	Urban to urban
United States	Authoritarian	Primary	25[20]	41[32]	14[25]
		Secondary	18[17]	8[25]	18[45]
	Democratic	Primary	8[25]	19[21]	10[30]
		Secondary	5[38]	9[46]	8[113]
Italy	Authoritarian	Primary	59[67]	75[41]	66[97]
		Secondary	64[13]	65[20]	57[55]
	Democratic	Primary	60[37]	65[18]	71[44]
		Secondary	46[22]	65[20]	56[56]

Note: Percentages are again shown for cells with less than 20 cases.

With age, adult status, and parent-youth relations statistically controlled similar results were obtained (see Table 7).[47] In three nations (the Mexican sample did not include persons living in rural areas), autocratic ideology appears to occur most frequently among migrants from rural areas. This orientation is least common to respondents with a stable urban pattern in the United States and West Germany. Note that variations by residential patterns are negligible for Great Britain, the most urbanized of the five countries.

Occupational Status and Work Setting. The rewards, stresses, and values which characterize work settings and have relevance for the way males view family relations are indexed by the status of the work role and by the nature of

autonomy and control in the work setting. We hypothesized that an intolerant and domineering approach toward youth would be inversely related to occupational status. Self-reliance, initiative, and independent judgment are more valued in high status jobs, and rewards from work, both intrinsic and extrinsic, are greater. Secondly, we hypothesized that coercive supervision on the job should induce a more intolerant and controlling approach toward others, and in particular toward youth.

Table 7 shows the percentage of autocratic males by six occupational levels with all other variables except education controlled.[48] The degree of overlap between education and occupation prevented statistical control of the former. In most nations, an autocratic ideology is least common among professionals. Differences in ideology among professionals in the five nations are small in relation to cross-national comparisons in other occupational groups. If Italy is excluded, the percentage variation is about 18 per cent. Manual workers, farmers, and small businessmen are generally more likely to be autocratic than white collar workers and professionals. In fact, across the five nations, small businessmen and farmers are virtually as likely to be autocratic as skilled and unskilled workers, a finding which corresponds to results obtained

---

[47] In Tables 6 and 7, a technique of multivariate analysis which permits the use of test factors with categorical response classes is used to control statistically for extraneous variables such as age. This technique enables the simultaneous control of all test factors in the analysis by statistically adjusting subclass percentages simultaneously for the effects of all other variables and their interrelations. No assumption concerning the linearity of the effects of each factor are required. It provides estimates of the main effects of each factor. See Alan B. Wilson, "Analysis of Multiple Cross-Classifications in Cross-Sectional Designs," a revision of a paper presented to the American Association for Public Opinion Research, Excelsior Springs, Missouri, May 9, 1964.

[48] *Ibid.*

Table 6

Percentage of males autocratic in family ideology by supervision in work setting with occupational status, parent-youth relations, age, and residence controlled

Control in the work setting	United States		Great Britain		West Germany		Italy		Mexico	
	Non-Manual	Manual	Non-Manual	Manual	Non-Manual	Manual	Non-Manual	Manual	Non-Manual	Manual
Self-employed	$12^{(26)}$	*	$42^{(52)}$	*	$36^{(50)}$	*	$56^{(66)}$	$60^{(53)}$	$50^{(67)}$	$47^{(70)}$
Benevolent Control	$8^{(54)}$	$20^{(67)}$	$34^{(52)}$	$43^{(107)}$	$28^{(47)}$	$49^{(70)}$	$55^{(28)}$	$76^{(19)}$	$39^{(52)}$	$47^{(84)}$
Coercive Control	$20^{(35)}$	$32^{(62)}$	$47^{(26)}$	$32^{(117)}$	$31^{(22)}$	$43^{(79)}$	$70^{(34)}$	$70^{(83)}$	$44^{(88)}$	$57^{(77)}$

Note: Farmers and farm workers are excluded from the analysis. Starred cells contain less than 20 cases.

on political ideology. Extremist and intolerant political sentiments tend to be particularly strong among these entrepreneurs.[49]

Self-employment and two types of supervision, benevolent and coercive, were measured by three questions. Workers were described as "under benevolent supervision" if they felt free to complain when they strongly disagreed with a decision, if they believed that their complaining did some good, and if they felt that management considered their needs and interests.[50] The remainder were considered to be under more *coercive* supervision. Farmers and farm workers have been deleted from this analysis. The effects of age, residential pattern, parent-youth relations, and religion are statistically controlled.

Comparison of men by type of supervision indicates that autocratic ideology is likely to occur more widely among middle-class men who work under coercive management. Differences are very inconsistent among manual workers; in three nations, manual workers with benevolent supervision are more apt to be autocratic. In sum, these data provide tentative support for the hypothesized effects of different types of work supervision only among nonmanual workers.

Among nonmanual workers, the self-employed

resemble coercively supervised workers in ideology. Fairly similar proportions espouse an autocratic view regarding participation in family decision-making on the part of youth. In addition, the manual and nonmanual self-employed tend to differ very little in ideology. This lack of difference is surprising since free professionals and small businessmen have achieved a higher average level of education than the self-employed craftsman.

An Overview. We have examined the effects of age, parent-youth relations, education, residential patterns, religion, occupational status, and supervision in work setting on autocratic ideology. Parent-youth relations and formal education are significant factors in the formation of an individual's idea system. Religious affiliation, as an index of the cultural orientation of the home, is also associated with autocratic ideology. With education controlled, Protestants are generally less likely to espouse an autocratic approach in the United States and West Germany than are Catholics. Movement from one sociocultural system to another may lead either to adoption and assimilation of new beliefs, or to retrenchment and a heightening of threatened beliefs. The likelihood of each of these outcomes depends in large part, we hypothesized, on experiences and predispositions acquired in the parent-child relationship. Another stimulus to acceptance of beliefs was explored in the occupational role and in supervision in the work setting. Nonmanual workers with benevolent supervision on the job, and professionals, as well as white collar workers, were least inclined toward autocratic ideology.

[49] See Lipset, "Working-Class Authoritarianism," *op. cit.*, and Martin Trow, "Small Businessmen, Political Tolerance, and Support for McCarthy," *American Journal of Sociology*, **64** (November, 1958), pp. 270–281.

[50] A clearer test of the consequences of coercive and benevolent supervision would require a more precise specification of coercion which the number of cases do not permit, and an item or two on how the foreman or supervisor reacted to trouble, workers' mistakes, etc. See Hamblin, *op. cit.*

Table 7

Percentage of males autocratic in family ideology by sociocultural factors in five nations: adjusted percentages for sub-classes in a multiple classification analysis

Sociocultural factors	United States	Great Britain	West Germany	Italy	Mexico
1. Age					
a. 18–30	16[89]	37[96]	36[104]	59[133]	50[155]
b. 31–50	20[141]	37[206]	40[173]	59[197]	42[200]
c. 51 +	26[175]	53[158]	45[172]	72[140]	56[109]
2. Residential Pattern					
a. Rural-rural	22[100]	43[63]	42[143]	55[123]	*
b. Rural-urban	25[120]	42[32]	48[63]	68[79]	—
c. Urban-urban	20[155]	43[300]	39[202]	62[194]	—
3. Religion					
a. Protestant	20[261]	44[324]	41[226]	—	—
b. Catholic	31[92]	44[52]	40[187]	—	—
4. Parent-Youth Relations					
a. Authoritarian	28[167]	55[178]	53[209]	69[238]	56[265]
b. Democratic	16[201]	34[237]	26[171]	56[158]	34[138]
5. Occupation					
a. Professional	20[53]	26[40]	34[47]	47[29]	38[18]
b. White Collar	14[85]	46[58]	28[49]	65[71]	45[78]
c. Small Business	24[33]	54[33]	40[36]	65[42]	59[61]
d. Farmer or farm worker	32[33]	*	46[41]	68[78]	*
e. Skilled	24[89]	40[151]	46[123]	62[84]	50[196]
f. Unskilled	26[98]	42[92]	46[56]	68[86]	47[36]
Grand per cent	22	43	41	64	48
Total N	405	460	449	470	464

Note: Starred cells have less than 20 cases. Since the Mexican sample was drawn from urban areas, a delineation of residential patterns is not possible. Some of the frequency distributions will not equal the total number of cases due to the exclusion of non-responses, don't know, and other responses.

These independent variables were assessed more or less serially without an attempt to present a complex multivariate picture. Table 7 shows the main effects of each of the independent variables except education. Since education and occupation overlap to some extent, it was not possible to assess meaningfully the main effects of each factor by using this statistical technique. The main effects of supervision in the work setting were shown in Table 6.

The downward trend in the occurrence of autocratic ideology with decreasing age is still evident in each nation, although the decline shown in Table 1 is substantially reduced. In the three most industrialized nations—United States, Great Britain, and West Germany—the four independent variables markedly reduce the trend by age group: in each nation, the percentage difference between the youngest and oldest age groups is halved or nearly halved. These same factors are much less effective in accounting for age variations in Mexico and Italy, the two nations in which autocratic ideology is most prevalent.[51]

Religious affiliation and parent-youth relations, as indexes of familial environment, con-

[51] Level of educational attainment was added to the independent variables listed in Table 7 in an analysis to determine whether variation in ideology by age could be more completely explained. The results showed no appreciable reduction in the unexplained variance. In exploratory analyses the crude indexes of educational attainment and occupational status appear to account for a similar proportion of the variance in autocratic ideology.

tinue to be associated with autocratic ideology when all other factors are controlled. Protestant-Catholic differences are pronounced only in the United States with Catholics more apt to be autocratic than Protestants. As in previous analyses, parent-youth relations are strongly related to ideology in each of the five nations. Variations by this index are greater than by any other factor examined.

The Relation Between Autocratic and Democratic Orientations in Family and Other Ideological Domains

Ideological consistency in different social and political areas was hypothesized as most likely among middle-class persons. We shall test this hypothesis among males in three nations: the United States, West Germany, and Italy. The need to simplify the analysis, and controls on social class and sex, necessitated the deletion of Great Britain and Mexico.[52]

Overall, men in the three nations who believe that youth should not have a voice in family decisions are not inclined to think that it is a good idea for students to have some part in running secondary schools, are more apt to be distrustful of others,[53] are less inclined to follow political events,[54] know political leaders[55] and be involved in the political process,[56] and are more likely to have a pessimistic view toward improvement of economic status in the future. The percentage of men autocratic and democratic in family ideology who gave autocratic responses to indicators of the variables listed above were compared within 34 nation and class subgroups. Thirty-three of these comparisons show percentage differences in the expected direction; most of the Q coefficients range between .3 and .5. These results generally show a positive relationship between the orientations of these respondents in family ideology and their views in four other domains: education, intergroup relations, politics, and economics.

In order to provide an adequate test of the consistency hypothesis it is necessary to determine the extent to which individuals who are autocratic in family ideology give autocratic responses to one, two, or more indicators of ideological orientation in other domains. A summated index of autocratic responses to four scales was constructed for this purpose. Respondents with a score of four (the highest score) are high on distrust, never follow political events, are low on political competence and involvement, and feel that their economic situation will not improve in the future. The education item is not included in the index because it is not available in the West German data. The indicator of knowledge of national political leaders is not included since political orientation is covered by two indices. The rela-

---

[52] Middle- and working-class are measured by non-manual and manual occupations respectively. Farmers and farm laborers were not included in this analysis. Respondents who for various reasons did not give an occupation were classified according to the interviewer's rating of the respondent's social class status.

[53] Distrust in people was measured by an index composed of five items which Morris Rosenberg included in his Faith in People scale: "No one is going to care much what happens to you, when you get right down to it"; "If you don't watch yourself, people will take advantage of you"; "Most people can be trusted"; "Most people are more inclined to help others than to think of themselves first"; and "Human nature is fundamentally cooperative." Distrust responses were given a score of 1. High distrust is measured by scores of 4 and 5. See Morris Rosenberg, *Occupations and Values*, New York: The Free Press of Glencoe, 1957.

[54] "Do you follow the accounts of political and governmental affairs: would you say you follow them regularly, from time to time, or never" Low political knowledge is indicated by "never."

[55] "We are also interested in how well known the national leaders of the various political parties are in this country." The percentage who named correctly five or less out of a possible seven is defined as low political knowledge.

[56] Passivity in political issues was measured by responses to the following four items (these items were included in a measure of subjective political competence in *The Civic Culture*, p. 231): "How about the local issues in this town or part of the country? How well do you understand them If such a case arose, how likely is it that you *would actually* do something about it If you made an effort to change this regulation, how likely is it that you would succeed Have you ever done anything to try to influence a local regulation." A "mastery" response to each of the four items was scored "1," while all other responses were given a score of "0." Scores of 0–2 are considered indicative of low political competence and involvement.

Table 8

Relation between family ideological orientations and autocratic views in intergroup relations, politics, and economics among American, German, and Italian men with social class controlled

Nation	Social class	Type of family ideology	Percentage of responses on an index of autocratic responses in three domains*			Total per cent
			Low (0–1)	Moderate (2)	High (3–4)	
United States	Middle Class	Autocratic	47	39	14	100[(28)]
		Democratic	68	24	8	100[(143)]
	Working Class	Autocratic	41	39	20	100[(51)]
		Democratic	59	30	11	100[(137)]
West Germany	Middle Class	Autocratic	47	22	31	100[(55)]
		Democratic	55	31	14	100[(98)]
	Working Class	Autocratic	22	46	32	100[(114)]
		Democratic	35	36	29	100[(124)]
Italy	Middle Class	Autocratic	43	38	19	100[(103)]
		Democratic	63	22	15	100[(65)]
	Working Class	Autocratic	21	28	51	100[(136)]
		Democratic	35	33	32	100[(60)]

* Gamma coefficients for United States middle- and working- class, .38 vs. .32; for West German middle- and working-class, .23 vs. .15; and for Italian middle- and working-class, .31 vs. .33.

tion between this index and orientations in family ideology is shown in Table 8.

In the United States and West Germany ideological consistency appears to be greater among middle-class men; no meaningful class difference in consistency is obtained between middle-class and working-class Italian men (see gamma coefficients at the bottom of Table 8). The inconclusive results among Italian men may be partially a function of socio-religious norms which advocate hierarchical relations between parents and youth. These norms conceivably represent a major source of cultural support for the exclusion of youth from family decision-making in middle-class Italian families. In one study in the United States, for instance, Catholic parents were found to be more controlling in relation to their adolescent offspring than Protestant families at each class level.[57]

These results tentatively add support to our initial assumption that ideological consistency among middle-class persons should be more a function of personality than of environment. Adherence to autocratic orientations among working-class men should be influenced more by traditional cultural patterns. An illustration of the influence of normative support for a belief is shown in the relation between prejudice and personality in the United States North and South. "In both the North and the South, there is a generalized anti-minority prejudice, and this is associated with authoritarianism. But the socially reinforced norms of prejudice in the South are expressed by many non-authoritarian persons who would be unprejudiced in the North."[58]

The effect of social class on ideological consistency is greatest generally for men who are autocratic in family ideology. Middle-class autocrats are much less likely to give one or no autocratic responses to the four scales comprising the summated index. This class difference is most pronounced between middle-class and

[57] Glen H. Elder, Jr., "Structural Variations in the Child Rearing Relationship," *Sociometry*, 25 (September, 1962), pp. 241–262.

[58] Williams, *op. cit.*, p. 91; see also Thomas F. Pettigrew, "Regional Differences in Anti-Negro Prejudice," *The Journal of Social Psychology*, **59** (July, 1959), pp. 28–36.

working-class Italians; 51 per cent of the working-class autocrats in family ideology gave autocratic responses to at least three indicators of orientations in other domains compared to only 19 per cent of the middle-class autocrats.

Differences between nations in the relation between family ideology and the index of autocratic orientation are greatest in the working-class. On the other hand, the proportion of middle-class autocrats and democrats who are low on autocratic responses is relatively similar in each nation, a result which corresponds to the observed cross-national resemblance of professionals in their tendency to hold autocratic views on the involvement of youth in family decision-making (see Table 7).

Political passivity and an aversion toward complex issues among men with autocratic views are expressed in other ways as well. Compared to equalitarians, autocrats in each nation are more inclined to agree that "politics and governments are so complicated that the average man cannot really understand what is going on," and to feel that they do not understand important national and international issues facing their country. Consistent with an inability to name major national leaders, autocrats are less able to name people in cabinet positions or in ministries. The subjective social isolation of autocrats is supported on the behavioral level by their lack of secondary ties; they are less likely to be involved in formal and informal associations.

The social-psychological orientations of men who believe that youth should have little or no voice in family decisions seem to describe a "constricted self," characterized by belief in a strict and unquestioning obedience of children to parents, by moralistic condemnation of deviation, by a generalized distrust of others, by uneasiness in meeting strangers, by feelings of personal frustration, and by a lack of secure group attachments[59]. A contrasting personality type appears to be most characteristic of the middle-class equalitarians. They are least likely to be domineering, distrustful, politically inactive, anti-intellectual, and pessimistic toward the future. On these characteristics they re-

semble the ideal-type democratic personality sketched by Inkeles:

> The citizens of a democracy should be accepting of others rather than alienated and harshly rejecting; open to new experiences, to ideas and impulses rather than excessively timid, fearful, or extremely conventional with regard to new ideas and ways of acting; able to be responsible with constituted authority even though always watchful, rather than blindly submissive to or hostilely rejecting of all authority; tolerant to differences and of ambiguity, rather than rigid and inflexible; able to recognize, control, and channel his emotions, rather than prematurely projecting hostility and other impulses on to others.[60]

In sum, these data tentatively suggest that an individual's consistency across ideological domains is apt to be maximized when the effects of environmental conditions on the expression of personal orientations are minimized. Hence, we find greater consistency among middle-class males in two of three nations than among working-class males.

Summary

Ideology defining the extent to which youth should be involved in family decision-making is partially acquired in parent-child role patterns in childhood and adolescence and is reinforced or modified by education, status changes, and work relationships in adulthood. Feelings of ego security, self-confidence, trust in others, sense of competence, and a broadening of intellectual horizons are intially acquired within a family characterized by an openness in parent-child relations, by consistent emotional support, by consistent and corrective discipline, and by mutual trust and understanding. These self-other orientations may be modified or reinforced by formal education, migration, occupational role, and by work setting. Data from Americans, Britons, West Germans, Italians, and Mexicans, as well as findings obtained by other studies, indicate role experiences to be important in both the formation and support of

---

[59] Williams, *op. cit.*, pp. 109–110.

[60] Alex Inkeles, "National Character and Modern Political Systems," in Francis L. K. Hsu, *Psychological Anthropology*, Homewood, Ill.: The Dorsey Press, 1961, p. 198.

autocratic or democratic family ideology. Sociocultural variations also affect the acquisition and reinforcement of ideological orientations. This is most evident in Mexico and Italy, two nations which are characterized by substantial cultural and institutional support for autocratic family ideology. Role experiences accounted for substantially less variation in ideology in these countries.

The association of democratic and autocratic orientations on adolescent involvement in family decision-making with ideological perspectives in intergroup relations, education, politics, and in economic matters was examined among males in the United States, West Germany, and Italy. Ideological consistency was most evident among middle-class males. Autocrats in family ideology were inclined to exclude youth from responsible positions in secondary school, were more apt to be distrustful of others, to be low on knowledge and involvement in politics, and were more likely to be pessimistic concerning their economic future.

Chapter 8

The Nuclear Family:
Solidarity among Members
and Liaisons with Other Groups

Liaisons with other groups affect the nuclear family whether by strengthening or by weakening its solidarity. This introductory statement first enumerates some of the concepts used to describe solidarity and then mentions a few problems evolving from liaisons with nonfamily groups in modern industrial society.

Family Solidarity. Most writers who discuss solidarity in the nuclear family use concepts such as companionship, complementarity of interests and of personality needs, and "mutuality." For example, Burgess perceives the family group in contemporary society as increasingly held together by "companionship" because most former functions have been distributed to other institutions.[1] Zelditch views the solidarity of the contemporary family as based on a complementary division of labor with the father the instrumental leader, responsible for the relationship of the family to the social structure, and the mother the social-emotional leader, responsible for the relationships between family members.[2] Winch regards the complementarity of personality needs of husband and wife as the basis for solidarity.[3] Wynne views the ability of the family members to adapt to their mutual needs as evidencing solidary relationships. In contrast, the family with rigid rules for interaction is not involved in truly reciprocating relations; instead, it betrays a pseudo-mutuality.[4] Each of these views on solidarity has value in explaining marital adjustment, role adaptations, mate selection, and mental health.

Liaisons with Other Groups. The traditional image of modern society suggests that economic and political relationships are established and maintained for familial

---

[1] Ernest W. Burgess, Harvey J. Locke, and Mary Margaret Thomes, *The Family from Institution to Companionship*, New York: American Book, 1963.
[2] Morris Zelditch, Jr., "Role Differentiation in the Nuclear Family: A Comparative Study," in Talcott Parsons and Robert F. Bales, *The Family, Socialization and Interaction Process*, New York: Free Press, 1955.
[3] Robert F. Winch, *Mate-Selection: A Study of Complementary Needs*, New York: Harper, 1958.
[4] Lyman C. Wynne, Irving M. Ryckoff, Juliana Day, and Stanley I. Hirsch, "Pseudo-Mutuality in the Family Relationships of Schizophrenics," *Psychiatry*, 21 (1958), pp. 205–220.

reasons. Contemporary economic and political institutions are often considered instrumental (or secondary) and are utilized for furthering personal interests. Conversely, the family is considered an existential (or primary) institution in which membership is established by birth in the family of orientation and by marriage and parenthood in the family of procreation.

This image of society is based on the idea that familial ties are permanent, whereas economic and political ties shift with potential economic and status gains. However, in a society in which families of orientation can easily be forgotten and avoided and in which marital ties can be broken readily, this model does not seem appropriate. When both familial and economic ties can be broken easily, personal gratification can be attained either in public (economic and political) spheres or in private familial relationships. With no permanent commitments, ties can be broken in any relationship. Thus competition is established among all groups in which the individual participates.

In past generations the competition between extrafamily and family groups has been greater for men than for women. Traditionally, the husband has been responsible for relationships between the family and the community (through work and community status). The situation is now changing because of the increase in the number of working mothers in middle-class as well as lower-class homes. The wife, too, is facing this competition between commitment to the family and participation in extrafamily groups.

With competition for commitment between public (economic and political) and intimate groups, the character of interpersonal relations changes in all spheres of activity. When an individual can positively identify relations in one group as "primary" and in another group as "secondary," he can easily allocate his emotionally invested acts to the primary group and his affect-free acts to the secondary group. However, as deep personal commitments become possible in both groups, neither can be affect-free. There is then less differentiation in the activities of the public and private groups. Family relationships become more like those in economic and political institutions. Personal involvement and commitment in the family cannot be so complete and certain as they are when sharp distinctions are made between behavior in the private intimate group and the large bureaucratic structure. At the same time, relationships in large bureaucratic structures become more family-like.

This decline in differentiation between large-scale and intimate group interaction may represent a stage in the social process described by Schelsky in the chapter on Open and Closed Families. Shelsky suggests that, with the disillusionment resulting from large-scale organizations, the intimate group becomes overloaded with emotional charge and tensions that must be eventually released in the larger community. The decrease in differentiation of style of interaction implies that the period of great emotional stress in the small nuclear family has passed. The large-scale organization now competes with the nuclear family for commitment.

The bilateral sibling group acts as a possible buffer between the nuclear family relations and the larger social structure in this competition bilateral kinship group can act as a buffer since it provides a permanent identity with siblings but does not make great demands on the individual for services or financial commitments. Moreover, it provides a large degree of freedom in that it is an age-graded group and hence does not require strong ties to the past. Since the position taken in this book is that nuclear-family solidarity can best be viewed in the setting of the kinship system, nuclear-family solidarity has been discussed along with sibling solidarity, kinship bilaterality, mate-lover roles, and closedness in family interaction. The readings in this chapter will focus on conflicts in commitments growing out of liaisons with other groups.

Readings on Solidarity in the Nuclear Family and Liaisons with Other Groups

These papers are related to those in the chapter on open and closed families. The readings on open and closed families viewed family structure from the perspective of broad social change; the readings in this chapter reflect the perspective of family members themselves.

The first paper, by Kirkpatrick, enumerates some dilemmas families face. The alternatives in these dilemmas chosen by the family members determine the major goals emphasized and the character of family integration.[5]

The second paper, by Lois Wladis Hoffman, indicates more specifically how choices made in other groups influence patterns of family integration. Her study shows the effects of the employment of mothers on marital power relations and the division of household tasks. Her findings suggest that, although maternal employment influences family division of labour directly, there is a modification of power structure only when the mothers are not certain whether there should be male dominance. The working mothers in the sample studied who were certain that there should be (or would not be) male dominance, however, had more power in the marital relationship than did the nonworking mothers. The Hoffman investigation also found that when husbands had low-income occupations their wives were more likely to be employed and to have high power in the marital relationship.

The paper by Tomasson, in discussing fertility trends, emphasizes the relationship between motherhood and conceptions of employment-role. Comparing fertility practices among American and Swedish women, his paper indicates that the difference in conception of employment is one of the major factors in variations in fertility and in age at marriage in Sweden and the United States. The Swedish woman sees her work as a profession, whereas the American woman regards hers as a job to help the husband. Thus for the American woman the household role is given priority, whereas in Sweden the occupational role is considered first.

The fourth paper, by Lincoln Day, deals with a comparison of divorce in Australia and the United States. Although Australia, like the United States, exhibits a steady secular trend in the increase of the ratio of divorces to marriages, Australian marriages are generally more stable. Divorce in Australia occurs later and is more likely to involve children than in the United States. In Australia divorce has been difficult to obtain during the first three or four years of marriage because of a long waiting period. Day suggests that alternatives to divorce are developed as solutions to marital

---

[5] See discussion of the Kirkpatrick dilemmas in Bernard Farber, *Family: Organization and Interaction*, San Francisco: Chandler, 1964, pp. 287–288.

difficulties and attributes the difference in marital stability partly to separate male and female friendship groups in Australia somewhat like the Amigo system described in the paper by De Hoyos and De Hoyos. The friendship groups provide emotional intensity lacking in marriage and thus reduce the amount of potential conflict between husband and wife. Day's discussion implies that, unlike problems developed by the Amigo system, those marital problems emerging from conflict between family and same-sex friends in Australia are inconsequential.

26. Cultural and Personal Dilemmas in Family Experience

BY CLIFFORD KIRKPATRICK

THE PURSUIT OF GOALS, whether by an individual or by a culture as an impersonal entity, demands a price. The familiar axiom that one does not get something for nothing is a fundamental principle of human experience. The concept of dilemma needs definition, exploration, and application.

Meaning of the Dilemma

It is not easy to make precisely clear what is meant by dilemma. There are certain dilemmas that have a formal, logical quality. Let us assume, for example, that there are two goals, (a) luxury and (b) economy. These goals are antithetical. In proportion as there is a pursuit of (a) luxury, there is a price to be paid, namely, economy. On the other hand, in proportion as there is pursuit of goal (b), economy, there is a price to be paid, namely, the loss of (a) luxury. This is a formal conception of a dilemma which approaches a platitude. Another more flexible way of considering the concept is to regard it as the choice between alternative goals, each of which demands a contrasting price. The formula then reads: goals (a) and (b) with a price (P_a) to be paid for (a) and a price (P_b) to be paid for (b). This broader con-

SOURCE: *From pp. 89–95, Clifford Kirkpatrick,* The Family: as Process and Institution, *Second Edition, Copyright 1963 The Ronald Press Company.*

ception of a dilemma implies merely that it is difficult to have both (a) and (b) and that corresponding prices (P_a) and (P_b) tend to be different and contrasting. Dilemmas can vary as to generality. There are some which pervade all human experience, the family dilemma being merely a specific aspect of the general principle. Other dilemmas are more specific to the family institution.

Ten Dilemmas Pertaining to the Family as Institution and Group

There follows a discussion of ten dilemmas roughly arranged in the order of decreasing generality with reference to firmness of cultural regulation, parenthood, focus of emotional identification, and timing of mate selection.

1. The defining of a particular family institution involves the dilemma of (a) freedom in family experience versus (b) order and efficiency. The goal (a) implies the possibility of adlibbing roles rather than acting in accordance with cultural definitions. It implies varied interaction and expression of age, sex, and individual potentialities according to the individual's own conception. It implies the freedom to choose a mate for love unhampered by family control or guidance.

The price (P_a) of freedom in family experience is confusion, clash of interests, and perhaps

311

immature behavior. In proportion as individuals are free to play family roles there is an interference of roles and confusion as to role choice. Absence of a clear-cut pattern of authority means a certain unpredictability of behavior. A homely example might be use of the family automobile. Complete freedom for the individuals comprising the family would mean confusion, interference, irritation, and uncertainty as to when the car would be available to a particular person. Freedom may mean irrationality, impulsiveness, and tragic mistakes in courtship possibly leading to divorce.

The goal (b), order and efficiency, implies clarity, predictability of behavior, and a coordination of roles. There may be an efficient division of labor, team work, and the simplicity of conformity to cultural categories.

The price (P_b) of order and efficiency is some degree of frustration. The teeth in a rigid cultural container may hurt. The price may include repression of individuality, denial of creativity, depression of initiative, and distortion of personality by conformity. There may be injustice when varied needs, abilities, and tastes are considered. There is strain when square pegs are forced into round holes. There may be misjudgment on the part of outsiders and diagnoses of a deep love as a mere infatuation.

2. A second dilemma may be expressed as (a) work achievement versus (b) the love-reproduction function. There is a natural desire for (a) work achievement in the sense of doing one's work in the world, accumulating money, getting ahead, and making a name for oneself in regard to whatever values a particular group esteems. The price (P_a) of exercising the work achievement function may be delayed, incomplete, or inadequate family life. A marriage may be postponed because of professional preparation. Life may be ill-balanced because of failure to have love experience. Even assuming love, marriage, and parenthood, concentration upon the work function in life may undermine the intimate, cooperative, affectionate aspects of family interaction. A father writing a book may be too busy for the comradeship of a fishing trip with his ten-year-old son. By the time the book is done, the son prefers a comrade from his own age group.

The (b) love-reproduction function in the sense of participating in love, marriage, and reproduction is worthy and understandable, but it is not without cost. The price (P_b) for the love-reproduction goal may include poverty because of early marriage or numerous children. There may be a denial of special talents, especially in the case of women, who are more closely bound by the love-reproduction function. A man may decline a better job because his family does not want to move. Persons of ability may fail to contribute to progressive social changes because of their preoccupation with romantic and family activities. Big business and the armed forces mitigate this dilemma as they deal increasingly with a family rather than with an individual employee. Every student is faced to some extent with this dilemma in proportion as dating, courtship, and plans for marriage cut into study activities and vocational preparation.

3. A third dilemma may be expressed as (a) personal self-expression versus (b) devoted child rearing. One goal is (a) personal self-satisfaction in the sense of gratification of innumerable adult desires other than work achievement, which involve time, energy, money, and movement to a particular place. The price (P_a) of personal self-expression may be a neglect of the more subtle needs of children. A sudden trip to the movies may mean insecurity for infants; money spent on books does not go for toys. Foreign travel may be at the expense of children's interests. Preoccupation with personal interests may mean failure of the child to identify with the parent and hence loss of effective parental control. Parental selfishness can bring the penalty of personality defects in offspring.

The goal (b) of devoted child rearing implies adequate socialization of children and the shaping of their personalities by close and intimate contact so that they may take their place as well-equipped adults in the community. This goal is socially worthy and personally rewarding. The price (P_b) to be paid for adequate child-rearing is personality frustration in certain areas. Unmarried college students often wave aside the prospect of frustration and quite properly view devoted child rearing as a supreme form of personal self-expression. Thus they eliminate in their minds the dilemma. Experienced parents, on the other hand, grant the impact of child rearing and recognize that travel, recreation, and fulfillment of aesthetic tastes are all affected by the imperatives of devoted child rearing. They recognize that privacy and free use of time with convenient flexibility are both hampered by the presence of children. Friendships with adults and marital interaction may suffer from the obligations of devoted child rearing. The intellectual life is not furthered by reading "Peter Rabbit" for the fortieth time.

4. One can think of (a) flexible, general training versus (b) rigid, specific as a dilemma pertaining to the cultural regulation of child rearing. In the atomic age with its many insecurities, a parent might well seek the goal of generalized preparation in rearing his children. The thought might be, "Nobody knows what is going to happen—let's have our children ready for anything." In regard to a girl, the resolution might be, "Let us train her so that she may obtain a husband and have children; but let us also train her so that she may earn her own living if there is a failure to marry or if something goes wrong with the family adjustment. Just to be on the safe side we will make her both loving and aggressive." The penalty (P_a) for (a) flexible, general training may be confusion. To be prepared for everything is to be prepared for nothing. To be trained for countless different roles is to lack incentive for any particular role.

The other goal, (b), rigid and specific training, is more characteristic of a sacred than of a secular society. Much can be said for setting up clear-cut expectations and shaping the formative years of childhood with reference to a specific role, as for example that of wife and mother. There is a price (P_b), however, which includes the possibility of failure if the specific training fails to meet the circumstances that exist at maturity. Again there may be frustration when the expectations established in the course of a rigid, specific training fail to be realized. A girl trained for motherhood may fail to marry.

A generation of American youth was trained to abhor war and to prepare itself specifically for peaceful pursuits; these expectations were violated with the outbreak of World War II. Boys trained to participate in family life upon attaining maturity found themselves forced to do without normal family life. A boy trained for vigorous self-assertion found himself as a soldier in an authoritarian situation which demanded submissive inhibition.

5. The phrase (a) high aspiration level for children versus (b) realistic expectations represents another dilemma pertaining to parenthood. It is well to tell children to hitch their wagons to stars. It is well to provide them with love and security in expectation of roles which involve the giving and receiving of love. There is a price (P_a), however, for any high aspiration level, and certainly for high familial aspirations developed in early childhood. The price includes frustration and disillusionment. Family satisfactions may not be maintained in marriage or seem at variance with the easier satisfactions derived as privileged children. There may be a shock at the rupture of ties with loving and indulgent parents. Disillusionment may result from the unfavorable contrast between family members and persons with whom the children have contact as adults. The good family can be too good to prepare children for a harsh world.

Realistic expectations (b) prepare offspring for sudden changes, for troubles, difficulties, and insecurity in family life. A story is told of a father who encouraged an infant to jump from a table into his arms by "Daddy will catch you." Then he let the child fall with a warning, "That will teach you not to believe what you are told." Extremes aside, there is a price (P_b) to be paid for shaping the more somber, realistic expectations. There may be cynicism or withdrawal from situations because of the expectation that they are dangerous. Protective mechanisms may be set up in order to avoid emotional risks. There may be lack of motivation to participate in life patterns which have not been favorably described in the process of shaping expectations. Again, there may be indecision in that alternatives seem unattractive because of the influence of prior training. If a child comes to regard life as a grim game, he may refuse to play it fully, richly, and with distinction as an adult.

6. The next dilemma may be expressed by the phrase (a) family loyalty versus (b) community loyalty. This dilemma pertains to the focus of emotional identification. The goal of loyalty to kinfolk is commendable and highly

esteemed in many cultures. Like the horns of other dilemmas, it demands a price. The price (P_a) of family loyalty includes the consequences of evading civic duty. Ancient China, a country once noted for its family loyalty, was also characterized by corruption and nepotism in government. The conspicuous illustration from American culture would be the refusal to perform military service in the interest of family support or the maintenance of family relationships. An additional price of family loyalty is a narrowness of outlook.

The contrasting goal of community loyalty (b) is traditionally associated with patriotism. Culture regulates the community as well as the family in the interest of coordinated functioning and group survival. This goal of community loyalty may mean a severe price (P_b) in the sense of violation of kinship ties by separation, financial restrictions, and even the denouncing of kinfolk to legal, political, or military authorities. In recent decades millions of American men and no small number of women placed the goal of community loyalty above family loyalty, with resulting family losses, deprivation for children, bereavement, and financial sacrifices. Not uncommonly a postponement of marriage or perhaps the denial of marriage and the experiences associated with family life is the price which must be paid for community loyalty.

7. A similar dilemma may be labeled (a) extensive, casual association versus (b) restricted, intensive association. This dilemma in its broadest term involves spreading as compared with concentrating the risks implied in association with others. The price (P_a) of extensive, casual association is superficiality in social relationships. The kindred, lineage, and extended family are groups which do not give the emotional intensity expressed between husbands and wives, parents and children.

The price (P_b) of restricted, intensive association as found in the nuclear family is, in essence, vulnerability. Bacon remarked that "He who hath wife and children hath given hostages to fortune." No relations are more meaningful than those between husband and wife, parent and child. Yet the very meaningfulness of these relationships in the nuclear family exposes persons to risk. The slender tie of affection between husband and wife may be broken by divorce. Bereavement is a traumatic experience in proportion to love for the departed family member.

8. A very general dilemma concerning focus of emotional identification may be labeled (a) love experience versus (b) love safety. Love experience can be regarded as a desirable goal in terms of intensity, romanticism, and adventure. The price (P_a) of giving one's self freely to love experience is essentially the risk of getting hurt by failure or loss. Furthermore, a profound love commitment makes it difficult to become emotionally detached. Devotion merges into crippling fixations which make it difficult to terminate a relationship which is unsatisfactory, unwise, or immature.

The alternate goal of (b), love safety, implies a self-protection from painful intensity of experience. It implies a minimizing of the shocks that come from bereavement, from other ruptured love relationships, and from the servitude which results from any deep emotional commitment. The price (P_b) of pursuing a goal of love safety is impoverishment of emotional experience and a superficiality in the design for living.

The dilemma here discussed is really part of the larger pleasure-pain dilemma. To be an animal with a nervous system capable of recording pleasure means the capacity for pain. The contented cow does not know ecstasy, but it does not suffer the pangs of a broken heart. In the emotional sphere, one can play for high stakes or for low stakes.

9. A ninth dilemma reads (a) free sex expression versus (b) sex restraint in support of family values. Free sex expression (a) implies experience for wise mate selection and a check upon sexual compatibility in marriage. This goal is associated with release of sex tension and the thrills of love adventure. The price (P_a) includes the weakening of marriage as a relationship implying exclusive sex privileges. The choice of this horn of the dilemma permits avoidance of marriage and accent on a recreational aspect of sex to the neglect of the reproductive aspects. Furthermore, there may be insecurity, social stigma, and emotional superficiality.

The alternative (b), sex restraint in support of

family values, gives vitality, continuity, and integration in family living. Marriage has a monopoly on sex expression and is correspondingly unique and important. The price (P_b) of channeling sex exclusively into the marital relationship implies frustration and a rather narrow range of sex expression. Theoretically, except for death or remarriage, there would be sex expression with only one person. The fact of frustration implies secondary effects such as, for example, substitute sex outlets. The price also includes mate selection without adequate knowledge of probable sex compatibility in marriage. Sex tension may prompt a hasty and unwise marriage. Furthermore, there may be a handicap in competition for mates because of sex restraint.

10. A final dilemma reads (a) early marriage versus (b) mature, discriminating mate selection. This dilemma pertains to the timing of mate selection. The choice of (a) early marriage implies approved sex expression following biological maturity and, furthermore, the possibility of parenthood while still young. The choice implies quick success in competition for mates and more years of marriage as an approved social status. There is pleasure of course in acting upon impulse. The price (P_a) of early marriage is inadequate economic and educational preparation. A hasty marriage may be an unwise marriage leading to divorce and tragic consequences to self and children. Persons marrying young face the possibility of growing apart because of unequal maturation.

The goal of (b) mature, discriminating mate selection implies wise choice of a mate and proper preparation for marriage. Maturity brings an awareness of alternatives, a sense of time perspective, and perhaps a better prospect of marital stability. Maturity and discrimination mean a richer companionship in marriage. The price (P_b) includes delay in finding a mate and perhaps failure to marry. In a long search for a straight stick, perhaps the forest ends without a straight stick being found. Furthermore there may be sex frustration, assuming adherence to existing taboos upon premarital sex expression. Parenthood may be unduly delayed and there may be impatience, self doubts, and perhaps a decline of adaptability.

27. Effects of the Employment of Mothers on Parental Power Relations and the Division of Household Tasks[*]

BY LOIS WLADIS HOFFMAN

THE EMPLOYMENT OF MOTHERS may be seen as part of a general trend toward a decrease in the differentiation of sex roles. Other variables that might be included in this trend are: the increased participation of fathers in routine household tasks, a change in power relations from male dominance toward husband-wife equality, and corresponding changes in ideology about sex roles in the family.

Each of these variables can be seen as mutually reinforcing. For example, the mother's outside employment may exert a pressure toward the father's increased participation in household tasks. The increased participation of the father, on the other hand, makes the mother's employment more feasible by lessening the demands of her conventional homemaking role. In addition, the holding of a favorable ideology would seem to contribute to the occurrence of both events; while their occurrence, for what-

ever reason, should stimulate the development of a legitimizing ideology.

Husband-wife power relations might be similarly interrelated. Thus, it seems likely that employment would increase a woman's power vis-à-vis her husband because of the socially defined importance of the monetary contribution; while a woman who already had high power would be more likely to go to work because of greater motivation, greater control over her own decisions, and greater success in obtaining her husband's participation in household tasks. Finally, the endorsement or rejection of a male dominance ideology might affect both the woman's employment and her power, and be affected by each of these variables in turn.

These four variables, then, might be seen as a system in which a change in one effects change in the others. However, at any given time, and particularly in periods of rapid social change, they may exert counterpressures and work against each other, since each can be separately affected by variables external to the system. For example, a wife may be forced to seek employment even though her husband is dominant, takes no part in household tasks, and there is ideological support for both these conditions. While it is true that such a family might resist mother employment longer than other families, the monetary advantages might eventually override this resistance. What happens in this situation? Does the mother's employment exert

SOURCE: Marriage and Family Living, *Volume 22 (February, 1960), pp. 27–35. Reprinted by permission of the National Council on Family Relations.*

* This paper is based on a doctoral dissertation, submitted to the University of Michigan in 1958. The data were collected as part of a larger project supported by the Foundation's Fund for Research in Psychiatry and supplemented by a grant from the National Institute of Mental Health. Some of the analyses reported here were made possible by a grant from the Horace H. Rackham Graduate Student Research Fund.

changes in the family structure despite the existing ideology, or must the ideology be supportive for employment to have such an effect? This problem is the focus of the present study.

Treating the mother's employment as the independent variable, this study deals with its effects on the husband's and wife's household participation and on the husband-wife power relationship *when the relevant ideologies are held constant*. The question essentially is this: is the mother's employment, unabetted by ideology, sufficient to induce these changes in family structure? The specific hypotheses are as follows:

Hypothesis 1. The employment of the mother outside the home will function to decrease her participation in household tasks and to increase that of her husband.

Hypothesis 2. The employment of the mother outside the home will function to decrease her decision-making in household tasks (activity control) and to increase that of her husband.

Hypothesis 3. The employment of the mother outside the home will function to increase her power vis-à-vis her husband.

The assumption behind the first hypothesis is simply that the stress of working, in terms of the time and effort it takes on the part of the mother, makes it necessary for the husband to take over some of her household tasks in order to maintain the smooth functioning of the household. Of the three hypotheses, this one would appear to be the most mechanical and direct in nature.

The second hypothesis is closely related to the first. Most household decisions are rather trivial and are usually made routinely by the person who performs the activity in question, e.g., what will be made for supper is apt to be decided by the person who cooks. It follows that if the mother's employment brings about a decrease in her household task participation and an increase in that of her husband (as stated in Hypothesis 1), there should be corresponding changes in household decision-making or activity control. Further, it seems likely that the working mother would be more willing to relinquish her activity control, not only in order to gain her husband's help with tasks, but also because of the alterna-

tive gratification she may receive from having one sphere, her outside job, which is her own.

The third hypothesis deals with the power aspect of the husband-wife relationship. Power is quite different from activity control. Whereas the latter concerns the sheer volume of decisions made, most of which are of relatively little concern to other persons, power involves decisions which may have important effects on others. As a simple approximation of "importance," power will be considered here as the extent to which one person decides over the other's behavior. The prediction that the mother's employment will function to increase her power vis-à-vis her husband is based on three assumptions: (a) money is an important basis of power so that the control of money leads to the possession of power; (b) a person has more control over the money he earns himself than other persons have; (c) the role of wage earner in our society carries with it greater opportunites for developing feelings of achievement, competence, and contribution than does the role of housewife. The theory is that by her employment the mother obtains control of a certain amount of money, thus gaining greater control over financial decisions. This financial control may also enable her to gain more extensive familial power. Furthermore, because she is working and earning money, she gains a new concept of her own worth and thus becomes more assertive. In short, both the husband and the wife are more likely to accept the legitimacy of the working woman's claim to power.

It can be seen that the hypothesis regarding power is more complex than the others since it involves intervening ideational processes between the mother's employment and the dependent variable.

Method

Sample. The total sample included 324 intact families with at least one child in the third through sixth grades of three elementary schools in Detroit, Michigan. The schools were selected so that the sample drawn would represent Detroit socio-economically, but would be relatively homogenous with respect to ethnic factors, excluding Negroes and families living in neighborhoods associated with particular ethnic groups.

Within this sample were eighty-nine families with working mothers, and eighty-nine families with nonworking mothers who were closely matched to them with respect to those characteristics, both ideological and situational, which seemed most likely to relate to the independent and dependent variables. *The matched sample was used to test the three hypotheses presented earlier;* i.e., scores obtained by the "working" families on the dependent variables were compared with those obtained by the matched "nonworking" families.

The total sample of 324 families was used initially to assess the importance of the ideology controls. It was then kept in reserve for purposes of making *post hoc* analyses should the hypotheses not be confirmed, and it therefore became necessary to ascertain which of the matching controls were responsible for nullifying relationships.

Control on Ideology. Two ideological variables were used in matching the respondents:

1. Mother's attitude about the extent to which men should not participate in household tasks— to be called *traditional sex role ideology.*

2. Mother's attitude about the extent to which men should hold superordinate positions over women—to be called *male dominance ideology.*

Endorsement of the traditional sex role and male dominance ideologies was expected to relate to low household participation by the husband and to husband dominance, respectively. Such endorsement was also expected to be negatively related to the mother's employment as discussed earlier; i.e., the ideologies and the behavioral patterns they imply would operate against her employment. Therefore, if these ideologies were not controlled, any relationship found between mother employment and family structure might be the spurious result of ideology and the corresponding behavior patterns existing before employment, instead of reflecting a true effect of employment. By controlling these variables, then, they can be eliminated as selective factors, and any differences found between the working and non-

working families can more readily be attributed to the independent operation of the employment variable. It should be pointed out, however, that instituting these controls makes for a strict test of the hypotheses, because any changes in ideology *and the corresponding behavior patterns* that might have resulted from mother employment by the time the data were collected would also be eliminated.[1]

Situational Controls. Matching, with respect to situational factors, was greatly facilitated by the homogeneity of the total sample. Thus, as already indicated, it was possible to remove the following as extraneous factors: absence of a parent; rural and ethnic factors; and, to some extent, stage in the family cycle. In addition, three situational variables were used in setting up the eighty-nine matched pairs: husband's occupation, number of children under thirteen years of age, and age of oldest child. Husband's occupation and age and number of children are known to be related to women's employment status.[2] Age and number of children, in addition, seemed likely to affect the division of labor in that having many young children should increase the work load, while having one's oldest child near maturity would provide potential assistance with the housework. Furthermore, by controlling on both of these variables the control on family cycle—felt to be potentially related to power—is more effective than merely relying on the presence of an elementary school child. Finally, the husband's occupation also seemed likely to relate to both dependent variables— division of labor and power.[3]

Measures. Data reported here were gathered from two sources: paper and pencil interviews with the children and mailed questionnaires

[1] This is particularly true, since matching on ideology was precise; i.e., actual scores were used rather than general high-low distinctions.

[2] National Manpower Council, *Womanpower,* New York: Columbia University Press, 1956.

[3] After the data were collected it was discovered that a number of families included persons who were not members of the conjugal family. Such persons were disproportionately represented in the families with working mothers ($\chi^2 = 5.57$; $p < .02$). Accordingly, as a final control all such families were excluded from the analyses dealing with the division of labor and activity control.

answered by the mothers. The children's interviews were used for measuring the dependent variables, while the mothers' questionnaires were used for measuring the independent and control variables.

The questions used in the child interview were similar in form to those developed by Herbst.[4] There were thirty-three paired items in all, the child being asked in each case which family members *do* a particular routine household activity and which members *decide* about that activity. For example, one item pair was as follows:

Who cooks the evening meal?
Who decides what to cook for the evening meal?

These questions were read to the child, who indicated his response by *encircling or underlining* the appropriate answers from a list of household persons. Circles were used to designate major actors, and underlines to designate minor ones. It was clearly indicated that the interviewer was interested in the child's particular family rather than general social norms.

TASK PARTICIPATION. The task participation scores were computed for mothers and for fathers by scoring two points when the parent was reported to have a major role in *doing* a given household activity, one point when he was reported to have a minor role, and zero when he was reported to have no role. Each parent was thus given a total activity participation score based on the child's responses to all the thirty-three *doing* questions. In addition subscores were computed. For example, each parent was given a score for participation in Mother's Household Area. This was based only on those items which asked about activities that are conventionally done by mothers. Similarly, task participation scores were computed for Father's Household Area, Common Household Area, and Child Care Area, the last being differentiated not by the conventional performer of the role but by the content of the activity inself.[5]

ACTIVITY CONTROL. Whereas the measure of task participation used only the *doing* questions in the child interview, the measurement of decision-making participation or activity control used only the *deciding* questions. Each family was assigned two activity control scores, each based on the total thirty-three items. One score represented the mother's activity control and the other, the father's. In addition to differentiating major from minor actors (as in the task participation measure), these scores took into account the exclusiveness of the deciding role.

POWER RELATIONSHIP. In using the child interview responses to measure the power relationship between the mother and father, both the *doing* and *deciding* questions were used, a pair of questions constituting the coding unit. In assigning weights to these responses in order to yield a measure of power, the assumption was made that when the child reports that one parent performs an act and the *other* parent makes the decision about the act, he is telling something about the power relationship between his parents. Underlying this assumption are the notions that (a) power is expressed in the extent to which one parent decides over the other's behavior; (b) when a child gives such a response, he may or may not be reporting the actual situation regarding that particular act, but his over-all pattern of responses to the total set of questions reflects his general picture of the mother-father relationship. Thus, for example, a child who responded to all the items by indicating that his father alone did all of the tasks but that his mother alone did all of the deciding about these tasks, would have a general picture of his father as being low-powered in relation to the mother. Finally, it is felt that (c) the child is an observer of the family scene, and, while a given child may perceptually distort the picture somewhat, the scores in the aggregate are valid.

To state the operational definition of power simply: power is the extent to which one parent decides over the other parent's behavior more than the other decides over his behavior. The specific weighting system is reported in Table 1. Since only the over-all scores are seen as valid indicators of power, as indicated above, it was felt that small differences in scores should not

[4] P. G. Herbst, "The Measurement of Family Relationships," *Human Relations*, 6 (1953), pp. 3–30.
[5] The total participation score is more than the sum of the four subscores because some of the thirty-three items did not fit the four household area categories.

Table 1

Scoring system for parental power measure

Child's response	Weight
Mother decides, father does	3
Mother decides, both do	2
Both decide, father does	1
Mother decides, mother does; father decides, father does, both decide, both do; neither parent decides, neither parent does	0
Both decide, mother does	−1
Father decides, both do	−2
Father decides, mother does	−3

be stressed. Therefore, the distribution of power scores was split at the midpoint for purposes of making statistical tests.

TRADITIONAL SEX ROLE IDEOLOGY. The scores used in matching on sex role ideology were based on the degree of agreement the mothers indicated with the following items:

1. Raising children is much more a mother's job than a father's.

2. Except in special cases, the wife should do the cooking and house cleaning, and the husband should provide the family with money.

3. If the man is working to support the family, his wife has no right to expect him to work when he's at home.

4. A man who helps around the kitchen is doing more than should be expected.

5. A man ought to feel free to relax when he gets home from work.

All items were answered on a four point scale: *agree a lot, agree, disagree, disagree a lot.* The greater the agreement, the greater the endorsement of traditional sex role ideology.

To assess the importance of sex role ideology as a control, the scores on this measure for the total sample were related to the father's participation in Mother's Household Area and in Total Activities. Both of these relationships were significant, endorsement of traditional sex role ideology being associated with low father participation in Mother's Household Area ($x^2 = 6.61$; $p < .006$)[6] and with low father

participation in Total Activities ($x^2 = 12.38$; $p < .0004$). Traditional sex role ideology also related significantly to mother's working status; nonworking women being more likely to endorse it than working women ($x^2 = 5.82$; $p < .007$). Thus, it would appear that sex role ideology is an important variable to control in studying mother employment and the division of labor in the home.

MALE DOMINANCE IDEOLOGY. The scores used in matching on male dominance ideology were based on the degree of agreement mothers indicated with the following items:

1. Some equality in marriage is a good thing, but by and large the husband ought to have the main say-so in family matters.

2. It goes against human nature to place women in positions of authority over men.

3. A wife does better to vote the way her husband does, because he probably knows more about such things.

4. Men should make the really important decisions in the family.

Items were answered and scored in the same way as the sex role items.[7]

It was found that scores on this measure for the total sample did not relate to the power scores nor to mother's working status. Further analysis, however, revealed that although the expected relationship did not exist for the working group, endorsement of male dominance was associated with low mother power for the nonworking group ($x^2 = 2.55$; $p < .06$).[8] These findings seem to suggest the possibility of some unanticipated interaction between male dominance ideology and mother's working status. This point will be taken up in more detail in the discussion of the power findings.

[6] All chi-squares reported in this paper have one degree of freedom. Where direction is predicted, the chi-square is converted to a *t*-score for purposes of making one-tailed tests of statistical significance.

[7] Ideology questionnaires were also answered separately by fathers. The correlations between mothers' and fathers' scores on traditional sex role ideology and male dominance ideology were .32 and .36 respectively, both being significant at better than the .01 level. Only the mother's ideology was used in the present study.

[8] This finding also occurred with fathers' responses. Endorsement of male dominance by the father is associated with low mother power in the working-mother families ($x^2 = 4.14$; $p < .03$), but not in families where the mother does not work.

Results and Discussion

Hypothesis 1—Task Participation. Significance tests were made comparing the matched pairs on father's participation and mother's participation, in each of the four household areas and in the total activities. The results are reported in Table 2.

Table 2

Mother's working status and household task participation of mother and father

Household area	Direction of relationship	T-scores	p less than
Mother's participation			
Mother's	W < NW*	2.50	.007
Father's	W < NW	2.07	.02
Common	W < NW	2.92	.002
Child-care	W < NW	—	—†
Total activities	W < NW	—	—
Father's participation			
Mother's	W > NW	—	—
	(FT > NW)‡(2.09)		(.02)
Father's	W > NW	—	—
Common	W > NW	1.70	.05
Child-care	W > NW	—	—
	(FT > NW)(2.39)		(.01)
Total activities	W > NW	2.46	.03

Note: N = 75. This includes only families which do not have servants or outside relatives as regular household participants.

* W = working; NW = nonworking.

† In all tables T-scores and p values are not reported if the latter exceeds .10.

‡ The numbers in parentheses refer to comparisons which included only full-time working mothers (FT) and the nonworking mothers matched to them, 45 pairs in all.

It can be seen that all results are in the predicted direction, with employed mothers participating less and their husbands participating more in all areas. The findings are significant for the mother's participation in Mother's, Father's, and Common Household Areas. This pattern is unchanged when full-time workers are differentiated from part-time workers. The significant differences in father's participation involve the Common Household Area, Total Activities, and, when the comparison is made between families with full-time working mothers and matched families with nonworking mothers, the Mother's Household and Child Care Areas.

If one views the mother and father participation scores as complements of one another, the over-all pattern of the data clearly supports the hypothesis that the employment of mothers functions to decrease their participation in household tasks and increase that of the fathers.

It should be noted that when these same comparisons were made using the total sample all differences except one were significant. The single exception, father's participation in Father's Household Area, may have resulted from the low ceiling of the particular measure; that is, most fathers had maximum participation scores in Father's Household Area.[9]

Hypothesis 2—Activity Control. Hypothesis 2 receives strong support from the data (Table 3). Working mothers have significantly less activity control than nonworking mothers and their husbands have significantly more, thus confirming the hypothesis.

Table 3

Mother's working status and activity control

Activity control	Direction of relationship	T-scores	p less than
Mother's control	W < NW	2.98	.002
Father's control	W > NW	2.66	.004

Note: N = 75. This includes only families which do not have servants or outside relatives as regular household participants.

Hypothesis 3—Power. Hypothesis 3 was tested by comparing power scores for the matched pairs of working and nonworking women. *No difference was found.* When the *total* sample was examined, however, it was found that working

[9] Although not germaine to the present analysis, it is interesting to note that maximum effects occur when ideology and employment operate in the same direction. That is, the husband's participation is highest when the wife is employed and the ideology is nontraditional, lowest when neither of these conditions exist, and in-between when only one of them exists.

mothers did have more power than nonworking mothers ($\chi^2 = 2.43$; $p < .06$).[10] *This difference was apparently completely washed out by the matching.*

Matching on male dominance ideology alone, however, cannot account for the washing out of the relationship, since, as already noted, endorsement of this ideology relates to high mother power only in the nonworking group. It will be recalled, however, that the two groups were also matched on husband's occupation, number of children under thirteen years of age, and age of oldest child. To throw further light on the relationship between mother's employment status and power, the total sample was examined to see how much each of the ideological and situational control variables, alone and in various combinations, related to employment status and to power.

The results of these analyses showed that the most effective controls were (a) husband's occupation and (b) the other two situational controls —number of children under thirteen and age of oldest child—which, acting in combination, resulted in a control on having only one child. Where the husbands had low income occupations, the wives were more likely to be employed ($\chi^2 = 5.57$; $p < .02$)[11] and also to have high power ($\chi^2 = 2.32$; $p < .15$).[12] This means that in the total sample the working group included relatively more women from lower income families, and, since in lower income

families the woman's power is higher, the correlation between the woman's employment and power was thereby heightened. Women with only one child were more likely to be employed than other women ($\chi^2 = 18.57$; $p < .001$) and more likely to have high power ($\chi^2 = 3.78$; $p < .06$).[13] This means that in the total sample the working group included more women with only one child than the nonworking group—actually 25 per cent as compared to 7 per cent; and, since having only one child relates positively to a mother's power, the correlation between mother's employment and power was heightened.

If the correlation obtained between working and power in the total sample was thus affected by the relationship of each of these variables to husband's occupation and family composition, it would seem to follow that a relationship between mother employment and mother power found in the total sample here, as well as in other studies, is merely the spurious result of failing to institute the necessary controls. Yet, there is considerable theoretical basis for assuming that outside employment does exert a pressure toward increasing a woman's power. At least four general theories predicting this can be inferred from the existing literature.

1. The person who receives wages in exchange for services has more control over this money than other family members; and this control can be used, implicitly or explicitly, to wield power in the family.

2. Society attaches greater value to the role of wage earner than to that of housewife and thus legitimizes for both parents the notion that the former should have more power.

3. An independent supply of money enables the working woman to exert her influence to a

---

[10] The small size of the relationship between mother employment and power is probably due partly to the homogeneity of the total sample. The Detroit Area Study (University of Michigan), which used a more heterogeneous sample, found a much stronger relationship ($\chi^2 = 15.22$). But when a sample similar in makeup to the one used here was pulled out, the relationship was comparable to that found here ($\chi^2 = 3.79$).

[11] This probability and all that follow are based on the two-tailed test.

[12] The positive association between social status of husband's occupation and his dominance has also been reported in M. Gold, *American Sociological Review*, **23** (1958), pp. 64–74; and in D. Heer, *Social Forces*, **36** (1958), pp. 341–347. It is interesting that although the present study shows this same pattern it also shows high social status of father's occupation to be associated with rejection of male dominance ideology by both mothers ($\chi^2 = 5.75$; $p < .02$) and fathers ($\chi^2 = 10.30$; p. $< .01$).

[13] The Detroit Area Study found similarly that mothers of only one child were more active than other mothers in making important family decisions. The relationship was not continuous, there being no further differences as the number of children increased beyond one. Heer (*Ibid.*), using only actively affiliated Catholics as subjects, found a continuous relationship, the mother's power varying inversely with the number of her children. He also reported that standardizing scores for number of children diminished but did not eliminate power differences between working and nonworking wives.

greater extent because she is less dependent on her husband and could, if necessary, support herself in the event of the dissolution of the marriage.

4. Working outside the home provides more social interaction than being a housewife. This interaction has been seen as leading to an increase in the wife's power because of: (a) the development of social skills which are useful in influencing her husband; (b) the development of self-confidence; (c) the greater knowledge of alternative situations that exist in other families; and (d) the more frequent interaction with men, which may result in the feeling that remarriage is feasible.

Certain of these theories appear to be somewhat limited. For example, "3" as well as "4d" assume a rather tenuous marriage. Furthermore, it may be argued that the assumption underlying "4a" that the development of social skills is important implies that family decisions are based on arguing and wit rather than on the simple assertion of power, as may often be the case.

Theories "1," "2," and "4b" are those which provided the theoretical basis presented earlier for the hypothesis that the mother's outside employment increases her power. These particular theories in combination seem too sound to be readily dismissed despite the fact that the analysis thus far raises serious doubt about the existence of a relationship between employment and power. Because of the face validity of these theories, and because of the sheer predominance of theories predicting a relationship between the mother's employment and power, further examination of the relationship was undertaken.

EMPLOYMENT, IDEOLOGY, AND POWER. A possible explanation for the discrepancy found between theory and data is as follows: the mother's employment does exert a force in the direction of increasing her power in the home, but there is a counterforce that prevents the effects from taking place in a simple one-to-one fashion. Such a counterforce might be the prevailing male dominance ideology. Perhaps the notion that men should be dominant is so deeply ingrained that any threat to the assymetric balance of power in the marriage relationship is warded off because a certain amount of husband dominance is essential for the wife to feel adequately feminine, for her husband to feel adequately masculine, and for the integrity of the marriage.[14]

To explore this idea further, the relationship between a mother's working status and parental power was analyzed within ideology groups. It was found (Table 4) that women who endorsed

Table 4

Mother's male dominance ideology and the relationship between mother's working status and parental power—total sample

Mother's position on male dominance ideology scale	Relationship found between working status and mother's power	N	χ^2	p less than*
Endorsement of male dominance (top half)	Working mothers have *more* power than non-working mothers	179	4.77	.05
Reserved rejection of male dominance (third quartile)	Working mothers have *less* power than non-working mothers	78	7.39	.01
Complete rejection of male dominance (fourth quartile)	Working mothers have *more* power than non-working mothers	67	6.07	.02

* The probabilities reported in this table are two-tailed.

male dominance, as well as those who completely rejected it, showed the originally hypothesized positive relationship between the

[14] The implication here that wife dominance is dysfunctional to the marriage relationship is borne out by data reported by D. Wolfe, "Power and Authority in the Family," *Studies in Social Power*, D. Cartwright, (ed.) Ann Arbor, Mich.: Institute for Social Research, 1959. Wolfe reports that wives in wife-dominant families are less likely to indicate marital satisfaction than are wives in either husband-dominant or equalitarian families.

mother's working status and power. However, women who indicated reserved rejection of male dominance, i.e., those who rejected it but not completely or consistently, showed an inverse relationship. For this group, mother's employment is associated with having low power.

The matched sample showed a similar pattern (Table 5), although for purposes of the statistical analysis it was necessary to combine the "endorsement" and "complete rejection" groups.[15] To see further if this pattern resulted from spurious factors, the "reserved rejection"

Table 5

Mother's male dominance ideology and the relationship between mother's working status and parental power—matched sample

Mother's position on male dominance ideology scale	Relationship found between working status and mother's power	No. of pairs*	t†	p less than‡
Endorsement of male dominance; and	Working mothers have *more* power than non-working mothers	49	1.81	.07
Complete rejection of male dominance		14		
Reserved rejection of male dominance	Working mothers have *less* power than non-working mothers	21	1.86	.06

* The number of pairs does not total eighty-nine because five pairs of respondents were dropped when both respondents did not fall within the same ideology grouping.

† t-test for correlated proportions.

‡ The probabilities reported in this table are two-tailed.

[15] Combining was necessary because the "complete rejection" group in the matched sample included so few subjects that the expected frequency of the cells was less than required. It was warranted because the expected as well as the obtained direction of the relationship was the same in the two groups.

group was compared with the other two on all of the control variables as well as education of parents, duration of mother's employment, and whether the mother worked part or full time. The "reserved rejection" group did not differ from the others on any of these characteristics.

Since the pattern reported in Tables 4 and 5 does not appear to be spurious, it provides interesting material for *post hoc* speculation and has implications for further research. Possibly the male dominance ideology is so deeply imbedded in American culture and personality structure, that *unless strongly rejected*, it operates as a counterforce to the pressure exerted by the mother's working. It is possible that the mother's employment not only exerts pressure toward increasing her power through giving her greater monetary control, a more legitimized claim to power, and greater self-confidence; but that her employment in and of itself may be a threat to the status quo of the marriage relationship. *Thus, whereas working may exert a pressure toward her increased power in the family, the male dominance ideology might lead her to become actually less dominant than before in order to compensate for the threat offered by the sheer fact of her employment.* To restore the former assymetric balance the wife may be compelled to express less power in direct interaction than before she went to work.

The relationships found for the "reserved rejection" and "complete rejection" groups may be understood in these terms. That is, in the latter group there is no counterforce and the effect of employment can operate unabated; whereas in the former group the working women respond to the threat of their employment by becoming less dominant than before in interacting with their husbands.[16]

If this explanation is accepted, however, the group *endorsing male* dominance needs further consideration, since the working women in this group do have more power. Three alternative explanations are here set forth that attempt to explain why these women may exempt their own

[16] This same theory and the unusual interaction between male dominance ideology, employment, and power explain the failure, reported earlier, to find a relationship between endorsement of male dominance and low mother power for the working women.

husbands from the right to deference which they accord men in general.

1. When women who endorse male dominance go to work, it is more likely to be out of economic necessity. Going to work under these conditions may lead them to perceive their husbands as failures and, therefore, undeserving of the deference due men in general.

2. Even if women endorsing male dominance do not go to work out of economic necessity, they may be more likely than other women to consider the economic role as the legitimate basis of power, since this is in keeping with a male dominance ideology. If this were true, the fact of their working, for whatever reason, would lead them to exempt their own situation from that which they consider generally appropriate.

3. Women who endorse male dominance may have a perception of masculinity which is so exaggerated that their husbands must fall short of this ideal. When they go to work, the counteracting force of the ideology is negated and does not block the power increments that result from employment. The counterforce is negated because these women consider their own husbands as inadequate compared to their ideal of masculinity and, hence, not deserving of deference. Neither do they feel their femininity threatened by employment, because, compared to their conceptions of masculinity, they are quite feminine.

Adequate tests of these *post hoc* hypotheses could not be made with the data at hand. However, two inferences drawn from the first hypothesis were tested using interview data obtained from the mothers. The first inference is that women who report they are working because of economic necessity will have more power than women who report they are working for other reasons. This was tested and confirmed ($\chi^2 = 4.48$; $p < .05$). The second inference is that women who endorse male dominance should be more likely to report that they are working because of economic necessity than women who reject male dominance. This was tested, but the data indicated no such tendency. An inference from the second hypothesis that women endorsing male dominance would consider earning money as the main basis of power, was not supported by the interview data. These women were no more likely than others to consider earning money as the basis of power in the home. None of the available data had a bearing on the third hypothesis. The lack of any test is unfortunate, because this hypothesis might not only explain the pattern of findings under discussion but is particularly rich in implications for the study of male-female interaction in general.[17]

Summary and Conclusions

This study investigated the effects of the mother's outside employment on task participation, routine decision making (activity control), and power structure in the family. The total sample included 324 intact Detroit families having at least one child in elementary school. To highlight mother's employment as the independent variable, eighty-nine of the working women in this group were matched to eighty-nine nonworking women on ideologies about sex roles and male dominance, husband's occupation, number of children under thirteen years of age, and age of oldest child. These eighty-nine matched pairs were used to test the hypotheses.

The results were as follows:

1. Working mothers participated less than nonworking mothers in household tasks, and their husbands participated more.

2. Working mothers made fewer decisions about routine household matters than nonworking mothers, and their husbands made more.

3. There was no difference in husband-wife power between working and nonworking women in the matched sample, although in the

[17] It is possible that certain of the employment-power theories listed earlier are more valid for one ideology group than another. For example, one of these theories holds that the mother's wish to be more assertive is restrained only by the fear that doing so might lead to the dissolution of the marriage, and, further, that the economic security resulting from her employment is sufficient to permit the expression of assertiveness. This theory assumes a minimum of affectional ties between husband and wife; therefore, it would be more applicable to the women endorsing male dominance, if these women do, in fact, have greater marital dissatisfaction as suggested in this paper.

total sample working women did have more power than nonworking. Analysis suggested that controls on husband's occupation and on age and number of children accounted for the washing out of the relationship when the matched groups were compared. Further subgroup analyses found the expected positive relationship between employment and power among women who endorsed the male dominance ideology and among women who consistently rejected it; the opposite relationship held for women who showed a reserved rejection of this ideology. This pattern was found both for matched groups and for the total sample. *Post hoc* hypotheses were advanced to account for it.

It may be concluded that a mother's employment leads her husband to assume some of her former household tasks and to become more active in making the corresponding decisions even when ideology is held constant.

The results also suggest that women's employment does not affect family power structure directly but only in interaction with the pre-existing ideologies and personalities of the actors. It seems that power relationships, unlike division of labor, are either too deeply intertwined with psychological needs to respond readily to an outside stimulus, or that mother's employment is too weak a stimulus. The several recent attempts to show the presence or absence of a relationship between mother employment and the husband-wife power, therefore, seem to be oversimplifications of what should be studied as a complex and multivariate phenomenon.

28. Why has American Fertility been so High?

BY RICHARD F. TOMASSON

BETWEEN THE END OF WORLD WAR II and 1963 the population of the United States increased by an average of 1.7 per cent a year. This is more rapid growth than any industrialized nation in Europe had during this period and almost as rapid growth as that of some underdeveloped nations such as India and Iran. The "temporary" high birth rates of the immediate postwar years continued through the 1950's. However, the birth rate has declined each year between 1957 (the highest rate since 1947) and 1963, from 25.3 to 21.6 births per 1,000 population. Other more sensitive measures show that the crude rate reflects a "real" and substantial decline in fertility since 1957.[1] Yet even the relatively low rate for 1963 is higher than that generally reported among the industrialized nations of Europe for a number of years.[2] This paper has been written with two questions in

mind: why has American fertility been so high over the past two decades? And, does the recent decline reflect a downswing in average family size among younger American couples? I want to stress that these are deceptively simple questions and that any attempt to answer them adequately by rigorous standards is impossible.

Sociologists and demographers have verified in detail the commonplace observation that families have become larger than formerly. The most extensive documentation of the changing patterns in family size are the national fertility studies made in 1955 and 1960 by the Scripps Foundation of Miami University together with the Survey Research Center of the University of Michigan.[3] From interviews with over 6,000 wives born between 1916 and 1942 they have found that a peak in family size will be reached by wives born in the years 1931–1935 (aged 25–29 in 1960). They have calculated that these wives will average *at least* 3.3 children by the time they have passed through the childbearing years.[4] (It is important to keep in mind, however, that "expectations" and actual births are

---

[1] "The declining trend in fertility is reflected in almost all measures of period fertility. The crude birth rate, 25.3 live births per 1,000 population in 1957, dropped to 22.4 in 1962. Both the general fertility rate and the total fertility rate declined by 8 per cent during this period. The decline was experienced among both white and nonwhite women bearing children of almost all birth orders from first to fifth." This quotation is from U.S. Department of Health, Education, and Welfare, National Center for Health Statistics, *Natality Statistics Analysis: United States—1962,* Series 21 (No. 1), October, 1964, p. 4.

[2] Iceland might be considered as an exception to this statement. In recent years the birth rate of this small society has been around 28 per thousand.

[3] The 1955 survey is reported in Ronald Freedman, Pascal K. Whelpton, and Arthur A. Campbell, *Family Planning, Sterility, and Population Growth,* New York: McGraw-Hill, 1959. The report on the 1960 survey is being prepared by Whelpton, Campbell, and John Patterson; it will probably be published in 1965. Some of the findings of the 1960 Study, however, have been reported in various places.

[4] Science Service press release, (December 13, 1962).

not the same, but the former appear a good approximation of the latter in the aggregate.[5]) This represents a sizable increase over the 2.4 children their mothers' generation had, married women born in the years 1906–1910.[6] These women (aged 50–54 in 1960) had smaller families than women born in any earlier or later period in our history up through the late 1930's. Their daughters will average almost as many children as did their grandmother's generation. Married women born in the years 1886–1890 (aged 70–74 in 1960) had an average of 3.5 children.[7]

A difference between 2.4 and 3.3 children is tremendous in its growth implications. With a continuation of our present high marriage rates and fairly low death rates an average of 2.2 children per couple would insure something close to a stable population. With an average of 2.4 children, the population would grow slowly, by a fraction of one per cent a year. With an average of 3.3 children it would double in less than 40 years. At this rate, by the time my young children are in their 90's, there would be a billion of us.

But the recent steady decline in the birth rate and other evidence I will touch on later indicate quite clearly that this will not occur. Although our fertility in all likelihood will continue at a relatively high level into the foreseeable future compared with that of the generation born in the decade and a half before World War I or compared with that of western European nations, our birth rate has passed its high-water period (the years 1947 through 1957) and the tide is subsiding.

There are two common beliefs about our high fertility that perhaps deserve comment. The first is that we returned to the large families of the past after World War II. This is not so. In fact, few American wives want large families, if by large we mean more than four children. Only one out of ten American wives want five or more children, and six out of seven want two, three,

or four.[8] On the other hand, few wives want only one child, and the number who want to remain childless has become negligible.

What has happened since the 1930's is that more couples, especially in the middle classes, are having three or four children and fewer are having only one or are remaining childless. Among white wives born in the years 1906–1910, 40 per cent have had only one child or are childless.[9] Of the 17 per cent who are childless, more than half are voluntarily so if we accept the estimate of 8 per cent as an upper limit of sterility among American couples.[10] The virtual disappearance of deliberate childlessness and the sharp decrease in one-child families among couples born after World War I are evidence, I think, of a basic value reorientation in our culture.

That the Depression is the main reason why middle-aged couples had so few children is a second belief that needs to be questioned and reinterpreted. Certainly many couples did not want to have children in the 1930's with husbands out of work; but the wives who had the smallest families, women born around 1909, were only about 30 when the Depression was over and prosperity began to return. The most the Depression explains is why birth rates were so low through the 1930's. There are, in fact, some demographers who deny even this. They point out that fertility declined more rapidly in the prosperous 1920's than during the Depression 1930's. They interpret the fertility decline of the early 1930's as a continuation of a long-term decline that began in the 1890's and that would have continued even without a depression. In any case, the Depression does not suffice as a full explanation of why voluntary childlessness and one-child families are so prevalent among couples, who are at present middle-aged.

Social scientists have been analyzing our changed fertility patterns in detail over the past

[5] See Arthur A. Campbell, Pascal K. Whelpton, and Richard F. Tomasson, "The Reliability of Birth Expectations of U.S. Wives," *International Population Conference: New York 1961*, Vol. I, London, 1963, pp. 49–58.
[6] Freedman, et al., *op. cit.*, p. 340.
[7] Freedman, et al., *op. cit.*, p. 340.

[8] The Scripps-Michigan Studies and the other studies conducted in the last decade all report that the overwhelming majority want two, three, or four children.
[9] Wilson H. Grabill, Clyde V. Kiser, and Pascal K. Whelpton, *The Fertility of American Women*, New York: Wiley, 1958, p. 346.
[10] Wilson H. Grabill and Paul C. Glick, "Demographic and Social Aspects of Childlessness: Census Data," *Milbank Memorial Fund Quarterly*, XXXVII, (January, 1959), pp. 60–86.

decade, but only a few of them have attempted the more arduous task of explaining these new patterns. The following paragraphs might be thought of as notes toward this end.

Economist Gray S. Becker has suggested that more leisure and a greater amount of discretionary income have encouraged younger Americans to have more children than their parents.[11] He maintains that, to a degree, children can be viewed as consumer durables, like appliances and automobiles, they demand a long term outlay of money, but they provide continuing psychic income.

Becker supports his view by pointing to the evidence that among those who are successful in planning the size of their families the prosperous have more children than the less prosperous. This is characteristic of the more educated half of the younger population (those who have at least graduated from high school) where number of children, like number of automobiles and appliances, is *directly* related to income. In high status categories fertility does appear to be higher. A study made by sociologist E. Digby Baltzell found 25 per cent of a sample of upper class Philadelphia fathers in the depression years to have four or more children.[12] Studies of Harvard, Yale, and Princeton graduates show a direct relation between income and number of children.[13] Data that I have recently collected on the fertility patterns of younger University of Illinois faculty couples indicate that the sons of fathers who are professionals or business executives are more likely to have four or more children than are those whose fathers have lower middle- or working-class occupations.

Another economist, Richard A. Easterlin, has offered an explanation of the high fertility of the 1950's based on the employment situation for males in the family-building years.[14] The great

merit of this theory is that it reconciles recent events with earlier trends. Easterlin focuses his analysis on the native-born urban white population, the segment of the population which has practiced effective family planning longest and among whom the baby boom has been most pronounced. Surprisingly, he found the fertility of this group to have been stable over the first three decades of this century. (From one important point of view this is a spurious stability. There was an increasing proportion of Catholics to Protestants in the urban native-born population over this period. Both Protestants and Catholics could have had declining fertility, but these trends could be obscured by the increasing proportion of higher fertility Catholics.) While it is true that there was a marked decline in total white fertility over this period, it was centered among the foreign-born and among the rural elements of the native born. During the early 1930's, however, the fertility of all segments of the population declined. In the 1940's the fertility of all groups increased and remained high throughout the 1950's. But the increase of the native-born urban whites, the largest sector of the population, was the most substantial. Easterlin's explanation for this increase rests on the concurrences of three factors: the great expansion of the economy from 1940 on, the virtual disappearance of young immigrants, and a low rate of young people entering the labor force. The simultaneous occurrence of these events created a uniquely favorable job market for those in the family-building ages and resulted in great acceleration in the formation of families.

Between 1890 and the 1950's the median age at first marriage declined more than three years for grooms, from 26 to under 23, and almost two years for brides, from 22 to just over 20. The rate of decline, however, was most rapid through the 1940's. The economic prosperity and optimism of the young is indicated by the fact that for a number of years a majority of couples have had all their children while still in their 20's. In recent years the median age of wives at the birth of their last child has been between 26 and 27, for husbands around 29.

The declining fertility of recent years in conjunction with the poorer employment opportunities for the young provide support for

[11] Universities-National Bureau Committee for Economic Research, *Demographic and Economic Change in Developed Countries*, Princeton: Princeton University Press, 1960, pp. 209–231.

[12] E. Digby Baltzell, "Social Mobility and Fertility within an Elite Group, "*Milbank Memorial Fund Quarterly*, XXXI (October, 1953), pp. 411–420.

[13] Frederick Osborn, *Preface to Eugenics*, rev. ed., New York: Hasper, 1950.

[14] Richard A. Easterlin, "The American Baby Boom in Historical Perspective," *American Economic Review*, **51** (December, 1961), pp. 869–911.

Easterlin's theory. The number of young people entering the labor force has increased substantially as a result of the sharp upswing in the birth rate after 1940. The employment situation for young untrained labor in particular has become worse as a result of increasing automation.

The theories of Becker and Easterlin, however, are limited in their generality. They do not appear applicable to the recent experience of some western European nations. Throughout the 1950's Sweden and France have had burgeoning full employment economies together with a declining age at marriage, yet both have had declining crude birth rates. The Swedish birth rate declined from 15.5 per 1,000 population in 1950–1954 to a low of 13.7 in 1960 under conditions of a full employment economy.[15] The French birth rate declined from 19.5 in 1950–1954 to 17.8 in 1962 during a period of extraordinary economic expansion. The United Kingdom, on the other hand, the most sluggish of the major economies of western Europe in this period, has undergone a steady increase in the birth rate from 15.5 in 1950–1954 to 18.0 in 1962. The economically booming German Federal Republic behaves according to the theory, with a birth rate that has increased from 16.1 in 1950–1955 to 18.1 in 1962.

Economic explanation has only a limited power to explain fertility differences and trends within and among advanced societies. Material well-being and security allow many couples to support adequately three or four children; it does not explain why fewer or more chose to do so in different societies and in different segments of the same society. Why not better vacations or a higher standard of living?

Will Herberg, William F. Whyte, and other commentators on American culture and character have stressed the return of Americans to the traditional institutions of home and organized religion.[16] The upper-middle-class style setters of the last generation, unlike their children, were not so involved in the search for the good and full personal life as such. They were more concerned with their work and getting ahead, making money and maintaining a front, and with politics and other causes. Seldom did they want more than two children and the majority did not want to have their first until a few years after marriage. In the postwar period, however, our style setters have become increasingly involved in bureaucratic organizations characterized by high security and regular promotion. The decline of the work ethic and a high degree of mobility have perhaps resulted in attempts to find a new fulfillment in the sustenance of human relationships and in the "good life." A spiritual and physical return to the institutions rooted in home and family allegedly has occurred. While I don't know of any evidence to support this, I think these values have taken on increased strength for all levels of the population.[17]

Related to this is the concurrent development of what Betty Friedan has called "the feminine mystique,"[18] The new version of the old ideology that has overwhelmed the feminine protest of the 1920's and 1930's. It maintains that women are fundamentally different from men in their basic needs and that they can find satisfaction only through marriage and in bearing and raising children. The mother-wife-as-fulfilled-woman view of women has permeated the women's magazines since the mid-40's and has once again become the only conventionally acceptable role for women in American society.

Recent studies of college undergraduates evidence the pervasiveness of this neo-traditional role for women.[19] Consider, for example, the conclusions of John H. Bushnell as to the future role identities of Vassar undergraduates of the mid-50's, an unusally intelligent academic sample of young women:

... the validation of femininity and a full realization of the potential of womanhood is thought to reside almost exclusively in the realm of marriage and family. . . . That the female should

---

[15] All of the birth rates in this paragraph are from *Population Index*, **29** (July, 1963), pp. 323–325.

[16] See, for example, Will Herberg, *Protestant, Catholic, Jew*, rev. ed., New York: Doubleday Anchor, 1960; and William H. Whyte, Jr., *The Organization Man*, New York: Simon and Schuster, 1956.

[17] That this has occurred among the English working classes is indicated by Ferdynand Zweig, *The Worker in an Affluent Society*, London: Heinemann, 1961, pp. 205–212.

[18] Betty Friedan, *The Feminine Mystique*, New York: Norton, 1963.

[19] *Ibid.*, pp. 150–181.

attempt, in their thinking, to usurp the preroga-
tives of the male is a distasteful notion which
would seriously disrupt their own projected role
of helpmate and faithful complement to the man
of the house. For these young women, the
"togetherness" vogue is definitely an integral
theme of future family life, with any opportunities
for independent action attaching to an Ivy League
degree being willingly passed over in favor of the
anticipated rewards of close-knit companionship
within the home that-is-to-be.[20]

In sharp contrast to this role definition of
academically talented American college girls is
the following observation by the Danish
sociologist Kaare Svalastoga on the role expectation for middle-class Scandinavian women:
"But even if she excels in all these respects
(being a good housekeeper and hostess, a loving
mother, and an attractive spouse), she will reap
slight social esteem, because dominant middle-
class opinion will insist on the superior values of
choosing a career outside the home and of
cultivating literary and artistic interests."[21]

Studies by the economist John B. Parrish have
shown a marked decline in the proportion of
upper managerial and professional positions
occupied by American women over the past
thirty years.[22] The proportion of all doctorates
awarded to women has declined from around 15
per cent in the early 1930's to around 10 per cent
in recent years. Law degrees awarded to women
have declined from 6 to 3 per cent over this
same period. The percentage of M.D.'s has
averaged around 5 per cent for several decades.
Four-year engineering degrees going to women
have never exceeded one-third of 1 per cent.
Parrish cites further evidence of the relative
decline of women with careers in the percentage
of women listed in *Who's Who in America;* the

1902 edition listed 8.5 per cent, the 1958 edition
4 per cent. He notes similar declines in specialized directories like *American Men of Science.*

The proportions of professional and upper
level managerial positions occupied by women
is one measure of the diversity of role possibilities for women in an industrial society. It is an
important observation, and perhaps a paradoxical one, that the proportion of married
women who work in a society is not much
related to this. Some examples will make this
clear. France probably has the highest proportion of married women working of any western
society, yet, outside of Paris, women make up
only a small percentage of the free professions
(yet higher than in the United States), and
women did not get the right to vote until after
World War II.[23] Switzerland, too, has a high
proportion of married women in the labor force,
yet only a small proportion of the professions
are made up of women, and there is still no
female suffrage in most of the cantons. In
Sweden, on the other hand, where there are
many job possibilities for women, a lower proportion of married women work compared with
France, Great Britain, Switzerland, or the
United States, but a relatively *high* proportion
of dentists, doctors, and lawyers are women. In
all of these societies, regardless of the proportion
of women who work, only small percentages are
found outside of certain "female" and "neuter"
types of work in clerical and kindred occupations, light manufacturing, service occupations,
school teaching, social work, and nursing.

In a comparative study of labor force participation of women in the United States, Great
Britain, France, and Sweden, Alva Myrdal and
Viola Klein express surprise at ". . . how small
the range of professional jobs is that are open to
women in the United States (or to which
American women aspire?)."[24] The proportion of
women in the traditional "learned professions,"
for example, is just a small fraction in America
compared to what it is in these other three
countries. But what is more interesting is that
these proportions have declined in the United

[20] John H. Bushnell, "Student Culture at Vassar," in
Nevitt Sanford (ed.), *The American College,* New
York: Wiley, 1962, pp. 509–510.

[21] "The Family in Scandinavia," *Journal of Marriage
and Family Living,* **16** (November, 1954).

[22] See John B. Parrish, "Professional Women as a
National Resource," *Quarterly Review of Economics
and Business,* I (February, 1961), pp. 54–63; "Top
Level Training of Women in the United States,
1900–1960," *Journal of the National Association of
Women Deans and Councelors,* XXV (January, 1962),
pp. 67–73, "Women in Top Level Teaching and
Research," *Journal of the American Association of
University Women* (January, 1962).

[23] Many of the facts in this paragraph come from
Alva Myrdal and Viola Klein, *Women's Two Roles,*
London: Routledge & Kegan Paul, 1956, pp. 42–77.

[24] *Ibid.,* p. 63.

States over recent decades, while they have increased in these other societies. I take this as evidence for the increased strengthening and pervasiveness of the neo-traditional role for women in American society.

Children, several children, have become part of the ideology of the good life in America. Having no children or only one child was perhaps taken as a mark of middle-class prudence in the 1920's and 1930's, while now such a state is regarded as unfortunate. After a few years of marriage a couple without children or with only one child become objects of curiosity to their friends. They themselves frequently feel the need to explain their unfamilial behavior. A generation ago ads with family pictures and movies with "typical" families almost always had a boy and girl; now they usually show three or four children. (More than two children might even be viewed in Veblenesque terms as a new form of conspicuous consumption.) The belief that being an only child is detrimental to wholesome development is widely held by American wives according to the Scripps-Michigan studies.[25] This is despite much evidence that extremely gifted children, leading scientists, and persons successful in other areas are disproportionately only children.[26] The extensiveness of the belief in the necessity of children for the good life is the key, I think, to explaining the virtual disappearance of voluntary childlessness in our society. Americans perhaps have more in common with the people of traditional societies than those of most industrial societies in the extent and intensity with which they regard children as essential to a woman's fulfillment.

Not all sections of the population have contributed equally to our rapid growth. As a matter of fact differential fertility has existed since Colonial times.[27] It was not however, until the first two decades of this century that sharp differences in average family size appeared. This is the period when family planning became widespread among the urban middle and upper classes. In the years since, these practices have diffused out into the rural areas and have trickled down in the class structure. During the 1920's, when family planning had become common, fertility differentials were probably at a maximum because the middle classes had become extremely effective family planners and the working classes had not. In *Middletown* in the mid-20's, all of the business class wives interviewed on family planning planning knew some method of birth control and favored its use.[28] Among the working-class wives, on the other hand, the majority interviewed were either totally ignorant of any method, were opposed to using any method, or were using ineffective methods. Since the onset of World War II knowledge of birth control methods has become thoroughly diffused throughout the population down through the bottom levels of American society: the unskilled, the uneducated, the poor. While there is great inability to control family size effectively here, the reasons are now rarely ignorance of techniques. Rather, it is the result of a lack of motivation to exert control and an absence of communication between husband and wife on such subjects rooted in the prudery of the traditional relationship between the sexes.[29] This underdog segment of American society (say, the bottom 15 per cent) is the only part of the population where unwanted pregnancies are recurrent.

The conventional fertility differentials that have been studied for decades, such as income, occupation, education, and place of residence, have been shrinking for many years. Some demographers believe we are passing through a transition to a direct relation between status level and fertility. This may or may not be the case, but there is no doubt that most of these differentials have become slight, always, however, excluding the underdog segment. Recent studies point to religion and race as the most significant sources of contemporary differential fertility.

[25] This is my impression based on answers to the question of why they want to have or have had a given number of children. This material has not been studied in any systematic way.
[26] Seymour Martin Lipset and Reinhard Bendix, *Social Mobility in Industrial Society*, Berkeley and Los Angeles: University of California, 1960, pp. 238–245.
[27] Wilson H. Grabill, et al., *The Fertility of American Women, op. cit.*, pp. 5–25.

[28] Robert S. Lynd and Helen Merrell Lynd, *Middletown*, New York, Harcourt, Brace, 1929, pp. 123–126.
[29] See Lee Rainwater, *And the Poor Get Children*, Chicago: Quadrangle Books, 1960.

According to the first of the Scripps-Michigan Studies, Catholics wives born in 1931–1935 (aged 20–24 in 1955) expected an average of 3.8 children by the time they completed their childbearing; non-Catholic wives of similar age expected an average of 2.9 children.[30] A panel study made by the Office of Population Research at Princeton University of urban wives who already had two children found somewhat smaller, but still sizeable religious differences.[31] Catholic wives "desired" (a somewhat different concept from "expected") 3.6 children, Protestant wives 3.0, and Jewish wives 2.7. Even when Catholic and non-Catholic wives with similar income and education are compared these large differences are maintained.

There are several reasons why Catholics have such relatively high fertility in the United States. The Roman Catholic Church regards the use of the highly effective mechanical and chemical methods of birth control as mortal sin; the less effective methods of *coitus interruptus* and douching are equally condemned. Only periodic abstinence (the rhythm method) or total abstinence are acceptable and then only when not used to avoid children for "selfish reasons." An occasional priest, however, forbids his flock the use of the rhythm method, and it is not at all uncommon for priests to discourage its use.[32] The moral inaccessability of the more effective means of contraception is certainly a factor encouraging high fertility. It leads to expecting and probably even to wanting larger families. There is also the strong family-centered tradition in the Church and in Catholic culture, along with the exalted position of the Virgin Mary as the Mother of Jesus, an unequivocal emphasis on the reproductive purpose of marriage, and perhaps the persistence of peasant traditions that encourage large families. Important also is the observation that American Catholics are "better" Catholics than those of most European societies. For example, André Maurois estimated in 1956 that only about one fifth of French Catholics attended church regularly.[33] A substantial majority of American Catholics, on the other hand, attend church regularly; and they evidence little anticlericalism, and almost certainly adhere to the teachings of the Church to a greater degree than the Catholics of most European societies.[34]

If we exclude the underdog segment again, there appears to be a strong tendency for the more educated American Catholics to have larger families than the less educated. The Scripps-Michigan Study found Catholic wives aged 18–39 in 1955 who had some high school to expect a total of 3.1 children, those who had graduated from high school to expect 3.3, and those who had some college to expect 3.9.[35] The Princeton Study found desired family size for these three educational levels of 3.4, 3.7, and 4.4 children.[36] No such clear-cut pattern characterizes non-Catholics in either study.

Among American Catholics, however, there are sharp differences in family size by nationality background. Among the major Catholic groups, the Irish are the least likely to get married, but when they do, they have the largest families. The Princeton study found wives of Irish background to want 4.1 children, while those of Italian background wanted only 3.3 children.[37] German and Slavic Catholics fall between these extremes. The higher fertility of the Irish appears related to their "better" Catholicism, they are more likely than the Italians to attend Church regularly, go to confession, attend parochial schools, and follow the teachings of the Church and the priests. The Italians, on the other hand, are the least attentive Catholics of the major nationality groups. They are traditionally anticlerical and show much independence of Church teachings. Father John V.

---

[30] Freedman, et al., *op. cit.*, p. 275.

[31] Charles F. Westoff, Robert G. Potter, Jr., Philip C. Sagi, and Elliot G. Mishler, *Family Growth in Metropolitan America*, Princeton: Princeton University Press, 1961, p. 180. (See, also, *The Third Child*, Princeton: Princeton University Press, 1963.)

[32] The second Scripps-Michigan Study asked all Catholic wives about the attitudes of their priests on the rhythm method and its use.

[33] *A History of France*, New York: Straus and Cudahy, 1956, p. 565.

[34] In the Scripps-Michigan Study 67 per cent of the Catholic wives attended church "regularly." See Freedman, et al., *op. cit.*, p. 161. In the Princeton Study 69 per cent attended church "at least once a week." See Westoff, et al., *op. cit.*, p. 205.

[35] Freedman, et al., *op. cit.*, p. 286.

[36] Westoff, et al., *op. cit.*, p. 219.

[37] Westoff, et al., *op. cit.*, p. 203.

Tolino, a close student of Italian-Americans, estimated in 1939 in the *Ecclesiastical Review* that only one third were "good" Catholics, that is, attended Church regularly and went to confession. At the other extreme, he estimated a sixth had received no religious instruction and were completely outside the Church. The remaining half had received partial instruction in the traditions of the Church, but did not attend Church or confession regularly.[38] Interestingly, the Princeton Study found the Italians to be far more effective than the Irish in planning family size. Though the authors of this report do not give information on the matter, I suspect the Italians are more likely than the Irish to violate Church doctrine by using forbidden methods of birth control.

The Princeton study points out that it is not nationality that explains these fertility differences, but rather differences in the religiosity of the varying groups. When religiosity among Catholics is measured by extent of education in Catholic schools and colleges, it emerges as a powerful determinant of intra-Catholic fertility.[39] Among wives all of whose education had been in Catholic schools, desired family size is 4.2 children; among those who have been to college it is a whopping 5.1. Among those with no parochial school education, desired number of children is 3.4. The final differences in completed family size will in all probability be greater than these figures indicate because the parochial school wives not only have shorter intervals between births but are less successful family planners than those Catholic wives without such education. A large share of the difference between the desired family size of wives of Irish and Italian background can be explained in terms of the greater education of Irish wives in parochial schools.

However, Catholicism does not *necessarily* have such a positive effect on fertility. France, Italy, and Austria are all predominantly Catholic countries with fertility as low or lower than most Protestant countries. Some of the provinces of northern Italy may have the lowest birth rates in the world. On the other hand, Catholics in Canada, Holland, West Germany, Switzerland, and Australia, like those in the United States, have higher fertility than non-Catholics. I would speculate that Catholics in all these countries abide by the teachings of the Church to a greater extent than in the predominately Catholic countries, Ireland being the most notable exception. Catholics have a greater religious self-consciousness when they are a minority, and there are few issues where this is more apparent than that of birth control. French and Italian clergy, I have the impression, say little publicly on the question compared to the American clergy.

Differences in fertility between whites and Negroes have not been getting smaller over recent years, as might be expected from the shrinking statistical gaps in education, white-collar employment, and certain other measures of socio-economic well-being. In fact, since the early 1930's the Negro population has been growing at an increasingly faster rate than the white population. In recent years the white population has been increasing by 1.6 per cent a year while the Negro population has been increasing by 2.4 per cent. What has been happening over the past three decades is a decrease in the differential between the average number of children among whites and Negroes *who have children*, which has been obscured by a greater increase among Negroes in the *proportion* having children. Childlessness among Negro wives, especially in urban areas has been high.[40] More than 35 per cent of urban Negro wives born before 1915 are childless. Most of this childlessness has been involuntary and much of it has probably been due to the sterilizing effects of syphilis and gonorrhea. The victory over venereal disease, aided perhaps by a decrease in family disorganization and an increased acculturation of Negroes into the dominant culture, has greatly changed the fertility patterns of Negroes. Among younger urban Negro wives, the incidence of childlessness is now even lower than among whites. As Negroes make further economic and status gains, there will almost certainly be a decline in Negro-white fertility differences.

[38] On the attitudes of urban Italian-Americans toward the Church, see Herbert Gans, *The Urban Villagers*, New York: Free Press of Glencoe, 1962, pp. 110–115.

[39] Westoff, et al., *op. cit.*, p. 219.

[40] Grabill and Glick, *op. cit.*, p. 9.

Within no American ethnic, racial, or religious group is there greater variation in family size than among Negroes. Those in the rural South average around five children while those in cities probably average between three and four. Upper middle-class Negroes, however, have lower fertility than any segment of the American population. For example, one recent study of 300 Negro professionals in medicine, dentistry, law, and college teaching in Washington D.C., by sociologist G. Franklin Edwards of Howard University, found those who were married to have an average of 1.2 children.[41] This is extremely low fertility for a group in which the average age is 46.

In Britain, Scandinavia, West Germany, Austria, France, and Italy married couples average almost one child less than American couples.[42] The Netherlands, which has the highest birth rate of any industrialized nation in Europe, had a crude birth rate that ran around 10 per cent below ours in the 1950's. Even some of the least industrialized nations of Europe, Greece and Spain, for example, have birth rates below that of the United States. Canada, New Zealand, and Australia, on the other hand, resemble us in their high birth and growth rates. The fertility dynamics of these other "born free" industrial societies seem to be similar to those that encourage our high fertility. Comparing United States and Australian birth rates, Coale and Zelnik have commented that the "similarity is startling. Since 1917, the two birth rates have rarely differed by more than one point (one birth per 1,000 persons)."[43]

A comparison of certain characteristics of Swedish society should be especially useful in helping us understand some of the reasons for our high fertility. This Scandinavian democracy is more like the United States than any European country in its high standard of living yet has had one of the lowest, if not the lowest, national birth rate in the world each year since the early 1930's. In 1960 the Swedes had 14 births per thousand population compared with 24 per thousand among Americans. Recent population projections suggest that the Swedish population will increase by only around 10 per cent between 1960 and 1975 while ours will increase by 25 or 30 per cent. and the Swedish projections allowed for a relatively greater net immigration.[44]

Swedish wives born in the 1930's will probably have an average of 2.2 or 2.3 children by the time they complete the childbearing years, compared with a minimum estimate of 3.3 children for their counterparts in America (and 3.0 children for those who are not Catholic.)[45] This lower fertility of the Swedes is not because of any great difference in ability to control family size. A substantial majority of both non-Catholic Americans and Swedes are effective users of contraceptives. Nor are economic factors the heart of the matter. In fact it might be argued that the relative cost of rearing a child in America is greater than in Sweden, where an expanding system of welfare legislation has provided increasing financial benefits to mothers and children. This aid began in the 1930's to spur the low birth rate which for several years ran below replacement level.

All Swedish mothers, married or not, now receive a grant of $180 when a child is born, as well as free delivery and confinement, grants for postnatal health care for mother and child, and an allowance of $180 per year for each child up to the age of sixteen.[46] There are no tax exemptions for children, but the married pay a lower tax rate than the single. Comprehensive national health insurance makes the child's medical bills negligible and complete dental care is available

[41] G. Franklin Edwards, *The Negro Professional Class*, Glencoe, Ill.: Free Press, 1959.

[42] This is only a rough estimate. The only non-U.S. study of expected family size that I am aware of is that of Ronald Freedman, Gerhard Baumert, and Martin Bolte, "Expected Family Size and Family Size Values in West Germany," *Population Studies*, XIII (November, 1959), pp. 136–150.

[43] Ansley J. Coale and Melvin Zelnik, *New Estimates of Fertility and Population in the United States*, Princeton: Princeton University Press, 1963, p. 27.

[44] For Sweden see *Statistical Abstract of Sweden*, Stockholm: Central Bureau of Statistics, 1963, p. 24. For U.S. see *Current Population Reports: Population Estimates*, U.S. Bureau of the Census, Series P-25, No. 279 (February 4, 1964).

[45] This figure of 2.2 is an estimate based on the Swedish birth rate, which is just barely over replacement level.

[46] The Swedish Institute, et al., *Social Benefits in Sweden*, Stockholm, 1963, pp. 13–15.

to all children in the schools. Housing allowances to large families and paid holidays for children are given to those parents with low-incomes. Housing, though in relatively short supply, costs substantially less than in the United States, though food and most manufactured goods cost somewhat more. Swedish parents do not need to be as concerned as American parents about paying for their children's education since through the university level tuition is free and there are generous scholarship and loan programs to meet students' living costs. Beginning in 1965 stipends of $350 per year were granted to all full-time undergraduate students. Employers are forbidden by law to discharge a woman employee who gets married or becomes pregnant. She is entitled to six months' maternity leave with pay, and her job must be held open for her for an additional three months. With these inducements one would expect Swedish fertility to exceed ours.

There are, however, certain differences in Swedish and American values, behavior patterns, and housing situations which may help us to understand the different fertility behavior of the two societies. Of some importance is the fact that Swedes marry at older ages than Americans. During the 1950's they were three to four years older. The median age at first marriage for Swedish men in the 1950's was between 26 and 27 and for women between 23 and 24.[47] Americans, on the other hand, marry earlier than the people of any other industrialized nation in the world. Very young couples have a longer period of fecundity, more energy to deal with the rigors of child-rearing, and a less realistic picture of the burdens of parenthood than those who marry later. It is also probably true that a girl who goes to marriage directly from her parents' home or the college dormitory adjusts more easily to the confining role of motherhood than one who has had several years of bachelor freedom. Also early marriage tends to canalize a girl's interests into the traditional roles of wife and mother before competing role possibilities have a chance to develop.

[47] See *Befolkningsrörelsen*, Stockholm: Central Bureau of Statistics for appropriate years.

The importance of age at marriage is quite difficult to assess. In Sweden there has been a decline in average age of first marriage of women between 1940 and 1960 of 2.2 years from age 25.0 to 22.8, compared with a decline of 1.3 years in the United States, from age 21.5 to 20.2. Yet there has been only a slight increase, if there has been any increase at all, in the average number of children married women have. The increase in the Swedish birth rate that occurred after the 1930's appears to be mainly the result of a marked increase in the proportion of women who married and to having babies in the 1940's who were postponed from the 1930's. (Of the women who became 30 in 1940, 30.1 per cent had never married; of those who turned 30 in 1960 only 13.5 per cent had never married.) The point is that the increase in average family size that has occurred in America between women born around 1910 and women born in the decade around 1930 has no counterpart in Sweden.

Most American wives have worked outside their homes before marriage, a majority do so again some time after marriage, but few—even among college graduates—can be said to have careers.[48] In Sweden, on the other hand, a high proportion of middle-class wives have relatively uninterrupted working lives and there are far more women in the traditional male occupations than in America. In Swedish universities in 1961–1962 women were a quarter of the students of medicine, theology, and the natural sciences, a third of the students of dentistry, and 16 per cent of those in law. A majority of the pharmacy students were women. As I indicated earlier, in all these fields in the United States the proportion of women is small or negligible and has tended to decrease since the 1930's. In Sweden these proportions have been increasing since the 1930's.

As I suggested earlier, the proportion of women in the professions and in the traditionally male occupations is an indicator of the general

[48] According to a 1959 U.S. Bureau of the Census Study only one out of twelve mothers who had any children under six and whose husbands earned over $6,000 a year had any employment. See Paul C. Glick and David M. Heer, "Joint Analysis of Personal and Family Characteristics," *International Population Conference: New York*, 1961, London, 1963, pp. 217–228.

role possibilities open to women in a society. I further suggest that the contraction in conventional role possibilities that has occurred in American society as indicated by the decline in the proportions of higher status career professions occupied by woman will be a crucial part of any explanation of the increase in average family size in America. That prosperity and an increased standard of living in a highly advanced society is not a satisfactory explanation of our increased fertility is suggested by Sweden where there has been a corresponding prosperity (though at not quite so high a level), without any marked change in average family size and with an actual decline in the birth rate over the 1950's, and in spite of a declining average age at marriage and an increasing proportion of women who marry. What is significantly different in the two societies is the increase in acceptable role possibilities for women that has occurred in Sweden over the past generation. The neo-traditional role for women has few spokesmen in the Swedish press and mass media compared to the United States. The feminism that became abortive in the United States about the time of World War II continued unabated in Sweden and has had far reaching effects in the society. Typical views of Swedish university students on women's roles are less differentiated and more egalitarian than those of the Vassar students earlier referred to. The minimizing of sexual differentiation and the maximizing of sexual equality in education are guiding principles in the radical school reform in Sweden in the postwar years. For example, all boys in the elementary schools are now required to have a certain number of periods in textile handicraft and all girls a certain number of periods in woodworking.

There is, however, one major factor in Swedish society that acts as a kind of brake on fertility: the generally small living quarters. Family size in the advanced societies is affected to some extent by type and size of living quarters. Apartment living and small quarters discourage families of more than two children. About three-fourths of non-farm Swedish families live in apartment houses and most families with children do not have more than two bedrooms.[49]

The fact that Americans have so much living space and do not hesitate to spend a large portion of their income on housing is a basic difference between Sweden and the United States. Statistically, Americans are more urbanized than the Swedes, but unlike them we are essentially anti-city. Most American parents with children prefer to live in sprawling suburbs of one family houses. Even if a Swede lives in a suburb, he is more likely to live in an apartment than a single family dwelling.

I think it is suggestive that more Swedish wives regard two children as "ideal" than any other number (48 per cent compared with 19 per cent of American wives), whereas more American wives so regard four children than any other number (41 per cent).[50] Actually, the Swedish wives will average more than two children and the American wives less than four. This fertility conservatism of the Swedes is understandable when it is noted that for most couples only one bedroom is available for children. Add this to the chronic housing shortage and the great emphasis that is placed on maintaining a well appointed home (where no one sleeps in the living room, and having a third child becomes virtually unthinkable to a large segment of the population, especially the urban middle classes. Having a third child in America rarely means that someone will have to sleep in the living room.

What about the future? I think we can predict that the 1960's will see a decline in fertility compared with the 1950's as measured by annual birth rates and average family size, even with a continuation of national prosperity. The job situation of the young without specialized training has become progressively worse through the 1960's and will depress fertility in a large segment of the child-bearing population. The Scripps-Michigan Studies indicate that wives who were aged 20–24 in 1960 had lower birth expectations than wives of similar age when interviewed in 1955. Most compelling, however, is the steady decline in the birth rate over the years 1957–1963 which in my opinion will be

[49] See *Statistical Abstract of Sweden*, 1963, *op. cit.*, pp. 206–214.

[50] Swedish data from a national survey of 617 families with children reported in *Dagens Nyheter*, April 29, 1964, p. 9. U.S. data from Freedman, Whelpton, and Campbell, *op. cit.*, p. 223.

reflected in a decline in the average number of children that wives born in the second half of the 1930's and early 1940's will have compared to those born in the decade 1926–1935. It is important to note, however, that data collected from two national samples in 1962 and 1963 by the University of Michigan Population Studies Center failed to detect such a decline in "mean total children expected" among white women of any age compared with the Scripps-Michigan studies of 1955 and 1960.[51]

No matter to what levels of affluence we go in future years, I doubt that it can have any more positive effects on fertility than it has had on those women born in the decade around 1930. The amount of time and energy mothers (and fathers) have is a constant, and household help is one item that becomes harder to get and relatively more expensive as national level of living increases. Also, there are interests besides children that will compete for the time and interest of our increasingly sophisticated population.

Wives born in the early 1930's will probably turn out to be the fertility champions among those born in the first half of the twentieth century. The high fertility of these women is the result of a concurrence of factors that has not yet been adequately explained.

The underdog segment of the population is where the future will see the sharpest decline in fertility. The present situation in industrial Europe and the past trend in this country both indicate this section of the population will become more effective in restricting the size of their families. We know that they do not *want* more children than the more fortunately situated.

Two groups in the population probably will not follow this general fertility decline: middle-class Negroes and Catholics. The fertility of the Negro bourgeosie is now so low it is doubtful if it can go anywhere but up. As their numbers increase, a lessening of their alienation and status insecurities should occur that will in time, perhaps, increase their extremely low fertility. The Catholics will be fascinating to watch. My guess is that Catholic fertility will remain at its present high level or even increase. The basis for this prediction is the strikingly high relation between education and adherence to Church doctrine on birth control among American Catholics. With the progressive increase in the level of education among Catholics, and the increasing proportion educated in parochial schools, there will be an increase in the higher status and higher fertility segments of the Catholic population. On the other hand, if the Church should accept the oral contraceptive as not contrary to natural law, following Dr. John Rock and certain Catholic theologians who maintain it is not, the fertility behavior of Catholics in the industrialized societies may become less divergent from that of non-Catholics.

[51] See *Population Index*, **30**, No. 2 (April, 1964), pp. 171–175.

29. Patterns of Divorce in Australia and the United States*

BY LINCOLN H. DAY

The incidence and patterning of divorce in Australia differs substantially from that in the United States: Australians resort to divorce less frequently than do Americans, and generally only after a much longer duration of marriage. It is suggested that this arises from differences between the two countries in (1) the availability of divorce (in both existential and normative senses), (2) the availability of alternative "remedies" for marital disharmony, and (3) the extent of marital disharmony itself.

This is a particularly appropriate time to report on divorce in Australia. The federal marriage and divorce law recently enacted in Australia offers an incentive to summarize what can be determined of previous patterns of divorce in order to create a basis for future comparisons with patterns following its establishment. This new law, the Matrimonial Causes Act 1959 (which took effect on February 1, 1961), is not only the first such law to apply to the entire Australian Commonwealth, but also in certain respects a more liberal one than any of the State or Territorial laws that preceded it. In addition, the wealth of American material now available as a result of the Jacobsons' work gives us the opportunity to make a much-needed comparison of divorce patterns in two Western countries of similar culture.[1]

Available Data

Students of divorce will find the Australian data unusually comprehensive. Combining registration data with materials collected in the various census enumerations permits analysis according to: duration of marriage, number of children, age, and relative ages of husbands and wives. In addition, Australian data are presented in enough detail to permit analysis by two types of cohort: age and marriage.

There are some distinct drawbacks, however. The usefulness of the cohort method of analysis is limited for the present by the fact that the necessary data can be obtained only for the period since 1950. As time goes on, of course,

SOURCE: American Sociological Review, *Volume 29 (August, 1964), pp. 509–522. Reprinted by permission from the author and the American Sociological Association.*

* For their perceptive criticisms of an earlier version of this paper I should like to thank Professor J. A. Barnes and Dr. Reginald T. Appleyard, both of the Australian National University, and my wife, Alice Taylor Day. This study was carried out while I was a Visiting Fellow in Demography at the Institute of Advanced Studies, The Australian National University, Canberra.

[1] Since the emphasis in this paper is on Australian divorce patterns, American data will be introduced only to highlight the Australian materials. For a comprehensive discussion of the nature and sources of the comparable American data, see Paul H. Jacobson and Pauline F. Jacobson, *American Marriage and Divorce*, New York: Rinehart, 1959.

this deficiency will, by its very nature, become increasingly less important.[2] Moreover, there are currently no tabulations with which to analyze Australian divorce patterns by socio-economic groupings—in which respect, incidentally, Australia is no worse off than most countries.[3] Since establishment of the new Matrimonial Causes Act, however, the Commonwealth Bureau of Census and Statistics has been collecting for each marriage not only the usual information on ages, dates, (and for divorce actions) duration of marriage, grounds, and number of living children, but also such information as the following: religious denomination of marriage ceremony, conjugal condition of each party to the marriage, number of times divorced, place of birth, year of arrival in Australia (if foreign-born), occupation and father's occupation at time of marriage. If and when these data become available, it will probably be possible to know more about divorce in Australia than in any other country in the world.

The main sources of data on divorce in Australia are: (1) the censuses of the Commonwealth and, for 1901, of the State of New South Wales; (2) the various state statistical registers and yearbooks; and (3) the Commonwealth Bureau of Census and Statistics annual,

Demography Bulletin.[4] The last contains registration data on the number of divorces back to 1891, the number of divorces by age and sex back to 1946, and the number of divorces by duration of marriage and number of children back to 1950. Except for the state breakdowns by grounds for dissolution, however, the data in *Demography Bulletin* are confined to the Commonwealth as a whole.

Information on divorce recorded in the various state and territorial registers lacks uniformity. There are no data whatever for Western Australia and the Northern Territory. And though the other four states have collected for varying intervals of time what can truly be termed a fascinating variety of information, in only a few instances are data on the characteristics of the total population (as against only that portion of it obtaining a divorce) sufficient to permit an assessment of the relevance of these attributes to the patterning of divorce.

Of all the state divorce tabulations, only those for New South Wales extend back beyond the census year 1947. Hence, the calculation of rates for a time series requires that the census data to be used as denominators be subdivided by state, so that data for New South Wales can be isolated from those for the remainder of the Commonwealth. Such state breakdowns are available in the 1947 and 1921 Commonwealth censuses and, of course, in the 1901 census of New South Wales. They are also available, in unpublished form, from the 1933 census of the Commonwealth, but not for the censuses of 1954 and 1911 nor, as yet, for the census of 1961. Trend analysis of differentials must therefore be confined not only to the State of New South Wales, but also to the period 1901–1947.

The Pattern of Divorce in Australia

To study any social phenomenon is to ask three general questions concerning it: (1) What

---

[2] This is discussed in more detail, and the experience of the 1952 marriage cohort presented, in Lincoln H. Day, "A Note on the Measurement of Divorce, with Special Reference to Australian Data," *The Australian Journal of Statistics*, **5** (November, 1963), pp. 133–142.

[3] Such analyses for whole countries have been attempted, but in nearly every instance these have been based on a misuse of census data: differences between proportions enumerated as currently occupying the status "divorced," have been taken to represent differences in the rate of divorce itself, despite the fact that socio-economic differences in rates of remarriage or in the interval of time between divorce and remarriage could seriously affect the relative sizes of these ratios. See, e.g., A. J. Nixon, *Divorce in New Zealand*, Auckland, N.Z.: Auckland University College, Bulletin No. 46, Sociology Series No. 1, 1964, Tables II and III, and William J. Goode, "Marital Satisfaction and Instability: A Cross-Cultural Class Analysis of Divorce Rates," *International Social Science Journal*, **14** (1962), pp. 507–526. Also see Lincoln H. Day, "Letter," *International Social Science Journal* (forthcoming).

[4] The data necessary to trace any trends in divorce in the whole Commonwealth are obtainable only for the period since 1947. For earlier years, the necessary data are available only for New South Wales, for which they extend back to 1901. (In 1901, the State of New South Wales contained 36 per cent of Australia's total population.)

Table 1

Divorce rates for selected years: Australia and the United States (Divorces per 1,000)

Year	Population		Marriages in existence (i.e., married women)	
	Australia	U.S.	Australia	U.S.
1956	.69	—	—	—
1957	.73	—	3.19	9.47
1950	.91	2.54	—	10.19
1947	1.16	3.44	5.01	14.00
1937	.41	1.93	—	8.65
1933	.30	1.31	1.52	6.11
1921	.28	1.47	1.50	7.19
1911	.11	.95	.70	4.91

Sources: Australia: Calculated from data in *Demography Bulletin*. Divorce numerator includes nullities of marriage and judicial separations (about 1 per cent of the total).

U.S.: Calculated from data in Paul H. Jacobson and Pauline F. Jacobson, *op. cit.*, Tables 42, A6, and A22. Divorce numerator includes annulment and dissolution of marriage decrees (about 3 per cent of the total).

Table 2

Divorce rates per 1,000 marriages

	(a) Divorces in specified year x per 1,000 marriages in the same year		(b) Divorces in specified year x per 1,000 marriages in Σ [(year $x-5$) + (year $x-6$) + (year $x-7$)]/3
Year	Australia	U.S.	Australia
1891	8.0	60.0	8.9
1901	14.4	82.2	18.3
1911	13.1	93.4	17.8
1921	32.0	134.5	34.7
1931	50.3	173.1	42.0
1936	42.9	167.7	57.9
1941	44.6	168.5	60.2
1946	91.0	264.4	100.0
1951	94.8	230.4	104.5
1956	90.4	233.0	86.2
1960	88.9	—	94.0

Sources: Australia: Calculated from data in *Demography Bulletin*. Column (b) presents rates calculated with denominators adjusted to bring them into closer alignment with the Australian divorce pattern: few divorces occur before the fourth year of marriage, and divorce is actually not very likely to occur before about the sixth year of marriage.

U.S.: Calculated from data in Jacobson and Jacobson, *op. cit.*, Tables 2 and 42 (excluding annulments and New York dissolution of marriage decrees).

is its incidence? (2) Has this undergone any change over time? and (3) What causes it? So far as the third question is concerned, analysis of the data on divorce made available by census enumeration and the registration of vital events can do little more than limit the range of conjecture and suggest some of the more worthwhile lines of endeavor for inquiries based on other types of evidence. But answers to the first two questions must come, if at all, from enumeration and registration data, whether they be derived from official reports or (as has been done with certain small and nonliterate societies)[5] through the exertions of the investigator himself.

1. Trends. I have already noted that analysis over time is seriously limited, but such calculations as are possible do show a general upward movement in Australia's divorce rates, with the all-time high occurring in the period immediately following World War II. The drop in rates since then, while substantial, has by no means been enough to reduce levels to those of the prewar years. This movement, along with comparative data for the United States, is shown in Tables 1 and 2.

Precise determination of the magnitude of these changes is impossible. Nevertheless, it is quite clear that this secular increase in the frequency of divorce has not been without its fluctuations. The probability of divorce was somewhat lower during the depression years of the 1930's than under the relatively good economic conditions of the 1920's, while the record high rates of the post-World War II period were perhaps as much as 40 to 50 per cent above the levels reached in the following decade.

The American divorce rate—however measured—has been consistently higher than the Australian. Although the gap between them has narrowed over the years, the respective duration —specific rates of 1954, were they to remain in effect indefinitely, would result in the dissolution by divorce of some 10 to 12 per cent of all marriages in Australia[6] and more than twice this

proportion in the United States. Apart from this difference in magnitude, however, the general pattern of movement in the two countries' *overall* divorce rates has been essentially the same. Both have undergone a secular increase, and both experienced a decline in the depression years and an all-time high in the period immediately following World War II.

2. Duration of Marriage. More detailed information on the character of these trends is available in the data on divorce by duration of marriage. One might reasonably suppose that an increase in the frequency of divorce would be accompanied by a shift in incidence toward the earlier years of marriage; that as divorce became more common less opprobrium would be attached to it, with the result that couples would resort to it earlier in marriage. But as Table 3 shows, this has not happened in Australia.

There have been some fluctuations, to be sure: the post-World War II upsurge involved new marriages to a greater extent than it did those of longer standing, while the general decline in rates after this peak period did not extend to couples married 20 or more years. For the present, however, it seems safe to conclude that there has been little tendency in Australia for divorce to occur either earlier or later in the course of a marriage.[7]

The Australian pattern of divorce by duration of marriage differs substantially from that in the United States. Not only is the Australian rate lower than the American, overall, it is also lower than the American at each duration of marriage (though the difference lessens with increasing duration). Moreover, while the distribution of American divorce rates by duration of marriage is markedly leptokurtic—showing a sharp peak in the second and third years, followed by steady declines with increasing duration—the distribution of the Australian

---

[5] See J. A. Barnes, "Measures of Divorce Frequency in Simple Societies," *Journal of the Royal Anthropological Institute,* **79** (1949), pp. 37–62.

[6] The proportion would be only about 3 to 4 per cent if the Australian rates in effect at the turn of the

century had continued, instead. For a discussion of the calculation of this proportion, see Day, "A Note on the Measurement of Divorce," *op. cit.*

[7] Once certain 1961 census data become available, it will be possible to determine whether this apparent anomaly in the higher durations was but a temporary phenomenon or representative, instead, of an actual change in the patterns of divorce by duration.

Table 3

Divorces per 1,000 wives, by duration of marriage: New South Wales, 1901–1947; sum of New South Wales, Victoria, South Australia, and Queensland, 1947; and Australia and the United States, 1954

Duration (years)	New South Wales				N.S.W., Vic., S. Aust. & Queensland	Australia	U.S.
	1901[a]	1921[b]	1933[c]	1947[d]	1947[e]	1954[f]	1954[g]
Under 5	.61	.46	.64	3.64	3.45	1.61	21.8
5–9	2.26	2.58	3.89	10.75	9.30	5.60	13.3
10–14	1.90	3.34	2.86	9.07	8.36	4.69	8.1
15–19	1.40	2.24	2.32	7.56	6.68	3.69	6.3
20–24	—	—	1.83	4.49	—	3.27	5.2
20–29	.70	2.49	1.52	3.87	2.65	2.77	4.5
25–29	—	—	1.08	3.14	—	2.23	3.7
30–39	.34*	.84	.50	1.27	1.13	1.14	2.0

* Calculated on the basis of only 12 divorces.

[a] Denominator calculated from *New South Wales Census of 1901*, Table XV.

Numerator $= \dfrac{\text{divorces for 1899} + \text{divorces for 1900}}{2}$; includes nullities of marriage and judicial separations.

Source of numerator: *Wealth and Progress of New South Wales*, 1898–99, pp. 584–585, and 1900–01, pp. 975–975.

[b] Denominator calculated on the assumption that the duration-specific distribution of couples not enumerated together (N = 58,380 = 15 per cent of all couples) was the same as that of couples who *were* enumerated together. Source of denominator: *1921 Census of Commonwealth*, Vol. I, Part viii, Table 12, and Vol. II, Part xxvii, Table 18, p. 1978.
Numerator = divorces for 1922, exclusive of nullities of marriage (n = 5) and judicial separations (n = 8). Source of numerator: *Official Yearbook of New South Wales*, 1923, pp. 247–248.

[c] Denominator from unpublished data from the 1933 census of the Commonwealth furnished by the Bureau of Census and Statistics. Estimated on the assumption that durations not stated are distributed in the same way as the durations stated and that durations of couples *not* enumerated together are distributed in the same way as those of couples who *were* enumerated together. Numerator consists only of divorces. Source of numerator: *Official Yearbook of New South Wales*, 1932–33, p. 730.

[d] Denominator calculated from *1947 Census of the Commonwealth*, Vol. III, Part xxviii, Table 3, on the assumption that the distribution by age and duration of those with *duration* not stated was the same as for those with duration stated. Numerator consists only of divorces. Source of numerator: *Statistical Register of New South Wales*, 1946–47, p. 585.

[e] Denominator: See note d.
Numerator consists only of divorces. Sources of numerator: *Statistical Register of New South Wales*, 1946–47, p. 585; *Victorian Yearbook*, 1946–47, p. 154; *Statistical Register of South Australia*, 1947–48, p. I-6; and *Queensland Yearbook*, 1948, p. 87.

[f] Denominator calculated on the assumption that the duration-specific distribution of couples *not* enumerated together (n = 23,325 = 1 per cent of all couples) was the same as that of couples who *were* enumerated together. Source of denominator: unpublished results of family tabulation from census of 1954. Numerator consists only of divorces. Source of numerator: *Demography Bulletin*, 1954, Table 59.

[g] Derived from Jacobson and Jacobson, *op. cit.*, Table 44, and Tables A21 and A22.

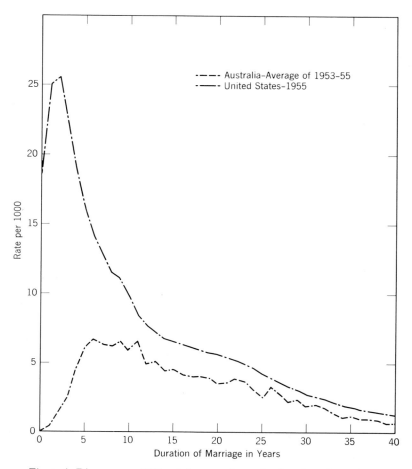

Figure 1. Divorces per 1000 existing marriages: by duration of marriage

rates, after the first three to four years, is essentially platykurtic (see Figure 1.). As I shall show presently, the very low Australian rates in the earliest durations of marriage may be largely attributed to the relatively long waiting period required by that country's divorce laws. Yet, if legal requirements create a build-up of demand during the early duration-years, it apparently does not result in any great rush to the divorce courts, once these requirements have been met. To be sure, the highest incidence of divorce in Australia occurs in the fifth to ninth years of marriage. Yet the rates in these duration-years differ little from the rates at the next higher durations (10–14 years), which in turn differ little from those at the next higher durations (15–19 years), and so on.

3. Children. One consequence of these differences in divorce rates by duration of marriage is that Australian divorces are more likely than American to involve children. In 1954, for example, children had been born to 57 per cent of the Australian couples who obtained a divorce at marriage durations of 0 to 14 years, and to 78 per cent of those who obtained one at durations of 15 to 19 years. The corresponding proportions among Americans were 40 and 62 per cent, respectively. Nevertheless, because the divorce rate is lower, the proportion of *all* children affected by divorce is substantially lower in Australia than it is in the United States. For example, if the Australian rates of 1954 and the American rates of 1948[8] were to hold throughout the first 14 years of a child's life, some 2 per cent of all Australian children and some 8 per cent of all American children would be directly affected by divorce before reaching their fifteenth birthdays. Admittedly, American rates were unusually high in 1948 (although lower that year than in the four preceding years), but the difference between the two countries is far greater than could be accounted for by either a sudden, and temporary, rise in American rates or a similarly sudden and temporary decline in Australian rates.

Although most of this difference between Australia and the United States in the proportion of children affected by divorce appears to be due to differences in the timing of *divorce*, a portion of it could also be due to differences in the timing of *childbearing*. The Australian generally marries at a later age than the American. But once married, he tends to let less time elapse before the commencement of childbearing: the proportion still childless after but *five* years of marriage in Australia (in 1954) was no higher than the proportion still childless in the United States (in 1950) after fully 10+ years of marriage.[9]

But even though Australian divorces are more likely than not to involve children, divorced couples have had, nevertheless, a consistently higher incidence of childlessness and a consistently lower average family size (even when the calculation excludes childless couples) than has the married population generally. This has been true of each marriage duration. The importance of calculating on the basis of year of separation instead of year of divorce (if the necessary data are available—which they seldom are) has been amply demonstrated.[10] Yet, even under the quite extreme assumption that cohabitation ceases an average of five years before the date of divorce— i.e., that the number of children born to divorcing couples of, say, 10–14 years' marriage duration would be more appropriately compared with that of non-divorcing couples of only 5–9 years' duration—couples whose marriages ended in divorce would still have a substantially lower average issue; and a substantially higher proportion of them would still have remained childless. Divorce involves many young children in Australia, but the number affected is smaller than it would be if divorcing couples had the same childbearing patterns as non-divorcing couples. (See Table 4).

Table 4 shows that both fertility and the extent of childlessness among couples obtaining a divorce were quite stable between 1921 and 1954. This is in direct contrast to the extensive fertility declines experienced by the total population over the same period.[11] The only exceptions to the stability of these figures for divorcing couples occurred at durations of 15–19 years in 1933 and 0–9 years in 1947; these are attributable to the separation of spouses during World Wars I and II, which doubtless increased the extent of involuntary childlessness and postponed second and higher-order births.

Why should these figures for divorcing couples show so little change over the period under consideration, while those for the total population show so much? Perhaps the answer can be found in the underlying conditions associated with the increased incidence of divorce. From the fact that more couples resort to

[8] This is the only year for which these data are available for the United States. See Jacobson and Jacobson, *op. cit.*, Table 61.

[9] Limiting our calculation to wives resident with their husbands whose current marriages occurred before the age of 30, the figure is 12.7 per cent for the Australians (Australian-born) and 12.6 per cent for the Americans. For white Americans only it is 11.8 per cent. Australian figure calculated from special tabulations of 1954 census; United States figure, from U.S. Bureau of the Census, *U.S. Census of Population: 1950*, Vol. IV, *Special Reports*, Part 2, Chapter E, "Duration of Current Marital Status," Washington, D.C.: U.S. Government Printing Office, 1955, Tables 4 and 8.

[10] See Thomas P. Monahan, "When Married Couples Part: Statistical Trends and Relationships in Divorce," *American Sociological Review*, **27** (October, 1962), pp. 625–633.

[11] Data that would show whether the total population experienced similar declines in the extent of childlessness by duration are not available.

Table 4

(1) Average issue, by duration of marriage: couples obtaining a divorce in specified years compared with all couples, New South Wales only

Duration of Marriage (Years)	Average issue							
	1921		1933		1947		1954	
	Divorcing couples	All couples	Divorcing couples	All couples	Divorcing couples	All couples	Divorcing couples	All couples
0–4	.41	.82	.38	@	.23	@	.23	.75
5–9	.76	2.18	.74	@	.64	@	.75	1.82
10–14	1.26	3.14	1.27	@	1.28	2.24	1.23	2.27
15–19	1.87	3.88	1.53	@	1.75	2.68	1.67	2.54
20–24	2.26	4.43	2.20	@	2.06	2.95	1.98	2.69
25–29	—	—	2.67	@	2.49	3.23	2.13	2.73
30+	—	—	—	—	3.29	4.14	2.74	3.47
0–14	.93	1.94	.91	@	.77	@	.87	1.60
0–19	1.10	2.26	1.03	@	.93	@	1.02	1.78

Table 4

(2) Per cent childless, by duration of marriage: couples obtaining a divorce in New South Wales in specified years, and all Australian-born couples in the Commonwealth in 1954

Duration of Marriage	New South Wales				Commonwealth 1954		
	(a)	(b)	(c)	(d)	(e)	(f)	
	Divorcing couples				Divorcing couples	All Australian-born couples	Ratio: * Col. (e) ÷ Col. (f)
	1922	1933	1947	1954			
0–4	62	67	78	68	68	44	1.54
5–9	46	45	51	47	45	17	2.71
10–14	29	32	30	31	30	14	2.25
15–19	16	31	19	20	22	12	1.85
20–24	14	12	12	14	17	12	1.44
25–29	—	13	11	11	16	12	1.39
30+	—	—	10	13	..	..	..
0–14	42	42	49	44	43	25	1.71
0–19	37	40	44	40	39	22	1.74

— Too few cases for comparison: N less than 40.
@ Not available.
.. Not calculated.
* Calculated from percentages carried to one decimal place.

Sources: 1921–22 Data for all couples calculated from *1921 Census of Australia*, Vol. II, Part xxviii, Tables 14 and 17. Data for couples obtaining a divorce are for 1922, *not* 1921. Calculated from Government of New South Wales, *Statistical Register of New South Wales*, 1922–23, Table 36.
1933 Data available only for couples obtaining a divorce. Calculated from Government of New South Wales, *Statistical Register of New South Wales*, 1933–34, Table 93.
1947 Data for couples obtaining a divorce calculated from Government of New South Wales, *Statistical Register of New South Wales, 1946–47*, Table 9. Data for all couples calculated from *1947 Census of Australia*, Vol. III, Part xxviii, Tables 2 and 8.
1954 Data for couples obtaining a divorce calculated from Government of New South Wales, *Statistical Register of New South Wales, 1953–54*, Table 9. Data for all couples are for the entire Commonwealth, *not* merely New South Wales. Rates for New South Wales in previous years are virtually identical with those for the Commonwealth, however, so there should not be much difference between them in 1954, either. Calculated from Commonwealth Bureau of Census and Statistics, *Census of 1954*, Vol. 8—*Australia*, "Statistician's Report," pp. 318, 324.

divorce, one can infer—though not prove—that divorce has become socially more acceptable. To the extent that this is so, one can hypothesize that those who resort to divorce are less likely than formerly to be deviant in other ways. At least so far as fertility is concerned, couples whose marriages ended in divorce in 1922 were generally a deviant group. But their deviance— toward lower fertility—was in the direction being taken (a few steps behind) by the population as a whole. Divorcing couples, on the average, simply arrived there first. As the pattern of lower fertility has diffused throughout Australian society, the fertility gap between divorcing couples and all other couples has also narrowed appreciably.

4. Age. Because divorce is so clearly related to duration of marriage, the most meaningful analysis of age-specified divorce rates would use data standardized for duration. Unfortunately, the materials currently available for Australia do not permit such standardization. The only age-specific rates that can be calculated are of the kind presented in Table 5.

As one would expect from the pattern of divorce by duration of marriage, the pattern of divorce by age takes a generally platykurtic form around the ages which couples are most likely to have been married some six to 15 years. The differences between the male and female rates can be accounted for entirely in terms of the general difference between the sexes in age at marriage.

5. Relative Ages of Husband and Wife. If age is classified in single years, only 10 per cent of the husbands and wives enumerated together in the Australian census of 1954 were of the same age at last birthday. Expressing age in 5-year intervals, instead, raises this proportion to only 40 per cent. Among all couples enumerated together the average age difference was 3.3 years.

Are these age differences likely to be reflected in differential divorce rates? From the available evidence it appears that they are. The numbers of divorces by relative ages (in single years) of husband and wife at time of divorce have been published in *Demography Bulletin* for each year since 1950. Relating the 1954 frequencies obtained from this source to the number of couples in each 5-year relative age classification recorded in the 1954 census (that is, relating them to the respective populations "at risk") discloses a definite pattern of divorce differentials: (a) The lowest divorce rates are for couples whose ages fall within the same 5-year age category. (b) Irrespective of age, a higher divorce rate occurs with each increase in intervals between the ages of husband and wife. Two examples of this relationship are given in Table 6, the first of which is based on the age of the husband; the second, on the age of the wife.

A possibly serious deficiency in these data is the fact that age is recorded as of the time of *divorce*, not *marriage*. Age differences of, say, 5 to 10 years are doubtless of far greater importance to couples who marry in their teens or twenties than to those who marry in their

Table 5

Annual number of divorces occurring per 1,000 married persons, by age and sex: Australia, 1947 and 1954*

	15–19	20–24	25–29	30–34	35–39	40–44	45–49	50 and over
				Males				
1954	—	2.1	4.8	5.1	4.9	4.1	3.4	1.5
1947	—	2.9	6.9	7.8	6.8	5.4	3.9	1.4
				Females				
1954	1.3	3.4	5.5	5.1	4.6	3.8	2.9	1.1
1947	1.2	4.8	8.0	7.2	5.9	4.5	2.9	1.0

*Numerators $= \dfrac{\Sigma(\text{age and sex-specific divorces in 1946-48})}{3}$ and $\dfrac{\Sigma(\text{age and sex-specific divorces in 1953-55})}{3}$,

respectively.

Source: Calculated from data in censuses and *Demography Bulletin*.

Table 6

Examples of divorce ratios for couples with ages in different 5-year age categories as a percentage of divorce ratios for couples with ages in the same 5-year category: Australia, 1954.

Age of husband last birthday	Age of wife, last birthday					
	25–29	30–34	35–39	40–44	45–49	
35–39	131	101	100	107	146*	
Age of wife last birthday	Age of husband, last birthday					
	30–34	35–39	40–44	45–49	50–54	55–59
40–44	226	137	100	102	109	113

* Based on fewer than 20 divorces. (No calculation made where divorces numbered fewer than 15.)

thirties or forties. Another deficiency is that neither duration of marriage nor number of children is taken into account. Nevertheless, our findings may be taken as highly suggestive of the relevance to divorce rates of age differences between spouses.

Such differences may well indicate divergencies in interests and personalities, giving rise to friction between husband and wife. But they may also indicate the extent to which the parties to a marriage conform to the norms of the society, an interpretation that recieves some support from the fact that the differences tend to be smaller when the husband is older than the wife (a condition more in keeping with the norm) than when the wife is older than the husband. As long as divorce remains outside the bounds of fully acceptable behavior, we could expect it to be more common among those whose marriages were formed, in the first place, somewhat outside the range of full social acceptance. Marriages involving substantial age differences between husband and wife would seem to be just "abnormalities."

Discussion

To account for differences in the incidence of divorce, either between separate jurisdictions or over time in the same jurisdiction, one must assess the relative importance of three interlocking determinants: (1) the availability of divorce, (2) the availability of alternatives to divorce, and (3) the extent of marital discord.[12]

[12] Cf. William J. Goode, op. cit., pp. 512–513, 516–517, 525.

Marital discord itself is probably ubiquitous. Whether it results in divorce, however, is determined, first, by the availability of this particular "remedy" for it and, second, by the availability of alternative remedies. By "availability" I mean not only the actual existence of divorce or other "remedy," but the extent to which the divorced person can adjust to the condition of being divorced, together with the extent to which the various remedies for marital discord are acceptable to the parties concerned.[13] "Availability" has, then, both existential and normative components.

Although it is not altogether clear just what the *positive* existential extreme would be with respect to divorce, it is obvious that some Catholic countries—Portugal, Spain, the Republic of Ireland, for example—by allowing no divorce at all, occupy a position at the *negative* extreme of the continuum.[14] Yet, even in countries where divorce is allowed, access to it is ordinarily so restricted as to justify the claim that "Society seems not to be vitally concerned with the happiness of individuals in marriage. It would much prefer that couples remain married, though unhappy, rather than be divorced."[15]

A very partial idea of the range of acceptability can be gained from a comparison of the

[13] For an example of the consequences of differences in "availability" see Judson T. Landis, "Social Correlates of Divorce or Nondivorce among the Unhappily Married," *Marriage and Family Living*, **25** (May, 1963), pp. 178–180.
[14] Portugal, however, does permit divorce for the small number of non-Catholics within its borders.
[15] Ray H. Abrams, "The Concept of Family Stability," *Annals*, **272** (November, 1950), p. 5.

various laws regulating divorce. So far as we know, for instance, mutual dislike—or, for that matter, mutual indifference—is nowhere in the Western world, save in Norway,[16] a sufficient legal ground for dissolving a marriage. But adultery, especially on the part of the wife, is one of the commonest grounds of all. In some jurisdictions (e.g., New York) it is the only ground.

We have seen that patterns of divorce in Australia are substantially different from those in the United States. Though research into the origins of these differences needs still to be undertaken, it is possible to enumerate, on the basis of our trinity of casual elements, some of the more fruitful lines of approach such research could take.

1. Is Divorce Less "Available" in Australia than in the United States? I have combined the various state statistics for both Australia and the United States as though each country were legally homogeneous; but actually, of course, divorce laws over the period under consideration varied substantially within both countries—particularly the United States. In certain American states these laws were more liberal than any in Australia, while in others they were far more stringent. Nevertheless, in 1950, a year when the overall American divorce rate (i.e., per 1,000 existing marriages) was only 73 per cent of what it had been in 1947 (and only 56 per cent of what it had been in the peak year, 1946), the divorce rate in all but five states of the Union was higher than in Australia in the latter's *peak* year, 1947. Thirty-eight of the states exceeded this peak Australian figure by at least 35 per cent; 35 of them, by at least 50 per cent.[17] Only New York had a rate as low as the 1954 Australian rate, and this is hardly indicative of the actual resort to divorce by New York residents. For legal limitations on divorce in that state are so stringent that the number getting decrees outside the state is estimated to have fluctuated

between a figure 30 to 200 per cent as high as the number obtaining them within it.[18]

Legal differences may, however, account for some of the differential in rates at the early marriage durations. Generally speaking, the waiting period is shorter in the United States than in Australia. What in Australia must in many instances have been (until the establishment of the new divorce law) a period of voluntary separation while the spouses awaited expiration of some minimum time period (usually three years), was in most American states accorded, instead, the sanction of a final divorce decree. That this accounts at most for only a portion of the difference between American and Australian rates at the early marriage durations, however, is suggested by data for the Australian states of New South Wales, Tasmania, and South Australia. Before institution of the Matrimonial Causes Act 1959, New South Wales offered the possibility of somewhat earlier divorce by admitting as a ground the failure to comply, for a period of not less than one year, with a decree for restitution of conjugal rights. But despite this greater liberality so far as the duration of marriage was concerned, the proportion granted divorces on grounds of desertion (which included failure to comply with a decree for restitution of conjugal rights) was no higher in New South Wales than in the other Australian states, where the laws were essentially the same in other respects. In Tasmania, where a wife could petition for a divorce on the grounds of her husband's desertion for a period of two years (as against three years elsewhere), one might expect a higher proportion of all divorces to have been for desertion, but as it happened, the proportion in Tasmania was roughly the same as elsewhere: some years a little higher; some years a little lower. In South Australia the more liberal ruling on what constituted legal cruelty did result in a substantially higher proportion using this as a ground for divorce action (apparently, in view of the percentage distribution, almost entirely as an alternative to

---

[16] Carl Jacob Arnholm, *Familierett* (3rd ed.), Oslo: Johan Grundt Tanum, 1958, pp. 278–279.
[17] Calculated from U.S. Bureau of the Census, *Statistical Abstract of the United States: 1959*, Washington, D.C., Table 38, and Paul H. Jacobson and Pauline F. Jacobson, *op. cit.*, Table A19.

[18] Paul H. Jacobson and Pauline F. Jacobson, *op. cit.*, p. 116, and Paul H. Jacobson, "Marital Dissolutions in New York State in Relation to Their Trend in the United States," *Milbank Memorial Fund Quarterly*, 28 (January, 1950), p. 42.

desertion). Yet, in 1947, the only year for which this comparison can be made, the divorce rate for the first five years of marriage was no higher in either New South Wales or South Australia than it was in Victoria, where these more liberal provisions were not in effect.[19]

Differences between the laws of the two countries, then, were probably of little importance in creating the differences in their divorce patterns, except so far as they served to prevent Australians from obtaining divorces within the first three years of marriage. This doubtless accounts for much of the difference in their rates at durations of less than five years, but it can not account either for the differences between them at durations of five or more years, or for the fact that the American rates are higher than the Australian at *every* duration. Thus, differences in law would seem to account for only a limited amount of the overall difference between Australian and American patterns of divorce.

Because divorce rates declined during the depression of the 1930's, we might reason that the monetary cost of divorce is itself a factor of some importance in determining the level of divorce rates at any one time. The specific effect of monetary factors is not easily assessed, however. Depression may leave fewer couples able to afford the requisite legal charges, the expenses of separate maintenance, and the like, but it is also possible that depression deters a certain number of wives from seeking a divorce because of the difficulties they expect to encounter in attempting to support themselves.

With respect to legal expenses themselves we have only very partial evidence for Australia, and virtually none at all for the United States. No study has been made of the costs of divorce action in Australia, but inquiries directed to two members of the law faculty at the Australian National University (one of whom had a sizeable divorce practice before he entered academic life), to a leading law firm in the Capital Territory, and to civil servants in the governments of both the Commonwealth and the state of New South Wales, revealed considerable agreement that the typical fee for an undefended case is between £A125 and £A140 ($280–315)

for both parties combined, though some lawyers were known to charge as little as £A70 ($160), while fees for defended cases might run as high as £A1,000 ($2,250), or even more. My informants felt that costs might be a bit higher in the state of Queensland, a bit lower in Victoria, and quite a bit lower in the three other states— South Australia, Western Australia, and Tasmania. Since only a small proportion of cases are defended,[20] the great majority cost the parties no more than about £A140 and in most instances considerably less.

Just how this compares with the American situation has been impossible to determine. From their admittedly limited experience with it my Australian informants felt that although the range of charges was probably greater in the United States, the majority were doubtless higher than in Australia. However, this is not borne out by a Kansas study involving interviews with 32 lawyers. Though there was little agreement about legal costs of divorce actions among these lawyers, the minimum figures mentioned were in most instances little different from those current in Australia. Some cited $150, but most named $250, $300 or $350 as the minimums in their respective localities. All agreed, however, that the actual fee would exceed the minimum, depending on the ability to pay, the amount of property, and the amount of legal work involved;[21] thus the proportion who pay more than the minimum is probably far higher in the United States than it is in Australia. Where they occurred, the court awards in the 40 divorce actions considered in this Kansas study varied between $150 and $425.[22]

That these Kansas figures may be relatively

[19] Unfortunately, there are no data by which to make a comparison with the 1947 Tasmanian rate.

[20] Tentative figures supplied us by Mr. Norman Brown, Deputy Registrar in Divorce, State of New South Wales, show that of the 3,337 divorces occurring during the 12-month period October 1, 1962– September 30, 1963, only 255 (7 per cent) were defended, and only 112 others involved disputes over custody of children, maintenance, or property division that required a court judgment for settlement.

[21] Dan Hopson, Jr., "The Economics of a Divorce: A Pilot Empirical Study at the Trial Court Level," *The University of Kansas Law Review*, **11** (October, 1962), p. 142.

[22] *Ibid.*, p. 143.

low is suggested by the few figures mentioned in passing in an article concerned with allowing counsel fees to the wife in matrimonial actions. For what appeared to involve relatively little legal work, the courts mentioned made awards ranging from $400 to $1,000.[23]

Neither of these studies supplies any information on costs that is of much practical interest to us, however. If divorce is either more or less expensive in Australia than in the United States, it has yet to be demonstrated.

With respect to the other non-legal determinants, however, divorce does indeed seem to be less available in Australia than in the United States, as its lower frequency, and its timing, strongly suggest. Since there are fewer divorces, and since when divorce occurs it is less likely to be concentrated within a relatively narrow age group, one is apt to know fewer divorced (or divorcing) persons. Divorce is less "in the air"; and as a consequence, perhaps, less likely to come to mind as a suitable "solution" to one's current troubles. Moreover, the relative difficulty of getting a divorce within the first three years of marriage may serve as a "cooling off" factor. And it is possible, too, that religious opposition is stronger in Australia than in the United States.[24]

To the possibility of greater normative restrictions in Australia must be added the possibility of greater restrictions from other sources: the generally shorter interval between marriage and birth of the first child; the seemingly fewer economic opportunities for women[25] (which might make a wife more hesitant to abandon a relationship in which she and her children received financial support for one in which the burden of support would devolve upon her, instead); and the generally later age at marriage (which might persuade the potential divorcee

that her chances of remarriage were only negligible).[26]

2. Are alternatives to divorce more "available" in Australia than in the United States? Is it easier for the unhappily married Australian to find alternative relationships or activities which, without necessitating a complete dissolution of his marriage, provide some compensation for what he finds unsatisfactory in that marriage? To ask such a question is, of course, to imply that the more available such substitutes are, the less will be the need to resort to divorce. This may not be altogether valid. If we take as "alternatives" such things as concubinage, adultery, desertion, the opportunity to form close friendships with persons of the opposite sex, the consequences could be in either direction: lowering the divorce rate by meeting needs unmet within marriage; or raising it by providing an inducement to dissolve one relationship in order to form another.

An important exception—an "alternative" that, while offering one kind of adjustment to an unhappy marital situation, seems to offer no counterbalancing incentive to divorce (at least for husbands)—is the Australian pattern of male "mateship." This is a very widespread civilian counterpart of the "buddy system" that exists among enlisted men in the American armed forces. With roots that are said to go back to the extremely harsh physical conditions facing the pioneers, and also to the trenches of World War I, "mateship" seems by now to have evolved into a largely recreational phenomenon. Far more than his American counterpart, the Australian male appears to obtain his recreation in the company of other men—whether at one

[23] Arlyss Welch Spence, "Counsel Fees in Matrimonial Actions," *Nebraska Law Review*, **38** (May, 1959), pp. 771, 777, 778.

[24] Though Roman Catholics comprise approximately a quarter of the adult population in both countries, a far higher proportion of the Australian non-Catholic population claims membership in the Protestant denominations (notably the Anglican) that seriously restrict divorce.

[25] See Norman MacKenzie, *Women in Australia*, Melbourne: F. W. Cheshire, 1962, esp. Part 3.

[26] Nor is this likely to be offset in the Australian situation by any attributes of the sex ratio. In 1954, the sex ratio was more favorable to the marriage (or remarriage) of women than of men within each single-year age grouping below the age of 55. But if the ratio of men age x to women age x–3 (a ratio more in keeping with the actual Australian pattern of age differences between spouses) is taken, instead, the women's favored position disappears by age 32, reappearing briefly at ages 35–38, and then only occasionally at higher ages. (Calculated from *1954 Census of Australia*, Vol. VIII, Part 1, "Cross-Classifications of the Characteristics of the Population." Table 4.)

of the ubiquitous "pubs" (from which women are virtually excluded), at the Returned Servicemen's League, the movies, or watching a game of "Australian Rules." "Mateship" is by no means limited to the unhappily married. Yet, in "mateship" men in this unenviable state have a ready-to-hand source for many of the satisfactions that a society characterized by more companionable marriages would expect them to obtain primarily in the company of their wives.

3. *Is there less marital discord in Australia than in the United States?* This is difficult to answer, whether we measure discord in terms of incidence or intensity. Much could be gained from comparative research into what Australian and American couples expect out of marriage. Much could also be gained from comparative research into the degree of specialization in the respective roles of husband and wife. One gets the impression from personal observation and from the rather scant literature on this aspect of the Australian family[27] that in terms of companionship and the fulfillment of emotional needs Australians expect rather less from marriage than do Americans. If less is, indeed, expected of a marriage, then discord is less likely to arise from disappointment in it. Perhaps what has been noted of Australian attitudes toward work applies as well to the Australian family: the Australian "would prefer to reduce his needs in order that they may be fulfilled."[28]

It seems likely, also, that the "partnership" type of marriage is less common in Australia than in the United States. The strength of such marriages is that they permit richer, fuller relations between a husband and wife well suited to one another; their weakness, that they maxi-

mize the chances of difficulty arising between those who are not.[29] Compared with American couples, the Australian husband and wife seem to share fewer activities and to participate less often in joint decision-making.[30] The consequence is a reduction in the opportunities for friction.

It is possible, too, that the generally older marriage age in Australia, by at least permitting a longer period of courtship, reduces the risk of mismatching and hence of marital disharmony.[31]

Finally, we might look to the Australian environment itself for an explanation of the lower Australian divorce rate. In terms of relative material prosperity, freedom from anxiety occasioned by international and domestic crises, climate, and general ease of living, Australia appears to present fewer day-to-day problems— or, at least, to offer more opportunity to adjust to them, if by no other means than resort to various mechanisms of withdrawal, including "mateship." Although the population is largely concentrated in five metropolitan areas, residential crowding is rare, the magnificent beaches are easily reached and completely free of charge, and ready access can be had to seemingly limitless open space inland. Moreover, the generally mild, sunny weather is conducive to outdoor

[27] See, e.g., W. D. Borrie, "The Family," in George Caiger (ed.), *The Australian Way of Life*, London: William Heinemann, 1953; Jean I. Martin, "Marriage, the Family and Class," Harold Fallding, "Inside the Australian Family," and Morven S. Brown, "Changing Functions of the Australian Family," in A. P. Elkin (ed.), *Marriage and the Family in Australia*, Sydney: Angus and Robertson, 1957; Frank A. Doczy, *Australian Women*, Melbourne: W. & J. Barr, 1957; O. A. Oeser and S. B. Hammond, *Social Structure and Personality in a City*, London: Routledge and Kegan Paul, 1954.

[28] Jeanne MacKenzie, *Australian Paradox*, Melbourne: F. W. Cheshire, 1961, p. 108.

[29] See A. Joseph Brayshaw, "The Stability of Marriage," *Eugenics Review*, **44** (July, 1952), pp. 88–89, and Leo Zakuta, "Equality in North American Marriages," *Social Research*, 30 (Summer, 1963), pp. 164–167.

[30] The American situation is summarized in Robin M. Williams, Jr., *American Society: A Sociological Interpretation*, New York: Alfred A. Knopf, 1951, pp. 55–61, 73–74, and also in Talcott Parsons, "Age and Sex in the Social Structure of the United States," *American Sociological Review*, **7** (October, 1942), and in Leo Zakuta, *op. cit.* The contrasting Australian pattern has been noted by a number of observers. See, e.g., D. H. Lawrence, *Kangaroo*, London: Martin Secker, 1923; Jeanne MacKenzie, *op. cit.*, especially Chs. 8 and 9; Sidney J. Baker, *The Drum: Australian Character and Slang*, Sydney: Currawong Publishing Co., 1959, Ch. 4; and John Douglas Pringle, *Australian Accent*, London: Chatto and Windus, 1958, Ch. 2.

[31] The widely held belief that younger marriage ages necessarily lead to more divorce, however, receives no confirmation in calculations we have made (on the basis of marriage "cohorts") of Australian divorce rates in the 1950's. See Lincoln H. Day, *op. cit.*

recreation all year round. If frequent escape into the out-of-doors can render a not-so-happy marriage more tolerable (or create a more favorable setting for sharing recreational and other interests), Australian couples would seem to have an environment less conducive to divorce than that available to most Americans.

All things considered, then, I would suggest that divorce is less frequent in Australia than in the United States partly because it is less available (largely in the non-legal sense), partly because at least one alternative "remedy" for marital disharmony (viz., "mateship") is more available, and partly because there is less marital disharmony. But these are only impressions as to the causal elements involved. The differences in patterns of divorce between Australia and the United States are firmly established. It is accounting for these differences that now poses the challenge to research.

Chapter 9

Socialization
and Permanent Availability

The relationship between social structure and socialization may be viewed in either of two ways. One perspective suggests that socialization practices and personality are determined by social structure. In this view, as changes occur in social structure, socialization practices are modified. For example, Miller and Swanson argue that when the number of business enterprises in the United States was increasing at a rapid rate middle-class children were socialized to become successful entrepreneurs. This meant the development of child-rearing practices which would produce highly individualized, self-reliant, self-disciplined persons willing to take risks. As the social structure changed to one dominated by large-scale bureaucracies, the individual entrepreneur became a misfit. In a bureaucracy competence in interpersonal relations became important, and parents began to emphasize this quality in their child-rearing practices.[1]

An alternative view is that the large social structure exists as a projection of the individuals' needs; that is, individuals project on society those norms and values consistent with their personality needs. These personality needs develop in the primary institutions, especially the family. From a series of conflicting societal norms and values, the individual selects those that accord with his personality needs. If the child has been raised in a family characterized by benevolent child-rearing, his views on economic structure and religion will reflect this benevolence. On the other hand, if the parental treatment has been harsh or punitive, this view will also be projected on society.[2]

The position taken in this book on the role of social structure is that certain kinds of changes in kinship arrangements affect family interaction and influence the socialization of children. Why do kinship arrangements change? Many factors may be responsible; first, the kinship organization may have to be modified to coexist with

---

[1] See selection by Miller and Swanson in this chapter.
[2] Abram Kardiner, "The Concept of Basic Personality Structure as an Operational Tool in the Social Sciences," in Ralph Linton (ed.), *The Science of Man in World Crisis*, New York: Columbia University Press, 1945, pp. 107–122.

a given economic, political, and religious social structure (e.g., capitalism, democracy, Protestant society). Second, the proportions of population segments may change so that what was formerly a minority (e.g., urban population) may become the majority. Third, the immigration of diverse ethnic groups may produce new traditions. Fourth, the age and sex structure of the population may shift (e.g., increase in life-span and in surviving males). Some of these factors have been mentioned in earlier chapters as facilitating the increase in bilaterality in kinship relations in American society.

Bilateral kinship systems influence the socialization of children in ways appropriate to permanent availability for marriage. In societies in which bilateral kinship predominates, there is substitutability of personnel in kinship relations (as indicated in the papers by Farber and by Cumming and Schneider in this volume). Substitutability implies that in the kinship organization itself no particular individual or group is assigned the specific responsibility or authority for stabilizing kin relationships. This absence of responsibility is sustained by the primacy of the sibling-group bond in bilateral kinship. There is a general equality of status among brothers and sisters in the unity of the bilateral sibling group. Any sibling's rights and obligations are interchangeable with those of any other (except for minor distinctions between older and younger siblings in some bilateral societies).

The importance of sibling bonds in the bilateral system and the apparent incorporation of the spouse into the sibling group implies that the spouse himself (or herself) is a substitute sibling. This interpretation of the spouse's role in the sibling group is consistent with the finding by Habenstein and Coult among Kansas City couples that same-sex siblings tend not to report each other's spouses as close or intimate.[3] Their study suggests that the incest taboo is extended to all consanguine and affinal members of the sibling group.

Although the presence of sex relations differentiates the husband-wife from the brother-sister relationship, much husband-wife interaction is concerned with nonsexual matters in spouse-parent roles, including housekeeping, community, and domestic activities, interaction with or concerning children, and participation with relatives and friends. In nonsexual matters siblings can act (and often have acted) as substitutes for the spouse, either in emergencies or sometimes in a mutual assistance pact. Moreover, when assistance is needed, there is no obligation to secure this help from any particular brother or sister, for all siblings have an equal status. Financial assistance can be sought from one sibling and household assistance from another. Close relationships can be established with one sibling at one time and with a different sibling at another time. Because cousins can be substituted for siblings, a sufficient number of siblings and cousins is usually available to establish a workable sibling like group. If the spouse is regarded as a quasi-sibling, then he (or she) is also considered substitutable.

The individual well-adjusted to a situation of substitutability of persons in intimate relationships is one who is facile in creating and breaking intimate ties. This is the same kind of competence required in bureaucratic structures, according to Miller and Swanson. Such competence rests on a norm requiring commitment in intimate

---

[3] Robert W. Habenstein and Allan D. Coult, *The Function of Extended Kinship in Urban Society*, Kansas City, Missouri: Community Studies, 1965.

relationships only as long as they supply personal gratification. To the extent that intimate relationships are sustained for personal satisfaction they are instruments to further specific ends rather than expressions of sentiments. Being instrumental, they make inoperative such views as one true love, marriage until death, or the sacredness of the particular marital relationship. Instead, concern with possible exploitation, emphasis on individual expression, the idea that each member of the family can act autonomously and still be accepted for "himself," and individual happiness as a criterion for marriage are consistent with the predominance of substitutability (or permanent availability) in the marriage system. Above all the individual strives for competence in formation and dissolution of intimate relationships.

Competence in intimate interpersonal relations (e.g., in mate-lover roles) is not sufficient to maintain a high availability in the marriage market. Divorce and re-marriage is facilitated when persons have considerable competence in economic institutions. A woman who can sustain herself economically between marriages is more likely to obtain a divorce than one who must face a severe reduction in standard of living. A man who is successful in his career can readily afford to pay for the support of children from a previous marriage while forming a new one. Moreover, economic success is a symbol of competence in a variety of areas and of being in the prime of adulthood. Therefore, to flourish, a marriage system based on permanent availability must emphasize economic success in socializing the child.

A note of clarification should be interjected here. The topic of concern is the flourishing of permanent availability in middle-class sectors of society. In lower socioeconomic classes other factors than competence facilitate permanent availability. Lower-class emphasis on immediate gratification and lack of sacredness in marriage provides sufficient motivation for maintaining permanent availability. The spread of permanent availability to the middle class requires different socialization practices that sustain a style of life associated with affluence but emphasize the impermanence of a specific marital relationship.

Readings on Socialization Appropriate to Permanent Availability

Study of socialization appropriate to permanent availability should focus on the development of sophistication in establishing and breaking intimate relationships. There has been little investigation of the development of sophistication in inter-personal relations. For example, Goffman describes how an experienced girl "cools out" a boy friend by according him a status as a friend; Goffman does not, however, indicate how she develops this skill. Various discussions, however, do suggest demands and facilities of the adult and adolescent cultures that enable the child to develop sophistication in making and breaking informal, intimate interpersonal relationships.

In the first paper Miller and Swanson describe the adaptation of child-rearing practices in a society moving from entrepreneurial to bureaucratic economic organization. They suggest that entrepreneurial social organization requires people who are "inner directed," authoritarian, and disciplined in the pursuit of goals, whereas the bureaucratic social organization requires individuals who are warm, friendly, and supportive of others. Their discussion indicates that bureaucratic families socialize children in ways that emphasize "selling one's self" to others and the maintenance of supportive, friendly relationships even in situations commonly defined as instrumental. Intimate relationships then no longer have the connotation of permanence.

Although Miller and Swanson do not differentiate between family and nonfamily relationships, their entrepreneurial versus bureaucratic family typology is consistent with the discussion in the introduction of Chapter 8. That discussion suggested a decline in the differentiation between the affective quality of family behavior and nonfamily interaction in bureaucratic structures. Frequently, entrepreneurs make a sharp distinction between family interaction and business behavior. Customers and employees are considered as outsiders to be exploited, whereas family relationships are supposed to be warm and protective. In bureaucratic structures, cooperation rather than exploitation is expected; with the shift to cooperative interaction, there is no longer the need to make a sharp distinction between family and extrafamily (especially economic) interaction. Both classes of interaction require some degree of personal commitment. Under these conditions, styles of behavior in familial and non-familial groups tend to merge.

The second paper, taken from the study of social climates in ten Midwestern high schools by James Coleman, describes adolescent culture through the characteristics admired in the leading cliques of the schools. Criteria for clique membership include "personality," personal attractiveness, and reputation. (Note that reputation is less prominent than personal characteristics.) These cliques control styles of dating and intimate interaction beyond their own members and provide other students with models for behavior and norms for informal, couple interaction.

The third paper, prepared by Meyerowitz and Farber, contrasts with the other papers by emphasizing the importance of the family's socioeconomic position in the community for the socialization of the child as a competent adult. The investigation reported in their paper dealt with families with six-year-old children, some of whom had been diagnosed as educable mental retardates (IQ 56–85). Isolation, lack of resources, and inattentiveness (contrasted with the situation of children in bureaucratic families or of the adolescents in leading cliques) create personalities unable to sustain stable and resourceful family relationships.

30. Changes in Society and Child Training in the United States

BY DANIEL R. MILLER AND GUY E. SWANSON

DISTINCTIVE FEATURES OF CHILD training in the recent American past and in the emerging future are now spread before us. How can the differences between the past and that developing future be explained?

The methods of child care of the first forty years of this century closely resemble the broad spirit and meaning of a style of life long associated with the older kinds of middle-class families in this country. Many of those methods can be found in use by middle-class parents over the last two hundred years. On the other hand, the parental practices that we believe are becoming conspicuous since 1940 look as if they were peculiarly in harmony with the values and ideas—with the way of life—of a new kind of middle-class person whose numbers are rapidly increasing.

We do not distinguish the "older" and "newer" middle classes by the age of their members. They differ in that the occupations in which the older middle classes are found have existed for a long time, whereas the occupations of the newer middle classes have opened up for large number of persons only within the past fifty years or so. These older and newer classes also differ in the opportunities and problems afforded by the occupations they hold.

SOURCE: The Changing American Parent, *New York: John Wiley and Sons, Inc., 1958, pp. 30–60. Reprinted by permission of the authors and publisher.*

In this chapter we want to describe the older and the newer middle-class occupations, the way of living associated with them, and how it is that each produces a distinctive pattern for the training of children. Reflecting what we believe is the most important difference between them, we shall call these two types of middle classes "individuated-entrepreneurial" and "welfare-bureaucratic"—or, for brevity, entrepreneurial and bureaucratic. We do not say that the differences between them account for all the recent changes in child care; we do want to claim that their differences are one important source of those changes.

The explanations for trends in child rearing which we develop here and in succeeding chapters require us to make many judgments and interpretations. Not all of these can be firmly substantiated with data from our study.

Fortunately, we can draw upon some fifty years of work by historians and social scientists as we try to picture recent historical changes in America. Our footnotes reflect only a small portion of our indebtedness to this previous scholarship. We have, however, projected explanations for differences in child care which cannot always be verified by referring to earlier studies. As a result, both our explanations and our findings should be considered as only suggestive of the reasons behind historical changes in methods of rearing youngsters. Predictions implied by our explanations find support in our results. Beyond that, as in any scientific enterprise, we must look to further research if the plausible is to become increasingly definitive. It will be for the sake of an uncluttered presentation, and not because we are insensitive to the preliminary state of our work, that we speak in this chapter and the next without constant qualifications and counter-arguments. Later chapters examine some explanations other than those we give here.

The Middle Classes in an Individuated and Entrepereneurial Society

The way of life of the older middle classes in the United States is best understood if we see it as growing out of the opportunities and difficulties such people experience. The way children are trained is partly set by that style of life and springs from the same sources. We shall try to explain methods of child rearing in such terms.

From their beginning, the middle classes were creatures of the rise of commerce and industry and of the cities burgeoning with these new methods of enterprise. Their fate was bound up with the classes above and below them. Middle-class persons—both older and newer—who operate a business are generally distinguished from the upper classes, by the fact that middle-class enterprises are local rather than regional or national in scope. Further, as compared with upper-class families, middle-class households do not have enough surplus income to save more than they spend. Their incomes are more likely to be in the form of salaries, wages, or profits rather than from dividends on investments. As a group, they are more likely than the upper classes to have a high school rather than a college education. Their skills are those of coordinating and recording and of providing specialized advice, but not those of controlling large organizations.

It is useful to distinguish between upper and lower middles. Upper middles are typically the owners or the managers of considerable enterprises. Or they may be persons with special skills, usually achieved through the completion of training at a college level, that enable them to take part in the planning and designing of work on which others will pass at a policy level. Or, as in the case of such independent professions as law and medicine, they have skills that enable them to deal, as no one with lesser training can, with the complexities of problems that are recurrent and most severe for the larger part of the population. As a result of the continuous demand for their skills, whether administrative or professional, such people have considerable job security and sufficient income to enable appreciable savings, while maintaining a level of life that assures plentiful food, home ownership, extended education for the children, and the maintenance of these benefits into the years after the husband has retired from active participation in the economy.

The lower middles are in much less favorable positions. They may have ownership or administrative duties in small enterprises. They may be the communicators and recorders of events— the secretaries and bookkeepers, accountants, clerks, and salesmen—in large concerns, working at a skill level requiring perhaps a high school education. Or, they may be the teachers in the public schools having, at best, an education directed toward producing very specific skills but lacking in the provision of any profound understanding of the philosophical and scientific bases of the tasks performed. Income is most likely to be in the form of salaries. They can save, but this has to be done at the expense of the current standard of living. Furthermore, that standard probably cannot be preserved after retirement. One child in the family might be given a college education or staked to a beginning in business, but most of the children would have to make their own way in life. Finally, since the skill levels of lower middles are modest and the number of such people often is large in relation to demand, their job security is not great.

We can better understand the middle-class family's life if we compare its position with that of the lower classes. Since we will include information about lower class families when we present the findings of our study, these few remarks will serve as background for that later discussion as well as for our immediate purpose of highlighting the characteristics of middles by comparing them with other social classes.

The lower classes are typically distinguished from the middle by working in occupations in which the contribution of the worker comes from manual skills or the use of muscle power. Income is in the form of wages, often on a piecework basis, but rarely on a plan like that of the annual salary which gives some guarantee of the amount that will be earned if the job continues.

The upper lower is the skilled laborer. His training in the schools may vary somewhat, but there is almost certainly a training for the job in an apprentice capacity that involves from two to four years of supervised experience. Until the period of the Second World War, the incomes of upper lowers as a group were usually somewhat lower than those for lower middles. The job security of upper lowers was comparable to that of lower middles if they worked for someone else. Their chances for moving into the upper middle or upper classes were significantly less.

This last point is often overlooked when, as we find in Detroit today, the incomes of upper lowers are slightly higher than those of lower middles. The top positions of power in our society require conceptual and administrative skills. These are not simple to acquire. The individual, usually his family as well, must come to value them and to practice them constantly so that he becomes thoroughly familiar with their uses. Further, this practice requires special education and the postponement of immediate opportunities to earn a living at jobs which, in the beginning, often afford a higher rate of pay. The individual and his family must have some incentive for that kind of sacrifice and some resources to permit its being made instead of devoting their energies to helping support the family. This is why it seems to take at least two generations for a lower-class family to shift into the middle classes with enough stability so that it becomes unlikely that it will return again to a manual labor type of job.

Along with this greater possibility for lower middles rather than upper lowers to advance to the topmost positions of the society, go at least three related advantages. First, there is the greater likelihood of being in a position to meet upper middles and upper-class persons and, having attracted their attention, to gain their help in further advancement, if not for themselves, then for their children. A second advantage of the lower middle over the upper lower is that he has developed a style of life that enables him to capitalize on such contacts and other opportunities that may open up a higher status for him. Finally, the kind of work he does is such that individual advancement, rather than the kind of collective advance that comes through the negotiations of the employee group, is more likely. These advantages have been somewhat lessened by the developments discussed under bureaucratization in the next section of this chapter, but they are still potent.

The lower lowers are the semiskilled and unskilled laborers. Their training is minimal, often requiring but a few hours on the job to equip them for work. When there is a downward trend in the business cycle or an oversupply of labor, theirs are the first jobs to be stripped of security. Such hopes as they have for advancement tend, even more than for upper lowers, to depend on political action or on worker organizations. However, since lower lowers have considerably less in the way of resources and since the road to security through these means is long and involved, they often have little incentive either for the union or for politics.

We have been highlighting the characteristics of all middle-class people by comparing them with the lower and upper classes. Now we turn to consider some features distinctive of the *older* middle classes.

In addition to having the characteristics just described, the older middle classes are entrepreneurial. This is the case not because all their members are businessmen, but because, whether owner, manager, or employee, most of their members jobs are sharply affected by the risks and vicissitudes of the market place. The entrepreneur is a man who gages how well a product or service will sell and what resources must be spent to produce and market it. His income depends on the accuracy of these judgments. Other occupations become entrepreneurial as they too are affected by these risks and dependent on the accuracy of these judgments. Such effects and dependencies were heightened for most while-collar workers by several aspects of business and industry more prevalent in the nineteenth and early twentieth centuries than today.

First, we must remember that most white-collar employees in that earlier period worked in small establishments. It is true that great enterprises could be found. It is also true, however, that they required relatively few middle-class workers. They were commanded and coordinated by a small corps of white-collar employees at the top, and manned primarily by large numbers of unskilled laborers on the production lines. The elaborate and vast clerical, managerial, engineering, sales, and accounting staffs of present-day corporations are a later development. Far larger proportions of middle-class workers found employment in small stores and workshops than is presently the case. Retailing and the "service" occupations, like manufacture, were more often on a small scale. Large department stores and chain stores did not appear in an important way until the early 1900's.

The small enterprise is highly susceptible to market fluctuations. It lacks resources to tide it over the declines of the business cycle or the difficulties created by the misjudgment of its operators. Its employees, like its managers, become very sensitive to risk and to the impact of the current success of the business on their income.

The second sense in which the older middle classes are entrepreneurial is that risk taking and the creation of enterprise is valued as the highest of economic activities. Financial success as well as financial failure is always possible. Their children prize entrepreneurship as the ideal occupation. Home and school praise and train for it. The heroes of fiction succeed through it. Religion commends it to man as the will of God.

But we say these older middle classes are individuated as well as entrepreneurial. What does that mean?

Individuated people lack close and continuing contacts with each other. They are like the heroes and heroines of so much of recent American fiction, who walk alone through a world crowded with other wanderers. What they have of the world's goods they win for themselves. If they have nothing, it means they have not been able to appropriate what they desired.

Increasingly, they lack friends and firmly held convictions and a sense of common humanity with their fellows. They are isolated and lonely.

To be individuated is not to be individualistic. The individualistic person has a personal, private life that he cherishes. Like that notable individualist, Thomas Jefferson, he pursues his own interests with zest, convinced of their importance. He sees other people as like himself in possessing personal interests. He believes that they should be encouraged to develop those interests, to pursue those interests, and to be protected and supported in what they choose to do. To him, each person is important as a living, creative being, sharing with him a common human condition.

City life makes people individuated. The very size of cities makes it difficult for them to know most of those whom they see on the streets. At the same time, urban conditions sap the strength of kinship ties. The urban worker depends on his wage or salary from a job that does not put him to work with his relatives. He must, in a dynamic economy, be ready to move his residence to obtain work. Each child must find his own way without the secure reserve or the patrimony of the family farm. Urbanites become impersonal with relatives as well as with strangers.

The diversity of people and values drawn to, and produced by, city life makes it still more difficult for people to meet one another in close relations. Diversity, like size, isolates people from one another.

Wirth gives an admirable sketch of the individuating results of urban conditions:

Characteristically, urbanites meet one another in highly segmental roles. They are, to be sure, dependent upon more people for the satisfactions of their life-needs than are rural people and thus are associated with a greater number of organized groups, but they are less dependent upon particular persons, and their dependence upon others is confined to a highly fractionalized aspect of the other's round of activity. . . . The contacts of the city may indeed be face to face, but they are nevertheless impersonal, superficial, transitory, and segmental. The reserve, the indifference, and the blasé outlook which urbanites manifest in their relationships may thus be regarded as devices for immunizing themselves against the personal claims and expectations of others.

The superficiality, the anonymity, and the transitory character of urban social relations make intelligible, also, the sophistication and the rationality generally ascribed to city-dwellers. Our acquaintances tend to stand in a relationship of utility to us in the sense that the role which each one plays in our life is overwhelmingly regarded as a means for the achievement of our own ends. Whereas, therefore, the individual gains, on the one hand, a certain degree of emancipation or freedom from the personal and emotional controls of intimate groups, he loses, on the other hand, the spontaneous self-expression, the morale, and the sense of participation that comes with living in an integrated society.

.   .   .

In a community composed of a larger number of individuals than can know one another intimately and can be assembled in one spot, it becomes necessary to communicate through indirect mediums and to articulate interests by a process of delegation. . . . The individual counts for little, but the voice of the representative is heard with a deference roughly proportional to the numbers for whom he speaks.

.   .   .

. . . as Simmel has suggested, the close physical contact of numerous individuals necessarily produces a shift in the mediums through which we orient ourselves to the urban milieu, especially to our fellow men. Typically, our physical contacts are close but our social contacts are distant. . . .

. . . The competition for space is great, so that each area generally tends to be put to the use which yields the greatest economic return. Place of work tends to become dissociated from place of residence.

. . . persons of homogeneous status and needs unwittingly drift into, consciously select, or are forced by circumstances into, the same area. The different parts of the city thus acquire specialized functions. The city consequently tends to resemble a mosaic of social worlds in which the transition from one to the other is abrupt. The juxtaposition of divergent personalities and modes of life tends to produce a relativistic perspective and a sense of toleration of differences which may be regarded as prerequisites for rationality and which lead toward the secularization of life.

The close living together and working together of individuals who have no sentimental and emotional ties foster a spirit of competition, aggrandizement, and mutual exploitation. To counteract irresponsibility and potential disorder, formal controls tend to be resorted to. Without rigid adherence to predictable routines a large compact society would hardly be able to maintain itself. The clock and the traffic signal are symbolic of the basis of our social order in the urban world. Frequent close physical contact, coupled with great social distance, accentuates the reserve of unattached individuals toward one another and, unless compensated for by other opportunities for response, gives rise to loneliness. The necessary frequent movement of great numbers of individuals in a congested habitat gives occasion to friction and irritation. . . .

. . . The heightened mobility of the individual, which brings him within the range of stimulation by a great number of diverse individuals and subjects him to fluctuating status in the differentiated social groups that compose the social structure of the city, tends toward the acceptance of instability and insecurity in the world at large as a norm. This fact helps to account, too, for the sophistication and cosmopolitanism of the urbanite. . . .

.   .   .

. . . There is little opportunity for the individual to obtain a conception of the city as a whole or to survey his place in the total scheme. Consequently he finds it difficult to determine what is to his own "best interests." . . .[1]

These individuating experiences can be intensified by two additional conditions. The first is the absence, in the city, of active and effective institutions that bind people together. The second is the fact of coming to urban ways from the small town or countryside as a stranger who must learn to live in this new and difficult world. The American experience has included both of these conditions. The second still persists for many city dwellers.

As cities grew, the old institutions of government and religion, of education and charity had neither the ability nor the experience to function with such large and diverse populations, to bind them together for effective joint action or to give them common purpose. It took time for these organizations and others such as trade associations, unions, service clubs, and political parties to grow sufficiently in resources and skill to undertake the job. And, as they did, the narrow and isolated experiences of urban life were reduced in number and importance. Of course they were not obliterated, only diminished in scope and frequency.

Again, even today, some citizens find urban life especially trying because they or their

[1] Louis Wirth, "Urbanism as a Way of Life," *The American Journal of Sociology*, **44** (July, 1938), pp. 1–24.

parents have come from the farm and have different expectations from those appropriate for the city. The industrial cities of the United States were fed by migrations of people from the small towns and the countryside. In they came by thousands and tens of thousands. The ties of kinship were broken. The familiar world of town and country was left behind. Bonds to fellow workers or employers were weak. And, with all this, the vastness and strangeness and impersonality of the city made it seem a wilderness. In 1906 Upton Sinclair, speaking for the immigrant to the city, could call his life history "The Jungle." Over and over run the themes: Men come to fear each other. They are strangers. The common law and the common morality corrode. People treat each other as means, not ends. A man in trouble is isolated from the help of kin or clergy or friend. This kind of society in which people live near each other, compete with each other, work with, for, and against each other, yet do not get to know each other with close, sympathetic understanding, as in the smaller community, is a shocking experience to many newcomers within its labyrinth of streets.

When we speak of individuated-entrepreneurial experiences, we refer to a characteristic way in which people are integrated with others in their society. Social classes are said to represent the way people are ranked in a hierarchy of power—are stratified—in a society. We may speak of a particular social class as a man's "stratification position." Correspondingly, we shall want to speak of an entrepreneurial or bureaucratic setting as a man's "integration position" or "integration setting."

Entrepreneurial Organization and Child Training

If the foregoing are the sources of individuated and entrepreneurial experiences, how do such experiences affect the way middle-class families rear their children? The answer, though speculative, is probably twofold. First, they are an important part of the kind of world in which those children will have to live. Only foolish or irresponsible parents will fail to train them for it. Second, they determine many of the values

and hopes and expectations of the parents with the result that they treat their children, as they treat themselves and most other people, in terms of those values and expectations. Thus, both purposely and unwittingly, these individuated and entrepreneurial experiences are involved in the socialization of the child.

Just how do such middle-class parents find the world? We must look at several features of their experience.

To begin with, there is the matter of self-control. A person with some prospects for personal advancement, or, at least, for maintaining such of the good things of life as he has, but with limited resources, has to learn wise management. In the present, he has to be ever-conscious of his future, husbanding his time and contacts and savings and skills for use at the most propitious moment. His behavior, like his money, is capital for investment. Doing and saying the right things at the correct places can hold or improve his social position. Slender resources of prestige as of money do not permit many bad investments without a loss of status. Such conditions put a premium on controlled, rational behavior, on ignoring the impulse of the moment in the interest of long-range prospects.

But there are other features of the older middle's position that are conducive to the same pattern of behavior. He has to look out for himself. No longer can the close ties of kinship hold security for him. He has to rely on his own profits or salary to take care of his wife and children. In the metropolis, friends on whom he might call in time of stress are scarce. Individuation as well as entrepreneurship places a premium on self-control.

Despite their differences, one continuing theme from Susannah Wesley to the time of John Watson is that the child must be taught self-denial, rationality, and a firm control over his current impulses. This is precisely the theme we have just sketched as a product of the experiences of the older middle classes and we want to suggest that it is as their numbers decrease that this theme declines in manuals of advice on child care.

A mother can begin to train her child in self-control and self-denial at a tender age if she will. She can require him to stop nursing before he desires to do so. She can ignore his wails when he is thwarted and upset, leaving him, in crying himself to sleep, to start toward the discovery that all that he wants cannot be had. In feeding him on a schedule which she sets and in putting him on the toilet and rewarding him for having his bowel movements when and as she chooses, she lays a foundation for teaching him that giving up immediate pleasures can lead to future gains. By punishing him when she herself is calm and controlled, she sets an example on which his own conduct can be modeled. By comparing his misconduct to objective standards of goodness, by threatening future punishment for misbehavior that is not amended, by providing deprivations that extend over several hours or days—by any of these instead of through an immediate spanking or slapping, painful at the moment but also something with which she and the child are over in a short time, the mother can underscore the importance of the child's directing himself, counting the costs in the future, and guiding his behavior accordingly.

There is, however, still another individuated-entrepreneurial theme concerning the way to point a child. It runs through the course of more than two hundred years. It is the notion that a youngster must be able independently to go out into the urban world, to capitalize on such opportunities as it may present, to carve out a life for himself which, in a rapidly changing society, may well require different tasks to be performed than were required of his parents. His is to be an active, manipulative approach to people and things. He must learn, as we see in the preceding discussion of urban life, that what he wants he will have to get for himself. Watson closes his book on that note.

. . . I believe that the internal structure of our American civilization is changing from top to bottom more rapidly and more fundamentally than most of us dream of. Consequently today less than ever before, is it expedient to bring up a child in accordance with the fixed molds that our parents imposed upon us. We have tried to sketch . . . a child *as free as possible of sensitivities to people* and one who, almost from birth, is *relatively independent of the family situation.*

Above all, we have tried to create a problem-solving child. We believe that *a problem-solving technique* (which can be trained) *plus boundless absorption in activity* (which can also be trained) are behavioristic factors which have worked in many civilizations of the past and which, so far as we can judge, will work equally well in most types of civilizations that are likely to confront us in the future.[2] (Italics supplied).

How might such an emphasis on active, independent behavior actually appear in training the child? We feel that it could appear very early in a prohibition of activities in which the child would learn to get satisfactions from his own body or from passive behaviors that did not require him to march upon his world and shape the environment to his own needs. This, we feel, is why such autoerotic activities as thumb-sucking and masturbation have been looked upon with genuine horror and disgust in previous times. We must not underestimate the violence of that disgust. It is not simply from considerations of the care of the teeth or the dangers of infection that children were prohibited from sucking their fingers. Such objective matters might be phrased in terms of dangers to health, but hardly in words like "odious habit," "disgusting practice," and the others that were commonly used. Violent adjectives suggest strong feelings, and our judgment is that those feelings represent, in part, a revulsion at the passivity of these pleasures of the child.

Although touching the genitals may be prohibited in order to prevent the child from becoming sexually stimulated (and we shall have more to say of that later), such prohibitions also prevent his gaining satisfaction from his own body. We believe the older middle classes find it an important element in their indictment of masturbation.

There are, of course, many other kinds of evidence of training the child to be active and independent. Such training appears in purposely breaking the ties to the parents by exposing the child early to other children and to the care of strange adults, and deliberately confronting the child with problems to be solved on his own and without parental assistance.

[2] John B. Watson, *Psychological Care of Infant and Child*, New York: W. W. Norton and Co., 1928, pp. 186–187.

Under these two themes of child care—training for self-control and the teaching of active and independent behavior—are subsumed many of the specific methods of training youngsters that now are undergoing change. Why are those changes occurring?

One source of an individuated society, and of techniques of rearing children related to it, lay in the conditions of urban living. Surely the proportion of urbanites has not declined. More people than ever live in cities and metropolitan areas, and the movement from the farms proceeds at a rapid pace. Further, even those families still living in small towns and in rural areas increasingly find their experiences set by the urban centers that dominate the American scene.

It is true that urbanism continues and swells in importance, and that many of its salient features as already outlined persist up to the present. It is also true, however, that city life has been modified and the entrepreneurial experiences known to the older middle classes—the uncertainties of the man of modest resources who must use them with care and caution—have been altered in drastic ways. We cannot be certain that these modifications in the form of the bureaucratization of American life are the only source of the newer styles of rearing children, but we feel they are an important source of the newer developments and quite consistent with the results in child and adult behavior that those styles seem to produce. It is to the origins and nature of this modification that we now turn. First, we describe the sources and characteristics of welfare bureaucracy. Then we examine its impact on the way parents train their children.

The Middle Classes and Welfare Bureaucracy

Toward the end of the nineteenth century and the beginning of the twentieth, new organizational trends appeared that were to transform much of the life of all Americans and to produce a new kind of middle class. These new trends are modifying the older and more individuated society of the United States just as the latter took the place of village and rural ways of life. For this emerging pattern of social life, we shall use the term "welfare bureaucracy." This new pattern of life is bureaucratic because it is characterized by large organizations employing many kinds of specialists and coordinating their activities by supervisors who follow a codified set of rules of practice. Its flavor is that of "welfare" bureaucracy because it can and must provide a large measure of security for its participants. Since the white-collar workers—the middle classes—are more likely to be highly specialized than the blue-collar employees, they are also more likely to be the first to feel the impact of these new conditions. Our purpose here is to describe these conditions, to contrast them with those of a more individuated period, and to show some of their effects on parents and children.

As we see it, four essential conditions are bringing about the change from individuated-entrepreneurial to welfare-bureaucratic (or, as we shall speak of it, bureaucratic) organization. These are: (a) the increase in the size of the organization of production, (b) the growth of specialization in organizations, (c) the great increase in the real incomes of the population, and (d) the enlarged power in the hands of lower-middle and lower-class workers.[3]

The increase in the size of organizations and in the proportion of their personnel who are specialists of some kind are the two defining characteristics of bureaucracy. Organizations are bureaucratic to the extent that they exhibit these features. Much that we shall have to say about the newer methods of child care will be explained as flowing from the experiences which parents encounter in a bureaucratized society.

We feel that American prosperity and the enlarged power of the lower middle and lower classes are important for our story because these two developments provide crucial aspects of the setting in which we expect bureaucratic influences to modify techniques of rearing children. These two conditions underlie our conception of welfare bureaucracy. Prosperity not only represents greater income, but it means, in our day,

[3] The development of automation may have as profound effects on the organization of American life as any of these, but its role is in the future and has no consequences for our present study.

that there is a considerable shortage of workers. That shortage, in turn, forces employers to give active attention to the problem of keeping their personnel happy and satisfied. We shall try to show how this makes an important modification in the amount of impersonality and insecurity experienced by bureaucratic employees.

The political strength of the American people, like prosperity, seems to us to affect the consequences of bureaucratization. It has forced the creation of governmental welfare measures which, like prosperity, enhance the economic security of the labor force. And, like prosperity, it provides a measure of freedom for employees that enables them to make demands of the organizations for which they work to the end that mutual respect and satisfaction are underwritten between employer and worker.

Each of these four conditions of welfare bureaucracy will now be discussed. Then we shall turn to the way of life and the methods of rearing children we believe to be consistent with them.

Increased Organizational Size. The decline of small business in all fields of endeavor and the shift toward larger and larger units have many sources. The population has been growing. Larger scale manufacturing and commerce can serve that population with greater economies on each unit sold than can small concerns. Because such large-scale concerns are working over vast regional, national, and international markets, they are not so susceptible to the ill effects of purely local drops in purchasing power; their profits are more stable. Not only can they compete successfully for existing markets, but they can create new ones through their ability to sponsor research, conduct massive advertising campaigns, and produce a greater variety of goods and services tailored to the desires of small, but significant, groups of purchasers. All of these potential advantages have been helped on their way to reality by the continuing development of machinery that increases the amount that can be produced and by such organizational inventions as assembly-line production, the corporation, and the holding company. By breaking production into small parts, the assembly line permits a considerable

increase in the volume of work turned out. The corporation, owned by large numbers of investors, with each liable for its debts only to the extent of his investment, allows for gigantic increases in the amount of capital available to start and expand production.

We have spoken of the growth of factories before the twentieth century as a growth of large organizations. In relative terms this is true. It was experienced as such by the people at the time. Yet, in a modern sense, most of these factories would not be considered large. The difference may be illustrated this way. It is estimated that the typical American urban manufacturing concern in the first half of the nineteenth century employed from fifty to one hundred persons. We may contrast this situation with estimates for 1948. Based on reports from establishments paying wages taxable under the Old-Age and Survivor's Insurance plan, a program covering the vast majority of employees in manufacturing concerns, we find that 75 per cent of all employees in manufacturing were employed in firms having 100 or more persons. Some 47.5 per cent worked in firms numbering 500 or more employees, and 34.9 per cent were in establishments of 1,000 or more workers.[4] For manufacturing, Table 1[5] is a summary of increases in organizational size since the turn of the century.[6]

[4] Wladimir S. Woytinsky and others, *Employment and Wages in the United States*, New York: The Twentieth Century Fund, 1953.

[5] The sources of the data in this table are the volumes of the United States *Census of Manufactures*. The respective years reported in the table and the dates of publication of the census reports in which they are found are:

  1909—*Census of Manufactures*, 1913, Vol. 3, p. 185.
  1919—*Census of Manufactures*, 1923, p. 85.
  1929—and 1939—*Census of Manufactures*, 1942, Vol. 1, p. 120.
  1947—*Census of Manufactures*, 1950, p. 97.
  1951—*Annual Survey of Manufactures: 1951*, 1953, p. 126.

The use of evidence here and elsewhere for manufacturing establishments as symptoms of bureaucratization should not be taken to mean that this trend fails to appear elsewhere in the economy. Data for manufacturing happen to be more complete on many points than are those from other enterprises.

[6] The argument is sometimes advanced that, since the percentage of the American labor force employed

Growth of Specialization. Luther Gulick has given a succinct statement of the causes of specialization:

1. . . . men differ in nature, capacity, and skill.
2. . . . no man can be in two places at the same time.
3. . . . no man can do two things at the same time.
4. . . . no man knows everything.[7]

Most of the jobs that have become specialized did so for one of the first three reasons listed by Gulick. The classic illustration is the establishment of assembly-line procedures.

Specialization has made important changes in the characteristics of the labor force. Table 2 shows the major differences.[8] Several important trends have appeared since the 1890's. Especially striking are the decline of laborers and the steady rise of semiskilled workers and of "clerks and kindred" types of employees. The percentage of professional and semiprofessional persons increases steadily but slowly in the non-farm labor force. Skilled workers and foremen showed a decline of similar proportions.[9] Servants and the broad group of proprietors, managers, and officials held relatively steady positions over these years.

These changes sharpen our picture of the results of a growth in the size and specialization of economic enterprise. Increasingly, machines have provided skills that in an earlier period would have been found in the talents of workmen. The machine tender, a semiskilled worker, does not have the kind of technical knowledge that he can take with him from job to job. His skill lies in "his ability to adjust quickly to the sequence and timing of his operation and to the attainment of an acceptable volume and quality of output."[10] Simultaneously, however, technological development has opened new jobs for skilled workers, and the demand for their services has shown only a slow decline.

Greater size and specialization of organizations have meant somewhat different things for white-collar employees. First, the proportion of white-collar workers has risen sharply. Second, although their numbers are small in relation to the total work force, increased demands for specialized skills have produced a rise in the

---

in service occupations is growing more rapidly than the proportions engaged in agriculture and manufacturing, it is likely that the number of small enterprises and the proportion of persons employed by them will evidence a sharp increase. If this trend is in the making it has not yet appeared in any dramatic fashion in the official government statistics. An examination of the United States *Census of Business* for the years 1929 through 1948, and including retail, wholesale, and service occupations as the data for each become available, shows that there has been an increase in the average number of employees working for each of these types of enterprise. Although it is true that, among retail stores, fewer outlets are centrally controlled by the managements of the very largest grocery chains, it also is true that the total number of persons employed by chain stores has increased over the period for which data exist. In the face of a somewhat declining number of stores operated by chain management, this means that the size of each remaining store under such control is larger than before.

Even if future studies show that there is an increase in the number of small enterprises in the retail, wholesale, and service fields, it may well be that the character of such enterprise will be substantially different from that which we have considered typical of an entrepreneurial society. These small businesses will operate in a society in which bureaucratized manufacturing provides a kind of security and stability that should serve to reduce the risks and isolation of the small shopkeeper and other minor businessmen even as it has that effect on its own employees.

[7] Luther Gulick, "Notes on the Theory of Organization," in Luther Gulick and L. Urwick (eds.), *Papers on the Science of Administration*, New York: Institute of Public Administration, Columbia University, 1937, p. 3.

[8] Data for 1870 are adapted from Wladimir S. Woytinsky, *Labor in the United States: Basic Statistics for Social Security*, Washington, D.C.: Social Science Research Council, 1938, p. 270. Statistics for the years 1910 through 1940 were computed from a report in: United States Bureau of the Census, *Historical Statistics of the United States: 1789–1945*, Washington, D.C.: United States Government Printing Office, 1949, p. 65. The information for 1950 was taken from A. J. Jaffe and Charles D. Stewart, *Manpower Resources and Utilization: Principles of Working Force Analysis*, New York: John Wiley and Sons, Inc., 1951, p. 146.

[9] Because of the nature of the categorization of data by the United States Census, it is likely that this trend should not be applied to skilled laborers. There is evidence that the proportion of skilled laborers in the urban labor force is rising.

[10] Harry Ober, "The Worker and His Job," *Monthly Labor Review*, **71** (July, 1950), p. 15.

Table 1

Percentage of wage workers in manufacturing industries by size of organization

Number of wage workers in reporting unit	Year			
	1909	1919	1929	1939
1–50	26.0	19.4	19.8	19.2
51–100	11.8	9.8	10.3	10.8
101–250	19.0	17.4	18.1	18.7
251–1000	27.9	27.0	27.9	29.1
1001 or more	15.3	26.4	24.0	22.4
Total	100.0	100.0	100.1	100.2
	per cent	per cent	per cent	per cent
Number	6,615,046	9,096,372	8,369,705	7,886,567

Number of wage workers in reporting unit*	Year	
	1947	1951
1–49	15.9	38.6†
50–99	9.1	
100–249	15.6	
250–699	26.6	27.0
1000 or more	32.8	34.4
Total	100.0	100.0
	per cent	per cent
Number	14,294,304	15,612,619

* The published groupings of the Census of Manufactures changed for 1947 and 1951. So slight is the change, that it will hardly account for the major shifts described in this table.

† The published report of the 1951 *Annual Survey of Manufactures* gives only this summary figure for firms employing from 1 to 249 wage workers.

Table 2

Non-farm labor force: social-economic group of the employed civilian labor force for 1950, of the experienced labor force for 1940, and of gainful workers for 1870 to 1930 (for persons fourteen years old and over)*

Socioeconomic group	Year					
	1870	1910	1920	1930	1940	1950
Professional persons	6.2	6.3	6.6	7.7	7.8	8.6
Wholesale and retail dealers	⎤ 8.7	4.8	4.5	4.6	4.7	⎤ 12.4
Other proprietors, managers, and officials	⎦	4.7	4.5	4.9	4.5	⎦
Clerks and kindred workers	4.7	14.8	18.3	20.7	20.7	22.4
Skilled workers and foremen	⎤	17.0	18.0	16.4	14.2	14.5
Semiskilled workers	50.3	21.3	21.4	20.8	25.4	32.3
Laborers	⎦	21.2	19.4	16.3	12.9	6.1
Servant classes	14.7	9.8	7.2	8.7	9.7	3.7
Total	84.6	99.9	99.9	100.1	99.9	100.0
	per cent	per cent	per cent	per cent	per cent	per cent
Number	6,578,156	25,731,890	30,990,994	38,395,379	43,037,126	51,648,000

* The data for 1870 do not add to 100 per cent since the basic tables include a group numbering 15.3 per cent of the labor force that is called "unclassified."

Table 3

Percentage of persons employed in manufacturing establishments, by occupation

Occupation	Year*						
	1899	1904	1909	1919	1929	1939	1947
Proprietors and members of the firm		3.6	3.6	2.5	1.4	1.2	
Salaried officers of corporations	7.7†	1.0	1.1	1.2	1.6	1.3	16.5‡
All other salaried employees		7.4	9.2	12.2	11.6	14.2	
Wage earners	92.3	88.0	86.1	84.1	85.5	82.4	82.5
Total	100.0	100.0	100.0	100.0	100.1	100.1	99.0
	per cent	per cent	per cent	per cent	per cent	per cent	per cent

* The data for 1899 through 1919 include reports for establishments with products valued between $500 and $5000. More recent data do not include these small manufacturers.

† Information for 1899 grouped salaried persons together and did not include statistics for proprietors and members of the firm.

‡ Information for 1947 grouped together all administrative, supervisory, sales, technical, office, and all other clerical personnel. It is not clear whether it does or does not include information for proprietors and members of the firm.

proportion of professional workers in the population. In Table 3 we find, similarly, that there has been an increase in the percentage of salaried corportion officers and a decline in the proportion of proprietors and members of firms in the total labor force.[11] This last pair of tendencies reflects the larger requirements of big organizations for specially trained management. This growing separation of ownership and administration has been dramatized as the "managerial revolution."

Broad data from the census mask some of the sharpness of the increase in managerial and other professionals as a proportion of the labor force. If, for example, we look only at some professions most closely connected with economic production, the change is clearer. Thus, from 1890 to 1940 the number of gainful workers per college-trained engineer employed in manufacturing, mining, construction, transportation, and public utilities dropped from about 300 to less than 100.[12]

Increase in Real Income. One of the phenomenal differences between the lot of most Americans in the nineteenth and those of the twentieth centuries is the rise in income, not only in terms of dollars, but of buying power. Despite a great depression and the inflation that accompanied two global wars, there has been a steady rise in the buying power of the American people at about the rate of 2 per cent a year.[13] Even over shorter periods, the rise in real income is most impressive. From 1929 to 1951, real income rose 131 per cent.[14] Another way to see the size of American prosperity is to compare real income in the United States with that in other Western, industrial countries. In 1949 real income was $1450 *per capita* in the United States.[15] By contrast, it was $870 in Canada, $780 in Sweden, $770 in the United Kingdom, and $230 in Italy. Asian and African peoples fared even less well by comparison. For example, the estimated figure for Korea is $35, for Japan, $100, for Communist China, $30, and for

[11] Data for the years 1899 through 1939 were obtained from United States Bureau of the Census, *Census of Manufactures*, Vol. 1, Washington, D.C.: United States Government Printing Office, 1942, p. 67. Data for 1947 come from the *Census of Manufactures* for that year and published in 1950. See page 69 of that report.

[12] Employment Outlook for Engineers," *Monthly Labor Review*, **69** (July, 1949), p. 15.

[13] See, for example, Elizabeth E. Hoyt and others, *American Income and Its Use*, New York: Harper and Bros., Publishers, 1954, pp. 87–91; and William F. Ogburn, "Technology and the Standard of Living in the United States," *The American Journal of Sociology*, **60** (January, 1955), pp. 380–386.

[14] Hoyt, *op. cit.*, xvi.

[15] *Ibid.*, xii.

Ethiopia, Kenya, Liberia, and Northern Rhodesia, $40.

Again, it is impressive that in recent years the percentage increase in American incomes has been greatest for those in the lower income groups. On every hand are signs that there has been a progressive equalization of income within the population through the rise in the amount of money in the hands of the least well paid.[16]

Enlarged Power of the Lower-Middle and Lower Classes. The final condition that has led to what we call welfare bureaucracy is the increased power in the hands of lower-middle and lower-class people in the United States.[17] The sources of this trend are complex, but its presence is reflected in the progressive enfranchisement of all the American people, and in the greater sensitivity of the Federal government to their needs and wishes. The trend is also mirrored in the success of such organizations as the labor unions which (whether or not actually providing the forces responsible for the rise in workers' incomes) seem to have gained greater job security for their members, to have helped them mobilize for political action, and to have represented them as effective pressure groups in the nation's councils.

We have been looking at the changes from an individuated-entrepreneurial to a welfare-bureaucratic society as if they happened in smooth transitions without overlap or conflict. This is not the case. An English economic historian could say that his country at the turn of the century embodied most of the previous economic systems of her history with sizable portions of the population employed in each organizational setting.[18] It is easy to find examples of such a variety of economic patterns in contemporary America. The small business-man still exists. The unorganized worker in fields oversupplied with labor can be found. The employee in the small establishment, depending on his employer's good will and clinging precariously to the uncertain fortunes of the little store or shop lives in the same towns as do the employees of welfare bureaucracies. Sons and daughters from both backgrounds often work in the same establishments and, with their very different expectations of the future and interpretations of the present, find it difficult to understand one another.[19] We shall find integrations of both the entrepreneurial and bureaucratic varieties in the Detroit area.

The Demands of Bureaucratic Organizations

The whole development of welfare bureaucracy changes the world for the middle-class citizens who join its ranks. No longer need they struggle and strive so hard. They must still be circumspect and respectable, but their incomes do not depend on manipulating a host of risks and investments.

The early picture that observers had of the likely consequences of bureaucratization for the middle classes took its cues primarily from the educational and governmental bureaucracies of Europe and the United States where this form of organization first matured. The employee in a bureaucratic situation should, it was felt, be more secure than his fellow in an individuated situation. The large organization had resources enabling it to continue operation without becoming disorganized through the minor ups and downs of the business cycle. Therefore it could provide job security.

Bureaucracies also embodied other sources of employee security. It takes time to train a man for a specialized type of work. To lose trained men costs money. They are hard to replace. Large organizations could keep their employees by providing them with tenure and pension plans and by guaranteeing them advancement on the basis of seniority.

[16] *Ibid.*, pp. 132–135.
[17] For the story of this change see Richard Hofstadter's *The American Political Tradition and the Men Who Made It*, New York: Alfred Knopf, Inc., 1948. Also useful are: Charles A. and Mary R. Beard, *The Rise of American Civilization*, New York: The Macmillan Company, 1930 and their *America in Midpassage*, New York: The Macmillan Co., 1939.
[18] George Unwin, *Industrial Organization in the Sixteenth and Seventeenth Centuries*, Oxford: The Clarendon Press, 1904, pp. 1–15.

[19] David Riesman and others, *The Lonely Crowd: A Study of the Changing American Character*, New Haven: Yale University Press, 1950, pp. 3–35.

Seniority not only worked to keep employees with a particular company, but it solved another problem of bureaucracies as well. A large, complex organization requires the continued, faithful performance of duties. Payrolls must come out. A product must flow from the production lines. A sales force has to be advised, stimulated, and coordinated. And these functions must be performed on an hourly and daily basis. They do not allow for drastic or continuous tampering. Steady morale must underlie steady performance. An employee with unusual imagination and energy who tries to institute drastic changes can cause the whole complex machine to grind to a halt. Such enterprising efforts are desirable, but need to be kept under control. To retain a high level of staff morale and to discourage excessive drive and ambition, a regular system of promotion through seniority provides an answer.

Just as size and complexity of organization can lead to employee security, they also exact a price from their personnel. The ideal worker must be precise and conscientious in performance. He must keep to his assigned task and not stray off into the provinces of others even if he has some new ideas for the performance of their work. He must always "clear" ideas and problems "through channels" with his superiors. Because he may leave the company or die, his work and plans must be reported on paper so that someone else may take his place and continue where he left off. He must, like the individuated middle-class worker, be rational, looking to the consequences of his action and curbing momentary desires until their consequences can be examined and evaluated. He must not be aggressive or too ambitious for these qualities disturb the organizations' course.

Thus it is clear, even though entrepreneurial and bureaucratic organizations make some similar demands of their personnel, they also differ in critical ways. In particular, bureaucratic organizations find unnecessary or undesirable the rather extreme self-control and self-denial and the active, manipulative, ambition that entrepreneurial organizations exalt. This difference is one that we expect to find influential in determining how children are reared.

This takes us a little ahead of our story. There is one feature of bureaucracy as described by the early writers on European and American developments that we feel has undergone considerable modification in the contemporary United States. Because the interpretation of this feature of bureaucracy makes a difference in the account of how the newer middle classes rear their children, we shall take it up in some detail. It is the stress in the earlier accounts on the theme that bureaucratic organizations force people to deal impersonally with one another.[20]

Those accounts say that the size and complexity of bureaucratic organizations force employees to see each other, the organization's clients, and themselves as parts of an organization, not as people. Bureaucratic personnel, these descriptions asserted, must learn to treat each other, not as living, feeling flesh that might make demands for special treatment or that might have idiosyncratic needs, but as human machines who might legitimately require only those things necessary for playing their parts in the organization. Each participant, these accounts continued, has a job to do, with limited but compulsory responsibilities and requirements. Other considerations must not be allowed to interfere with this impersonal order.

If these early descriptions of bureaucracy were correct about the unadulterated impersonality of the human relations in such organizations, we would have to conclude that bureaucracy exacerbates rather than relieves the individuating tendencies of urban life. In its impersonality it would be yet another way of isolating people from one another and should promote a wary self-control. However accurate these early accounts may have been as descriptions of the governmental and military bureaucracies on which they are based, we feel that they do not describe the growing spirit of large organizations in the United States today. This is the reason that we speak not simply of "bureaucracy" but of "welfare bureaucracy" as characterizing our place and time.

What difference does that adjective "welfare" make? We use it to represent developments having the effect of reducing impersonality; of

[20] For a convenient summary of the literature describing bureaucratic characteristics, see: Robert K. Merton and others (eds.), *Reader in Bureaucracy*, Glencoe, Illinois: The Free Press, 1952.

doing much toward transforming the relation of employees to their employers and to each other from one based on a formal job contract to one based on a shared moral relationship. All of this has consequences for the interpretation we want to make of the newer developments in child care, so we shall elaborate our meaning before presenting that interpretation.

The language of employer-employee relations tells much of the story. In the entrepreneurial organization and in the earlier and more authoritarian bureaucracy, management defined its relations to the work force in terms of employee discipline. It was assumed that the worker came haltingly to his tasks. He was seen as resisting or lazy or stubborn and the problem of the supervisor was that of providing him with direct and effective rewards and deprivations which would force him, in his own self-interest, to behave as desired. It was also implicit that supervisors had the power to perform such a task. One magazine much favored among entrepreneurs still describes its model for labor relations with the telling analogy of the donkey that can be persuaded only by the proper, but minimal, rewards of the carrot and, simultaneously, proper and judicious prods from the master's stick. But even *Time* is not always timely. The day of forcing the worker to his desk or machine passed. The day of fitting him to the job took its place.

Shortly before the First World War, a student of industrial management, Frederick J. Taylor, published his epochal *The Principles of Scientific Management*.[21] He pointed out that workers "soldiering" on the job hurt their company's competitive position. Labor discontent was costly. Taylor urged on management the adoption of procedures that would minimize such discontent. If unruly impulses could not be eliminated, they could be managed. The way to do it was to fit the worker's needs to his job by a program of determining the demands the job would make, by simplifying jobs through breaking them into tasks "anyone" could perform, and by hiring employees who would find these jobs congenial. This theory became a great modern impetus for the personnel man—a man

defined as one who could analyze jobs and administer tests to find workers whose personalities and skills fitted the work situation.

However, even Taylor's scientific management was not adequate to the newer problems of contemporary organization. It assumed a degree of managerial dominance that was already passing in his time. The latest step has been the adaptation of the job to the worker. Pressures for such a move were inherent in welfare bureaucracy. They were, as we remarked earlier, enhanced by the growing political power of employees and by their prosperity. From the assumptions of the disciplining of labor, the social relations of management moved to adapting the worker to his tasks, and from that to the maintenance of his morale. This last step needs some elaboration.

A concern with worker morale suggests that managerial skills are now directed toward enlisting worker desires and aspirations. But it also assumes that it is in the worker's power to grant or to refuse such enlistment. If he refuses, management will have to continue trying to gain his support. Within the limitations set by technology, the worker's loyalty can be had by adjusting the conditions of work to his desires. The word "loyalty" is central. He must be prevented from disturbing the routines of production by transferring to another company. If he is highly specialized in tasks such as those of business operation or design or sales or any of the pyramiding number of others in which there is no clear and rapid index available by which his performance may be judged, supervision is extremely difficult. He must be self-supervised. He must want to perform with high proficiency. An essential part of that performance is set by the way he gets along with other people. For many reasons the older conceptions of control and decision-making in giant organizations have broken down.[22] Again, there is required a devotion to the welfare of the enterprise and a satisfaction with its procedures if the irritations of human interaction are to be minimized. No

---

[21] *The Principles of Scientific Management*, New York: Harper and Brothers, 1911.

[22] A book written largely in the course of attempts to identify the newer problems of organizational functioning is Herbert A. Simon and others, *Public Administration*, New York: Alfred A. Knopf, Inc., 1950.

known techniques of supervision could compel such behavior.[23]

This kind of natural loyalty and devotion does not come solely from good pay and a feeling of dominance over one's employer. It represents the experience of a fundamentally moral relationship. Morals, in turn, are the code of social rules that grow up to preserve a situation in which people find each other's presence to be so mutually rewarding and, simultaneously, so lacking in threat, that they feel wholly comfortable and spontaneous and seek to preserve their happy and productive state. The problem of management is to establish such a moral relationship with its workers without losing its authority over them. There has been a persistent and analogous problem for parents in dealing with their children—how to be both authority and benefactor. The management solution, like that of many parents, is one of seeking avidly for benefits it can give without jeopardizing control. The pastel-colored washrooms, the coffee breaks, the use of first names on the job, the company banquet, the employee picnic, the practice of consultation with employees on those decisions where a crucial management position will not be compromised are examples of the important devices to be used. The change of the personnel man and the vice-president in charge of employee relations from, respectively, giving tests and settling disputes on a legal, contractual basis to the roles of counselors and liaison men is part of the same movement. What once was accomplished in small informal groups in the little communities and in the countryside now is the subject of planning and of the construction of elaborate formal organizational devices. Moral relations in large institutions, like the daily quota of parts produced, must be planned.

The benefits, not the planning, must be the conspicuous thing in the worker's experience. He must feel that what was done occurred because management was genuinely interested

in his welfare, not because the benefits would result in higher productivity. Since there are always suspicions of management's motives, there are persistent tests of the genuineness of the employer's concern. The limits of his willingness to fraternize and spend time on non-productive employee interests are sought. Walk-outs that seem irrational to workers, union leaders, and supervisors alike may occur to determine whether management will be punitive or understanding. Morale may be the overt subject of discussion, but morality is its central object.

These paragraphs on the moral nature of relations in a welfare bureaucracy have been broad and descriptive. They have sought, in the absence of more systematically gathered evidence, to bring together a picture of a new and potent and, in good measure, incipient style of life. They emphasize our view that the competitive and amoral world of the individuating metropolis is being changed. The consequence, we believe, is yet another force that makes striving and extreme and rigid self-control less necessary than before. Further, it seems to us that the reestablishment of moral relations makes such striving and self-control less desirable than formerly for they interfere with the development of supportive and moral relations among employees. Now we must examine some of the effects of moralization and the other features of welfare bureaucracy on the training of children.

Bureaucracy and Child Training

Bureaucratized parents train their children for this new world and treat them in terms of its values. For most parents, this will not be a matter of self-conscious planning. Their methods of child care will simply reflect the values these mothers and fathers have learned from living in a bureaucratized society.

In the previous chapter we summarized some of those values in the questions, "Is it natural?" and "Is the child old enough?" In the more relaxed and secure atmosphere of a society whose tone is set importantly by welfare bureaucracy, the child, like the adult, is free to enjoy the present, to express his feelings. Not only is

[23] A summary of many studies of the relation of the newer attempts at supervision to overcome this problem appears in Edward A. Shils' article "The Study of the Primary Group," in Daniel Lerner and Harold D. Lasswell (eds.), *The Policy Sciences: Recent Developments in Scope and Method*, Stanford University Press, 1951, pp. 44–69. See also: Riesman and others, *op. cit.*

he free, but the confident, smooth social relations of the great organizations of which he must become a part will require him to get along well with other people and to take their feelings as well as his own into account with skill and confidence.

This child will need to be taught that superiors are not hateful figures to be challenged, but men of skill and feeling, whom he should emulate, and with whom he can cooperate. As William Henry puts it in his study of workers who win high executive appointments:

The successful executive posits authority as a controlling but helpful relationship to superiors. He looks to his superiors as persons of more advanced training and experience, whom he can consult on special problems and who issue to him certain guiding directives. He does not see the authorities in his environment as destructive or prohibiting forces.

.   .   .

In general the mobile and successful executive looks to his superiors with a feeling of personal attachment and tends to identify himself with them. . . .[24]

The adult, as the child, must be warm, friendly, and supportive of others. The child will not develop in this way if his family provides too little nurturance or too cold and objective and difficult an environment for him. It is a plea for just such high and continued nurturance that characterizes the advice to parents by Spock and other "authorities" on child care in our time. The powerful ambitions and desires for independence cherished by our middle classes for two centuries would unfit a youngster for participation in a society that requires him to be relaxed and cooperative—a willing subordinate to the policies of a great organization. Such passive enjoyments as thumb-sucking not only fail to incapacitate the child for future independence, but may actually be one way of teaching him valuable skills. They may give him practice in an accommodative approach to life. They may teach him to relax and be content when under pressure rather than to make demands on other people for a change in his environment.

[24] William E. Henry, "The Business Executive: The Psychodynamics of a Social Role," *The American Journal of Sociology,* **54** (January, 1949), pp. 288, 290.

By contrast, teaching the child self-control and self-denial at a very early age through such devices as bowel training in the first six months of life, or requiring him to give up the breast or bottle at such an age, or refusing to pay attention to him if he cries "just to get attention" not only is made unnecessary by the lesser demands of bureaucratic life but may actually disturb the baby's confidence in people. It may shake his firm sense that, as Spock puts it, he belongs to them and they to him.

The bureaucratization of adult experience does not lead to a lack of discipline in training children. It does not mean that highly "passive" or "dependent" persons are desired. It means that discipline takes "external" forms such as spanking rather than "internal" forms such as appeals to conscience, and that more passivity and dependence are tolerated and, on occasion, encouraged than would have been true under individuated conditions.

When parents expected that their children would be relatively unsupervised and isolated from others as they moved into adult activities, they needed to train their youngsters by means which would insure that strong consciences were acquired. Armored with a powerful conscience, a man might be expected to obey the social codes even when surrounded by the opportunities and temptations afforded by the anonymity and heterogeneity of an entrepreneurial society. However, when parents can feel that their children will grow up in a closely knit and moral society in which, as members of great organizations, their behavior will be guided and supervised through daily contacts with others, there is less need for fathers and mothers to provide the child with a stern, self-propelling conscience. For reasons we elaborate as we present our finding, such external punishments as spankings may be expected to occur more frequently under bureaucratic than under entrepreneurial conditions, whereas entrepreneurial families, to develop and reinforce a vigorous conscience in the child, will be more likely to make use of such disciplines as deprivation of privileges and parental lectures that make the child feel he is responsible for his own misdeeds and that make him feel guilty when he disobeys.

Thus we expect that two themes of child care

emphasized under entrepreneurial conditions— the themes of self-control and of an actively manipulative orientation toward the world— will receive less stress in a bureaucratic society. We have argued, further, that greater dependence is placed on continuing and external controls exercised on the individual by his fellows and his superiors in the bureaucratic situation while a more accommodative orientation toward the world is actually encouraged.

Intrigued by the seeming consistencies and affinities between the values of the newer middle classes and the methods now being advocated for rearing children, we have concluded that the bureaucratization of the American people is an important source of the recent emphases in child care. Although the picture given in this chapter pays special attention to those whose involvement in that change is best understood, the middle classes, lower-class Americans and their children certainly are affected by these same trends. We will describe the social situation of lower-class families as we present findings about them as well as about the middle-class parents in our study.

Summary

At this point we bring together some of the observations in this chapter. We have described two types of integration setting, the entrepreneurial and bureaucratic, and have associated them with certain methods of child care.

The term entrepreneurial has referred to organizations having these features: small size, a simple division of labor, a relatively small capitalization, and provision for mobility and income through risk taking and competition. Social situations were called individuated if they isolate people from one another and from the controlling influence of shared cultural norms. Children reared in individuated and entrepreneurial homes will be encouraged to be highly rational, to exercise great self-control, to be self-reliant, and to assume an active, manipulative stance toward their environment.

The term bureaucratic has referred to organizations which are large and which employ many different kinds of specialists. It is typical that the capitalization of such enterprises is substantial and that participants' incomes are in the form of wages or salary. Mobility comes through specialized training for a particular position rather than through success in taking risks once on the job. A welfare bureaucracy is one in which the organization provides considerable support to the participants in meeting their personal crises and offers the security of continuity of employment and income despite some fluctuations of the business cycle. Children reared in welfare-bureaucratic homes will be encouraged to be accommodative, to allow their impulses some spontaneous expression, and to seek direction from the organizational programs in which they participate.

31. Leading Crowds in Ten Midwestern High Schools and Emphasis upon Personality and Attractiveness

BY JAMES S. COLEMAN,
WITH THE ASSISTANCE OF
KURT JONASSOHN, AND W. C. JOHNSTONE

THE SCHOOLS ARE ALL LOCATED in northern Illinois, but are not intended to be "representative" of this section. On the contrary, they were selected with diversity in mind. For example, it is likely that there are more similarities between Executive Heights, a well-to-do Chicago suburb, and Scarsdale, New York, and more similarity between Green Junction and a farm town of 5,000 population in Oregon, than there are between Executive Heights and Green Junction. The results of the study, then, are not intended to apply to "schools in northern Illinois," but to all schools encompassed within the range of community composition exhibited by these schools. This range, roughly, is from prosperous farming or farming and industrial community (the five smallest schools) to working-class parochial boy's school in the center of a large city (St. Johns), to new working class suburb (Newlawn) to small cities (Millburg—heavy industry; Midcity—light industry) to well-to-do suburb (Executive Heights).

Some parts of the analysis examine all schools together; other parts deal with each school separately; thus the common characteristics of the adolescent culture are examined, along with those which vary from one kind of school to another.

SOURCE: Social Climates in High Schools, OE-33016 Cooperative Research Monograph No. 4: Washington: U.S. Government Printing Office, 1961, pp. VIII–IX and 19–33.

Leading Crowds in the Schools

Just what does it take to "rate" in these schools, with one's own sex, and with the other sex? What does it take to be in the "leading crowd" in school? This question, of course, presumes something to which some might object: that there *is* a leading crowd in the school. And, to be sure, when students were asked such a question, some, particularly in the smallest school, did object to the idea that there was a leading crowd. Yet this kind of objection is in large part answered by one of the boys in another small school, Maple Grove, in a group interview, when his friend denied that there was any leading crowd at all in the school, and he responded: "You don't see it because you're in it." Another boy in the same school had this to say in an interview:

Q. What are some of the groups in school?
A. You mean like cliques? Well, there's about two cliques. There's one that's these girls and boys—let's see, there's —— —— ——. I'm in it, but as far as I'm concerned. I'm not crazy about being in it. I tell you, it wasn't any of my doing, because I'm always for the underdog myself. But I'd rather be with a bunch like that, you know, than have them against me. So I just go along with them.
Q. What's the other clique?

A. Well, I don't know too much about it, it's just another clique.

Q. Kind of an underdog clique?

A. Sort of.

Q. Who are some of the kids in it?

A. Oh—I couldn't tell you. I know, but I just can't think of their names.

Q. How do you get in the top clique?

A. Well, I'll tell you, like when I came over here, I had played football over at ——. I was pretty well known by all the kids before I came over. And when I came there was —— always picking on kids. He hit this little kid one day, and I told him that if I ever saw him do anything to another little kid that I'd bust him. So one day down in the locker room he slammed this kid against the locker, so I went over and hit him a couple times, knocked him down. And a lot of the kids liked me for doing that, and I got on the good side of two or three teachers.

Q. What are the differences between these two cliques?

A. Well, I'll tell you, I don't like this top clique, myself. Just to be honest with you, they're all scared of me, because I won't take anything off of them, and they know it. I've had a run-in with this one girl, she really thinks she's big stuff. And I don't like her at all, we don't get along, and she knows it and I know it, and they don't say nothing. But a lot of them in the big clique, they're my friends. I get along with them real good and then I try to be real nice to the underdogs, the kids that haven't got—not quite as lucky—they haven't got as much money. They have a hard time; maybe they don't look as sharp as some of the others.

Q. What are the main interests of the top clique?

A. Just to run everything, to be the big deal.

Q. Are most of the boys in athletics?

A. Yeah—you couldn't really say that in this town, though. The really good athletes, a couple of them may be in the clique—the clique's a funny thing, it's just who they want to be in it. They don't want to have anybody in there they think might give them trouble. They want to rule the roost.

Q. Do most of them have fathers that have good jobs, are they well-to-do?

A. Most of them. They come from families that have money.

Q. Would this be the main thing that divides the top clique from the others?

A. Could be, very easily, it sure could.

Q. What does this underdog clique have in common?

A. Well, you might say they just stick together, for self-protection. And they do things together.

Q. And there are both boys and girls in the cliques?

A. Yeah.

Q. And they all go around together?

A. Um-hm.

Q. In a party, would——.

A. Now there you go. The big-deal clique, that's all that's there. None of the underdogs are there at all. They won't invite——I've got some graduation pictures here now, and we can get some names from that. Now she's not in the clique.

Q. What's her name?

A. Now this girl here, she's Joyce. She's real sweet, not very sharp-looking or nothing, and I sat by her in home room. And I talked with her and stuff like that, and she really—I mean, I think she thinks a lot of me. And this is a girl who sort of sticks to herself, more or less. She's a very nice girl, but I don't think she's in the clique. And she's not in the clique and neither is ——.

Q. And they aren't in the other clique either?

A. No. Well, yeah, they're probably—I'll tell you, some of them—see, the big clique rules the roost, and this underdog clique, you might say, is just there to give the other one a little competition, just to know there is another one. And a lot of them are not in it. I was just automatically put in it, you might say. I didn't ask to be in it or nothing.

This account of the leading crowd in one school gives a vivid picture of how such crowds function. This is not to say, of course, that the leading crowd in every school functions in just the same way. Most interviews in other schools suggested a somewhat less closed circle than in this school, yet one which is not greatly different.

In every school, most students saw a leading crowd, and were willing to say what it took to get in it. This should not be surprising, for every adult community has its leading crowd, though adults are less often in such close and compelling communities. Yet laymen and educators as well are often blind to the fact that the teenagers in a high school *do* constitute a community, one which *does* have a leading crowd. Consequently adult concern tends to be with questions of better ways to teach "the child" viewed as an isolated entity—whether it is the "gifted child" or the "backward child."

How to Get In. In order to see more systematically what it takes to be in the leading crowd, every student was asked in the questionnaire:

What does it take to get into the leading crowd in this school?

The major categories of response to this question about the leading crowd are shown in Figure 1. Consider first the girls' responses. Most striking is the great importance of "having a good personality." Not only is this mentioned most often in the overall study, but it is mentioned most often in seven of the nine schools.

The importance of having a good personality, or, what is a little different, "being friendly" or "being nice to the other kids," in these adolescent cultures is something which adults often fail to realize. Adults often forget how person-oriented children are: they have not yet moved into the world of cold impersonality in which many adults live. This is probably due to the limits on their range of contacts; for in the limited world of grade school, a boy or girl *can* respond to his classmates as persons, with a sincerity which becomes impossible as one's range of contacts grows. One of the transitions for some children comes, in fact, as they enter high school and find that they move from

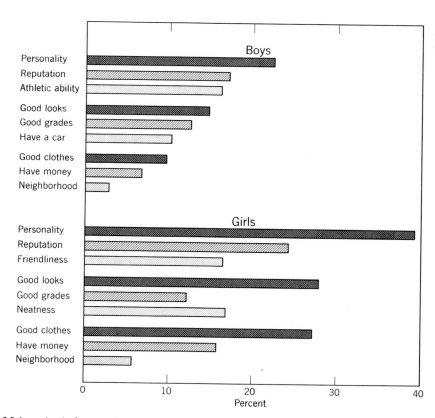

Figure 1. Major criteria for membership in the leading crowds of 9 schools of the study: Percent of boys and girls mentioning each.

classroom to classroom and have different classmates in each class.

After a good personality come a wide range of attributes and activities. A flavor of this is indicated by the collection of responses listed below—some hostile to the leading crowd (and in their hostility, often seeing it as immoral), others friendly to it (and in their friendliness attributing positive virtues to it).

What does it take to get into the leading crowd in this school?
Wear just the right things, nice hair, good grooming and have a wholesome personality.
Money, clothes, flashy appearance, date older boys, fairly good grades.
Be a sex fiend—dress real sharp—have own car and money—smoke and drink—go steady with a popular boy.
Have pleasant personality, good manners, dress nicely, be clean, don't swear, be loads of fun.
A nice personality, dress nice without overdoing it.
Hang out at ——'s. Don't be too smart. Flirt with boys. Be cooperative on dates.

Among these various attributes, the graph shows "good looks," phrased in some fashion, to be second to "personality" in frequency for the girls. Having nice clothes, or being well-dressed, is the third most frequent item mentioned. What it means to be well-dressed differs sharply in a well-to-do suburb and in a working-class school, of course. Nevertheless, whether it is the number of cashmere sweaters a girl owns, or simply having clean and attractive dresses, the matter of having good clothes is an important one in the value systems to which these girls pay heed. This importance of clothes appears to derive in part from the fact that clothes symbolize family status. But in part also, it appears to derive from the same source that gives importance to "good looks": these items are crucial in making a girl attractive to boys. Thus in this respect the values of the girls' culture are molded by the presence of boys—and by the fact that success with boys is itself of overriding importance.

Another element in the constellation of attributes required if one is to be in the leading crowd is indicated by the class of responses labeled "having a good reputation," which was fourth in number of times mentioned. In all

these schools, this item was often mentioned, though in each school, some saw the leading crowd as composed of girls with bad reputations and immoral habits; and in some schools the leading crowd was less interested in a good reputation than in others.

A girl's reputation is crucial among adolescents. A girl is caught in a dilemma posed by the importance of good looks on the one hand, and a good reputation on the other. A girl must be popular with the boys, says the culture, but in doing so the must maintain her reputation. In some schools, the limits defining a good reputation are stricter than in others; but in all the schools, the limits are there to define what is "good" and what is "bad." The definitions are partly based on behavior with boys, but they also include drinking, smoking, and other less tangible matters—something about the way a girl handles herself, quite apart from what she actually *does*.

It is not such an easy matter for a girl to get and keep a good reputation, particularly if her mother is permissive in letting her date whom she likes as a freshman or sophomore. Junior and senior boys often date freshman and sophomore girls, sometimes with good intentions and sometimes not. One senior boy in Green Junction, in commenting upon the "wildness" of the leading girls in his class, explained it by saying that when his class was in the eighth grade, it was forced to go to school in the high school building because of a classroom shortage. A number of the girls in the class, he explained, had begun dating boys in the upper classes of high school. This, it seemed to him, was where the problem began.

Another criterion by which a girl gets into the leading crowd or fails to get in is expressed by a girl who said simply, "Money, fancy clothes, good house, new cars, et cetera: the best."

These qualities are all of a piece; they express the fact that being born into the right family is a great help to a girl in getting into the leading crowd. It is expressed differently in different schools and by different girls, sometimes as "parents having money," sometimes as "coming from the right neighborhood," sometimes as "expensive clothes." These qualities differ sharply from some of those discussed above, for they are not something a girl can *change*.[1] Her position in the system is ascribed according to her parents' social position, and there is nothing she can do about it. If criteria like these dominate, then we would expect the system to have a very different effect on the people in it than if other criteria, which a girl or boy could hope to achieve, were the basis of social comparison—just as in the larger society a caste system has quite different effects on individuals than does a system with a great deal of mobility between social classes.

It is evident that these family-background criteria play some part in these schools, but—at least according to these girls—not the major part. (It is true, however, that the girls who are *not* in the leading crowd more often see such criteria, which are glossed over or simply not seen by girls who are in the crowd.) Furthermore, these criteria vary sharply in their importance in different schools.

Another criterion for being in the leading crowd is scholastic success. According to these girls, good grades, or "being smart" or "intelligent" has something to do with membership in the leading crowd. Not much, to be sure—it is mentioned less than 12 per cent of the time, and far less often than the attributes of personality, good looks, clothes, and the like. Nevertheless, doing well in school apparently counts for something. It is surprising that it does not count for more, because in some situations, the "stars," heroes, and objects of adulation are those who best achieve the goals of the institution. For example, in the movie industry the leading crowd is composed of those who have achieved the top roles—they are by consensus the "stars." In a graduate school, the "leading crowd" of students ordinarily consists of the bright students who excel in their studies. Not so for these high school girls. The leading crowd seems to be defined primarily in terms of *social* success: their personality, desirability as dates, clothes—and in communities where social success is tied closely to family background, their money and family.

[1] To be sure, she sometimes has a hard time changing her looks or her personality; yet these are her own personal attributes, which she can do something about, except in extreme situations.

Different Criteria for Boys. What about boys? What were their responses to this question about criteria for the leading crowd? Figure 1 also shows the boys' responses, in somewhat the same categories used for the girls. The first difference between these and the girls' responses is the overall lower frequency. The girls sometimes set down in great detail just what is required to get in the leading crowd—but the matter seems somewhat less salient to the boys.

For the boys, a somewhat different set of attributes is important for membership in the leading crowd. The responses below give some idea of the things mentioned.

> A good athlete, pretty good looking, common sense, sense of humor.
> Money, cars and the right connections and a good personality.
> Be a good athlete. Have a good personality. Be in everything you can. Don't drink or smoke. Don't go with bad girls.
> Athletic ability sure helps.
> Prove you rebel against the police officers. Dress sharp. Go out with sharp freshman girls. Ignore senior girls.
> Good in athletics; "wheel" type; not too intelligent.

By categories of response, Figure 1 shows that a good personality is important for the boys, but less strikingly so than it is for the girls. Being good looking, having good clothes, and having a good reputation are similarly of less importance. Good clothes in particular are less important for the boys than for the girls. Similarly, the items which have to do with parents' social position—having money, coming from the right neighborhood, and the like, are less frequently mentioned by boys.

What then are the criteria which are more important for boys than for girls? The most obvious is, as the graph indicates, athletics. Of the things that a boy can *do*, of the things he can *achieve*, athletic success seems the clearest and most direct way to gain membership in the leading crowd.

Having good grades, or doing well academically, appears to be a less sure path to the leading crowd than is athletics (and sometimes it is a path away, as the final quotation listed above suggests). It does, however, sometimes constitute a path, according to these responses. The path is apparently stronger for boys (where scholastic achievement is fifth in frequency) than for the girls (where it is eighth in frequency) This result is a little puzzling, for it is well known that girls work harder in school and get better grades than boys do. The ambivalence of the culture concerning high achievement among girls will be examined in some detail later. At this point, it is sufficient to note that such achievement is apparently less helpful to a girl for getting into the leading crowd than it is for a boy.

An item which is of considerable importance for the boys, as indicated on the bar graph, is a *car*—just having any car, according to some boys, or having a *nice* car, according to others— but whichever it is, a car appears to be of considerable importance in being part of the "inner circle" in these schools. In four of the five small-town schools—but in none of the larger schools —a car was mentioned more often than academic achievement. When this fact is coupled with the fact that the response included not only juniors and seniors, but also freshmen and sophomores, who were too young to drive, the place of cars in these adolescent cultures looms even larger.

As a whole, how do the criteria for the leading crowd among boys differ from the criteria for girls? Several sharp differences are evident. Family background seems to matter less for boys; it is apparently considerably easier for a boy than for a girl from the wrong side of the tracks to break into the crowd. Clothes, money, and being from the right neighborhood hold a considerably higher place for the girls.

The same appears to be true for personal attributes such as personality, reputation, good looks—all of the things which define what a person *is*. In contrast, the criteria for boys include a much larger component of what a person *does*, whether in athletics or in academic matters. Such a distinction can be overdrawn, for a girl's reputation and her personality are certainly determined by what she does. Yet these are not clear-cut dimensions of achievement in which a person can actively do something; they are far less tangible. Furthermore, they are pliable in the hands of the leading crowd itself, whose members can define what constitutes a good reputation or a good personality but cannot

ignore football touchdowns or scholastic honors. Numerous examples of the way the leading crowd can shape reputations were evident in these schools. For example, a girl reported:

It is rumored that if you are in with either —— or —— that you've got it made. But they are both my friends. You've got to be popular, considerate, have a good reputation. One girl came this year with a rumor started about her. She was ruined in no time by —— especially.

The girl who had been "ruined" was a top student and a leader in school activities, but neither of these things was enough to give her a place in the leading crowd. At the end of the school year she was just as far out of things as she was at the beginning, despite her achievements in school.

The matter is different for boys. There are fewer solid barriers, such as family background, and fewer criteria which can be twisted at the whim of the in-group, than there are for girls. To be sure, achievement must be in the right area—and athletics is by far the area which is more right than any other—but achievement *can* in most of these schools bring a boy into the leading crowd, which is more than it can do in many instances for girls.

Again there is the suggestion that the girls' culture is in some fashion derived from the boys: The girl's role is to sit there and look pretty, waiting for the athletic star to come for her. A girl must cultivate her looks, be vivacious and attractive, wear the right clothes, but then wait—until a football player, whose status is determined by specific achievements, comes along to choose her. This is, of course, only part of the matter, for in a community where the leading crowd largely reflects the "right families" in town, or in a school where "activities" are quite important, the girls have more independent power. Also, the fact that girls give the parties and determine who is invited puts a tool in their hands which the boys do not have.

It is as if the adolescent culture were a Coney Island mirror, throwing back a reflection of the adult society, distorted but recognizable. And just as there are variations in different places in the adult society, there are variations in different schools in the adolescent society. Their existence should be kept in mind, in order not to make the serious mistake of seeing the "adolescent culture" as all of a piece, as a single invariant entity.

Popularity with Own or Opposite Sex. In the questionnaire, boys were asked what it takes to be popular with other boys, and then, in a separate question, what it takes to be popular with girls. Girls were asked a similar pair of questions about popularity with their own sex and popularity with the opposite sex.

A comparison of the pair of questions shows an interesting result: "good grades," or doing well in school counts for something with one's *own* sex, but for very little in popularity with the opposite sex. In contrast, out-of-school activities and attributes (a boy's having a car, or a girl's having good clothes) count for much more in popularity with the opposite sex. The differences are especially great for a girl's popularity. Doing well in school is of some value in making a girl popular with other girls, but it has little or no value in her popularity with boys.

Perhaps these results are to be expected. Yet their implications are not so obvious. Let us suppose that the girls in a school valued good grades more than the boys did. One might naively expect this to mean that the presence of these girls would be an influence on the boys toward a higher evaluation of studies. Yet these data say that is *not* the case; they say that a boy's popularity with girls is based less on doing well in school, more on such attributes as a car, than in his popularity with other boys. Similarly for girls—their popularity with boys is based much less on academic studies than is their popularity among members of their own sex.

The standards men and women use to judge each other have always included a large component of physical attractiveness and a smaller component of the more austere criteria they use in judging members of their own sex. Yet adults seem to ignore that this is just as true in high schools as it is in business offices, and that its cumulative effect may be to deemphasize education in schools far more than they realize. In the normal activities of a high school, the relations between boys and girls tend to increase the importance of physical attractiveness, cars, and clothes, and to decrease the importance of achievement in school activities. Whether this *must* be true is another question; it may be that the school itself can shape these relations so that they will have a positive effect rather than a negative one on the school's goals.

The general research question is this: What kinds of interaction among the boys and girls could lead each sex to evaluate the other less on grounds of physical attraction, and more on grounds which are not so superficial? It seems likely, for example, that in some private schools such as the Putney School, the kinds of common work activities of boys and girls lead to different bases for evaluating the opposite sex than do the usual activities surrounding a public high school. The question of practical policy, once such a research question has been answered, is even more difficult: What can a school do to foster the kinds of interactions and activities which lead the judgments of the opposite sex to be made on grounds which implement the school's goals?

It is commonly assumed, both by educators and by laymen, that it is "better" for boys and girls to be in school together during adolescence —if not better for their academic performance, then at least better for their social development and adjustment. But this may be not at all true— the benefits may depend wholly upon the kind of activities within which their association takes place. Coeducation in some high schools may be inimical to *both* academic achievement *and* social adjustment. Again, we should emphasize that the dichotomy often forced between "life-adjustment" and "academic emphasis" is a false one, for it forgets that most of the teenager's energy is not directed toward either of these goals. The relevant dichotomy is instead cars, clothes, and the cruel jungle of rating and dating versus school activities, whether of the academic or life-adjustment variety.

Perhaps this is where the emphasis *should* be among girls: on making themselves into desirable objects for boys. Perhaps physical beauty, nice clothes, and an enticing manner are the attributes which should be most important among adolescent girls. Yet in none of the roles in adult life that most girls will occupy are physical beauty, an enticing manner, and nice clothes as important for performing successfully as they are in high school. Even receptionists and secretaries, for whom personal attractiveness is a valuable attribute, must carry out their jobs well, or they cannot survive. Comparable performance is far less important in the status system of the high school. A girl can survive much longer on personal attractiveness, an enticing manner, and nice clothes.

The adult activities of women in which such attributes *are* most important are of a different order from those of wives, citizens, mothers, career women, secretaries: they are the activities of chorus girls, models, movie and television actresses. In all these activities, women serve as *objects of attention* for men, and even more, objects to *attract* men's attention. These attractions are quite different from the attributes of a good wife, which involve less superficial qualities. If we want our high schools to inculcate the attributes which make girls successful as objects to attract men's attention, then these values of good looks and nice clothes discussed above are just right; if not, then the values are quite inappropriate.

A second answer to the question, "What is wrong with these values?" is this: Nothing is wrong with such values, so long as they do not completely pervade the atmosphere. The values are all right, as long as there are also *other* ways a girl can become popular and successful in the eyes of her peers. And there are other ways, as indicated by the emphasis on "a nice personality" in the questions discussed above. Yet these two questions suggest that in adolescent cultures, these superficial, external attributes of clothes and good looks do pervade the atmosphere to the extent that girls come to feel that this is the only basis or the most important basis on which to excel.

Effect on Girls of Emphasis on Attractiveness

There are several sets of reponses in the questionnaire which indicate that girls do feel that the attributes of attractiveness are most important. One is the response to the question in which more girls checked "model" as the occupation they would like than any of the

other three: "nurse," "schoolteacher," or "actress or artist." As suggested before, a model is one of the few occupations which most embodies the attributes of beauty and superficial attractiveness to men.

Further consequences of this emphasis in high school on being attractive to boys are indicated by responses to a set of sentence-completion questions. Comparing the boys' responses and the girls' will give some indication of the degree to which the high school culture impresses these matters upon girls. The tabulation below shows the proportion responding in terms of popularity or relations with the opposite sex. These questions were asked in a supplementary questionnaire, filled out by the 6,289 students in the nine schools who completed the basic fall questionnaire early.

Sentence-completion responses related to popularity

	Boys per cent	Girls per cent
More than anything else, I'd like to * * *		
Responses involving popularity with opposite sex	5.4	10.8
Responses involving popularity, unspecified	5.3	11.4
Total codable responses	(2,343)	(2,776)
The best thing that could happen to me this year at school would be * * *		
Responses involving relations with opposite sex	4.5	20.7
Responses involving relations with others, unspecified	3.2	9.0
Total codable responses	(2,222)	(2,702)
The most important thing in life is * * *		
Responses involving popularity with opposite sex	6.3	7.4
Responses involving popularity, unspecified	4.6	7.9
Total codable responses	(2,151)	(2,737)
I worry most about * * *		
Responses involving popularity with opposite sex	9.2	13.9
Responses involving personal attributes related to popularity (weight, hair, figure, etc.)	2.7	8.6
Total codable responses	(2,201)	(2,803)

To each one of these sentence-completion questions, girls gave far more responses involving popularity with the opposite sex than the boys did. The responses suggest that the emphasis of these cultures on a girl's being an object of attention for boys has powerful consequences for the girl's attitudes toward life and toward herself. A further indication that success with boys is tied to rather superficial external qualities is shown by the greater proportion of girls who say they worry most about some personal characteristic (most often an external attribute such as weight or figure or hair or skin, but also including such attributes as shyness).

One might suggest, however, that girls' concern with popularity with boys, and with physical attributes which help make them popular, would be just as strong in the absence of the adolescent culture. A simple comparison of these four sentence-completion questions suggests that this is not so. The question in which girls *most* often give responses involving relations with the opposite sex is the one which refers directly to the school life: "The best thing that could happen to me this year at school would be.***" When the question refers to life in general (The most important thing in life is ***), then the boy-girl differential is sharply reduced. This suggests that it is the system itself, the social system of adolescents, which makes relations with boys, and physical attractiveness, so important to girls.

These values which feature a girl as an object of a boy's attention have other effects on the girls, of which we have only the barest knowledge. One of the effects is on her self-conception. One would expect that if a girl found herself in a situation where she was not successful in "the things that count," she would be less happy with herself, and would want to change, to be someone different; on the other hand, the more successful she was in the things that counted, the more she would be satisfied with herself.

We have no measure of the objective beauty of girls, and we are not able to single out those who are particularly unattractive in dress or beauty, to see the impact that these values have upon their conceptions of themselves. However,

it is possible to pick out the girls who are, in the eyes of their classmates, the best-dressed girls, to allow an indirect test of the effect of the emphasis on clothes and on being attractive to boys. In the questionnaire, every girl was asked:

Of all the girls in your grade, who is the best dressed?

The girls who were named most often by their classmates were at one end of the continuum— better dressed than their classmates. Thus, if this is an important attribute to have, these girls should feel considerably better about themselves than do their classmates. The following tabulation shows that they did, and that those named most often felt best about themselves.

If I could trade, I would be someone different from myself:

	Per cent	No.
All girls who agreed	21.2	3,782
Girls named 2–6 times as best dressed	17.0	282
Girls named 7 or more times as best dressed	11.2	98

The effect of being thought of as "best dressed" by her classmates was striking, reducing by half the likelihood of a girl's wanting to be someone different. Or to put it differently, the effect of *not* being thought of as "best dressed" by her classmates more than doubled a girl's likelihood of wanting to be someone different.

To see the strength of this effect, relative to the effect of competing values, it is possible to compare these responses with those of girls who were highly thought of by their classmates, but in other ways. The following questions were asked along with the "best-dressed" question:

Of all the girls in your grade, who
—is the best student?
—do boys go for most?

The girls who were named most often by their classmates on these two questions and the previous one can be thought of as "successful" in each of these areas—studies, relations with boys, and dress. Insofar as these things count, they should make the girls feel happier about themselves—and conversely, make the girls who are not successful less happy about themselves.

The degree to which these three values count in making a girl happy or unhappy about herself can be seen in Figure 2. It is apparent that all have some effect. Being successful with boys apparently has most effect, being thought of as best dressed (which seem to be important in large part because it contributes to being successful with boys) is somewhat less effective, and being thought of as best student is apparently the least effective of the three. The results of the companion questions for boys are shown along with those for the girls, to indicate that this result is not simply due to the personality of those popular with the opposite sex. For boys, it is athletics which is apparently most effective more so than popularity with girls.

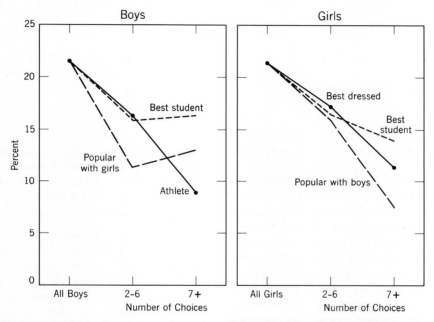

Figure 2. Per cent wanting to be someone else among all boys or girls and those chosen as outstanding on three criteria.

32. Family Background of Educable Mentally Retarded Children*

BY JOSEPH H. MEYEROWITZ AND BERNARD FARBER

MUCH HAS BEEN WRITTEN about effects of cultural deprivation upon intellectual functioning (Hunt, 1961; Masland, Sarason, and Gladwin, 1958; Kirk, 1958; and Riessman, 1962). Cultural deprivation implies an inaccessability to the vocabulary (Bernstein, 1961), the values and motivation (Schneider and Lysgaard, 1953), conceptual apparatus (Inhelder and Piaget, 1958), and ways of acting (Miller and Riessman, 1961) which are required for successful participation in the major institutions of the society, such as school, government, and economic enterprise. This culture is sometimes designated as middle-class culture, the formal culture, the public culture, or the culture transmitted in the schools. Regardless of the name applied, there is a general consensus that when access to this culture is impeded, intellectual development is somehow stultified. The investigation of family backgrounds of the educable mentally retarded children in the study was undertaken to determine the presence of factors which appear to be related to the phenomenon of cultural deprivation. Since previous investigations have indi-

cated that cultural deprivation is associated with socioeconomic level, the investigation was designed to study influences other than socioeconomic factors in mental retardation.

The following characteristics of family life were investigated in three Illinois counties:

1. Integration of the family in the community. If children are to have access to the content of the dominant culture, the parents should be integrated into the formal and informal groups which reflect this culture. Community relationships which appear to reflect integration into the community of the families of the retarded were studied. These community relationships included (a) participation in formal organizations, such as voluntary associations and religious institutions, and (b) informal relationships, such as contact with neighbors and friends. In addition, residential mobility of the family was investigated.

2. Resources in the home. Ordinarily, the family is expected to provide children with an introduction to the content of the dominant culture. Accordingly, personal, cultural, and economic resources of the families to provide this cultural content were studied. These resources included education of the parents, income, dependence upon welfare agencies, health of the mother, presence of a telephone, and exposure to mass communications, such as movies, magazines, and newspapers.

SOURCE: *Appendix B in Herbert Goldstein, James W. Moss, and Laura Jordan,* The Efficacy of Special Class Training on the Development of Mentally Retarded Children, *Cooperative Research Project No. 619, U.S. Office of Education, Urbana: Institute for Research on Exceptional Children, University of Illinois, 1965, pp. 152–182.*

* Data collection by Joseph H. Meyerowitz.

3. Family relationships. Studies of maternal deprivation have suggested that warm, stable relationships in the family are conducive to the child's personal development (Hunt, 1961; Casler, 1961). Various factors which may affect the stability of relationship between parents and their children were studied. These factors included extent of divorce and remarriage, birth of the retarded child outside the present marriage, age of the parents, birth order of the retarded child, and degree of crowding in the home.

4. Motivation by parents. Finally, those parent-child relationships which are relevant to the motivation of the child in school were investigated. These were (a) the parents' aspirations with regard to the child's ultimate educational attainment, and (b) the extent to which parents experience difficulty in handling the child.

The majority of the 120 educable mentally retarded children in the study came from homes in which there was a low income and in which the parents were engaged in unskilled, or semiskilled occupations. Integration of the family in the community, resources in the home, stability of family relationships, and parental motivation are all associated with socioeconomic variables. A comparison between families of the retarded children with families in a representative sample from the community would therefore not reveal those factors which are themselves related to mental retardation. However, many families with socioeconomic characteristics like those of the retarded children do not produce retarded children. Hence, in the investigation a sample of 60 families of comparable income and occupational status with normal children was selected for comparison with the families with retarded children. The person interviewed was the mother or her surrogate (usually the grandmother).

The comparison group of families with normal children was selected from the same areas in which the families with retarded children resided. The normal children were in the same schools as the retarded children. The distribution by income and occupation of families in both groups is presented in Table 1.

Table 1 indicates that the weekly income of

Table 1

Weekly income and father's occupation in families with retarded child and in comparison group families with normal children

Income and occupation	Retarded	Normal
	per cent	per cent
Weekly family income		
less than $35	21.5	21.3
$36 to $85	70.0	66 0
more than $85	8.5	12.7
Father's occupation		
Professional, managerial	11.2	21.8
Skilled	19 6	10.9
Semiskilled	24.3	29.1
Unskilled	44.9	38.2

the families of the retarded group was approximately the same as that of the families of the normal group. However, while proportions in semiskilled and unskilled occupations were similar for the two groups, the proportions in the professional and skilled worker categories were not. The professional and managerial category had approximately 10 per cent more fathers from the normal group than from the retarded group. On the other hand, the skilled category had about 10 per cent more fathers from the retarded group. With these exceptions, socioeconomic characteristics of the two groups were comparable.

Integration of the Family in the Community

One of the tasks in family life is to socialize children so that they can develop into mature, responsible adults. To do so, however, the family must be sophisticated about adult society. Moreover, since modern society is very complex and changing, a family must participate constantly in the institutions of the society to perform its socialization task adequately. Deutsch (1960) and others (e.g., Fraser, 1959), have indicated that family isolation from major institutions in the society affects scholastic achievement. This isolation may also affect the intellectual functioning of children. This section describes findings on formal and informal community participation of the parents of the educable mentally retarded children.

Formal Organizations. The participation of the parents of the retarded children in two kinds of formal organization were investigated. These were membership in voluntary associations and religious organizations.

Voluntary associations are those formally organized groups, such as clubs, unions, athletic teams, and other organizations which ordinarily have a definite charter or by-laws, a definite membership, and a set of officers. The findings pertaining to membership in voluntary associations are presented in Table 2. About half of the parents of the retarded children, as compared with less than one-fourth of the parents of the normal children, did not belong to any voluntary associations. Moreover, almost one-third of the parents of normal children, but very few parents of the retarded, belonged to three or more voluntary associations. Table 2 clearly indicates that there is a greater tendency of parents of normal children than parents of retarded children to belong to voluntary associations.

Table 2

Number of voluntary associations to which parents belong

Number of associations	Retarded	Normal
	per cent	per cent
0	49.2	22.4
1–2	44.1	44.8
3+	6.7	32.8

The data on participation in religious institutions were analyzed in terms of denomination and church attendance. The findings are presented in Table 3. The results on membership in religious denominations indicate a tendency for the parents of normal children to belong to the traditional denominations, such as Catholic or Protestant groups, to a greater extent than parents of the retarded. More parents of the retarded were classified in the residual category of religious organizations. The residual category consists mainly of small sects. These religious sects may represent small, unstable groups which are isolated from the major religious traditions of the society. Their isolation from these traditions prevents the integration of

Table 3

Religious affiliation and church attendance of the parents

Religious characteristics	Retarded	Normal
	per cent	per cent
Religious denomination		
Protestant	67	79
Catholic	7	14
Jewish	0	0
Others	26	7
Church attendance		
Attended at least once		
per month	51	85
Less than once per month	21	5
Did not attend	28	10

individuals into those institutions which reflect the dominant culture of the society (Yinger, 1957; Lipset, 1960).

The second analysis on religion concerned church attendance. Although 85 per cent of the parents of the normal children reported that they attended church services at least once a month, only 50 per cent of the parents of the retarded did so. Over one-fourth of the parents of the retarded did not attend church at all, while only one-tenth of the parents of the normal children were non-attenders.

In summary, the data on religion revealed that the parents of the normal children were more often members of the major denominations in the society, while the parents of the retarded children were more often members of deviant religious sects. In addition, the parents of the normal children reported more often that they attended church regularly. Together with the findings on membership in voluntary associations, in the two groups the data on religion indicate a greater tendency of the parents of normal children to participate in formal organizations in the community.

Informal Community Activities. The extent to which the parents of the mentally retarded children participated in informal activities in the community was indicated by their interaction with friends and with neighbors. Interaction with friends was indicated by (a) the extent to which visits are exchanged, and (b) amount of recreational activities with friends.

Interaction with neighbors was determined by the parent's response to a scale of neighborliness developed by Wallin (1953).

The extent to which visits were exchanged with friends is shown in Table 4. Parents of the retarded reported less exchange of visits than did parents of the normal. Although only 3 per cent of the parents of the normal children reported that they never exchanged visits with friends, 14 per cent of the parents of the retarded did so. Whereas 47 per cent of the parents of normal children reported that they often exchanged visits, only 30 per cent of the retarded gave this response.

Table 4

Exchange of visits with friends

Response	Retarded	Normal
	per cent	per cent
Never	14.4	3.4
Sometimes	55.9	50.0
Often	29.7	46.6

Findings on attendance at recreational activities with friends were similar to those on exchange of visits. The findings on recreational activities are presented in Table 5. Fourteen per cent of the parents of the retarded but only 3 per cent of the parents of the normal responded "never." Twenty per cent of the parents of the retarded and 35 per cent of the parents of the normal responded "often." Thus, the findings on interaction with friends clearly indicate that parents of the normal children interacted to a greater extent with friends than did parents of the retarded children.

Table 5

Attendance by parents at recreational activities with friends

Response	Retarded	Normal
	per cent	per cent
Never	14.4	3.4
Sometimes	40.7	44.8
Often	19.5	34.5

The findings on neighborliness are presented in Table 6. Over one-fourth of the parents of the retarded scored low on neighborliness whereas less than one-fifth of parents of the normal were low. On the other hand, only one-fourth of the parents of the retarded were high in neighborliness but almost half of the parents of the normal children were high. The results relating to neighborliness and friendships indicate that generally the parents of the normal children participate more in informal community activities than do parents of mentally retarded children.

Table 6

Extent of neighborliness of parents[a]

Neighborliness	Retarded	Normal
	per cent	per cent
Low	29.5	17.3
Moderate	45.6	35.7
High	24.9	47.0

[a] See P. Wallin, A Guttman scale for measuring women's neighborliness. *Amer. J. Sociol.*, **59**, 1953, pp. 243–246.

Mobility. The findings on residential mobility suggest that the lesser community integration of the parents of the mentally retarded children as compared to the parents of the normal children is occasioned in part by high residential mobility. In both groups, about 60 per cent of the families were descended from grandparents born in Illinois. Approximately 37 per cent of the mothers and 27 per cent of the fathers were born within the area in which they were living at the time of the interview. Over half of the grandparents were sufficiently close by to be visited at least once a month. In spite of the general stability of the families within the area of the study, however, there was more residential mobility on the part of the parents of the retarded. Thirty-five per cent of the families of the retarded, as compared with 14 per cent of those with normal children, had lived at their current address for less than a year. [For the United States, about 20 per cent of the population move each year (Statistical Abstracts, 1963).] Presumably families with educable mentally retarded children who had not moved in the previous year were also relatively more mobile than the parents whose children are of normal intelligence. Residential mobility, like low participation in formal and informal community activities, suggests a lack of integration of many families with retarded children into the major community institutions.

Family Resources

If a child is to be socialized to become a responsible adult in society, the family must have various personal, cultural, and economic resources to provide him with the intellectual tools that he will need. Educated, healthy parents with a high income generally provide their children with the means for learning the intellectual and social behavior associated with the dominant culture of the society. Conversely, the absence of these resources would interfere with the socialization of the child. Accordingly, those family resources which were studied included education of the parents, income per family member, dependence upon welfare agencies, health of the mother, and mass communication media available.

Table 7

Parents' education: last grade completed

Grade	Mothers		Fathers	
	Retarded	Normal	Retarded	Normal
	per cent	per cent	per cent	per cent
6th or less	7.7	3.4	18.6	8.6
7–9	50.8	31.0	49.2	37.9
10–12	38.1	60.3	29.7	50.0
College	3.4	5.3	2.5	3.5

Education of Parents. Table 7 shows the last grade in school completed by the mothers and fathers of both retarded and of normal children. About two-thirds of the mothers of normal children had finished at least 10 grades in school. In contrast, the majority of the mothers of retarded children had completed nine grades or less. For the fathers, the results were similar. Over two-thirds of the fathers in the retarded group completed nine grades or less as compared with almost half the fathers in the normal group. There was clearly a tendency for parents of

normal children to have completed more years of school than parents of the retarded.

Table 8

Income per person in family per week

Income	Retarded	Normal
	per cent	per cent
—$12	43.2	32.8
$13 to $24	42.4	36.2
$25 +	14.4	31.0

Income per Family Member. Table 8 shows the amount of income per week per family member. Although total family income for the families with a mentally retarded child and for the families with a normal child showed little difference, the two groups did differ on income per person. For the normal group, 31 per cent of the families had a weekly income of 25 dollars or more per person, whereas in the retarded group only about 15 per cent had an income of 25 dollars or more. Moreover, over 40 per cent of the retarded group, as compared with about 30 per cent of the normal group, had an income of less than 12 dollars per week per person. These findings indicate that families with a retarded child had fewer financial resources for each child.

Dependence upon Welfare Agencies. Although the common stereotype of families with mentally retarded children is one of a "problem family" constantly on welfare roles, an examination of the files of county and social agencies revealed that few of the families within the study were known to these agencies. The most frequent bases for aid were unemployment insurance, workmen's compensation, and old age assistance as opposed to ordinary relief payments. However, especially in Kankakee, most families without a husband-father were on ADC rolls. More families with a retarded child than with a normal child appeared on welfare records.

Health of Mother. The health of the mother can be regarded as a resource in the socialization of the child. The mother who regards herself as being in poor health can ordinarily not be expected to put forth the amount of effort needed to provide children with the means for facilitating

Table 9

Reported health of the mother

Response		Retarded	Normal
		per cent	per cent
1. Good health?	No	15	8
2. Bothered by special condition?	Yes	20	20
3. Sought help?	Yes	18.5	9
	No	6	14

their socialization. In fact, past evidence suggests that mothers who regard themselves as being in ill health use this personal condition to avoid responsibilities (Farber, 1960). Table 9 presents findings related to the health of the mother. The mothers were asked:

1. Are you in good health?

2. Since —— was born, have you been bothered by any special conditions or problems?

3. If yes to 2, have you sought any kind of help?

Fifteen per cent of the mothers of retarded children as compared with eight per cent of the mothers of normal children responded that they were not in good health. Although the percentage of mothers who responded that they were bothered by a special condition in both groups was the same (20 per cent), almost all of the mothers of retarded children sought assistance to remedy their condition. However, less than half of the mothers with a special condition in the normal group sought assistance. This finding suggests various interpretations: (a) mothers of the retarded children are less self-reliant, (b) they seek confirmation by outsiders that they are not in good health, or (c) they have more serious health problems.

All of the findings relating to personal, economic, and social resources of parents indicate that the parents of the retarded children have fewer resources for effective socialization than do parents of normal children.

Mass Communication Media. Three questions were asked to elicit information on the extent of family contact with mass communication media. These media can be a source of knowledge about society even when individuals are generally isolated. The questions asked were: (1) How often do you go to the movies; (2) Do you subscribe to or purchase any newspaper or magazine; and (3) Do you have a telephone. Because many of the respondents lived in rural areas far from television stations, they were not asked about television watching.

Table 10

Exposure to mass communication media

Communication media	Retarded	Normal
	per cent	per cent
Go to movies once per month	15	15
Go to movies less than once per month but at least on "holidays"	41	57
Never go	44	28
No magazine or newspaper enters home on regular basis	21	12
No telephone in home	33	22

The findings on exposure to mass communications media are presented in Table 10. Forty-four per cent of the families with retarded children as compared with 28 per cent with normal children never go to movies. Over half of the families of the normal but a little under half of the families of the retarded go occasionally. A small percentage (15 per cent) in both groups goes at least once a month. The families in the normal sample thus were exposed to a somewhat greater extent to the content of American culture as shown in movies. The results were similar for magazine and newspaper purchasing. About 20 per cent of the families with a retarded child do not receive a magazine or newspaper on a regular basis; only a little over 10 per cent of the families with a normal child are not exposed to a magazine or newspaper regularly. The findings on a telephone in the home are in the same direction. A third of the families with a retarded child do not have a telephone in the home, while about one-fifth with a normal child are without a telephone.

In general, the findings indicate a lesser exposure to mass communication media by the families with a retarded child. Since the movies, magazines, newspapers, and telephones all involve a money expediture, the smaller amount of money available per person in the families of the retarded probably affects their exposure to mass communications media. The lower educational level of the parents of mentally retarded children is probably a factor in their lesser inclination to read magazines and newspapers regularly. Moreover, if the families with retarded children participate less with friends and neighbors, they have less need for a telephone. The lower exposure of families with a retarded child to mass communications media would serve to further isolate them from the major institutions in the community.

Family Relationships

The ideal family life in the United States is one characterized by stability, companionship, and lack of friction. Ideal parents are those who shower affection and attention on their children but at the same time promote the development of children as independent beings. This section describes characteristics of the parents and of the household as they may affect family relationships.

Parents. Information concerning the parents included responses to questions on marriage and age of the parents. The findings are presented in Table 11. The material on marriage in Table 11 indicates that, on the average, families with a retarded child had been married slightly longer than families with normal children. However, one-fifth of the marriages in the retarded group were of a duration less than the age of the child. In contrast, only one-twentieth (5 per cent) of the marriages in the normal group were of such short duration. Thus, 20 per cent of the retarded children have known a parent other than their current set of parents. Most important to note with regard to stability is that parents in families with a retarded child showed a greater tendency to have been remarried (presumably divorce and remarriage) than parents with normal children. Hence, there is less stability indicated in families which have a retarded child.

Further indication of unstable family relationships is suggested by data on age of parents in

Table 11

Marital status and age of parents

Marital status and age	Retarded	Normal
	per cent	per cent
Marital status		
Unmarried at time of interview (mothers)	15.0	15.0
Married other than to first husband	20.0	20.0
Married fewer years than age of child (6.5 years)	20.0	5.0
Married up to 10 years	18.0	18.0
Married 11–16 years	33.0	52.0
Married more than 16 years	14.0	9.0
Families with either spouse remarried	32.0	24.0
Fathers remarried	22.0	11.0
Age of parents		
Age of mother		
25 years or less	25.0	13.0
26 to 35	63.0	64.0
36 to 40	12.0	23.0
Age of father		
25 years or less	15.0	5.0
26 to 40	53.0	61.0
41 to 45	11.0	26.0
46 or over	21.0	8.0

Table 11. Although the mothers of the retarded children were generally younger than mothers of the normal children, the reverse was true for the fathers. Twenty-five per cent of the mothers of retarded children were aged 25 or less, whereas only 13 per cent of the mothers of normal children were in that age range. However, 21 per cent of the fathers of the retarded children were over 45 whereas only 8 per cent of the fathers of the normal children were so classified. This finding suggests that there is a greater age spread between the husband and wife in families with a retarded child than in families with a normal child. The long term trend in the United States toward marriages in which the husband and wife are similar in age has been accompanied by a continual increase in equalitarian, companionate relationships in marriage (Burgess, Locke, and Thomes, 1963). When the husband is considerably older than the wife, an authoritarian relationship will more likely be

established. An authoritarian marital relationship will probably affect the personal development of children (Adorno, Frenkel-Brunswik, Levinson, and Sanford, 1950). In addition, since one-fourth of the mothers in the retarded group were still under 25 at the time of the study, they were teenagers when the child was born and may have been ill-prepared as teenagers to cope with the raising of children. Considered together, the findings on marriage and age of parents suggest that the families with a retarded child are less stable and that the relationship between the parents is apparently less equalitarian and less companionate.

Table 12

Number of rooms in dwelling unit

Number of rooms	Retarded	Normal
	per cent	per cent
4 or less	36	21
5	24	39
6 or more	40	40

Household. The second group of family characteristics studied were attributes related to the amount of attention and affectionate behavior which the parents can provide for each of their children. Table 12 indicates a lack of privacy in homes of families of the retarded. Thirty-six per cent of these families, as compared with 21 per cent of families with normal children, lived in dwelling units with 4 or less rooms. However, as shown in Table 13, regardless of the number of rooms in the house, homes of families with

Table 13

People living in dwelling unit

Number of rooms in dwelling	Average number of people per dwelling		Persons per room	
	Retarded	Normal	Retarded	Normal
2	5.5		2.75	
3	6.1	4.5	2.04	1.50
4	6.1	4.9	1.52	1.22
5	6.7	5.8	1.33	1.15
6	7.1	6.5	1.17	1.09
7	8.4	6.3	1.20	0.89
8+	9.6	4.8	1.06	0.78

mentally retarded children were more densely populated than homes of families with normal children. Even when there were 8 or more rooms in the dwelling unit, the density in the retarded group was over twice that in the normal group. In the households studied, residents included not only members of the nuclear family (husband, wife, and children), but also boarders, more distantly related children, and other relatives. Under these conditions, noise and lack of privacy would interfere with the attentive behavior desired in parent-child interaction.

Table 14

Birth order and number of younger siblings

Birth order and younger siblings	Retarded	Normal
	per cent	per cent
Birth order		
Only child	3.5	3.5
Oldest child	27.0	20.0
Youngest child	20.0	40.0
Other	50.0	36.0
Number of younger siblings		
0, 1	52.5	77.6
2, 3	36.5	20.7
4+	11.0	1.7

Family relationships appear to be complicated further by the birth order of the children. Table 14 presents information on birth order. Half of the retarded children were middle-children rather than the eldest or youngest child. By comparison, only slightly over a third of the normal children were middle-children. In a large family, the youngest child is usually the recipient of more attention and affectionate behavior than other children (Bossard and Boll, 1956). It is therefore significant that 40 per cent of the normal children as compared with 20 per cent of the retarded children were the youngest in the family. The lack of attention given to the retarded children is further suggested by information on the number of siblings who are younger than the retarded child. Almost 50 per cent of the retarded children had 2 or more younger siblings whereas only about 20 per cent of the normal children had more than one younger sibling. Thus, the data on birth order as well as that on over-crowdedness suggest that the retarded children receive less attention from their parents than the children in normal families. The age discrepancy between parents and the instability of marriage are consistent with this interpretation of lack of attention and affectionate behavior in the case of the retarded children.

Parental Motivation

One of the complaints about children who are regarded as culturally deprived is that they lack motivation in school. Therefore, one of the important questions to be raised is: to what extent do parents provide academic motivation for the child? Two parts of the interview relating to family background may shed light on this problem. First, each mother was administered a scale which described the extent to which a child constitutes a problem to her. This scale, developed by Farber (1960) for his study of families with severely retarded children, is described in Table 15. (See also Farber, Jenne, and Toigo, 1960). A study by Vogel and Bell (1960) suggests that parents frequently project their difficulties upon one of their children and, as a result, this child develops a variety of personality or intellectual difficulties. A second element in parental motivation is their aspiration with respect to the educational attainment of their child. The higher the attainment expected by parents, the more they would generally attempt to inject this motivation into their children. However, probably in a lower socioeconomic class sample, although high educational aspiration may be verbalized, little may be done to make it a reality.

The information on the extent to which the mother regards the child as a problem is presented in Table 15. According to the table, there is a tendency for mothers of retarded children to regard them as more of a problem than mothers of normal children. In addition, responses to the scale by mothers with a child in the special class were compared with responses by mothers with children in the control group of retarded children. There was little difference between these two groups. The finding suggests

Table 15

Extent to which mother regards child as a problem (by scale type)

Scale Type[b]	Retarded	Normal
	per cent	per cent
0	32.2	53.5
1	20.3	20.7
2	18.6	10.3
3	17.8	8.6
4	11.1	6.9

Note: Results from the population of the project were compared with those which Farber had derived upon 450 mothers of severely retarded children (1960).[a] The coefficient of reproducibility exceeded 90 per cent for Farber's sample, exceeded 89 per cent for the parents of EMR children and 88 per cent for the parents of the normal children. The instrument was thus applicable to the population of this project. Other data were gathered which tended to indicate that the meaning of the scale items was essentially the same for the mothers of the normal educable and severely retarded children. Statistical analysis indicated that the impact of the child upon the mother varied directly with the severity of the child's retardation.

[a] B. Farber, Perceptions of crisis and related variables in the impact of a retarded child on the mother. *J. Hlth. Human Behav.*, **1**, 1960, pp. 108–118.

[b] Scale Types based on agreement with statements:

    a. (Child's name) needs patience and understanding.

    b. (Child's name) is hard to handle.

    c. I feel worn out from taking care of (Child's name).

    d. My life revolves around (Child's name).

Scale types computed as follows:

    0 – answered no to a, b, c, and d.
    1 – answered yes to a.
    2 – answered yes to a and b.
    3 – answered yes to a, b, and c.
    4 – answered yes to a, b, c, and d.

that the school's labeling the child as a "problem child needing special attention" has little bearing upon the mother's attitude toward the child. Apparently, the child had been making greater demands on the mother even before the official designation. Under these conditions, it seems reasonable that the mother will not attempt to motivate the child highly toward intellectual academic achievement.

Table 16

Parents' educational expectations for children

Expectations	Retarded	Normal
Less than high school	9.3	
High school graduate	69.5	55.2
College attendance	21.2	44.8

The second factor related to achievement was parental aspirations with respect to the child's educational achievement. Findings related to educational aspiration are presented in Table 16. About 10 per cent of the parents did *not* expect their mentally retarded children to graduate from high school, while all of the parents of normal children expected their child to be at least a high school graduate. Unexpectedly, about 70 per cent of the parents of the retarded thought their child *would* graduate from high school. Since most of the parents in the retarded group are not themselves high school graduates, they may not realize the academic expectations in high school. The interpretation of lack of awareness is supported by the report of 21 per cent of the parents of retarded children who expected their child to attend college. This lack of awareness was further indicated in the course of the interview by parents of retarded children who expected their children to enter professional occupations. These parents apparently were unable to comprehend the requirements of these occupations and their educational prerequisites. Since these parents do not seem to understand the nature of the educational process required for high school or college graduation, it is unlikely that they can provide the motivation to stimulate their children in academic and intellectual pursuits.

Summary and Conclusion

An investigation was made of the family background of the 120 mentally retarded children in Illinois. To indicate possible social and cultural factors in the development of mental retardation, these children were compared with the 60 normal children of comparable socio-economic status living in the same neighborhoods. Findings indicated that families with retarded children showed a lower level of integration into the community, provided less adequate resources in the home, were characterized by family relationships reflecting instability, inattentiveness, and over-crowding, and were less capable of motivating the children intellectually and academically.

The lower level of integration of the retarded families in the community was indicated by (a) less participation in voluntary associations, (b) membership in isolated religious sects rather than in major denominations, (c) less church attendance, (d) less contact with friends and neighbors, and (e) greater residential mobility.

The inadequacy of parental resources in the retarded group was indicated by (a) low level of education of the parents, (b) low income per family member, (c) slightly greater reliance upon welfare agents, (d) poorer health of the mother, and (e) less exposure to mass communications media such as movies, magazines, and newspapers, as well as (f) the lack of a telephone in the home.

The inadequacy of family relationships in the retarded sample was suggested by (a) greater amount of remarriage, (b) frequency of birth of the retarded child prior to the current marriage, (c) large age discrepancy between husband and wife, (d) the greater tendency for the mother to be a teenager when the child in the study was born, (e) overcrowdedness of the home, and (f) the tendency to be a middle-child with several younger siblings rather than an oldest or youngest child.

Finally, inadequate motivation by the parents was suggested by (a) the tendency for the mother to regard the retarded child as a problem child, and (b) either the expectation of low academic achievement for the child or aspirations which indicate that the parent does not comprehend the nature of the educational process.

The findings suggest that at least a large number of the educable mentally retarded children in the study can be characterized as culturally deprived with respect to the dominant culture of the society. However, the label of cultural deprivation does not exclude other factors from involvement in the mental retardation nor should it suggest that these families exist without a culture. It merely indicates that these families are not active participants in the institutions which reflect the dominant culture in our society. In conclusion, the discussion has emphasized the major trends of the data. At the same time, the tables reflect much variation in the retarded sample on all characteristics described. Thus, while the tendencies toward cultural deprivation exist, many of the families are involved in at least some of the institutions which reflect the dominant culture of the society.

REFERENCES

Adorno, T. W., Frenkel-Brunswik, E., Levinson, D. J., and Sanford, R. N., *The Authoritarian Personality*, New York: Harper, 1950.

Bernstein, B., "Social Structure, Language and Learning," *Educ. Res.*, **3**, 1961.

Bossard, J. H. S., and Boll, Eleanor S., *The Large Family System*, Philadelphia: Univer. of Pennsylvania Press, 1956.

Burgess, E. W., Locke, H. J., and Thomes, M. M., *The Family from Institution to Companionship*, New York: American Book, 1963.

Casler, L., "Maternal Deprivation: A Critical Review of the Literature," *Monogr. Soc. Res. Child Develpm.*, **26**, 1961, No. 2 (Serial No. 80).

Deutsch, M., "Minority Group and Class Status as Related to Social and Personality Factors in Scholastic Achievement," *Monogr. Soc. appl. Anthrop.*, 1960, No. 2.

Farber, B., "Perceptions of Crisis and Related Variables in the Impact of a Retarded Child on the Mother," *J. Hlth. Human Behav.*, **1**, 1960, pp. 108–118.

Farber, B., Jenné, W. C., and Toigo, R., "Family Crisis and the Decision to Institutionalize the Retarded Child," *Res. Monogr. Council except. Child.*, NEA., 1960, Series A., No. 1.

Fraser, Elizabeth, *Home Environment and the School*, London: University of London Press, 1959.

Hunt, J. McV, *Intelligence and Experience*, New York: Ronald Press, 1961.

Inhelder, Bärbel, and Piaget, J., *The Growth of Logical Thinking from Childhood to Adolescence*, (Translated by Anne Parsons and S. Milgram), New York: Basic Books, 1958.

Kirk, S. A., *Early Education of the Mentally Retarded*, Urbana: University of Illinois Press, 1958.

Lipset, S. M., *Political Man: The Social Bases of Politics*, New York: Doubleday, 1960.

Masland, R. L., Sarason, S. B., and Gladwin, T., *Mental Subnormality*, New York: Basic Books, 1958.

Miller, S. M., and Riessman, F., "The Working Class Subculture: A New View," *Soc. Problems*, **9**, 1961, pp. 86–97.

Riessman, F., *The Culturally Deprived Child*, New York: Harper, 1962.

Schneider, L., and Lysgaard, S., "The Deferred Gratification Pattern: a Preliminary Study," *Amer. Sociol. Rev.*, **18**, 1953, pp. 142–149.

U.S. Bureau of the Census, *Statistical Abstract of the United States: 1963*. (84th ed.) Washington, D.C.: Government Printing Office, 1963.

Vogel, E. F., and Bell, N. W., "The Emotionally Disturbed Child as the Family Scapegoat," in N. W. Bell and E. F. Vogel (eds.), *A Modern Introduction to the Family*, New York: Free Press, 1960, pp. 382–397.

Wallin, P., "A Guttman Scale for Measuring Women's Neighborliness," *Amer. J. Sociol.*, **59**, 1953, pp. 243–246.

Yinger, J. M., *Religion, Society and the Individual*, New York: Macmillan, 1957.

Chapter 10

Change in Family Life

Most attempts to conceptualize change in family life involve analogies between family relationships and other social and biological processes. For instance, sociologists frequently introduce similarities between family life and the theater or drama to illuminate their discussions.[1] Major dramatic elements include plot, staging, scenes, organization of roles, backstage action, characterization, and acting. Changes in the family drama emerge through intentional modification, through lack of agreement on specific definitions or dramatic elements, or through ignorance or carelessness in the handling of any of these elements. Sometimes sociologists discuss the family in economic terms. Thus perceived, family interaction is described by such concepts as role bargaining, exploitation, side bets, the marriage market, production of children, ritualistic exchange, and reciprocities.[2] Changes in family relationships occur through general revisions of societal values through shortages (or surpluses) of potential marriage mates or children, or though circumstances that require reallocation of time, money, or emotional commitment. At times, sociologists have used analogies from biology to develop theories of family organization and change. The rest of this introduction concentrates on organic and genetic biological analogies.

Organic Analogies

The analogy between an organism and human society appeared early in the development of sociology. The specialization, integration, and self-regulation of the

---

[1] Erving Goffman, *Presentation of the Self in Everyday Life*, Garden City, N.Y.: Doubleday, 1959; Clifford Kirkpatrick, *The Family as Process and Institution*, New York: Ronald Press, 1963.

[2] Claude Levi-Strauss, "The Principle of Reciprocity," in Lewis A. Coser and Bernard Rosenberg, *Sociological Theory*, New York: Macmillan, 1964, pp. 74–86; William J. Goode, "A Theory of Role Strain," *American Sociological Review*, **25** (August, 1960), pp. 483–496; Howard S. Becker, "Notes on the Concept of Commitment," *Americal Journal of Sociology*, **66** (July, 1960), pp. 32–40; Willard Waller, *The Family, a Dynamic Interpretation*, New York: Dryden, 1938.

elements that make up an organism suggest analogous parts and processes in human society. Herbert Spencer made use of the organic analogy in his view of society as an entity becoming increasingly differentiated.[3] He saw in this movement a marked increase in the specialization and complexity of social organization.

A more sophisticated form of the Spencerian organic analogy is the basis for Talcott Parsons' concept of the contemporary family.[4] Parsons sees the increase in role differentiation and specialization of function as a major trend in modern family life.[5] He sees a decline in emphasis on extended-family relationships beyond the nuclear family as part of this general pattern. Usually Parsons considers the nuclear family as an organ rather than as an organism. This organ depends on the rest of society for its sustenance and, in turn, contributes to society through its special functions: reproduction, sex regulation, and socialization of children.

Those sociologists who use the organic analogy also appear to view institutional change similarly to Neo-Lamarckian biologists. Lamarck, who is considered the founder of evolutionary thought, formulated laws of organic change. The Neo-Lamarckians regard the second law as a central principle of change.[6] This law says, "the production of a new organ in an animal body results from a new need (*besoin*) which continues to make itself felt, and from a new movement that this need brings about and maintains."[7] This law is interpreted by the Neo-Lamarckians to mean that, if the relationship between an organism and its environment changes so that a new organ is needed, that organ will come into existence. As long as the modified environment persists, continued use of that organ will be required and will appear in succeding generations.

Note that the genes themselves do not change; it is the information processed by the genes that changes in its significance for the organism as the environment is modified. As the environmental change impinges on the organism, the organism reacts as a whole to maintain its internal equilibrium. Simultaneously, it must also preserve its equilibrium with the environment. In reacting to both, the organism produces an adaptation in the form of a new or modified organ.

There is much similarity between the Neo-Lamarckian view and that expressed by structural-functionalists. According to structural-functionalists, if the relationship between the family and its environment changes so that a new role is needed,

---

[3] Herbert Spencer, *The Principles of Sociology*, Vol. I, pp. 471–489, New York: Appleton-Century-Crofts, 1897. Reprinted in Lewis A. Coser and Bernard Rosenberg, *Sociological Theory*, New York: Macmillan, 1964, pp. 617–623.

[4] Talcott Parsons and Robert F. Bales, *Family, Socialization and Interaction Process*, New York: Free Press of Glencoe, 1955; Jesse R. Pitts, "The Structural Functional Approach," in Harold T. Christensen (ed.), *Handbook of Marriage and the Family*, Chicago: Rand McNally, 1964, p. 56.

[5] For Parsons, the differentiation implies a movement in society from "particularistic" norms based on ascribed status to "universalistic" norms. He suggests universals in social evolution, proceeding from kinship to stratification and cultural legitimation of new statuses and then on to administrative bureaucracy and to money and markets. Talcott Parsons, "Evolutionary Universals in Society," *American Sociological Review*, **29** (1964), pp. 339–357.

[6] H. Graham Cannon, *Lamarck and Modern Genetics*, Springfield, Ill.: Charles C. Thomas, 1959. Neo-Lamarckians, while accepting the empirical findings in modern genetics, nevertheless believe that new species emerge in the reaction of the total organism to environmental changes. They argue that ordinarily mutations are recessive and generally reduce fitness.

[7] *Ibid.*, p. 51.

that role will come into existence. As long as the modified environment persists, the continued use of that role will be required, and it will appear in succeeding generations. This change in role will occur insofar as the family as an organization of roles reacts as a whole to maintain its internal equilibrium. The potentialities for change are considered almost unlimited. This modification in role structure, however, does not imply that the family will lose its major functions in the society; it will continue to act as the social unit responsible for reproduction, socialization of the young, and regulation of sex relations.

In the organic analogy society is seen as a system that endures over a series of human generations and thus, according to the Neo-Lamarckian position, change in society occurs as a response to change in the environment so that the organism can maintain its equilibrium. Because the organism responds as a whole to a disturbance in the environment, there is no need to seek specific mechanisms that determine stability or change in the make-up of the organism. As long as the environment remains the same, no further change is induced in the organism no matter how many human generations pass. In the Neo-Lamarckian view the single human generation is not an important phenomenon.

Genetic Analogy

Opposed to the view of society as an organism enduring over a series of human generations is the theory that society must renew itself with each generation and that there is much variation in family norms and values (especially in modern industrial societies). The almost ubiquitous existence of generational differences in ideas and interests, of conflict between generations, and of difficulties in the socialization of children suggest a temporal discontinuity.[8] The many differences in families within a society suggest also some functional autonomy of kinship groups. Instead of people existing as body cells in an organism, each generation (indeed, each kinship group) takes the cultural accruments of the previous generation and sifts, interprets, and modifies them, retaining selected portions. If each generation is considered separate the analog of an enduring organism does not seem appropriate. Instead, institutions can be more adequately seen as analogous to species. From this perspective the family is a species that can be identified through the specific norms and values governing a given generation. The society then becomes a collection of coexisting institutions. From the perspective of a societal ecology the particular institutions (such as the family, government, school, and factory) have a symbiotic relationship with one another. They compete for human resources, they engage in cooperative and conflict behavior, and they coexist as do the flora and fauna in a "natural" habitat.

Genetic Problems. Viewing the family as a species rather than as an organ produces a shift in problems for investigation. The important questions about family organization become those related to genetic processes instead of to the structure and function

---

[8] See, for example, Bennett M. Berger, "How Long is a Generation " *British Journal of Sociology*, **11** (1960), pp. 10–23; Karl Mannheim, *Essays on the Sociology of Knowledge*, New York: Oxford University Press, **1952**.

of organs.[9] If the emphasis in sociological investigation of the family is to be on the survival and modification of the species, investigations must focus on genetically relevant topics.

The first concern in the study of genetics is the process by which information about the organization of the parent organisms is transmitted to offspring. The second concern is how the offspring survive in a given environment.[10] Biologists have investigated genetic codes to determine how information is transmitted. Except for mutations, a genetic code remains untouched from one generation to the next; the total genetic information capable of being transmitted from parent to offspring is the genotype. This information guides development of the offspring. The characteristics of the genotype are generally inferred by comparisons between organisms with common ancestors and organisms with different ancestors, on the basis of phenotypic characteristics of the organisms. A phenotype is the total of the organism's characteristics developed through the interaction among tendencies induced by genetic information and environmental factors.[11] Mutations in genetic codes do not seem to occur at random but take place either in the deterioration or modification of genes in the parent or on errors in the process of transmitting the genetic information to the offspring.[12] Often mutations are recessive and are not readily observed.

Geneticists view the influence of environment as twofold. First, certain environments may impede the development inherent in the genotype and have a lethal effect on the organism. Second, environments may stimulate or interfere with the use of genetic information so that certain organs are elaborated in development. The probability of lethals in a given environment determines the fitness of the organism in that environment. A favorable environment is one in which there is a low probability that lethals will occur.[13]

The Family and the Genetics Analog. In family sociology the genetic analog raises questions about the nature of social genotypes (or sets of genetic codes) and the fitness of these in specific environments. The concept of social genotype is similar in some ways to the ideal type described by Max Weber[14]: both are logical constructs meant to characterize a social phenomenon as if no disturbing influences were introduced by historical circumstances. These historical circumstances introduce many complexities

[9] See Talcott Parsons, "A Note on Some Biological Analogies," in Parsons and Bales, *op. cit.* Appendix A, pp. 395–399.

[10] J. Bronowski, "Introduction," in Michael Banton (ed.), *Darwinism and the Study of Society*, Chicago: Quadrangle Books, 1961, pp. ix–xx.

[11] John L. Fuller and W. Robert Thompson, *Behavior Genetics*, New York: Wiley, 1960.

[12] See Howard B. Newcombe and Olwyn G. Tavendale, "Effects of Father's Age on the Risk of Child Handicap or Death," *American Journal of Human Genetics*, **17** (1965), pp. 136–178; W. J. Schull and J. V. Neel, "Radiation and the Sex Ratio in Man; Sex Ratio among Children of Survivors of Atomic Bombings Suggests Induced Sex-Linked Mutations," *Science*, **128** (1958), pp. 343–348.

[13] Julian Steward, *Theory of Culture Change*, Urbana: University of Illinois Press, 1955, suggests that in anthropology, "the orthodox view now holds that history, rather than adaptive processes, explains culture." (p. 35) He opposes the "widely accepted anthropological position" that environmental factors "may be permissive or prohibitive of culture change but are never causative." (p. 34).

[14] Max Weber, *The Methodology of the Social Sciences*, New York: Free Press of Glencoe, 1949 (translated and edited by Edward A. Shils and Henry A. Finch).

and, by their uniqueness, evoke special adjustment patterns characteristic of the phenotype. In his writings Weber sometimes considered the ideal type as a genetic construct[15] and advocated the application of an ideal-type description to a specific historical event. Whenever the ideal-typical construct provided a close fit to the historical circumstances, Weber saw the situation described in the ideal type as a reflection of the crucially significant elements of reality. The ideal type could then provide a causal explanation for the historical situation.

However, more can be expected of a genotypic explanation. The concept of genotype provides a distinction between the ways by which family norms and values are sustained in a given generation and the mechanisms for replicating them in the next generation. A kinship genotype is a program for action which the parent generation transmits to the succeeding generation through the inculcation of certain norms and values. If characteristics either inherent in the genotype or dominant in the environment interfere with this replication, then (although the pattern can be maintained in the parent generation) the genotype will be especially prone to produce mutations in the following generation.

The genetic analogy focuses on the requisites in norms and values about nuclear- and extended-family positions for the maintenance of any given form of kinship organization. Bilateral, patrilineal, matrilineal, and bilineal kinship systems can be seen as alternative genotypic forms of kinship. Such characteristics as inheritance systems, kinship corporate structures, or marriage systems may be viewed as expressions of the genotypes in specific types of environments. Investigation should reveal whether certain norms and values in these kinship genotypes are necessary for their reproduction over a series of generations.

Change in Kinship Organization. Changes in kinship organization may be considered analogous to modifications of genotypes. This book suggests that sibling solidarity, incorporation of a married couple into a bilateral kinship group, emphasis on mate-lover roles, and permanent availability as a spouse in future marriages are characteristics of the bilateral kinship system. That these are internally consistent genotypic features does not imply that opposing tendencies are absent in bilateral kinship. There is an interplay of such tendencies as permanent availability for marriage and orderly replacement of norms and values from one generation to the next. This interplay provides a basis for variation in kinship systems in different societies without assuming that these variations necessarily emerge as adaptations to different environments. Instead, the presence of oppositions within the genotype may itself create a potentiality for change along certain lines.

Suppose that in a given society permanent availability became so prevalent that the orderly replacement of family norms and values from one generation to the next was seriously impeded. Because the new generation did not have direct experience with the older norms for sustaining orderly replacement, it would regard them as obsolete and unworkable and would probably invent a new form. For example, the new generation might create a nonmarrying kinship "priesthood" responsible for replication of family norms and values. The priests as kin-group entrepreneurs could be given guardianship over family property to provide them with power in kinship

---

[15] See, for example, *ibid.*, pp. 93–94.

matters.[16] Given the current technology of contraceptives, the kinship priests could be sexually active but not bound by formal personal commitments either inside or outside the kinship group.

Although the invention of kinship priests may seem farfetched, this example indicates how, given the dominance of permanent availability for marriage, new family forms may be invented (or, in the genetic analog, mutated) to sustain family continuity. The genetic model thereby provides a means of explaining immanent change in family organization without positing a continual increase in specialization of functions. Indeed, family functions may sometimes expand.[17]

Genotype, Phenotype, and Environment

The characterization of a kinship system as a social genotype raises questions about the fitness of the system in various environments. Probably all modern societies contain bilateral, patrilineal, matrilineal, and bilineal kinship groups in varying proportions. The Neo-Lamarckian organic-system analogy suggests that, as industrialization and urbanization proceed, there will be an increasing similarity in family and kinship norms and values among different societies. The major differences in family organization among them occurs because of divergent general societal values.

Empirically, however, strong similarities in prevalent kinship characteristics exist in societies with great differences in nonfamily institutions. For example, there are many similarities in marriage and family relationships in urban areas between the United States and the U.S.S.R. The two societies differ widely in patterns of ownership and inheritance of property, social stratification, composition of the population both ethnically and in age-sex structure, and economic and ideological systems. Yet in both societies there is emphasis in the middle-class population on companionate marital relations, equal status for men and women, bilaterality in kinship relations, and relatively easy divorce and remarriage. The basis for the origin and survival of these similarities is not clear; possibly, the similarities may have resulted from the reaction in both societies to the overthrow of an hereditary-based ruling class (the English nobility isolated from the Americans by distance and the Russian nobility inaccessible to the mass of the population).

At the same time cross-cultural analysis of societies with generally similar nonfamily institutions reveal differences in kinship organization among comparable social classes. Although some sociologists contend that strong, corporate kinship groups cannot readily survive in modern, industrial society, there is evidence of their persistence in wealthy segments of both European and American society. The patrician family described in an earlier chapter by Saveth represents a flourishing of well-organized, extended-kinship groups in American society.

The analysis of upperclass American society by Baltzell indicates that patrician families tend to be patrilineal (i.e., emphasize the male line).[18] Still, patrilineal kinship

---

[16] Compare with statement about "political entrepreneurs" in S. N. Eisenstadt, "Institutionalization and Change," *American Sociological Review*, **29** (1964), p. 237.

[17] S. N. Eisenstadt, "Social Change, Differentiation and Evolution," *American Sociological Review*, **29** (1964), pp. 375–386.

[18] E. Digby Baltzell, *Philadelphia Gentlemen*, New York: Free Press of Glencoe, 1958.

does not seem to be the only system compatible with high socioeconomic status in an industrial society. In his description of the French bourgeoisie, Pitts suggests that the emphasis on accumulating or maintaining family-owned property strengthens the extended-family relationships on one side. He indicates that among the affluent French bourgeoisie the nuclear family tends to ally itself with either the husband's or the wife's kin. The choice of alliance depends on the amount of property controlled by each set of kin. Despite expressions of equalitarianism and individualism, inter-generational bonds are sustained by an emphasis (both in the nuclear family and by the extended-family leaders) on authority and sense of responsibility to kin.[19] A close alliance with one lineage rather than both, however, is typical of bilineal rather than bilateral kinship.[20] (As expressed in other societies, bilineal kinship is characterized by the incorporation of the married couple into a unilateral sibling group rather than a bilateral group and by an emphasis on parent-spouse roles.[21])

Although both the patrician class in the United States and the wealthy French bourgeoisie emphasize family property, marital stability, and unilineal alliances, they appear to express different "genotypes." The American patrician class had its historical roots and models in English and German societies, where the wealthy bourgeoisie was generally incorporated into the aristocracy (with its patrilineal tendencies).[22] In France, with a greater cleavage between aristocracy and bourgeoisie and with a history of "lip-service" equalitarianism, patrilineal kinship was not able to flourish. Yet, maintenance of family property from one generation to the next does provide a condition more conducive to bilineal than bilateral kinship. Wealthy French bourgeoisie society thus favors dominance of bilineality over either patri-lineage or bilaterality in its family traditions. Insofar as the social origins of the patrician or wealthy bourgeoisie class determine family and kinship organization, genotypic factors rather than Lamarckian-like system adaptations clearly pre-dominate.

Organic Versus Genetic Analogs

Both organic and genetic models are unable to explain fully changes in family norms and values. Some of the limitations of the organic analog are that (a) it cannot explain immanent change of somewhat autonomous institutions, (b) it does not account for variations of kinship organization in similar environments nor for similar

---

[19] Jesse R. Pitts, "Continuities and Change in Bourgeois France," in Stanley Hoffman, et al., *In Search of France*, Cambridge: Harvard University Press, 1963, pp. 235–304. (See also the reading by LePlay in Chapter 1.)

[20] Pitts reports that alliances are never fixed but can be revised. Because of this impermanence it would be necessary to retain a congenial relationship with both the husband's and wife's kin. This situation sustains a balance of power between husband and wife in the nuclear family. (Compare with paper by Farber in Chapter 2.)

[21] See, for example, J. D. Freeman, "The Iban of Western Borneo," in George P. Murdock. (ed.), *Social Structure in Southeast Asia*, New York: Wenner-Gren Foundation, 1960, pp. 65–87.

[22] See discussion of recent caste-like trends in the American patrician class in E. Digby Baltzell, *The Protestant Establishment*, Philadelphia: University of Pennsylvania Press, 1964.

family norms and values in different environments, and (c) the interaction of elements of the system may produce a reduction in specialization of function.[23]

The similarity between human genetics and cultural transmission is also limited. Unlike cultural transmission, human genetics is characterized by: (a) the production of an embyro as a single recognizable event, (b) two and only two biological parents, (c) the gene, as the agent of transmission, as apparently a finite entity, and (d) the selection of genes from the father and mother generally by a random procedure.[24] Thus it can be seen that the organic and genetic models are analogs and not theories.

In the final analysis the controversies over adaptational-organic models of the structural-functionalists and genetic models may have no real resolution.[25] Both models reflect distinct tendencies in the change (or stability) of social organization. The adaptational-organic models emphasize the constraints of functions and the adaptability of family structures, whereas the genetic models stress the constraints of structures and flexibility of functions. Insofar as they focus on different constraints, both adaptational-organic and genetic analogs are useful in the development of theory, and resolution is possible only through the formulation of a model that integrates them.

Readings on Change in Family Life

The papers on revisions in family life reflect some of the problems deriving from the view of the family as a species of social organization. According to the genetic analogies, these papers are concerned with fitness of forms of family organization, the development of phenotypic variations given certain constraints in organization, and, finally, kinds of organization of family life conducive to producing effective mutations.

In the first paper Greenfield presents evidence that the small nuclear family was the basic kinship unit in both Great Britain and the United States before the period of industrialization. Although Barbados is not highly industrialized, Greenfield also characterizes its basic household unit as the nuclear family. He then shows that the extended family is not inimical to modern industrial society. His paper implies that various forms of family and kinship organization prevalent throughout the world indicate a high degree of fitness for many different industrial environments.

The second paper, by Bruner, describes the persistence of strong kinship groups in Medan, a large urban center in Indonesia. His discussion also points out modifications that are taking place: Membership in urban clan associations is voluntary; the nuclear family joins the clan associations of both the husband and wife; with neolocal residence in the city, the nuclear family tends to be more isolated physically from kin. These developments may portend a shift from patrilineal to bilateral kinship organization, but they do not indicate a dramatic decline of kinship as a factor in interaction. In the future, formal corporate kinship associations may provide much control over the

---

[23] Compare with *ibid.* See also Pitirim A. Sorokin, *Contemporary Sociological Theories*, New York: Harper, 1928, pp. 194–218.

[24] C. H. Waddington, "The Human Evolutionary System," in Michael Banton, ed., *Darwinism and the Study of Society*, Chicago: Quadrangle Books, 1961, pp. 63–81.

[25] Compare with Pierre L. van der Berghe, "Dialectic and Functionalism: toward a Theoretical Synthesis," *American Sociological Review*, **28** (1963), pp. 695–705.

nuclear family and inhibit the practice of divorce and remarriage, or they may operate mainly as welfare agencies in time of difficulty or crisis. With neolocal residence of the nuclear family and with voluntary membership in the clan associations, welfare functions rather than control will probably predominate.

The paper by Farber shows how families in a crisis situation can select alternative strategies to maintain their integrity. He proposes that social scientists view the ways in which families act in crisis situations as analogous to a game of strategy. His model takes into account both the planning activities of family members and the constraints on their freedom of action. These constraints are conceptualized as the "moves" permitted to the players. These moves, from which strategies are developed, are based on existing norms and values of family life. The environment, as the opposing player in the game, provides the countermoves as difficulties to be overcome. His model suggests the constraints on action required if a specific kind of family and kinship system is to be maintained. Certain strategies maintain the integration of the family unit, whereas others are lethal.

In the final paper Foote and Cottrell delineate the personal requisites for the development of strategies of family organization. This delineation, which has many implications for education programs, emphasizes competence in interpersonal relations. Foote and Cottrell give a high priority to research on the development of intelligence, health, empathy, autonomy, judgment, and creativity, in the belief that they will provide a foundation for effective family planning in a rapidly changing society. In terms of the genetic analogy, Foote and Cottrell provide a series of prescriptions for the development of mutations with a high degree of fitness in modern society.

33. Industrialization and the Family in Sociological Theory

BY SIDNEY M. GREENFIELD

ABSTRACT

When the hypothesis that the small nuclear family of western Europe and the United States is a functional consequence of the urban-industrial revolution is examined cross-culturally, it is established that urbanization and industrialization may exist without the small nuclear family and fragmented kindred, and that the small nuclear family exists without industrialization and urbanization. An alternative hypothesis, hence, is that the specific social system that grew up around machine technology in Western civilization may result from the fact that the small nuclear family existed in Europe and the United States before the industrial revolution.

I

The small nuclear family found in western Europe and the United States is generally viewed in sociological theory as a consequence of the urban-industrial revolution. The present paper questions the hypothesis and suggests alternative lines of thinking.[1]

As Western society continues to disseminate its distinctive technology to the remainder of the world, both theoretical and practical consideration must be given to the changes in social organization that accompany the introduction of the machine and the market-exchange economic system. The specific task of the sociologist and cultural anthropologist here is to seek empirically founded generalizations about cultural process, causality, and functional interdependence. For policy-makers and administrators in foreign affairs and international relations have been applying ill-founded generalizations uncritically: they reason that, if certain types of social organization and urban-industrial technology and the market-exchange economic system are interrelated, they must inevitably accompany Western technology, and as consequence, they support action programs designed to establish and foster these forms.

The dominant sociological hypothesis relating technology and social organization postulates a functional interdependence between industrialization and urbanization, the techno-economic system, with the small nuclear family as the unit of social organization. Hypotheses of functional interdependence, however, take several forms, each with different implications. As Nagel has pointed out, statements phrased in functional terms are the equivalent of those phrased in non-functional terms and any statement in one terminology can be translated into the other: "The difference between a functional and a non-functional formulation," he states, "is one of selective emphasis; it is quite comparable to the

SOURCE: American Journal of Sociology. *Volume 67 (November, 1961), pp. 312–322. Reprinted by permission of University of Chicago Press (Copyright, 1961).*

[1] A portion of this paper was presented under another title at the annual meeting of the American Anthropological Association, Minneapolis, Minnesota, November, 1960.

difference between saying that B is the effect of A, and saying that A is the condition (or cause) of B."[2]

There are, however, two contrasting ways of conceptualizing sociocultural phenomena that result in significantly different meanings for statements of functional relationships. In one formulation the functional statements have approximately the same meaning as conventional casual statements while, in the other, a special type of causal implication is rendered. The most widely adopted formulation of functionalism found in social science is based upon the organic analogy. Sociocultural systems are likened to living organisms in being goal-directed, self-righting systems in which all of the parts "function" to maintain the whole in a state of equilibrium. As phrased by Radcliffe-Brown:

The concept of function involves the notion of a *structure* consisting of a *set of relations* amongst *unit entities*, the continuity of the structure being maintained by a *life process* made up of the *activities* of the constituent units.

Such a view implies that a social system (the total structure of a society together with the totality of social usages in which the structure appears and on which it depends for its continued existence) has a certain kind of unity, which we may speak of as functional unity. We may define it as a condition in which all parts of the social system work together with a sufficient degree of harmony or internal consistency, i.e., without producing persistent conflicts which can neither be resolved nor regulated.[3]

Maintenance of the state of equilibrium, then, is likened to the continuance of life in the organism; the destruction of the equilibrium is analogous to death. The system is closed, and change in the total configuration is ruled out by the basic assumptions. The state of equilibrium is based upon the efficient integration of all of the parts, each of which functions to maintain the continuing existence of the whole. As long as the system continues, then, each part is necessarily functional and its relationship vis-à-vis any other part is one of functional inter-

dependence—all of the parts operating to achieve the goal or purpose of the whole: maintenance of the state of equilibrium. Given this self-maintaining system, we can say that both parts and whole are functionally interrelated and interdependent. By varying our perspective, however, we may view each as a functional consequence of the other, that is, any part is a functional consequence of the operation of the total system, or the whole is a functional consequence of the operation of all the parts.

In the terminology of cause and effect there may also be two perspectives: Starting from the parts, we may say that they are the cause of the whole, which is the effect of their activity, since they maintain the totality in a given state. On the other hand, however, the whole is also the cause of the parts, since the latter operate in accord with the pattern of the former, thereby becoming its effect. In this formulation, however, no causal statements can be made about relations among the parts themselves; that is, one part cannot be the cause of any other since all, taken cumulatively, are either the cause of, or are caused by, the whole. The only relationship that can exist among the parts of a self-regulating, functionally integrated, equilibrium system is that of functional interdependence.[4]

The alternative formulation of functional theory in social science modifies the assumption of equilibrium and discards the organic anology. To those who hold this position, the empirical evidence suggests the conclusion that sociocultural systems are never in a state of complete equilibrium. They are always changing and, consequently, equilibrium is a state relative to a given period of time and, at best, only approximated. In the long run, all sociocultural systems appear to be in continuous flux and both the parts and the whole can and do change. Adherents of this opinion, then, do not generally conceptualize sociocultural systems as self-regulating and goal-directed; consequently, the specialized set of functional statements used to

[2] Ernest Nagel, "A Formulation of Functionalism," in *Logic without Metaphysics*, Glencoe, Ill.: Free Press, 1956, p. 251.

[3] A. R. Radcliffe-Brown, *Structure and Function in Primitive Society*, Glencoe, Ill.: Free Press, 1952, pp. 180, 181.

[4] Associated with the notion of functional interdependence of parts is that of functional alternatives. This refers to a limited range of parts that can perform the same function as the given part in the total system and consequently may be considered as substitutes for the given part since the equilibrium will still be maintained after the exchange.

analyze self-regulating systems are not necessary. Functional statements in this formulation are thus the direct equivalent of causal statements, and a causal relationship is implied whether the terms "functional consequence" or "functional interdependence" are used. The term "functional consequence," however, may be read as necessary and sufficient cause while "functional interdependence" is the equivalent of sufficient cause alone.

In accord with this view the possible relationships between part and whole and part and part differ from those possible in the prior formulation. Since equilibrium is not assumed, the cause of the total system being maintained in its given state is not the functioning of the parts, nor is the cause of the operations of the units taken to be the achievement of the goal of the whole. Here the total system tends to be viewed as resulting from a process of change and adjustment among the parts. Thus, one part can and does, as the interpretation is made, exert a causal effect on the other parts and by implication on the whole. It is only after the parts have had their effect on the other units that the parts may be thought of as being functionally interrelated—the term being taken to mean operating in a state of harmony with each other for a given time. So conceptualized, the locus of the causal nexus is the part-part relationship rather than the part-whole relationship, as is the case in the alternative formulation.

II

Many students in both Europe and the United States have studied the historical conditions that have produced the distinctive modern form of the family. We select Ogburn and Nimkoff because they present the generally accepted point of view. They distinguish three basic types—the consanguineous, the stem, and the conjugal family in that temporal order. "The consanguine family and the clan," they state, "tended to break up in the course of time. . . . The family [then] took on the pattern found in historical Europe and colonial America. The consanguine family tended to disappear, especially in the western world, and the conjugal family became the predominant type." The

stem family is seen as a transitional form. "With increasing industrialization," however, it "tends to be superseded by the conjugal family."[5]

For the United States, the base line used in the study of the family is the nineteenth century and the focal type is the rural farm family.

The American family is not a European institution transplanted to a new environment and slightly changed by this transferring. Instead it represents an original development which so reconstructed the contributions of European culture as to bring forth a family type in its characteristics clearly distinctive from the original European institution.[6]

The industrial revolution, starting in the nineteenth and going into the twentieth century, is seen as the force that changed the farm family and is basically responsible for the "modern American family." Industrialization had several immediate consequences:

Industrial organization eventually outgrew the family. The trend was in this direction as the inventions used in handicrafts manufacture multiplied and the use of windmills increased. But with cheaper iron and steel, and the use of streams as a source of power applied to tools, more space was needed and more workers were required than were to be found in the household. The steam boiler was too big for the home and the power generator required more space for the machine. The factory instead of the homestead became the unit of production. The factory was too large to be manned even by a very large family.[7]

Thus, the adoption of the machine resulted in sweeping changes in social organization: factories needed laborers who could be more readily obtained in cities than on farms; urbanism and industrialization worked hand in hand to change the structure of American society; industry needed laborers and the cities grew to provide them.

In addition to ecological and demographic changes, there were significant structural-functional changes in the social system, primary among them being the expansion of the indus-

[5] William Ogburn and Meyer F. Nimkoff, *Sociology*, Boston: Houghton Mifflin Co., 1950, p. 469.
[6] Ernest Groves and Gladys Groves, *The Contemporary Family*, Philadelphia: J. B. Lippincott Co., 1947, p. 140.
[7] Ogburn and Nimkoff, *op. cit.*, p. 473.

trial factory system to assume most of the tasks formerly handled by the isolated farm family. At first, industry was only a new techno-economic system transforming methods of production. But along with the new technology there developed a set of social relations with its own specific principles of organization and stratification, and its own way of patterning interaction between individuals, into which rural people were assimilated as they moved into the cities to work.[8] One aspect of all this was the small nuclear family with its distinctive form and means of social articulation.

The argument here is concerned with social and cultural change, and a state of equilibrium is therefore not assumed. In fact, it precludes the existence of a self-regulating system since the family is being analyzed in terms of change occurring in it, in the total system, and in the other parts of the system. In formal terms the argument is that the small nuclear family found in the United States takes its present form because of the national industrialization and urbanization. Within a system in a state of change then, one part is the cause of the new form taken by another part.

Once the change is completed, however, and all of the causal factors achieve their effects, a new equilibrium in the total system is commonly assumed. For the present scholars tend to view the small nuclear family as being in a state of functional interdependence with industry and the other parts of what may be loosely called the American form of Western civilization. The family now is functional in that it operates to maintain the new equilibrium.

In Europe, the best example of this line of thinking is presented by Max Weber who, in his *General Economic History*, for example, states the reasons for viewing the changes in the family as a function of its changing economic position that, in turn, is a function of the changes in the total society that stemmed from the industrial revolution. The concluding paragraph of Part I of the book summarizes a part of the argument:

With the dissolution of the manors and of the remains of the earlier agrarian communism through consolidation, separation, etc., private property in land has been completely established. In the meantime, in the course of the centuries, the organization of society has changed in the direction described above, the household community shrinking, until now the father with his wife and children functions as the unit in property relations. Formerly, this was simply impossible for physical reasons. The household has at the same time undergone an extensive internal transformation, and this in two ways; its function has become restricted to the fields of consumption, and its management placed on an accounting basis. To an increasing extent, the development of inheritance law in place of the original complete communism has led to a separation between the property of the men and the women, with a separate accounting. This two-fold transformation was bound up with the development of industry and trade.[9]

A fuller reading of this and his other works completes the presentation which, though more scholarly and sophisticated, is the same in theory as is argued in the United States. Though Weber seems to imply functional interdependence of the small family and industrialization, the conceptual formulation he uses in explaining the changes in the family is the one in which parts in a dynamic system may be construed to have a causal impact on other parts. It is only after industrialization is accomplished and the new whole is created that he postulates an equilibrium in which the causal nexus is between part and whole and the parts are only interdependent.

III

In a recent paper Erwin H. Johnson questioned the hypothesis that the small nuclear family is caused by industrialization and urbanization. After examining the data from modern Japan, he concludes that the stable stem family, which is at least four hundred years old there, "is sufficiently generalized in its nature to conform to the needs of the changing technology of Japan." He then goes on to say that the traditional family, in fact, had not and "does not have to give way under ... urban or industrial influences."[10]

[8] Wirth, in his "Urbanism as a Way of Life," *American Journal of Sociology*, XL (July, 1938), pp. 1–24, argues that the modern small nuclear family is a function of city living.

[9] Trans. Frank H. Knight, Glencoe, Ill.: Free Press, 1950, p. 111.

Modern Japan, then, provides us with a case of both urbanization and industrialization with a family other than the small nuclear form. Garigue reports extensive kinship networks among urbanized, industrialized French-Canadians in Montreal. These extended networks of "urban French-Canadian kinship," he writes, "are no new development, but seem to have been in existence since the period of New France." He concludes:

The collected evidence indicates no trend toward transformation of the present French-Canadian urban kinship system into the more restricted system reported for the United States. While difficulties were reported in maintaining a united domestic family or an integral kin group, there is no reason to suppose that these difficulties were caused primarily by urban living. Moreover, many cases were reported where the kin group re-formed after a period of disunity. There are many reasons for believing that the present system will continue. Far from being incompatible, kinship and urbanism among French-Canadians seem to have become functionally related.[11]

In a recent paper on Luso-Brazilian kinship patterns, Wagley, after examining data on the *parentela*—a bilateral kindred—from seven Brazilian communities, writes: "It is evident from the data provided . . . that kinship plays an important role in social, economic and even political affairs."[12] The *parentela*, he adds, operates in both rural and urban areas. In the cities, kinsmen tend to purchase apartments in the same building to facilitate the working out of kinship obligations. The studies by Firth, Young, Shaw, and Townsend in London show further evidence of the extension of kinship in urbanized, industrialized areas.[13]

Additional evidence is presented here to question the hypothesis of functional interdependence and implied causality between urban-industrial technology and the small nuclear family, challenging that part of the generally accepted hypothesis in which the diachronic formulation of sociocultural events is used. The position which assumes a static equilibrium in which functional interdependence within a closed, stable system is assumed a priori will not be argued other than to stress that even here there may be a range of family forms that can serve as functional alternatives to the small nuclear family in urbanized, industrialized systems. The additional evidence is found in an analysis of the family on the island of Barbados where the small nuclear family and fragmented kindred are present in the same form and functionally articulated with the larger society in the same way as in industrialized Western society, but without industry and machines.

We shall, then, have examples from the ethnographic record in which urbanization and industrialization are present without the small nuclear family and fragmented kindred, and the nuclear family is found in the same form and with the same functions as in industrialized Western society but without industrialization and urbanization. Taken together, these combinations seriously question a hypothesis that has received general acceptance in sociological theory before being tested by the comparative evidence.

IV

Barbados is a small, densely populated island, twenty-one miles long and fourteen miles wide, located in the Caribbean Sea at the eastern rim of the Lesser Antilles. It was first colonized by Great Britain at the beginning of the seventeenth century, and, in contrast with her other Caribbean possessions, has remained a British colony from the time of its settlement until 1956, when, with nine other English Caribbean dependencies, it became part of the Federation of the West Indies.

Today, Barbados is not a folk or peasant society. On the other hand, it is not highly

---

[10] "The Stem Family and Its Extensions in Modern Japan" (paper presented at the Annual Meeting of the American Anthropological Association, Minneapolis, Minnesota, 1960), p. 13.
[11] Philip Garigue, "French Canadian Kinship and Urban Life," *American Anthropologist*, LVIII (December, 1956), pp. 1098–1099.
[12] Charles Wagley, "Luso-Brazilian Kinship Patterns" (unpublished manuscript, 1960).
[13] Raymond Firth, *Two Studies of Kinship in London*, London: Athlone Press, 1957; Michael Young, "Kinship and Family in East London," *Man*, LIV, No. 210 (September, 1954), pp. 137–139; L. A. Shaw, "Impression of Family Life in a London Suburb," *Sociological Review*, III (December, 1955), pp. 175–195.

mechanized and industrialized. Its economy, which is based upon agriculture, is best not considered underdeveloped since the application of additional capital has not, and, at present, cannot lead to a profitable expansion of productivity and employment opportunities for its very large population.

At present, Barbados—only 166.3 square miles in area—is one of the most densely populated areas in the world: its inhabitants numbered approximately 230,000 at the end of 1956—a density of almost 1,380 persons per square mile—and were increasing at a rate of about 2 per cent per year. Overpopulation has long been recognized as a major problem on the island.

How is this myriad of human beings supported? While its economy is based upon agriculture, in contrast with most of the world's densely populated rural areas where subsistence as well as cash crops are raised, Barbados is almost exclusively dependent upon a single cash crop—sugar. As emphasized in a recent national accounts study of the economy of Barbados,[14] agriculture, in which the growing of sugar cane predominates over all other forms of agricultural activity, is the most important contributor to the island's gross domestic product in which the processing of sugar and molasses accounts for more than half the total contribution of manufacturing. Sugar, to quote the authors of Barbados' ten-year development plan, is truly "the blood of the island."[15]

Barbadians, then, are not subsistence farmers. The island's agricultural activities are organized around the production of sugar, which is cultivated because it provides more revenue per acre than any other crop which could be grown on the island and for which a world market exists.[16] Individuals earn their livelihood in the form of wages; they produce very little for their own consumption.

[14] Jeanette Bethel, "A National Accounts Study of the Economy of Barbados," *Social and Economic Studies*, IX, Special No. (June, 1960), pp. 127–128.
[15] *A Ten Year Development Plan for Barbados, 1946–56*, Bridgetown, Barbados: Advocate Press, n.d., p. 11.
[16] Lord Simon of Wythenshawe, *Population and Resources of Barbados*, Bloomcroft: Disbury, 1954, pp. 1–2.

Barbados, as has already been mentioned, is not an industrialized society in the general sense of the term. The concept of industrialization, however, as it is used in sociological discussions is ambiguous. The specific referent is technological—machines and factories. In general, however, it refers also to the system of social relations that organize human populations in the management of the machines. The use of one term to refer to both the technology and the social structure is regrettable since it leads to thinking of the two as inseparable: that is, the student finds it difficult to think of machine technology without the specific social patterns that have developed in Western civilization. This double referent, however, reveals more of the causal assumptions made by the early students of industrialization: the causal impact of machine technology was considered to be so great that the social relations governing the use of the machines was conceptualized as a necessary consequence of it. Both referents of industrialization must be considered independently, at least until some evidence is presented to demonstrate that there is only one way to organize a population in the use of machines.

This inadequate conceptualization is crucial, however, in the analysis of the data from Barbados since many of its social structural forms are those generally associated with machine technology in North America and Europe, although there are few factories and machines are little used except for a handful of instances in the sugar industry. This situation, itself, however, provides an additional challenge to the hypothesis which claims that industrialization—which at the beginning, at least, was purely technological—is the cause of social organization, since the consequence is present without the cause.

V

The elementary family in Barbados, as in most of the islands of the West Indies, takes two basic forms—one conjugal or nuclear, the other subnuclear and generally matrifocal. As used here, matrifocality refers to the form of the family in which the mother-child relationship is stronger and more durable than the conjugal (husband-wife) bond. It is characterized by (1) a marginal role for the husband-father; (2) high percentages of female heads of households; (3) easy adoption and high ratios of children per household; (4) high rates of illegitimacy (by European and American standards); and (5) low rates of "legal" marriages. The conjugal or nuclear family, on the other hand, is based upon the husband-wife relationship and is characterized by the converse of the features of the matrifocal family.

The household, which generally contains at least one of the elementary kinship units, is variable. Ideally, it is composed of an isolated nuclear family which lives in a separate shelter, usually provided by the adult male. This, however, is rarely achieved by most of the population. When not composed of an isolated nuclear family, the household may consist of a number of alternative forms. The first is a nuclear family in which a mature child, invariably a daughter, has begun to have a family—often she is unmarried—before establishing a firm conjugal relationship in a separate dwelling. This extended family group, or "multi-family" household, is of three generations and is composed of one nuclear family plus one or more matrifocal units of unwed mother and children, all sharing the same house. An alternative appears when a woman and her children become established in an independent dwelling unit without an adult male. This occurs either when the members of the conjugal group separate— the male leaving—or when a woman obtains a dwelling, usually through inheritance, and occupies it with her children but without a mate. An infrequent variant of this denuded family occurs when a man is left alone with his children in a household without an adult female. These denuded family households can become extended when the children mature and begin to have offspring while they are still living at home. Here we find a three-generation unit which, generally, is composed of a woman and her children, including mature daughters and their offspring. This form, which is found throughout the Caribbean, is usually referred to as the "grandmother family." A household then, can consist of one of four alternative forms which are found distributed in the same frequencies in

both the rural and urban areas: (1) a nuclear family, (2) a nuclear extended family, (3) a denuded or subnuclear family (male or female, but usually female-centered), and (4) a denuded or subnuclear extended family (male or female but again usually female-centered).

In form and functional integration with the total society—an at least temporary state of equilibrium is assumed for the purpose of analysis—the ideal nuclear group found in Barbados is very similar to the nuclear family found in the United States and described by Parsons.[17] The tendency toward structural and spatial isolation appears in both places; the importance of the mother in the process of the child's socialization and in the development of his personality are similar; the role of the adult male within the family as "breadwinner," responsible for supporting the entire group, is likewise analogous. More significantly, even the relationship between the individual and the larger society is the same. Individuals are all members of families linked to the larger society through the adult male who occupies a place in the local occupational system, and in both cases, the position of the latter member in the occupational system is a primary determinant of the position of the others in the social hierarchy.

Other similarities can be found in patterns of descent: Both systems are bilateral. In Barbados, illegitimacy is common, it is usual for parents to leave wills bequeathing their property to all of their children.[18] Relations with ascending and descending generations show no tendency toward structural bias in favor of any one line of descent. Both Barbados and the United States, therefore, can be described as symetrically multilineal.

In both cases, the tendency toward structural isolation is reinforced by the relationship between the family and the occupational system, particularly with reference to social mobility.

[17] Talcott Parsons, "The Kinship System in the Contemporary United States," *American Anthropologist*, XLV (January, 1943), pp. 22–38. See also Talcott Parsons and Robert Bales, *Family, Socialization and Interaction Process*, Glencoe, Ill.: Free Press, 1955.
[18] Sidney M. Greenfield, "Land Tenure and Transmission in Rural Barbados," *Anthropological Quarterly*, XXXIII (October, 1960), pp. 165–176.

Each nuclear family is ascribed a place in the system of stratification which is based upon the social class of the family of orientation of its adult male subject to the mobility he may achieve in his occupational pursuits. Mobility is a driving force in both societies. Kinship relationships are generally divorced from the occupational system, thus permitting conjugal units to be socially mobile, independent of kinship ties. Nuclear families striving for mobility are often best able to do so by almost total denial of kinship claims, which, of course, leads to the isolation of the conjugal family. In Parsons' terms, then, both the Barbadian and American nuclear families can be characterized as "bilateral, structurally isolated, open, multi-lineal, conjugal systems."[19] The alternative forms of the household discussed above are all variants of the isolated nuclear unit produced by factors relating directly to the integration of family and society.

The primary functions of Barbadian society are performed through a highly stratified system of occupational statuses; the hierarchically ranked positions, however, provide their occupants with wages that vary considerably. The insular system of social stratification is tied directly to these ranked occupational positions since they are the primary determinant of an individual's social class. Families are articulated with the larger society through adult males who are members of both a family and the occupational system simultaneously: the male role is defined in terms of supporting women and children; he is also expected to hold a position in the occupational system. In the latter system he holds one of a series of ranked positions from which he receives money and prestige; in the family he holds a position that calls for the contribution of income obtained in the occupational world. Women and children, who, in the ideal, are outside the dominant institutional complex,

are linked to it through reciprocal role obligations to a male within the family. Satisfactory performance of the adult male role within the family requires an individual to hold a position in the occupational system that provides him with income sufficient to support a family.

The occupational system in Barbados, however, is so constituted that many, if not most, of the positions at the lower end of the hierarchy provide neither the prestige nor the income necessary for the support of a family. The occupants of these low-ranked positions are not able to fulfil the role expectations of adult male within the family, and if they cannot improve their occupational status after a period of time they tend to leave the household, thereby creating a denuded, subnuclear, matrifocal or mother-oriented group. The extended family households, both nuclear and denuded, appear when the fathers of the children born to girls living in parental households have not been able to attain an occupational position with rewards sufficient to purchase a house and to establish the new family as an isolated nuclear group.

The importance of a man to his family and his relationship to the others, therefore, will vary directly with the income and status he earns in the occupational world. Consequently, we may expect both the family and the household to take different forms of varying socioeconomic levels. Whether the unit is nuclear or matrifocal is, therefore, a function of the system of social stratification and the way in which adult males link the family to society. Where adult males hold positions that provide rewards sufficient for the support of a nuclear family, the nuclear group is isolated in a separate household; where not, a subnuclear, matrifocal group appears, causing the household to take one of the forms outlined above.

On the tiny sugar-growing island of Barbados, then, we find the same small nuclear family, articulated with the larger society in precisely the same way as we find in industrialized Western society, but without urbanization and industrialization. The industrial revolution, in fact, has not yet come to the island.

The existence of an industrialized and urbanized society in Brazil, French Canada, England, and Japan with an extended family, and the

[19] The most significant difference between the Barbadian and the American nuclear family is size. This difference, however, most critically effects the socialization and personality development of the children and not the form of the family or its articulation with the larger society (Parsons and Bales, *op. cit.*, p. 18). It is, therefore, excluded from the present comparison.

small nuclear family—identical in form and function to the nuclear family of industrialized Western society—in Barbados without industrialization or urbanization provides evidence to question the hypothesized causal relationship between urban-industrial technology and the family. The explanation for the similarity in family form and function in Barbados and in industrialized Western society, however, may provide us with a new perspective with which to re-analyze the historical data used to support the old hypothesis.

VI

Barbados was settled by colonists who came in family groups from Great Britain. Though African slaves were later introduced to work on the sugar plantations, significant numbers of English and Irish families remained and their descendents are still there today. The institutionalized form of family now found in Barbados was brought to the island by the first settlers and later, adopted by the Negroes when integrated into the larger society through the occupational system immediately following Emancipation.[20]

The small nuclear family, the *famille particulariste* of Le Play, which is native to North Europe,[21] is known to have existed in England in the seventeenth century, prior to the colonization of the New World. Specialists in the culture of the Old World (Europe, Mediterranean, Middle East), in fact, believe it to be much older, "as old as the Vikings or older" according to Arensberg.[22] If this is the case, it antedates both urbanism and machine technology in England and the United States. Perhaps its contemporary place in modern, urban, industrial-

ized society is related to its temporal priority to machine technology.

If, at the very beginning of the urban-industrial revolution, the inventors of machine technology already lived in small nuclear families, it is no small wonder that this form became functionally integrated with industrial technology as a new equilibrium was achieved. As North European man developed the social forms to go with the machine, it is quite probable that he reworked the social institutions with which he was already familiar. If so, the relationship between the small nuclear family and industrialization is better interpreted as one of the temporal priority of the former and not a necessary functional consequence or cause and effect in which the latter is the determinant. Further investigation of the historical material, then, may indicate that the two are related because the small nuclear family was there first. Subsequent social institutions, such as the occupational system, that went with the machine were probably adapted to, and therefore fitted with, a society organized in small families. One wonders what organizational forms urban-industrialized society might have today if these early North Europeans lived in extended families.

Some might argue that wage labor more than

---

[20] It is significant to note that the family form has remained the same even though it has been transferred from one ethnic group to another.

[21] Frederic Le Play, Focillon, and DeLaire, *L'Organisation de la famille*, (Tours, 1884) (see also Edmond Demolins, *Comment la Route Crée de type social*, Paris: F. Didet, n.d., 1890?, 2 vols.; and Carle C. Zimmermann and Merle Frampton, *Family and Society*, New York: D. Van Nostrand & Co., 1937, pp. 97 ff.).

[22] Conrad M. Arensberg, "Discussion of Methods of Community Analysis in the Caribbean by Robert Manners," *Caribbean Studies: A Symposium*, Mona,

Jamaica: Institute of Social and Economic Studies, 1957, p. 97. An example of what might have happened in the total society is found at the upper end of the occupational ladder where a given individual can earn enough to support more than one family.

With the acquisition of great wealth and property, we find the development of extended families, with the income-earning property accumulated by one generation providing support and prestige for several other generations. These extended families, usually patrilineages in Europe, North America, and the West Indies, develop around family property that provides income and status to all who can establish a valid genealogical connection therein.

At the lower end of the occupational scale, jobs do not provide sufficient income for a man to support even one family and the prestige rating is so low as to deny status either for himself or his family. It is here that women and children must enter the labor force to help out. The jobs available to them, however, are also at the bottom of the hierarchy. As the primary feature of the division of labor is destroyed, so is the strength of the conjugal bond. It is then that the subnuclear, matrifocal family appears.

machine technology is the cause of the distinctive Western family. If one uses the equilibrium formulation, there is no doubt that wage labor and the small family are functionally interrelated and interdependent. The question, however, is whether a system of wage labor is a necessary and sufficient cause for the small family when an entire sociocultural system is in the process of change.

The crucial relationship between wage labor and the form of the family concerns the scale of remunerations. In the systems of North America, Europe, and Barbados, with the exception of the relative few who hold positions at the top of the hierarchy, workers earn only enough for the support of a nuclear group. While variability in wages is considerable, we rarely find a job paying enough to support more than one nuclear family. Since men are the principal wage-earners—this probably being based upon a prior cultural definition of the sexual division of labor in North Europe—they are expected to provide money for the kinship unit. The degree of possible extension of the kin group is thus related to the income earned by men. Since each nuclear unit also is expected to have its own wage-earner, it is economically independent, which brings about a weakening of reciprocal relations between members and kinsmen outside the group. Within the nuclear family, however, there is relative equality, each member having a right to a share of the income of the adult male or the goods or services it can buy.

Were the occupational system so organized as to pay one individual enough to support a larger group or to enable him to provide employment for such a unit, extended families might arise to engulf or submerge the nuclear group. Perhaps,

if extended families had existed in England when the complex took its present form, the remuneration scale of modern industrial society would be very different.

In the United States, industrialization started in the Northeast, a section appropriately called New England. With reference to the family in New England, Arensberg writes, "The brittle, easily split 'nuclear' or 'democratic' ('Eskimoan') family, . . . came with [the] Yankees from England and fitted well with their egalitarian, unstratified farmer-artisan towns."[23] The small nuclear family, then, was brought to the United States from Great Britain by its earliest settlers. Therefore, it was present before the industrial revolution began in the United States. We suggest that it was reworked, as it had been several centuries earlier, in England, to provide the foundation for the new system of social organization that developed and spread with the industrial revolution. Here again, it was not the industrial revolution that produced the small nuclear family; in fact, the opposite may be true. The prior existence of the small nuclear family as the basic kinship unit of the people who industrialized both Great Britain and the United States may have been responsible for the very forms of social organization that developed along with the machines.

Furthermore, the data from Barbados demonstrates that the small nuclear family can diffuse without urbanization and industrialization just as the latter seems to be able to diffuse without the small nuclear family.

In conclusion, then, an examination of both the comparative and historical evidence indicates that, developmentally, there is no necessary and sufficient causal relationship, whether expressed in terms of necessary functional interdependence or consequence, between the small nuclear family and urbanization and industrialization. Any relationship that exists most probably results from the presence of the small family in North Europe prior to the industrial revolution.

[23] Conrad M. Arensberg, "American Communities," *American Anthropologist*, LVII (December, 1955), p. 1149.

The close functional adjustment between the isolated nuclear family and this form of stratified occupational system is related to the organization of the latter system. Since most jobs pay enough to support one family, the total system functions best when one wage-earner links one family to the social system through his wage contribution. His income and status are identified with the members of the nuclear group until the children are old enough to establish their own nuclear families, each with its own adult male wage-earner.

34. Medan: The Role of Kinship in an Indonesian City*

BY EDWARD M. BRUNER

OVER A CENTURY AGO Sir Henry Maine told us that kinship, the basis of primitive social organization, declines in importance in more advanced societies. The proposition has been widely accepted and has been restated in one form or another by many scholars during the last hundred years. Most recently, for example, Julian Steward (1960) writes that internal specialization, social classes, and state institutions come to supersede kinship groups, and Leslie White (1959, p. 141) goes so far as to suggest that the transformation from primitive to civil society entails "the loss of kinship."

Criticisms have been made of Sir Henry's proposition on the grounds that not only kinship but also territorial groups and age-sex groupings are significant in the social life of many primitive peoples, and on the grounds that kinship often plays a crucial role in some urban social systems. These points are well taken; nevertheless if we take the long view, and especially if we compare carefully selected societies at extreme ends of the developmental continuum, Sir Henry's generalization appears to be essentially correct. It is perfectly clear that kinship was more prominent among Australian aborigines of the last century than it is today in urban centers of the Western nations.

The generalization is less clear, however, if we focus on intermediate level societies, those that are neither truly primitive nor fully urbanized, or if we focus on societies that have recently been exposed to modernizing influences and are currently undergoing rapid culture change. In many of these societies even a preliminary analysis of the role of kinship takes us far beyond the confines of Sir Henry's proposition. I agree with Oscar Lewis (1962) that the distinction between kinship-based versus nonkinship-based societies simply does not tell us enough for purposes of comparative analysis. We now have field studies of the processes of kinship change and of the details of the sequence in which change occurs, and on the basis of these data we must formulate theoretical distinctions finer than those proposed by Sir Henry. His generalization and other similar evolutionary propositions were and are important advances, but rather than repeat or defend them, we must aim for more sophisticated formulations which take account of the more complete data now being gathered by anthropologists from a wider range of societies.

This brief paper is more limited in scope. It explores the role of kinship among the Toba Batak located in the modern coastal city of Medan, Indonesia; demonstrates the inadequacy

SOURCE: Pacific Port Towns and Cities, A Symposium, edited by Alexander Spoehr, Honolulu: Bishop Museum Press, 1963, pp. 1–12. Reprinted with permission of the author.
* I am indebted to my colleagues, Joseph B. Casagrande, Alan H. Jacobs, and Oscar Lewis, for helpful suggestions.

418

of broad statements to the effect that kinship declines in importance, is superseded, or even "lost" in urban societies; and presents some tentative conclusions which may be applicable in other similar situations.

Historical and Ethnographic Background

The Toba Batak are a Malayo-Polynesian speaking people whose traditional homeland is in the interior mountain region of North Sumatra. Wet-rice agriculture in terraced fields is the major economic activity. The society is patrilineal, patrilocal, and includes a segmentary lineage system and affinal alliances.

In the mid-nineteenth century the heaviest concentration of population was in the interior highlands. The coastal lowlands to the east were a dense tropical rain forest and hence sparsely settled, although Batak communities were located along the banks of the larger rivers. The rivers originated in the mountains and flowed through the lowlands into the Malacca Strait. At the mouths of the navigable rivers were a series of small port towns. The language spoken in these towns was Malay, the religion was Islam, and the economy was based upon trade, fishing, and the collection of tribute. Batak traders came to the port towns for salt, cloth, dried fish, and manufactured goods in exchange for forest products and benzoin from the hinterland.

The situation began to change radically in the 1860's, with the arrival of Europeans. There were two major streams of contact; one was the penetration of German missionaries and Dutch administrators to the Batak highlands, and the other was the establishment of Western plantations in the lowlands. Almost the entire lowland region of North Sumatra was eventually cleared and transformed into a vast estate area in which tobacco, rubber, palm oil, tea, coconut, and other agricultural products were cultivated. These developments, however, did not extend into the Batak homeland; no plantations were established there, and the land remained under the control of village and kinship groups. It was not until 1907, in fact, that the interior was finally brought under the complete jurisdiction of the Dutch colonial government.

European contact brought about considerable cultural change, even for those Toba Batak who remained in their villages. Trade between the interior and the coast was increased through improved means of communication and transportation. A railroad extended to the edge of the highlands and roads were built throughout the Batak area. The missionaries succeeded in converting many hundreds of thousands to Christianity and, with financial help from the government, opened a series of village schools, some in rather remote areas. Many Toba Batak obtained at least the rudiments of a Western elementary school education and some went on to high school and even to universities in Java and Holland. Today there are Batak poets, artists, doctors, lawyers, engineers, and university professors, the majority of whom received their training since the end of World War II. Before the war, most Batak with the desire and opportunity for education and advancement could realistically aspire to positions no higher than that of teacher, clerk, or lower-level administrator.

By the 1900's, educated Batak, as individuals and as family groups, began migrating from the villages to seek their fortunes on the plantations and cities located in the coastal lowlands. From the migrant's point of view there had been both a push and a pull; on the one hand he wished to escape from poverty, overpopulation, and scarcity of terraced rice fields in the highlands, and on the other, he desired the opportunity to increase his standard of living and to enjoy the excitement, greater wealth, and higher social position offered by life in the city.

Many Batak migrants went to Medan, a city strategically located 14 miles from the sea at the junction of an inland highway and the Deli River. Medan was founded in the latter part of the nineteenth century as a commercial center to serve the interests of European planters, but it rapidly became the administrative, military, and cultural center of North Sumatra. Today, it is the primary regional metropolis in Sumatra and the second largest Indonesian city outside of Java (Withington, 1962).

Medan has increased in population from 14,000 in 1905, to 76,000 in 1930, and to 360,000 in 1959, according to official figures (*Statistical*

Pocketbook of Indonesia, 1960). The most recent population figure is an estimate, since no accurate census was taken after 1930, and most authorities feel it is too conservative. There may well be as many as half a million people in the larger Medan area.

The city has been characterized by notable shifts in ethnic composition. In the late nineteenth century, Medan was populated primarily by indigenous Malay, European administrators and planters, and a few Chinese traders. The first wave of migration was a consequence of the need for agricultural laborers on the plantations. Rather than recruit labor locally, company agents located in Java, Singapore, and Hong Kong brought in Javanese and Chinese workers. After the expiration of their three-year contracts many of these laborers left the estate to settle permanently in the city. Thus in Medan in 1930, out of a total population of 76,000, there were 27,000 Chinese, 21,000 Javanese, 4,000 Europeans, and 4,000 others of foreign descent. The combined nonindigenous population was 74 per cent of the total. Approximately three out of every four persons in the city were comparatively recent migrants, in that they or their parents had not been born in the area.

In the recent period the number of Europeans has decreased so drastically that today they may be counted in the hundreds rather than the thousands, and there has also been a decrease in the rate of Chinese population growth. The rapid increase in total population has been due to the migration of rural Sumatrans from many different ethnic groups in the highlands who have settled in the city. The Toba Batak are simply one group among many. Some are third-generation urbanites whose grandparents left their highland village, but most are recent arrivals.

The urban migrant finds himself in a radically different physical and social environment. The rural villages are approximately 3,000 feet above sea level and hence are considerably cooler than the coastal city. The villages lack electricity, running water, telephone service, and paved streets, while the city has all of these and more, including restaurants, hotels, hospitals, department stores, banks, theaters, publishing houses, daily newspapers, universities, a medical school,

and other facilities normally associated with a busy metropolitan center and regional capital. The language spoken in the village is Toba Batak, while in the city it is Indonesian; the two are mutually unintelligible. Almost all village men, even those who are teachers or government employees, are at least part-time farmers, and village women regularly work in the fields along with their husbands. Most urban men work in an office and neither they nor their wives engage in any agricultural activity. But possibly the most significant difference is that in the village everyone is not only a Toba Batak but also a close relative, while in the city one's immediate neighbors are most likely to be strangers.

In sum, Medan is a relatively new city, characterized by a constant influx of migrants, by rapid growth, high population density, ethnic diversity, and cultural heterogeneity. The Batak migrant leaves his familiar village world or kinsmen to settle among strangers in an alien environment. It is in this context that we inquire into the role of kinship in the city.

The Role of Kinship

The Toba Batak residing in Medan are part of a single kinship community, in that every person is bound by multiple ties in a widely ramifying kinship network. The urban Batak are very aware of their relationships to kinsmen; they employ kinship terminology in daily life, and the kinship system is symbolized at all life-crisis rites and ceremonials.

Kinship ties are based on both descent and marriage. Let us consider each in turn. The Batak descent system is a patrilineal one which operates on many levels of segmentation. At the highest level the Toba Batak form a single super-patrilineage, since they consider themselves to be descendants of one man, Si Radja Batak, who existed, they say, about 25 generations ago. Below the super-patrilineage are groupings of clans, named exogamous clans, maximal and minimal lineages. Every Batak, living and dead, has a place on the tribal genealogy and persons in different descent lines are always able to determine their proper relationship to one another by tracing their social distance from a common male ancestor. In addition to the descent system, relationships are also reckoned through affinal ties, as every Batak marriage binds two or more lineages or clans. When a man is married, not only he, but every member of his descent group immediately becomes related to all members of the bride's lineage. These affinal bonds are always significant in social life as they involve a status relationship, ceremonial obligations, and the exchange of money, goods, and services. They may be further reinforced by additional marriages in subsequent generations, thus creating affinal alliances which have structural continuity over time. Every descent group, at any given time, has a series of affinal alliances or more transitory ties to those lineages to whom they have given wives and to those from whom they have received wives. Thus in Batak society there is a kind of kinship grid binding all individuals vertically through descent lines and horizontally through affinal bonds.

The system operates somewhat differently in village and city. In the village, kinship relationships are known from childhood, but in the city they have to be established, a consequence of the mobility and high rate of in-migration which characterizes the urban condition. Since there are approximately a million Toba Batak, and since migrants come to Medan from different rural areas, the urban Batak frequently find themselves in the position of meeting other Batak for the first time in the city. On these occasions the parties involved almost invariably determine their respective positions in the kinship grid before any extended interaction. There are, in fact, words in the Batak language for this procedure, *martarombo*, meaning literally "to genealogize," and *martutur*, to engage in the process of establishing a kinship connection. It is not always an easy or rapid procedure, because the correct kinship bond between any two individuals may not be readily apparent and there are often alternate possibilities. Then too, the Batak frequently prolong these preliminary discussions about kinship, since they find many satisfactions in the process. It is for them what the weather or baseball is for us—something to talk about—and it provides an opportunity to

exchange gossip about mutual acquaintances, which most Batak thoroughly enjoy. Once established, the kinship relationship structures all subsequent interaction; the individuals involved relate to one another as kinsmen.

In order to establish a kinship connection to every other Batak whom he may meet, a man must possess fairly extensive genealogical knowledge and he must be aware of recent marriages in his own and related lineages. In the rural areas most men have acquired the necessary information by the time they become adults, but this is not so in the city, especially among the younger generation. There are, however, various short cuts for determining kinship connections. An urban youth who does not know how to relate to someone will simply ask his parents or possibly one of the genealogical specialists. The latter are older men who have distinguished themselves by their knowledge of Batak customs and genealogies; they are often consulted by the parents themselves as to the proper procedures for various ceremonies. Another short cut employed by the urban Batak is to reckon descent by reference to the number of generations a person is removed from a clan ancestor, without going through the intermediate descendants. A man will be told, for example, that he is sixteen generations removed from the founder of his clan; with this information, and a knowledge of how the system works, it is possible for him to determine his relationship to others with a minimum of consultation. Another procedure is for two persons to work out their kinship connection by reference to a known relationship to a third person. There are other procedures. The important point is not which particular procedure is utilized, but rather that all Batak have techniques enabling them to key into the system by one means or another.

The urban Batak form a kinship community, but the quality of interaction among kinsmen is different from that in the village. As we have pointed out, migrants come to the city from various highland areas, they represent many different descent lines, and there is a larger number of Toba Batak in Medan than in any comparable rural area. The city man has more relatives distributed more widely in the kinship network than his village counterpart, but he interacts with them less frequently, in more restricted situations, and for shorter periods of time. Kinship sentiment decreases concomitantly. The affective component of kinship is dispersed; intimacy and depth of feeling are sacrificed for a wider and larger circle of relationships. In this sense, the range of the kinship system has been extended in the city, a situation notably unlike that in other areas of the world, where the kinship system has narrowed in range under modern conditions.

It will be instructive to examine the predicament of an urban man of wealth and power who finds himself in a subservient position in the kinship system to a distant relative of low status, since it is precisely this situation which is often seen as leading directly to the breakdown of kinship ties. Our wealthy Batak urbanite wants to preserve his capital and he must guard against excessive demands on his time, but he dares not offend his poor relative, particularly at public gatherings, because this would lead to widespread criticism from the entire urban community. It is not just criticism that he fears; he realizes that if his situation changes in the future he may need the support of his kin group. He is also aware that any flagrant violation of the Batak social and ceremonial system may lead to severe economic, political, or social sanctions. If he is a merchant, those who have been offended will not make purchases at his establishment; if he needs a political favor or a government loan, it might be denied; his wife may be ostracized by other women of the community; and it might be difficult to arrange a good marriage for his son. To ignore Batak tradition can hurt him economically and socially, so he naturally tries to avoid the application of these adverse sanctions.

My data indicate that the wealthy man plays the game according to the rules, but makes excuses when kinship demands become excessive. He attends the necessary rituals, contributes toward the cost of a clansman's ceremonial, and, in most situations, conforms to the requirements of his kinship role. If he behaves in this way, then his distant kinsmen will be less inclined to make demands upon him in situations in which it would be inappropriate—in the market place, a business office, or a government

bureau. If, however, a request is made which exceeds the normal expectations of the kinship relationship, he will express great sympathy but claim that unfortunately he is not in a position to comply with the request; for example, he may say that he has suffered financial reverses, or that he has to repay a bank loan, or that he has to accumulate funds to pay for his son's marriage feast. His motives may be questioned by some, but no sanctions will be employed against him. The predicament of wealthy high-status urbanites is often a difficult, but not an impossible one; they generally handle conflicting sets of role expectations so as to minimize conflict, and some do so with considerable skill and finesse.

The attitude toward particularly close relatives is less calculating and impersonal. Those who are members of the minimal lineage, who trace their origin to the same highland village, and who are descendants of one grandfather or great-grandfather, do continue to constitute a corporate group and may cooperate economically. One wealthy urbanite contributed heavily toward university education of his brother's son; another permitted his father's brother's son to work his rice fields in the village without requesting a share of the harvest; and on the affinal side, still another paid the hospital expenses of his son's father-in-law who was recuperating from a long illness. Other examples of cooperation among lineage mates and close affinals could be cited from village or city. Most well-to-do urban families have had a succession of young people from their rural village reside in their homes. It is a reciprocal arrangement, in which the village youth assists in household tasks while the family provides room and board, and pays the cost of his attendance at one of the institutions of higher learning in Medan. The important consequence of this practice is that, in effect, the lineage invests in the education of its most promising young members; in Indonesia today this is an excellent capital investment.

The minimal lineage is a descent group, not a residence group. Some members of the lineage have remained in their village of origin, others have moved to new villages in the highlands, while still others have migrated to Medan; nevertheless they meet for all important ceremonies, assist one another in times of need, participate in the administration of lineage property, and visit each other fairly frequently. Residence in an urban environment does not necessarily mean that a man severs connections with his rural relatives or even that be becomes "urbanized." Some urbanites are, in fact, closer to their lineage mates in the highlands than to their next-door neighbors in the city.

Over a century ago the unity of the lineage was based upon common ownership of terraced rice fields—the key productive property in Batak society—and also upon the necessity for defense, since intervillage warfare, slavery, and cannibalism are reported to have been characteristic of the old culture. The lineage co-operated economically, fought together, and avenged insults to any fellow member. Today the rice fields are less important, particularly to urban businessmen; and warfare, slavery, and cannibalism were effectively stamped out by the Dutch colonial administration.

Why then does the lineage continue to constitute a meaningful corporate group? The lineage is a less closely knit group today than it was in the last century, and the functions it now performs are different from those performed in the past, but it still serves essential economic and defensive needs.

It would be beyond the scope of this paper to present a full analysis of the contemporary functions performed by the Batak lineage and the reasons why it has been maintained, but the bare outline of the argument will be presented (Cf. Bruner, 1961, for additional data). Indonesia is a new nation that lacks a strong central government, political stability, a rapidly developing economy, and a wide extension of welfare services. Without minimizing the tremendous strides made by Indonesia since its independence was gained, most observers and Indonesians alike would agree that the country still has a long way to go before achieving the degree of progress and modernization desired by all. In this context, kinship groups continue to serve important functions that in the established Western nation have been taken over by the state or other organizations. Further, there are a series of local conditions which have led to the maintenance of kinship ties in the city and

which, to some extent, have strengthened them. The Toba Batak are a Christian minority in a predominantly Islamic society; their migrations to Medan have been comparatively recent and there is a constant influx of new migrants to the city; and Medan itself is populated by many different ethnic groups which compete with one another for economic and political power. Within recent times there have been knife fights between younger members of different ethnic groups, and the attitude of most Toba Batak toward other Indonesians in Medan, such as the Javanese, the Minangkabau, the Atjehnese, and the Karo, is one of suspicion and distrust. One response of the urban Batak to residence in an alien and sometimes hostile environment has been to solidify lineage and kinship ties.

Another response to the urban environment is the emergence of a new form of social organization in the city that has no exact counterpart in village society. The urban Batak form clan associations, *dongan samarga* (Bruner, 1959). Some associations have established scholarships and a revolving loan fund; all have officers and periodic meetings and serve as a corporate mutual aid and welfare society. Members assist one another in times of misfortune, but their primary function is to take responsibility for the organization of life-crisis rites that are performed on such occasions as a birth, a wedding, a house construction, or a funeral.

The clan association is simultaneously a residence group, a descent group, and a voluntary association. In order to join, a man must live in Medan, must be a descendant of the clan ancestor, and must choose to apply—membership is neither obligatory nor automatic. An additional criterion is that the applicant must pay the initiation fee and, to maintain membership, he must pay the nominal monthly dues.

The emergence of the clan association implies a need in the city for a social group intermediate in size between the minimal lineage and the larger community. In Medan there are, of course, occupational groups, restricted social clubs, labor unions, and political parties; but the clan association is a distinctly Toba Batak institution which cross-cuts occupation, social class, and political affiliation. It is a product of the city, but it utilizes structural principles inherent in the traditional Batak descent system. In the village the clan is a descent category, whose members own no property in common, have no political headmen, and reside in non-contiguous areas; but in the city the clan association becomes a corporate social group.

Social affiliation is further extended because each nuclear family customarily joins both the clan association of the husband and that of the wife. The unmarried children become members of the two associations, and may participate in the affiliated youth groups. To put it another way, each urban clan association is open to both the male and the female members of the clan and their spouses, which doubles the membership and widens the scope of relationships.

In effect, it is the nuclear family rather than the individual, or even the minimal lineage, which joins an urban clan association. Husband and wife participate together. This is but one indication of the fact that the nuclear family, although important in the village, has become even more significant in the city. To a large extent this is a consequence of residence patterns.

In the rural areas today most households are occupied by a single nuclear family, but the family is located in a lineage context. A cluster of households forms a hamlet, and a series of hamlets, separated from one another by the rice fields, constitutes a village community. The core of each hamlet is a localized patrilineage, as patrilocal residence is followed in almost 90 per cent of the cases. Thus a man's immediate neighbors in the hamlet will be his lineage mates; that is, his father, brothers, father's brothers, or father's brother's sons, with their spouses and children.

Residence in the city is neolocal, and there is no one section of Medan occupied exclusively by the Toba Batak. A newly married couple may select a home, which they either rent or buy, in any part of the city; their choice of location is dictated by such factors as personal preference, convenience, and cost. In most cases, the nuclear family will be physically isolated from lineage mates or other close relatives; a man's immediate neighbors are likely to be distantly related Batak or members of other Indonesian ethnic groups.

The physical isolation of the nuclear family in the city does not lead to the breakdown of unilineal descent groups, as indicated by the continued importance of the minimal lineage and the emergence of the urban clan association. All three social units, family, lineage, and clan, are meaningful corporate groups which serve somewhat different but significant functions for the urban Batak.

The aim of this paper has been to examine the extent to which kinship has declined in importance in an urban environment, and we are primarily interested in drawing conclusions about the direction of change. Thus we need a base line for purposes of comparison. Rather than compare the contemporary urban system with a reconstructed "aboriginal system" floating in a hypothetical "ethnographic present," the reference point for each statement about the changing role of kinship in the city will be the contemporary village system. My data support the following series of propositions:

1. The urban Batak form a single kinship community, and the sense of ethnic identity is stronger among Toba Batak in the city than in the village.

2. The range of the kinship system has been extended more widely in the city to encompass a larger number of more distantly related persons.

3. Social relationships among urban kinsmen are generally less personal, intimate, and familial than in the village.

4. The minimal lineage, which includes some members who reside in the village and others who live in the city, continues to be a meaningful, cooperative, corporate group.

5. The urban Batak form clan associations, a corporate unit intermediate in size between the lineage and the community, which serve many social and ceremonial functions not performed by the village clan system.

6. The nuclear family is more important in the city than in the village.

Discussion

The major conclusions of this paper is that for the Toba Batak, kinship has not been superseded or lost in an urban environment. Some authorities on the evolution of social organization apparently present us with a choice between a completely kinship-oriented society on the one hand and the absolute breakdown of all extended kinship ties, even the loss of kinship, on the other; and every system between is termed "transitional." The Batak data, in my opinion, do not support this position, with its implication that, as non-Western peoples become progressively modernized, they will eventually—and inevitably—develop a bilateral European type of family organization in which kinship plays a relatively minor role.

Clearly, the urban Batak kinship system has changed in comparison with the village, and it is highly probable that it will change even more in the future, in response to changing conditions in Medan and in Indonesia generally. There is an inherent conflict in the urban system between loyalty to the nuclear family and loyalty to the minimal lineage; most urban men prefer to pass on their property to their daughters rather than to their brother's sons. But the increasing importance of the nuclear family does not necessarily imply the complete dissolution of all extended kin groups beyond the personal kindred.

The emergence of the urban clan association among the city Batak supports my thesis. The clan association is a new and creative adaptation to the conditions of urban life, the reverse of breakdown and decline. It is not, strictly speaking, a unilineal descent group, since membership is not based exclusively upon birthright. I choose to call the clan association a "voluntary descent group," although it could also be regarded as a descent-based voluntary association. In any case it is a kinship group, in which all members are related to one another by consanguineal or affinal ties.

Indications of kinship breakdown should be more readily apparent among those segments of the urban community who occupy higher positions in the stratification system. Those who are wealthy, better educated, and who have lived in Medan the longest should have changed the most. A traditional, poorly educated, recent migrant is, in effect, a transplanted villager. The urban Batak community is stratified, but rather

than study the differences between various groupings within the city, I was primarily concerned with a rural-urban comparison. In order to differentiate more clearly between village and city, I focused upon the wealthy elite and the upper classes of Medan; my aim was to contrast extremes. Thus the data on the urban system were gathered from among those who were the most modern and upwardly mobile in the city. If extended kin ties were in process of breakdown, I should have found it within this social segment; the fact that I did not lends further support to my position.

Nevertheless, the generalizations of the evolutionists may prove to be valid in the long run; possibly I have simply described one stage in the urbanization process. If this is so, then I am not entirely sure how long one has to wait for the process to complete itself: the customary one or two generations, or perhaps one or two centuries, or even longer. It is my feeling, however, that the creative adaptation to the city made by the Batak of Medan is neither unique nor transitory. The Batak clan groups bear some similarity to the clan associations of the overseas Chinese, to the urban tribal association of West Africa, and to the *zaibatsu* of industrial Japan. I suspect that future research on changing kinship systems among societies of the middle range now undergoing rapid cultural change, and among the newly urbanized peoples of Asia and Africa, will disclose not only the maintenance of existing kinship ties, but also the development of novel and stable recombinations based upon traditional structural principles.

REFERENCES

Bruner, Edward M., 1959, "Kinship Organization Among the Urban Batak of Sumatra," *Trans. New York Acad. Sci.*, **22** (2), pp. 118–125.
1961, "Urbanization and Ethnic Identity in North Sumatra," *Amer. Anthropologist*, **63** (3), pp. 508–521.
Lewis, Oscar, 1962, "Further Observations on the Folk-Urban Continuum and Urbanization with Special Reference to Mexico City," Paper presented at 35th Congress of Americanists, Mexico City.

Statistical Pocketbook of Indonesia, 1960, Djakarta: Biro Pusat Statistik.

Steward, Julian H., 1960, "Evolutionary Principles and Social Types," in Sol Tax (editor), *Evolution After Darwin*, Vol. 2, pp. 169–186. Chicago: University of Chicago Press.

White, Leslie A., 1959, *The Evolution of Culture*, New York: McGraw-Hill.

Withington, William A., 1962, "Medan: Primary Regional Metropolis of Sumatra," *J. Geography*, **61**, pp. 59–67.

35. A Research Model: Family Crises and Games of Strategy

BY BERNARD FARBER

A FAMILY CRISIS CAN BE DEFINED as the breakdown of patterns of conduct and values which had been developed to guide activities of family members through the family's life-cycle. The crisis can be either limited or general in its severity. For example, having a first child in any family disrupts previous family routines and modifies the values held by the parents. The parents, however, can usually maintain most of their occupational, friendship, and kinship commitments. In contrast, having a severely mentally retarded child frequently creates a situation of utter chaos. In interviews, parents of severely mentally retarded children have remarked:

I had the feeling that everything in the world had ended and stopped for me. Nothing worse could happen. It would be better if the whole family could be wiped out. I used to dream that it wasn't real and didn't happen.

They explained to me that he would never be normal mentally. It was a complete trauma and shock to both of us—the horror was equal. I got hysterical. It's something you just don't get over, but I am feeling a lot better in many ways.

If you have dreamed all your life of having a child and watching him grow up and go through life and then have it smashed all at once, it's pretty rough on you. It's crushing.

SOURCE: "*Family Organization and Crisis: Maintenance of Integration in Families with a Severely Mentally Retarded Child*," Monographs of the Society for Research in Child Development, *Volume 25 (1960), Serial 75, pp. 5–15. Reprinted with permission of the Society for Research in Child Development.*

Although the emotional impact of having a severely retarded child is generally great, the parents do meet the challenge which the retarded child presents. They do not stop living. Family roles and values are revised. Decisions are made to handle successive problems that arise.

Several questions can be asked with respect to the ability of the family to withstand the disruptive influence of the retarded child:

1. What are the conditions or circumstances which influence the potential severity of the disintegrative effects of the retarded child on the family?

2. What are the effective courses of action which the family may take in order to maintain its integrity?

3. As specific courses of action, (a) Is it necessary to place the retarded child in an institution? (b) How does interaction between normal and retarded siblings affect the normal children?

To suggest answers to these questions, a study was undertaken of effects on family integration of the presence of a severely mentally retarded child. The results reported in this monograph pertain to 233 families living in the Chicago metropolitan area.

The data in the study were analyzed in two phases. The first phase of the analysis was concerned primarily with conditions which influenced the effect of the severely retarded child on family integration. Findings of the first phase of analysis were reported in an earlier monograph. The present monograph is based on the results of the second phase of analysis, which dealt with courses of action developed by the family to maintain its integrity.

To make explicit the assumptions underlying the second phase of analysis and to provide a framework for integrating specific hypotheses, a research model was developed. This model was based upon the theory of games as described by economists. The discussion below, however, pertains only to the model as used in the present study. In the model the activities of husband and wife in a crisis situation are considered as analogous to their acting in concert as a player in a game of strategy.

As a research instrument, the model specifies the relationship between the investigator and his subject matter. While the subjects of the research are considered as participants in a game of strategy, the investigator is regarded as the judge who (a) defines the rules of the game insofar as his conceptual scheme and instruments permit him and (b) evaluates the outcome. Over a period of time, the judge or investigator can approach a *theory* of games of strategy only as his knowledge of all the pertinent moves of the players becomes perfect.

Any game consists of a set of admissible moves which, combined in certain ways, result in a resolution of a contest. A move is defined as a single alternative in the set of acts specified in the rules of the game. In playing the game, the participants choose a number of these moves (either at the same time or in sequence) to resolve the contest. A strategy is regarded as a specific combination of moves.

The problems of the judge or investigator are (a) to gain a perfect knowledge of all effective moves and strategies possible in the game and (b) to obtain *full* information regarding the development of strategies by the players. The judge's ability to perform these tasks is limited by the present state of research technology and organization of theoretical concepts. In doing research, the judge's task is then to expand upon both research technology and theoretical constructs.

Games of Strategy and the Prediction of Family Behavior

Decision-making, whether in economic institutions or government, seems to imply a problematic situation or a critical event. The family crisis presents a situation which requires solution, and any stage in the family cycle produces its own set of crises. Several severe crises in the family have been investigated (e.g., unemployment, mental illness, alcoholism, and the presence of a severely mentally retarded child). In each of these crises the decisions made determined the eventual integration or disintegration of the family. Thus, the problem of prediction of subsequent events is introduced. Since the games of strategy analogy is so closely allied with prediction problems, it seems reasonable to view the application of the games analogy to family crises within the framework of a prediction research model.

The analogy in the discussion below is based upon a two-person zero-sum game in the theory of games of strategy. A zero-sum game means merely that the amount lost by one player is gained by the other. In the following sections a general statement is made concerning the players, the rules of the game, and conditions for playing the game.

The Players. Generally, the game model permits the methodological opposition of factors which are controllable by the marital partners and those which are uncontrollable. For example, demographic and community factors are beyond the control of individual families and certain of these factors can be assumed to "play against" the marriage. The married couple must counteract the effects of these attributes, and certain parts of their interaction operate to overcome the unfavorableness of the demographic and community attributes.

Resorting to anthropomorphism in order to create a "methodological" adversary in a strategy model has been found a useful fiction. For example, Toynbee's concept of challenge-and-response implies an environment, either human or physical, with evil motives, attempting to prevent self-determination and growth. In addition, the family in crisis itself often regards Nature as an antagonist. Parents of severely mentally retarded children have described their problem as follows:

It was an act of God.

Raymond is like a small pair in poker—too good to throw in—hoping it will improve—while throwing money in.

I was stunned that it was my boy that this had happened to—you know it can always happen to someone else's kid and you say, "My, that's a shame." I wasn't ashamed or bitter—I was more disappointed—I wanted him to be normal and be able to play ball and stuff like that.

People told me that if I got pregnant, the next one would be the same (retarded). Then when I got pregnant, I was afraid; but my husband told me not to be afraid—just take that chance.

There was complete amazement—that isn't the right word—from self-pity—why did this have to happen to us, wondering about ourselves and each other—whether there's something wrong with us. Nothing like this ever happened before in either of our families.

Aside from providing a stimulus for action, the anthropomorphic fiction provides a framework for evaluating whether or not the action of Nature is favorable or unfavorable for the development of the group. The valuational framework facilitates the grouping of various kinds of situations. Without the grouping, we would have to resort to a descriptive classification of situations. This would mean eliminating many details and significant combinations of circumstances from the descriptions in order to maintain homogenous groupings. With Nature as a challenger in a game, however, the many combinations of circumstances which may go into defining "unfavorableness" can be grouped, and the married couple's responses to various degrees of "unfavorableness" can be studied.

In the application of the theory of games to economics, the assumption of rational behavior is made. By rational behavior is meant the logical deduction by the actor of the amount of pay-off accruing from given deliberate conduct. To require "rational behavior" (as defined above) in counteracting family crises implies that the strategies which enable the family to meet crises without loss of mutual commitment of family members or decrease in personal integrity are conscious and voluntary. Earlier

studies of the reaction of families to crises have shown, however, that the ability to overcome crisis is influenced by the pre-crisis family organization. Emotional elements achieve importance in meeting crisis. Thus, the extent to which the actor is deliberate in his development of strategies is not pertinent to the efficacy of a given strategy. The strategy itself is the unit of study. The normative object of the research is to enable families in a crisis to make a rational choice *between* strategies.

Rules of the Game. The rules of the game of strategy include an enumeration of the strategies and moves permitted in the game and a description of the system of pay-offs. A full description of the rules of the game would provide a theoretical basis for describing given strategies and circumstances "favorable" or "unfavorable" to marital integration.

MOVES AND STRATEGIES. Moves and strategies (including circumstances) can be classified in three ways: (a) the amount of their value or utility, (b) whether or not the moves are permitted in the game under study, and (c) conditions affecting the value of the moves.

In the application of the theory of games in economics, the concept of strategy involves a plan of specific moves to be made in every possible situation. The "value" of each strategy is the amount of pay-off units obtained through the application of that strategy. With the assumption of rational behavior, minimum and maximum pay-off accruing from the strategy can be foreseen by the player. The player can then make choices which would maximize his gains with the least amount of risk. If, however, the assumption of rationality in the development of strategies is dropped then the basis for defining the player's strategies must be derived by the investigator from theoretical consideration or results of past research.

In prediction, the background or crisis circumstances—the factors over which the individual or group now has no control—can be regarded as the moves of his opponent (Nature) in the game. That is, the individual's or group's crisis circumstances challenge him (or the group) by acting to maximize the social *costs* in a marriage (i.e., trying to bring about personal disorganization, unhappiness, divorce, or at least heightened conflict). It is assumed that some combinations of background factors or crisis circumstances are more efficient in increasing social costs than are others. In only a few cases are *all* crisis circumstances favorable or unfavorable. Usually, both favorable and unfavorable factors are present. The degree of unfavorableness of the combination of circumstances determines the "value" or "utility" of that set of crisis circumstances for the game.

In order to minimize the probability of personal disorganization, unhappiness, conflict, or divorce, the individuals must make certain choices from a set of alternative moves. Making choices which minimize social costs would therefore be more urgent under a very severe challenge of circumstance than under a less severe challenge. One task of prediction research on the family can be to determine the rank-order of the effectiveness of strategies used by married couples to counteract unfavorable circumstances. The purpose of the first sample studied is to determine pay-off matrices for various strategies. Succeeding samples are then needed to verify these pay-off matrices.

Regardless of their value or utility, only certain moves are considered legitimate in the rules of the game. In the theory of games the game with an infinite number of possible strategies is included. Given the limits of research method or technique, however, it seems expedient to restrict the game under study to a small number of strategies and place all other choices by subjects and their circumstances into a residual category. In the game analogy players' moves not enumerated in the rules as defined by the judge are regarded as "cheating"; e.g., making chess moves in a game of checkers. Pay-offs in games are made only in accordance with legitimate moves.

In research the investigator has no power to disallow a marriage integration score because a strategy was applied which was not included in the rules of the game as he had defined them. "Cheating" in the context of the game analogy in research is defined from the judge's, not the player's, point of view. From a legal or moral perspective the conduct regarded as "cheating" may be highly acceptable. The investigator

must either ignore the "cheating" or revise his rules to legitimate the strategy in question.

For example, in a sample of parents with retarded children a married couple using strategies which generally are favorable to marital integration among couples with a similar background received a low marital integration score. Further investigation of the case, however, revealed that the husband also showed many indications of paranoia. The child had been conceived to prevent the wife from "running around." The husband was actually pleased that the child was almost completely dependent and kept his wife fully occupied. The case served to emphasize that the prediction instrument was valid only for nonpsychotic persons. In bringing what seemed like paranoia to the marriage, the husband introduced a move to the game that was not included in the prediction instrument.

By examining deviant cases, the investigator is sensitized to discern ways of "cheating" by the couples studied. If the same kind of "cheating" takes place in many instances, the investigator can change the rules to legitimate these moves in future use of the prediction instrument. In changing the rules of his game, the investigator must revise his conceptual scheme to include the newly legitimated strategies or circumstances of families. Hence, with the game analogy, items cannot be added to the prediction battery arbitrarily. The new items, regarded as strategies, must also be integrated into the admissable rules of the game.

Because of the great complexity surrounding the lives of most people, however, it would be impossible to legitimize all "cheating" with respect to the rules of the prediction instrument. Arbitrarily, in the evaluation of strategies already hypothecated, it is assumed that "cheating" occurs in an idiosyncratic manner in each family and that the effect of this "cheating" on marital integration score is randomly distributed throughout the population. If the scores on marital integration for a sample of families are restricted to a given range and the distribution of scores tends toward a normal curve, any effects of "cheating" would operate as a regression toward the mean integration score. Hence, the *mean* integration score for sub-categories of circumstances and strategies would be used to evaluate predictions made (along with appropriate tests of statistical significance) on the basis of certain specified strategies.

Regarding "cheating" as idiosyncratic unfortunately eliminates (in practice) the saddle-point or minimax solution in evaluating a "legitimate" strategy. The saddle-point indicates the choice which will permit a maximum gain at a minimum possible cost and assumes a specific value in terms of the pay-off for each strategy. However, if the opposing player can "cheat" in his move, we can never be certain of our minimum possible cost. Since "cheating" is not a predictable move in playing the game, we cannot make a choice with the expectation of being "cheated." Hence, in evaluating predictions, we act as if only strategies within the rules of the game will be used. Only in the ideal case where there is no "cheating" can we expect to obtain the exact marital integration for couples faced with critical characteristics of a certain severity. Actually, because of "cheating" by the families, strategies can have only mean "value" or utility.

Strategies can be classified not only in terms of their values and legitimacy but also in terms of conditions affecting their consequences for pay-offs. Some strategies may be capable of overcoming any kind of opposition; other strategies may be restricted in their usefulness to given situations. In the absence of a saddle-point solution, this classification may be important. A general strategy would tend to be effective regardless of the circumstances under which it was used. A specialized strategy would tend to be effective only under given combinations of circumstances. For example, placing the retarded child in an institution may serve to increase the marital integration of parents faced with unfavorable circumstances regarding the sex of the retarded child, social class, religion, and birth order of the retarded child. However, if a family with favorable circumstances surrounding the retarded child placed that child in an institution, the marital integration of the parents may actually decrease. Hence, strategies can be ranked in order of the generality of their appropriateness.

SYSTEM OF PAY-OFF. The marital integration score as the commodity to be maximized in family crises constitutes the major pay-off in the game. The securing of marital integration scores, which are obtained in the course of the research, does not terminate the game. The scores merely define the status of the game; the rules of marriage provide that the game can only be stopped by legal proceedings, desertion, or by the death of one spouse at any time.

Marital integration is defined as (a) the consensus of husband and wife on their ranking of domestic values and (b) the effective coordination of domestic roles. Failure to coordinate domestic roles is defined negatively as tension in the system of roles. The definition of marital integration, furthermore, assumes that in the integrated marriage (a) there is a clear-cut focus or coherence of the domestic values on a single aspect of family life—the development of the children, the welfare of the parents, or the promotion of the home and (b) the specific moves are so organized as to direct the interaction of family members consistently toward gratification of this aspect of family life. The specific organization of the moves into integrative family orientations represents the development of strategies which are considered as consistent in attaining gratification for the parents in a given, focused aspect of family life. Hence, the integrative family orientations reflect a utility for the parents. This utility, from the perspective of the pay-off in a game of strategy, is objectified in the index of marital integration.

Although marital integration is regarded as the major pay-off, there are other consequences resulting from the reaction of the family to crises. In fact, one of the problems in prediction is that of multiplicity of consequences of circumstances and strategies. While a given kind of strategy may tend to result in high marital integration, it may also produce personality problems in children.

One solution to the problem of multiple criteria of family success is to apply an average weight to each criterion (e.g., personal adjustment, happiness, sex adjustment, extent of love, and emotional interdependence) on the basis of a factor analysis or a canonical correlation. The weighting is performed on an empirical basis.

With the introduction of the analogy of the game of strategy, an alternative procedure for handling secondary criteria of success becomes available. In games of strategy the participants can make "side bets" in terms of highly restricted rules. For example, in chess or checkers the players may bet not only on who will win but also on whether the person may win within a certain number of moves or whether certain pieces will be "taken." There can be several side bets during the course of a single game. A player can win many of the side bets, but lose the game.

In the study of families in crisis situations, if the pay-off for the game is the degree of marital integration, the pay-off in side bets can be such criteria as the extent of adjustment of the children, the involvement between parents and grandparents, the fertility of the parents, or the place of the family in the community. The rules of the game would be formulated on the basis of the pay-off of the primary criterion of success, but side bets (or secondary criteria) could be introduced at any point in the game. The decision as to whether a given criterion is primary or secondary would have to be made on the basis of either theoretical or practical considerations, but not on the empirical grounds of degree of predictability.

Because of the close relationship between specific parts of the games and side bets, the secondary criteria would be evaluated only for specific moves considered pertinent to them. For example, in the study of families with mentally retarded children, the use of normal siblings as parent surrogates in caring for the retarded child could be evaluated not only as it affected the marital integration of the parents but also as it influenced the personality development of the normal children involved.

Conditions for Playing the Game. From a theoretical viewpoint the games-of-strategy model presented seems to supplement the dramaturgical analogy of social relationships. The dramaturgical analogy vividly describes the situation of well-defined expectations in which, so to speak, the "script" (mutual understanding) carefully defines each person's role. The dramaturgical analogy fails as soon as someone "gives the show away" or another unanticipated event occurs which is not accounted for in the "script." At that point, the number of alternatives increase and decisions must be made; new strategies must be devised; a new tentative "script" must be introduced.

These alternatives, however, are not infinite in number. It is impossible for an actor to be guided in every muscular movement by the script so that he is completely restricted to a single set of acts by the script. Similarly, it would be impossible to choose alternative innovations if there were an infinite number of potential strategies and no rules for their selection. Probably, social relations can be placed on a continuum with the dramatic or completely restricted kind of social relations at one extreme and strategic or infinite kinds of social relations at the other. Specific social relations can then be described as tending toward the dramatic or the strategic. In some instances, the dramatic analogy would serve as a more appropriate model and, in other instances, the games of strategy analogy seems a more appropriate model.

Generally, we may assume that each family is motivated to solve its strategic problems and to act out its own plot. The normal plot in family life is ordinarily described as its life-cycle. Family life as a game of strategy is therefore descriptive of the process by which the family members define or "write the script for" the family life-cycle when a disturbance in the original or normal script occurs.

An Evaluation of the Games of Strategy Analogy

In stating that the family in crisis acts like a participant in a game of strategy, we imply merely that by superimposing the assumptions and attributes of the game of strategy upon the family situation we can make a variety of interrelated predictions about family relations. The usefulness of the game model lies in its predictive power rather than in its reflection of the "reality" or "essence" of the family in crisis. Hence, problems such as whether the family conceives of itself as playing a game against Nature are not pertinent to the adequacy of the model. Only the ability of the game analogy applied to the family in crisis to explain variation in family relations is the criterion of adequacy.

It is anticipated that one of the gains in prediction research procedure to be made through using the games of strategy analogy is a narrowing of the gap between theoretical formulations of marital interaction and the development of prediction devices. The increased reliance on theory is accomplished through the need for making explicit a description of the players and the rules of the game. Hence, in describing the players and the rules, we discuss assumptions about the personal attributes of the players and the nature of interaction.

The games-of-strategy model in the study of family crisis makes explicit the following assumptions:

1. The motivation of individuals is to maximize the probability of their attaining certain values or goals at a minimum of risk of social costs.

2. In the face of uncertainty the family members are motivated to get together to define a "script" pertaining to the attainment of their ideal family cycle. The general hypothesis is that an internally consistent pattern of relationships focussed on a given aspect of family life must be developed to maintain family integrity.

3. Critical situations and critical circumstances can be ranked as to the severity of their impact upon the family in its life-cycle development. The ranking of strategies by their severity provides a framework for the development of some specific hypotheses. The model sensitizes the investigator to determine (a) whether there exists a general desired "script" as defined in the community, (b) the severity of a given crisis as it affects the family's actual "script," (c) the strategies which the family members develop to counteract the crisis, and (d) the effectiveness of various strategies in counteracting a crisis of a given severity.

4. Various attributes can be regarded as clustered or cumulative in the form of strategies. This assumption facilitates the handling of a large number of variables in specific combinations rather than by average weights. Thus, the procedure enables prediction by combination of attributes rather than "prediction score" and

increases the power of explanation of prediction instruments.

5. In prediction research the aim of the investigator is to select or develop a procedure which (a) provides the least amount of error in prediction for the population as a whole and (b) minimizes social costs. That is, first, the investigator must find a means which, in marriage, maximizes the proportion of the total variance of marital success scores explained by the predictors; secondly, he must find a prediction instrument which specifies decisions which will produce the highest amount of social utility (and, at the same time, the least social cost). The games of strategy analogy takes into account both error in prediction and concepts of social cost and utility.

6. Research related to prediction is an iterative process. (The model makes a provision for reducing "cheating" by families in crisis by its rule that strategies previously regarded as idiosyncratic can be legitimated. By this rule of serendipity, the predictive power of the research instrument can be increased without revising the general model itself.)

7. By its provisions for major pay-offs and side bets, the model permits analysis in terms of specific combinations of scores pertaining to criteria of success in meeting crises.

The game analogy also seems appropriate for a variety of practical situations. For example, the application of the results of a study may require a coalition between the family members and a therapist. The game in the research would then become more than a two-person game. The situation covered by the model employed, however, includes not only the evaluation of alternatives which the family can apply, but also the process by which this family tries to apply the strategy as a second game.

A problem which may arise in a counseling situation is that the success of previous, tested strategies may exert a conservative influence. That is, instead of being encouraged to keep exploring for new integrative strategies, the family would be encouraged to use a strategy already devised. The decision, which itself can be handled within the framework of the theory of games of strategy, however, is one for the family and its therapist to make.

36. Interpersonal Competence

BY NELSON N. FOOTE AND LEONARD S. COTTRELL, JR.

COMPETENCE IS A SYNONYM for ability. It means a satisfactory degree of ability for performing certain implied kinds of tasks. Each of the abilities described below as components of interpersonal competence is found to some degree in any normal person, regardless of his previous experience. Nevertheless, as with virtually all human abilities by practice and purposeful training wide differences result. In this sense, interpersonal competence although based upon inherited potentialities, and directly contributing to self-conceptions, may be compared to acquired skills. To conceive of interpersonal relations as governed by relative degrees of skill in controlling the outcome of episodes of interaction is to diverge greatly from some other explanations of characteristic differences in behavior.

Some Possible Misunderstandings

The term "social skills" is now quite widely used. It might seem more advantageous and less awkward to employ it, rather than "interpersonal competence." Unfortunately, however, it has already accumulated a number of connotations which hinder its conveying what is intended here. Thus social skill often indicates

SOURCE: Identity and Interpersonal Competence, *pp. 36–60. Reprinted by permission of University of Chicago Press (Copyright, 1955).*

correct etiquette or polish. At other times it means success in achieving popularity through display of coveted virtues.

Social skill is also used instead of a word such as rhetoric. In some of the numberless books on self-help and human relations readers are initiated into the various tricks and routines for persuading others—into the sort of skills that are necessary for salesmanship and supervision. While selling and supervision are legitimate activities, and success in these no doubt makes some use of interpersonal competence, skill in influencing others would be a very limited and limiting objective to impose upon family life.

Countless educational media—though ostensibly not commercially or manipulatively minded—likewise profess to furnish training for leadership, which is described in the language of social skill. Again, however, their emphasis tends to be on institutional ends, to the relative neglect of self-realization in day-to-day family living. But it is fairly often observed that a person can function quite successfully in his job or committee post, though his behavior as a husband or father is unsatisfactory to all concerned. Conversely, even the development of extraordinary competence in interpersonal relations—though it may help—cannot guarantee success in business or politics.

Despite these warnings against confusing interpersonal competence with the social skills of success literature, a word can be said in defense of the impulse which moves writers and readers of self-help books on human relations. Immense numbers of our fellow-citizens feel inept in their interpersonal relations; they sense narrow limits to their ability to influence or even to conciliate others. Their belief that something can be done about their ineptitude is hopeful and constructive. Were they to adopt the pessimistic alternative, and construe their fate as recalcitrant to all thought or effort, the result would undoubtedly be grave for them and the community at large.

Certainly no professional person in the field of family relations can lightly condemn the millions who read the endless stream of books, pamphlets, and columns upon marital and child-rearing problems. Yet this too is a kind of self-help literature. The mounting demand for functional courses in marriage and parenthood may be interpreted in part as a response to the fact that knowledge and skill in these matters can no longer be simply absorbed through watching one's parents. The motives which inspire this demand are not merely intended to repair a deficit. More often the reader is confident that better practices are to be found than tradition affords; or he explicitly declares that he wants to do a better job than his parents did. In nearly all such expressions the assumption is evident that differing outcomes depend upon relative degrees of competence.

Among experienced educators in the family field, there is general agreement that mere rules and prescriptions cannot give this eager audience the competence they desire. Applied inappropriately, the most intelligent advice can have untoward results. What the advice-seeking public requires in addition is the resource to utilize general knowledge effectively in varied circumstances. Moreover, as such adaptability of response develops, the craving for categorical rules frequently, as in other fields of learning, abates; the second baby is less likely to be raised from the book. To be sure, the need for straight information on technical matters cannot be gainsaid. But specifically with regard to the intimate interpersonal episodes of family life, general information and abstract principles are of minor effect in enhancing competence;

demonstration and practice are superior means of changing behavior.

The possible sources of confusion about the meaning of competence are less troublesome than a moral issue which the term may evoke. In his earliest book, Sullivan spoke forthrightly of the achievement of power in interpersonal relations.[1] Negative reactions to the connotations of the word "power" appear to have convinced him that more was to be gained by dropping than by keeping it. Yet perhaps a later generation of readers can suspend judgment long enough to consider afresh the ambiguity of attitudes toward power in society, at least at the level of the family. This might enable us to dispose of any lingering notion that interpersonal competence implies the mechanical manipulation of others.

The philosopher Bertrand Russell in his book *Power: A New Social Analysis* defines power simply as the ability to produce intended effects, a definition which might also stand for competence. The resistance sometimes engendered by referring to power in interpersonal relations can be traced back to a fear of one person controlling another. Implied in this fear is the assumption that the dominated person will be exploited or forced to serve ends of which he disapproves. Where dominator and dominated are assumed to seek the same goals, the question of domination is less often raised.

The democratic values of freedom and equality imply plurality of values and presume that the values of some shall not be imposed upon others. In government, protection against domination by the stronger is approached through distributing power as widely as possible, and by various checks and balances for maintaining this distribution. It is logically absurd to speak of eliminating power; the threat of domination is countered by equalizing power. Some self-styled realists claim that power is never restrained except by equal and opposite power, and that to expect any self-restraint by the powerful is to think wishfully. Yet, if some self-restraint by fathers and husbands, as well as

[1] Harry Stack Sullivan, *Conceptions of Modern Psychiatry*, Washington: The William Alanson White Psychiatric Foundation, 1947, pp. 6–11. From lectures given in 1940.

majorities vis-à-vis minorities, could not be counted upon, the powers of the weaker parties could never develop sufficiently to match the strength of their potential oppressors. Thus, even if power is taken to be the relative strength to dominate or resist, there is every reason to learn how to control the conditions of its growth.

As the pragmatist philosophers have pointed out, power (in Russell's sense) is the means of access to all other values. Power may be employed to realize favored or opposed values, to suppress or to foster the development of other persons. The mere fact of possessing power is not evil per se. There is no way of increasing power which guarantees against its misuse, and one cannot realize good ends if one is powerless.

So construed, the pursuit of power in interpersonal relations is ethically neutral. In proposing the enhancement of interpersonal competence we are not advocating any one set of institutional values as against any other.

The analogy to free public education is fairly exact. Unless citizens are equipped with the knowledge and the skill with which to communicate and judge public policy they cannot participate equally in governing the commonwealth. The purpose of free (and compulsory) public education has always been to make all citizens competent to exercise their voice in making public decisions. In a country where only a small class is literate, self government is hardly feasible, and so the lifting of educational levels generally has become a democratic value. In this same sense, the diffusion of interpersonal competence is a democratic value. It can be employed for good or evil, yet from the standpoint of any one person, it is good to have more of it. As an anti-democrat, a person would at least want it for himself, but as a democrat, he would logically want to see everyone at least as competent as himself. As a program, therefore, the development of interpersonal competence could well be regarded as a proper extension of the value of free public education.

The neutral or general value of interpersonal competence, considered as a prerequisite for the achievement of any other values of personality and family life, appeals to neo-Freudians as well as to pragmatists. Alfred Adler was perhaps the

earliest to stress the incessant effort by the person from infancy onward to gain control of his world. And Adler also saw from the outset that the "power-seeker"—the neurotic individual who deliberately maneuvers to dominate others —is a person who, having been unsuccessful in winning their favorable response by normal means, strives to construct a situation in which he can extort involuntary deference.[2] Erich Fromm says the same of self-love and selfishness. Karen Horney, though denying the derivation of her thoughts from Adler, repeats almost the identical theme throughout her several works. Erik Erikson postulates the quest for mastery as a virtually universal motive. Yet none of these thinkers could be accused of advocating the domination or manipulation of others, not even of children by parents. All are advocates of some variant of self-realization. And all recognize the dependence of optimal development along self-chosen lines upon one's social relations with others.

At the level of common sense observation, people are seen to differ markedly in their aptitude or ineptitude for dealing satisfactorily with others. At the level of theoretical speculation, interpersonal competence as a general phenomenon appears to be based on what certain existentialist philosophers call transcendence.[3] This term summarizes the uniquely human processes of suspended action, memory, revery, foresight, reflection, and imagination, by means of which a person from birth onward escapes progressively from the control of his immediately given environment and begins to control it. It is by this freedom from the irresistible instincts and external stimuli, which chain the responses of lower animals, that the human being is enabled to modify his surroundings, to plan and create, to have a history and a future. His detachment from the present situation provides both the opportunity and the

[2] Alfred Adler, "The Family Constellation," *Understanding Human Nature*, Cleveland: The World Publishing Company, 1941.

[3] Ortega y Gasset, "The Self and the Other," *Partisan Review*, XIX, No. 4 (July-August, 1952). Simone de Beauvoir, *The Second Sex*, New York: Alfred A. Knopf, Inc., 1953. Robert Ulich, *The Human Career: A Philosophy of Self-transcendence*, New York: Harper and Brothers, 1955.

necessity for him to declare his own indentity and values as an adult.

This capacity for transcending the immediately given and thus affecting and reconstructing it invites several levels of explanation, ranging from neurology to prehistory. The explanation most relevant here is the one based on man's ability to use symbols. Symbolization affords representation at will of that which is not present, and recombination of its elements—whether in language, dreams, art, or play. It is more than possible that inquiries into the abstract realms of symbolic processes will produce findings more potent in the development of interpersonal competence than the more proximate behavioral hypotheses ventured in the next chapter. It takes wings of greater breadth than the authors' however to fly in such thin air. We applaud those who will make the attempt while sticking closer to earth ourselves.

Instead of attempting, therefore, to further elaborate a general concept of the origins of interpersonal competence, our main strategy of definition will be analytical, to name its parts, as manifested in observable behavior. These we take to be: (1) health, (2) intelligence, (3) empathy, (4) autonomy, (5) judgment, and (6) creativity. The final number and order of these components, as well as the names assigned to them, are the result of reflection, as well as extensive reference to previous literature and current discussion. Nonetheless they arose initially in quite different form through intensive pondering of what qualities distinguish inept from competent performance in interpersonal relations.

It may seem somewhat inconsistent to take pains to distinguish interpersonal competence from social skills and to insist upon the unfamiliar phrase, while on the other hand assigning to the components of competence terms which have acquired competing meanings and interpretations in previous research. It is advantageous, however, to utilize terms with established significance, and to draw upon the treasuries of previous research, even if both are somewhat wide of the target erected; in this case, these advantages outweigh those of neologism. Given that the general notion of interpersonal competence sets the framework for defining

each of its components, it is hoped that each component will be interpreted as an acquired ability for effective interaction, rather than in some other context. To illustrate, creativity may refer elsewhere to artistic talent or scientific genius, but here it is confined to resourcefulness in devising new and effective responses to problematic interpersonal situations. Each component will be separately and more fully defined below, but each is conceived as a component of total competence. In any performance all six aspects of competence are manifested simultaneously, though one may be more obviously put to test than another. And the degree to which each can be cultivated independently remains an empirical question.

The abilities designated are possessed by individual family members in varying degrees, however much they may derive from common family experience or affect family structure and functioning. Nor is this the only reason for speaking of interpersonal rather than family competence. By including all intimate relationships such as fiancé, chum, or sibling long absent, futile controversy over who is a family member is avoided. Since our dependent variable is personality development, every significant other in the family constellation must be taken into account; and, as will be seen in a later chapter, the concept of quasi-families arises both to explain certain suggestive developments in urban sociability and to suggest self-conscious experimentation with identity-forming small groups.

Some Prior Formulations

A number of theorists have endeavored broadly to classify the relationships among people according to the motives these relationships are said to express. Many years ago, for example, Albion W. Small designated the six basic interests which he believed to generate all human associations:[4] health, wealth, sociability, knowledge, beauty, rightness. Among the many schemes for classifying motives which have been proposed, this early list is of special interest

[4] Albion W. Small, *General Sociology*, Chicago: The University of Chicago Press, 1905.

because, as has been called to our attention by Mr. Howard Stanton, Small's list is nearly cognate with the elements of interpersonal competence. Why such resemblances should occur is itself an inviting topic for speculation.

An intriguing coincidence of the same order was also discovered in the 1952 Annual Report of the Superintendent of Schools of New York City, which lists "what we want for our children" as: (1) adequate knowledges and skills, (2) good social character for living in a democracy, (3) good health, (4) sound thinking, (5) creative expression and appreciations, (6) adjustment of the world of work. And Miss Ethel Kawin, Director of the Parent Education Project at the University of Chicago, in a progress report dated March 31, 1954, presented what an advisory panel of qualified scholars had approved as "the major essential characteristics of mature, responsible citizens," and what such citizens require for "competent participation of the individual in a democratic social system": (1) feelings of security and adequacy, (2) understanding of self and others, (3) democratic values and goals, (4) problem-solving attitudes and techniques, (5) self-discipline, responsibility, and freedom, (6) constructive attitudes toward change.

Beyond the obvious differences and similarities of these lists and the elements of competence, two less visible assumptions involved deserve emphasis: that their authors aspired to completeness in the range of species under the genus imputed, and that the motives of persons and the goals of institutions do, can, or ought to congrue.

Some other writers, more therapeutically and less educationally oriented, have attempted to define analytically the characteristics of mental health. At the 1953 National Conference on Social Work, for example, Dr. Marie Jahoda grappled with this quite metaphorical concept before an interdisciplinary symposium on the family.[5] She first criticized previous conceptions which confused psychological health with (1) the absence of disease, (2) statistical normality, (3) psychological well-being (happiness), or (4)

successful survival. These criteria were inappropriate, she asserted, because they neglected the social matrix of human behavior:

It follows that we must not conceive of psychological health as the final state in which the individual finds himself, for this state is dependent upon external events over which he has no control. Rather we should think of it as a style of behavior or a behavior tendency which would add to his happiness, satisfaction, and so on, if things in the external world were all right. Psychological health, then, manifests itself in behavior that has a promise of success under favorable conditions.

Although Dr. Jahoda only adumbrated two tentative examples of the positive criteria she recommends, she did set another basic question for family research: What are the psychologically relevant attributes of an environment which permit the manifestation of psychologically healthy behavior? This research task differs markedly from the etiology of mental disease.

Dr. Albert Dorfman, a pediatrician at the University of Chicago, in a 1952 seminar at the Family Study Center, pointed out that any systematic effort to define normality in child development must include, even for small children, not only physical well-being, but such aspects of their behavior as effectiveness, originality, adaptability, trust, and confidence in self. He sought the assistance of social scientists in constructing precise measures of these variables, so that their development might be more readily traced.

In his major work to date,[6] Erik H. Erikson

The entire symposium, reported in this same issue, is of especial interest as a notable step toward redefinition of the aims of the caseworker. A highly contemporary statement of aims by one authority was: "to help clients with their struggles to master difficult life situations." When this is linked with the classical vocabulary of Mary E. Richmond, one of the founders of social work, who held that the special field of the caseworker is "the development of personality through the conscious and comprehensive adjustment of social relationships," it appears that the earliest and latest periods of social work may be more like each other in this respect than the middle period was to either. Perusal of Miss Richmond's *What Is Social Casework?* New York: Russell Sage Foundation, 1922, especially Chapter v, fortifies this impression.

[5] Marie Jahoda, "The Meaning of Psychological Health," *Social Casework*, XXXIV, No. 8 (October, 1953), pp. 349–354.

[6] Erik H. Erikson, *Childhood and Society*, New York: W. W. Norton and Co., 1950.

promulgates a scheme of eight stages in personality development from infancy to maturity. This scheme is far more profound than the many which simply cut up the process of development into chronological intervals. Erikson entitles each of his stages according to the favorable or unfavorable personality characteristics in which they result. These emerge from successful or unsuccessful negotiation of the problems peculiar to each stage: (1) trust versus basic mistrust, (2) autonomy versus shame and doubt, (3) initiative versus guilt, (4) industry versus inferiority, (5) identity versus role diffusion, (6) intimacy versus isolation, (7) generativity versus stagnation, (8) ego integrity versus despair. Without committing themselves completely to Erikson's apparatus of stages, the editors of the fact-finding report of the Midcentury White House Conference on Children and Youth adapted the favored products for designating the attributes of healthy personality. The cultivation of these products is set forth as an implied objective for the various social institutions making up the community: (1) the sense of trust, (2) the sense of autonomy, (3) the sense of initiative, (4) the sense of duty and accomplishment, (5) the sense of identity, (6) the sense of intimacy, (7) the parental sense, (8) the sense of integrity.[7] That the concept of interpersonal competence converges with certain other trends of current thought is thus as evident as that it diverges from certain lines of conceptualization.

What Competence is Not

Not all researchers agree that it is desirable to set up as their major dependent variable some central measure of family functioning. Among those who do think so, a considerable variety of variables is favored. Some appear to refer to attributes of the family as a kind of reified entity, as for example, solidarity. But upon examination it usually turns out that such a

[7] *Personality in the Making: The Fact-Finding Report of the Mid-century White House Conference on Children and Youth*, Helen L. Witmer and Ruth Kotinsky (eds.), New York: Harper and Brothers, 1952.

measure is applied to the behavior of individuals defined as family members, and then their scores are more or less arbitrarily combined as a family score. Other measures explicitly refer to individual behavior, but in ways that relate it to the behavior of others in familial or other interpersonal relations. The most widely employed measures of this type are happiness, adjustment, and emotional maturity. To approach family behavior in terms of interpersonal competence is a fairly substantial reorientation from these more established ways of interpreting family interaction.

To speak of competent personalities is not to refer to ingrained virtues or fixed traits. What is generally meant by a personality trait is not some constantly evident attribute like blue eyes, but a standardized response to standardized situations. Nevertheless it is usually described adjectivally as if it were a constant, the presence of which transcends or pervades the actor's behavior in all situations. Actually, this is what competence does, and in that limited sense competence answers the notion of a trait better than what are usually called traits, e.g., authoritarianism.

The trait concept, as commonly formulated in psychological literature, is inadequate as a theory of behavior; to attempt directly to inculcate some desired trait is therefore frequently unworkable in practice, and indoctrination is improper as an end. Any notion of molding personalities to fit preconceived standards is likely to construe human beings as things or objects, passively subject to manipulation by superior authorities who stand upon some detached pedestal. Behavior, however, is dynamic, episodic, situationally specific.

Traits, as descriptive categories for distinguishing recurrent aspects of behavior, are applied by some people to other people, and imply a relationship between observer and observed; it is thus that in social life they serve to regularize expectations, though they can do so only roughly and incompletely, for the contingencies are too variable. Reciprocal attributions and imputations are subject to unceasing diversification and disagreement. They are stable bases for reliable prediction only to the extent that the representative situations which evoke them are stabilized through implicit commitments of all the parties involved. Every person repeatedly steps beyond the range of standard expectation in the course of his development; in a dynamic social world novel situations are pandemic. Outside those situations in which conventional responses are appropriate, trait psychology is as ineffectual in guiding the observer or experimenter as rigid iteration of previous responses would be frustrating to an actor.

There is something to be said for the trait notion from the standpoint of an actor's effort to create a harmonious style of life, but this conception—of a more or less self-conscious pattern of decisions—is quite removed from what is normally meant by traits; style of life is a holistic notion, employing themes to relate items or events.

One of the more plausible versions of trait psychology as applied to the study of the family is its incorporation in the idea of compatibility. In its most common form, as applied to marital selection, the traits of one partner are seen as ideally fitting those of another, analogous to the way in which a key fits a lock. In this interpretation the relationship between two people is put either in terms of similarity or complementarity, and it is explained as the predictable product of matching or mismatching of attributes. This is the simplest and most static view which could be taken; actually theories based upon this original notion are woven principally of qualifications and auxiliary hypotheses intended to account for the numerous negative cases. How, for example, do ostensibly compatible people become incompatible, and vice versa? And how do incompatible people marry to begin with?

Contradictions particularly multiply when the matching notion is applied to children and parents. The latter have presumably instilled their own traits into their offspring, yet incompatibilities arise. The emphasis on matching is sometimes carried to extreme lengths in adoption cases, though this has no warrant from research. To suppose that happy marriage and successful parenthood depend upon felicitous concurrence of compatible traits, and that wise selection can avert the hazards of family life, is

neither a logical nor an empirical conclusion. Most of the important questions lie in areas that this approach cannot reach, or where it cannot be experimentally tested.

Out of the reaction against the atomistic and static approach of trait psychology, there has arisen a more holistic and dynamic concept—adjustment. This became, and for the present still remains, predominant in both research and practice. There are many measures of adjustment, differing so widely that proponents of each can no doubt with some validity deny the applicability of any general criticism of this concept. Nonetheless the various usages of adjustment can probably for present purposes be sufficiently distinguished from competence by pointing out certain of their most common meanings.

One usage has the "contented cow" overtones of adjustment terminology; the implication is that human beings react only to disturbances which upset their putative equilibrium, and that the objective of all action is the restoration of tensionless rest. Another usage which has come in for increasing attack is the one that implies reliance upon others to provide instigations to action. If each lets himself be directed by others, critics ask, who guides the whole, and, for that matter, who is responsible for each? The so-called environment to which the individual is assumed to be adjusting is mainly a social environment; are the good adjusters to subordinate themselves to the poor adjusters? A third implication which is being currently challenged is the notion of immediate happiness and security as ultimate values, and the rejection of trial, sacrifice, and risk as evils. One of the most recent standard textbooks on the family defines maladjustment as consisting of conflict, frustration, disapproval, and deprivation; by this view Romeo and Juliet were totally maladjusted.

Logically, the concept gets into insuperable difficulties as soon as its users commence to speak of good adjustment and poor adjustment; all pretense of its being a value-neutral term vanishes at this point. The critics allege that adjustment as either an imputed or recommended end masks a conservative ethic; and this cannot be removed without abandoning the use of the term as a means of differentiating desired from undesired states of affairs, or else plainly adopting a value position other than defense of some given status quo.

The practical motive for research on adjustment seems to be the attainment of a state of affairs having a specific behavioral and emotional content deemed "good." But one man's happiness is another man's gloom. We reject such a formulation because (*a*) while we no doubt share the middle-class norms which are idealized, they too often imply a sort of subcultural ethnocentrism that neither can nor should be forced upon other segments of society, (*b*) it treats conflict as evil in itself, and conceives it unrealistically as unnatural and expungeable, and (*c*) by setting up a stable state of affairs as the end of action by family agencies, it dooms such action to inevitable futility, while closing the door to the exploration and the discovery of new experience and forms in family life. Joint involvement in constructive activity is much more than absence of disagreement.

Quite apart from the intricate and unresolved methodological problem of getting operational definitions and objective measures of adjustment and maladjustment, the basic concept seems to have passed the peak of its popularity a decade or so ago. Research devoted to determining the conditions of adjustment in families evokes less and less interest, while critics multiply. The historian of ideas may eventually associate it with the period of the depression, while the notion of traits may perhaps be associated with a still earlier period in which a man's character was alleged to be his fate, a fate predestined because impervious to change.

Thus interpersonal competence is neither a trait nor a state. Competence denotes capabilities to meet and deal with a changing world, to formulate ends and implement them. The incessant problem of equipping human beings to handle their affairs and to progress toward the discovery of new values and new means is not solved by authoritarian indoctrination of static attributes and beliefs. To rely upon such methods would not only be subversive of the most fundamental of American democratic values but would ultimately result in failure of the system which sought to maintain itself by these means.

On the other hand, there are no grounds for assuming that human nature will "unfold" into competent personalities if merely given freedom. Somewhere between these extremes lies a conception of personalities not inflexibly bound to and molded by the past, nor by utopian absolutists eager to sacrifice the present generation, but capable of utilizing past experience and future aspirations in an effective organization of present effort; not dependent upon direction from without but capable of integrating their goals with those of others and collaborating in their realization; in short, able to cope with their world whether the formulas devised by predecessors fit or not.

The developmental approach, while considerably more suitable than concepts of compatibility and adjustment for evaluating family functioning, is still somewhat encrusted with earlier associations. The notion of maturity, for example, is a rather ambiguous term, which deserves scrutiny. In the normal physical development of a child from infancy to adulthood, the final stage of growth is usually called maturity. When applied to the development of the child's personality, however, the idea of maturity frequently becomes a misleading organic analogy. And when a phrase like "emotional maturity" begins to be used as an epithet by which some adults pronounce moral judgments upon others, its utility has almost vanished.

From the standpoint of interpersonal behavior, personality development is a continuous process. Not only must there be intermittent adaptation to those conditions beyond the control of the person, but a person must constantly set himself a fringe of new objectives. This is especially so in a dynamic society, for it is only thus that a person can resist the welter of conflicting influences which play upon him daily, and organize a more or less unified scheme of autonomous action.

The confusion of age norms with stages of growth is one of the more harassing connotations of the maturity concept because of its incomplete emergence from biology and child psychology. This confusion is especially acute in the more rivalrous subcultures of the American community, where children's progress relative to other children is watched with a jealous eye by their parents. An adequate concept of personality development recognizes the full potential range of qualitative differentiation; it requires the measurement of development of a child or an adult against his previous self or his authentic peers, rather than against extraneous competitive norms. To impose competitive norms in a punitive manner is often discouraging or destructive for development, though intended to be motivating.

As central concepts in family research, adjustment has not superseded compatibility, nor has maturity outdated adjustment, in any neat and clear-cut manner; at most there has been a series of successive emphases. This is particularly true in connection with the concept of adaptability, which was first used effectively in family research by Robert C. Angell in the early 1930's, yet has recently been more fully elaborated by Burgess and Wallin,[8] as particularly appropriate to companionate family relationships. Despite its early use, adaptability appears to be a concept which is transitional from adjustment to competence as a way of looking at family behavior. As used by Burgess and Wallin, it partakes also of a realistic developmental approach: persons do not automatically, if their development is unimpeded, become adapted to a wide range of situations; rather, they acquire adaptability through formulating diverse ways of coping with problematic situations, and if conditions do not permit this kind of learning, they may acquire instead quite maladaptive modes of performance.

There are other terms current in the research literature which might be compared and contrasted with the idea of competence, but we prefer to leave their further consideration to another place or to other writers, while we return now to the further exploration of the elements which compose our central variable.

The Components of Competence

Each of the component aspects of competence in interpersonal relations can be considerably elaborated and investigated. The decision as to how far to go in any particular instance depends on the particular project in mind and the amount of resources available. Here it is deemed suitable only to outline roughly a recognizable conceptual definition of each component, and not to attempt definition or the construction of any measures. We can then go on to consider some hypotheses about the purposeful development of the six components of competence.

1. Health. In this component we include much more than mere absence of disease. Rather it signifies the progressive maximization —within organic limits—of the ability of the organism to exercise all of its physiological functions, and to achieve its maximum of sensory acuity, strength, energy, co-ordination, dexterity, endurance, recuperative power, and immunity. A popular synonym is "good physical condition." In some medical research circles, there is, in this positive sense, considerable discussion of the better operational criteria of health to take the place of such crude indices as, for example, gain in weight among children. Research in psychiatry and psychosomatic medicine has been finding not only that sexual competence and fertility depend on psychosocial development, but also physical health in general.[9] But the relationship runs in both directions.

Without good health, interpersonal episodes often diverge in outcome from wanted ends. Fatigue is a common example of this. While it can be and often is a symptom of complications in living, with certain other people it may also originate new difficulties. The overworked mother will lose her patience unless her reserve of energy, her ruggedness of physique, can carry her through the critical periods. The ailing person of either sex may find his dependence is not only a burden to others but means that he cannot complete the tasks that he formerly

[8] Robert C. Angell, *The Family Encounters the Depression,* New York: Charles Scribner's Sons, 1936; Ernest W. Burgess and Paul Wallin, *Engagement and Marriage,* Chicago: J. B. Lippincott and Co., 1953, Chaps. xviii and xix.

[9] Henry B. Richardson, *Patients Have Families,* New York: The Commonwealth Fund, 1948. Also, Metropolitan Life Insurance Company, *Statistical Bulletin,* XXXVI, New York: Metropolitan Life Insurance Company, 1955, published monthly. Innes H. Pearse, M.D., and Lucy H. Crocker, *The Peckham Experiment,* New Haven: Yale University Press, 1945.

could. Endurance of strain makes physical demands, but the capacity to bear strain is not a constant; it can be cultivated in advance of its use. A striking example is the frequent recovery from despair and breakdown of interpersonal relations through vacation and rest, hygiene and recreation. On the positive, nontherapeutic side —in terms of optimal development—a benevolent spiral seems to extend from radiant health to a cheerful mien, from a cheerful mien to a friendly response, and back again to competence. The physiological substrates of interpersonal acts have been little studied within each social context; the body-mind dualism lingers on in the choice of research problems; by treating health as an element of competence, fresh possibilities arise, for the physiologist as well as the social psychologist.

Efficient criteria of health which are appropriate to the various developmental periods are needed, and so are economical devices for measuring these criteria. Also needed are hypotheses where the health component is regarded as a consequent as well as an antecedent, and finally there should be programs to test these hypotheses. Such hypotheses can of course range over the entire social, biological, and physical environment. For purposes of this report we limit our definition of the field to the relation of families or quasi-families to the development and maintenance of this component of competence.

2. Intelligence. Since this component has been studied continuously and widely for over two generations, it would be presumptuous to elaborate upon it here. Scope of perception of relationships among events; the capacity to abstract and symbolize experience, to manipulate the symbols into meaningful generalizations, and to be articulate in communication; skill in mobilizing the resources of environment and experience in the services of a variety of goals; these are the kinds of capacities included in this category. It is significant that the construction of measures of intelligence is as controversial as ever, and that in any particular research project, the appropriateness and validity of the measure adopted is always a question of judgment.

The research implications of this component

are toward appraisals of the findings of past research within the competence frame of reference and the design of research to fill the gaps in relevant knowledge. Of special interest will be the study of the interrelations of this component with the others we list.

In the planning-action context, the most promising line will be the appraisal of the effectiveness of present programs in creating the relevant antecedent conditions for maximizing the intelligence component, and the design of new sets of conditions which will strengthen or replace those currently operative. The conception of intelligence as a variable subject to planned development is exemplified in certain previous research studies[10] and a number of ambitious experimental programs of action, e.g., the X. G. project of the New York City public schools.

Health and intelligence have been far less often assumed to be variables subject to change through experimental programs than the remaining components of competence, yet they are no less psychosocial in their development. Research and action in respect to the following four components of competence may be less hampered by the weight of previous assumptions.

3. Empathy. People appear to differ in their ability correctly to interpret the attitudes and intentions of others, in the accuracy with which they can perceive situations from others' standpoint, and thus anticipate and predict their behavior. This type of social sensitivity rests on what we call the empathic responses.[11] Empathic responses are basic to "taking the role of the other" and hence to social interaction and the communicative processes upon which rests social integration. They are central in the development of the social self and the capacity

[10] Harold M. Skeels, Ruth Updegraff, Beth L. Wellman, and Harold M. Williams, "A Study of Environmental Stimulation: An Orphanage Preschool Project," *University of Iowa Studies in Child Welfare*, Vol. XV, No. 4, New Series, No. 363, December 1, 1938, Iowa City: University of Iowa, 1938.
[11] For a fuller treatment, see: Leonard S. Cottrell, Jr., and Rosalind F. Dymond, "The Empathic Processes," *Psychiatry*, XII, No. 4 (November, 1949), pp. 355–359.

for self-conscious behavior. No human association, and least of all democratic society, is possible without the processes indicated by this term. For this reason we must include empathic capacity as one of the essential components of interpersonal competence. The sign of its absence is misunderstanding; to measure its presence in the positive sense is a task now being attempted by a few investigators.

The kind of interaction experienced in the family as well as in other groups appears to depend heavily upon the degree to which empathic capacity develops, but experimental research on fluctuations in this element of competence has hardly begun. This lack in research is paralleled by a lack of explicit programs in action agencies aimed at the development of this type of skill. Yet it is so fundamental to social life of every kind that some social psychologists have come close to defining their field as the study of empathy.

4. Autonomy. In the conception of the competent personality which we are defining in terms of its components, one essential element is perhaps best denoted by the word "autonomy," though the ordinary usage of the term does not include all the significance we shall assign to it here. Our present referents, expressed as aspects, are: the clarity of the individual's conception of self (identity); the extent to which he maintains a stable set of internal standards by which he acts; the degree to which he is self-directed and self-controlled in his actions; his confidence in and reliance upon himself; the degree of self-respect he maintains; and the capacity for recognizing real threats to self and of mobilizing realistic defenses when so threatened. That is, autonomy is taken to be genuine self-government, construed as an ability, not a state of affairs. A narrower definition, close to operational, is ease in giving and receiving evaluations of self and others.

Commencing with Piaget in the 1920's, the number of writers who have attempted to deal with autonomy has been growing steadily, but the process of making clearer what is meant by this term (or its near-equivalents like ego-strength and integrity) has as yet produced no satisfactory agreement upon its referents. Some

writers treat it as a trait, some as a value, some as a set of rules for behavior, and some as a highly subjective, desired state of affairs.[12] We believe that progress in definition and measurement of this obviously very important though subtle complex will come most rapidly if definition is sought in terms of an acquired ability for handling those kinds of problematic interpersonal situations where self-esteem is threatened or challenged.

5. Judgment. While critical judgment has long been understood to be acquired slowly with experience, more or less according to age, its operational definition and measurement is still a difficult task. Certain of the educational psychologists have perhaps gone furthest in differentiating this ability from intelligence, and in analyzing the conditions by which an educational or other agency may cultivate judgment among its pupils.[13]

Judgment refers here to the ability which develops slowly in human beings to estimate and evaluate the meaning and consequences to one's self of alternative lines of conduct. It means the ability to adjudicate among values, or to make correct decisions; the index of lack of judgment (bad judgment) is mistakes, but these are the products of an antecedent process, in which skill is the important variable. Obviously

[12] Andras Angyal, *Foundations for a Science of Personality*, New York: The Commonwealth Fund, 1941. Erik H. Erikson, *Childhood and Society*, New York: W. W. Norton and Co., 1950. Joanna Field (pseud.), *A Life of One's Own*, Harmondsworth, Penguin Books, 1952. Erich Fromm, *Man for Himself: An Inquiry into the Psychology of Ethics*, New York: Rinehart, 1947. Robert Lindner, *Prescription for Rebellion*, New York: Rinehart, 1952. Rollo May, *Man's Search for Himself*, New York: W. W. Norton and Co., 1953. Henry A. Murray, et al., *Explorations in Personality*, Cambridge: Harvard University Press, 1938. Jean Piaget, *The Moral Judgment of the Child*, Glencoe: The Free Press, 1948. David Riesman, *The Lonely Crowd*, New Haven: Yale University Press, 1950.

[13] E.g., R. B. Raup, K. D. Benne, B. O. Smith, and G. E. Axtelle, *The Discipline of Practical Judgment in a Democratic Society*, 28th Yearbook of the National Society of College Teachers of Education, Chicago: University of Chicago Press, 1943. Also, Edward M. Glaser, *An Experiment in the Development of Critical Thinking*, New York: Bureau of Publications, Teachers College, Columbia University, 1941.

neither small children nor incapacitated adults can make sound decisions in the sense indicated; and it is equally obvious that among normal adults there is wide variation in this ability. Some persons acquire reputations for unusually good judgment, and some others become conspicuous for the opposite. It is therefore highly proper to conceive of judgment as an acquired critical ability differing in degree among individuals.

Currently among several of the social sciences, though notably in economics, the study of decision-making and of value-choices is receiving much emphasis. Generally speaking, however, the various studies and seminars under way focus upon the outcome or the product of this process—upon ethics, logic, or some highly abstract calculus of contingencies and relative utilities; rarely do they focus upon the choosers, their identities, and the conditions under which their critical abilities develop. A thoroughly interpersonal concept of judgment, appropriate for studying its development, probably therefore must include the skill involved in getting others to be reasonable in discussion, and to handle criticism in a way that utilizes its value.

6. Creativity. This component is perhaps the least amenable to precise definition and division into manageable variables which can be measured. It is ironical that the so-called tough-minded scientists and hard-headed practical people are inclined to look askance at this category as a proper object of scientific study, and yet all of these people demand appraisals of this quality in prospective associates on whom heavy responsibility for leadership and initiative will fall.

The idea of creativity is commonly associated with artistic and intellectual activities. We define it here as any demonstrated capacity for innovations in behavior or real reconstruction of any aspect of the social environment. It involves the ability to develop fresh perspectives from which to view all accepted routines and to make novel combinations of ideas and objects and so define new goals, endowing old ones with fresh meaning, and inventing means for their realization. In interpersonal relations, it is the ability to invent or improvise new roles or alternative

lines of action in problematic situations, and to evoke such behavior in others. Among other things it seems to involve curiosity, self-confidence, something of the venturesomeness and risk-taking tendencies of the explorer, a flexible mind with the kind of freedom which permits the orientation of spontaneous play. While this is a none too satisfactory delineation of creativity, we can begin here and invite help in the search for a more satisfying one. In interpersonal relations, the uncreative person is continually found in dilemmas and impasses—"at his wits' end"—but the valid indices of creativity are harder to discover. Rigidity obtrudes upon attention more than flexibility, for obvious reasons, but that is not to say it deserves more scientific attention.

Why Six Components of Competence?

This brief outline of our conception of the essential components of interpersonal competence is offered with no illusions as to its adequacy or finality. If we have succeeded in giving to the reader at least a rough working idea of the content and meaning the term has for us, and have stimulated critical thinking on its contemporary relevance or implications, our purpose for the moment has been served. Perhaps such reflection will result in the discovery of other skills and qualities which should be added to this list. For the present we are unable to offer additions or corrections, and have some reasons for assuming its completeness.

Readers of George Herbert Mead[14] will recall his distinction between the "me" and "I" phases of the self in personality development and social interaction. Looking at the elements of competence, three correspond roughly to the "me" phase and three to the "I" phase:

Me:	Intelligence	I:	Health
	Empathy		Autonomy
	Judgment		Creativity

The former refer to the vested and organized experience of the community as incorporated within personal conduct; the latter, to the active,

[14] George H. Mead, *Mind, Self, and Society*, Chicago: The University of Chicago Press, 1934.

assertive, and emergent features of human behavior, not reducible to standard roles in conventional situations. But while Mead, like Dewey, relied heavily upon biological explanation for the impulsive and unpredictable character of human development, it had nonetheless been his intention to show the emergence of novel identities within the process of interaction. The concepts of interpersonal autonomy and interpersonal creativity may help to complete his task. In any social act—any episode of interaction—all six capacities are and must be employed, though their prominence varies from phase to phase.

The cultural anthropologists have offered many attempts to classify the full range of human culture. These range from the classic division into technology, social organization, and ideology, through Lowie's "universal pattern of culture" and Malinowski's six-category analysis of institutions, to the extremely elaborate Yale cross-cultural index. It seems significant that the classical tripartite scheme can be detected underlying each of its more sophisticated successors. From quite a different angle, this old division seems to gain a vague additional warrant from Morris' division of the study of meaningful verbal relationships into semantics, syntactics, and pragmatics.[15] Considering the fondness of Western thinkers for indicating completeness by schemes of three elements and opposition by schemes of two, it is difficult to distinguish chicken from egg in trying to account for the recurrence of such schemes, i.e., do they describe reality, or is social reality not the precipitate of such linguistic constructions?

Probably neither metaphysics nor intellectual history has to be called on for defense of either the number or order of the elements of competence, however intriguing it is to speculate about their resemblance to previous schemes. Health and intelligence refer to the factual world of physical events and overt experience; both principally afford rational and efficient manipulation of the objects of the environment. Em-

[15] Charles Morris, *Signs, Language and Behavior*, New York: Prentice-Hall, Inc., 1946.

pathy and autonomy, by contrast, have to do with the relationships of selves and others, not as objects, but as human subjects with whom each person is engaged in the plots of the human drama. Judgment and creativity refer to the symbolized realm of not-present relationships, to the extent that these can be distinguished from the social and instrumental realms of immediate experience.

As mentioned at the outset of this chapter, the six elements of competence were arrived at principally through reflection upon previous research and upon the observable content of interpersonal behavior, and not from play with hyper-abstractions. If further abstraction, however, could demonstrate the completeness of a scheme that is made open-ended by the inclusion of creativity as its final element, then it would seem logical to suppose that our list of six would be lengthened by the addition only of subcategories, rather than by the addition of a seventh or eighth component.

With regard to order, the list is thought to proceed from the most given to the least given features of any interpersonal performance. Also, as will be seen in ensuing chapters, the order adopted is cognate with an order which appears not only empirically convenient in presenting types of family agencies and types of play, but also productive of further useful meditation about reciprocal implications. It would deprive the reader of some pleasant speculation to explore these exhaustively here; we prefer only to suggest the avenues which may be used to order and traverse the vast territory confronting us.

It appears to us that a community which organizes its activity so that it maximizes the number of healthy, intelligent, self-directing citizens, capable of viewing situations from perspectives other than their own, of weighing alternatives and making decisions, of defining new goals and inventing ways of achieving them, is in fact a democratic community and is producing members who can sustain it against all more pessimistic theories of human nature and the social order.

Name Index

Subject Index